PATERNOSTER BIBLICAL MONOGRAPHS

The Christological Witness Function of the Old Testament Characters in the Gospel of John

PATERNOSTER BIBLICAL MONOGRAPHS

SERIES PREFACE

One of the major objectives of Paternoster is to serve biblical scholarship by providing a channel for the publication of theses and other monographs of high quality at affordable prices. Paternoster stands within the broad evangelical tradition of Christianity. Our authors would describe themselves as Christians who recognise the authority of the Bible, maintain the centrality of the gospel message and assent to the classical credal statements of Christian belief. There is diversity within this constituency; advances in scholarship are possible only if there is freedom for frank debate on controversial issues and for the publication of new and sometimes provocative proposals. What is offered in this series is the best of writing by committed Christians who are concerned to develop well-founded biblical scholarship in a spirit of loyalty to the historic faith.

SERIES EDITORS

I. Howard Marshall, Honorary Research Professor of New Testament, University of Aberdeen, Scotland, UK

Richard J. Bauckham, Professor of New Testament Studies and Bishop Wardlaw Professor, University of St Andrews, Scotland, UK

Craig Blomberg, Distinguished Professor of New Testament, Denver Seminary, Colorado, USA

Robert P. Gordon, Regius Professor of Hebrew, University of Cambridge, UK

Tremper Longman III, Robert H. Gundry Professor and Chair of the Department of Biblical Studies, Westmont College, Santa Barbara, California, USA

Stanley E. Porter, President and Professor of New Testament, McMaster Divinity College, Hamilton, Ontario, Canada

PATERNOSTER BIBLICAL MONOGRAPHS

The Christological Witness Function of the Old Testament Characters in the Gospel of John

Sanghee M. Ahn

WIPF & STOCK · Eugene, Oregon

Wipf and Stock Publishers
199 W 8th Ave, Suite 3
Eugene, OR 97401

The Christological Witness Function of the Old
Testament Characters in the Gospel of John
By Ahn, Sanghee M.
Copyright©2014 Paternoster
ISBN 13: 978-1-4982-0079-0
Publication date 6/13/2014
Previously published by Paternoster, 2014

To Judy, my God-given companion,
מֵיְהוָֹה אִשָּׁה מַשְׂכָּלֶת

CONTENTS

Acknowledgements	xiii
Preface	xv
List of Abbreviations	xvii
List of Tables	xxix

Chapter 1 Introduction	**1**
The Two Testaments and "Biblical Theology" Movement	1
Canonical Approach	3
Tradition-Historical Approach	4
Christology within Jewish Conceptual Bounds	8
Centrality of Christology in the Fourth Gospel	9
Johannine Christology from the Vantage Point of the Jewish Context	15
The Main Thesis	19
History of Research	20
Theios Aner Theory	20
Johannine Christology and the Jewish Messianic Figures	22
T.F. Glasson	22
Wayne Meeks	23
J. Louis Martyn	24
Marinus de Jonge	27
Georg Richter, Francis Grob, and Wolfgang Bittner	30
Marie-Émile Boismard	31
Margaret Daly-Denton	31
Eric M. E. Wallace	32
Recent German Contributions with a Particular Emphasis on Scripture as Christological Witness	33
Martin Hengel	34
Andreas Obermann	34
Christian Dietzfelbinger	35
Wolfgang Kraus	35
M.J.J. Menken	37
William Loader	38
Klaus Scholtissek	39
Michael Labahn	40
Hans-Josef Klauk	41
Michael Theobald	41
Justification for the Present Study	42
Scripture as Christological Witness	42
Lack of study on the Old Testament characters	43
Legitimacy of tradition-historical approach	43
Methods	44

Diachronic and Synchronic Approaches	44
Intertextuality	48
Category of intertextuality	48
Implication of orality	52
Religious Comparative Analysis	54
Chronological boundaries of early Judaism	55
Terms	56
Typology and Prefiguration	56
Messiah and Christ	56
Contributions	58
Old Testament Characters as Christological Witnesses	58
Affinity between Early Judaism and John	58
Competency of Redactor/Author of the Fourth Gospel	59
Scope	62
Limitations	63
Chapter 2 The Jewish Patriarchs	**65**
Introduction	65
Jacob	66
Allusions to the Bethel Theophany: John 1:51	66
Narrative context	67
Excursus 1: The "Son of Man" in John 1:51	68
Jacob-Jesus typology	71
Ladder-Jesus typology	72
Contents of theophany	74
Summary	77
Jacob, the Provider of Water: John 4:10-14	77
Narrative context	77
Jacob's well	80
The contrast of Jacob's water with Jesus'	82
Summary	83
Abraham as Christological Witness: John 8:51-58	84
Narrative Context	85
Excursus 2: The Johannine Antagonists	86
Immortality of Jesus and of Abraham	87
Abraham's Witness of the Pre-Existent Jesus	91
Temporal Priority of Jesus over Abraham	93
Summary	94
Conclusion	95
Chapter 3 Elijah	**97**
Introduction	97
Elijah in Second Temple Judaism	98
Eschatological Reconciliation Ministry	99

Malachi	99
Sirach	100
Apocalyptic Militant Subjugation	101
Sibylline Oracles and the Coptic Apocalypse of Elijah	101
The Nag Hammadi Library	102
The Qumran Documents	103
4Q521	104
Scribal Expectation of Elijah's Return	106
Elijah in the Synoptic Gospel	108
Elijah in John's Gospel	109
Jesus as Elijah	110
Cullmann, Schnackenburg, and Robinson	110
J. Louis Martyn	112
Excursus 3: John Meier's Eschatological Prophet Paradigm	114
John the Baptist as Elijah	114
Marinus de Jonge	114
Etienne Trocmé	115
John the Baptist Not as Elijah	117
Markus Öhler	117
High view of John the Baptist	119
Anachronism and the textual testimony	120
Narrative Function of John the Baptist in Fourth Gospel	120
Witness	120
Divine Provenance	123
Analogy with and Comparison to Jesus	123
Mediator	125
Recapitulation of the Old Testament	125
Conclusion	126
Chapter 4 David	**128**
Introduction	128
David in the Old Testament and in the Second Temple Period	128
Ideal Ruler	129
Exemplary Jew	131
Davidic Messianic Expectations in the Old Testament	131
Davidic Messianic Expectations in the Second Temple Judaism	134
1 Maccabees and Sirach	134
Psalms of Solomon	135
4 Ezra	136
4Q252	137
Summary	138
David in the Synoptic Gospels	139
Messianic Role of David in John	141
Daly-Denton	142

Jesus as the Replacement of the Temple: John 2:17	143
Jesus as a Davidic Posterity?: John 7:42	148
Jesus as Davidic King of Israel?: John 12:13	152
Passion as a Messianic Qualification	155
Judas' betrayal as foreshadowed in David: John 13:18	159
Irony of Jewish persecution: John 15:25	162
Allocation of Jesus' clothes: John 19:24	163
Jesus' thirst: John 19:28	165
Not breaking of the legs: John 19:36-37	167
Piercing of the side: John 19:37	169
Conclusion	171
Chapter 5 Moses	**173**
Introduction	173
Mosaic Images in the Old Testament and in Early Judaism	175
Moses as Authority Figure with Particular Emphasis on	
Law-Giving and Legitimatizing	176
The Old Testament	176
Sirach, the Assumption of Moses, and 1 Esdras	180
4 Maccabees	182
2 Maccabees	183
Qumran	185
Excursus 4: The Letter of Aristeas and Moses	190
Moses as Prophet with Particular Emphasis on	
Intercession and Miracle-Working	191
The Old Testament	191
Sirach, 2 Maccabees, the Wisdom of Solomon	193
The Assumption of Moses	194
Qumran	196
Moses as Royal Figure	200
The Old Testament	200
God language of Moses in Exodus, Sirach, and Philo	205
The *Exagoge* of Ezekiel	209
The Sibylline Oracle	211
Philo	212
Josephus and Qumran	214
Moses as Eschatological Prophet	214
Deuteronomy 18:15	214
Rabbinic tradition	217
Samaritan tradition	219
Excursus 5: Schism between Jews and Samaritans	221
Qumran tradition	223
Summary	230
Moses in the New Testament	231

Contents xi

Moses in the Gospel of John 231
  Law through Moses, Grace through Jesus: John 1:16-17 232
    Structure of the prologue 235
    Syntax 238
    Semantics 241
    Summary 244
  Serpent of Moses: John 3:14 245
    Context 246
    T.F. Glasson 247
    Critique of Glasson 249
    Summary 250
  Witness and Accusation of Moses: John 1:45, 5:37-39, 46 251
    Controversial context 252
    A series of witnesses 253
    An allusion to the Sinai account 254
    Klaus Scholtissek and the majority view 254
    Bertold Klappert 257
    Marie-Émile Boismard 258
    Summary 261
  Allusions to the Exodus Events: John 6:14-15, 32-33 262
    Narrative unity 263
    Thematic link between John 5 and 6 264
    Wayne Meeks 265
    Critique of Meeks 267
    John Dennis 268
    Critique of Dennis 269
    Summary 273
Conclusion 274

Chapter 6 Concluding Reflections **276**
Summary of Foregoing Observations 276
Research Results 278
Implications for Study of John's Gospel 279

Appendix 1: Messianism/Christology in the Old Testament and in the Fourth
    Gospel 281

Appendix 2: *Religionsgeschichte* and the Fourth Gospel 289
  Importance of Religionsgeschichte 289
  Bickermann/Hengel Theory 290
  Hellenistic (especially Gnostic) Influence 291
  C.H. Dodd 295
  Semitic Linguistic Features 296
  Recent Archaeological Discoveries 297

Conceptual Affinities	299
After Dodd	300
Appendix 3: The Old Testament in John	305
Significance of the Old Testament	305
Fulfillment Motif in the Passion Narratives	308
Appendix 4: The Internal Well of Living Water in John 7:38	311
Appendix 5: Explicit Old Testament Materials in John	312
Appendix 6: Important Sources on the Study of the Old Testament and the Early Jewish Literature in the Gospel of John	317
The Hebrew Old Testament	317
The Greek Old Testament	317
The Greek New Testament	318
The Old Testament Apocrypha	318
The Old Testament Pseudepigrapha	318
The Qumran Literature	319
Early rabbinic Literature	320
The Samaritan Pentateuch	320
Hellenistic Writings	321
Miscellaneous secondary sources	321
Appendix 7: The Use of Rabbinic Materials for New Testament Studies	323
Bibliography	**325**
Primary Sources	326
Books	328
Articles	347
Dissertations	387
Author Index	**388**
Scripture Index	**399**
Index for Other Ancient Sources	**406**

ACKNOWLEDGEMENTS

This book is in no way a product of one individual's labor. I want to take this space to acknowledge those who have collaborated on seeing this study coming in print. Between 2009 and 2013, I was privileged to work with three different academic institutions as adjunct instructor: the Southern Baptist Theological Seminary, Louisville, KY, USA, Southwestern Baptist Theological Seminary, Fort Worth, TX, USA, and the American Theological Institute, Abidjan, Côte d'Ivoire. Since May 2012, Golden Gate Baptist Theological Seminary, Mill Valley, CA, has hired me as Associate Professor of New Testament and associate director of the KEB program. Before and concurrent to serving at these seminaries, I was involved in a local church ministry as Senior Pastor of All Nations Baptist Church, Arlington, Texas, USA, between October 2006 and April 2012. It has been truly an honor and blessing beyond description to serve the Lord along with the people of God in these institutions. Pastoral and academic experiences I had at these places challenged me to realize intellectual and spiritual inadequacies on my part. At the same time, they also stimulated and shaped me to grow in maturity. As such, I have incurred a profound debt of gratitude to a number of individuals.

Dr. John Polhill, my *doctor vater*, at Southern Seminary was gracious to accept a weakling under his wings to nurture and train. It is not only his keen awareness and broad knowledge in linguistics and other areas of theological discourses but his warmth, kindness and love for the body of Christ that have left a long-lasting imprint in me. Dr. Robert Stein, for whom I had privilege to work as his graduate assistant, instilled in me the virtue and the beauty of precision in critically theological inquiries. Initially, I started a doctoral dissertation project with him. It is very regretful, however, that the project couldn't reach completion. Even after a half-year of research in the area of Markan eschatology, my interest in the relationship between the Old Testament, early Judaism and John's Gospel did not become abated and only remained rising. The topic stuck with me from the beginning of the doctoral study at Southern. Professors Mark Seifrid and Robert Plummer (SBTS) collaborated on this project as second readers. I am especially grateful to the former for the kind endorsement and some insightful suggestions he shared with me. Dr. Andreas Köstenberger of Southeastern Baptist Theological Seminary offered invaluable advice and even corrected me on several fronts as an external reader. Finally, I must mention a dear colleague and a German friend, Dr. Lars Kierspel, now teaching at Shiloh University, who has thoroughly read an earlier draft. Had he not rendered his service for me with his usual eyes of hawk, I would have been even more humbled. He saved me from a number of embarrassing mistakes that I made earlier and some of his suggestions and guidance have proven very helpful. These scholars contributed to this book significantly so now it stands much better in form and content. But, of course, all the shortcomings despite their assistance fall entirely upon myself.

The Kim professional development fund of Golden Gate Baptist Theological Seminary partially underwrote the book purchase expenses that were necessitated by this writing project. I extend my appreciation to Mr. & Mrs. David Kim for endowing this grant.

Dr. Michael Parsons, the commissioning editor of Paternoster also deserves appreciation for accepting this work into their monograph series and guiding me through sometimes what would have demanded patience at his end.

My family and in-laws in Korea, parents and the parents-in-law, supported the years of my study in the United States through their earnest prayer and sacrificial financial assistance. They are exemplary Christians and should be proud of this work because this is a small token of pouring out of their lives in upbringing their children in a godly way. My daughter, Grace, was born during my doctoral study and she sustained me on course with her precious smiles and presence. My wife, Judy, encouraged and prayed for me, and beyond the fair portion of any wife endured my absence with her typical very cheerful spirit. She is a genuine example of God's unfailing grace upon me, a sinner forgiven. It is to her that I dedicate this humble piece of study in the revelation of the divine mercy and salvation through his Son, Christ, the God incarnate.

S. Michael Ahn
2013

PREFACE

This book is a revised and significantly updated version of a doctoral dissertation previously submitted to and defended at the Southern Baptist Theological Seminary, Louisville, KY, USA, in 2006. For this revision, pertinent studies appeared since its initial publication have been added into discussion and the wordings have been slightly smoothed out from its original draft. In addition, most of the French and German citations are translated into English except, only on a few occasions, the original wordings stand better untranslated.

This book sets out on an inquiry into the Christological function of the major Old Testament characters as described in the Gospel of John. In addition, possible connections between the Christology of the Gospel and the messianism of the early Jewish traditions are explored. It is primarily these two questions that this book tries to answer critically and exegetically.

It has become customary or even virtuous that recent theological monographs take on such lengthy discussions. Thus, it is daunting and has become almost impossible to read cover to cover most recent theological academic books in short breath. This study is structured in a way that the flow of the main argument is kept to the minimal and precision as much as possible for the purpose of speedy reading on the first encounter. However, plenty of in-depth discussions, side-notes, and concomitant references are offered in the footnotes. Also, readers are advised to turn to appendices where some important background issues are addressed such as the relationship between messianism and Christology, and early Judaism and the Fourth Gospel. With such an arrangement, it is hoped that serious students and researchers may use this book as a reference tool and a point of departure for further inquiries into the topics under discussion.

For the matter of format, the Turabian and the SBL styles have been eclectically adhered to as they deem appropriate (Kate Turabian et al., eds., *A Manual for Writers of Research Papers, Theses, and Dissertations*, 8th ed. [Chicago: University of Chicago Press, 2013]; Patrick H. Alexander et al, eds., *The SBL Handbook of Style: For Ancient Near Eastern, Biblical, and Early Christian Studies* [Peabody, MA: Hendrickson, 1999]). For abbreviations, the guideline set forth by the Society of Biblical Literature was consulted and generally followed. The Hebrew and Greek fonts are employed from Microsoft Word©. For the English translation, *New Revised Standard Version* was cited throughout unless noted otherwise.

LIST OF ABBREVIATIONS

4QFlor	4Q174 (Florilegium) or 4QEschMidr (*Midrash on Eschatology*)
4QpIsa^a	4Q161 (*Commentary on Isaiah*)
11QPs^a	J. Sanders, ed. *The Psalms Scroll of Qumran Cave 11*
AASF	Annales Academiae scientiarum fennicae
AASGE	Auctoritate Academiae Scientiarum Göttingensis editum
AB	The Anchor Bible
ABD	D.N. Freedman, ed. *Anchor Bible Dictionary*
ABIG	Arbeiten zur Bibel und ihrer Geschichte
Abot	*Aboth*
Abr.	Philo *De Abrahamo* (On Abraham)
ABR	*Australian Biblical Review*
ABRL	The Anchor Bible Reference Library
AbrN	*Abr-Nahrain*
ACCS	Ancient Christian Commentary on Scripture
AGAJU	Arbeiten zur Geschichte des antiken Judentums und des Urchristentums
Ag. Ap.	Josephus *Against Apion*
ÄgAT	Ägypten und Altes Testament
AGSU	Arbeiten zur Geschichte des Spätjudentums und Urchristentums
AnBib	Analecta biblica
ANRW	*Aufstieg und Niedergang der römischen Welt*
Ant.	Josephus *Jewish Antiquities*
ANTC	Abingdon New Testament Commentaries
ANTJ	Arbeiten zum Neuen Testament und Judentum
Anton	*Antonianum*
AOAT	Alter Orient und Altes Testament
AOTC	The Apollos Old Testament Commentary
APF	*Archiv für Papyrusforschung und verwandte Gebiete*
Apo. Ab.	*Apocalypse of Abraham*
Apo. El. (C)	Coptic *Apocalypse of Elijah*
ArBibM.	McNamara, ed. The Aramaic Bible
As. Mos.	*Assumption of Moses*
ATANT	Abhandlungen zur Theologie des Alten und Neuen Testaments
AThR	*Anglican Theological Review*
ATLABS	The ATLA Bibliography Series
AUSS	*Andrews University Seminary Studies*
AUSDDS	Andrews University Seminary Doctoral Dissertation Series

AYBRL	The Anchor Yale Bible Reference Library
b.	I. Epstein, ed. *The Babylonian Talmud*
Bar	Baruch
BAR	*Biblical Archaeology Review*
B. Bat.	*Baba Batra* (Babylonian Talmud)
BBB	Bonner biblische Beiträge
BBET	Beiträge zur biblischen Exegese und Theologie
BBR	*Bulletin for Biblical Research*
BDAG	W. Bauer et al., eds. *A Greek-English Lexicon of the New Testament and Other Early Christian Literature*. 3rd ed.
BDB	F. Brown, S.R. Driver, and C.A. Briggs, eds. *Hebrew and English Lexicon of the Old Testament*
BDF	F. Blass, A. DeBrunner, and R.W. Funk, eds. *A Greek Grammar of the New Testament and Other Early Christian Literature*
BECNT	Baker Exegetical Commentary on the New Testament
Ber.	*Berakot*
Ber. R.	*Beršit Rabbati*
BETL	Bibliotheca ephemeridum theologicarum lovaniensium
BevT	Beiträge zur evangelischen Theologie
BFCT	Beiträge zur Förderung christlicher Theologie
BG	Biblische Gestalten
BHS	R. Kittel et al., eds. *Biblia Hebraica Stuttgartensia*. 5th ed.
Bib	*Biblica*
BibInt	*Biblical Interpretation*
BIS	Biblical Interpretation Series
BiW	Bible World
BJRL	*Bulletin of the John Rylands University Library of Manchester*
BJS	Brown Judaic Studies
BK	*Bibel und Kirche*
B. Mes.	*BaBa Mesia*
BN	*Biblische Notizen*
BNTC	Black's New Testament Commentaries
BP	Bibliothèque de la Pléiade
BRev	*Bible Review*
BRLJ	Brill Reference Library of Judaism
BRS	Biblical Resource Series
BS	The Biblical Seminar
BSac	*Bibliotheca Sacra*
BSR	Biblioteca di scienze religiose
BTB	*Biblical Theology Bulletin*
BTF	*Bangalore Theological Forum*

List of Abbreviations xix

BThSt	Biblisch-theologische Studien
BTZ	*Berliner theologische Zeitschrift*
BU	Biblische Untersuchungen
BWANT	Beiträge zur Wissenschaft vom Alten und Neuen Testament
BZ	*Biblische Zeitschrift*
BZAW	Beihefte zur Zeitschrift für die alttestamentliche Wissenschaft
BZNW	Beihefte zur Zeitschrift für die neutestamentliche Wissenschaft und die Kunde der älteren Kirche
CBC	Cambridge Bible Commentary
CBET	Contributions to Biblical Exegesis and Theology
CBQ	*Catholic Biblical Quarterly*
CBQMS	Catholic Biblical Quarterly Monograph Series
CBSS	Continuum Biblical Studies Series
CCR	Cambridge Companions to Religion
CD	The Damascus Document
CEJL	Commentaries on Early Jewish Literature
CGLP	The Coptic Gnostic Library Project
CH	*Church History*
CJA	Christianity and Judaism in Antiquity
CIS	Copenhagen International Seminar
CM	Christianity in the Making
CNT	Companions to the New Testament
CIS	Copenhagen International Seminar
COQG	Christian Origins and the Question of God
CovQ	*Covenant Quarterly*
CQS	Companion to the Qumran Scrolls
CRBR	*Critical Review of Books in Religion*
CREJ	Collection de la Revue des Études juives
CRINT	Compendia rerum iudaicarum ad Novum Testamentum
CRTP	*Cahiers de la revue de théologie et de philosophie*
CTR	*Criswell Theological Review*
CurBS	*Currents in Biblical Research* (formerly *Currents in Research*)
CV	*Communio viatorum*
DCLS	Deuterocanonical and Cognate Literature Studies
DCLY	Deuterocanonical and Cognate Literature Yearbook
DDD	B. Becking, P.W. van der Horst, and K. van der Toorn, eds. *Dictionary of Deities and Demons in the Bible*
Det.	Philo *Quod deterius potiori insidari soleat*
DJD	Discoveries in the Judaean Desert
DJG	J.B. Green, S. McKnight, and I.H. Marshall, eds. *Dictionary of Jesus and the Gospels*

DNP	H. Cancik and H. Schneider, eds. *Der neue Pauly*
DNTB	C.A. Evans and S. E. Porter, eds. *Dictionary of New Testament Background*
DPHL	G.F. Hawthorne, R.P. Martin, and D.G. Reid, eds. *Dictionary of Paul and His Letters*
DRev	*Downside Review*
DSD	*Dead Sea Discoveries*
DSS	F.G. Martínez and E.J.C. Tigchelaar, eds. *The Dead Sea Scrolls*
DTT	*Dansk teologisk tidsskrift*
EBib	Etudes bibliques
ECDSS	The Eerdmans Commentaries on the Dead Sea Scrolls
EDNT	H. Balz and G. Schneider, eds. *Exegetical Dictionary of the New Testament*
EDSS	L.H. Schiffman and J.C. VanderKam, eds. *Encyclopedia of the Dead Sea Scrolls*
Eduy.	*Eduyyot*
EHPR	Études d'histoire et de Philosophie Religieuses
EHS	Europäische Hochschulschriften
EJIL	Early Judaism and Its Literature
ErIsr	*Eretz-Israel*
Esdr	Esdras
EstB	*Estudios bíblico*
ETL	*Ephemeridum theologicarum lovaniensium*
ÉTR	*Études théologiques et religieuses*
ETSS	Evangelical Theological Society Studies
EuroJT	*European Journal of Theology*
EvT	*Evangelische Theologie*
EvQ	*Evangelical Quarterly*
ExpTim	*Expository Times*
Ezek. Trag.	Ezekiel the Tragedian
FAT	Forschungen zum Alten Testament
FB	Forschung zur Bibel
FBBS	Facet Books Biblical Series
FM	*Faith and Mission*
FoiVie	*Foi et vie*
FRLANT	Forschungen zur Religion und Literatur des Alten und Neuen Testaments
FSC	Faith and Scholarship Colloquies
FTS	Frankfurter theologische Studien
FZPhTh	*Freiburger Zeitschrift für Philosophie und Theologie*
GAP	Guides to the Apocrypha and Pseudepigrapha
Gen. Rab.	*Genesis Rabbah*
GNT	Grundrisse zum Neuen Testament

GP	Gospel Profiles
GTA	Göttinger theologische Arbeiten
GTS	Gütersloher Taschenbücher Siebenstern
GTJ	*Grace Theological Journal*
HALOT	L. Koehler and W. Baumgartner. *The Hebrew and Aramaic Lexicon of the Old Testament: Study Edition*
HBIS	History of Biblical Interpretation Series
HBS	Herders biblische Studien
HBT	*Horizons in Biblical Theology*
HCS	Hellenistic Culture and Society
HDR	Harvard Dissertations in Religion
Hen	*Henoch*
HNT	Handbuch zum Neuen Testament
HO	Handbuch der Orientalistik
HSS	Harvard Semitic Studies
HTCNT	Herder's Theological Commentary on the New Testament
HTR	*Harvard Theological Review*
HTS	Harvard Theological Studies
HTSTS	*HTS teologiese Studies*
HvTSt	*Hervormde teologiese Studies*
HUCA	*Hebrew Union College Annual*
IBS	*Irish Biblical Studies*
ICC	The International Critical Commentary
ICS	*Illinois Classical Studies*
IDS	*In die Skriflig*
IJST	*International Journal of Systematic Theology*
Int	*Interpretation*
IR	Iconography of Religions
IRT	Issues in Religion and Theology
ISFCJ	International Studies in Formative Christianity and Judaism
JAC	Jahrbuch für Antike und Christentum
JBL	*Journal of Biblical Literature*
JBLMS	Journal of Biblical Literature Monograph Series
JBQ	*Jewish Bible Quarterly*
JBT	Jahrbuch für Biblische Theologie
JCHS	Jewish and Christian Heritage Series
JCPS	Jewish and Christian Perspectives Series
JDS	Judean Desert Studies
Jdt	Judith
JETS	*Journal of the Evangelical Theological Society*
JHS	*Journal of Hebrew Scriptures*
JJS	*Journal of Jewish Studies*

JPSTC	The JPS Torah Commentary
JQR	*Jewish Quarterly Review*
JR	*Journal of Religion*
JRR	*Journal from the Radical Reformation*
JSHJ	*Journal for the Study of the Historical Jesus*
JSHR	Jüdische Schriften aus hellenistisch-römischer
JSJ	*Journal for the Study of Judaism in the Persian, Hellenistic and Roman Period*
JSJSup	Supplements to the Journal for the Study of Judaism
JSNT	*Journal for the Study of the New Testament*
JSNTSup	Journal for the Study of the New Testament Supplement Series
JSOT	*Journal for the Study of the Old Testament*
JSOTsup	Journal for the Study of the Old Testament Supplement Series
JSP	*Journal for the Study of the Pseudepigrapha*
JSPSup	Journal for the Study of the Pseudepigrapha Supplement Series
JSRC	Jerusalem Studies in Religion and Culture
JSS	*Journal of Semitic Studies*
JTI	*Journal of Theological Interpretation*
JTS	*Journal of Theological Studies*
J.W.	Josephus *Jewish War*
KD	*Kerygma und Dogma*
KEK	Kritisch-exegetischer Kommentar über das Neue Testament
KJV	The King James Version
KohlT	Kohlhammer Taschenbücher
KST	Kohlhammer Studienbücher Theologie
KT	Kaiser Taschenbücher
KuI	*Kirche und Israel*
L.A.B.	*Liber antiquitatum biblicarum* (Pseudo-Philo)
Lan	*Landas*
LCL	Loeb Classical Library
LD	Lectio divina
LDSC	The Literature of the Dead Sea Scrolls
Let. Aris.	Letter of Aristeas
LHBOTS	The Library of Hebrew Bible/Old Testament Studies
Liddell & Scott	H.S. Jones, ed. *A Greek-English Lexicon*
Liv. Pro.	*The Lives of the Prophets*
LKW	*Lutherische Kirche in der Welt*
LNTS	The Library of New Testament Studies
LSTS	The Library of Second Temple Studies
LTR	*Lutheran Theological Review*

List of Abbreviations xxiii

LumVie	*Lumière et Vie*
LUOSA	*Leeds University Oriental Society Annual*
LXX	A. Rahlfs, ed. *Septuagint*
m.	H. Danby, trans. *The Mishnah*
Macc	Maccabees
MdB	Monde de la Bible
Meg.	*Megillah*
Midr. Pss.	W.G. Braude, trans. *The Midrash on Psalms*
Migr.	Philo *De migratione Abrahami*
MNTC	The Moffatt New Testament Commentary
MNTS	McMaster New Testament Studies
Mos. (*Moses*)	Philo *De vita Mosis* (Philo *On the Life of Moses*)
MP	Myth and Poetics
MScRel	*Mélanges de Science Religieuse*
MT	The Masoretic Text
MTZ	*Münchener theologische Zeitschrift*
Mut.	Philo *De Mutatione Nominum* (*the Change of Names*)
NA	Nestle-Aland, *Novum Testamentum Graece*. 28th ed.
NABPRSSS	NABPR Special Studies Series
NAC	The New American Commentary
NASB	The New American Standard Bible
NCB	The New Century Bible
NCamBC	The New Cambridge Bible Commentary
NEA	*Near Eastern Archaeology*
NEchtB	Neue Ecter Bibel
NEchtBAT	Neue Ecter Bibel zum Alten Testament
NEchtBNT	Neue Ecter Bibel zum Neuen Testament
NEchtBT	Neue Ecter Bibel Themen
Neot	*Neotestamentica*
NET	Neutestamentliche Entwürfe zur Theologie
NGWG	*Nachrichten von der königlichen Gesellschaft der Wissenschaften zu Göttingen*
NHMS	Nag Hammadi and Manichaean Studies
NIB	L.E. Keck, ed. The New Interpreter's Bible
NICNT	The New International Commentary on the New Testament
NICOT	The New International Commentary on the Old Testament
NIDNTT	C. Brown, ed. *New International Dictionary of the New Testament Theology*
NIDOTTE	W.A. VanGemeren, ed. *New International Dictionary of the Old Testament Theology & Exegesis*
NovT	*Novum testamentum*
NovTSup	Novum testamentum Supplement

NRSV	The New Revised Standard Version
NRTh	*La nouvelle revue théologique*
NTA (1963)	E. Hennecke and W. Schneemelcher, eds. *New Testament Apocrypha*
NTA (1991)	W. Schneemelcher, ed. *New Testament Apocrypha*
NTAbh	Neutestamentliche Abhandlungen (new series)
NTD	Das Neue Testament Deutsch
NTL	New Testament Library
NTM	New Testament Monographs
NTOA	Novum Testamentum et Orbis Antiquus
NTS	*New Testament Studies*
NTSI	The New Testament and The Scriptures of Israel
NTT	New Testament Theology
NTTS	New Testament Tools and Studies
NTTSD	New Testament Tools, Studies and Documents
Num. R.	*Numbers Rabbah*
OBO	Orbis Biblicus et Orientalis
ÖBS	Österreichische biblische Studien
ÖTKNT	Ökumenischer Taschenbuch-Kommentar zum Neuen Testament
OTL	The Old Testament Library
OTP	J.H. Charlesworth, ed. *The Old Testament Pseudepigrapha*
OtSt	Oudtestamentische Studiën
PBM	Paternoster Biblical Monographs
PEGLMBS	*Proceedings, Eastern Great Lakes and Midwest Biblical Societies*
Pesah.	*Pesahim*
Pesiq. Rab Kah	*Pesiqta de Rab Kahana*
PFTUN	Publications de la Faculté de Théologie de l'Université de Neuchâtel
PG	Patrologia Graeca (Paris: J.–P. Migne, 1857-66)
PIRSB	Publications de l'Institut romand des sciences bibliques
PNTC	The Pillar New Testament Commentaries
POC	*Proche Orient Chrétien*
Post.	Philo *De posteritate Caini*
PPSSHJ	Princeton-Prague Symposia Series on the Historical Jesus
Praem.	Philo *De praemiis et poenis*
Prob.	Philo *Quod Omnis Probus Liber sit*
ProEccl	*Pro Ecclesia*
ProtoBib	*Protokolle zur Bibel*
PRSt	*Perspectives in Religious Studies*
Ps.-Clem. *Recog.*	Pseudo-Clementine *Recognitions*

PSJCO	Princeton Symposium on Judaism and Christian Origins
Pss. Sol.	*Psalms of Solomon*
PThSt	Paderborner theologische Studien
PTM	Paternoster Theological Monographs
PTMS	Princeton Theological Monograph Series
PTS	Patristische Teste und Studien
PTSDSSP	The Princeton Theological Seminary Dead Sea Scrolls Project
QC	*Qumran Chronicle*
QD	Quaestiones disputatae
RB	*Revue biblique*
RBS	Resources for Biblical Study
RCT	*Revista Catalana de Teología*
Rech	Recherches
RevExp	*Review and Expositor*
RevQ	*Revue de Qumran*
RevScRel	*Revue des sciences religieuses*
RGG	H.D. Betz, ed. *Religion in Geschichte und Gegenwart*. 4th ed.
RHPR	*Revue d'histoire et de philosophie religieuses*
RHR	*Revue de l'histoire des religions*
RivB	*Rivista biblica*
RSR	*Recherches de science religieuse*
RTL	*Revue théologique de Louvain*
RThom	*Revue Thomiste*
RTP	*Revue de théologie et de philosophie*
RTR	*Reformed Theological Review*
Sanh.	Sanhedrin
SANT	Studien zum Alten und Neuen Testament
SubBi	Subsidia biblica
SBAB	Stuttgarter biblische Aufsatzbände
SBB	Stuttgarter biblische Beiträge
SBEC	Studies in Bible and Early Christianity
SBFLA	*Studii biblici Franciscani liber annuus*
SBLDS	The Society of Biblical Literature Dissertation Series
SBLEJL	The Society of Biblical Literature Early Judaism and Its Literature
SBLRBS	The Society of Biblical Literature Resources for Biblical Study
SBLSCS	The Society of Biblical Literature Septuagint and Cognate Studies Series
SBLSP	*The Society of Biblical Literature Seminar Papers*
SBLSS	The Society of Biblical Literature Symposium Series
SBLTT	The Society of Biblical Literature Texts and

	Translations
SBS	Stuttgarter Bibelstudien
SbT	Studienbücher Theologie
SBT	Studies in Biblical Theology
SBTS	Sources for Biblical and Theological Study
ScEccl	*Sciences ecclésiastiques*
ScEs	*Science et Esprit*
SCHNT	Studia ad corpus hellenisticum Novi Testamenti
SCJ	*Stone-Campbell Journal*
ScrBi	*Scripta biblica*
ScrTh	*Scripta Theologica*
SCS	Sino-Christian Studies
SCSS	Septuagint and Cognate Studies Series
SeptCS	The Septuagint Commentary Series
SDSSRL	Studies in the Dead Sea Scrolls and Related Literature
SEÅ	*Svensk exegetisk årsbok*
SECA	Studies on Early Christian Apocrypha
SecCent	*Second Century*
SFSHJ	South Florida Studies in the History of Judaism
SHC	Studies in Hellenistic Civilization
SHJ	Studying the Historical Jesus
SHR	Studies in the History of Religions
Sib. Or.	*Sibylline Oracles*
SIJD	Schriften des Institutum Judaicum Delitzschianum
Sir	Sirach
SJ	Studies in Judaism (Studia Judaica)
SJLA	Studies in Judaism in Late Antiquity
SJOT	*Scandinavian Journal of the Old Testament*
SJT	*Scottish Journal of Theology*
SK	*Skrif en Kerk*
SNTSMS	Society for the New Testament Studies Monograph Series
SNTSU	*Studien zum Neuen Testament und seiner Umwelt*
Somn.	Philo *De Somniis* (On Dreams)
SP	Sacra Pagina
SPAW	*Sitzungsberichte der preussischen Akademie der Wissenschaft*
Spec.	Philo *De specialibus legibus*
SPhiloA	*Studia philonica Annual*
SPhilo	*Studia philonica*
SS	Studia Samaritanan
SSSGA	Septuaginta Societatis Scientiarum Gottingensis auctoritate
SSEJC	Studies in Early Judaism and Christianity

ST	*Studia theologica*
STDJ	Studies on the Texts of the Desert of Judah
STI	Studies in Theological Interpretation
StPB	Studia Post-Biblica
Str-B	H.L. Strack and P. Billerbeck. *Kommentar zum Neuen Testament aus Talmud und Midrasch*. 6 vols.
StudBibTh	*Studia Biblica et Theologica*
StudMonR	*Studia Montis Regii*
StudPat	*Studia Patavina*
SUNT	Studien zur Umwelt des Neuen Testaments
Sus	Susanna
SVTP	Studia in Veteris Testamenti Pseudepigrapha
SVTQ	*St. Vladimir's Theological Quarterly*
TANTZ	Texte und Arbeiten zum neutestamentlichen Zeitalter
TBS	Tools for Biblical Study
TCBAI	Transactions of the Casco Bay Assyriological Institute
TDNT	Kittel, ed. *Theological Dictionary of the New Testament*
TDOT	G.J. Botterweck, H. Ringgren, and H.-J. Fabry, eds. *Theological Dictionary of the Old Testament*
Tehar.	*Teharot*
ThGl	*Theologie und Glaube*
Tg. Ps.	*Targum of Psalms*
Tg. Yer. I	*Targum Yerušalmi*
Tg. Yer. II	*Targum Yerušalmi I*
Them	*Themelios*
THKNT	Theologischer Handkommentar zum Neuen Testament
ThR	Theology and Religion
THS	Tyndale House Studies
ThTo	*Theology Today*
TI	Theological Inquiries
TJT	*Toronto Journal of Theology*
TK	*Texte & Kontexte*
TKNT	Theologischer Kommentar zum Neuen Testament
TLZ	*Theologisch Literaturzeitung*
Tob	Tobit
TP	*Theologie und Philosophie*
TQ	*Theologische Quartalschrift*
TranseuSup	Supplément à Transeuphratène
TRE	H.R. Balz, ed. *Theologische Realenzyklopädie*
Treat. Res.	*Treatise on the Resurrection*
TRev	*Theologische Revue*
TRu	*Theologische Rundschau*
TS	*Theological Studies*
TSAJ	Texte und Studien zum antiken Judentum

TTZ	*Trierer theologische Zeitschrift*
TUGAL	Texte und Untersuchungen zur Geschichte der altchristlichen Literatur
TW	Theologische Wissenschaft
TxCrSt	Text-Critical Studies
TynBul	*Tyndale Bulletin*
TZ	*Theologische Zeitschrift*
UBIW	Understanding the Bible and Its World
UBS	B. Aland et al., eds. *The Greek New Testament*. 4th ed.
UNDCSJCA	University of Notre Dame Center for the Study of Judaism and Christianity in Antiquity
UNT	Untersuchungen zum Neuen Testament
UTB	Uni-Taschenbücher
VE	*Verbum et Ecclesia*
VF	*Verkündigung und Forschung*
Virt.	Philo *De virtutibus*
Vita	Josephus *Vita*
VT	*Vetus testamentum*
VTSup	Vetus Testamentum Supplements
WBC	Word Biblical Commentary
WF	Wege der Forschung
Wis	Wisdom of Solomon
WMANT	Wissenschaftliche Monographien zum Alten und Neuen Testament
WTJ	*Westminster Theological Journal*
WUNT	Wissenschaftliche Untersuchungen zum Neuen Testament
WW	*Word & World*
y.	J. Neusner, ed. *The Talmud of the Land of Israel*
YJS	Yale Judaica Series
YPR	Yale Publications in Religion
ZAW	*Zeitschrift für die alttestamentliche Wissenschaft*
ZBKNT	Zürcher Bibelkommentare zum Neuen Testament
ZDPV	*Zeitschrift des deutschen Palästina-Vereins*
ZKT	*Zeitschrift für katholische Theologie*
ZNT	*Zeitschrift für Neues Testament*
ZNW	*Zeitschrift für die neutestamentliche Wissenschaft und die Kunde der älteren Kirche*
ZTK	*Zeitschrift für Theologie und Kirche*
ZWT	*Zeitschrift für wissenschaftliche Theologie*

LIST OF TABLES

Table 1	Escalating Faith in Christ in John 4	78
Table 2	Comparison of Gen 12:6-7 between the Samaritan & Masoretic Texts	80
Table 3	Comparison of the Syriac and Latin versions of Ps.-Clem. *Recog.* on John the Baptist	116
Table 4	The Witness Function of John the Baptist in John 1	121
Table 5	Chiastic Structure surrounding the Triumphant Entry	155
Table 6	Comparison of 1 Esdras, Ezra, and 2 Chronicles	182
Table 7	Comparison of Deuteronomy and 2 Maccabees on Mosaic loyalty to the Law	185
Table 8	Contents of 4Q175	228
Table 9	Various Structural Analyses of the Prologue	236
Table 10	Four witnesses on behalf of Christ's mission and identity	255
Table 11	Direct Quotations with Introductory Formulae	313
Table 12	Direct Quotations without Introductory Formulae	316
Table 13	Introductory Formulae without Explicit Quotations	316
Table 14	OT Allusions Discussed in the Present Study	317

CHAPTER 1

Introduction

The Two Testaments and "Biblical Theology" Movement
The bipartite nature of the Christian Bible has been recognized not only as a central issue of biblical theology, but a source of a perennial dilemma for biblical theologians for a long time.[1] One of the reasons for such a quandary lies in the considerable measure of incongruity that the two Testaments display with one another (and within themselves), notwithstanding a certain degree of commonality.[2] In the face of this observation, one group of scholars, especially some historical critics, has expressed skepticism toward the unity of the Old and New Testaments and further argued that "biblical theology" is possible only within certain confessional circles, reflecting reductionistic and positivistic methodology and *a priori* theological presuppositions.[3] Along with the inherent flaws,

---

[1] James K. Mead, *Biblical Theology: Issues, Methods, and Themes* (Louisville: Westminster/John Knox, 2007), 63; Edward W. Klink, III and Darian R. Lockett, *Understanding Biblical Theology: A Comparison of Theory and Practice* (Grand Rapids: Zondervan, 2012), 17-18.

[2] This question of disparity or diversity is at issue not only concerning the relation between the two Testaments but within the scope of the respective Testament. For the case of the New Testament, see James D.G. Dunn, *Unity and Diversity in the New Testament: An Inquiry into the Character of Earliest Christianity* (London: SCM, 2006). However, Dunn seems to have slightly shifted his stress from the diverse to the synthetic witness of the New Testament writings in his more recent work. Some of his observations are noteworthy: first, the impact the historical Jesus made upon his disciples was the formative force in shaping the present New Testament witnesses. Second, the oral communication environment facilitated a considerably conservative transmission process. Thus, he suggests the close connection between the first and third life settings. James D.G. Dunn, *Jesus Remembered* (Grand Rapids: Eerdmans, 2003), 882-84. Dunn's observation on the diversity (in the former book) indicates the difficulty inherent in the undertaking of "biblical theology." For a survey of attempts to construct "biblical theology" in the sense of "übergreifende Thematik (overarching theme)," see Ferdinand Hahn, *Theologie des Neuen Testaments: Die Vielfalt des Neuen Testaments, Theologiegeschichte des Urchristentums* (Tübingen: Mohr Siebeck, 2011), 1:1-28.

[3] Jon Douglas Levenson, *The Hebrew Bible, the Old Testament, and Historical Criticism: Jews and Christians in Biblical Studies* (Louisville: Westminster/John Knox, 1993), 106-26; Wolfhart Pannenberg, "Problems in a Theology of (Only) the Old Testament," in *Problems in Biblical Theology: Essays in Honor of Rolf Knierim*, ed.

some prominent biblical theologians also assessed the demise of "biblical theology" as inevitable. In the previous generation, Brevard Childs assessed the meagre beginning of this approach and foresaw its imminent ending:

> The [biblical theology] movement was strongly Protestant in its orientation and directed consciously toward the needs of the Christian Church. Its influence spread widely beyond these borders, but the center of the movement remained concentrated in a limited area of the Protestant spectrum. The movement had a rather closely definable beginning and an approximate ending.[4]

However, such a judgment has proven not to be entirely correct because "biblical theology" continues to be a subject of much discussion as evidenced by the recent installment of journal series, monographs, and commentaries that closely address this topic.[5] A significant number of biblical theologians are optimistic about the possibility of constructing a critically-analytical "biblical theology."[6]

Henry T.C. Sun and Keith L. Eades (Grand Rapids: Eerdmans, 1997), 275-80. From a New Testament scholar, see Hans Hübner, *Biblische Theologie des Neuen Testaments: Prolegomena* (Göttingen: Vandenhoeck & Ruprecht, 1990), 1:28.

[4] Brevard S. Childs, *Biblical Theology in Crisis* (Philadelpha: Westminster, 1970), 1. A working definition of "biblical theology" is worthy of mention. Scobie defines "biblical theology" as "the ordered study of what the Bible has to say about God and his relation to the world and to humankind." Charles H.H. Scobie, *The Ways of Our God: An Approach to Biblical Theology* (Grand Rapids: Eerdmans, 2003), 4-5.

[5] In addition to the monographs mentioned in this section, recent installments of such a prestigious series of monographs, journals, and commentary series signal rather the growing interest in the issues that the two-part-nature of the Bible generates. Cf. *Biblical Theology Bulletin*; Overtures to Biblical Theology (Minneapolis: Fortress, 1977-); *Horizons in Biblical Theology* (Pittsburgh: Pittsburgh Theological Seminary, 1979-); Biblical Encounters (Nashville: Abingdon, 1981-); *Jahrbuch für biblische Theologie*, ed. Ingo Baldermann et al. (Neukirchen-Vluyn: Neukirchener, 1986-); New Studies in Biblical Theology, ed. D.A. Carson (Downers Grove: InterVarsity, 1995-); The Two Horizons New Testament Commentary, ed. Joel B Green and Max Turner (Grand Rapids: Eerdmans, 2005-). Cf. Scobie, *The Ways of Our God*, 42-45.

[6] John J. Collins, *Encounters with Biblical Theology* (Minneapolis: Fortress, 2005), 11-44; John Barton, "Biblical Theology: An Old Testament Perspective," in *The Nature of New Testament Theology: Essays in Honour of Robert Morgan*, ed. Christopher Rowland and Christopher Tuckett (Oxford: Blackwell, 2006), 18-30. Therefore, they disregard the sharp disjunction between the "what it meant" and the peripheral "what it means" proposed by Krister Stendahl, "Biblical Theology, Contemporary," *IDB* 1:418-32. For more scholars who stress the differences in terms of a balanced tension or unity between the two Testaments, see David L. Baker, *Two Testaments, One Bible: The Theological Relationship between the Old and New Testaments* (Downers Grove: InterVarsity, 2010); K. Koch, "Two Testaments—One Bible: New Trends in Biblical Theology," *BTF* 28 (1996): 38-58; Steve Motyer, "Two Testaments, One Biblical Theology," in *Between Two Horizons: Spanning New Testament Studies and Systematic Theology*, ed. Joel B. Green and Max Turner (Grand Rapids: Eerdmans, 2000), 143-64; Bernd Janowski, "The One God of the Two Testaments: Basic Questions of a Biblical Theology," *ThTo* 57 (2000): 297-324; idem, "Biblical Theology," in *The Oxford Handbook of Biblical Studies*, ed. J.W. Rogerson and Judith M. Lieu (Oxford:

Introduction

In this context, various attempts have been undertaken along this line. For the sake of space, only two of more popular approaches in this rubric of movement can be mentioned as samplings: canonical and tradition-historical approaches.

Canonical Approach

On the one hand, the enterprise of "biblical theology" has received more criticism than welcome in certain studies. For instance, the canonical approach, one of the more prominent approaches to "biblical theology" is most popularly advocated by B.S. Childs, who points to the importance of the present form of the biblical canon as it was received and interpreted within the early church.[7] His assumption and methodology, however, have been frequently criticized for the ambiguity of his hermeneutical program and general ignorance of the original historical contexts.[8] Furthermore, the paucity of this type of study in New Testament scholarship obliquely bears testimony to the exegetical obstructions

---

OUP, 2006), 716-31; Mead, *Biblical Theology*, 8-10; Daniel J. Trier, "Biblical Theology and/or Theological Interpretation of Scripture?" *SJT* 61 (2008): 16-31.

[7] Childs, *Biblical Theology in Crisis*; idem, *Introduction to the Old Testament as Scripture* (Philadelphia: Fortress, 1979), idem, *Old Testament Theology in a Canonical Context* (Minneapolis: Fortress, 1985); idem, *Biblical Theology of the Old and New Testaments: Theological Reflection on the Christian Bible* (Minneapolis: Fortress, 1993); idem, *The Struggle to Understand Isaiah as Christian Scripture* (Grand Rapids: Eerdmans, 2004); idem, *The Church's Guide for Reading Paul: The Canonical Shaping of the Pauline Corpus* (Grand Rapids: Eerdmans, 2008). Another well-known proponent of canonical criticism is found in: James A. Sanders, *Canon and Community: A Guide to Canonical Criticism* (Philadelphia: Fortress, 1984); idem, *From Sacred Story to Sacred Text: Canon as Paradigm* (Philadelphia: Fortress, 1987); idem, *Torah and Canon* (Eugene: Cascade, 2005). For those who positively welcome Childs' approach, see Mark G. Brett, *Biblical Criticism in Crisis?: The Impact of the Canonical Approach on Old Testament Studies* (Cambridge: CUP, 1991); Paul R. Noble, *The Canonical Approach: A Critical Reconstruction of the Hermeneutics of Brevard S. Childs* (Leiden: Brill, 1995); Christopher R. Seitz, *The Character of Christian Scripture: The Significance of a Two-Testament Bible* (Grand Rapids: Baker, 2011), 27-91.

[8] For critical responses to Child's approach, see James Barr, *Holy Scripture: Canon, Authority, Criticism* (Philadelphia: Westminster, 1983), 49-104; Dale A. Brueggemann, "Brevard Childs' Canon Criticism: An Example of Post-Critical Naiveté," *JETS* 32 (1989): 311-26; John Barton, *Reading the Old Testament: Method in Biblical Study* (Louisville: Westminster John Knox, 1996), 77-103; Collins, *Encounters with Biblical Theology*, 15-16; H. Frankemölle, "'Biblische' Theologie: Semantisch-historische Anmerkungen und Thesen," in *Studien zum jüdischen Kontext neutestamentlicher Theologien* (Stuttgart: Katholisches Bibelwerk, 2005), 1-22. Also, Brueggemann designates Childs' canonical approach as pre-critical and massively reductionistic. Walter Brueggemann, *Theology of the Old Testament: Testimony, Dispute, Advocacy* (Minneapolis: Fortress, 2005), 91-93. Barr evaluates Childs' terminology, "canonical intention," as "mystical phrase." James Barr, "Childs' Introduction to the Old Testament as Scripture," *JSOT* 16 (1980): 13.

intrinsic to pursuing such a venture.⁹ Finally, the advocates of such an attempt often place emphasis on the principal hermeneutical role of the receptive community. This reader-oriented tendency renders the canonical approach less attractive to the practitioners of the traditional historical-grammatical approach.¹⁰

Tradition-Historical Approach
This is a more positively received attempt than canonical criticism along the line of biblical theology, at least for the exegetes standing in the historical-critical tradition, is the tradition-historical approach, which seeks to find an overarching motif that weaves together the texts of the Old and New Testaments.¹¹ Hartmut Gese and Peter Stuhlmacher are usually associated with this systematic reading of the two Testaments through "Zion," or "Torah" leitmotifs.¹² Gese argues, for instance, that successive Hebrew and Christian communities re-worked the previous generation's doctrine of the law in the face of the present life setting. Thus, he finds several phases of the Hebrew belief in the law differently understood throughout the history of Israel. This reinterpreted law is the final product for the community of the time, but is fully comprehensible in light of the ultimately re-read law, the New Testament.¹³ Some students of Gese and Stuhlma-

---

⁹ For example, Reumann notes the dearth of such an attempt by New Testament exegetes, see John H.P. Reumann, "Profiles, Problems, and Possibilities in Biblical Theology Today Part I," *KD* 44 (1998): 61-85; idem, "Profiles, Problems, and Possibilities in Biblical Theology Today Part II: New Testament," *KD* 44 (1998): 145-69. His observation and the survey of James Barr (*The Concept of Biblical Theology: An Old Testament Perspective* [Minneapolis: Fortress, 1999]) indicate the difficulty of establishing a framework of biblical theology from a viewpoint of New Testament studies.

¹⁰ For examples of reader-oriented nature of this approach, see Walter Brueggemann, "Biblical Theology Appropriately Postmodern," in *Jews, Christians, and the Theology of the Hebrew Scriptures*, ed. Alice Ogden Bellis and Joel S. Kaminsky (Atlanta: Society of Biblical Literature, 2000), 97-108; idem, *Theology of the Old Testament*; Christine Helmer and Christof Landmesser, eds, *One Scripture or Many?: Canon from Biblical, Theological and Philosophical Perspectives* (Oxford: OUP, 2005). The essays in the latter anthology amply demonstrate that various Christian and Jewish traditions have interpreted their canons in different terms. However, an important hermeneutical question is neglected in their discussions, i.e., whether or how the different interpretations of the various traditions and times exegetically and logically cohere with the meanings inherent in the texts discussed in their studies.

¹¹ Scobie, *The Ways of Our God*, 42-43.

¹² Hartmut Gese, *Vom Sinai zum Zion* (Munich: Kaiser, 1974); idem, "The Law," in *Essays on Biblical Theology*, trans. Keith Crim (Minneapolis: Augsburg, 1981), 60-92; Peter Stuhlmacher, "Das Gesetz als Thema biblischer Theologie," *ZTK* 75 (1978): 251-80. Stuhlmacher's ground for the continuous unity of the Christian Bible is due to the historical fact that the early church closed the both Testaments at the same time. Idem, *Biblische Theologie des Neuen Testaments* (Göttingen: Vandenhoeck & Ruprecht, 2005), 1:5.

¹³ Hartmut Gese, *Essays on Biblical Theology*, trans. Keith Crim (Minneapolis: Augsburg, 1981), 15-25. However, the program of Gese has been criticized for some rea-

cher and other scholars have taken up this program, and put on a new dress, the "exile-and-restoration" theme.[14] Of course, Gese and Stuhlmacher, on the one hand, and the proponents of the "exile-and-restoration" theme, on the other, do not overlap exactly in their theological presuppositions and exegetical conclusions, but they do share much in common as far as their methodological presupposition is concerned. That is, a unifying theme visibly runs through the Old and New Testaments and exegetes can unpack it without inflicting violence to the texts.

Despite the considerable degree of enthusiasm with which a number of biblical students received these types of studies, these studies seem to possess both strengths and weaknesses.[15] One of the positive contributions would be their recognition of the presence of a unifying theme woven together in the two Testaments. However, several negative upshots are inherent in this history-of-traditions approach. First, the theme of exile-restoration is surprisingly sparse in a great number of the books in the scripture. Second, it does not seem to appropriately take into account the scope of the divine redemptive plan which

---

sons, one of which is his hypothetical reconstruction of historical settings. Gerhard F. Hasel, "Biblical Theology: Then, Now, and Tomorrow," *HBT* 4 (1982): 66-67; John Haralson Hayes and Frederick C. Prussner, *Old Testament Theology: Its History and Development* (Atlanta: John Knox, 1985), 244, 262; Henning Graf Reventlow, *Problems of Old Testament Theology in the Twentieth Century* (Philadelphia: Fortress, 1985), 150-54.

[14] James M. Scott, ed., *Exile: Old Testament, Jewish, and Christian Conceptions*, (Leiden: Brill, 1997); idem, ed., *Restoration: Old Testament, Jewish, and Christian Perspectives* (Leiden: Brill, 2001); idem, "Jesus' Vision for the Restoration of Israel as the Basis for a Biblical Theology of the New Testament," in *Biblical Theology: Retrospect and Prospect*, ed. Scott J. Hafemann (Downers Grove: InterVarsity, 2002), 129-43; idem, *On Earth as in Heaven: The Restoration of Sacred Time and Sacred Space in the Book of Jubilees* (Leiden: Brill, 2005), Scott Hafemann, "Paul and the Exile of Israel in Galatians 3-4," in *Exile: Old Testament, Jewish, and Christian Conceptions*, ed. James Scott (Leiden: Brill, 1997), 329-71; idem, "Paul's Argument from the Old Testament and Christology in 2 Cor 1-9: The Salvation-History/Restoration Structure of Paul's Apologetic," in *Corinthian Correspondence*, ed. Reimund Bieringer (Louvain: Leuven University Press, 1996), 277-303. For a helpful survey of the topic, see Nicholas Perrin, "Exile," in *The World of the New Testament: Cultural, Social, and Historical Contexts*, ed. Joel B. Green and Lee Martin McDonald (Grand Rapids: Baker, 2013), 25-37.

[15] This exile and restoration theme has been also implemented in John with particular attention to the allusions to the Exodus events in John 6. Diana M. Swancutt, "Hungers Assuaged by the Bread from Heaven: 'Eating Jesus' as Isaian Call to Belief, the Confluence of Isaiah 55 and Psalm 78 (77) in John 6:22-71," in *Early Christian Interpretation of the Scriptures of Israel: Investigations and Proposals*, ed. Craig A. Evans and James A. Sanders (Sheffield: Sheffield, 1997), 218-51; Andrew C. Brunson, *Psalm 118 in the Gospel of John: An Intertextual Study on the New Exodus Pattern in the Theology of John* (Tübingen: Siebeck, 2003), 153-79; John Dennis, "The Presence and Function of Second Exodus-Restoration Imagery in John 6," *SNTSU* 30 (2005): 105-21.

covers the whole world, not the nation of Israel. Third, a great portion of the scripture emphasizes personal piety upon which the eternal security of souls hinges.[16] Finally and most directly contingent upon the thesis of this book, it undercuts or misrepresents the insurmountable centrality of God.[17] In other words, they lose sight of the principal thrust of the Christian Bible. That is, the main agent of salvation history is differently put forth in the two Testaments. This peculiarity is, however, seldom or inadequately addressed in both canonical and tradition-historical approaches.[18] What is fundamentally lacking in their studies is an aggressive engagement with the fact that the first Testament is deeply steeped in a scrupulous promotion of monotheism *vis-à-vis* Yahweh worship, whereas the second Testament is ditheistically oriented with a disproportional emphasis on the second person of the God-head, Jesus Christ. The statement of Seitz is pertinent on this perspective:

> The Bible is not one continuous tradition history, like a novel with a beginning, a middle and an end. Something stops, and a history of effects is set in motion that testifies to the form of the original canon and the differentiation of traditions, of various sorts, form it. . . . The problem for the early church was not what to do with the OT. Rather, in the light of Scripture whose authority and privileged status were everywhere acknowledged, what was one to make of a crucified messiah and a parting of the ways?[19]

---

[16] For the second and third points, see Mark A. Seifrid, "The 'New Perspective on Paul and Its Problems," *Them* 25, no. 2 (February 2000): 8-12. Seifrid's critiques are leveled against N.T. Wright, Frank Thielman, and James Scott, but the caveats are relevant to the tradtion-historical approach as well (N.T. Wright, *The New Testament and the People of God* [Minneapolis: Fortress, 1992], 268-79; Frank Thielman, *Paul and the Law: A Contextual Approach* [Downers Grove: InterVarsity, 1994], 48-68; James Scott, "Restoration of Israel," *DPHL*, 796-805). Seitz also recognizes irreconcilable incongruities between the two Testaments and the critical exegetical misrepresentation on the part of the tradition-historical approach. Christopher R. Seitz, "Two Testaments and the Failure of One Tradition History," in *Biblical Theology: Retrospect and Prospect*, ed. Scott J. Hafemann (Downers Grove: InterVarsity, 2002), 195-211. Also, a similar caution is expressed in G. Barth, "Biblische Theologie: Versuch einer vorläufigen Bilanz," *EvT* 58 (1998): 384-99.

[17] Cf. A. Andrew Das and Frand J. Matera, eds., *The Forgotten God: Perspectives in Biblical Theology, Essays in Honor of Paul J. Achtemeier on the Occasion of His Seventy-Fifth Birthday* (Louisville: Westminster/John Knox, 2002), 1.

[18] Seifrid also points out the grave oversight of the New Perspective. That is, it misses the Christo-centric emphasis of the New Testament writings. Mark A. Seifrid, "Paul's Use of Habakkuk 2:4 in Romans 1:17: Reflections on Israel's Exile in Romans," in *History and Exegesis: New Testament Essays in Honor of Dr. E. Earle Ellis for His 80th Birthday*, ed. Sang-Won Son (London: T & T Clark, 2006), 133-49.

[19] Seitz, "Two Testaments and the Failure of One Tradition History," 205-10. Also, Wilckens recognizes that the unity of the resurrected Jesus with God is what legitimized the Christian reading of the Old Testament, not the historical reading of the Scripture. Urlich Wilckens, "Monotheismus und Christologie," in *Der Sohn Gottes und seine Gemeinde: Studien zur Theologie der Johanneischen Schriften* (Göttingen:

These two varying portraits of the two God-heads constitute one of the most vexing questions posed upon biblical theologians, and they call for serious consideration. One of the more oversimplistic responses to this question has been undertaken by a group of scholars who played down the testimonies of the Old Testament while stressing the uniquely elevated place of New Testament Christology.[20] The history of the biblical theology movement, however, generally disagrees with the sharp wedge that this movement has driven between the two Testaments, especially their presentation of the God-head.[21]

Vandenhoeck & Ruprecht, 2003), 131-34. For a survey on the Johannine redefinition of the Jewish traditional monotheism in the person of Jesus Christ, see Richard Bauckham, "Monotheism and Christology in the Gospel of John," in *The Testimony of the Beloved Disciple: Narrative, History, and Theology in the Gospel of John* (Grand Rapids: Baker, 2007), 239-52. For a helpful survey of the Jewish monotheism, see Nathan McDonald, "Monotheism," in *The World of the New Testament: Cultural, Social, and Historical Contexts*, ed. Joel B. Green and Lee Martin McDonald (Grand Rapids: Baker, 2013), 77-84.

[20] Marcion, Rudolf Bultmann, and Friedrich Baumgärtel can be classified under this category. Earl E. Ellis, "Foreword," in *Typos: The Typological Interpretation of the Old Testament in the New*, Leon Goppelt, trans. David H. Madvig (Grand Rapids: Eerdmans, 1982), xi-xiv; Baker, *Two Testaments, One Bible*, 36, 64-66, 79-83. Not entirely on the same track, Dunn speaks of a "parting of the ways" in which, the Johannine Christianity took a significant departure from its strict Jewish monotheistic conceptual bounds. James D.G. Dunn, "Let John Be John: A Gospel for Its Time," in *The Gospel and the Gospels*, ed. Peter Stuhlmacher (Grand Rapids: Eerdmans, 1991), 304, 315-19; idem, *The Partings of the Ways: Between Christianity and Judaism and Their Significance for the Character of Christianity* (London: SCM, 2006), 298-30.

[21] Three other significant attempts along the lines of "biblical theology movement" can be mentioned here. First, Francis Watson notes the artificial gap present between Old Testament, New Testament, and systematic theological studies. These "three autonomous interpretive communities" are "ideologically motivated" and their academic products "systematically distort their subject matter," which is the God of the gospel revealed in Jesus Christ as witnessed to by the Christian canonical Scriptures. Francis Watson, *Text and Truth: Redefining Biblical Theology* (Grand Rapids: Eerdmans, 1997), 6-7. Also, refer to his others propositions, idem, *Text, Church, and World: Biblical Interpretation in Theological Perspective* (Grand Rapids: Eerdmans, 1994); idem, "Authors, Readers, Hermeneutics," in *Reading Scripture with the Church: Toward a Hermeneutic for Theological Interpretation*, ed. A.K.M. Adam et al (Grand Rapids: Baker, 2006), 95-118; idem, "Hermeneutics and the Doctrine of Scripture: Why They Need Each Other," *IJST* 12 (2010): 118-43. Watson's studies are full of sound judgments and a great number of scholars would heartily share his concerns. However, how practically his points can be applied in theological discussions seems uncertain. See Christopher R. Seitz, "Christological Interpretation of Texts and Trinitarian Claims to Truth: An Engagement with Francis Watson's Text and Truth," *SJT* 52 (1999): 209-26. Another important stream of thought in the line of "biblical theology" is the salvation historical perspective, most popularly associated with Oscar Cullmann. Once widely criticized, this approach has been revived recently. Robert W. Yarbrough, *The Salvation-Historical Fallacy?: Reassessing the History of New Testament Theology* (Leiden: Deo, 2004); Roy E. Ciampa, "The History of Redemption,"

Christology within Jewish Conceptual Bounds

A more considerate attempt to account for this disparity has traced back the origin of Christology from the conceptual strands attested in the Old Testament and the subsequent Jewish traditions.[22] This approach can be further divided into two sub-groups. The first sub-group, more popularly represented by Richard Bauckham, William Horbury, and others, maintains that New Testament Christology can be understood within the bounds of Jewish monotheism. Although in much different measure, they both postulate that Christian Christology is somewhat an organic outgrowth from perculiar Jewish monotheism.[23] However, as Hurtado has pointed out, "the binitarian" theology of early Christians differs significantly from the conventional Jewish monotheism. Accordingly, the Jesus event (not the Jewish heritage of nascent Christianity) must have been the principal impetus for the early Christian worship of the second God-head.[24]

---

in *Central Themes in Biblical Theology: Mapping Unity in Diversity*, ed. Scott J. Hafemann and Paul R. House (Downers Grove: InterVarsity, 2007), 254-308; Jörg Frey, Stefan Krauter, and Hermann Lichtenberger, eds., *Heil und Geschichte: Die Geschichtsbezogenheit Des Heils* (Tübingen: Mohr Siebeck, 2009). Finally, Hans Hübner argues that the Old Testament quotations in the New must be the starting-point and focus of "biblical theology." Hans Hübner, *Biblische Theologie des Neuen Testaments*, 3 vols. (Göttingen: Vandenhoeck & Ruprecht, 1990-95). Especially important is the first volume, "prolegomena," which deals with the methodology and rationale for his thesis. Cf. Hans Hübner and Antje and Michael Labehn, *Vetus Testamentum in Novo*, 2 vols. (Göttingen: Vandenhoeck & Ruprecht, 1997-2002).

[22] See appendix 2 (*"Religionsgeschichte* and the Fourth Gospel") for the legitimacy of inquiry into the provenance of Christian Christology (esp. that of Johannine) from the Jewish background instead of its Hellenistic counterpart.

[23] J.C.O'Neill, "The Trinity and the Incarnation as Jewish Doctrines," in *Who did Jesus Think He Was?* (Leiden: Brill, 1995), 94-114; Loren T. Stuckenbruck, *Angel Veneration and Christology: A Study in Early Judaism and in the Christology of the Apocalypse of John* (Tübingen: Mohr Siebeck, 1995); Charles A. Gieschen, *Angelomorphic Christology: Antecedents and Early Evidence* (Leiden: Brill, 1998); William Horbury, *Jewish Messianism and the Cult of Christ* (London: SCM, 1998); idem, *Messianism among Jews and Christians: Twelve Biblical and Historical Studies* (London: T & T Clark, 2003); John Lierman, *The New Testament Moses: Christian Perceptions of Moses and Israel in the Setting of Jewish Religion* (Tübingen: Mohr Siebeck, 2004), 258-88; Loren T. Stuckenbruck and Wendy E.S. North, eds., *Early Jewish and Christian Monotheism* (London: T & T Clark, 2004); Richard Bauckham, *God Crucified: Monotheism and Christology in the New Testament* (Grand Rapids: Eerdmans, 1998); idem, *Jesus and the God of Israel: God Crucified and Other Studies on the New Testament's Christology of Divine Identity* (Grand Rapids: Eerdmans, 2008); Timo Eskola, *Messiah and the Throne: Jewish Merkabah Mysticism and Early Christian Exaltation Discourse* (Tübingen: Mohr Siebeck, 2001); James F. McGrath, *The Only True God: Early Christian Monotheism in Its Jewish Context* (Urbana: University of Illinois Press, 2009).

[24] Larry W. Hurtado, *One God, One Lord: Early Christian Devotion and Ancient Jewish Monotheism* (London: T & T Clark, 1998); idem, *Lord Jesus Christ: Devotion to Jesus in Earliest Christianity* (Grand Rapids: Eerdmans, 2003); idem, *How on Earth Did*

The other group has explored certain Jewish concepts (such as Son of Man, wisdom, or even angels[25]) and heroic protagonists, such as Moses, Elijah, or David, in an attempt to ascertain if they were seen as dormant messianic icons which were later translated into Christian Christology.[26] This type of approach to New Testament Christology has found its way into the study of John's Gospel, as well as into studies of other parts of the New Testament corpus. The present study aims primarily at assessing the value of the latter approach for understanding of the Gospel of John and its Christology in particular, by means of evaluating the Johannine texts that allegedly contain the traces of thought reflecting a Christology of Jewish heroes in view of the pertinent intertestamental Jewish writings that point to a *redivivus* eschatology.

Centrality of Christology in the Fourth Gospel

A serious student of the Fourth Gospel is immediately confronted with widely divided scholarly opinions on various issues surrounding John.[27] There is,

---

Jesus Become a God?: Historical Questions about Earliest Devotion to Jesus (Grand Rapids: Eerdmans, 2005), 111-204.

[25] Recently, Stuckenbruck and others have proposed the angelomorphic messianic tie between early Judaism and early Christianity. J. Alexander Cunningham, "Christology and the Angel of the Lord," *JRR* 6 (1997): 3-15; Darrell D. Hannah, *Michael and Christ: Michael Traditions and Angel Christology in Early Christianity* (Tübingen: Mohr Siebeck, 1999); Gary Simmers, "Who is 'The Angel of the Lord?'" *FM* 17 (2000): 3-16; Jonathan Knight, "The Origin and Significance of the Angelomorphic Christology in the *Ascension of Isaiah*," *JTS* 63 (2012): 66-105; Phillip Muñoa, "Raphael, Azariah and Jesus of Nazareth: Tobit's Significance for Early Christology," *JSP* 22 (2012): 3-39. A good number of scholars, however, are hesitant to accept the proposition. See James D.G. Dunn, *Christology in the Making: A New Testament Inquiry into the Origins of the Doctrine of the Incarnation* (Grand Rapids: Eerdmans, 1989), 149-59; Aquila H.I. Lee, *From Messiah to Preexistent Son: Jesus' Self-Consciousness and Early Christian Exegesis of Messianic Psalms* (Tübingen: Mohr Siebeck, 2005), 19-21.

[26] One example is Andrew Chester, *Messiah and Exaltation: Jewish Messianic and Visionary Traditions and New Testament Christology* (Tübingen: Mohr Siebeck, 2007). For a detailed review of various approaches to Jewish monotheism and Christian Christology, see McGrath, *The Only True God*, 1-22.

[27] Convenient and helpful surveys of the recent developments on various issues in the Johannine scholarship abound. The following list provides in an alphabetical order of the last names of the authors on the topic: Paul N. Anderson, "Beyond the Shade of the Oak Tree: The Recent Growth of Johannine Studies," *ExpTim* 119 (2008): 365-73; Roland Bergmeier, "Fragen zur Interpretation der johanneischen Schriften: Homogenität und Widersprüche," *TZ* 60 (2004): 107-30; Yves-Marie Blanchard, "Les écrits johanniques: Une communauté témoigne de sa foi," *EspVie* 116 (2006): 10-15; 154 (2006): 11-16; 155 (2006): 14-21; James H. Charlesworth, "From Old to New: Paradigm Shifts concerning Judaism, the Gospel of John, Jesus, and the Advent of 'Christianity,'" in *Jesus Research: An International Perspective, The First Princeton-Prague Symposium on Jesus Research, Prague 2005*, ed. James H. Charlesworth

and Petr Pokorný (Grand Rapids: Eerdmans, 2009), 56-72; Jörg Frey, "Grundfragen der Johannesinterpretation im Spektrum neuerer Gesamtdarstellungen," *TLZ* 133 (2008): 743-60; Konrad Haldimann and Hans Weder, "Aus der Literatur zum Johannesevangelium 1985-1994, Erster Teil, I: Historische Situierung und diachrone Analysen," *TRu* 67 (2002): 328-48; idem, "Aus der Literatur zum Johannesevangelium 1985-1994, Erster Teil, II: Historische Situierung und diachrone Analysen," *TRu* 67 (2002): 425-56; idem, "Aus der Literatur zum Johannesevangelium 1985-1994, Zweiter Teil: Synchrone Analysen," *TRu* 69 (2004): 75-115; idem, "Aus der Literatur zum Johannesevangelium 1985–1994, Dritter Teil: Theologische Akzentuierungen (I)," *TRu* 71 (2006): 91–113; Robert Kysar, *Voyages with John: Charting the Fourth Gospel* (Waco: Baylor University Press, 2006), 43-146; Francis J. Moloney, "Where Does One Look?: Reflections on Some Recent Johannine Scholarship," *Anton* 62 (2000): 223-51; idem, "Recent Johannine Studies, Part One: Commentaries" *ExpTim* 123 (2012): 313-22; idem, "Recent Johannine Studies, Part Two: Monographs," *ExpTim* 123 (2012): 417-28; Michèle Morgen, "Bulletin d'exégèse du Nouveau Testament: La littérature johannique," *RSR* 84 (1996): 277-303; idem, "Bulletin johannique," *RSR* 89 (2001): 561-91, idem, "Bulletin johannique," *RSR* 95 (2007): 281-310; idem, "Les écrits johanniques," *RSR* 93 (2005): 291-324; idem, "Bulletin johannique," *RSR* 97 (2009): 605-32; idem, "Bulletin johannique," *RSR* 100 (2012): 127-59; Helge Kjær Nielsen, "Johannine Research," in *New Readings in John: Literary and Theological Perspectives Essays from the Scandinavian Conference on the Fourth Gospel in Århus 1997*, ed. Johannes Nissen and Sigfred Pedersen (Sheffield: Sheffield, 1999), 11-30; Silke Petersen, "Das andere Evangelium: Ein erster Wegweiser durch die Johannesforschung," *ZNT* 12 (2009): 2-11; Andrianjatovo Rakotoharintsifa, "Chronique johannique," *ÉTR* 75 (2000): 81-102; idem, "Chronique johannique II," *ÉTR* 78 (2003): 79-95; Walter Schmithals, *Johannesevangelium und Johannesbriefe: Forschungsgeschichte und Analyse* (Berlin: de Gruyter, 1992), 3-214; Udo Schnelle, "Perspektiven der Johannesexegese," *SNTSU* 15 (1990): 59-72; idem, "Ein neuer Blick: Tendenzen der gegenwärtigen Johannesforschung," *BTZ* 16 (1999): 29-40; idem, *Einleitung in das Neue Testament* (Göttingen: Vandenhoeck & Ruprecht, 2002), 479-555; idem, "Aus der Literatur zum Johannesevangeium 1994-2010. Erster Teil: Die Kommentare als Seismographen der Forschung," *TRu* 75 (2010): 265-303; Klaus Scholtissek, "Johannine Studies: A Survey of Recent Research with Special Regard to German Contributions," *CurBS* 6 (1998): 227-59; idem, "Johannes auslegen I: Forschungsgeschichtliche und methodische Reflexionen," *SNTSU* 24 (1999): 35-84; idem, "Neue Wege in der Johannesauslegung: Ein Forschungsbericht I," *ThGl* 89 (1999): 263-95; idem, "Johannes auslegen II: Methodische, hermeneutische und einleitungswissenschaftliche Reflexionen," *SNTSU* 25 (2000): 98-140; idem, "Johannine Studies: A Survey of Recent Research with Special Regard to German Contributions II," *CurBS* 9 (2001): 277-305; idem, "Neue Wege in der Johannesauslegung: Ein Forschungsbericht II," *ThGl* 91 (2001): 109-33; idem, "Johannes auslegen III: Ein Forschungsbericht," *SNTSU* 27 (2002): 117-53; idem, "The Johannine Gospel in Recent Research," in *The Face of New Testament Studies: A Survey of Recent Research*, ed. Scot McKnight and Grant R. Osborne (Grand Rapids: Baker, 2004), 444-72; idem, "Johannes auslegen IV: Ein Forschungsbericht," *SNTSU* 29 (2004): 67-118; Giuseppe Seglla, "L'orizzonte attuale della teologia giovannea," *StudPat* 54 (2007): 593-608; Gerard S. Sloyan, *What Are They Saying about John?: Johannine Scholarship 1965-2005* (New York: Paulist, 2006); Tom Thatcher, "The New Current through John: The Old 'New Look' and the New Critical Orthodoxy," in *New Cuurents through John: A Global Perspective*, eds. Francisco Lozada, Jr. and

however, one aspect that seems to enjoy unanimity, that is, that Christology stands at the heart of the Gospel.[28] It may not be a coincidence that one of the most explicit Christological statements in the entire New Testament corpus is placed literally at the center of the Fourth Gospel: "I and the Father are one" (John 10:30).[29] In this respect, one can come to good terms with Eduard Schweizer's observation that "everything in John is radically concentrated on Jesus."[30] Similarly, Otto Schwankl also notes that all other aspects of John's theological concerns are subsumed under the rubric of Christology:

> An important characteristic of the Gospel of John is the enormous concentration on Christology. In contrast, other subjects of theology, for instance, ecclesiology and ethics, are withdrawn. Those subjects are subsumed under or marginalized by Christology.[31]

He further goes on to spell out the centrality of Jesus in John in seven points: the Gospel's concentration on Jesus, concentration on his words, Christological

---

Tom Thatcher (Atlanta: Society of Biblcial Literature, 2006), 1-26; idem, ed., *What We Have Heard from the Beginning: The Past, Present, and Future of Johannine Studies* (Waco: Baylor University Press, 2007); Franz G. Untergaßmair, "Das Johannesevangelium: Ein Bericht über neuere Literatur aus der Johannesforschung," *TRev* 90 (1994): 91-108; Jean Zumstein, "Interpréter le quatrième évangile aujourd'hui: Questions de méthode," *RHPR* 92 (2012): 241-58.

[28] For surveys of recent approaches to the Johannine Christology, see Paul N. Anderson, *The Christology of the Fourth Gospel: Its Unity and Disunity in the Light of John 6* (Tübingen: Mohr Siebeck, 1996), 1-32; James F. McGrath, *John's Apologetic Christology: Legitimation and Development in Johannine Christology* (Cambridge: CUP, 2001), 3-47.

[29] Hans Weder, "Die Menschwerdung Gottes: Überlegungen zur Auslegungsproblematik des Johannesevangeliums am Beispiel von Joh 6," in *Einblicke ins Evangelium: Exegetische Beiträge zur neutestamentlichen Hermeneutik* (Göttingen: Vandenhoeck & Ruprecht, 1992), 391; Udo Schnelle, *Theologie des Neuen Testaments* (Göttingen: Vandenhoeck & Ruprecht, 2007), 629. This statement recurs in other places of the Fourth Gospels as well: John 17:11, 22. Richard Bauckham, "Biblical Theology and the Problems of Monotheism," in *Jesus and the God of Israel: God Crucified and Other Studies on the New Testament's Christology of Divine Identity* (Grand Rapids: Eerdmans, 2008), 104-06.

[30] Eduard Schweizer, *Jesus Christus: Im vielfältigen Zeugnis des Neuen Testaments* (Gütersloh: Gütersloher, 1976), 154.

[31] Otto Schwankl, "Aspekte der johanneischen Christologie," in *Theology and Christology in the Fourth Gospel: Essays by the Members of the SNTS Johannine Writings Seminar*, ed. Gilbert van Belle, Jan G. van der Watt, and P.J. Maritz (Leuven: Peeters, 2005), 349. Also, see C.K. Barrett, "Christocentric or Theocentric?: Observations on the Theological Method of the Fourth Gospel," in *Essays on John* (Philadelphia: Westminster, 1982), 1-18; Marinus de Jonge, "Christology, Controversy and Community in the Gospel of John," in *Christology, Controversy and Community: New Testament Essays in Honor of David R. Catchpole*, ed. David G. Horrell and Christopher M. Tuckett (Leiden: Brill, 2000), 209; Raymond E. Brown, *An Introduction to the Gospel of John*, ed. Francis J. Moloney (New York: Doubleday, 2003), 249.

self-understanding of Jesus, Christological confessions, Christological titles, missionary Christology, and the I-am sayings.[32]

Even without entering into a meticulous discussion on such notions, however, this centrality of Christology simply makes a compelling case at least on two grounds. First, structurally speaking, the introductory prologue (1:1-18) and the concluding purpose statement (20:30-31) constitute an *inclusio* and stand out as pivotal points in John's overall narrative schemes.[33] The Johannine prolog elucidates in clear terms the pre-existence of Jesus and his participation in the creation of the universe with God the Father in terms of wisdom Christology. Labahn rightly observes that the Johannine prologue is programmatically placed at the beginning so as to unfold the unity of the Father and the Son for the rest of the Gospel.[34] The purpose statement placed at the end of the Fourth Gospel also points to the provenance of Jesus and his identity as the fulfillment of the old covenant:[35]

> But these are written so that you may come to believe that Jesus is the Messiah, the Son of God, and that through believing you may have life in his name." (John 20:31)

---

[32] Schwankl, "Aspekte der johanneischen Christologie," 348-61.

[33] Saeed Hamid-Khani, *Revelation and Concealment of Christ: A Theological Inquiry into the Elusive Language of the Fourth Gospel* (Tübingen: Mohr Siebeck, 2000), 151-53; C. Koch and K. Huber, "Konzentrisches Erzählkonzept im Johannesevangelium: Skizze eines Strukturierungsvorschlags," *ProtoBib* 12 (2003): 129-42. Becker posits that the Johannine prologue is a later interpolation by the final redactor because the incarnation theme is neither repeated nor explicated in the rest of the Gospel. Jürgen Becker, "Ich Bin die Auferstehung und das Leben: Eine Skizze der johanneischen Christologie," *TZ* 39 (1983): 138-51. See also Appendix 3: The Significance of the Old Testament for the Fourth Gospel. His judgment suffers from a serious exegetical oversight in view of John's overall attitude towards the Old Testament. The evangelist repeatedly manifests a keen interest in presenting Jesus' identity and action in commensurate terms with the word of God, i.e., the fulfillment of the scripture. For instance, the bread speech in chapter 6 is sensible only when Jesus is taken to be the realized Word of God in view of Peter's confession in v. 68 which concludes the pericope ("Lord, to whom shall we go? You have the words of eternal life").

[34] Michael Labahn, "Jesus und die Autorität der Schrift im Johannesevangelium: Überlegungen zu einem spannungsreichen Verhältnis," in *Israel und seine Heilstraditionen im Johannesevangelium: Festgabe für Johannes Beutler SJ zum 70. Geburtstag*, ed. Michael Labahn, Klaus Scholtissek, and Angelika Strotmann (Paderborn: Schöningh, 2004), 188; similarly, Robert H. Gundry, "How the Word in John's Prologue Pervades the Rest of the Fourth Gospel," in *The Old Is Better: New Testament Essays in Support of Traditional Interpretations* (Tübingen: Mohr Siebeck, 2005), 324-62.

[35] It seems that the fourth evangelist is not interested in the fulfillment of particular passages of the Old Testament. Rather, he portrays that the life of Jesus as a whole is the fulfillment of the entire scripture. Johannes Beutler, "Der Gebrauch von 'Schrift' im Johannesevangelium," in *Studien zu den johanneischen Schriften* (Stuttgart: Katholisches Bibelwerk, 1998), 297.

Along with Martha's confession in the middle (John 11:27), both sections speak of Christology in the highest terms possible in Jewish thought patterns, i.e., Jesus is portrayed as being equal to God (5:18; 10:30, 33).[36] Secondly, the content of the Fourth Gospel points to Jesus whose origin, divine and human nature, and works are constantly brought to the forefront throughout John.[37] This Christo-centric characteristics of the Fourth Gospel is in good accords with the rest of the New Testament writings. Frank Thielman judiciously sums up this perspective.

> For all the distinctiveness of its discrete textual witnesses, the New Testament is remarkably homogenous in its commitment to these basic themes. It offers a compelling vision of reality . . . and it invites those who read its various texts sympathetically to adopt its Christ-centered vision of the universe as their own.[38]

Similarly, Ferdinand Hahn states that the crucial point of reference for the entire New Testament traditions is the divine revelation in the person of Christ, from which all the questions concerning the New Testament derive:

---

[36] Klaus Scholtissek, "Neues Testament," in *Der Messias: Perspecktiven des Alten und Neuen Testaments*, ed. Hans-Joachim Fabry and Klaus Scholtissek (Würzburg: Echter, 2002), 88; idem, "'Ich und der Vater, wir sind eins' (Joh 10,30): Zum theologischen Potential und zur hermeneutischen Kompetenz der johanneischen Christologie," in *Theology and Christology in the Fourth Gospel: Essays by the Members of the SNTS Johannine Writings Seminar*, ed. Gilbert van Belle, Jan G. van der Watt, and P. Maritz (Leuven: Peeters, 2005), 333-39; Andrew T. Lincoln, *A Commentary on the Gospel according to St. John* (London: Continuum, 2005), 69. Nonetheless, this statement is not to underestimate the sense in which Jesus is also presented as subordinate to God in John as the missionary Christology most prominently indicates. Wilhelm Thüsing, "Die johanneische Theologie als Verkündigung der Grösse Gottes," *TTZ* 74 (1965): 321-31; C.K. Barrett, "'The Father is Greater Than I' (Jo 14, 28); Subordinationist Christology in the New Testament," in *Essays on John* (Philadelphia: Westminster, 1982), 19-36; Anderson, *The Christology of the Fourth Gospel*, 267; Christopher Cowan, "The Father and Son in the Fourth Gospel: Johannine Subordination Revisited," *JETS* 49 (2006): 115-35.

[37] For discussions on the crucial importance of Christology for New Testament theology, see Bo Reicke, "Unity and Diversity in New Testament Theology," in *Good New in History: Essays in Honor of Bo Reicke with a Contribution by Professor Reicke*, ed. E.L. Miller (Atlanta: Scholars, 1993), 177; Peter Stuhlmacher, *How to Do Biblical Theology* (Allison Park: Pickwick, 1995), 15-29, 87-88; Earl E. Ellis, "Jesus' Use of the Old Testament and the Genesis of New Testament Theology," in *Christ and the Future in New Testament History* (Leiden: Brill, 2000), 20-37; Morna Hooker, "The Nature of New Testament Theology," in *The Nature of New Testament Theology: Essays in Honour of Robert Morgan*, ed. Christopher Rowland and Christopher Tuckett (Oxford: Blackwell, 2006), 75-92; Richard Bauckham, "Historiographical Characteristics of the Gospel of John," in *The Testimony of the Beloved Disciple: Narrative, History, and Theology in the Gospel of John* (Grand Rapids: Baker, 2007), 93-112.

[38] Frank Thielman, *Theology of the New Testament: A Canonical and Synthetic Approach* (Grand Rapids: Zondervan, 2005), 725.

The crucial point of reference throughout the New Testament tradition is the revelation of God in the person of Jesus Christ. Jesus' preaching and ministry stand necessarily at the beginning of the early Christian theological history. But now many problems are connected with the Jesus tradition and its place within a New Testament theology.[39]

Recently, Dunn asserted that early Christianity was more God-oriented than Christ-oriented. However, the disproportional emphasis on the personhood of Christ and the way the New Testament describes the second God-head stand in stark difference from those of the Old Testament. It seems, therefore, justifiable to elevate the place of worship in Christ in modern Christianity.[40] In that sense, penetrating to the point is Martin Hengel's assessment of Wrede whose theological framework downplayed the messianism but rather overemphasized the formative history of the early Christian communities. Hengel points to four aspects in which Wrede's postulation is at fault: his denial of historicity of Peter's confession at Caesarea Philippi, his misinterpretation of the Passion narratives, the disciples' sudden change of faith in Jesus from unmessianic to heavily messianic, and the inadequate recognition of the Galilean-Jewish origin of Jesus and his first hearers and disciples.[41] In a similar vein, Ferdinand Hahn critiques the history-of-religions program of Heikki Räisänen for he ignores the theological unity of the New Testament in its emphasis on "theo-logy" and Christology and the early Christian approval of such a concept.[42]

The recent insights gained from the genre-critical analysis of the four Gospels also call for an urgent need for Gospel scholarship to refocus upon the main character (i.e., Jesus) rather than the developmental history of the communities which are allegedly responsible for the shaping of the present canonical Gospels:[43]

---

[39] Ferdinand Hahn, "Das Zeugnis des Neuen Testaments in seiner Vielfalt und Einheit: Zu den Grundproblemen einer neutestamentlichen Theologie," in *Grundsatzfragen, Jesusforschung, Evangelien*, vol. 1 of *Studien zum Neuen Testament*, ed. Jörg Frey and Juliane Schlegel (Tübingen: Mohr Siebeck, 2006), 168.

[40] Cf. James D.G. Dunn, *Did the First Christian Worship Jesus?: The New Testament Evidence* (Louisville: Westminster John Knox, 2010).

[41] Martin Hengel, "Jesus, der Messias Israels: Zum Streit über das 'messianische Sendungsbewußtsein' Jesu," in *Messiah and Christos: Studies in the Jewish Origins of Christianity, Presented to David Flusser on the Occasion of His Seventy-Fifth Birthday*, ed. Ithamar Gruenwald, Shaul Shaked, and Gedaliahu G. Stroumsa (Tübingen: Mohr Siebeck, 1992), 160.

[42] Ferdinad Hahn, "Eine religionswissenschaftliche Alternative zur neutestamentlichen Theologie?: Ein Gespräch mit Heikki Räisänen," in *Grundsatzfragen, Jesusforschung, Evangelien*, vol. 1 of *Studien zum Neuen Testament*, ed. Jörg Frey and Juliane Schlegel (Tübingen: Mohr Siebeck, 2006), 151-62, esp. 159-60 for the fundamental and integral place of Christology in early Christian theology.

[43] Robert Guelich, "The Gospel Genre," in *The Gospel and the Gospels*, ed. Peter Stuhlmacher (Grand Rapids: Eerdmans, 1991), 173-208; Mark W.G. Stibbe, *John as Storyteller: Narrative Criticism and the Fourth Gospel* (Cambridge: CUP, 1992), 30-49; Richard Bauckham, ed., *The Gospels for All Christians: Rethinking the Gospel*

None of the four Gospels was written only for one particular community; far less do they simply reproduce the views of the one individual community. They give primarily the views of their authors.[44]

This point does not rest on whether or not the canonical Gospels took on their literary form from a certain antecedent literary genre. Rather, the point is that the recent debates about the literary genre of the Gospels call attention to the centrality of the main character, Jesus.

Johannine Christology from the Vantage Point of the Jewish Context

If another consensus is to be designated, it would be the prominence of the Jewish religious/cultural milieu, with which a large number of Johannine exegetes associate the formation of the Fourth Gospel.[45] The foremost reason for such a judgment is due to the recent recognition of Gospel scholarship that the

---

Audiences (Grand Rapids: Eerdmans, 1998), esp., idem, "For Whom Were Gospels Written?" 9-48; idem, "The Beloved Disciple as Ideal Author," in *The Testimony of the Beloved Disciple: Narrative, History, and Theology in the Gospel of John* (Grand Rapids: Baker, 2007), 73-92; David B. Capes, "*Imitatio Christi* and the Gospel Genre," *BBR* 13 (2003): 1-19; Richard A. Burridge, *What Are the Gospels?: A Comparison with Graeco-Roman Biography* (Grand Rapids: Eerdmans, 2004); idem, "Gospels," in *The Oxford Handbook of Biblical Studies*, ed. J.W. Rogerson and Judith M. Lieu (Oxford: OUP, 2006), 432-44; William Horbury, "'Gospel' in Herodian Judea," in *The Written Gospel*, ed. Markus Bockmuehl and Donald A. Hagner (Cambridge: CUP, 2005), 7-30; Martin Ebner, "'Evangelium,'" in *Einleitung in das Neue Testament*, ed. Martin Ebner and Stefan Schreiber (Stuttgart: Kohlhammer, 2008), 112-24; Justin Marc Smith, "About Friends, by Friends, for Others: Author-Subject Relationships in Contemporary Greco-Roman Biographies," in *The Audience of the Gospels: The Origin and Function of the Gospels in Early Christianity*, ed. Edward W. Klink, III (London: T & T Clark, 2010), 49-67. Recently, Burridge has mounted probably the most informidable argument for the genre of the four gospels as ancient Greek bios. His argument lies in the four similarities present between the former literary genre and the gospels: opening features, the subject of bios, external features, and internal features. See esp. Burridge, *What Are the Gospels*, 105-23. For a recent survey of the research history, see Johannes Beutler, "Literarische Gattungen im Johannesevangelium: Ein Forschungsbericht 1919-1980," *ANRW* 2.25:2506-68; Robert H. Gundry, "The Symbiosis of Theology and Genre Criticism of the Canonical Gospels," in *The Old Is Better: New Testament Essays in Support of Traditional Interpretations* (Tübingen: Mohr Siebeck, 2005), 18-48; Judith Diehl, "What is a 'Gospel'?: Recent Studies in the Gospel Genre," *CBR* 9 (2011): 171-91.

[44] Martin Hengel, *The Four Gospels and the One Gospel of Jesus Christ: An Investigation of the Collection and Origin of the Canonical Gospels* (Harrisburg: Trinity, 2000), 106-15, esp. 106-07 for the quote.

[45] Thomas Söding, "'Was kann aus Nazareth schon Gutes kommen?' (Joh 1.46): Die Bedeutung des Judeseins Jesu im Johannesevangelium," *NTS* 46 (2000): 21-41. This judgment should be self-evident due to the plain fact that John speaks of Jesus' identity exclusively in Jewish terms such as "Christ" and "Messiah." However, the dissensions of some scholars on this point require further discussion. See Appendix 2: "*Religionsgeschichte* and the Fourth Gospel."

historical genesis of the Jesus tradition is deeply rooted in Jewish contexts:

> The picture of Jesus that has [recently] emerged is more finely nuanced, more obviously Jewish . . . we read and read again the old Gospel stories and try to come to grips with the life of this remarkable Galilean Jew.[46]

On a negative note, for example, it has become passé to posit the provenance of Johannine dualism exclusively in terms of Hellenism. Since the discovery of the Qumran documents, it has provided a fertile conceptual backdrop for such a distinct Johannine trait, and subsequent researches reveal pervasive dualistic symbols, language, and worldview present in Palestine through various intertestamental Jewish literatures including the Qumran documents during the New Testament era.[47]

Unless a sharp bifurcation is to be placed between the first and the third life-settings (that is, between Jesus and his disciples, on the one hand, and the theoretical writer/redactor responsible for the present form of John's Gospel, on the other), one cannot fail to notice the pervasive Jewish elements of the Jesus tradition, which characteristic also has been frequently criticized as lacking in the previous quests for the historical Jesus:

> The third failure of previous quests [the Old and New Quests] has been the mistake of looking for a *distinctive* Jesus, distinctive in the sense of a Jesus *different* from his

---

[46] Craig A. Evans, "Assessing Progress in the Third Quest of the Historical Jesus," *JSHJ* 4 (2006): 54.

[47] Jörg Frey, "Different Patterns of Dualistic Thought in the Qumran Library: Reflections on Their Background and History," in *Legal Texts and Legan Issues: Proceedings of the Second Meeting of the International Organization for Qumran Studies Cambridge 1995, Published In Honour of Joseph M. Baumgarten*, ed. Moshe Bernstein, Florentino García Martínez, and John Kampen (Leiden: Brill, 1997), 275-335; idem, "Recent Perspectives on Johannine Dualism," in *Text, Thought, and Practice in Qumran and Early Christianity: Proceedings oft he Ninth International Symposium of the Orion Center fort he Study of the Dead Sea Scrolls and Associated Literature, Jointly Sponsored by the Hebrew University Center for the Study of Christianity, 11-13 January, 2004*, ed. Ruth A. Clements & Daniel R. Schwartz (Leiden: Brill, 2009), 127-57; James H. Charlesworth, "A Study in Shared Symbolism and Language: The Qumran Community and the Johannine Community," in *The Scrolls and Christian Origins*, vol. 3 of *The Bible and the Dead Sea Scrolls: The Princeton Symposium on the Dead Sea Scrolls*, ed. James H. Charlesworth (Waco: Baylor University Press, 2006), 97-152; Géza G. Xeravits, ed., *Dualism in Qumran* (London: T & T Clark, 2010); Paul N. Anderson, "John and Qumran: Discovery and Interpretation over Sixty Years," in *John, Qumran, and the Dead Sea Scrolls: Sixty Years of Discovery and Debate*, ed. Mary L. Coloe and Tom Thatcher (Atlanta: Soceity of Biblical Literature, 2011), 15-19. *Contra*, Richard Bauckham, "The Qumran Community and the Gospel of John," in *The Testimony of the Beloved Disciple: Narrative, History, and Theology in the Gospel of John* (Grand Rapids: Baker, 2007), 125-36.

environment. This failure also has a twin aspect: first, the determination to find a non-Jewish Jesus.[48]

Another reason for approaching Johannine Christology from Jewish viewpoints owes to the way in which the fourth evangelist portrays the main character of his Gospel.[49] That is, that Jesus is depicted primarily and exclusively in Jewish eschatological terms, i.e., "Messiah" (twice) and "Christ" (19 times), who was to fulfill the covenant promised in the Jewish scriptures.[50] "Messiah," which is a Greek transliteration of the Aramaic word "*Masiha*" (מָשִׁיחַ), occurs within the entire New Testament corpus only in John (1:41; 4:25).[51] The Greek translation (Χριστός) of this Semitic title does not connote any redeeming figure in the Hellenistic extra-biblical usages and it always refers to objects or abstract ideas. Not to mention the Semitic semantic provenance, therefore, the Greek epithet "Christ" was unintelligible to Gentiles in the Hellenistic cultural and/or religious contexts with reference to an eschatological overtone as denoted in the Fourth Gospel:[52]

> As far as tradition-historical considerations are concerned, all NT texts with Χριστός are related to the OT and Jewish traditions. There is no secondary influence from secular Greek usage, which never applied Χριστός to persons;[53] Basically the word [Χριστός] describes a thoroughly secular, everyday process, and has no sacral undertone at all.[54]

Therefore, Craig Keener comments that

> "Messiah" was a Jewish category, not Gentile, so it is hardly plausible that the title was invented by later Gentile Christians. "Christ" was a natural way to translate "Messiah" into Greek, and so it translates "anointed one" regularly in the LXX. . . . That John, writing in Greek, should explicitly translate "Messiah" as "Christ (1:41)," need not indicate Gentiles in his audience, as some have thought; quite the contrary, John is the

---

[48] James D.G. Dunn, *A New Perspective on Jesus: What the Quest for the Historical Jesus Missed* (Grand Rapids: Baker, 2005), 58 (italics original). An example of distancing these two *Sitz-im-Lebens* to a considerable extent is attested to in Eduard Lohse, *Grundriß der neutestamentlichen Theologie* (Stuttgart: Kohlhammer, 1998), 43-50. For a thorough critique of the New Quest and positive examination of the Third Quest, which locates the historical Jesus in the framework of Jewish apocalypticism, see N.T. Wright, *Jesus and Victory of God* (Minneapolis: Fortress, 1996), 28-124.

[49] The missionary Christology and the I-am sayings are particular traits of the Old Testament influence on John. Schwankl, "Aspekte der johanneischen Christologie," 356-61.

[50] David Rensberger, "The Messiah Who Has Come into the World: The Message of the Gospel of John," in *Jesus in Johannine Tradition*, ed. Robert T. Fortna and Tom Thatcher (Louisville: Westminster/John Knox, 2001), 17; F. Hahn, "Χριστός," *EDNT*, 3:484.

[51] W. Radl, "Μεσσίας, ου," *EDNT*, 2:412; *BDAG*, 634.

[52] W. Grundmann, "Χριστός," *TDNT*, 9:493-96.

[53] Hahn, *EDNT*, 3:485.

[54] K.H. Rengstorf, "Χριστός," *NIDNTT*, 2:334.

only NT writer to include the Semitic term at all.[55]

Finally, the Johannine narratives which inquire of Jesus' identity manifest repeatedly a tenacious recourse to the exclusive Jewish messianic ideas and expectations as forecast, according to John, in the utmost Jewish authority, the Old Testament. In this respect, Klaus Scholtissek's assessment is illuminating.

> The Johannine Christology is fundamentally biblical theology in the sense that the fourth evangelist reformulates the Old Testament view of God and the covenant . . . and applies it to Jesus the Nazarene in terms of Messiah. . . . Like the synoptic Gospels, it was also important for John to interpret the salvific events in the life of Jesus the Nazarene (the incarnation, the death, and resurrection) in terms of the Messiah. The messianic expectation of early Judaism . . . has gone through a Christian transformation process. Nevertheless, to John's Gospel, the incarnation of Jesus is to be understood messianically in the covenant history of Israel.[56]

This aspect is most tangibly felt in the passion narratives in which the fourth evangelist depicts the suffering of Jesus as fulfilling the messianic qualifications as expected of the Old Testament.[57]

As such, the aforementioned reasons lead one to conclude that Johannine Christology is dovetailed within the incipient Judaism, inclusive of the Old Testament. As a corollary, this judgment heuristically points to the ancient Jewish messianic antecedents as hermeneutically promising clues for a better understanding of Johannine Christology.[58] Although this perspective does not promote the sheer exclusion of Hellenistic divine mediator types or traditions, it must, however, be acknowledged that the Jewish religious traditions require a substantially much closer scrutiny than other religious-cultural variables with reference to the formation of the Johannine Christology. In this respect, the comment of Stephen Smalley is penetrating for the scope of this study.

> Our consideration of the Jewish influence on the background to the Fourth Gospel leads us to the conclusion that John's ethos is at root more in touch with Judaism than

---

[55] Craig S. Keener, *The Gospel of John: A Commentary* (Peabody: Hendrickson, 2003), 1:290; Lincoln, *A Commentary on the Gospel according to St. John*, 64.

[56] Klaus Scholtissek, "'Ich und der Vater, wir sind eins' (Joh 10,30): Zum theologischen Potential und zur hermeneutischen Kompetenz der johanneischen Christologie," in *Theology and Christology in the Fourth Gospel: Essays by the Members of the SNTS Johannine Writings Seminar*, ed. Gilbert van Belle, J.G. van der Watt, and P. Maritz (Leuven: Leuven University, 2005), 341-42; idem, "Neues Testament," 88. See also Appendices 1 and 2.

[57] See the section on the fulfillment themes of the Fourth Gospel in Appendix 3: The Significance of the Old Testament for the Fourth Gospel.

[58] For a methodological survey of the Jewish messianic types studies, see James R. Davila, "Of Methodology, Monotheism and Metatron: Introductory Reflections on Divine Mediators and the Origins of the Worship of Jesus," in *The Jewish Roots of Christological Monotheism: Papers from the St. Andrews Conference on the Historical Origins of the Worship of Jesus*, ed. Carey C. Newman, James R. Davila, and Gladys S. Lewis (Leiden: Brill, 1999), 3-18.

Hellenism . . . but if we accept the description of John's background as 'Jewish-Hellenistic' . . . we must also recognize that the contact with Judaism is primary. The Hellenistic features of the Fourth Gospel tell us more about its final audience, that is to say, than about the background of its author or its tradition.[59]

In contrast to the estimation of Bultmann, Otto Betz notes that the approach to the Gospel of John from Hellenistic frameworks is fatal to the interpretation of the Gospel despite its seemingly sparse citations of the Old Testament passages:

> According to Rudolf Bultmann, the Gospel of John is largely free from binding of the Old Testament and in sharp contrast to Judaism; quotations from the Old Testament are quite rare, and the Jews appear overall as opponents of Jesus, as a representative of the faithless and the ungodly world. The Fourth Gospel, therefore, is seen as a Hellenized testimony of faith in which various sources are: (for instance,) a "semeia source," which served chiefly the character of Jesus, a special source for the story of suffering and, in addition, this gnosticizing source (both are circulated widely), in which a pure heavenly revealer is proclaimed as the bringer of knowledge and truth, of light and life. But such hypotheses are disastrous for the right understanding of this gospel.[60]

The Main Thesis

In Judaism of the second temple period, Jewish messianic figures were often expected to play a *redivivus* role such as that of the king David, Moses, or the prophet Elijah. This heightened interest was often juxtaposed in the eschatological contexts. Such traits of thought, language or metaphor, however, are strikingly absent in John's Gospel. In view of this observation, therefore, this study sets out to make a case that the fourth evangelist presents the Old Testament characters primarily as witnesses to Jesus' messianic identity in contradistinction to conventional Jewish messianic hopes prior to or contemporary with the writing of the Gospel. This conclusion, however, does not entail a sharp break between the Jewish Scriptures and the Fourth Gospel. One of the more conspicuous reasons lies in John's belief that Jesus is the pivotal fulfillment of the Jewish Scriptures and that their validity is assured as a cogent testimony to the messianic characteristics of Jesus the Nazarene.[61]

---

[59] Stephen S. Smalley, *John: Evangelist and Interpreter* (Downers Grove: IVP, 1998), 74. For further justifications for this judgment, see also a discussion on the recent reassessments of the so-called Bickermann/Hengel theory in Appendix 2.

[60] Otto Betz, "Das Johannesevangelium und das Alte Testament," in *Wie verstehen wir das Neue Testament?* (Wuppertal: Aussaat, 1981), 87. Another important insight has been offered recently to add to this point. The final author/redactor oft he Fourth Gospel supposed the primarily intended reader(s) steeped in a form of early Judaism. Thus, the Christological exploration in the Johannine Gospel would be more fruitful over against such a cultural backdrop. Jörg Frey, "Diaspora-Jewish Background of the Fourth Gospel," *SEÅ* 77 (2012): 169-96.

[61] Labahn, "Jesus und die Autorität der Schrift im Johannesevangelium," 203-206.

History of Research
Theios Aner Theory

Before summarizing the past contributions which sought to account for the Johannine Christology in light of the traditional Jewish messianic figures, it is worthwhile to comment on some previous attempts to resolve this question from the Hellenistic context. Hans-Jürgen Kuhn, for example, found no conclusive evidence that the evangelist spoke of Jesus in terms of a prophet. Further, he went on to note the absence of a miracle-working messiah in Jewish tradition. Thus, he postulated a *theios aner* Christology for the Signs Source in which Jesus is referred to as "Son of God." Since the "Son of God" title is more akin to the Jewish context in his estimation, he dialectically came up with a merged conception of a Jewish "Son of God" and a Hellenistic miracle-working redeemer which he posited to be present in the Christology of the Signs Source in the Fourth Gospel.

> The term, "divine man," does not appear not only in John 1:35-42 and 44-50 but in the entire New Testament text. The Jewish Old Testament and Christian New Testament traditions do not use the adjective, "divine," for human characteristics. Nevertheless, the texts in John 1 display a tendency to characterize Jesus in terms of a divine-man, although it may not be explicitly apparent. An analysis of the texts in John 1 results in the following. Literary criticism is a valid method for the quesiton of the formation of the Gospel of John. The Jewish Old Testament tradition should be seen as a general influence in its entirety. If the question about the miracles in the New Testament, or especially in the Gospel of John, is concerned, the Hellenistic expressions must be taken into account.[62]

His point is that although the term, "theios aner" is explicitly stated nowhere in the New Testament, his analysis of the Fourth Gospel, and John 1:35-51 in particular, leads him to conclude that the Gospel reflects a fused expression, that of the Old Testament and Hellenistic myths, of a divine man with reference to Jesus in the latter traits.

Despite some measure of popularity since 1960s, the *theios aner* theory, however, has been deemed to be fraught with intrinsic methodical flaws.[63] John

---

[62] Hans-Jürgen Kuhn, *Christologie und Wunder: Untersuchungen zu Joh 1,35-51* (Regensburg: Pustet, 1988), 554-56.

[63] Variegated degrees of skeptical responses are found in the following studies: Martin Hengel, *The Son of God: The Origin of Christology and the History of Jewish-Hellenistic Religion* (Philadelphia: Fortress, 1976); Carl R. Holladay, *Theios Aner in Hellenistic Judaism: A Critique of the Use of This Category in New Testament Christology* (Missoula: Scholars, 1977); Gail P. Corrington, *The "Divine Man": His Origin and Function in Hellenistic Popular Religion* (New York: Peter Lang, 1986); Barry L. Blackburn, *Theios Aner and the Markan Miracle Traditions: A Critique of the Theios Aner Concept as an Interpretative Background of the Miracle Traditions Used by Mark* (Tübingen: Siebeck, 1991); Aage Pilgaard, "The Hellenistic Theios Aner—A Model for Early Christian Christology?" in *The New Testament and Hellenistic Judaism*, ed. Peder Borgen and Søren Giversen (Aarhus: Aarhus University Press, 1995),

Polhill, for instance, offers a three-tiered caution.[64] First, the major sources cited to advocate the theory date back to from as early as the early third century A.D. onward. Thus, a serious anachronistic nature of the comparative approach hampers the alleged influence of the Hellenistic divine myths on Johannine Christology.[65] The advocates of the *theios-aner* theory usually claim the necessity of incipient oral traditions prior to their written stages. Granted that the existence of the extended period of an oral stage is certainly possible, however, it is precarious to pursue a scientific query solely on the basis of speculative oral traditions without any tangible evidence.

Second, the general characteristics of divine man myths are also problematic. In other words, the picture of a divine man is an artificially constructed one in that a number of recurring features are compiled from a number of sources so as to create a composite ideal figure. Polhill points out this shortcoming:

> The concept "theios aner" is certainly freely used but seldom defined, and when it is defined, then so broadly that all figures rising out of antiquity might be subsumed under it.[66]

Similarly, Scott laments an uncritical use of different ancient traditions:

> In fact, many of the figures in Bieler's exhaustive collection of ancient sources were never called θεῖος ἀνήρ by an ancient author. This recognition has given rise to ques-

---

101-22; Erkki Koskenniemi, *Apollonios von Tyana in der neutestamentlichen Exegese: Forschungsbericht und Weiterführung der Diskussion* (Tübingen: Mohr Siebeck, 1994); idem, "Apollonius of Tyana: A Typical Theios Aner?" *JBL* 117 (1998): 455-67; idem, *The Old Testament Miracle-Workers in Early Judaism* (Tübingen: Mohr Siebeck, 2005); Udo Schnelle, *Das Evangelium nach Johannes* (Leipzig: Evangelische Verlagsanstalt, 1998), 17-19; Ian W. Scott, "Is Philo's Moses a Divine Man?" *SPhiloA* 14 (2002): 87-111.

[64] John B. Polhill, "Perspectives on the Miracle Stories," *RevExp* 74 (1977): 389-99. Polhill traces the theological impetus of this movement back to Richard Reitzenstein, *Hellenistische Wundererzählungen* (Stuttgart: Teubner, 1906) and Ludwig Bieler, *Theios Aner: Das bild des "göttlichen Menschen" in Spätantike und Frühchristentum*, 2 vols. (Wien: Oskar Höfels, 1935-36). Ian Scott ("Is Philo's Moses a Divine Man?," 87) notes further developments and affirmations of the view in the following: Gillis P. Wetter, *"Der Sohn Gottes": Eine Untersuchung über den Charakter und die Tendenz des Johannes Evangeliums, zugleich ein Beitrag zur Kenntnis der Heilandsgestalten der Antike* (Göttingen: Vandenhoeck & Ruprecht, 1916); Hans Windisch, *Paulus und Christus: Ein biblisch-religionsgeschichtlicher Vergleich* (Leipzig: J.C. Hindrichs, 1934); Rudolf Bultmann, *Theology of the New Testament* (London: SCM, 1951), 1:130; idem, *History of the Synoptic Tradition* (New York: Harper & Row, 1963), 218-44; and Otto Weinreich, "Antikes Gottmenschentum," in *Römischer Kaiserkult*, ed. Antonie Wlosok (Darmstadt: Wissenschaftliche Buchgesellschaft, 1978), 55-81.

[65] A glance at other anachronistic presuppositions in modern Johannine studies is offered in Charles E. Hill, *The Johannine Corpus in the Early Church* (Oxford: OUP, 2004).

[66] Gerd Petzke, *Die Traditionen über Apollonius von Tyana und das Neue Testament* (Leiden: Brill, 1970), 161. The translation is Polhill's. Polhill, "Perspectives on the Miracle Stories," 391.

tions about how much Bieler's influential picture of a single, defined "archetype" for divine men was in fact created by his indiscriminate use of a single (anachronistic and imposed) title. . . . Bieler himself compounds so many features of the "type," many of which are represented by only one or two (often anachronistic) members, that the very notion of a unified figure begins to seem forced.[67]

It is thus doubtful as to whether the divine man image of Kuhn was created at his fingertips or it was actually circulated among the first century Mediterranean religio-cultural backdrops.

Finally, the history of religions approach, which Polhill labels as reductionistic, appears to assume an immense logical leap with great ease. Differently put, even if there are some parallel imageries and symbols between the miracle accounts of the Fourth Gospel and certain Hellenistic literature, they do not automatically necessitate a literary or social-cultural dependence between them (unless of course one document claims such relationship, for instance, as the Gospel of John evinces a direct dependence on the Old Testament which is attested ostensibly in the fulfillment formulae). These alleged parallels might simply suggest the universal nature of hope for a miraculous and gracious redemption from the common human ordeals experienced in the majority of cultures.[68] Thus, Polhill writes that

> [t]here are parallels to nearly every detail of the Gospel miracles in the ancient literature—both as to form and content. This should come as no surprise. It is mere testimony to the fact that the miracle stories belong to the literary and social milieu of the first-century. One should expect an affinity with that milieu.[69]

For the reasons discussed above, the juxtaposition of Johannine Christology with non-Jewish Hellenistic literature does not seem hermeneutically promising. Rather, a more obvious provenance of Johannine messianism is observed in references to the Old Testament symbols and figures, with which the fourth evangelist plainly and repeatedly associates.

Johannine Christology and the Jewish Messianic Figures

A number of studies sought to address the correlation between the Johannine Christology and the major Old Testament protagonists in John's Gospel. A brief chronological overview of selective studies on such topics will provide us with a glimpse into the development of the scholarly assessment of the issue.[70]

T.F. Glasson. Thomas F. Glasson published one of the seminal modern

---

[67] Scott, "Is Philo's Moses a Divine Man?" 89-90.
[68] Cf. Samuel Sandmel, "Parallelomania," *JBL* 81 (1962): 2-13; Terence L. Donaldson, "Parallels: Use, Misuse and Limitations," *EvQ* 55 (1983) 193-210.
[69] Polhill, "Perspectives on the Miracle Stories," 392.
[70] For another overview of the history of interpretation of the Old Testament figures and John, refer to Stan Harstine, *Moses as a Character in the Fourth Gospel: A Study of Ancient Reading Techniques* (Sheffield: Sheffield, 2002), 3-11.

book-length treatments that located a thematic linkage of John's Christology with an Old Testament messianic figure, Moses.[71] He argued that Jesus is presented as a second (or new) Moses based on the typological parallels found in the Gospel and in some Jewish literature (the Old Testament and rabbinic documents). His study, however, has drawn some criticism, especially for his excessive recourse to typology. For example, A.J.B. Higgins, in a critique of Glasson's association of the brazen serpent and Jesus, comments as follows: "The kind of exegesis offered here is in danger of becoming excessively typological. Not all the resemblances which Dr Glasson sees between Moses and Christ were necessarily or even probably present in the evangelist's own mind."[72] Furthermore, his uncritical use of the rabbinic materials (especially without regards to their dating issues) eclipses the value of this otherwise fine study on the role of Moses in the Gospel of John.

Wayne Meeks. Wayne Meeks' doctoral dissertation accepted at Yale University in 1965 was in many ways truly a ground-breaking attempt to account for Johannine Christology in terms of the Jewish expectation of the prophet like Moses, whom Meeks assesses to be regarded as the prophet-king *par excellence* in Judaism of the Second Temple period.[73] According to Meeks, the fourth evangelist reveals a multi-layered understanding of Jesus. At first, he fulfills the functions expected of Moses (thus, Jesus being the true Moses). Then, the Christ does this in such a superior and exclusive way that Moses is stripped of those messianic functions and presented, not as a messianic type, but merely as a messianic witness to Jesus (thus, discounting Glasson's thesis significantly).[74]

---

[71] T. Francis Glasson, *Moses in the Fourth Gospel* (London: SCM, 1963). Glasson's thesis is positively affirmed in Günter Reim, *Jochanan; Erweiterte Studien zum alttestamentlichen Hintergrund des Johannesevangeliums* (Erlangen: Der Ev.-Luth. Mission, 1995), 110-54; Paul Trudinger, "A Prophet Like Me (Deut 18:5): Jesus and Moses in St John's Gospel, Once Again," *DRev* 113 (1995): 193-95; Dietmar Neufeld, "And When That One Comes?: Aspects of Johannine Messianism," in *Eschatology, Messianism, and the Dead Sea Scrolls*, ed. Craig A. Evans and Peter W. Flint (Grand Rapids: Eerdmans, 1997), 127-28, 132-33. J.L. Martyn also sees the Mosaic typology as the starting point of genuine faith. J.L. Martyn, "From the Expectation of the Prophet-Messiah like Moses . . . ," in *History and Theology in the Fourth Gospel* (Louisville: Westminster/John Knox, 2003), 101-43.

[72] A.J.B. Higgins, "review of T. F. Glasson, *Moses in the Fourth Gospel*," *SJT* 18 (1965): 233. Glasson's book will be further scrutinized in detail in ch. 5.

[73] Wayne A. Meeks, *The Prophet-King: Moses Traditions and the Johannine Christology* (Leiden: Brill, 1967). For a recent reaffirmation of Meeks' thesis, see John Lierman, *The New Testament Moses: Christian Perceptions of Moses and Israel in the Setting of Jewish Religion* (Tübingen: Mohr Siebeck, 2004), 79-123.

[74] This unparalleled or contrastive nature of Moses and Jesus is supported by a number of scholars, for instance, John Painter, *The Quest for the Messiah: The History, Literature, and Theology of the Johannine Community* (Nashville: Abingdon, 1993), 253-86; Peder Borgen, "John 6: Tradition, Interpretation and Composition," in *From Jesus to*

From this notion, he advances to postulate the *Sitz-im-Leben* of the alleged Johannine community as one standing in tension with a Moses-revered Jewish community. What distinguishes Meeks' study from the previous scholarship is that he understands Moses not in separate terms but in the combination of both prophet and king. Meeks' original dissertation postdates Glasson's study by two years, but he is not aware of the latter work.

Criticism of Meeks' study can be unfolded in three respects. First, his reconstruction of the Johannine community employs a problematic mirror-reading based on oversimplistic deductions. It is not entirely clear as to why a certain Johannine interpretation should not have derived from the first *Sitz-im-Leben* (that of Jesus) instead of the third (that of the early church). Second, the broad scope and meticulous examination of relevant materials evident in his study is commendable. Meeks examines an extensive range of materials for his research. Along with the Old Testament and the Fourth Gospel, both Jewish and non-Jewish literature of the intertestamental period, later rabbinic documents, and the Samaritan and Mandaean sources are carefully examined in order to locate possible Mosaic parallels with the Gospel. The latter aspect, offering a broad overview on the Mosaic estimation in the intertestamental Judaism on the one hand, however, casts a shadow on his conclusion. The reason is because he bases his thesis (that Jesus is the prophet-king Moses) disproportionately upon the Jewish literary evidences outside the Gospel of John. He investigates primarily two Johannine pericopae, John 7:37-52 and 18:28–19:22, devoting about 70 pages, while the examination of the extra-canonical literature takes up 220 pages. As a result, a reader suspects that Meeks has superimposed the idea of the extra-canonical sources onto the Johannine text. The final criticism has to do with his heavy dependence upon non-mainstream Jewish sources, for example, some later Samaritan, Mandaean, and late rabbinic texts. The late dates of these writings significantly diminish the value of the parallels that Meeks finds in their texts. The direction of influence is more likely from John onto those Jewish texts with datings taken into account. Furthermore, conceptual affinities are too great a factor to ignore between John and some of its contemporary literatures. Especially problematic is John's connection with the Mandaean sources, which is largely refuted in recent Johannine scholarship (see Appendix 2: "*Religionsgeschichte* and the Fourth Gospel"). Nevertheless, this work of Meeks has broken afresh ground and has exerted a lasting impact on the subsequent Johannine studies that bear relevance to the identity and historical setting of the so-called Johannine community.

J. Louis Martyn. Similar to Wayne Meeks and Raymond E. Brown, J. Louis

---

John: Essays on Jesus and New Testament Christology in Honour of Marinus de Jonge, ed. Martinus C. de Boer (Sheffield: JSOT, 1993), 269-71.

Martyn marks a watershed point in the history of Johannine research.[75] His contribution lies in the establishment of the Jewish hostility toward Jesus and his disciples as reflecting a historical reality of the later period.[76] Martyn was not the first one to recognize this point. Yet, he still deserves credit since he was one of the first ones to reconstruct systematically the historical setting of the so-called Johannine community based on the textual examination of John's Gospel.[77] This insight stands in stark contrast to his predecessors, who approached the Gospel in an abstract manner, for example, the existential interpretation of Bultmann. Based on his historical reading, Martyn further argued that the tension portrayed in the Gospel reflects not only that of the first *Sitz-im-Leben* but that of the third, that is, the life setting of the alleged Johannine community. Thus, "two-level drama" has become a popular entry framework for a study of John. Since the dual reflection of the first and third life settings was important for the understanding of the Gospel, Martyn came up with the Gospel's progressive portrayal of Jesus concerning the Mosaic prophet image. Differently put, although the earlier layers contain a positive Mosaic image of Jesus, the later editorial hands accentuate the faith in Jesus whose quality is far superior to that of Moses. Both Meeks and Martyn represent earlier form-critical attempts, which conveniently attributed the seemingly contradictory internal textual testimonies to different *Sitzen-im-Leben*. However, this deduction of the Johannine community has come under rigorous criticism due to its artificial conjecture of the reality of writing (that, it is usually an individual who writes a book), underestimation of the competence of the final author (or redactor who is usually capable of resolving contradictory theologies in the final draft of writing), and the lack of concrete historical evidences for such an isolated and exclusive Christian community.[78]

---

[75] Beside the work of Meeks reviewed above, see Raymond E. Brown, *The Community of the Beloved Disciple* (New York: Paulist, 1979).

[76] J. Louis Martyn, "From the Expectation of the Prophet-Messiah like Moses . . . ," in *History and Theology in the Fourth Gospel* (Louisville: Westminster John Knox, 2003), 101-23; idem, ". . . To the Presence of the Son of Man," in *History and Theology in the Fourth Gospel* (Louisville: Westminster John Knox, 2003), 124-43.

[77] For perceptive reviews of Martyn's contribution from the historical perspective of Johannine research, see D. Moody Smith, "The Contribution of J. Louis Martyn to the Understanding of the Gospel of John," in *History and Theology in the Fourth Gospel*, J. Louis Martyn (Louisville: Westminster John Knox, 2003), 1-18; idem, "Postscript for Third Edition of Martyn, *History and Theology in the Fourth Gospel*," in *History and Theology in the Fourth Gospel*, J. Louis Martyn (Louisville: Westminster John Knox, 2003), 19-23; idem, "The Gospel of John in Its Jewish Context: Why Begin with Judaism?" in *The Fourth Gospel in Four Dimensions: Judaism and Jesus, the Gospels and Scripture* (Columbia: University of South Carolina Press, 2008), 9-14. Historical reconstruction of the Johannine community has been undertaken extensively in a recent multi-volume work. See Urban C. von Wahlde, *The Gospel and Letters of John*, 3 vols (Grand Rapids: Eerdmans, 2010).

[78] For recent criticisms of Martyn's reconstruction of the developmental history of the Johannine community as reflected in the Johannine literature, see Peter Schäfer, "Die

The third point particularly deserves serious consideration. Since there is no explicit internal testimony to both early Christian and non-Christian records of the presence of such a community producing the Gospel of John, the burden of proof, therefore, rests entirely on those who argue for the writing of the Gospel by a certain sectarian group.[79] On the contrary, the early patristic witnesses, however, strongly point to an individual author by the name of John.[80]

---

sogannante Synode von Jabne," in *Studien zur Geschichte und Theologie des rabbinischen Judentums* (Leiden: Brill, 1978), 45-55; Reuven Kimelman, "Birkat ha-minim and the Lack of Evidence for an Anti-Christian Jewish Prayer in Late Antiquity," in *Jewish and Christian Self-Definition*, ed. E. P. Sanders, Albert I. Baumgarten, and Alan Mendelson (Philadelphia: Fortress, 1981), 2:226-44; Steven T. Katz, "Issues in the Separation of Judaism and Christianity after 70 CE: A Reconsideration," *JBL* 103 (1984): 43-76; Richard Bauckham, "The Audience of the Fourth Gospel," in *Jesus in Johannine Tradition*, ed. Robert T. Fortna and Tom Thatcher (Louisville: Westminster/John Knox, 2001), 101-06; Daniel Boyarin, "Justin Martyr Invents Judaism," *CH* 70 (2001): 427-61; Tobias Hägerland, "John's Gospel: A Two-Level Drama?" *JSNT* 25 (2003): 309-22; Robert Kysar, "The Expulsion from the Synagogue: The Tale of a Theory," in *Voyages with John: Charting the Fourth Gospel* (Waco: Baylor University Press, 2005), 237-46; idem, "The Whence and Whither of the Johannine Community," in *Life in Abundance: Studies of John's Gospel in Tribute to Raymond E. Brown, S.S.*, ed. J.R. Donahue (Collegeville: Liturgical, 2005), 65-81; Kåre Sigvald Fuglseth, *Johannine Sectarianosm in Perspective: A Sociological, Historical, and Comparative Analysis of Temple and Social Relationships in the Gospel of John, Philo, and Qumran* (Leiden: Brill, 2005), 373-74; Urban C. von Wahlde, "Archaeology and John's Gospel," in *Jesus and Archaeology*, ed. James H. Charlesworth (Grand Rapids: Eerdmans, 2006), 523-86; Paul N. Anderson, "Aspects of Historicity in the Gospel of John: Implications for Investigations of Jesus and Archaeology," in *Jesus and Archaeology*, ed. James H. Charlesworth (Grand Rapids: Eerdmans, 2006), 614-15; Edward W. Klink, *The Sheep of the Fold: The Audience and Origin of the Gospel of John* (Cambridge: CUP, 2007), 107-51; Brian J. Capper, "John, Qumran, and Virtuoso Religion," in *John, Qumran, and the Dead Sea Scrolls: Sixty Years of Discovery and Debate*, ed. Mary L. Coloe and Tom Thatcher (Atlanta: Society of Biblical Literature, 2011), 95-99; David A. Lamb, *Text, Context and the Johannine Community: A Sociolinguistic Analysis of the Johannine Writings* (London: T & T Clark, 2014).

[79] Klink, *The Sheep of the Fold*, 87-104; Michael F. Bird, "Sectarian Gospels for Sectarian Christians?: The Non-Canonical Gospels and Bauckham's *The Gospels for All Christians*," in *The Audience of the Gospels: The Origin and Function of the Gospels in Early Christianity*, ed. Edward W. Klink, III (London: T & T Clark, 2010), 27-48; Richard Bauckham, "Is There Patristic Counter-Evidence?: A Response to Margaret Mitchell," in *The Audience of the Gospels: The Origin and Function of the Gospels in Early Christianity*, ed. Edward W. Klink, III (London: T & T Clark, 2010), 68-110.

[80] Martin Hengel, *Die johanneische Frage: Ein Lösungsversuch* (Tübingen: Mohr Siebeck, 1993), 61-95; Richard Bauckham, "The Beloved Disciple as Ideal Author," in *The Testimony of the Beloved Disciple: Narrative, History, and Theology in the Gospel of John* (Grand Rapids: Baker, 2007), 73-92; Andreas J. Köstenberger and Stephen O. Stout, "'The Disciple Jesus Loved': Witness, Author, Apostle—A Response to Richard Bauckham's *Jesus and the Eyewitnesses*," *BBR* 18 (2008): 209-231.

Marinus de Jonge. Marinus de Jonge published a review article in which he considered the previously reviewed work of Meeks.[81] Regardless of some agreements with Meeks at a few points, he parts ways with Meeks at one important point. That is, the themes "king" and "prophet" (and even the epithet "Christ") are not central to John. Rather, the expressions "Son of Man" and "Son of God" are hermeneutical keys to Johannine Christology.[82]

Jonge's notion might be correct that the Christological titles could possess higher hermeneutical priorities in John's presentation of Jesus as Christ: "He is not simply a prophet like Moses as a second Moses, but the Son of God who came to do God's will, that is: to give eternal life to all who believe."[83] Nonetheless, he does not adequately address some important historical questions related to John's Christological presentation, namely, how the evangelist concretely used such ambiguous and fluid terms as those epithets and how he also anticipated without further explanation the immediate understanding on the end of his hearers or readers. For instance, the term "Son of Man" occurs only three times in the entire Jewish writings of the Second Temple Judaism: Daniel 7, 1 Enoch 37-71, and 4 Ezra 13. However, the evidence is comparatively clear that the Danielic text had a heavy influence on the latter two. It is generally accepted that there was no widespread "Son of Man" messianism in pre-Christian Judaism. Some exegetes arguably demonstrated a theological trait of "Son of Man" Christology in the Fourth Gospel. However, it still seems to remain a riddle as to how this alleged Johannine concept had been formulated, understood, and communicated in the first century Palestine setting.[84] Thus, Seyoon Kim writes

---

[81] Marinus de Jonge, "Jesus as Prophet and King in the Fourth Gospel," *ETL* 47 (1973): 160-77; idem, "Christology, Controversy and Community in the Gospel of John," in *Christology, Controversy and Community: New Testament Essays in Honor of David R. Catchpole*, ed. David G. Horrell and Christopher M. Tuckett (Leiden: Brill, 2000), 218-20.

[82] Similarly, the son of man and the son of God epithets as having messianic connotations, see Klaus Koch, "Messias und Menschensohn: Die zweistufige Messianologie," *JBT* 8 (1993): 73-102; William Horbury, "Messianic Associations of 'the Son of Man,'" in *Messianism among Jews and Christians* (London: T & T Clark, 2003), 125-56; Adela Yarbro Collins and John J. Collins, *King and Messiah as Son of God: Divine, Human, and Angelic Messianic Figures in Biblical and Related Literature* (Grand Rapids: Eerdmans, 2008), 178-87. In his programmatic essay, Keck, however, expresses his caution against the study of New Testament Christology concentrated only on the Christological titles. Leander E. Keck, "Toward the Renewal of New Testament Christology," in *From Jesus to John: Essays on Jesus and New Testament Christology in Honour of Marinus de Jonge*, ed. Martinus C. de Boer (Sheffield: JSOT, 1993), 321-40. For a review of the Johannine "son of man," see John F. McHugh, *John 1-4: A Critical and Exegetical Commentary* (London: T & T Clark, 2009), 170-75.

[83] Jonge, "Jesus as Prophet and King in the Fourth Gospel," 167-68.

[84] John Ashton suggests that the term merely functions to rouse the curiosity on the part of the reader concerning Jesus' heavenly origin. John Ashton, "Son of Man," in *Understanding the Fourth Gospel* (Oxford: OUP, 1991), 240-76. For studies on the

as following:

> Now, the question is whether there was an apocalyptic Son of Man messianism at the time of Jesus. Against the older assumption that there was in the pre-Christian Judaism an expectation for the Son of Man as the messiah, it has been rightly made clear recently that before the New Testament there was no such messianic *title* as "the Son of Man."[85]

Kim lists a number of scholars to support his statement: Moule, Schnackenburg, Leivestad, Marshall, Colpe, Lindars, Schweizer, and Fitzmyer. Kim belongs to the group of scholars which maintains the Son of Man Christology was influenced by the Danielic tradition. Through a complicated linguistic analysis, R. Buth also postulates the Danielic background of Jesus' self-designation, "Son of Man," as a "quasi-title." However, his proposal fails to take note of the destination or the intended audience of the Gospels, especially that of Mark. From his repeated explanations of Jewish customs and idioms, it is evident that the intended audience was not familiar with Semitic backgrounds. That such a courteous explanation is lacking with regard to the son of man phrase must have been mystifying to the original Markan reader, if the phrase were a quasi-title.[86]

Johannine Son of Man, see Sigfried Schulz, *Untersuchungen zur Menschensohn-Christologie im Johannesevangelium: Zugleich ein Beitrag zur Methodengeschichte der Auslegung des 4. Evangeliums* (Göttingen: Vandenhoeck & Ruprecht, 1957); Robert Maddox, "The Function of the Son of Man in the Gospel of John," in *Reconciliation and Hope: New Testament Essays on Atonement and Eschatology Presented to L. L. Morris on His 60th Birthday*, ed. Robert Banks (Grand Rapids: Eerdmans, 1974), 186-204; Francis J. Moloney, *The Johannine Son of Man* (Rome: Libreria Ateneo Salesiano, 1978); idem, "The Johannine Son of Man Revisited," in *Theology and Christology in the Fourth Gospel: Essays by the Members of the SNTS Johannine Writings Seminar*, ed. Gilbert van Belle, Jan G. van der Watt, and P. Maritz (Leuven: Peeters, 2005), 177-202; Delbert R. Burkett, *The Son of Man in the Gospel of John* (Sheffield: JSOT, 1991); Markus Sasse, *Der Menschensohn im Evangelium nach Johannes* (Tübingen: Francke, 2000); Walter Wink, "'The Son of Man' in the Gospel of John," in *Jesus in Johannine Tradition*, ed. Robert T. Fortna and Tom Thatcher (Louisville: Westminster/John Knox, 2001), 117-23; Benjamin E. Reynolds, *The Apocalyptic Son of Man in the Gospel of John* (Tübingen: Mohr Siebeck, 2008); idem, "The Use of the Son of Man Idiom in the Gospel of John," in *"Who Is This Son of Man?": The Latest Scholarship on a Puzzling Expression of the Historical Jesus*, ed. Larry W. Hurtado and Paul L. Owen (London: T & T Clark, 2011), 101-29.

[85] Seyoon Kim, *The Son of Man as the Son of God* (Tübingen: Mohr Siebeck, 1983), 19 (italics original). Bauckham also postulates that the son of man is a general self-designation in the gospels. Richard Bauckham, "The Son of Man: 'A Man in My Position' or 'Someone'?" in *The Jewish World around the New Testament: Collected Essays I* (Tübingen: Mohr Siebeck, 2008), 93-101.

[86] Randall Buth, "A more Complete Semitic Background for אשנא־רב, 'Son of Man,'" in *The Function of Scripture in Early Jewish and Christian Tradition*, ed. Craig A. Evans and James A. Sanders (Sheffield: Sheffield, 1998), 176-89. For a convenient survey on the son of man debate, see I.H. Marshall, "The Son of Man in Contemporary

Similarly, Geza Vermes reaches a four-fold conclusion concerning the use of the "son of man" based on his observation of the pertinent Jewish writings: (1) *bar nash* [in Aramaic uses] is a regular expression for 'man' in general, (2) *bar nash* often serves as an indefinite pronoun, (3) the Aramaic speaker often referred to himself, not as 'I', but as 'the son of man,' and (4) in none of the passages, not even in the Jewish messianic exegesis of Daniel 7, does the expression *bar nasha* figure as a title.[87] On the other hand, in intertestamental Judaism, the title "Son of God" referred to such a wide range of individuals that it is virtually impossible to speak of "Son of God" messianism (also, the link of "Son of God" with messianism is rather meager):

> "[S]on of God" was . . . understood metaphorically in Jewish circles. In Jewish sources its use never implies participation by the person so-named in the divine nature.[88]

The emphasis could have been on the function, not on the ontic aspect with regard to the epithet "Son of God." In other words, the title could have referred to

---

Debate," in *Jesus the Saviour: Studies in New Testament Theology* (Downers Grove: InterVarsity, 1990), 100-20; Mogens Müller, *The Expression Son of Man and the Development of Christology* (London: Equinox, 2008). Marshall takes the middle of the road position that both views are possible. Similarly, for those who argue that "Son of Man" refers to both divine and human natures of Jesus, see William O. Walker, "John 1:43-51 and 'The Son of Man' in the Fourth Gospel," *JSNT* 56 (1994): 31-42; Clay Ham, "The Title 'Son of Man' in the Gospel of John," *SCJ* 1 (1998): 67-84; Hahn, *Theologie des Neuen Testaments*, 1:630.

[87] Geza Vermes, "The Present State of the 'Son of Man' Debate," in *Jesus in His Jewish Context* (Minneapolis: Fortress, 2003), 82. Also, Joseph A. Fitzmyer, "The New Testament Title 'Son of Man' Philologically Considered," in *A Wandering Aramean: Collected Aramaic Essays* (Missoula: Scholars, 1979), 143-60, idem, *The One Who Is to Come* (Grand Rapids: Eerdmans, 2007), 56-59; Maurice Casey, *Son of Man: The Interpretation and Influence of Daniel 7* (London: SPCK, 1979); idem, "Corporate Interpretation of 'One Like a Son of Man' (Dan 7:13) at the Time of Jesus," *NovT* 18 (1976): 167-80; idem, "General, Generic and Indefinite: The Use of the Term 'Son of Man' in Aramaic Sources and in the Teaching of Jesus," *JSNT* 29 (1987): 21-56; idem, "Method in Our Madness, and Madness in Their Methods: Some Approaches to the Son of Man Problem in Recent Scholarship," *JSNT* 42 (1991): 17-43; idem, "Idiom and Translation: Some Aspects of the Son of Man Problem," *NTS* 41 (1995): 164-82; idem, "Aramaic Idiom and the Son of Man Problem: A Response to Owen and Shepherd," *JSNT* 25 (2002): 3-32; O. Michel, "The Son of Man," *NIDNTT*, 3:613-17; F. Hahn, "Son of Man," *EDNT*, 3:387-88; James D.G. Dunn, *Jesus Remembered* (Grand Rapids: Eerdmans, 2003), 760; Geza Vermes, "The Son of Man Debate Revisited (1960-2010)," *JJS* 61 (2010): 193-206. For "the son of man" as a mildly reverential designation, see Larry W. Hurtado, "Summary and Concluding Observations," in *"Who Is the Son of Man?": The Lastest Scholarship on a Puzzling Expression of the Historical Jesus*, ed. Larry W. Hurtado and Paul L. Owen (London: T & T Clark, 2011), 159-77.

[88] Geza Vermes, *Jesus in His Jewish Context* (Minneapolis: Fortress, 2003), 66.

the kind of individuals who do works in service of God.[89] Furthermore, it seems that it is, not the title ("Son of Man") that confers the Christological qualifications to Jesus, but the various conceptual images and the events which are closely associated with Jesus in the Johannine narrative contexts that constitute the Christological characteristics proposed by the advocates of "Son of Man" Christology theory. John Painter, for instance, concludes that "there is no Son or Son of Man Christology in John."[90] His judgment is based on his exegesis of the Johannine "Son of Man' texts, which demonstrate high Christology through various themes (i.e., "descent and ascent," "king and judge," "from giver to gift," "exaltation and glorification," and "Messiah"). Thus, it is these themes or traditions that constitute the Johannine Christology, not the epithet "Son of Man" in these texts. In short, the term contributes too little to the heavenly origin of Johannine Christology.[91]

It is, therefore, logical to assume that more concrete and definite messianic icons, such as David, Elijah, or Moses, would have more readily conveyed the messianic overtones of Jesus' signs to the first century Jewish audiences than would the opaque conceptions, such as "Son of Man" or "Son of God" (this is especially true in view of the advocates of "Son of Man" Christology who cannot explicate why the evangelist does little to explain such an obscure Semitic phrase to the Hellenistic audience).[92] Jonge appears to overstate his case by downplaying the way in which the messianic identity of Jesus is carried over through, and often in contrast to, the terms of the traditional Jewish messianic prefigures, as found at many junctures in the Fourth Gospel.

Georg Richter, Francis Grob, and Wolfgang Bittner. Georg Richter and Francis Grob concurred with Glasson by expressing their understanding of Jesus' identity as a miracle-working prophet-messiah like Moses. They based their

---

[89] Similarly, Richard Bauckham, "Jewish Messianism according to the Gospel of John," in *Challenging Perspectives in the Gospel of John*, ed. John Lierman (Tübingen: Mohr Siebeck, 2006), 56.

[90] John Painter, "The Enigmatic Johannine Son of Man," in *Four Gospels 1992: Festschrift Frans Neirynck*, ed. F. van Segbroeck et al. (Louvain: Leuven University Press, 1992), 1887.

[91] Idem, *The Quest for the Messiah: The History, Literature und Theology of the Johannine Community* (Nashville: Abingdon, 1993), 319-42. Also for the negation of "Son of Man" Christology in John, see Margareth Pamment, "The Son of Man in the Fourth Gospel," *JTS* 36 (1985): 56-66; Mogens Müller, "'Have You Faith in the Son of Man?' (John 9.35)," *NTS* 37 (1991): 291-94.

[92] "The most appropriate background of the term when applied to Jesus was the sense 'Messiah.'" Keener, *The Gospel of John*, 1:295. Cf. "Figural representation is . . . the basic recognition that the biblical authors employ images or figures familiar to their readers . . . to present their eschatological messages." M. Jay Wells, "Figural Representation and Canonical Unity," in *Biblical Theology: Retrospect and Prospect*, ed. Scott J. Hafemann (Downers Grove: InterVarsity, 2002), 113.

arguments on their exegesis of the "signs" passages in John (contra Kuhn).[93] Their thesis was taken up and broadened by Wolfgang Bittner, who included David in the scope of messianic precursors in the Gospel (as it was the most predominant messianic paradigm in antique Judaism). He argued that although miraculous signs are repeatedly and decisively linked with Jesus, John's Gospel refuses to associate Jesus with prophets. Rather, he is depicted as a prophet-messiah like Moses and David.[94]

Marie-Émile Boismard. Marie-Émile Boismard also joined the interpretive tradition which explicates Johannine Christology in terms of ancient Jewish messianic prefigurations. He based his thesis largely on his belief in John's indebtedness to the Samaritan tradition on Deuteronomy 18:18-19, and argued that the Moses-like messiah stands at the center of Johannine Christology:

> My interpretation of Johannine thought is at the opposite pole from that of Bultmann: the Johannine Christ is situated above all in the line of the prophets, and especially of Moses, who were sent by God to reveal his will to men.[95]

The majority and the most nascent redactional layers, according to him, speak of Jesus in terms of a new Moses or a prophet like Moses, although a small portion of the final redaction added the superiority of Jesus over Moses. The earlier redactional layers represent the attempt to evangelize the Samaritans while the latter the Jews, compelling the readers to choose between Moses and Jesus.[96]

Margaret Daly-Denton. Margaret Daly-Denton has broken new ground in the study of Johannine Christology. She is the first one to recognize a large scale correspondence between David and Jesus in John.[97] Her judgment is based on a

---

[93] Georg Richter, "Die Fleischwerdung des Logos im Johannesevangelium," *NovT* 13 (1971): 81-126; idem "Die Fleischwerdung des Logos im Johannesevangelium," *NovT* 14 (1972): 257-58; repr., in *Studien zum Johannesevangelium*, ed. Josef Hainz (Regensburg: Friedrich Pustet, 1977), 149-98. Richter especially concerntrates on Deut 18:15-20. Francis Grob, *Faire l'œuvre de Dieu: christologie et éthique dans l'Evangile de Jean* (Paris: Presses Universitaires de France, 1986).

[94] Wolfgang J. Bittner, *Jesu Zeichen im Johannesevangelium: Die Messias-Erkenntnis im Johannesevangelium vor ihrem jüdischen Hintergrund* (Tübingen: Mohr Siebeck, 1987). This evaluation of Richter, Grob, and Bittner is indebted to M.J.J. Menken, "The Christology of the Fourth Gospel: A Survey of Recent Research," in *From Jesus to John: Essays on Jesus and New Testament Christology in Honour of Marinus de Jonge*, ed. Martinus C. de Boer (Sheffield: JSOT, 1993), 311-15; and Neufeld, "And When That One Comes?" 135.

[95] Marie-Émile Boismard, *Moses or Jesus: An Essay in Johannine Christology* (Minneapolis: Fortress; Leuven: Peeters, 1993); trans., *Moïse ou Jésus: essai de christologie Johannique* (Leuven: Peeters: Leuven University Press, 1988), xiv-xv.

[96] The work of Boismard will be further assessed more in detail in ch. 5.

[97] Minor exceptions to this current include the following: T. Francis Glasson, "Davidic Links with the Betrayal of Jesus," *ExpTim* 85 (1974): 118-19; Paul Trudinger, "Da-

structural comparison of John (it is commonly argued that John has a bipartite structure) with the first two books of the Psalms to find close parallels between them. She then goes on to say that the structural analysis and some intertextual echoes demand an understanding of the Fourth Gospel in which Jesus fulfills and replaces the Mosaic institutions as the Davidic messiah.[98]

Eric M.E. Wallace. In contrast to the previous studies that sought to elucidate Moses in John as an arch-type of Jesus, Eric Wallace sets out his study in the jurisdiction setting, especially that of the Old Testament.[99] Over against the court narratives of the Pentateuch, he maintains that the fourth evangelist depicts Moses as a witness on behalf of Jesus. Two conclusions of his dissertation are particularly pertinent for the present research. First, the Pentateuch is intimately woven throughout the Gospel of John. Thus, the knowledge of the foundational Jewish traditions is a crucial hermeneutical prerequisite on the part of John's readers.[100] The second observation especially marks a watershed point in the study of Moses in the Johannine Gospel because Wallace points out the narrative

---

vidic Links with the Betrayal of Jesus: Some Further Observations," *ExpTim* 86 (1974-75): 278-79; idem, "Hosanna to the Son of David: St John's Perspective," *DRev* 109 (1991): 297-301.

[98] Margaret Daly-Denton, *David in the Fourth Gospel: The Johannine Reception of the Psalms* (Leiden: Brill, 2000). Although seemingly tenuous in John, the Davidic messiah theme is predominant from the viewpoint of the Old Testament and early Judaism. See F. Furman Kearley, "Davidic and Messianic Expectations in the Dead Sea Scrolls," in *Last Things: Essays Presented by His Students to Dr. W.B. West, Jr., upon the Occasion of His Sixty-Fifth Birthday*, ed. Jack P. Lewis (Austin: Sweet, 1972), 74-95; John Bowman, "David, Jesus Son of David and Son of Man," *AbrN* 27 (1989): 1-22; Cleon L. Rogers, Jr., "The Promises to David in Early Judaism," *BSac* 150 (1993): 285-302; Yehezkel Kaufman, "The Messianic Idea: The Real and the Hidden Son-of-David," *JBQ* 22 (1994): 141-50; Kenneth Pomykala, *The Davidic Dynasty Tradition in Early Judaism: Its History and Significance for Messianism* (Atlanta: Scholars, 1995), 42-271; John J. Collins, *The Scepter and the Star: The Messiahs of the Dead Sea Scrolls and Other Ancient Literature* (New York: Doubleday, 1995), 49-73; Rex Mason, "The Messiah in the Postexilic Old Testament Literature," in *King and Messiah in Israel and the Ancient Near East: Proceedings of the Oxford Old Testament Seminar*, ed. John Day (Sheffield: Sheffield, 1998), 338-64; Michael E. Fuller, "The Davidic Messiah in Early Jewish Literature," in *Spirit and the Mind: Essays in Informed Pentecostalism to Honor Dr. Donald N. Bowdle Presented on His 65th Birthday*, ed. Terry L. Cross and Emerson B. Powery (Lanham: University Press of America, 2000), 65-86; Daniel I. Block, "My Servant David: Ancient Israel's Vision of the Messiah," in *Israel's Messiah in the Bible and the Dead Sea Scrolls*, ed. Richard S. Hess and M. Daniel Carroll R. (Grand Rapids: Baker, 2003), 36-49. Chapter 4 will interact more in depth with Daly-Denton.

[99] Eric M.E. Wallace, "The Testimony of Moses: Pentateuchal Traditions and Their Function in the Gospel of John" (Ph.D. diss., Union Theological Seminary and Presbyterian School of Christian Education, 2004).

[100] Thus, Wallace construes that what Moses wrote about Jesus in the law and the prophets (John 1:45) refers to the Pentateuch.

contribution of Moses in terms of a witness role (not his typological prefiguration as often argued in the previous studies) in defense of Jesus who is "Son of God" and is also equated with Yahweh. Although Wallace does not seem to be cognizant of the recent German scholarship on this point as will be reviewed in the following section, his thesis stands in accordance with a number of Johannine scholars who understand the function of the scripture and the Old Testament characters primarily as witness in John.

This brief summary of the previous contributions manifests a mixed tendency toward identifying John's Christology. Concerning the comparative messianic prefigures, primarily Moses and/or David are often central to the discussions. In terms of the narrative role pertaining to Johannine Christology, views range between a typological prefiguration and a messianic witness. Regardless of the various opinions, they all seem to be unanimous in pointing out the important Jewish heroic figures as standing in close connection with the Christology of the fourth Gospel.

Recent German Contributions with a Particular Emphasis on Scripture as Christological Witness

The use of the Old Testament in the Gospel of John has recently drawn a great deal of scholarly attention. Some of these studies, especially written by German exegetes, have focused on the contribution of "Scripture" to the messianic identity of Jesus.[101] Their assessment of the role of "Scripture" more or less forms a

---

[101] Some significant recent German contributions on the issue of the Old Testament in John, which are not reviewed here are worthy of mention. Most of these studies will be closely interacted with in the following chapters. Bertold Klappert, "'Mose hat von mir geschrieben': Leitlinien einer Christologie im Kontext des Judentums Joh 5,39-47," in *Hebräische Bibel und ihre zweifache Nachgeschichte: Festschrift für Rolf Rendtorff zum 65. Geburtstag*, ed. Erhard Blum, Christian Macholz, and Ekkehard W. Stegemann (Neukirchen-Vluyn: Neukirchener, 1990), 619-40; Martin Rose, "Manna: Das Brot aus dem Himmel," in *Johannes-Studien: Interdisziplinäre Zugänge zum Johannes-Evangelium, Freundesgabe der Theologischen Fakultät der Universität Neuchâtel für Jean Zumstein*, ed. Martin Rose (Zurich: Theologischer Verlag, 1991), 75-107; Siegfried Kreuzer, "'Wo ich hingehe, dahin könnt ihr nicht kommen': Joh 7,34; 8:21; 13,33 als Teil der Mosetypologie im Johannesevangelium," in *Die Kirche als historische und eschatologische Grösse: Festschrift für Kurt Niederwimmer zum 65. Geburtstag*, ed. Wilhelm Pratscher and Georg Sauer (Frankfurt: Peter Lang, 1994), 63-76; Dieter Sänger,"'Von mir hat er geschrieben' (Joh 5,46): Zur Funktion and Bedeutung Mose im Neuen Testament," *KD* 41 (1995): 112-35; Matthias Gawlick, "Mose im Johannesevangelium," *BN* 84 (1996): 29-35; Andreas Lindemann, "Mose und Jesus Christus: Zum Verständnis des Gesetzes im Johannesevangelium," in *Das Urchristentum in seiner literarischen Geschichte: Festschrift für Jürgen Becker zum 65. Geburtstag*, ed. Ulrich Mell and Ulrich B. Müller (Berlin: Walter de Gruyter, 1999), 309-34; Michael Labahn, *Jesus als Lebensspender: Untersuchungen zu einer Geschichte der johanneischen Tradition anhand ihrer Wundergeschichten* (Berlin: Walter de Gruyter, 1999); idem, *Offenbarung in Zeichen und Wort: Untersuchungen zur Vorgeschichte von Joh 6,1-25a und seiner Rezeption in der Brotrede* (Tübingen:

consensus. That is, "Scripture" functions as Christological witness. As such, a review of these studies bears a direct relevance on the present discussion on the narrative role of the Old Testament characters as Christological witnesses. The following review will provide a point of departure for the present investigation as to the correlation between the functions of "Scripture" and the Old Testament characters.

Martin Hengel. In a lengthy essay on the role of the Scripture in the Fourth Gospel, Martin Hengel argues for a three-fold thesis. First, the role of the Scripture is so great that John's Gospel must be seen as both anti-docetic and anti-gnostic. Second, the Gospel presupposes one salvation history, and the picture of Israel is overshadowed in the present Jesus event, which the Old Testament figures accepted. Furthermore, they were content to be witnesses of this salvation history. Finally, the evangelist is to be understood as an original exegete of the Jewish texts better understood in view of Philo and Qumran.[102]

Andreas Obermann. In a dissertation inquiring into the use of the Old Testament in John's Gospel, Andreas Obermann reaches a six-fold conclusion. The Christological dimension is fundamental to John's understanding of the Scriptures. The Old Testament is an authoritative witness to Jesus as the Christ.[103] The Scriptures and Jesus mutually interpret each other in the working of Jesus in the Christological light. The glory of Jesus is indispensable for the Christological understanding of the Scriptures. This shift of understanding (from the conventional Jewish understanding of the Scriptures as the supreme authority and the source of life) is due to the evangelist's memory and the guidance of the Para-

---

Mohr Siebeck, 2000); Klaus Scholtissek, *In ihm sein und bleiben: Die Sprache der Immanenz in den Johanneischen Schriften* (Freiburg: Herder, 2000); Jean Zumstein, "Die Schriftrezeption in der Brotrede (Joh 6)," in *Israel und seine Heilstraditionen im Johannesevangelium: Festgabe für Johannes Beutler SJ zum 70. Geburtstag*, ed. Michael Labahn, Klaus Scholtissek, and Angelika Strotmann (Paderborn: Ferdinand Schöningh, 2004), 123-39; Heinz-Josef Fabry, "Mose, der 'Gesalbte JHWHs': Messianische Aspekte der Mose-Interpretation in Qumran," in *Moses in Biblical and Extra-Biblical Traditions*, ed. Axel Graupner and Michael Wolter (Berlin: Walter de Gruyter, 2007), 129-42.

[102] Martin Hengel, "Die Schriftauslegung des 4. Evangeliums auf dem Hintergrund der urchristlichen Exegese," in *"Gesetz" als Thema Biblischer Theologie* (Neukirchen-Vluyn: Neukirchen, 1989), 249-88. A condensed version of this article is accessible in English in idem, "The Old Testament in the Fourth Gospel," in *The Gospels and the Scriptures of Israel*, ed. Craig A. Evans and W. Richard Stegner (Sheffield: Sheffield, 1994), 380-95.

[103] This function of Scripture as a primary witness for Jesus' Christological identity is also recognized by Michael Labahn, "Scripture *Talks* because Jesus *Talks*: The Narrative Rhetoric of Persuading and Creativity in John's Use of Scripture," in *The Audience of the Gospels: The Origin and Function of the Gospels in Early Christianity*, ed. Edward W. Klink, III (London: T & T Clark, 2010), 133-56.

clete. Finally, John was a scriptural theologian and the Old Testament was an important background in the formation of his theology.[104]

Christian Dietzfelbinger. Christian Dietzfelbinger is one of the first, in recent years, to perceptibly recognize the unique Johannine presentation of the Scriptures. The typological rendering of the Old Testament characters does not stand out. Rather, the Scriptures as a whole remain exclusively as a witness for the Christological identity of Jesus. In contrast to the testimonies of the Old Testament, the Old Testament characters do not provide a typological prefiguration as a recipient of the divine revelation, which becomes available only through Jesus. The reason is because only he "looked at God; only he climbed up the heaven and down from it (3:13). Therefore, only he can give authentic information of God (1:18); in the Old Testament, however, such notion is not to be found."[105] The seemingly ambivalent stance toward the scripture, according to Dietzfelginger, is a result of editing that the Johannine redactor attempted to preserve two opposite opinions present in the Johannine community.[106] In addition, the evangelist explains the justification of the Jewish rejection of Jesus on the basis of Scripture's anticipation and pre-witness in John.

Wolfgang Kraus. On the other hand, Wolfgang Kraus explicates the Scriptures in the strongest antithetical terms of all the Johannine exegetes under review.[107] With attention both to explicit citations of the Old Testament and to statements about "Scripture" in the Fourth Gospel, the author makes nine observations (summarized in 18-19). First, in reference back to Genesis 1:1, John 1:1 equates the beginning of the Christ event (*Christusgeschehens*) with the beginning of the creation.[108] Second, according to John 1:17, Moses and Christ (in John's phrase, "law" and "grace and truth") represent the old and the new order respectively, standing with each other in an antithetical relationship, or, at least, the latter replaces

---

[104] Andreas Obermann, *Die christologische Erfüllung der Schrift im Johannesevangelium: Eine Untersuchung zur johanneischen Hermeneutik anhand der Schriftzitate* (Tübingen: Mohr Siebeck, 1996). A convenient summary of his dissertation is found in ibid., 425-30.

[105] Christian Dietzfelbinger, "Aspekte des Alten Testaments im Johannesevangelium," in *Geschichte-Tradition-Reflexion III, Frühes Christentum: Festschrift für Martin Hengel zum 70. Geburtstag*, ed. Hermann Lichtenberger (Tübingen: Mohr Siebeck, 1996), 208.

[106] Christian Dietzfelbinger, *Das Evangelium nach Johannes* (Zürich: Theologischer, 2001), 1:165-66.

[107] Wolfgang Kraus, "Johannes und das Alte Testament: Überlegungen zum Umgang mit der Schrift im Johannesevangelium im Horizont Biblischer Theologie," *ZNW* 88 (1997): 1-23.

[108] Also, Martin Hengel, "Die Schriftauslegung des 4. Evangeliums auf dem Hintergrund der urchristlichen Exegese," in *"Gesetz" als Thema Biblischer Theologie*, ed. Ingo Baldermann and Dwight R. Daniels (Neukirchen-Vluyn: Neukirchen, 1989), 283.

the former.[109] Third, the earlier νόμος ("law") does not apply to the Johannine community any longer. The bywords ("your" or "their law") indicate this aspect (cf. 8:5, 17, 10:34, 15:25, 18:31). Only the new order of stipulations, embodied in Jesus (13:34), is relevant to the Johannine community.[110] Fourth, the Passion accounts of the Gospels altogether, particularly that of the Johannine Gospel, are to be understood as "arch-typical cult reports" in an anti-thesis to the Peshah Haggada. Fifth, the verb πληρόω ("to fulfill") is used in 18:9 and 18:32 concerning the word of Jesus. Therefore, the word of Jesus and the "Scripture" stand in the same stage. Sixth, the outcry of Jesus in John 19:28 ("it is finished") indicates that the "Scripture" was completed. Seventh, the proper understanding for the "Scripture" is made possible only in view of the Jesus events, particularly the resurrection of Jesus (2:17, 12:15, 20:9).[111] Eighth, after the resurrection, the "Scripture" and the words of Jesus were fused with one another to become a unit (2:22 in the context of 2:18-22; see also 12:16, 20:8). Finally, in the bread of life discourse (John 6), it is not the scriptural quotations but the word of Jesus in verse thirty-five that occupies the central meaning.[112] The "Scripture" is subordinated to the words of Jesus thereby and possesses no independent relevance. Only in the light of the Jesus' words and in reference to the Jesus event, the "Scripture" becomes comprehensible.

Based on these observations, Kraus reaches a four-fold conclusion (19-21). John understands the Scripture as a witness to Jesus. He also regards the Christ event to be the "fulfillment" of Scriptures. Jesus brings the imperfect Scripture to a "termination (Abschluß)." Finally, the Jesus event moves up to the rank of "Scripture."[113] In addition to these four points, Kraus makes one more important comment along the same line in another article. That is, John sees the aban-

---

[109] Also, Obermann, *Die christologische Erfüllung der Schrift im Johannesevangelium*, 53-56.

[110] Also, Dieter Sänger,"'Von mir hat er geschrieben' (Joh 5,46): Zur Funktion und Bedeutung Mose im Neuen Testament," *KD* 41 (1995): 124, n. 52.

[111] Ulrich Luz, "Das Neue Testament," in *Gesetz*, ed. Rudolf Smend and Ulrich Luz, KT 1015 (Stuttgart: Kohlhammer, 1981), 120; Udo Schnelle, *Antidoketische Christologie im Johannesevangelium: Eine Untersuchung zur Stellung des vierten Evangeliums in der johanneischen Schule* (Göttingen: Vandenhoeck & Ruprecht, 1987), 44; Wolfgang Schräge, *Ethik des Neuen Testaments* (Göttingen: Vandenhoeck & Ruprecht, 1989), 288.

[112] Theobald, "Schriftzitate im 'Lebensbrot'-Dialog Jesu (Joh 6)," 309-49.

[113] For similar judgments related to the fourth notion, see Thomas Söding, "Die Schrift als Medium des Glaubens: Zur hermeneutischen Bedeutung von Joh 20:30f," in *Schrift und Tradition: Festschrift für Josef Ernst zum 70. Geburtstag*, ed. Knut Backhaus and Franz G. Untergassmair (Paderborn: Ferdinand Schöningh, 1996), 351-54; D. Moody Smith, "When Did the Gospels Become Scripture?" *JBL* 119 (2000): 3-20; Francis J. Moloney, "The Gospel of John as Scripture," *CBQ* 67 (2005): 454-68.

doning of the old redemptive program which was being carried out in Judaism, and the new salvific program is put into effect in Jesus.[114]

In addition to the assessment of the role of "Scripture," his brief notion of the function of the Old Testament characters is of direct relevance for the present study (21-22). Kraus posits that John employs the Old Testament characters (Abraham, Isaiah, Moses, and John the Baptist) paradigmatically. In the accounts of these figures, the reception of the word of God is self-evident in the Old Testament. However, the Johannine depiction of these figures manifests some degree of ambivalence. For instance, Abraham is an ancestor, but not the father. He is jubilant, not over the birth of his son Isaac as Jews would have believed, but over his witness of "the day of Jesus (8:56)." Isaiah is a witness for Christ (12:41), both for the Jewish rejection of Jesus and the unbelief of Israelites in his time. Moses passed down the law, which cannot be broken (10:34). However, the community possesses a new commandment (13:34). Moses prefigures the giving up of the life of Jesus (3:16). The law was given through him, but Christ replaces it (1:17). The contrast exists, thus, between "law" on the one hand and "grace and truth" on the other, not between Moses and Jesus, because Moses wrote about Christ (1:45, 5:39, 45). It is the law of Moses, by which Jesus is delivered to death (18:31, 19:7). It is a misconception, thus, to believe that Moses would have given the heavenly bread (6:32), which sustained the Israelites, but it was not the bread of life. Finally John the Baptist stands within the rank of the Old Testament figures in John's Gospel and plays an important witness role. However, he completely disappears as a person behind his witness for Christ (3:30). Kraus offers one of the more convenient overviews on John's portrayal of the Scriptures and the Old Testament characters with lucid insight, although he seems to interpret the texts oversimplistically at times. His article is primarily focused on the role of Moses, and it will be closely reviewed in chapter five.

M.J.J. Menken. The rest of this review on the recent German scholarly contributions will address two non-German exegetes. Although non-German by ethnicity, their contributions have come forward in significant interaction with the recent German contributions on the topic under discussion. Maarten Menken, a Catholic faculty member at the University of Utrecht, has contended in a way precisely analogous to the arguments mounted by some recent German exegetes as reviewed so far. He delivered a keynote address before the annual meeting of the New Testament Society of South Africa in 1999.[115] The kernel of his address

---

[114] Wolfgang Kraus, "Die Vollendung der Schrift nach Joh 19,28: Überlegungen zum Umgang mit der Schrift im Johannesevangelium," in *The Scriptures in the Gospels*, ed. Christopher M. Tuckett (Leuven: Leuven University Press, 1997), 635-36.

[115] M.J.J. Menken, "Observations on the Significance of the Old Testament in the Fourth Gospel," *Neot* 33 (1999): 125-43. A revised version of this article is found in *Theology and Christology in the Fourth Gospel: Essays by the Members of the SNTS Johannine Writings Seminar*, ed. G. van Belle, J.G. van der Watt, and P. Maritz (Leuven: Leuven University, 2005), 155-75.

is that the Scriptures and the Old Testament figures are employed in the Fourth Gospel as valid witnesses to the messianic identity of Jesus. In other words, their validity stands as far as they bear witness to the messianic identity of Jesus. However, they do not amount to the true revelation of God as revealed through Jesus, who according to the evangelist is the only true revelation (similar to Kraus' third and fourth conclusions).[116] This supporting role of the scripture is also summed up by Léon-Dufour:

> John presented Jesus as the one in whom God revealed himself as the Father of all humanity. In the process he showed that the law had genuine value, although this value was relative at the same time. It was a preliminary gift of God, whose role needed to be recognized and appreciated. One of its contributions was, in fact, to give birth to a new vocabulary by which the newness of Jesus could be expressed in relation to the law.[117]

William Loader. Although not a German but in substantial engagement with German scholarship, William Loader concurs with a number of other German exegetes on the point relevant to the thesis of this study.[118] His observation on the use of the Law in the Fourth Gospel enables him to posit several conclusions: first, "the Law [inclusive of more than the Pentateuch in the Fourth Gospel]

---

[116] Other significant contributions from Menken on the present subject are M.J.J. Menken, "The Christology of the Fourth Gospel: A Survey of Recent Research," in *From Jesus to John: Essays on Jesus and New Testament Christology in Honour of Marinus de Jonge*, ed. Martinus C. de Boer (Sheffield: JSOT, 1993), 292-320; idem, *Old Testament Quotations in the Fourth Gospel: Studies in Textual Form* (Kämpen: Kok Pharos, 1996); idem, "The Use of the Septuagint in Three Quotations in John: Jn 10,34; 12,38; 19,24," in *Scriptures in the Gospels*, ed. Christopher M. Tuckett (Louvain: Leuven University Press, 1997), 367-93; idem, "Interpretation of the Old Testament and the Resurrection of Jesus in John's Gospel," in *Resurrection in the New Testament*, ed. Reimund Bieringer et al. (Leuven: Leuven University Press, 2002), 189-205; idem, "The Minor Prophets in John's Gospel," in *The Minor Prophets in the New Testament: The New Testament and the Scriptures of Israel*, ed. M.J.J. Menken & Steve Moyise (London: T & T Clark, 2009), 79-96; idem, "Allusions to the Minor Prophets in the Fourth Gospel," *Neot* 44 (2010): 67-84.

[117] Xavier Léon-Dufour, *To Act according to the Gospel*, trans. Christopher R. Smith (Peabody: Hendrickson, 2005), 63.

[118] William Loader, "'Your Law'—the Johannine Perspective," in *". . . was ihr auf dem Weg verhandelt habt": Beiträge zur Exegese und Theologie des Neuen Testaments, Festschrift für Ferdinand Hahn zum 75. Geburtstag*, ed. Peter Müller, Christine Gerber and Thomas Knöppler, (Neukirchen-Vluyn: Neukirchener, 2001), 63-74. A slight revision of this article is also found in William Loader, "Jesus and the Law in John," in *Theology and Christology in the Fourth Gospel: Essays by the Members of the SNTS Johannine Writings Seminar*, ed. G. van Belle, J.G. van der Watt, and P. Maritz (Leuven: Leuven University, 2005), 135-54. This article in part grew out of a major section of the author's previous book-length study, William Loader, *Jesus' Attitude towards the Law: A Study of the Gospels* (Tübingen: Mohr Siebeck, 1997), esp. 432-91.

matters because it points forward to Christ."[119] The Scriptures [an equivalent of the Law in the Gospel] are not disparaged by any means because they were given by God with an implication that they bear divine authority. However, "generally there is replacement [theme]: of the temple and related laws not because of its destruction, but because . . . they have been taken up and replaced by Jesus."[120] In view of this estimation, "The role of the Old must now be redefined. Its role as the basis for cultic and ritual practice ceases. . . . Its role now is to testify through its words, stories and rituals to Christ."[121] That is to say that, "John affirms the Law only as testimony to Christ."[122]

> The exclusive Christology appears therefore to leave no room for a dual authority: the Son and the Law. What once was said of the Law now belongs exclusively to Christ. . . . the Law cannot be seen as anything more than supporting evidence, but at least this remains. The treatment of John the Baptist provides a helpful analogy. John is neither dismissed nor allowed to stand beside Jesus as a second authority.[123]

Klaus Scholtissek. In response primarily to Menken and other German exegetes, Klaus Scholtissek, one of the most prolific German writers of this generation on the Fourth Gospel, reconsiders various viewpoints on the function of the Old Testament in John's Gospel as proposed by Obermann, Menken, Kraus, Theobald, and Dietzfelbinger. He then goes on to classify them in three categories, namely, "the Christological fulfillment as abolition of the Scripture," "cancellation of salvation history," and "typological interpretation of Scripture."[124] Ultimately, Scholtissek is largely dissatisfied with these preceding views because they demonstrate a minimalistic appreciation of the Scriptures in view of the Johannine remark that "the law cannot be broken."[125]

His article is, however, unpersuasive at least on two fronts. On the one hand,

---

[119] Loader, "'Your Law'—the Johannine Perspective," 73.

[120] Ibid.

[121] Ibid.

[122] Ibid., 74. Similarly, "There seems to be a broad consensus that John sees the primary role of the Law as bearing witness to Christ." Idem, *Jesus' Attitude towards the Law*, 446.

[123] Loader, "Jesus and the Law in John," 152.

[124] Klaus Scholtissek, "'Die unaufulösbare Schrift' (Joh 10,35): Zur Auslegung und Theologie der Schrift Israels im Johannesevangelium," in *Johannesevangelium—Mitte oder Rand des Kanons?: Neue Standortbestimmungen*, ed. Thomas Söding (Freiburg: Herder, 2003), 146-77.

[125] The concern for anti-semitism seems to be a driving motive for Scholtissek's writings. Klaus Scholtissek, "Die Brotrede Jesu in Joh 6,1-71: Exegetische Beobachtungen zu ihrem johanneischen Profil," *ZKT* 123 (2001): 35-55; idem, "'Geschrieben in diesem Buch' (Joh 20,30): Beobachtungen zum kanonischen Anspruch des Johannes-evangeliums," in *Israel und seine Heilstraditionen im vierten Evangelium: Festgabe für Johannes Beutler SJ zum 70. Geburtstag*, ed. Michael Labahn, Klaus Scholtissek, and Angelika Strotmann (Paderborn: Schöningh, 2004), 207-26; idem, "'Ich und der Vater, wir sind eins' (Joh 10,30)," 315-46.

Scholtissek's interpretation of John 10:35 is misleading since the phrase (that "the law cannot be broken") was quoted to undergird the validity of the Scripture's testimony to Jesus' identity as "Son of God" in the immediate literary context as Menken's perceptive essay addresses the validity of the Scripture, that is, the Scripture is valid as far as it bears testimony to Jesus being Christ.[126] Second, he does not take into proper account the fourth evangelist's different use of the terms, λόγος ("word") and γραφή ("scripture"). The former refers to God incarnate while the latter points to the Mosaic writings. It is suspected that his judgment is largely driven by an extra-textual concern for Jewish-Christian dialogue rather than by the internal textual witness. This politically driven exegesis is also found in Bertold Klappert's study as it will be reviewed later more in detail in chapter five.[127]

Michael Labahn. A recent *Festschrift* to Johannes Beutler is devoted entirely to the questions concerning the Old Testament in the Fourth Gospel.[128] Some of the essays from this volume are particularly pertinent to the present discussion. Michael Labahn's essay addresses how the authority of Jesus supersedes that of the Old Testament. For him, Jesus is the hermeneutical key to Scripture, and the only passage to the true understanding of God:

> The Scripture and the incarnate Son stand qualified as one but they are not in the same relation. Jesus is the invisible and unheard hermeneutical key to the scripture. Without the incarnate Son, God is invisible and unheard. He and His glory is visible in Jesus.[129]

Labahn first recognizes that the recent German contributions to the theme of the

---

[126] Kraus, "Johannes und das Alte Testament," 22; Loader, "Jesus and the Law in John," 145-46.

[127] Bertold Klappert, "'Mose hat von mir geschrieben': Leitlinien einer Christologie im Kontext des Judentums Joh 5,39-47," in *Hebräische Bibel und ihre zweifache Nachgeschichte: Festschrift für Rolf Rendtorff zum 65. Geburtstag*, ed. Erhard Blum, Christian Macholz, and Ekkerhard W. Stegemann (Neukirchen-Vluyn: Neukirchener, 1990), 619-40.

[128] Michael Labahn, Klaus Scholtissek, and Angelika Strotmann, eds., *Israel und seine Heilstraditionen im vierten Evangelium: Festgabe für Johannes Beutler SJ zum 70. Geburtstag* (Paderborn: Schöningh, 2004). Other anthologies helpful for the understanding of John's historical backdrop are Jörg Frey and Udo Schnelle, eds., *Kontexte des Johannesevangeliums: Das vierte Evangelium in religions- und traditionsgeschichtlicher Perspektive* (Tübingen: Mohr Siebeck, 2004); Konrad Huber and Boris Repschinski, eds., *Im Geist und in der Wahrheit: Studien zum Johannesevangelium und zur Offenbarung des Johannes sowie andere Beiträge: Festschrift für Martin Hasitschka SJ zum 65. Geburtstag* (Münster: Aschendorff, 2008).

[129] Michael Labahn, "Jesus und die Autorität der Schrift im Johannesevangelium: Überlegungen zu einem spannungsreichen Verhältnis," in *Israel und seine Heilstraditionen im vierten Evangelium: Festgabe für Johannes Beutler SJ zum 70. Geburtstag*, ed. Michael Labahn, Klaus Scholtissek, and Angelika Strotman (Paderborn: Schöningh, 2004), 185-206, esp. 204 for the quotation.

Introduction   41

Old Testament in the Fourth Gospel are set within the notion of the complex unity of the Father and the Son (p. 186).[130] Within this unity, the Son is portrayed as the exclusive revelation of the Father. Thus, the Son possesses the revelatory superiority over Moses and the other Old Testament prophets chronologically, hermeneutically, and functionally. For Labahn, the hermeneutical key to Johannine Christology is, in this light, the concept of the pre-existent Logos, which legitimizes John's presentation of Jesus as the ultimate revelation of God himself.

There are two more essays from the *Festschrift* to Beutler that are pertinent to the present discussion. **Hans-Josef Klauck** advances nine distinct criteria by which Old Testament materials in the Gospel are to be identified: (1) marked quotations, (2) unmarked quotations, (3) allusions, (4) echo, (5) biblical language, (6) narrating figures and narrative example (pattern), (7) general statements about the Scripture, (8) Jewish interpretive traditions and techniques, (9) Christian reception.[131]

Michael Theobald, on the other hand, explores the perplexing question of the function of the Jewish Patriarchs who seem to be downplayed in John. The first point in his three-fold conclusion is particularly germane to the present discussion. That is, for the evangelist, Abraham is exclusively a witness for Christ.[132] In another study, Theobald reaches two other important conclusions: (1) this first observation does not imply the Johannine community being a "fatherless" society. Rather, the polemic is leveled against the synagogue of Jewish Christianity; and (2) a hermeneutical consideration pivotal for the Fourth Gospel is the past projection of the Johannine Christianity's self-denial suffered by the contemporary synagogue. Theobald made an important observation relating to the present discussion. His examination of the "bread speech" in John 6 reveals that Jesus is not the interpreter of the Scripture but is "the authoritative revealer" by which scripture can be properly understood. This understanding entails the rad-

---

[130] See also Michael Theobald, "Gott, Logos und Pneuma: 'Trinitarische' Rede von Gott im Johannesevangelium," in *Studien zum Corpus Iohanneum* (Tübingen: Mohr Sieberck, 2010), 349-88; Ulrich Wilckens, "Gott, der Drei-Eine: Zur Trinitätstheologie der johanneischen Schriften," in *Der Sohn Gottes und seine Gemeinde: Studien zur Theologie der Johanneischen Schriften* (Göttingen: Vandenhoeck & Ruprecht, 2003), 9-28; Udo Schnelle, "Trinitarisches Denken im Johannesevangelium," in *Israel und seine Heilstraditionen im Johannessevangelium: Festgabe für Johannes Beutler SJ zum 70. Geburtstag*, ed. Michael Labahn, Klaus Scholtissek, and Angelika Strotmann (Paderborn: Schöningh, 2004), 367-86.

[131] Hans-Josef Klauck, "Geschrieben, erfüllt, vollendet: die Schriftzitate in der Johannespassion," in *Israel und seine Heilstraditionen im vierten Evangelium: Festgabe für Johannes Beutler SJ zum 70. Geburtstag*, ed. Michael Labahn, Klaus Scholtissek, and Angelika Strotmann (Paderborn: Schöningh, 2004), 140-57.

[132] Michael Theobald, "Abraham—(Isaak—) Jacob: Israels Väter im Johannesevangelium," in *Studien zum Corpus Iohanneum* (Tübingen: Mohr Siebeck, 2010), 282-308.

ical paradigmatic hermeneutical shift in that the Old Testament loses the relevance for the history of Israel and has meaning only in relation to the Jesus event.[133]

Justification for the Present Study
Scripture as Christological Witness

A cursory review of the previous contributions shows that much has been already inquired of the role of the Old Testament messianic prefigures in the Fourth Gospel. However, three observations call for further research on the issue. First, for the last thirty years or so, important insights have emerged particularly among German scholarship concerning the role of the Scriptures and the prominent ancient Jewish figures in the Fourth Gospel. In their discussions, it is frequently acknowledged that Christology is an important hermeneutical key to John's interpretation of the Old Testament.[134] Moreover, the Scriptures and the Old Testament figures coherently play, as a whole (with some generalization), a witness function for the messianic identity of Jesus. Recent scholarly literature, especially written in the English language, however, has largely ignored these important contributions.[135] One of very few exceptions to this state is found in Paul Miller's brief article:

---

[133] Michael Theobald, "Schriftzitate im 'Lebensbrot'-Dialog Jesu (Joh 6): Ein Paradigma für den Schriftgebrauch des vierten Evangelisten," in *Studien zum Corpus Iohanneum* (Tübingen: Mohr Siebeck, 2010), 309-48.

[134] Cf. "John's school utilized the OT and Jewish wisdom tradition in a consistently christological fashion." Peter Stuhlmacher, "My Experience with Biblical Theology," in *Biblical Theology: Retrospect and Prospect*, ed. Scott J. Hafemann (Downers Grove: InterVarsity, 2002), 186.

[135] This oversight is attested to in Daly-Denton, *David in the Fourth Gospel*; Hamid-Khani, *Revelation and Concealment of Christ*; Diana M. Swancutt, "Hungers Assuaged by the Bread from Heaven: 'Eating Jesus' as Isaian Call to Belief, the Confluence of Isaiah 55 and Psalm 78 (77) in John 6:22-71," in *Early Christian Interpretation of the Scriptures of Israel: Investigations and Proposals*, ed. Craig A. Evans and James A. Sanders, JSNTSup 48 (Sheffield: Sheffield, 1997), 218-51; McGrath, *John's Apologetic Christology*; Stan Harstine, *Moses as a Character in the Fourth Gospel: A Study of Ancient Reading Techniques* (Sheffield: Sheffield, 2002); Jaime Clark-Soles, *Scripture Cannot Be Broken: The Social Function of the Use of Scripture in the Fourth Gospel*, (Leiden: Brill, 2003); Andrew C. Brunson, *Psalm 118 in the Gospel of John: An Intertextual Study on the New Exodus Pattern in the Theology of John* (Tübingen: Mohr Siebeck, 2003); Gary T. Manning, Jr., *Echoes of a Prophet: The Use of Ezekiel in the Gospel of John and in Literature of the Second Temple Period* (London: T & T Clark, 2004); Wallace, "The Testimony of Moses"; Susan Hylen, *Allusion and Meaning in John 6* (Berlin: Walter de Gruyter, 2005); Andrew Chester, *Messiah and Exaltation: Jewish Messianic and Visionary Traditions and New Testament Christology* (Tübingen: Mohr Siebeck, 2007) in the chronological order of their initial appearances.

But that Word is rightly understood only by those who see that it refers to the Logos who was manifested most completely in Jesus. In fact, Scripture is not really the direct self-disclosure of the Father, but testimony to the Son whom the Father has made known. The witness of Scripture, though true, cannot be anything but partial and provisional; and those who read it truthfully must realize that 'Moses and the prophets bear witness to Jesus.' . . . *Scripture is the enduring record of those who saw the activity of the divine Logos prior to its appearance in Jesus and then testified to what they had seen.*[136]

Lack of Study on the Role of the Old Testament Characters

Second, in spite of a plethora of studies on the messianic prefigurative role of the Old Testament characters in John, only selective personages (such as Moses or David) have been treated in isolation. No attempt has been made so far to probe into whether all the Old Testament figures that appear in John's Gospel play a coherent function in relation to his Christology. The absence of this type of comprehensive treatment is striking in light of the key importance of the Old Testament figures played in the intertestamental period. Maier, for instance, characterizes this period as having an increased interest in personalities within both Judaism and incipient Christianity: "It is general characteristic of this period a growing interest in personalities and characters."[137] Especially, the Abrahamic figure played an important apologetic role for the defense of Christianity.[138] Furthermore, a discussion on the messianic contribution of the Jewish patriarchs in the Gospel is virtually absent in recent Johannine scholarship, except for Theobald.[139]

Legitimacy of Tradition-Historical Approach

As a corollary to those two inquiries mentioned above, the propriety of the *traditionsgeschichtliche* approach for the Johannine Gospel should be reckoned, as it has become an almost accepted presupposition within certain academic circles

---

[136] Paul Miller, "'They Saw His Glory and Spoke of Him': The Gospel of John and the Old Testament," in *Hearing the Old Testament in the New Testament*, ed. Stanley E. Porter (Grand Rapids: Eerdmans, 2006), 127-51 (italics original). Also, John Painter, *The Quest for the Messiah: The History, Literature and Theology of the Johannine Community* (Nashville: Abingdon, 1993), 32. Miller also notes the coherent witness function of the Old Testament figures in the Gospel. Miller, "'They Saw His Glory and Spoke of Him,'" 137-48.

[137] Johann Maier, "Schriftrezeption im jüdischen Umfeld des Johannesevangeliums," in *Israel und seine Heilstraditionen im Johannesevangelium: Festgabe für Johannes Beutler SJ zum 70. Geburtstag*, ed. Michael Labahn, Klaus Scholtissek, and Angelika Strotmann (Paderborn: Schöningh, 2004), 56. Also, Marie-Françoise Baslez, "Écrire l'histoire dans le judaïsme hellénisé et le premier christianisme: Les galleries de figures ancestrales," in *Eukarpa: Études sur la Bible et ses exégètes en hommage à Gilles Dorival*, ed. Mireille Loubet and D. Pralon (Paris: Cerf, 2011), 191.

[138] Rainer Albertz, "Isaak II: Neues Testament," *TRE*, 16:296.

[139] Theobald, "Abraham—(Isaak—) Jacob: Israels Väter im Johannesevangelium."

that there was a continuous tradition of thoughts in Jewish writings of the intertestamental period bridging the two Testaments. This approach arose as a more positive alternative to the history of religions approach in view of the recent recognition of its limitations and legitimacy as an interpretive tool for the relationship between the two Testaments traditions. A Tübingen exegete expresses confidence in the history of traditions approach as following:

> The method by which the unity of the Bible is best suited is, I would describe, the history of traditions interpretation. It is important to follow the Scriptures of the Old Testament and its interpretation, first in early Judaism, whether Palestinian or Hellenistic, then in the New Testament and finally even in rabbinic literature that was written only after the New Testament period, but in its oral stage partially going back to the New Testament times. Hence, there are criteria for legitimacy and limit of the form-critical method.[140]

Here it should be also noted that Betz uses the terminologies with different definitions. As for him, "the form-historical method" designates the extreme history of religions assumptions, such as those maintained by Rudolf Bultmann. Similarly, another Tübinger bears testimony to such a view:

> Today, that the New Testament without the knowledge of contemporary Jewish history and religion remains largely incomprehensible is seldom challenged. But, the trend is being reversed. The New Testament times are gradually recognized as an important source for the study of Judaism.[141]

Thus, this approach adequately accounts for not only some particular expressions but the basic theological frameworks attested to in the canonical scope of the Christian Bible and other Jewish documents of the intertestamental period.[142] It seems to be an opportune juncture to reconsider the methodical legitimacy of the approach, at least for the Gospel of John, *vis-à-vis* an examination of the Gospel's self-claim on the messianic prefigurative and/or witness role of the Old Testament protagonists in view of their depictions in early Judaism.

Methods

Diachronic and Synchronic Approaches

There has been a tendency in biblical scholarship to bifurcate the approaches to New Testament studies into diachronic and synchronic studies, and to argue in

---

[140] Otto Betz, "Das Johannesevangelium und das Alte Testament," in *Wie verstehen wir das Neue Testament?* (Wuppertal: Aussaat, 1981), 14-20, especially 17 for this citation.

[141] Martin Hengel, "Das Johannesevangelium als Quelle für die Geschichte des antiken Judentums," in *Judaica, Hellenistica, et Christiana: Kleine Schriften II*, ed. Martin Hengel with Jörg Frey and Dieter Betz (Tübingen: Mohr Siebeck, 1999), 294-95.

[142] For instance, "a heavenly, transcendent Messiah was not a unique invention of the Christian community but the outgrowth of reflection that had its roots in Judaism." Neufeld, "And When That One Comes?" 140.

Introduction

favor of one at the expense of the other. For instance, Martin Hengel, in his inaugural address as the president of Society for New Testament Studies, expressed an outcry for the immediate need to return to a sound diachronic approach in the discipline of New Testament studies.

> New Testament scholarship must move beyond its current preoccupation with faddish methods (as evidenced by several variations of the so-called new literary criticism) and return to a solid grounding in history, primary source materials, archaeology, and competence in the pertinent languages.[143]

Some Johannine exegetes point out that narrative criticism neglects the formative historical aspects of the Fourth Gospel and the difference between fictional and non-fictional texts.[144] To give an example from the opposite pole, Larry Chouinard asserts that "the literary paradigm is logically prior to the historical analysis" in the inquiry of the Gospel Christology.[145]

The sharp schism between the two, however, has been lately recognized as artificial and unnecessary, and accordingly, some practitioners of historical criticism have adopted in some measure positive insights offered by literary critics.[146] That is, the extremely fragmentizing tendency of the diachronic approach (i.e., identifying multiple redactional layers resulting from various his-

---

[143] Martin Hengel, "Aufgaben der neutestamentlichen Wissenschaft (Presidential Address, SNTS, Chicago, August 1993)," *NTS* 40 (1994): 321-57; an English translation of the article is found in Martin Hengel, "Tasks of New Testament Scholarship," *BBR* 6 (1996): 67-86 (p. 67 for the quotation).

[144] John Ashton, "Narrative Criticism," in *Studying John: Approaches to the Fourth Gospel* (Oxford: OUP, 1998), 141-65; idem, "Second Thoughts on the Fourth Gospel," in *What We Have Heard from the Beginning: The Past, Present, and Future of Johannine Studies*, ed. Tom Thatcher (Waco: Baylor University Press, 2007), 1-18. For an example of studies that shows the benefit of historical critical method, see Jean-Louis Ska, "Les vertus de la méthodes historico-critique," *NRTh* 131 (2009): 705-27.

[145] Larry Chouinard, "Gospel Christology: A Study of Methodology," in *New Testament Interpretation and Methods: A Sheffield Reader*, ed. Stanley E. Porter and Craig A. Evans (Sheffield: Sheffield, 1997), 69. For other examples of strong proponents of synchronic approach for the study of the Fourth Gospel, see Adele Reinhartz, "Building Skyscrapers on Toothpicks: The Literary-Critical Challenge to Historical Criticism," in *Anatomies of Narrative Criticism: The Past, Present, and Futures of the Fourth Gospel as Literature*, ed. Tom Thatcher and Stephen D. Moore (Atlanta: Society of Biblical Literature, 2008), 55-76; Jean Zumstein, "Narrativité et herméneutique du Nouveau Testament: La naissance d'un nouveau paradigm," *RTL* 40 (2009): 324-40; James L. Resseguie, "A Narrative-Critical Approach to the Fourth Gospel," in *Characters and Characterization in the Gospel of John*, ed. Christopher W. Skinner (London: T & T Clark, 2013), 3-17.

[146] For examples of this tendency, see Robert H. Stein, *Studying the Synoptic Gospels: Origin and Interpretation* (Grand Rapids: Baker, 2001), 274-75; Edwin K. Broadhead, "Narrativity and Naiveté: Critical Reflections on Literary Analysis of the Gospels," *PRSt* 35 (2008): 9-24.

torical situations) probably does not accurately reflect the reality of writing. A recent insight into the Johannine literary structure militates against the suggested merits of a conventional literary investigation of the Fourth Gospel. For instance, Peter Ellis's analysis of the Johannine literary structure strongly suggests the pervasive orality at its writing stage of the Gospel.[147] With this orality as the most prominent communication factor at its formative stage, the former generation's form and redactional stages are called into serious question.[148]

As such, an individual document within the entire New Testament corpus should be treated as a coherent literary unity in view of its literary context:

> The result is stated: The question of the coherence must be preceded by the question of tensions and fractures. It is because the question of coherence is aimed at determining the form in the sense of a meaningful relationship. This pre-order means for the tradition-historical way of working that it must come more than ever from the unity of form and content and should therefore explain especially the relationship of the whole.[149]

Joanna Dewey also adds to this growing awareness in the oral nature of the first century communication pattern.

> Oral stories do not continue to circulate as isolated, independent units until they are drawn together in written texts, as form criticism has traditionally supposed. Rather, individual stories tend to aggregate into a larger, more or less coherent overall oral narrative focused on a hero or heroes, and such an oral narrative is likely to underlie the gospels. . . . Knowledge of first-century media culture suggests that such a written source [signs source] is improbable. . . . Furthermore . . . the level of FG [the Fourth Gospel]'s Greek suggests reliance on oral memory rather than use of written source texts.[150]

This notion entails the importance of considering the narrative flow. Although an excessive preoccupation with complex structural analysis must be equally avoided (such as reconstructing a sophisticated chiastic structure), a considerable measure of exegetical benefit can be gained by paying attention, first, to the immediate context that precedes and follows a pericope under discussion and,

---

[147] Peter F. Ellis, "Understanding the Concentric Structure of the Fourth Gospel," *SVTQ* 47 (2003): 131-54.

[148] For a convenient survey of various form, source, and redactional proposals for the Gospel of John in the earlier generation of critics, see Raymond E. Brown, *An Introduction to the Gospel of John*, ed. Francis J. Moloney (New York: Doubleday, 2003), 40-89. Markku Kotila observes the consensus of German Johannine scholarship (Bultmann, Becker, Schnackenburg, Schulz, and Gnilka) that assumes three redactional layers present in the Gospel of John. Markku Kotila, *Umstrittener Zeuge: Studien zur Stellung des Gesetzes in der johanneischen Theologiegeschichte* (Helsinki: Suomalainen Tiedeakatemia, 1988), 3.

[149] Klaus Berger, *Exegese des Neuen Testaments: Neue Wege vom Text zur Auslegung* (Wiesbaden: Quelle und Meyer, 1991), 32.

[150] Joanna Dewey, "The Gospel of John in Its Oral-Written Media World," in *Jesus in Johannine Tradition*, ed. Robert T. Fortna and Tom Thatcher (Louisville: Westminster/John Knox, 2001), 248-49. Parentheses are added for clarification.

second, to the overall literary schema of the entire document (i.e., the central message of the Fourth Gospel). Accordingly, recent biblical scholarship displays the increasing awareness of the exegetical benefits gained by combining the two approaches. This recognition results in the integration of these two methods, instead of their mutual exclusion, and seems to have provided a more productive venue for Gospel studies.[151] This trend generated a new approach, namely, "composition criticism," which recognizes the competence of the final author (the contribution of redaction criticism) and the importance of the final form of the Gospels (the contribution of literary criticism). Accordingly, the once seen irreconcilable approaches (synchronic and diachronic) appear to have converged into a more productive method of research.[152] With such a judgment in mind, this study utilizes an eclectic approach as it deems necessary and beneficial, but without excessively engaging with extereme historical reconstructions or sophisticated literary analyses.

> Thus, if the future of Johannine exegesis wants to design a contextual theology, and not as an interpretation disregard to time and place, we have to put diachrony and synchrony into a mutually reflective relationship as [scholars have endeavored on]

---

[151] For a notion of this tendency in general, see Adela Yarbro-Collins, "Narrative, History, and Gospel," *Semeia* 43 (1988): 145-53; David R. Catchpole, "Source, Form and Redaction Criticism of the New Testament," in *Handbook to Exegesis of the New Testament*, ed. Stanley E. Porter (Leiden: Brill, 1997), 167-88; Margaret M. Mitchell, "Rhetorical and New Literary Criticism," in *The Oxford Handbook of Biblical Studies*, ed. J.W. Rogerson and Judith M. Lieu (Oxford: OUP, 2006), 615-17; Ulrich Berges, "Synchronie und Diachronie: Zur Methodenvielfalt in der Exegese," *BK* 62 (2007): 249-52. For the Gospel of John in particular, see Martinus C. de Boer, "Narrative Criticism, Historical Criticism, and the Gospel of John," *JSNT* 47 (1992): 35-48; Stanley E. Porter, "Can Traditional Exegesis Enlighten Literary Analysis of the Fourth Gospel?: An Examination of the Old Testament Fulfillment Motif and the Passover Theme," in *Gospels and the Scriptures of Israel*, ed. Craig A. Evans and Wolfgang R. Stegner (Sheffield: Sheffield, 1994), 396-428; Steve Motyer, "Method in Fourth Gospel Studies: A Way out of the Impasse?" *JSNT* 66 (1997): 27-44; Smalley, *John*, 126-28; Helge Kjær Nielsen, "Johannine Research," in *New Readings in John: Literary and Theological Perspectives Essays from the Scandinavian Conference on the Fourth Gospel in Århus 1997*, ed. Johannes Nissen and Sigfred Pedersen (Sheffield: Sheffield, 1999), 12-14.

[152] The arbitrary nature of the previous redaction approach which inherited the context-downplaying tendency from form and source criticisms is noted in D.A. Carson, "Redaction Criticism: On the Legitimacy and Illegitimacy of a Literary Tool," in *Scripture and Truth*, ed. D.A. Carson and John D. Woodbridge (Grand Rapids: Zondervan, 1983), 119-46. The co-authored introduction to the New Testament by Carson and Moo is more favorable to redaction approach than the aforementioned Carson's article. D.A. Carson and Douglas J. Moo, *An Introduction to the New Testament* (Grand Rapids: Zondervan, 2005), 103-12.

those two approaches for quite some time.[153]

Intertextuality

Category of intertextuality. First of all, a recent notion of intertextual dynamics in the Fourth Gospel, which is primarily synchronic in its presupposition, will be taken into account. In order to meet this end, certain Old Testament materials contained in John need to be identified. In reality, however, it could be precarious to walk on that path due to the lack of clear demarcations for identifying the Old Testament traits. Porter, for instance, laments that previous researches into the New Testament use of the Old Testament have suffered from the imprecise usage of terminologies employed by different scholars.[154] Some of the New Testament exegetes have, therefore, recently suggested clearer and more specific sets of criteria to detect the presence of the Old Testament in the New. For instance, Anthony T. Hanson suggests five ways in which the Old Testament is utilized in the Gospel of John: (1) the use of written scriptural sources without formal introductions, (2) citations with formal indications (i.e., the so-called fulfillment formulae), (3) quotations without formal introductions, (4) Christological use of the scriptural concepts, and (5) the Old Testament influence on narrative style.[155] More precisely, I. Howard Marshall also identifies seven areas in which the New Testament writers made use of the Old Testament: (1) the influence of the language of the Old Testament; (2) the influence of the style of the Old Testament; (3) literal reference to events; (4) literal reference to commands; (5) literal reference to prophecies; (6) typological reference; and (7) allegorical reference.[156] A third example is from Hans-Josef Klauck, who suggests nine criteria by which to define the presence of the Old Testament in John's Gospel: (1) marked quotations, (2) unmarked quotations, (3) allusions, (4) echo, (5) Biblical language, (6) narrating figures and narrative example (pattern), (7) general statements about the Scripture, (8) Jewish interpretation traditions and

---

[153] Joachim Kügler, "Das Johannesevangelium," in *Einleitung in das Neue Testament*, ed. Martin Ebner and Stefan Schreiber (Stuttgart: Kohlhammer, 2008), 213. Brackets are included for clarification.

[154] Stanley E. Porter, "The Use of the Old Testament in the New Testament: A Brief Comment on Method and Terminology," in *Early Christian Interpretation of the Scriptures of Israel: Investigations and Proposals*, ed. Craig A. Evans and James A. Sanders (Sheffield: Sheffield, 1997), 79-96; Jean Zumstein, "Intratextuality and Intertextuality in the Gospel of John," in *Anatomies of Narrative Criticism: The Past, Present, and Futures of the Fourth Gospel as Literature*, ed. Tom Thatcher and Stephen D. Moore (Atlanta: The Society of Biblical Literature, 2008), 133-34.

[155] A.T. Hanson, "John's Technique in Using Scripture," in *The New Testament Interpretation of Scripture* (London: T & T Clark, 1980), 157-76.

[156] I. Howard Marshall, "An Assessment of Recent Developments," in *It is Written: Scripture Citing Scripture: Essays in Honour of Barnabas Lindars*, ed. D.A. Carson and H.G.M. Williamson (Cambridge: Cambridge University Press, 1988), 9-10.

techniques, and (9) Christian reception.[157]

The criteria of Marshall, however, seem more difficult (than that of Klauck's formal criteria) to apply because his categories demand *a priori* hermeneutical judgments, whereas those of Hanson are not comprehensive enough (for instance, the use of the conceptual symbols and Old Testament figures is not accounted for). As such, this dissertation will employ the criteria suggested by Klauck. However, a primary consideration will be given only to the first four categories (citations with an introductory formula, citations without an introduction, allusions, and echoes) with reference to the Old Testament characters while due attention will be also paid to the rest of the five aspects as deemed necessary.[158] In terms of Marshall's category, all but the first two are directly related to this study.

A word of caution, however, is in order at this juncture concerning the defi-

---

[157] Klauck, "Geschrieben, erfüllt, vollendet," 143-44.

[158] For the stylistic and linguistic influence of the Old Testament on the New, see Joseph A. Fitzmyer, *A Wandering Aramean: Collected Aramaic Essays* (Missoula: Scholars, 1979). Another example of criteria to discern the Old Testament quotations in the New includes the following: (1) introduction of the quotation by an explicit quotation formula; (2) an interpretative gloss accompanying the quotation, and (3) syntactical tension between the quotation and its New Testament context. Christopher D. Stanley, *Paul and the Language of Scripture: Citation Technique in the Pauline Epistles and Contemporary Literature* (Cambridge: CUP, 1992), 65-82. For more essays on the methodology of intertextuality and its implications for the study of the New Testament, see R.T. France, *Jesus and the Old Testament: His Application of Old Testament Passages to Himself and His Mission* (Vancouver: Regent College Publishing, 1982), 259-63; Steve Moyise, "Intertextuality and Biblical Studies: A Review," *VE* 23 (2002): 418-31; Stefan Alkier, "Dei Bibel im Dialog der Schriften und das Problem der Verstockung in Mk. 4: Intertextualität im Rahmen einer kategorialen Semiotik biblischer Texte," in *Die Bibel im Dialog der Schriften: Konzepte intertextueller Bibellektüre*, ed. Stefan Alkier and Richard B. Hays (Tübingen: Francke, 2005), 1-22; idem, "Intertextualität—Literatur in Auswahl," in *Die Bibel im Dialog der Schriften: Konzepte intertextueller Bibellektüre*, ed. Stefan Alkier and Richard B. Hays (Tübingen: Francke, 2005), 257-64; Dennis L. Stamps, "Use of the Old Testament in the New Testament as a Rhetorical Device: A Methodological Proposal," in *Hearing the Old Testament in the New Testament*, ed. Stanley E. Porter (Grand Rapids: Eerdmans, 2006), 9-37; R.T. McKay, "Biblical Texts and the Scriptures for the New Testament Church," in *Hearing the Old Testament in the New Testament*, ed. Stanley E. Porter (Grand Rapids: Eerdmans, 2006), 38-59; James H. Charlesworth, "Towards a Taxonomy of Discerning Influence(s) between Two Texts," in *Das Gesetz im frühen Judentum und im Neuen Testament: Festschrift für Christoph Burchard zum 75. Geburtstag*, ed. Dieter Sänger and Matthias Konradt (Göttingen: Vandenhoeck & Ruprecht; Fribourg: Academic, 2006), 41-54; G.K. Beale and D.A. Carson, "Introduction," in *Commentary on the New Testament Use of the Old Testament* (Grand Rapids: Baker, 2007), xxiii-xxviii; Robert. A. Kraft, *Exploring the Scripturesque: Jewish Texts and Their Christian Contexts* (Leiden: Brill, 2009); G.K. Beale, *Handbook on the New Testament Use of the Old Testament: Exegesis and Interpretation* (Grand Rapids: Baker, 2012).

nitions of "allusions" and "echoes." Although there is a general consensus that allusions encompass echoes, some scholars have sought to clearly demarcate between the two. For example, Richard Hays put forward seven tests to discern echoes: availability, volume, recurrence, thematic coherence, historical plausibility, history of interpretation and satisfaction.[159] He, thus, notes that echo is a subtler allusion:

> The concept of allusion depends both on the notion of authorial intention and on the assumption that the reader will share with the author the requisite 'popular library' to recognize the source of the allusion; the notion of echo, however, finesses such questions.[160]

However, some of these categories are quite difficult to define clearly, not to mention its practice in reality. It is virtually impossible, for instance, with a high degree of certainty to determine the availability (whether certain scriptural material was known to the reader) and history of interpretation (how a certain scriptural text was understood in the community to which the readers belonged) primarily because the business of identifying the so-called community of each New Testament writing is notoriously subjective.[161] While Hays himself recognizes the elusive nature of establishing objective criteria for allusions and echoes, nonetheless, he is concerned more with being too loose with his criteria than with being too restrictive:

> Although the foregoing texts are serviceable rules of thumb to guide our interpretive work, we must acknowledge that there will be exceptional occasions when the texts fail to account for the spontaneous power of particular intertextual conjunctions. Despite all the careful hedges that we plant around texts, meaning has a way of leaping over, like sparks.[162]

---

[159] Richard B. Hays, *Echoes of Scripture in the Letters of Paul* (New Haven: Yale University Press, 1989), 29-32.

[160] Hays, *Echoes of Scripture in the Letters of Paul*, 29.

[161] For a thorough critique of Hays' criteria to discern echoes, see Christopher Tuckett, "Paul, Scripture and Ethics," in *New Testament Writers and the Old Testament: An Introduction*, ed. John M. Court (London: SPCK, 2002), 71-97.

[162] Hays, *Echoes of Scripture in the Letters of Paul*, 32-33. Hays' application of his criteria is also somewhat obscure. "Echoes linger in the air and lure the reader of Paul's letters back into the symbolic world of Scripture. Paul's allusions gesture toward precursors whose words are already heavy with tacit implications." Ibid., 155. The arbitrary nature of Hays hermeneutical program is attested to in Richard Hays, "Can the Gospels Teach us How to Read the Old Testament?" *ProEccl* 11 (2002): 412-15. Here Hays is primarily concerned with the role of the original readers. However, in practice, his own theological agenda (or that of those who share his) overshadows his hermeneutics. In his interpretation of Psalm 69:9 alluded to in John 2:17, he colors his reading with the themes of vindication of Jesus and the restoration of Israel, both of which are not clearly indicated as the primary interest of the Gospel at least on the surface level in John 2 or in the rest of the Gospel. See "Thus, a reading of Psalm 69 after the passion and resurrection of Jesus would disclose that the Psalm is to be read as

Hays' observation of the difficulty to identify the intertextual dynamics is probably valid, but the scientific nature of biblical exegesis requires a particular nature of repeatability. That is, an exegete must be able to repeatedly demonstrate the intertextual dynamics in the crucible of exegesis by means of the available data, i.e., the Old Testament, the extant intertestamental Jewish documents, and the New Testament. Other exegetes, such as Greg Beale, point to the authorial intention as a valid criterion to demarcate allusions from echoes. Echoes, thus, differ from allusions in that they are the product of the author's sub-consciousness. He stresses a "reasonable or persuasive explanation of authorial motive" to discern the presence of allusion.[163] Although this notion seems to more closely reflect the reality of writing, it still does not completely avoid a sense of obscurity.[164] Therefore, echoes of the Old Testament scriptures will be taken into account with caution in the following investigation.

Once the relevant citations of and allusions (or references) to the Old Testament characters are identified, an inquiry will proceed as to how such appropriation of the Old Testament materials (or traditions) contributes to the Johannine Christology. In this respect, the criterion suggested by Zumstein are helpful: (1) the source of the Old Testament tradition (i.e., MT or LXX), (2) the exact nature of appropriation (i.e., citation, allusion, or echo), (3) the possibility of utilizing certain Jewish hermeneutical traditions (i.e., haggadah or targumic), (4) the social setting of the Old Testament appropriation (i.e., pre-Christian or Jewish theology), and finally (5) conservative or creative hermeneutical use of the Old Testament tradition. The present study is primarily concerned with the questions he raises with the exclusion of the third and fourth inquiries. Overall, however, the main question asked is the Christological contribution of the Old

---

a poetic depiction of the suffering and vindication of Jesus the Messiah, whose voice 'David' had anticipated. . . . One implication of such a reading is that the meaning of Jesus' resurrection is not to be understood apart from Israel's hope for deliverance and restoration." Hays, "Can the Gospels Teach us How to Read the Old Testament?", 413-14.

[163] G.K. Beale, *The Use of Daniel in Jewish Apocalyptic Literature and in the Revelation of St. John* (Lanham: University Press of America, 1984), 307-11; idem, *John's Use of the Old Testament in Revelation* (Sheffield: Sheffield, 1999), 62-67; Steve Moyise, "Intertextuality and the Study of the Old Testament in the New Testament," in *The Old Testament in the New Testament: Essays in Honour of J.L. North*, Steve Moyise (Sheffield: Sheffield, 2000), 18-19; idem, "Intertextuality and Historical Approaches to the Use of Scripture in the New Testament." *VE* 26 (2005): 447-58; Manning, *Echoes of a Prophet*, 13-14.

[164] This difficulty of identifying allusive presence of the Old Testament traditions is also noted in Martin Hengel, "Die Schriftauslegung des 4. Evangeliums auf dem Hintergrund der urchristlichen Exegese," in *"Gesetz" als Thema Biblischer Theologie*, ed. Ingo Baldermann and Dwight R. Daniels (Neukirchen-Vluyn: Neukirchen, 1989), 275, 282-87; Theobald, "Schriftzitate im 'Lebensbrot'-Dialog Jesu (Joh 6)," 309, n. 2.

Testament messianic prefigures in John.¹⁶⁵

Implication of orality. The observation of different criteria to discern the presence of the Old Testament in the New as reviewed above is in no way meant to disparage the contributions and insights certain scholars attempt to offer on the issue under discussion, but rather it is to demonstrate the complexities inherent in this type of study. Thus, it seems best to limit this study to citations and strong allusions so that the current investigation will remain as a feasible project. Faint allusions or echoes could be merely a creation of a reader's imagination, therefore, interfering with the results of this research. As such, overly subtle allusions and echoes will be excluded from serious consideration, although at times they will be briefly addressed when they seem relevant. With this remark, it must be also noted that this investigation is undertaken with certain exegetical predilections. That is, instead of a reader-oriented approach, this study is more interested in the authorial intention (which characterizes the diachronic orientation of this research) and the meaning inherent in the text.¹⁶⁶ The reason lies in an opinion that the attempts to retrieve the meaning of the author or the text better account for the first century Mediterranean communication pattern, namely, orality as its default mode.¹⁶⁷ At this juncture, John Ashton's bleak critique against read-

---

[165] Jean Zumstein, "Die Schriftrezeption in der Brotrede (Joh 6)," in *Israel und seine Heilstraditionen im Johannesevangelium: Festgabe für Johannes Beutler SJ zum 70. Geburtstag*, ed. Micahel Labahn, Klaus Scholtissek, and Angelika Strotmann (Paderborn: Ferdinand Schöningh, 2004), 123-24.

[166] For a review essay summarizing the last thirty years' growing awareness in and implications of the orality for the study of the Gospels, see Kelly R. Iverson, "Orality and the Gospels: A Survey of Recent Research," *CurBR* 8 (2009): 71-106. For an article that articulates the value of author-oriented hermeneutics, see Robert H. Stein, "The Benefits of an Author-Oriented Approach to Hermeneutics," *JETS* 44 (2001): 451-66. Also see the value of the author-oriented intertextual studies. Harstine, "The Functions of Moses as a Character in the Fourth Gospel and Responses of Three Ancient Mediterranean Audiences," 9-15. On the contrary, for a study that stresses the importance of readers who confer various meanings to the text, see Hieke Thomas, "Vom Verstehen biblischer Texte: Methodologisch-hermeneutische Erwägungen zum Programm einer 'biblischen Auslegung,'" *BN* 119-120 (2003): 71-89.

[167] For studies on the corollaries of the oral dynamics for New Testament scholarship, see Birger Gerhardsson, *Memory and Manuscript: Oral Tradition and Written Transmission in Rabbinic Judaism and Early Christianity with Tradition and Transmission in Early Christianity* (Grand Rapids: Eerdmans, 1998); idem, "The Gospel Tradition," in *Interrelations of the Gospels: A Symposium Led by M.-É. Boismard, W.R. Farmer, F. Neirynck, Jerusalem 1984*, ed. David L. Dungan (Louvain: Leuven University Press, 1990), 497-545; Paul J. Achtemeier, "Omne Verbum Sonat: The New Testament and the Oral Environment of Late Western Antiquity," *JBL* 109 (1990): 3-27; Henry Wansbrough, ed., *Jesus and the Oral Gospel Tradition* (Sheffield: JSOT, 1991); Samuel Byrskog, *Story as History—History as Story: The Gospel Tradition in the Context of Ancient Oral History* (Tübingen: Mohr Siebeck, 2000); Robert H. Stein, "Is Our Reading the Bible the Same as the Original Audience's Hearing It?: A Case Study

er-oriented interpretation is illuminating:

> Reader-response theorists do their best to guard their first-time readers from any knowledge that might sully the purity of their responses and prevent them from reacting to the text in the way that they (the theorists) have imagined. But ignorant as they are, they must know *something*, and *what* they know . . . will be prescribed by the theorists who are their only-begetters. It is hard to see this procedure as anything other than alegatory exegesis of the worst kind. . . . Why not face the fact that implied readers, as they are called, are simply doing the exegetes' job for them, but with one hand tied behind their back? Undo the knot and they are transformed into real readers, free to use whatever tools are lying to hand. These are the tools of historical criticism.[168]

The importance of orality in the first century Mediterranean communicative environment is increasingly recognized in recent Gospel scholarship, and it entails two important exegetical corollaries in particular. First, unlike visual communication models, such as reading, the orality in human communication is much less conducive for meditations on some literary devices, such as, complicated typology, subtle symbolism, and extended chiastic structures.[169] Second, orality and its concomitant eyewitness aspect reinforce the crucial role of individuals—especially those eyewitnesses of the original Jesus traditions—in the

---

in the Gospel of Mark," *JETS* 46 (2003): 63-78; Richard A. Horsley, Jonathan A. Draper, and John Miles Foley, eds., *Performing the Gospel: Orality, Memory, and Mark, Essays Dedicated to Werner Kelber* (Minneapolis: Fortress, 2006); Dennis C. Duling, "Memory, Collective Memory, Orality and the Gospels," *HvTSt* 67 (2011): 1-11. For expressions of such a caution more directly impinging upon the study of the Fourth Gospel, see Dewey, "The Gospel of John in Its Oral-Written Media World," 239-52; Ellis, "Understanding the Concentric Structure of the Fourth Gospel," 131-54. These studies in various degrees point to the reliability of the oral tradition and the important role of individual witnesses in transmitting and formulating the Gospel traditions.

[168] John Ashton, "Studying John," in *Studying John: Approaches to the Fourth Gospel* (Oxford: OUP, 1998), 199.

[169] James Dunn also notes the corollary of this nature of orality. The fluidity and flexibility of the original oral tradition makes implausible the recent confidence of complicated form and source reconstructions with regards to the Gospel of John. James D.G. Dunn, "John and the Oral Gospel Tradition," in *Jesus and the Oral Gospel Tradition*, ed. Henry Wansbrough (Sheffield: JSOT, 1991), 351-79; idem, "Jesus in Oral Memory: The Initial Stages of the Jesus Tradition," *SBLSP* 39 (2000): 287-326; idem, "Altering the Default Setting: Re-Envisaging the Early Transmission of the Jesus Tradition," *NTS* 49 (2003): 139-75; idem, *A New Perspective on Jesus: What the Quest for the Historical Jesus Missed* (Grand Rapids: Baker, 2005); idem, "The Gospels as Oral Traditions," in *The Living Word* (Minneapolis: Fortress, 2009), 21-36; idem, "John's Gospel and the Oral Gospel Tradition," in *The Audience of the Gospels: The Origin and Function of the Gospels in Early Christianity*, ed. Edward W. Klink, III (London: T & T Clark, 2010), 157-86. However, it must be also noted that the prevalence of orality does not necessarily exclude the possibility of the use of written traditions in the writing of John's Gospel as Paul Achtemeier seems to presume. Schuchard, *Scripture within Scripture*, xvi-xvii.

transmission and formulation of the Gospel traditions. As a consequence, they buttress the reliability of the Gospel traditions:

> If the Form Critics are right, the disciples must have been translated to heaven immediately after the Resurrection.... [Many eyewitnesses of the Gospel events] did not go into permanent retreat; for at least a generation they moved among the young Palestinian communities, and through preaching and fellowship their recollections were at the disposal of those who sought information.[170]

In conclusion, the significance of orality in the transmission and formation of the Fourth Gospel precludes the inclusion of subtle echoes and sophisticated analyses of literary devices in the Gospel.

Religious Comparative Analysis

In addition to the attention given to intertextual dynamics, the religious comparative analysis of early Judaism and John's Gospel, which is diachronic in its orientation, will be undertaken so as to shed light on the alleged affinity between the Fourth Gospel and its most closely related religio-cultural backdrop, namely, early Judaism (see Appendix 2 for the necessity and relevance of religious-historical discussions). This inquiry, however, does not seek traces of direct dependence between them. Rather, it attempts to demonstrate the presence and/or degree of theological backgrounds and climate of thoughts that are supposedly common to and probably available between both streams of religious expressions.[171] In the process of this comparative investigation, furthermore, the provenance of the intertestamental Jewish materials will be carefully weighed. Although it is commonplace to acknowledge the presence of variegated soundings within early Judaism, it is totally another matter to claim that the early Judaism of the diaspora settings (for example, that of the Egyptian context) and

---

[170] Vincent Taylor, *The Formation of the Gospel Tradition: Eight Lectures* (London: Macmillan, 1949), 41-42. Similarly, for the importance of orality and its corollary for the reliability of the Fourth Gospel, see Martin Hengel, *The Four Gospels and the One Gospel of Jesus Christ: An Investigation of the Collection and Origin of the Canonical Gospels* (Harrisburg: Trinity, 2000), 143; Arthur J. Dewey, "The Eyewitness of History," in *Jesus in Johannine Tradition*, ed. Robert T. Fortna and Tom Thatcher (Louisville: Westminster/John Knox, 2001), 59-70; Richard Bauckham, "The Eyewitnesses and the Gospel Traditions," *JSHJ* 1 (2003): 28-60; idem, *Jesus and the Eyewitnesses: The Gospels as Eyewitness Testimony* (Grand Rapids: Eerdmans, 2006); idem, "Historiographical Characteristics of the Gospel of John," in *The Testimony of the Beloved Disciple: Narrative, History, and Theology in the Gospel of John* (Grand Rapids: Baker, 2007), 93-112. For a brief review of the previous generation's skepticism over the historical reliability of the Fourth Gospel, see William Baird, *From Deism to Tübingen*, vol. 1 of *History of New Testament Research* (Minneapolis: Fortress, 1992), 311-19.

[171] For examples of such approaches, see Robert M. Wilson, "Philo and the Fourth Gospel," *ExpTim* 65 (1953): 47-49; Catherine Hezser, "Diaspora and Rabbinic Judaism," in *The Oxford Handbook of Biblical Studies*, ed. J.W. Rogerson and Judith M. Lieu (Oxford: OUP, 2006), 128-29.

Palestinian Judaism exerted influence to an equal degree on the formation of the Gospel. Due to spatial restraints, it cannot be fully discussed here, but it is assumed that the train of Jewish thought stemming from a Palestinian origin was much more at work in the birth of the Fourth Gospel than its counterparts in the wider pan-Mediterranean world: "That the Fourth Gospel has its roots in Palestine is virtually certain."[172] Scholars have proposed at least four ancient locations as the geographical provenance of the writing of the Fourth Gospel (Ephesus, Antioch, Alexandria, and Palestine).[173] However, a more formative factor should have been a conceptual provenance, rather than a geographical one. The primary and secondary sources frequently consulted in the course of this research include the materials listed in Appendix 6.

Chronological boundaries of early Judaism. Finally, another methodological caveat needs to be mentioned. This study takes into account the Jewish writings written in the period that ranges from 400 B.C. to A.D. 100. To indicate the Jewish conceptual currents of this period, three expressions will be used interchangeably without any significant distinction in meaning: early Judaism, intertestamental Judaism, and second temple Judaism. Some scholars have expressed reservation to restricting the scope of Jewish literature up to A.D. 100 because they believe that much later Jewish sources (usually early rabbinic literature) manifest coherent conceptual currents with the earlier documents (for the same reason, they disagree with the categorization of early Judaism or second temple Judaism).[174] However, the scientific nature of this inquiry requires concrete and tangible evidences. It seems necessary to restrict the material evidences taken into account so as to prevent interferences from overtly speculative deductions coming into play. The exegetical danger of comparing the body of literature from this period (from A.D. 200 onward) with the New Testament writings has been noted, especially in view of the possible Christian influence on later Jewish documents (for example, see the discussions on the use of the rabbinic and Samaritan writings in chap. 5 and Appendix 7: "The Use of the Rabbinic Materials for New Testament Studies").[175] Whenever the intertestamental

---

[172] Beasley-Murray, *John*, lxxx. For a detailed discussion of the importance of the Palestinian Jewish traditions for the formation of the Fourth Gospel, see appendix 2: *Religionsgeschichte* and the Fourth Gospel.

[173] For different locales as possible place for the writing of the Fourth Gospel, especially, the Gospel's interest in the eastern side of Jordan River for the possible locale of the writing, see Kügler, "Das Johannesevangelium," 217-18.

[174] William Horbury, "Rabbinic Literature in New Testament Interpretation," in *Herodian Judaism and New Testament Study* (Tübingen: Mohr Siebeck, 2006), 221-35.

[175] Morton Smith, "Comparison of Early Christian and Early Rabbinic Tradition," *JBL* 82 (1963): 169-76; Johann Maier, "Schriftrezeption im jüdischen Umfeld des Johannesevangeliums," in *Israel und seine Heilstraditionen im Johannesevangelium: Festgabe für Johannes Beutler SJ zum 70. Geburtstag*, ed. Michael Labahn, Klaus Scholtissek, and Angelika Strotmann (Paderborn: Schöningh, 2004), 79-88.

Jewish writings are referred to, thus, their date of writings, reception in early Judaism, and possible Christian influence will be taken into consideration.

Terms

Typology and Prefiguration

The importance of typology or prefiguration bears direct relevance upon the present study. In the wake of the rise of modern historical criticism, allegorical and typological studies encountered serious dismissal. On the other hand, some evangelical scholars sought to salvage the New Testament's figurative interpretations by carefully distinguishing between allegory and typology.[176] A common consensus within the current Johannine scholarship is that the Fourth Gospel does not display recourse to typology, in which an emphasis is placed on correspondences between events, persons, or institutions of the past and the present. The Fourth Gospel, however, rather presents the OT components in such radical terms that they simply foreshadow the reality of the New Testament revelation.[177] The exegetical inquiries of the present investigation will confirm the assessment of the current Johannine scholarship. At the present, suffice it to say that typology or prefiguration is understood in a broad sense as the ancients would probably have.[178] The definition of typology or prefiguration does not directly impinge upon the result of this study. However, for the sake of advancing a study as this one, a working definition is worth mentioning: A type is a biblical, person, or institution which serves as an example or pattern for other events, persons, or institutions.[179]

What concerns primarily in the present study is whether the fourth evangelist presents the Old Testament characters as messianic prefigurations and, if that be the case, how much and in what ways he lays the emphasis on such depiction.

Messiah and Christ

Another clarification of terms is related to "Messiah" and "Christ." As briefly discussed earlier and addressed more in depth in Appendix 1 (Messianism/Christology and the Gospel of John), these two nomenclatures do not overlap exactly in the domain of semantics. Probably, the epithet "Messiah" encompasses a larger range of referents than "Christ" does, but "Christ" also possesses a unique connotation. That is, he is the exclusively supreme divine being

---

[176] Leonhard Goppelt, *Typos: The Typological Interpretation of the Old Testament in the New*, trans. Donald H. Madvig (Grand Rapids: Eerdmans, 1982), 61-237; Baker, *Two Testaments, One Bible*, 169-89; Benjamin J. Ribben, "Typology of Types: Typology in Dialogue," *JTI* 5 (2011): 81-95.

[177] Hamid-Khani, *Revelation and Concealment of Christ*, 293.

[178] Moisés Silva, "Has the Church Misread the Bible?" in *Foundations of Contemporary Interpretation: Six Volumes in One*, ed. Moisés Silva (Grand Rapids: Zondervan, 1996), 44-57.

[179] Baker, *Two Testaments, One Bible*, 180.

and it carries an eschatological overtone. In earlier Hebrew traditions, "messiah" is only associated with historical figures such as kings, prophets, and priests.[180] However, later it was developed to connote more specifically an eschatological sense. Suffice it to point to the definition of Charlesworth for the present discussion:

> This eschatological figure [the Messiah] will inaugurate the end of all normal time and history. I, therefore, use the term "Messiah" in its etymological sense, to denote God's eschatological Anointed One, the Messiah.[181]

With this notion in mind, however, these two terms will be used interchangeably as the fourth evangelist identifies "Christ" with "Messiah". As this study proceeds, however, fuller semantic realms of the "messiah" in early Jewish tradition and the "Christ" in the incipient Christianity will be unfolded in detail in the following chapters. On a side note, what demarcates the Christian Christ from the Jewish messiah is succinctly put forth by Neusner and Chilton:

> Where Christianity parts company from all other religions, including Judaism, signifies the systemic center of Christianity—all Christianities. That point, of course, is Jesus Christ. What, in particular, about Jesus Christ matters (from the perspective of Judaism in particular) is not the claim that he was and is the Messiah, or that he was and is God incarnate, or that he taught and teaches Torah over and above the Torah of Sinai and in fulfillment of that first Torah. What matters is that Jesus Christ for Christianity uniquely is the Messiah, uniquely is God incarnate, uniquely reveals Torah against which all other Torah falls short. . . . After all, everyone knows, when it comes to mere mortal sages, we of holy Israel have hundreds who compare in wisdom and piety and supernatural insight; and prophets, priests, and martyrs to compare as

---

[180] Horbury, *Jewish Messianism and the Cult of Christ*, 7-13; John J. Collins, "Pre-Christian Jewish Messianism: An Overview," in *The Messiah in Early Judaism and Christianity*, ed. Magnus Zetterholm (Minneapolis: Fortress, 2007), 1-20; Joseph A. Fitzmyer, *The One Who Is to Come* (Grand Rapids: Eerdmans, 2007), 8-25; Adela Yarbro Collins & John J. Collins, *King and Messiah as Son of God: Divine, Human, and Angelic Messianic Figures in Biblical and Related Literature* (Grand Rapids: Eerdmans, 2008), 1. However, a non-historical messianic figure was also conceivable, see Shirley Lucass, *The Concept of the Messiah in the Scriptures of Judaism and Christianity* (London: T & T Clark, 2011), 144-57.

[181] James H. Charlesworth, "From Messianology to Christology: Problems and Prospects," in *The Messiah: Developments in Earliest Judaism and Christianity: The First Princeton Symposium on Judaism and Christian Origins*, ed. James H. Charlesworth (Minneapolis: Fortress, 1992), 4; idem, "Introduction: Messianic Ideas in Early Judaism," in *Qumran-Messianism: Studies on the Messianic Expectations in the Dead Sea Scrolls*, ed. James H. Charlesworth, Hermann Lichtenberger, and Gerbern S. Oegema (Tübingen: Mohr Siebeck, 1998), 1. Oegema's definition covers a wider range: "a priestly, royal or otherwise characterized figure, who will play a liberating role at the end of time." Gerbern S. Oegema, *The Anointed and His People: Messianic Expectations from the Maccabees to Bar Kochba* (Sheffiedl: Sheffield, 1998), 26.

well. What we do not have is God incarnate in one person only, and what we have not known is the Messiah in any one person-at least, not yet.[182]

Contributions

Old Testament Characters as Christological Witnesses

The main question this study seeks to answer is whether or not the Old Testament figures in the Fourth Gospel play a coherent role as Christological/messianic witnesses (as Scripture does), as some German exegetes have recently argued. Their thesis will be tested through conventional exegesis of the Johannine pericopae which either directly mention or allude to the traditional Jewish heroic figures. If the thesis stands intact, then it will be compared with the perception of the Old Testament figures pertaining to messianism in the Jewish literature of the second temple period. This comparison, however, will remain at a secondary level of investigation as the main focus of the research will be devoted to the role of the Old Testament characters within the canonical confines of the Johannine Gospel. The findings from this research are hoped to illuminate some of the hermeneutical and theological insights crucial for an appropriate appreciation of the New Testament and the Gospel of John in particular.[183] First, this study is expected to articulate theological claims the evangelist makes to his first century readers/hearers over against its Jewish background in his presentation of the Old Testament Jewish figures with reference to the Christology of the Fourth Gospel.

Affinity between Early Judaism and John

Second, this study will demonstrate the degree of affinity between the Gospel and the Jewish milieu of the Second Temple period. The conclusions adduced from this observation will point to somewhere other than the Old Testament or the Jewish intertestamental literature for the genesis of the Johannine Christology. Scholars have suggested the Jesus event[184] as the provenance (or more

---

[182] Jacob Neusner and Bruce D. Chilton, *Jewish-Christian Debates: God, Kingdom, Messiah* (Minneapolis: Fortress, 1998), 215-16.

[183] For its implication on "biblical theology" from an understanding of the Old Testament figures' role in the New, see Oda Wischmeyer, "Abraham unser Vater: Aspekte der Abrahamsgestalt im Neuen Testament," in *Biblical Figures in Deuterocanonical and Cognate Literature*, ed. Hermann Lichtenberger and Ulrike Mittmann-Richert (Berlin: Walter de Gruyter, 2009), 567.

[184] Kraus, "Johannes und das Alte Testament," 20; Mogens Müller, "Neutestamentliche Theologie als Biblische Theologie: Einige grundsätzliche Überlegungen," *NTS* 43(1997): 475-90; and Walter Schmithals, "Das Alte Testament im Neuen," in *Paulus, die Evangelien, und das Urchristentum: Beiträge von und zu Walter Schmithals*, ed. Cilliers Breytenbach (Leiden: Brill, 2004), 563-614; Schwankl, "Aspekte der johanneischen Christologie," 362-67. A colleague of mine, Lars Kierspel, deserves credit for directing me to the works of Müller and Schmithals.

specifically the post-Easter perspective)[185] or the inspiration of the Holy Spirit.[186] An implication of this second aspect will touch upon the legitimacy of *Traditionsgeschichte* as a proper interpretive method for the Gospel of John on the basis of the conclusions drawn from the first two inquiries.[187] As a corollary, a hermeneutical doubt is cast over the typological and/or simplistic salvation-historical approach to the New Testament vis-à-vis the function of Old Testament characters with reference to the Johannine Christology. So does Reim ward off the typological interpretation of the Old Testament messianic texts in John:

> For John, typology is not an end-time recurrence of the same event that happened in the ancient times. But, what happened in the ancient times is a reference to the event of the essential at the time of Christ.[188]

In this venue, some scholars have already expressed their skepticism over the history of traditions approach. For instance, Mogen Müller posits that the history of traditions approach undertaken by Stuhlmacher and Gese is in fact reading the Bible from the perspective of the Old Testament onto the New. That attempt, he believes, will naturally lead to where it came from, "Judaism."[189] Similarly, Seitz perceptively sets the issue under proper perspective when he writes,

> The problem for the early church was not what to do with the OT. Rather, in the light of a Scripture . . . , what was one to make of a crucified messiah and a parting of the ways? It is this dimension of early Christian use of the OT that is attenuated in tradition-historical approaches of the Gese-Stuhlmacher variety.[190]

Competency of Redactor/Author of John

Finally, if a coherent role of the Old Testament characters in the Gospel narratives is established, it will bolster, to some degree, the integrity of the final form of the Gospel text in contradistinction to the view that assumes various phases of a redactional process before the finalization of the present Gospel. The unity of the Fourth Gospel is closely tied to the question of authorship. Built upon the hypothesis of community production, some scholars have suggested various sources that are sort of coarsely woven into the present form of John's Gospel. Bultmann initiated the theory, and Fortna and Kotila have rendered by far the

---

[185] Scholtissek, "'Die unauflösbare Schrift' (Joh 10,35)," 166-67.

[186] Hengel, "The Old Testament in the Fourth Gospel," 389-91. The role of the Holy Spirit in shaping John's use of the Old Testament was first proposed by Albreght Thoma, "Das Alte Testament im Johannes-Evangelium," *ZWT* 22 (1879): 311, cited in Obermann, *Die christologische Erfüllung der Schrift im Johannesevangelium*, 5.

[187] For a convenient summary of Gese's methodological presuppositions, see Seitz, "Two Testaments and the Failure of One Tradition History," 195-211.

[188] Reim, *Jochanan*, 268.

[189] Müller, "Neutestamentliche Theologie als Biblische Theologie," 490.

[190] Seitz, "Two Testaments and the Failure of One Tradition History," 210-11.

most elaborate reconstruction of the source-and-form critical scheme.[191] Recently, Scholtissek and Zumstein have revived this topic by analyzing the inter-

---

[191] Rudolf Bultmann, *The Gospel of John: A Commentary*, trans. George R. Beasley-Murray (Louisville: Westminster, 1971), 113, 632-35, 681; Robert T. Fortna, *The Gospel of Signs: A Reconstruction of the Narrative Source Underlying the Fourth Gospel* (Cambridge: CUP, 1970); idem, *The Fourth Gospel And Its Predecessor: From Narrative Source to Present Gospel* (Philadelphia: Fortress, 1988); Kotila, *Umstrittener Zeuge*. On the other hand, clumsy Johannine editorial traces were allegedly detected first by Eduard Schwartz, "Aporien im vierten Evangelium," *NGWG* 14 (1907): 342-72; 15 (1908): 115-88, 497-560. The positions proposed by Bultmann, Fortna, and Schwartz, however, have been repeatedly refuted in the recent advancement of gospel scholarship which has expressed a serious caveat against the notion of the Gospels as the literary product of communities through an extended period of time with a result in theological tension apparently present in the Gospel. For such a concern in general for the Gospels, see Bauckham, *The Gospels for All Christians*; idem, *Jesus and the Eyewitnesses: The Gospels as Eyewitness Testimony* (Grand Rapids: Eerdmans, 2006); Michael F. Bird, "Bauckham's *The Gospel for All Christians* Revisited," *EuroJT* 15 (2006): 5-14. For the Gospel of John in particular, see Eduard Schweizer, *Ego Eimi: Die religionsgeschichtlich Herkunft und theologische Bedeutung der johanneischen Bildreden, zugleich ein Beitrag zur Quellenfrage des vierten Evangeliums* (Göttingen: Vandenhoeck & Ruprecht, 1939); D. Moody Smith, *The Composition and Order of the Fourth Gospel: Bultmann's Literary Theory* (New Haven: Yale University Press, 1965); George Mlakushyil, *The Christocentric Literary Structure of the Fourth Gospel* (Rome: Pontificio Istituto Biblico, 1987); Eugene Ruckstuhl, "Johannine Language and Style: The Question of Their Unity," in *L'Évangile de Jean: Sources, rédaction, théologie*, ed. Marinus de Jonge (Leuven: Leuven University Press, 1977), 125-48; Eugene Ruckstuhl and Peter Dschulnigg, *Stilkritik und Verfasserfrage im Johannesevangelium: Die Johanneischen Sprachmerkmale auf dem Hintergrund des Neuen Testaments und des zeitgenössischen hellenistischen Schrifttums* (Freiburg: Universitätsverlag, 1991); Barnabas Lindars, "Traditions behind the Fourth Gospel," in *L'Evangile de Jean: Sources, redaction, theologie*, ed. M. de Jonge (Leuven: Peeters, 1987), 107-24; Gary M. Burge, "The Literary Seams in the Fourth Gospel," *CovQ* 48 (1990): 15-25; Martin Hengel, *Die johanneische Frage: ein Lösungsversuch* (Tübingen: Mohr Siebeck, 1993); Gilbert van Belle, *The Signs Source in the Fourth Gospel: Historical Survey and Critical Evaluation of the Semeia Hypothesis* (Louvain: Peeters, 1994); and Hans-Joachim Schulz, *Die apostolische Herkunft der Evangelien: Zum Ursprung der Evangelienform in der urgemeindlichen Paschafeier* (Freiburg: Herder, 1997), 292-391; Earl E. Ellis, *The Making of the New Testament Documents* (Leiden: Brill, 1999), 147-83, 233-37; Thomas Popp, *Grammatik des Geistes: Literarische Kunst und theologische Konzeption in Johannes 3 und 6* (Leipzig: Evangelische Verlagsanstalt, 2001). Cf. Andreas Köstenberger, "Frühe Zweifel an der johanneischen Verfasserschaft des vierten: Evangeliums in der modernen Interpretationsgeschichte," *EuroJT* 5 (1996): 37-46. Recently, Hahn assessed the previous form critical approaches to the Gospel of John. In light of the literary unity of the Gospel, he construes that it is unnecessary to differentiate the tradition from redaction (against Jürgen Becker and Rudolf Schnackenburg). He further traces the core concept of the Gospel to the evangelist, not to the Johannine community (against Hartwig Thyen and Rudolf Bultmann). Hahn, *Theologie des Neuen Testaments*, 2:586-87.

play between interrelated texts ("reference text" and "reception text") by means of *relecture* and *réécriture* (re-reading/re-writing) in the formation of the Fourth Gospel. Observing this re-reading process (which leads to a creation of surplus meaning[s]), then, they proposes, enables the possibility of detecting different redactional layers.[192]

Some of the recent linguistic investigations of the Fourth Gospel, however, point out that the hypothetical sources and layers cannot be exhibited linguistically and the language of the Gospel is consistent throughout John. Therefore, contrary to the once popular assumption that the evangelist(s) was a clumsy editor who wittingly or unwittingly preserved various tensions between Jesus and the Old Testament figures (either from a history of religions or socio-political point of view), the consistent and coherent role of various ancient Jewish characters concerning Christology will, if proven, bear witness to the competent editorial ability of the final redactor. To this point, Jeffrey Staley adds:

> If redaction critics are correct to conclude that FG [the Fourth Gospel] reflects to fifty years of editing, it is remarkable that the current text also reflects an unusual rhetorical unity on the themes of "authority" and "witness." . . . a two-tiered motif of witnessing is reflected in the three major redactional stages in FG's composition history . . . .

---

[192] See Jean Zumstein, *Kreative Erinnerung: Relecture und Auslegung im Johannesevangelium* (Zürich: Theologischer, 2004); especially the first chapter, "Zur Geschichte des johanneischen Christentums," ibid., 1-14; idem, "Intratextuality and Intertextuality in the Gospel of John," in *Anatomies of Narrative Criticism: The Past, Present, and Futures of the Fourth Gospel as Literature*, ed. Tom Thatcher and Stephen D. Moore (Atlanta: Society of Biblical Literature, 2008), 121-36; idem, "Le processus de relecture et réception de l'Écriture dans le quatrième évangile," *ÉTR* 70 (2012): 37-54; and Klaus Scholtissek, "Relecture und réécriture: Neue Paradigmen zu Methode und Inhalt der Johannesauslegung aufgewiesen am Prolog 1,1-18 und der ersten Abschiedsrede 13,31-14,41," *TP* 75 (2000): 1-29. For examples of applying this hermeneutical insight into the Johannine texts, see Johannes Beutler, "Die Überleitung zu den johanneischen Abschiedsreden (Joh 13,31f.): Ein Beispiel der 'relecture,'" in *Studien zu Matthäus und Johannes: Festschrift für Jean Zumstein zu seinem 65. Geburtstag*, ed. Andreas Dettwiler and Uta Poplutz (Zürich: Theologischer, 2009), 221-31; idem, "Joh 6 als christliche 'relecture' des Pascharahmens im Johannesevangelium," in *Neue Studien zu den johanneischen Schriften*, ed. Rudolf Hoppe and Ulrich Berges (Göttingen: Vandenhoeck & Ruprecht; Bonn University Press, 2012), 165-81; Samuel Vollenweider, "Der Logos als Brüke vom Evangelium zur Philosophie: Der Johannesprolog in der Relektüre des Neuplatonikers Amelios," in *Studien zu Matthäus und Johannes: Festschrift für Jean Zumstein zu seinem 65. Geburtstag*, ed. Andreas Dettwiler & Uta Poplutz (Zürich: Theologischer, 2009), 377-97; Devillers Luc, "Le prologue du quatrième évangile: Clé de voûte de la littérature johannique," *NTS* 58 (2012): 317-30. A corrective to Zumstein's hermeneutical program is suggested by Ulrich Luz, "Relecture? Reprise!: ein Gespräch mit Jean Zumstein," in *Studien zu Matthäus und Johannes: Festschrift für Jean Zumstein zu seinem 65. Geburtstag*, ed. Andreas Dettwiler & Uta Poplutz (Zürich: Theologischer, 2009), 233-50.

Throughout FG, no one comes to Jesus without the assistance of another person . . . . the Signs Source exhibits a strategy remarkably similar to the one isolated earlier in the three "formative redactional periods" of the Johannine Community.[193]

One of the recent examinations of the Johannine characters also shares the same judgment based on a linguistic analysis of the Johannine texts:

> A third trend has been the work of Schweizer (1939) and Ruckstuhl (1951) due to the development of linguistic peculiarities, which distinguishes the Gospel of John from the Synoptic Gospels and other writings of the New Testament, and emphasizes that the hypothesis that deduced layers and sources are not linguistically analyzed, rather, the language of the Gospel of John is consistent and is strongly affected by the final redactor in all its parts.[194]

Scope

Unless one is prepared to venture upon the writing of a *magnum opus* on the historical Jesus (such as Dunn's *Jesus Remembered*), he/she will have to, at some points, presuppose and assume certain aspects instead of proving every statement with careful qualifications. This study proceeds in line with those who see Jesus as standing primarily in a Jewish messianic light.[195] Generally speaking, Johannine Christology has been investigated in two ways: one in the form of Jewish messianic prefigurations (David, Elijah, or Moses), and the other through abstract titles and symbols (Son of God, Son of Man, wisdom, etc.). It is the former that seems to have had closer affinities with ancient Judaism. The conceptions of the latter category in the intertestamental period are known to be notoriously slippery and elusive, not to mention their meager references in terms of messianology. Consequently, the comparison of the former category with its coun-

---

[193] Jeffrey L. Stalley, "What Can a Postmodern Approach to the Fourth Gospel Add to Contemporary Debates about Its Historical Situation?" in *Jesus in Johannine Tradition*, ed. Robert T. Fortna and Tom Thatcher (Louisville: Westminster/John Knox, 2001), 53-55. The outcome of this book reaches a similar implication of Culpepper's literary analysis of John that the Fourth Gospel contains a high degree of literary integrity. R. Alan Culpepper, *Anatomy of the Fourth Gospel: A Study in Literary Design* (Philadelphia: Fortress, 1983).

[194] Dschulnigg, *Jesus Begegnen*, 8.

[195] Likewise, Peter Stuhlmacher, *Jesus of Nazareth—Christ of Faith* (Peabody: Hendrickson, 1993); James D.G. Dunn, *Christology in the Making: A New Testament Inquiry into the Origin of the Doctrine of the Incarnation* (London: SCM, 2003); idem, *Jesus Remembered* (Grand Rapids: Eerdmans, 2003), 615-764; Marinus de Jonge, *Jesus, the Servant Messiah* (New Haven: Yale University Press, 1991); Markus Bockmuehl, *This Jesus: Martyr, Lord, Messiah* (Downers Grove: InterVarsity, 1996); N.T. Wright, *Jesus and the Victory of God* (Minneapolis: Fortress, 1996); and Gerd Theissen and Annette Merz, *Der historische Jesus: Ein Lehrbuch* (Göttingen: Vandenhoeck & Ruprecht, 2008). For a summary of other proposals that seek to account for the historical Jesus in terms other than a Jewish messiah, see Ben Witherington, *The Jesus Quest: The Third Search for the Jews of Nazareth* (Downers Grove: InterVarsity, 1997), 42-196.

terpart conceptions in the Fourth Gospel will reveal more evidently the points of contact between early Judaism and Johannine Christianity. There is certainly some degree of disparity between Christian Christology and Jewish messianism. Charlesworth correctly notes the danger of imposing New Testament Christology onto the Old Testament messianism. The former category unanimously identified Jesus with Christ, but the latter construed the idea via a variety of the so-called messianic figures, such as, prophets, priests, and kings.[196] This book intends to explore the possibility of early Christian appropriation of the early Jewish messianic hopes through Jewish heroic figures. The scope of this study includes Moses, David, Elijah (and John the Baptist), and two of the arch-patriarchs (Abraham and Jacob) of Israel. Not only do these figures emerge prominently on the surface of the Jewish literary structures but they were held in high esteem in early Judaism as messianic prefigures. For the latter reason, the prophet Isaiah is excluded from the scope of this research regardless of his conspicuous Christological witness role in John. Although Jacob and Abraham do not usually occur in the intertestamental Jewish eschatological contexts as messianic prefigures, they are included for their symbolic status as the heads of Israel.

Limitations

In spite of several considerable merits, there are also some limitations to this research. Although a comprehensive comparison of the perceptions of the Jewish heroic figures as a messianic prefiguration and/or witness in the Fourth Gospel and contemporary Judaism is highly desirable, the vast scope of such inquiry is hardly viable. Furthermore, an initial investigation has detected virtually no dominant point of contact between the two distinct Jewish spheres of religious expressions (this is especially due to the lack of the motif of the Jewish antique figures as messianic witness not to mention the dearth of a systematized understanding of the messianic prefigures in early Judaism). Therefore, the present study limits its scope within the understanding of the Jewish antique figures as presented in the Fourth Gospel.

Another limit of this study involves the method of the present inquiry, that is, that an investigation of the messianic paradigms of the Old Testament figures in early Judaism will take its point of departure primarily from the secondary literature due to the enormous purview of the primary sources which contain the messianic ideas and figures in the Jewish writings of the Second Temple period. The secondary literature on the Old Testament messianic figures will be played out as dialogue partners. From there on, then, further investigations will be

---

[196] James H. Charlesworth, "From Messianology to Christology: Problems and Prospects," in *The Messiah: Developments in Earliest Judaism and Christianity: The First Princeton Symposium on Judaism and Christian Origins*, ed. James H. Charlesworth (Minneapolis: Fortress, 1992), 3-35.

conducted to see the intertextual Christological dynamics of the Jewish messianic protagonists in view of their original texts and contexts.

CHAPTER 2

The Jewish Patriarchs

Introduction

The Gospel of John makes no mention of Isaac. It is not too surprising in view of the rare occurrence of his name in the entire corpus of the New Testament. Furthermore, even in the Old Testament and early Judaism, Isaac and Jacob are already subsumed under the arch-forefather, Abraham:

> The trend that is visible already in the Old Testament and continuing in early Judaism is fully observed that Abraham outpaced the other two progenitors.[1]

Not only the arch-patriarch occupied a crucial place for the matter of identity, he was also seen in a messianic prefigurative light in some early Jewish and Christian sources.[2] The portrayal of the Jewish patriarchs in John, however, differs

---

[1] Rainer Albertz, "Isaak II: Neues Testament," *TRE*, 16:296; Johann Maier, "Schriftrezeption im jüdischen Umfeld des Johannesevangeliums," in *Israel und seine Heilstraditionen im Johannesevangelium: Festgabe für Johannes Beutler SJ zum 70. Geburtstag*, ed. Michael Labahn, Klaus Scholtissek, and Angelika Strotmann (Paderborn: Schöningh, 2004), 56.

[2] For some of the discussions on the importance of Abraham in early Jewish and Christian sources, see G. Mayer, "Aspekte des Abrahambildes in der hellenistisch-christlichen Literatur," *EvT* 32 (1972): 118-27; Friedrich. E. Wieser, *Die Abrahamvorstellungen im Neuen Testament* (Bern: Peter Lang, 1987); Jeffrey S. Siker, *Disinheriting the Jews: Abraham in Early Christian Controversy* (Louisville: Westminster/John Knox, 1991); Rodney A. Werline, "The Transformation of Pauline Arguments in Justin Martyr's Dialogue with Trypho," *HTR* 92 (1999): 79-93; Craig A. Evans, "Abraham in the Dead Sea Scrolls: A Man of Faith and Failure," in *The Bible at Qumran: Text, Shape, and Interpretation*, ed. Peter W. Flint (Grand Rapids: Eerdmans, 2001), 149-58; Nancy Calbert-Koyzis, *Paul, Monotheism and the People of God: The Significance of Abraham Traditions for Early Judaism and Christianity* (London: T & T Clark, 2004), 6-84; Beate Ego, "Abraham's Faith in the *One* God—A Motif of the Image of Abraham in Early Jewish Literature," in *Biblical Figures in Deuterocanonical and Cognate Literature*, ed. Hermann Lichtenberger and Ulrike Mittmann-Richert (Berlin: Walter de Gruyter, 2009), 337-55; Oda Wischmeyer, "Abraham unser Vater: Aspekte der Abrahamsgestalt im Neuen Testament," in *Biblical Figures in Deuterocanonical and Cognate Literature*, ed. Hermann Lichtenberger and Ulrike Mittmann-Richert (Berlin: Walter de Gruyter, 2009), 567-85; H.G.M. Williamson, "Abraham in Exile," in *Perspectives on Our Father Abraham: Essays in Honor of Marvin R. Wilson*, ed. Steven A. Hunt (Grand Rapids: Eerdmans, 2010), 68-80. For a

slightly from these traditions in that the Samaritans seem to regard Jacob, not Abraham, as their progenitor (4:12), and for the Jews, of course, Abraham stands as the arch-patriarch (8:39, 53). Jesus as depicted in John, on the other hand, does not appear to acknowledge the significance of the typical Jewish perception of the Abrahamic fatherhood. "Abraham, your father" in John 8:56 seems to be reflective of Jesus distancing himself from the Jews (or at least the particular Jews were opposing him. In various places, the New Testament writings generally recognize the importance of Abraham in the divine redemptive plan even for the gentile believers.

> "He [God] has helped his servant Israel, in remembrance of his mercy, according to the promise he made to our ancestors, to Abraham and to his descendants forever." (Luke 1:54-55)
>
> "What then are we to say was gained by Abraham, our ancestor according to the flesh?" (Romans 4:1)

In contrast, the fourth evangelist does not seem to be eager to claim the spiritual lineage of the patriarchs for Christ.[3] Rather, the patriarchs serve as mere witnesses to Jesus' messianic and/or Christological identity, most remarkably of his pre-existence. This chapter will discuss the portrayals of the forefathers in early Judaism and how they are cast in different pictures in John. In light of the exegetical examination of the Johannine narratives that mention and allude to Abraham or Jacob, the latter part of this chapter will probe into their narrative function with particular regards to the Christology of John.

Jacob

One of the three Jewish forefathers, Jacob, appears twice in the major sections of John's Gospel, that it, alluded to in 1:51 and explicitly mentioned twice by name in 4:10-14. The first instance of his appearance is important since it encapsulates the programmatic prologue which reveals the messianic identity of Jesus and his calling. Also, this incident provides an ample opportunity to introduce readers to the following Book of Signs with an invitation, "you shall see greater things (John 1:50)."

Allusions to the Bethel Theophany: John 1:51

καὶ λέγει αὐτῷ· ἀμὴν ἀμὴν λέγω ὑμῖν, ὄψεσθε τὸν οὐρανὸν ἀνεῳγότα καὶ τοὺς

---

discussion on the messianic appropriation of the Abrahamic traditions, see Moshe D. Herr, "L'Herméneutique juive et chrétienne des figures bibliques à l'époque du deuxième Temple, de la Mishna et du Talmud," in *Messiah and Christos: Studies in the Jewish Origins of Christianity Presented to David Flusser on the Occasion of His Seventy-Fifth Birthday*, ed. Ithamar Gruenwald, Shaul Shaked, and Gedaliahu G. Stroumsa (Tübingen: Mohr Siebeck, 1992), 99-109.

[3] Christian Dietzfelbinger, *Das Evangelium nach Johannes* (Zürich: Theologischer, 2001), 1:261-65.

ἀγγέλους τοῦ θεοῦ ἀναβαίνοντας καὶ καταβαίνοντας ἐπὶ τὸν υἱὸν τοῦ ἀνθρώπου. (John 1:51, NA[28])[4]

And he said to him, "Very truly, I tell you, you will see heaven opened and the angels of God ascending and descending upon the Son of Man." (John 1:51, NRSV)[5]

Narrative context. Jacob, son of Isaac, is alluded to in John 1:51, which echoes the Bethel account in Genesis 28. Structurally speaking, v. 51 concludes the first chapter of the Gospel which is marked by a recurrent witness theme.[6] For example, John the Baptist carries out this "witness" motif in the first chapter. Vv. 7 and 8 of the first chapter of John mark a pivotal point in the Baptist's ministry of "witness": "He came as a witness to testify to the light, so that all might believe through him. He himself was not the light, but he came to testify to the light." The witness ministry of the Baptist for Christ is spelled out in the rest of the chapter. His testimony concerning Christ is first directed to "the Jews of Jerusalem" in vv. 19-28, first indirectly (vv. 19-24) and then directly (vv. 25-28).[7] He aims his next witness at "the people who came to hear him" in vv. 29-34. The next day, the Baptist's witness is extended to some of his own disciples in vv. 35-37. The eye-witness nature of the latter two pericopae enhances the level of credibility of John's witness.[8] In addition, the force of his witness is further

---

[4] The Greek New Testament is cited throughout this study from Kurt Aland et al, eds., *Novum Testamentum Graece* (Stuttgart: Deutsche Bibelgesellschaft, 2012).

[5] The English scriptural citations throughout this study are from *The Holy Bible: New Revised Standard Version* (Nashville: Thomas Nelson, 1989). For a survey of scholarship on John 1:51, see Francis J. Moloney, *The Johannine Son of Man* (Rome: Libreria Ateneo Salesiano, 1978), 23-41; Barnabas Lindars, *Jesus Son of Man: A Fresh Examination of the Son of Man Sayings in the Gospels* (Grand Rapids: Eerdmans, 1983), 145-57. For a survey of various suggestions for the religious background of the term "son of man" in this text, see Douglas R.A. Hare, *The Son of Man Tradition* (Minneapolis: Fortress, 1990), 80-81; Adela Yarbro Collins and John J. Collins, *King and Messiah as Son of God: Divine, Human, and Angelic Messianic Figures in Biblical and Related Literature* (Grand Rapids: Eerdmans, 2008), 183-87. Some exegetes construe the suffering servant traditions (e.g., Isa 42-53, Pss 78-80) behind the son of man in the present text. Hugo Odeberg, *The Fourth Gospel: Interpreted in Its Relation to Contemporaneous Religious Currents in Palestine and the Hellenistic-Oriental World* (Chicago: Argonaut, 1929; repr., Amsterdam: B.R. Grüner, 1968), 36; Stephen S. Smalley, "Johannine Son of Man Sayings," *NTS* 15 (1969): 288; F.F. Bruce, "The Background to the Son of Man Sayings," in *Christ the Lord: Studies in Christology Presented to Donald Guthrie*, ed. Harold H. Rowdon (Downers Grove: InterVarsity, 1982), 56-58.

[6] This structural analysis is indebted to George R. Beasley-Murray, *John* (Nashville: Nelson, 1999), 22-23; Udo Schnelle, *Das Evangelium nach Johannes* (Leipzig: Evangelische Verlagsanstalt, 1998), 56.

[7] Klaus Wengst, *Das Johannesevangelium* (Stuttgart: Kohlhammer, 2000), 1:86-94.

[8] The eye-witness motif is also an important characteristic in John. See Urban C. von Wahlde, "The Witnesses to Jesus in John 5:31-40 and Belief in the Fourth Gospel," *CBQ* 43 (1981): 385-404; Andrew T. Lincoln, "The Beloved Disciple as Eyewitness

evidenced in some of his disciples' (Philip and Nathanael) turning to Jesus upon departure from their first mentor in vv. 38-50. These preceding occurrences of the "witness" theme culminate in the concluding statement of v. 51, which is presented in the form of an affirmative answer to the new disciple's Christological confession, "you are the Son of God, you are the King of Israel" (v. 49).

Excursus 1: The "Son of Man" in John 1:51

In the pericope of John 1:35-51, where Jesus calls disciples, his identity is unfolded in four steps: rabbi (v. 38), son of God (v. 49), king of Israel (v. 49), and son of man (v. 51). Cordula Langner suggests that these four titles here proleptically function to summarize the mission and life of Jesus. That is, as a rabbi Jesus provides his teachings, as son of God he was condemned, as king crucified, and as son of man he was resurrected. As glaringly as it sounds, however, his interpretation seems to be without much textual support in this text or in view of the entire scope of the Gospel. In particular, it is doubtful whether Jesus was resurrected as "son of man."[9] The epithet, "son of man," in recently scholarly discussions, is taken to be more or less a general self-designation.[10] Yet, the Johannine son of man epithet is uniquely Johannine in contrast to the opaque presentation of such tile in the Synoptic Gospels.[11] The confession of Nathanael has been puzzling exegetes since it appears to be too mature at such an early stage of the Gospel narratives. Three interpretations have appealed to a number of exegetes. First, this confession is polemically directed at the unbelieving

---

and the Fourth Gospel as Witness," *JSNT* 85 (2002): 3-26; Richard Bauckham, "The Gospel of John as Eyewitness Testimony," in *Jesus and the Eyewitnesses: The Gospels as Eyewitness Testimony* (Grand Rapids: Eerdmans, 2006), 358-83; idem, "The Eyewitness of the Beloved Disciple," in *Jesus and the Eyewitnesses: The Gospels as Eyewitness Testimony* (Grand Rapids: Eerdmans, 2006), 384-411. For another contextual consideration of this pericope as a part of the first chapter of John, see Yves-Marie Blanchard, "Le fils de l'homme et l'échelle de Jacob: Réflexion sur l'intertextualité scripturaire et relecture de Jean 1,51, à la lumière de la Bible juive," in *Analyse narrative et Bible: Deuxième colloque international du Prenab, Louvain-la-Neuve, Avril 2004*, ed. Camille Focant and André Wénin (Leuven: Peeters, 2005), 186-87.

[9] Cordula Langner, "Was für ein König ist Jesus?" in *Israel und seine Heilstraditionen im Johannesevangelium: Festgabe für Johannes Beutler SJ zum 70. Geburtstag*, ed. Michael Labahn, Klaus Scholtissek, and Angelika Strotmann (Paderborn: Ferdinand Schöningh, 2004), 250.

[10] Jean-Marie Sevrin, "Le commencement du quatrième évangile: Prologue et prélude," in *La Bible en récits*, ed. Daniel Marguerat (Genève: Labor et Fides, 2005), 345; Richard Bauckham, "The Son of Man: 'A Man in My Position' or 'Someone'?" in *The Jewish World around the New Testament: Collected Essays I* (Tübingen: Mohr Siebeck, 2008), 93-101.

[11] Collins and Collins, *King and Messiah as Son of God*, 186-87. For the son of man in Jn 1:51 as the savior and pre-existent divine logos redefined from its Danielic origin, see J. Harold Ellens, "Exegesis of Second Temple Texts in a Fourth Gospel Son of Man Logion," in *Biblical Interpretation in Judaism and Christianity*, ed. Lsaac Kalimi and Peter J. Haas (London: T & T Clark, 2006), 131-49.

Jews.¹² Therefore, it must be read retrospectively from the end to the beginning. Alternatively, others posit that Nathanael's confessional statement is only provisional, that is, it merely reveals the amazed emotion of the new disciple.¹³ Finally, still some others point to the emphatic function of the confession in relation to the omnipotent supernatural divinity of Jesus.¹⁴ Contrary to their judgments, a natural reading of the present text and the immediate literary contexts does not seem to allow sufficient connections with the suffering servant motif or other Jewish eschatological expectations. It is not the title *per se*, but other literary devices that bring the eschatological overtone to the surface. "It is thus, the opened heaven and the movement of the angels that express the point of the verse not the name the 'son of man'; the latter merely serves to identify Jesus as the person who is related to heaven in this way."¹⁵

The prediction of Jesus is disclosed to Nathanael, a true Israelite (possibly a proto-example of the New Testament Christians):

> That is, Nathanael is a true Israelite. In him the eschatological salvation of the people of God exemplarily testified and promised by the prophets comes true proleptically. Nathanael is a true Israelite in such a way that he points to the eschatological existence of the people of God and the salvation through Yahweh. And, he teaches a whole number of the prophetic texts in a new eschatological context.¹⁶

Two analogous features call for this prophecy to be taken as an allusion to the Bethel account in Genesis 28:12.¹⁷ First, the beholders of the visions are called

---

[12] Ludger Schenke, *Johannes: Kommentar* (Düsseldorf: Patmos, 1998), 50; Joachim Gnilka, *Johannesevangelium* (Würzburg: Echter, 1999), 21-22.

[13] Wengst, *Das Johannesevangelium*, 1:94-97.

[14] Ekkehard W. Stegemann and Wolfgang Stegemann, "König Israels, nicht König der Juden?: Jesus als König im Johannesevangelium," in *Messias-vorstellungen bei Juden und Christen*, ed. Ekkehard Stegemann (Stuttgart: W. Kohlhammer, 1993), 47; Stefan Schreiber, "Rätsel um den König: Zur religionsgeschichtlichen Herkunft des König-Titels im Johannesevangelium," in *Johannes aenigmaticus: Studien zum Johannesevangelium für Herbert Leroy*, ed. Stefan Schreiber and Alois Stimpfle (Regensburg: Friedrich Pustet, 2000), 58-59.

[15] Hare, *The Son of Man Tradition*, 85. For a helpful survey on the topic of "the Son of Man" in John, see J. Harold Ellens, *The Son of Man in the Gospel of John* (Sheffield: Sheffield Phoenix, 2010).

[16] Johann A. Steiger, "Nathanael—Ein Israelit, an dem kein Falsch ist: Das hermeneutische Phänomen der Intertestamentarizität aufgezeigt an Joh 1,45-51," *BTZ* 9 (1992): 53; Schnelle, *Das Evangelium nach Johannes*, 56. For a positive understanding of Jacob in the Hellenistic writings, see Petra von Gemünden, "La figure de Jacob à l'époque hellénistico-romaine: L'exemple de Philon d'Alexandrie," in *Jacob: Commentaire à plusieurs voix de Gen. 25-36, mélanges offerts à Albert de Pury*, ed. Jean-Daniel Macchi (Geneva: Labor et Fides, 2001), 358-70.

[17] For an allusion to Ezek 1:1, see Gilles Quispel, "Nathanael und der Menschensohn (Joh 1 15)," *ZNW* 47 (1956): 281-83; Gary T. Manning, Jr., *Echoes of a Prophet: The Use of Ezekiel in the Gospel of John and in Literature of the Second Temple Period* (London: T & T Clark, 2004), 150-60. The brevity of the parallel phrase (viz., "heaven . . . opened"), however, makes it difficult to argue for a strong allusion between John and Ezekiel. For a survey of various later rabbinic interpretations of the

"Israel" and, second, the wordings of the vision in both accounts are noticeably identical ("you will see the heaven opened and the angels of God ascending and descending"). Therefore, exegetes commonly recognize an analogy present in the text, identifying the son of man as the anti-type. However, opinions vary as to the type, i.e., Jacob, the stone, the ladder, and the place, of which the proponents of Jacob and the ladder as an extension of the place represent two more popular views than others.[18] The Hebrew Scripture is somewhat ambiguous as to the antecedent of the third person singular masculine pronominal suffix, בּוֹ, since he/it could refer back to either Jacob or the ladder (סֻלָּם) upon which the traffic of angels took place.

וַיַּחֲלֹם וְהִנֵּה סֻלָּם מֻצָּב אַרְצָה וְרֹאשׁוֹ מַגִּיעַ הַשָּׁמָיְמָה וְהִנֵּה מַלְאֲכֵי אֱלֹהִים עֹלִים וְיֹרְדִים בּוֹ׃ (Gen 28:12, BHS[5])[19]

However, the Septuagint clarifies the antecedent of the demonstrative pronoun as it shifts the gender into feminine (ἐπ' αὐτῆς).[20] Thus, it is clearly upon the ladder where the angels were moving up and down.

καὶ ἐνυπνιάσθη, καὶ ἰδοὺ κλίμαξ ἐστηριγμένη ἐν τῇ γῇ, ἧς ἡ κεφαλὴ ἀφικνεῖτο εἰς τὸν οὐρανόν, καὶ οἱ ἄγγελοι τοῦ θεοῦ ἀνέβαινον καὶ κατέβαινον ἐπ' αὐτῆς. (Gen 28:12, LXX)[21]

Bethel accounts, see James L. Kugel, "The Ladder of Jacob," in *The Ladder of Jacob: Ancient Interpretations of the Biblical Story of Jacob and His Children* (Princeton: Princeton University Press, 2006), 9-35.

[18] For Jacob, see Dietzfelbinger, *Das Evangelium nach Johannes*, 1:61; David R. Kirk, "Heaven Opened: Intertextuality and Meaning in John 1:51," *TynBul* 63 (2012): 237-73; for the stone at Bethel, see Justin, "Dialogue with Trypho, a Jew," *ANF*, 86.2; J.C. O'Neil, "Son of Man, Stone of Blood (John 1:51)," *NovT* 45 (2003): 374-81; for the ladder as an extension of the place, see Craig S. Keener, *The Gospel of John: A Commentary* (Peabody: Hendrickson, 2003), 1:488-89; Robert H. Gundry, "New Wine in Old Wineskins: Bursting Traditional Interpretations in John's Gospel (Part 1)," *BBR* 17 (2007): 119-24; for the place (Bethel), see Rudolf Schnackenburg, *The Gospel according to St. John* (New York: Crossroad, 1982), 1:320; Barnabas Lindars, *The Gospel of John* (London: Marshall, Morgan & Scott, 1972), 122; Jürgen Becker, *Das Evangelium des Johannes* (Würzburg: Echter, 1991), 1:125; Schnelle, *Das Evangelium nach Johannes*, 56; Wengst, *Das Johannesevangelium*, 1:103-05; Andreas Köstenberger, *John* (Grand Rapids: Baker, 2004), 84-87.

[19] The Hebrew scriptural citations throughout this study are from Karl Elliger and Willhelm Rudolph, eds., *Biblia Hebraica Stuttgartensia* (Stuttgart: Deutsche Bibelgesellschaft, 1997).

[20] Another change from the MT is the shift of Hebrew participles to finite verbs in the imperfect tense. John W. Wevers, ed., *Genesis* (Göttingen: Vandenhoeck & Ruprecht, 1974), 271. In this respect, the Greek text of John follows more closely the Hebrew verb forms than those of the LXX. Both the MT and John use participles for the traffic of the angels. Johnson, "Our Father Jacob," 197.

[21] The Greek Old Testament scriptural citations throughout this study are from Alfred Rahlfs and Robert Hanhart, eds., *Septuaginta: Id est Vetus Testamentum graece iuxta LXX Interpretes*, rev. ed. (Stuttgart: Deutsche Bibelgesellschaft, 2006).

Jacob-Jesus typology. Taking the pronoun as referring to Jacob, however, some exegetes see a typology present between Jesus and Jacob. They typically detect John's intentional opting for the Hebrew tradition over the Greek.[22] This view is further argued for in view of some Jewish hermeneutical traditions, notably in Targum, Philo, and some of the early rabbinic interpretations of the present text.[23] Two conspicuous aspects stand out in these Jewish traditions. First, the traffic of the angels is inferred or explicitly stated to have taken place on Jacob and, second, these texts present Jacob as the focal point of the vision, promoting him into a rank of the righteous.[24]

For instance, midrashic *Genesis Rabbah* (composed in the fourth through fifth centuries A.D.) on Genesis 28:12 recounts Jacob's image engraved in heaven and the angels' ascending and descending upon him in order to examine his facial features.

> R. Hiyya the Elder and R. Yannai: One of them said, "'they were going up and coming down' on the ladder." The other said, "'they were going up and coming down' on Jacob." The one who says, "'they were going up and coming down' on the ladder,' has no problems. As to the one who says, "'they were going up and coming down' on Jacob," the meaning is that they were raising him up and dragging him down, dancing on him, leaping on him, abusing him. For it is said, "Israel, in whom I will be glorified" (Isa 49:3). [So said the angels,] "Are you the one whose visage is incised above?" They would then go up and look at his features and go down and examine him sleeping.[25]

---

[22] C.F. Burney, *The Aramaic Origin of the Fourth Gospel* (Oxford: Clarendon, 1922), 116; Johnson, "Our Father Jacob," 203-08.

[23] Hugo Odeberg, *The Fourth Gospel: Interpreted in Its Relation to Contemporaneous Religious Currents in Palestine and the Hellenistic-Oriental World* (Chicago: Argonaut, 1929; repr., Amsterdam: B.R. Grüner, 1968), 33-42; Martin McNamara, *Targum and Testament Revisited: Aramaic Paraphrases of the Hebrew Bible, a Light on the New Testament* (Grand Rapids: Eerdmans, 2010), 221-22; Craig A. Evans, "Old Testament in the Gospels," *DJG*, 588; Keener, *The Gospel of John*, 1:490-91; George J. Brooke, "The *Temple Scroll* and the New Testament," in *The Dead Sea Scrolls and the New Testament* (Minneapolis: Fortress, 2005), 106-10; Blanchard, "Le fils de l'homme et l'échelle de Jacob," 194. For a survey of such interpretive traditions, see Christopher Rowland, "John 1.51, Jewish Apocalyptic and Targumic Tradition," *NTS* 30 (1984): 498-507; William Loader, "John 1:50-51 and the 'Greater Things' of Johannine Christology," in *Anfänge der Christologie: Festschrift für Ferdinand Hahn zum 65. Geburtstag*, ed. Ferdinand Hahn, Cilliers Breytenbach, and Henning Paulsen (Göttingen: Vandenhoeck & Ruprecht, 1991), 255-74; Jerome H. Neyrey, "Are You Greater Than Our Father Jacob?: Jesus and Jacob in John 1:51 and 4:4-26," in *The Gospel of John in Cultural and Rhetorical Perspective* (Grand Rapids: Eerdmans, 2009), 86-106.

[24] Cf. Philo *De Somniis* 2.19 calls Jacob "the practiser [of virtue]."

[25] Jacob Neusner, *Genesis Rabbah: The Judaic Commentary to the Book of Genesis* (Atlanta: Scholars, 1985), 13. Similarly, *Midrash Rabbah: Genesis II*, trans. H. Freedman (London: Soncino, 1951), 626.

Targum Neofiti on Genesis 28:12 (the tenth through eleventh centuries A.D.) also follows the interpretive tradition of Jacob's image engraved in heaven.

> And he dreamed, and behold, a ladder was fixed on the earth and its head reached to the height of the heavens; and behold, the angels that had accompanied him from the house of his father ascended to bear good tidings to the angels on high, saying: "Come and see the pious man whose image is engraved in the throne of Glory, whom you desired to see." And behold, the angels from before the Lord ascended and descended and observed him.[26]

Targum Pseudo-Jonathan on this Genesis passage renders an analogous understanding of the Bethel account that the righteousness of Jacob and his image in heaven take the center stage in the discourse.[27]

> He had a dream, and behold, a ladder was fixed in the earth with its top reaching towards the heavens. And behold, the two angels who had gone to Sodom and who had been banished from their apartment because they had revealed the secrets of the Lord of the world, went about when they were banished until the time that Jacob went forth from his father's house. Then, as an act of kindness, they accompanied him to Bethel, and on that day they ascended to the heavens on high, and said, "Come and see Jacob the pious, whose image is fixed in the Throne of Glory, and whom you have desired to see." Then the rest of the holy angels of the Lord came down to look at him.[28]

In view of these rabbinic traditions, thus, there seems to be sufficient reason to posit a Jacob-Jesus typology.[29]

Ladder-Jesus typology. However, the interpretive judgment that sees a Jacob-Jesus typology in the present text under discussion poses a problem. The difficulty is two-fold. First, the advocates of such a view unfairly represent the rabbinic traditions which testify contradicting pictures within themselves, not to

---

[26] Martin McNamara, *Targum Neofiti 1: Genesis* (Collegeville: Liturgical, 1992), 140.

[27] The dating of this source is debated and the views are divergent. It ranges from the second to fifteenth centuries C.E. The majority view is the late medieval period, probably no later than 14th century C.E., due to the alleged anti-Islamic traits. However, recently, a much earlier dating is expressed around the second to third centuries C.E. Paul V.M. Flesher, "The Targumim," in *The Literary and Archaeological Sources*, part 1 of *Judaism in Late Antiquity*, ed. Jacob Neusner (Leiden: Brill, 1995), 60-62; Martin McNamara, *Targum and New Testament: Collected Essays* (Tübingen: Mohr Siebeck, 2011), 483-84.

[28] Michael Maher, *Targum Pseudo-Jonathan: Genesis* (Collegeville: Liturgical, 1992), 99-100.

[29] For the adherents of this view, see C.H. Dodd, *The Interpretation of the Fourth Gospel* (Cambridge: CUP, 1954), 245-49; McNamara, *Targum and Testament*, 147; Rowland, "John 1.51, Jewish Apocalyptic and Targumic Tradition," 498-507; Johnson, "Our Father Jacob," 202-03; John H.C. Neeb, "Jacob/Jesus Typology in John 1,51," *PEGLMBS* 12 (1992): 83-85; E. Earle Ellis, "Background and Christology of John's Gospel," in *Christ and the Future in New Testament History* (Leiden: Brill, 2000), 87; Kirk, "Heaven Opened," 237-56.

mention the anachronistic importation of the rabbinic materials onto the New Testament text (see Appendix 7: "The Use of the Rabbinic Materials in New Testament Studies"), and, second, they readily ignore the narrative context of the Johannine pericope (i.e., it is Nathanael and Jacob who behold the visions). For instance, *Genesis Rabbah* records the uncertainty among some rabbis concerning the place upon which the traffic of the angels took place. In addition, other Jewish texts, notably *the Ladder of Jacob* and *Targum Onkelos*, clearly state that it was upon the ladder where the angels traveled. These two texts also do not reveal the centrality of Jacob *vis-à-vis* his righteousness:[30] "There were twelve steps leading to the top of the ladder . . . . And while I was still looking at it, behold, angels of God ascended and descended on it."[31]

A greater number of more recent commentators, thus, correctly recognize a correspondence, not between Jacob and Jesus, but between the Son of Man and the ladder or Bethel, a place where God manifested himself to human beings.[32] Then the anti-type of Jacob is Nathanael. Hence v. 15 can be rendered as follows: "Like Jacob, you [Nathanael] will witness the divine theophany bestowed upon the Son of Man."[33]

---

[30] Moses Aberbach and Bernard Grossfeld, ed., *Targum Onkelos to Genesis: A Critical Analysis together with an English Translation of the Text* (New York: Ktav, 1982), 169.

[31] H.G. Lunt, "Ladder of Jacob," in *OTP*, 2:407.

[32] W.D. Davies, *The Gospel and the Land: Early Christianity and Jewish Territorial Doctrine* (Sheffield: JSOT, 1994; reprint, Berkeley, CA: University of California Press, 1974), 298; Michael Theobald, *Die Fleischwerdung des Logos: Studien zum Verhältnis des Johannesprologs zum Corpus des Evangeliums und zu 1 John* (Münster: Aschendorff, 1988), 288; idem, "Abraham—(Isaak—) Jacob: Israels Väter im Johannesevangelium," in *Studien zum Corpus Iohanneum* (Tübingen: Mohr Siebeck, 2010), 282-308; A.T. Hanson, *The Prophetic Gospel: A Study of John and the Old Testament* (Edinburgh: T & T Clark, 1991), 37-39; Michèle Morgen, "La promesse de Jésus à Nathanaël (Jn 1:51) éclairée par la hagaddah de Jacob-Israël," *RevScRel* 67 (1993): 16; William O. Walker, "John 1:43-51 and 'The Son of Man' in the Fourth Gospel," *JSNT* 56 (1994): 31-42; Walter Wink, "'The Son of Man' in the Gospel of John," in *Jesus in Johannine Tradition*, ed. Robert T. Fortna und Tom Thatcher (Louisville: Westminster/John Knox, 2001), 118-19; Paul M. Hoskins, *Jesus as the Fulfillment of the Temple in the Gospel of John* (Milton Keynes: Paternoster, 2006), 132-33; Andreas Köstenberger, "John," in *Commentary on the New Testament Use of the Old Testament*, ed. G.K. Beale and D.A. Carson (Grand Rapids: Baker, 2007), 430; J. Ramsey Michaels, *The Gospel of John* (Grand Rapids: Eerdmans, 2010), 136. In this respect, Philo's understanding of the ladder seems distant from that of John since he records that "by the ladder in this thing, which is called the world, is figuratively understood the air, the foundation of which is the earth, and the head is the heaven." Philo *Somn* 1.133. Some others still suggested that the ladder refers to the cross, see F.F. Bruce, *The Gospel of John* (Grand Rapids: Eerdmans, 1983), 88; Margaret Pamment, "The Son of Man in the Fourth Gospel," *JTS* 36 (1985): 58-66.

[33] Benjamin E. Reynolds, "The Use of the Son of Man Idiom in the Gospel of John," in *"Who Is This Son of Man?": The Latest Scholarship on a Puzzling Expression of the*

However, some commentators are still hesitant to accept the presence of a Jacob-Nathanael typology in the text. Schnackenburg, for instance, offers a three-fold skepticism.[34] First, the vision is promised not only to Nathanael but also to the disciples since the number of the verb ὄψεσθε ("you will see") in v. 51 is in the plural. Second, seeing Jesus being pierced and raised up (as some exegetes take the referent of this vision to be) is different from seeing the heaven opened. Third, John is taking only an element of Jacob's vision, namely, the image of the ladder and the ascending and descending of angels. As for Schnackenburg, thus, to find a large scale correspondence between the Bethel account and John 1:51 is to press the symbolism beyond what the textual evidences permit. However, his dismissal of the typology calls for a more nuanced examination of the present text. Literary devices such as imagery, symbolism, and typology should not be interpreted too literally, but rather in their own rights. Schnackenburg is certainly correct in insisting on inclusion of other disciple(s) as the recipients of the vision and in not limiting it exclusively to Nathanael. Nonetheless, it is hard to avoid the notion that Nathanael is depicted as an inclusive representative of the disciples and presented somewhat as a descendant and/or spiritual realization of Jacob (Israel) only without the fraudulent disposition characteristic of that forefather.[35] In addition, an attempt to find detailed one-on-one correspondences in an analogy is to misunderstand such a literary genre. It is the context of John 1:51 (i.e., a [true] Israelite seeing a vision) and the resemblance (or the verbatim quotation in the case of this text) of the language that warrant the presence of such an analogy.

Contents of theophany. Once the agents of the typology are established, the contents of the visions need to be clarified. From the Johannine text, on the one hand, it is clear that the Son of Man is the focus of the Johannine theophany. On the other hand, the exact nature of the theophany is uncertain. The cross event, Jesus' baptism, the subsequent signs, and the second coming have been variously

---

Historical Jesus, ed. Larry W. Hurtado and Paul L. Owen (London: T & T Clark, 2011), 114.

[34] Schnackenburg, *The Gospel according to St. John*, 1:322; similarly, Raymond E. Brown, *The Gospel according to John* (New York: Doubleday, 1966), 83. Michaelis also sees the verse as a mere reflection of the synoptic materials. Wilhelm Michaelis, "Joh 1:51, Gen 28:12 und das Menschensohn-Problem," *TLZ* 85 (1960): 564-66.

[35] Morgen, "La promesse de Jésus à Nathanaël (Jn 1:51)," 19; Hoskins, *Jesus as the Fulfillment of the Temple in the Gospel of John*, 132-33. Taking one individual representing a group of people is a Johannine literary device. For examples, one disciple for all (13:10; 14:5-7; 8:10), Nicodemus for all Jews (3:10-12), Jesus for all Jews (4:20), the Samaritan woman for all Samaritans (4:21-22). Michaelis, "Joh. 1,51, Gen. 28,12 und das Menschensohn-Problem," 563. For an argument for the integral part of 1:51 within its literary context, see Johnson, "Our Father Jacob," 194-97.

proposed but all seem to fall short of the concrete textual warrant.[36]

The most important aspect of this typology appears to concern the presence of a polemic over against the Old Testament and the contemporary Jewish traditions. In other words, in lieu of the well-known Johannine axiom that "no one has seen God" (John 1:18; 5:37; 6:46), an interesting exegetical question can be posed as to whether John is making a counter-claim that Jacob, the Johannine proto-type of a genuine Israelite, was a witness to the pre-existent Christ instead of God.[37] An affirmative answer to this question is possible since the Jewish traditions (OT, Targum, and Philo) on the Bethel account almost unanimously opt for Jacob's witness of God on the ladder.

> And behold there was a ladder firmly planted on the earth, and the Lord was standing steadily upon it; and he said, I am the God of Abraham thy father, and the God of Isaac, be not afraid. (Philo *Somn* 1.3)

> And he dreamed, and behold, a ladder was fixed in the ground, while its top reached towards heaven; and behold, angels of the Lord were going up and down on it. And behold, the Glory of the Lord was standing over him, and He said, "I am the Lord, the God of your father Abraham and the God of Isaac." (*Targum Onkelos to Genesis 28:12*)[38]

---

[36] For the cross event, see Peter Dschulnigg, "Die Berufung der Jünger Joh 1,35-51 im Rahmen des vierten Evangeliums," *FZPhTh* 36 (1989): 443-45; Wengst, *Das Johannesevangelium*, 1:105; for the ensuing signs, see Bultmann, *The Gospel of John*, 105-06; Brown, *The Gospel according to John*, 1:83; Herman Ridderbos, *The Gospel of John* (Grand Rapids: Eerdmans, 1997), 95; Köstenberger, *John*, 86; for Jesus' earthly life, see John B. Polhill, "John 1-4: The Revelation of True Life," *RevExp* 85 (1988): 449-50; for the second coming, see Hubert Windisch, "Joh i 51 und die Auferstehung Jesu," *ZNW* 31 (1932): 199-204; William Loader, "John 1:50-51 and the 'Greater Things' of Johannine Christology," in *Anfänge der Christologie: Festschrift für Ferdinand Hahn zum 65. Geburtstag*, ed. Ferdinand Hahn, Cilliers Breytenbach, and Henning Paulsen (Göttingen: Vandenhoeck & Ruprecht, 1991), 255-74.

[37] Jerome H. Neyrey, "The Jacob Allusions in Joh 1:51," *CBQ* 44 (1982): 594; Reim, *Jochanan*, 154-55; Dietzfelbinger, *Das Evangelium nach Johannes*, 1:61; Theobald, "Abraham—(Isaak—) Jacob," 287 (n. 28). Cf. Christian Dietzfelbinger, "Aspekte des Alten Testaments im Johannesevangelium," in *Geschichte-Tradition-Reflexion III, Frühes Christentum: Festschrift für Martin Hengel zum 70. Geburtstag*, ed. Hermann Lichtenberger (Tübingen: Mohr Siebeck, 1996), 208; and Michael Labahn, "Jesus und die Autorität der Schrift im Johannesevangelium: Überlegungen zu einem spannungsreichen Verhältnis," in *Israel und seine Heilstraditionen im Johannessevangelium: Festgabe für Johannes Beutler SJ zum 70. Geburtstag*, ed. Michael Labahn, Klaus Scholtissek, and Angelika Strotmann (Paderborn: Schöningh, 2004), 204.

[38] Aberbach and Grossfeld, *Targum Onkelos to Genesis*, 169-70. Also, this view that Jacob saw God at Bethel is commonly argued in recent Old Testament studies; for instance, see John Van Seters, "Divine Encounter at Bethel (Gen 28,10-22) in Recent Literary-Critical Study of Genesis," *ZAW* 110 (1998): 503-13; Michael Oblath, "'To Sleep, Perchance to Dream . . .': What Jacob Saw at Bethel (Genesis 28.10-22)," *JSOT* 95 (2001): 117-26; Kirk, "Heaven Opened," 238-42.

Then, this intentional and apparent shift or clarification would have made quite a stark impression on the audience familiar with the current Jewish traditions.

This observation is intriguing and will certainly strengthen the thesis of the present discussion since it infers Jacob's eyewitness of the pre-existent Son of Man as interpreted by some early church commentators.[39] Differently put, the confession of Nathanael is read back into Jacob's vision so that Jacob bears witness to the Christological identity of Jesus in terms of his pre-existence, the divine sonship, and the headship of Israel (John 1:49).[40] However, this construal remains in the realm of a reader-oriented hermeneutics, which often evades a reasonable exegetical control from the traditional historical critical point of view. Accordingly, it is more of a suggestive reading without definite certainty as being intended by the fourth evangelist.

A more natural reading of the present text, therefore, can be proposed here which bears, in our judgment, a more important bearing on the Johannine shift of the place of the angelic traffic, i.e., from on the ladder to on the Son of Man. In the Hebrew text of Genesis 28:12, Jacob is portrayed as a mere observer of the divine theophany. This passive aspect on the part of Jacob is further elaborated on by an extended divine promise in the following verses (Gen 28:13-15) since it is the divine providence that will enact the redemptive program through Jacob. On the other hand, in John 1:51, the focus of the vision motif is shifted onto Jesus (he even assumes the role preserved for God). The centrality of Jesus in this discourse is evidenced in the immediately preceding context, Nathanael's Christological confession, which is positively affirmed by this prediction of the Jacob theophany motif. In addition, another noteworthy change is the announcer of the theophany. In the Genesis account, it is God who reveals the unfolding of his own salvation historical plan. In the Johannine account, however, it is Jesus himself who discloses the theophany which captures a divine revelation of the Son of Man.[41] These two apparent shifts set forth the centrality of Jesus.

---

[39] For instance, Justin *Dialogus cum Tryphone Judæo* 86.2, in *Opera quae exstant omnia*, ed. B. de Montfaucon, rev. J.–P. Migne, PG, vol. 6 (Paris: J. –P. Migne, 1885), 680. For a more detailed study on the patristic interpretation of the Bethel account in John 1:51, see Willy Rordorf, "Gen 28,10ff und John 1,51 in der patristischen Exegese," in *Johannes—Studien: Interdisziplinäre Zugänge zum Johannes—Evangelium, Freundesgabe der Theologischen Fakultät der Universität Neuchâtel für Jean Zumstein*, ed. Martin Rose (Zürich: Theologischer, 1991), 39-46. By the second century, this interpretive tradition seems to have gained an even wider reception. See *b. Hullin* 91b & *b. Rabba* 68:12. Cf. Christopher Rowland, "John 1.51, Jewish Apocalyptic and Targumic Tradition," *NTS* 30 (1984): 502, 507, n. 15.

[40] For a study of Nathanael as a witness to a realization of the Old Testament messianic hopes, see Craig R. Koester, "Messianic Exegesis and the Call of Nathanael (John 1.45-51)," *JSNT* 39 (1990): 23-34.

[41] The angels are often used to depict the delivery of the divine revelation in Jewish traditions. Reim, *Jochanan*, 103, 255-56. "In this piece of elaborate typology Jesus corresponds to 'the Lord' in the Bethel vision, the Lord who stood at the top of the ladder: but he also corresponds to the ladder itself, since the point of the midrash is to

Summary. In conclusion, therefore, the aforementioned observations suggest that John 1:51 speaks of the christological characteristics of Jesus in the backdrop of Jacob's theophany motif which serves an affirmative function of Jesus' messianic identity as reflected in the mouth of a genuine Israelite, Nathanael. Moreover, the present Johannine text illuminates Jesus as the focal point of the divine revelation or the divine redemptive history in view of the immediate narrative context (that is, the immediately preceding Johannine prologue) and the Old Testament background, and it sets the stage for the unpacking of the replacement and/or contrast theme that follows in the subsequent chapters.[42]

Jacob, the Provider of Water: John 4:10-14

¹⁰ ἀπεκρίθη Ἰησοῦς καὶ εἶπεν αὐτῇ· εἰ ᾔδεις τὴν δωρεὰν τοῦ θεοῦ καὶ τίς ἐστιν ὁ λέγων σοι· δός μοι πεῖν, σὺ ἂν ᾔτησας αὐτὸν καὶ ἔδωκεν ἄν σοι ὕδωρ ζῶν. ¹¹ λέγει αὐτῷ [ἡ γυνή]· κύριε, οὔτε ἄντλημα ἔχεις καὶ τὸ φρέαρ ἐστὶν βαθύ· πόθεν οὖν ἔχεις τὸ ὕδωρ τὸ ζῶν; ¹² μὴ σὺ μείζων εἶ τοῦ πατρὸς ἡμῶν Ἰακώβ, ὃς ἔδωκεν ἡμῖν τὸ φρέαρ καὶ αὐτὸς ἐξ αὐτοῦ ἔπιεν καὶ οἱ υἱοὶ αὐτοῦ καὶ τὰ θρέμματα αὐτοῦ; ¹³ ἀπεκρίθη Ἰησοῦς καὶ εἶπεν αὐτῇ· πᾶς ὁ πίνων ἐκ τοῦ ὕδατος τούτου διψήσει πάλιν·¹⁴ ὃς δ᾽ ἂν πίῃ ἐκ τοῦ ὕδατος οὗ ἐγὼ δώσω αὐτῷ, οὐ μὴ διψήσει εἰς τὸν αἰῶνα, ἀλλὰ τὸ ὕδωρ ὃ δώσω αὐτῷ γενήσεται ἐν αὐτῷ πηγὴ ὕδατος ἁλλομένου εἰς ζωὴν αἰώνιον. (John 4:10-14, NA[28])

¹⁰Jesus answered her, "If you knew the gift of God, and who it is that is saying to you, 'Give me a drink,' you would have asked him, and he would have given you living water." ¹¹The woman said to him, "Sir, you have no bucket, and the well is deep. Where do you get that living water? ¹²Are you greater than our ancestor Jacob, who gave us the well, and with his sons and his flocks drank from it?" ¹³Jesus said to her, "Everyone who drinks of this water will be thirsty again, ¹⁴but those who drink of the water that I will give them will never be thirsty. The water that I will give will become in them a spring of water gushing up to eternal life." (John 4:10-14, NRSV)

Narrative context. The fourth chapter of the Gospel of John should be seen in a natural narrative tie with the second chapter. In this regard, Polhill's analysis of the present text is illuminating. He finds a natural development of narrative follow in this context that chapters two through four constitute a literary unity.

> Like much of the Fourth Gospel, its first four chapters are rather episodic, more a patchwork quilt than a seamless robe. It is recurrent themes rather than a continuous narrative that bind them together. To be sure, there is some narrative development. The prologue sets the stage for the Gospel story. The witness to the incarnate Word begins in 1:19-51. Two miracles, or "signs," both located at Cana (2:1ff. and 4:54ff.), bracket the following three chapters. Through these signs and the conversations with Nicodemus, John the Baptist, the Samaritan woman, and the disciples, the reader is led to an increasing understanding of Jesus as revealer and of the proper response to him.[43]

---

emphasise that Jesus is now the place where God is permanently to be found, both in heaven and on earth." Hanson, *The Prophetic Gospel*, 37.

[42] Theobald, "Abraham—(Isaak—) Jacob," 287.

[43] Polhill, "John 1-4," 445.

In addition to Polhill's observation, at least, two more features in particular warrant such judgment. First, the recurrent keyword μαρτυρία ("witness") and its cognate words weave together chs. 2 through 4 (John 2:25; 3:11, 26, 32; 4:39, 44). In those pericopae, the testimonies offered by the minor characters lead to the explicit manifestation of Jesus' christological identity, i.e., Mary's disclosing of Jesus' divine power, John the Baptist's verbal testimony of Jesus as Christ converting his disciples into Jesus', and the Samaritan woman's witness resulting in the Samaritans' confession of Jesus as the redeemer. In the present pericope, Jesus' discourse with the Samaritan woman leads her and others to escalating faith in Christ.

Table 1 Escalating Faith in Christ in John 4[44]

a Jew (v. 9) → greater than Jacob (v. 12) → a prophet (v. 19) → the Messiah (v. 26) → her leading the villagers to Jesus (v. 30) → the villagers' confession of Jesus as the savior of the world (v. 42)

Second, the replacement or contrast theme that permeates these texts requires these chapters to be seen as a narrative unit.[45] As the plain water for Jewish purification practices was changed into better wine (John 2:1-11), so the water of Jacob's well that quenches the human thirst only temporarily will be replaced with the water of Jesus that enlivens the human soul perennially (John 4:1-15). Also, as the old temple is replaced with the spiritual temple of Jesus' body (John 2:13-22), so the true worship will supersede the superficial old cultic rituals in

---

[44] R. Alan Culpepper, *Anatomy of the Fourth Gospel: A Study in Literary Design* (Philadelphia: Fortress, 1983), 91.

[45] Hoskins, *Jesus as the Fulfillment of the Temple in the Gospel of John*, 147-81. For a brief summary of the replacement theme in John, see D.A. Carson, "John and the Johannine Epistles," in *It Is Written: Scripture Citing Scripture: Essays in Honour of Barnabas Lindars*, ed. D.A. Carson and H.G.M. Williamson (Cambridge: CUP, 1988), 253-56; idem, *The Gospel according to John* (Grand Rapids: Eerdmans, 1991), 180-83; Frank Thielman, "Grace in Place of Grace: Jesus Christ and the Mosaic Law in John's Gospel," in *The Law and the New Testament: The Question of Continuity* (New York: Crossroad, 1999), 92-110; Andrew C. Brunson, *Psalm 118 in the Gospel of John: An Intertextual Study on the New Exodus Pattern in the Theology of John* (Tübingen: Mohr Siebeck, 2003), 147-49. For a study that interprets the Gospel as a whole in terms of the fulfillment and replacement of Jewish symbols and institutions, see John W. Pryor, *John: Evangelist of the Covenant People: The Narrative and Themes of the Fourth Gospel* (Downers Grove: InterVarsity, 1992); Christian Grappe, "Du sanctuaire au jardin: Jésus, nouveau et véritable Temple dans le quatrième évangile," in *Studien zu Matthäus und Johannes: Festschrift für Jean Zumstein zu seinem 65. Geburtstag*, ed. Andreas Dettwiler & Uta Poplutz (Zürich: Theologischer, 2009), 285-96.

Jerusalem and in Gerazim at the advent of the new age (John 4:19-26).[46] As the serpent of Moses was lifted, so "Jesus must be lifted so that everyone who believes in him may have eternal life" in contrast to the Israelites who did not live even to see the Promised Land (John 3:14-15).[47] This new redemptive paradigm is further marked by the breaking of the ethnic barrier. That is, the citizens of the new Kingdom of God now encompass beyond the exclusive boundary of Israel, as Jesus embraces these Samaritans into the saving knowledge in his ministry.[48]

Some exegetes note possible parallels in this anecdote to other incidents at the well recorded in the Old Testament, i.e., the encounters of Abraham's servant, Jacob, and Moses, with their future wives (or the master's wife in the case of Abraham's steward) coupled with the unfaithful wife of Hosea 2 and other analogous allusions in the Old Testament.[49] In view of some corresponding elements such as meeting a woman by a well or reunion of husband and unfaithful wife, these allusions are possible and the parallels will bolster the force of the contrast theme in the narrative. However, it seems a special pleading to argue that the fourth evangelist had those allusions in mind as such because those instances would not have been extremely sparse even in ancient times, especially encountering of male and female at a well.[50] So does argue Okure.

> There are no real parallels between the OT stories and the Samaritan narratives as it now stands . . . . A striking difference between the Johannine account and these OT stories lies in the centrality of marriage in the Patriarchal accounts. This is not clearly an issue in 4:1-42, even though Jesus is called "the bridegroom" in 3:29, and even though some notion of wooing (in the sense of persuading . . .) is clearly present.[51]

---

[46] This contrast and/or replacement theme is frequently noted in a number of commentaries on John, for example, Beasley-Murray, *John*, 58-59; for the theme related to this text, Benny Thettayil, *In Spirit and Truth: An Exegetical Study of John 4:19-26 and a Theological Investigation of the Replacement Theme in the Fourth Gospel* (Leuven: Peeters, 2007), 398-403.

[47] Keener, *The Gospel of John*, 1:590. Wengst also notes that the present pericope is in continuation with the comparison of John the Baptist with Jesus. Wengst, *Das Johannesevangelium*, 1:160.

[48] For the exclusive reception of the gift of God by Israel in Jewish literature, see Odeberg, *The Fourth Gospel*, 150-52.

[49] Neyrey, "Jacob Traditions and the interpretation of John 4:10-26," 425-26; Jean-Louis Ska, "Jésus et la Samaritaine (Jn 4): Utilité de L'ancien Testament," *NRTh* 118 (1996): 641-52; Keener, *The Gospel of John*, 1:586-91; Theobald, "Abraham—(Isaak—) Jacob," 294; Ton Veerkamp, "Die Frau am Jakobsbrunnen: John 4,4-42," *TK* 27 (2004): 71-96; Tina Dykesteen Nilsen, "The True and the False: The Structure of John 4,16-26," *BN* 128 (2006): 61-64; Mary L. Coloe, "The Woman of Samaria: Her Characterization, Narrative, and Theological Significance," in *Characters and Characterization in the Gospel of John*, ed. Christopher W. Skinner (London: T & T Clark, 2013), 182-96.

[50] Carson, *The Gospel of John*, 232-33; Lindars, *The Gospel of John*, 187.

[51] Teresa Okure, *The Johannine Approach to Mission: A Contextual Study of John 4:1-42* (Tübingen: Mohr Siebeck, 1988), 88.

Jacob's well. The Old Testament does not mention Jacob's ever digging a well, nor that he gave it to his son(s). Genesis 33:19; 48:22 and Joshua 24:32 only comment on the purchase of Shechem for Joseph, which is the locale of Jacob's well in John 4:5 (as it is addressed as Sychar in the Gospel). Sychar was situated at the foot of Mount Ebal in the Shechem valley.[52] Historically speaking, Sychar probably became the new center of Samaritan life after the destruction of Shechem in the second century B.C. The Samaritan Pentateuch changes the place of the sacrifice of Isaac from המריה ("Moriah": Gen 12:6-7; 33:20) to המוראה ("the place of vision"). The extant manuscripts of the Samaritan Pentateuch date to the fourth century A.D. However, it must have originated in the second century B.C. from the schism with the mainline Judaism.[53]

Table 2 Comparison of Gen 12:6-7 between the Samaritan & Masoretic Texts[54]

The Samaritan Text	The Masoretic Text
⁶And Abraam passed through the land as far as the site of Ashkem, to the **Alone moora**. And the Kaanannee was then in the land. 7And Shehmaa **envisioned** Himself to Abraam and said **to him**, To your seed I will give this land. And there he built an altar to Shehmaa who had **envisioned** unto him.	⁶And Abram passed through the land unto the place of Shechem, unto the **plain of Moreh**. And the Canaanite was then in the land. ⁷And Adonai **appeared** unto Abraam and sai . . . "Unto thy seed will I give this land"; and he builded there an altar unto Adonai who **appeared** unto him.

---

[52] H.M. Schencke, "Jacobs-brunnen-Josephsgrab-Sychar," *ZDPV* 84 (1968): 159; Zdravko Stefanovic, "Jacob's Well," *ABD*, 3:608; Martin Hengel, "Das Johannesevangelium als Quelle für die Geschichte des antiken Judentums," in *Judaica, Hellenistica, et Christiana: Kleine Schriften II*, ed. Martin Hengel with Jörg Frey and Dorothea Betz (Tübingen: Mohr Siebeck, 1999), 293-334; Urban C. von Wahlde, "Archaeology and John's Gospel," in *Jesus and Archaeology*, ed. James H. Charlesworth (Grand Rapids: Eerdmans, 2006), 556-59. For a brief introduction to Shechem and Jacob's well in Jewish history, see Wengst, *Das Johannesevangelium*, 1:164-65; John F. McHugh, *John 1-4: A Critical and Exegetical Commentary* (London: T & T Clark, 2009), 302-05. For an archaeological survey of the location in the time of Jesus, see Jürgen Zangenberg, "Between Jerusalem and Galilee: Samaria in the Time of Jesus," in *Jesus and Archaeology*, ed. James H. Charlesworth (Grand Rapids: Eerdmans, 2006), 416-18.

[53] Esther & Hanan Eshel, "Dating the Samaritan Pentateuch's Compilation in Light of the Qumran Biblical Scrolls," in *Emanuel: Studies in Hebrew Bible, Septuagint, and Dead Sea scrolls in Honor of Emanuel Tov*, ed. Shalom M. Paul (Leiden: Brill, 2003), 215-40.

[54] Benyamim Tsedaka and Sharon Sullivan, eds., *The Israelite Samaritan Version of the Torah: First English Translation Compared with the Masorectic Version* (Grand Rapids: Eerdmans, 2013), 27 (emphasis added).

This shift opens up a possibility that Isaac was sacrificed not in Jerusalem ("Moriah," 2 Chr 3:1) but in Shechem. As a result, all three patriarchs are related to the Samaritan territory.[55]

Another Jewish tradition composed in the eighth century records an interesting legend concerning Jacob and a well, such as, the traveling well and Jacob's performing a miracle of water surging itself to the surface of the well. *Pirqe Rabbi Eliezer* attests that "Jacob was seventy-seven years old when he went forth from his father's house, and the well went with him."[56] This well could have followed him to Shechem and it may well be the reason why the Samaritan woman associated the well with Jacob.

Another rabbinic tradition testifies to a similar picture, which could have been contrasted with Jesus' living water. In this narrative, Jacob is said to have the water surge to the top of the well and overflow. *Targum Neofiti* on Genesis, dating between the first through the fourth centuries A.D., notes the overflowing of Jacob's well as following:

> And the fourth miracle: the stone which all the pastors had come together to roll away from over the mouth of the well and could not, when our father Jacob came he raised it with one hand and gave to drink to the flock of Laban, his mother's brother. And the fifth: when our father Jacob raised the stone from above the mouth of the well, the well overflowed and came up to its mouth, and was overflowing for twenty years—all the days that he dwelt in Haran.[57]

Some exegetes also relate the Qumran documents with this "spring of living water": CD-A III 16-17, CD-A VI 4, 4Q418 103 II 6. Especially, the last one specifically includes a phrase "like a spring of living water."[58] This text led some

---

[55] Reinhard Pummer, *The Samaritans* (Leiden: Brill, 1987), 10. For a recent argument for the legitimacy of the Samaritan temple, see Etienne Nodet, "Israelites, Samaritans, Temples, Jews," in *Samaria, Samarians, Samaritans: Studies on Bible, History and Linguistics*, ed. József Zsengellér (Berlin: Walter de Gruyter, 2011), 121-72. Because of the seeming congeniality to Samaritans, some exegetes posited some type of Samaritan influence on this pericope. For an overview of such scholarly judgments, see Margaret Pamment, "Is There Convincing Evidence of Samaritan Influence on the Fourth Gospel," *ZNW* 73 (1982): 221-30. However, such a judgment suffers from the uncritical use of literature (see 168-71 of Nodet above). For a survey of the Samaritanism, see Magnar Kartveit, *The Origin of the Samaritans* (Leiden: Brill, 2009); Gary N. Knopper, *Jews and Samaritans: The Origins and History of Their Early Relations* (Oxford: OUP, 2013).

[56] *Pirqe Rabbi Eliezer* 35 in *Pirkê de Rabbi Eliezer (The Chapters of Rabbi Eliezer the Great) according to the Text of the Manuscript belonging to Abraham Epstein of Vienna*, trans. Gerald Friedlander (New York: Bloch, 1916), 263.

[57] Martin McNamara, *Targum Neofiti I: Genesis* (Collegeville: Liturgical, 1992), 139-40. Cf. José Ramón-Díaz, "Palestinian Targum and the New Testament," *NovT* 6 (1963): 75-80.

[58] Raymond E Brown, "The Qumran Scrolls and the Johannine Gospel and Epistles," in *The Scrolls and the New Testament*, ed. Krister Stendahl (New York: Harper & Brothers, 1957), 199-200; James H. Charlesworth, "A Study in Shared Symbolism and

exegetes to believe that this tradition sets the stage for Jesus' reply about his living water, i.e., springing or gushing out water in contrast to the stagnant water in Jacob's well.[59] However, the aforementioned rabbinic witnesses do not predate the second century A.D. Yet the contrast of the provisions of Jacob and Jesus still stands in the Johannine text. An echoing of this tradition may well have been intended in the text, but the insufficiency of the internal textual evidence leaves us uncertain.

The contrast of Jacob's water with Jesus'. Although various elements in the discourse of Jesus and the Samaritan woman are subject to dispute,[60] one aspect is certain, that is, the gift of Jesus (the gift of God in v. 10 is equivalent to the living water of Jesus in vv. 14-15) is greater than that of Jacob even in the face of the patriarch's impressive ability to supply abundantly for himself, his sons, their cattle, and even his descendants of generations later.[61] The Samaritan woman did

---

Language: The Qumran Community and the Johannine Community," in *The Bible and the Dead Sea Scrolls: The Princeton Symposium on the Dead Sea Scrolls*, ed. James H. Charlesworth (Waco: Baylor University Press, 2006), 3:138; Albert L. Hogeterp, *Expectations of the End: A Comparative Traditio-Historical Study of Eschatological, Apocalyptic and Messianic Ideas in the Dead Sea Scrolls and the New Testament* (Leiden: Brill, 2009), 198-99.

[59] McNamara, "The Targums and Johannine Literature," 145-46; Neyrey, "Jacob Traditions and the Interpretation of John 4:10-26," 423. Πηγὴ ὕδατος in John 4:14 literally means "gushing out, flowing, or springing" water. "πηγή, ῆς," *BDAG*, 810.

[60] Scholarly interpretations are divided over the meaning of "the gift" and the symbolic referent of "the water" in the discourse. It seems to refer to the living water and more specifically either the word of Jesus, the Logos (cf. Jer 2:13, Wengst, *Das Johannesevangelium*, 1:167-68, 170) and/or the Holy Spirit (Köstenberger, *John*, 150). The sacramental referent theory for the living water is ruled out due to its evident internalized characteristic in v. 14 (Polhill, "John 1-4," 454-55). For the eschatological connotation of the Johannine "living water," see Dale C. Allison, Jr., "The Living Water (John 4:10-14, 6:35c, 7:37-39)," *SVTQ* 30 (1986): 143-57. In view of John 7:38 where "the indwelling of the well" clearly refers to the Holy Spirit, the gift in this pericope should involve some elements of the Spirit as well. For the religious background of "living water," see Jeremiah 2:13, 17:13, Ezekiel 47, Isaiah 12:3, Sirach 15:3, 24:21, 1 Enoch 48:1. Dietzfelbinger, *Das Evangelium nach Johannes*, 1:104-05; Köstenberger, *John*, 152. Noteworthy is a possible polemic of Jesus' gift against the Torah, which is often depicted as "water" or "well" in the Second Temple Judaism (see Keener, *The Gospel of John*, 1:602-05). Then, the implication is that Jesus' water supplants the Torah since it is internal, eternal, and spiritual over against the opposite characteristics of the Torah. Such symbolic reading is attractive but still is without definite textual proofs.

[61] Dietzfelbinger, *Das Evangelium nach Johannes*, 1:102. Some scholars posit that the fourth evangelist incorporated the Samaritan Christian tradition into this text. George Wesley Buchanan, "Samaritan Origin of the Gospel of John," in *Religions in Antiquity: Essays in Memory of Erwin Ramsdell Goodenough*, ed. Jacob Neusner (Leiden: Brill, 1968), 163. The argument is refuted by Margaret Pamment, "Is There Convincing Evidence of Samaritan Influence on the Fourth Gospel," *ZNW* 73 (1982): 221-30.

not expect this to be true (because of her use of the negative particle μή in front of her question in v. 12) but Jesus' answer to her question comes as a surprise in three ways.[62] First, Jacob's well meets only a temporary human need for a while whereas the water of Jesus quenches the human thirst perennially. Second, Jacob was able to offer an external provision which men had to visit over and over again, but the gift of Jesus is internalized in the heart of men so as to remain effective continuously (also see Appendix 4).[63] Lastly and most importantly, the gift of Jesus essentially supersedes that of Jacob in that the former leads to spiritual rejuvenation (this internalized well refers to the incoming of the Holy Spirit later, see 7:38-39).[64] This last aspect stands in stark contrast to the earthly oriented nature of the woman's interest which is symbolically reflected in her history with six men. This manner in which the provision of Jesus surpasses that of Jacob rhetorically illustrates the overall superiority of Jesus, i.e., the magnitude of the new redemptive plan is far greater through Jesus than through the Jewish heroic figure. This theme occurs repeatedly and permeates throughout the Gospel of John, for instance, with Jacob in chapter 4, Abraham in chapter 8, and Moses in 1:17, 6:32, 35.[65]

Summary

Some conclusions can be induced from the observations noted above concerning the narrative function of Jacob for Jesus' christological identity. In only a couple of pericopae in which the forefather is mentioned or alluded to (John 1:51; 4:10-14), he provides a point of comparison to connote the prominence of Jesus. Jesus and Jacob share a common ground in that they take part in the redemptive program. However, the points of contrast surpass the common denominator in these pericopae: Jesus is the focal point of the divine revelation and salvific program while Jacob remains at the fringe merely as a witness in the first pericope; in the latter, whereas Jacob provides an earthly and tentative means to sustain life, the gift of Jesus offers an efficient resource for eternal spiritual transformation.

---

[62] Udo Wilckens, *Das Evangelium nach Johannes* (Göttingen: Vandenhoeck & Ruprecht, 1998), 82.

[63] The internalized gift of Jesus is far superior to the gift of Jacob since the latter is restricted by its locality. The same is true for the following comparison of the place for the true worship, which transcends the limitation of locality (whether Jerusalem or Samaria). Thielman, "Grace in Place of Grace," 94-96.

[64] Wengst, *Das Johannesevangelium*, 1:169; Dietzfelbinger, *Das Evangelium nach Johannes*, 1:103-105. O. Betz notes the theme of worship in spirit and truth and argues that this text echoes Joshua 24, in which Israelites are summoned to returned to true worship. His judgment is based on the semantic synonyms of Jesus and Joshua. Otto Betz, "Das Johannesevangelium und das Alte Testament," in *Wie verstehen wir das Neue Testament?* (Wuppertal: Aussaat, 1981), 103-05. The visibility of allusions, however, seems to be subject to question.

[65] Dietzfelbinger, *Das Evangelium nach Johannes*, 1:103.

Briefly put, these two texts portray the magnificent divine redemptive ministry being unfolded through Jesus. In light of such revelation, Jacob is presented as a witness who foreshadows it. The inauguration of this new divine redemptive history takes on such a radically different level from that of the previous age, that is, of Jacob or of the Old Testament that the theme of "replacement" is probably adequate to characterize this shift, especially in John 4. Yet a sense of contact-points still remains since Jacob's involvement in the redemptive history echoes, foreshadows, and, bears a valid testimony to this new progression of the centuries-old program first exclusively put forth in Israel and now expanded to embrace the broader ethnic boundary with the incoming of Jesus into human history[66] As such, Jesus is not a new Jacob nor is the patriarch a messianic prefiguration. He is more of a qualified witness to the realization of the salvation history only hinted at in the life of the forefather. In this respect, the comment of Theobald on this this text is illuminating:

> Through inserting vv. 10-15, the evangelist uniquely transforms what the basic story quietly resonates with its scene from Jacob's well. Of course, it excludes any idea of "salvation historical" continuity. Jesus is not a new Jacob. He and his *gift* are entirely *different* in quality. Something Jacob could *not* "*give*" breaks out in him.[67]

Abraham as Christological Witness: John 8:51-58

[51] ἀμὴν ἀμὴν λέγω ὑμῖν, ἐάν τις τὸν ἐμὸν λόγον τηρήσῃ, θάνατον οὐ μὴ θεωρήσῃ εἰς τὸν αἰῶνα. [52] εἶπον [οὖν] αὐτῷ οἱ Ἰουδαῖοι· νῦν ἐγνώκαμεν ὅτι δαιμόνιον ἔχεις. Ἀβραὰμ ἀπέθανεν καὶ οἱ προφῆται, καὶ σὺ λέγεις· ἐάν τις τὸν λόγον μου τηρήσῃ, οὐ μὴ γεύσηται θανάτου εἰς τὸν αἰῶνα. [53] μὴ σὺ μείζων εἶ τοῦ πατρὸς ἡμῶν Ἀβραάμ, ὅστις ἀπέθανεν; καὶ οἱ προφῆται ἀπέθανον. τίνα σεαυτὸν ποιεῖς; [54] ἀπεκρίθη Ἰησοῦς· ἐὰν ἐγὼ δοξάσω ἐμαυτόν, ἡ δόξα μου οὐδέν ἐστιν ἔστιν ὁ πατήρ μου ὁ δοξάζων με, ὃν ὑμεῖς λέγετε ὅτι θεὸς ἡμῶν ἐστιν, [55] καὶ οὐκ ἐγνώκατε αὐτόν, ἐγὼ δὲ οἶδα αὐτόν. κἂν εἴπω ὅτι οὐκ οἶδα αὐτόν, ἔσομαι ὅμοιος ὑμῖν ψεύστης· ἀλλ' οἶδα αὐτὸν καὶ τὸν λόγον αὐτοῦ τηρῶ. [56] Ἀβραὰμ ὁ πατὴρ ὑμῶν ἠγαλλιάσατο ἵνα ἴδῃ τὴν ἡμέραν τὴν ἐμήν, καὶ εἶδεν καὶ ἐχάρη. [57] εἶπον οὖν οἱ Ἰουδαῖοι πρὸς αὐτόν· πεντήκοντα ἔτη οὔπω ἔχεις καὶ Ἀβραὰμ ἑώρακας; [58] εἶπεν αὐτοῖς Ἰησοῦς· ἀμὴν ἀμὴν λέγω ὑμῖν, πρὶν Ἀβραὰμ γενέσθαι ἐγὼ εἰμί. (John 8:51-58, NA[28])

[51] Very truly, I tell you, whoever keeps my word will never see death." [52] The Jews said to him, "Now we know that you have a demon. Abraham died, and so did the prophets; yet you say, 'Whoever keeps my word will never taste death.' [53] Are you greater than

---

[66] "The question asked in John 4:12, 'Are you greater than our father Jacob?' formally resembles the one put to Jesus in 8:53, 'Are you greater than our father Abraham?' Together the two questions belong to a theme in the Gospel which asserts Jesus' superiority to the founding fathers of traditional Jewish religion. The thrust of the questions suggests that Jesus not only replaces Jacob, Abraham, and Moses vis-à-vis God's revelation, but that an absolute claim is made on his behalf: he is greater than these, he supplants them with new revelation, a new cult and a new covenant." Neyrey, "Jacob Traditions and the interpretation of John 4:10-26," 420-21.

[67] Theobald, "Abraham—(Isaak—) Jacob," 295 (italics original).

our father Abraham, who died? The prophets also died. Who do you claim to be?" ⁵⁴ Jesus answered, "If I glorify myself, my glory is nothing. It is my Father who glorifies me, he of whom you say, 'He is our God,' ⁵⁵ though you do not know him. But I know him; if I would say that I do not know him, I would be a liar like you. But I do know him and I keep his word. ⁵⁶ Your ancestor Abraham rejoiced that he would see my day; he saw it and was glad." ⁵⁷ Then the Jews said to him, "You are not yet fifty years old, and have you seen Abraham?" ⁵⁸ Jesus said to them, "Very truly, I tell you, before Abraham was, I am." (John 8:51-58, NRSV)

Narrative Context

Commentators frequently note that the Gospel of John breaks into two parts: the book of Signs (1:19-12:50) and the book of Glory (13:1-20:31) with the prologue (1:1-18) and the epilogue (21:1-25) sandwiching them in-between.[68] Indeed, the first book is replete with miraculous signs: turning water into wine (2:1-12), the healing of royal official's son (4:43-54) and of the lame man (5:1-47), the feeding of the multitude (6:1-71), the healing of the blind man (9:1-41), and the climactic raising of Lazarus from death (11:1-57). These signs serve to reinforce the messianic identity and divinity of Jesus as the crowd attests in John 7:31: "Yet many in the crowd believed in him and were saying, 'When the Messiah comes, will he do more signs than this man has done?'"

In addition, lengthy speeches and controversies with Jews are interspersed between these signs materials. Just as the signs serve to expose the messianic identity of Jesus, these extended discourses also engender the messianic faith in Jesus on the part of the hearers of the dialogues: "When they heard these words, some in the crowd said, 'This is really the prophet.' Others said, 'This is the Messiah'" (7:40-41a).[69] In brief, the previous signs and discourses (chs. 2-7) stir the prolonged argument with Jews (ch. 8), in which the identities of Jesus and his interlocutors are called into question. In the course of these debates, Abraham is brought into the fore as a vehicle by which the status of Jesus is measured. Also, it is in this context of dispute for Jesus' messianic identity that the Old Testament texts are explicitly cited and alluded to. Thus, the primary function of the

---

[68] The existence of the book of signs was first proposed by Rudolf Bultmann, *Das Evangelium des Johannes* (Göttingen: Vandenhoeck & Ruprecht, 1986); trans., *The Gospel of John: A Commentary*, trans. George R. Beasley-Murray (Louisville: Westminster, 1971). His hypothesis is taken up and elaborated by Raymond Brown, *The Community of the Beloved Disciple: The Life, Loves, and Hates of an Individual Church in New Testament Times* (New York: Paulist, 1979). The existence and use of such a written material in the writing of the fourth Gospel, and the subsequent historical reconstruction of the so-called Johannine community are widely disputed. However, a bi-partite structural insight originated from Bultmann is largely accepted. For instance, see Köstenberger, *John*, 10-11.

[69] Urban C. von Wahlde, "'You Are of Your Father the Devil' in Its Context: Stereotyped Apocalyptic Polemic in John 8:38-47," in *Anti-Judaism and the Fourth Gospel: Papers of the Leuven Colloquium, 2000*, ed. Reimund Bieringer, Didier Pollefeyt, and Frederique Vandecasteele-Vanneuville (Assen: Royal Van Gorcum, 2001), 419-20.

scripture is to validate Christology of Jesus from the Jewish vantage point.[70]

With regard to Abraham, the eighth chapter of John contains three disputes (8:31-38; 39-47; 48-59) between Jesus and his opponents. The first two of the three concern the status of Jesus' interlocutors, namely, whether or not they are descendants of Abraham. It is the last debate (8:51-58) that leads explicitly to the revealing of Jesus' identity in comparison with the quality of the patriarch. This pericope can be further broken down into two parts: (1) the immortality of Jesus and of Abraham (vv. 52-55); (2) and Abraham's witness to the pre-existent Jesus (vv. 56-58).

Excursus 2: The Johannine Antagonists

The Johannine interlocutors are consistently designated as Ἰουδαῖοι 4 times in this pericope (31, 48, 52, and 57). This ethnic description has generated a plethora of debates.[71] A somewhat classic description of the referent argues for the residents of the Roman Judaean province.[72] Wengst identifies this group of Jews as apostate former-Christian Jews whereas Schnelle classifies them as simple "dialogue partners" which group represents one of the eight categories he identifies as the uses of "Jews" in John.[73] Von Wahlde takes it to mean the Jewish rulers in Jerusalem.[74] Caron construes

---

[70] Michael Labahn, "Deuteronomy in John's Gospel," in *Deuteronomy in the New Testament: The New Testament and the Scriptures of Israel*, ed. Maarten J.J. Menken and Steve Moyise (London: T & T Clark, 2007), 97.

[71] Helpful discussions are found in the following: Reimund Bieringer, Didier Pollefeyt, and Frederique Vandecasteele-Vanneuville, eds., *Anti-Judaism and the Fourth Gospel: Papers of the Leuven Colloquium, 2000* (Assen: Royal Van Gorcum, 2001); Angus Paddison, "Christology and Jewish-Christian Understanding: Reading the Fourth Gospel as Scripture," in *Christology and Scripture: Interdisciplinary Perspectives*, ed. Andrew T. Lincoln and Angus Paddison (London: T & T Clark, 2007), 41-57. For the research history on the topic, see, Jörg Augenstein, "Jesus und das Gesetz im Johannesevangelium," *KuI* 14 (1999): 164-65; Reimund Bieringer and Didier Pollefeyt, "Open to Both Ways . . . ?: Johannine Perspectives on Judaism in the Light of Jewish-Christian Dialogue," in *Israel und seine Heilstraditionen im vierten Evangelium: Festgabe für Johannes Beutler SJ zum 70. Geburtstag*, ed. Michael Labahn, Klaus Scholtissek, and Angelika Strotmann (Paderborn: Schöningh, 2004), 11-32; Jörg Frey, "Das Bild 'der Juden' im Johannesevangelium und die Geschichte der johanneischen Gemeinde," in *Israel und seine Heilstraditionen im vierten Evangelium: Festgabe für Johannes Beutler SJ zum 70. Geburtstag*, ed. Michael Labahn, Klaus Scholtissek, and Angelika Strotmann (Paderborn: Schöningh, 2004), 33-54; Raimo Hakola, *Identity Matters: John, the Jews and Jewishness* (Leiden: Brill, 2005), 10-16, 225-31; Wendy E.S. North, "'The Jews' in John's Gospel: Observations and Inferences," in *Judaism, Jewish Identities and the Gospel Tradition: Essays in Honour of Maurice Casey*, ed. James G. Crossley (London: Equinox, 2010), 207-26.

[72] Malcolm F. Lowe, "Who Were the 'Ioudaioi,'" *NovT* 18 (1976): 101-30.

[73] Wengst, *Das Johannesevangelium*, 1:338-39; Schnelle, *Das Evangelium nach Johannes*, 164. Somewhat similar to Wengst, Jonge construes this group as recent Christian converts who are threatened to the point of apostasy. Henk Jan de Jonge, "'The Jews' in the Gospel of John," in *Anti-Judaism and the Fourth Gospel*, ed.

"Jews" representing "pseudo-Judaism."[75] Lars Kierspel associates the "Jews" with the unbelieving world, and his view has a precedent in Eduard Lohse.[76] Recently, Hunn identifies the term referring to various groups.[77] One of the more convincing views is expressed by Bennema who identifies the Jews as a non-ethnic referent but a religious group who adheres to Judaism in the ancient Mediterranean region.[78] None of the views suggested above is without difficulty and all of them have been contested. The precise referent of the term "Jews" in John may be difficult to attain both in the first and third *sitzen-im-Leben*, but the epithet is not used in a pejorative sense. Thus, some exegetes suggest that it simply is a literary device which functions to point to all those who are antagonists of Jesus.[79]

Immortality of Jesus and of Abraham

Jesus' emphatic exclusive claim (i.e., the immortality of the ones who keep Jesus' words in v. 51) provokes the Jews' comparison of Jesus with their identity figures, Abraham and the prophets (vv. 52-53). Abraham stands out in three ways in the Old Testament: the father of Jewish people, the original source of blessing for the Jewish people, and the identity figure of the Jewish people in his epithet, "the God of Abraham." Abraham is further developed in four respects in the following intertestamental Jewish traditions: a tenacious monotheist, a receiver of the divine covenant, possession of virtues, and finally his intercession and ascension to heaven.[80] In relation to the comparison of Abraham and Jesus in the present text, the expression "to taste death" does not occur either in the Hebrew or Greek Old Testament versions. However, some other ancient Jewish writings contain such an idiom, for example, *Pseudo-Jonathan Targum* on Deuteronomy

---

Reimund Bieringer, Didier Pollefeyt, and Frederique Vandecasteele-Vanneuville (Louisville: Westminster/John Knox, 2001), 121-40.

[74] Urban C. von Wahlde, "The Johannine 'Jews': A Critical Survey," *NTS* 28 (1982): 33-60.

[75] Gérald Caron, *Qui sont les Juifs de l'Evangile de Jean?* (Quebec: Bellarmin, 1997), 260-73.

[76] Lars Kierspel, *The Jews and the World in the Fourth Gospel: Parallelism, Function, Context* (Tübingen: Mohr Siebeck, 2006); Eduard Lohse, *Grundriß der neutestamentlichen Theologie* (Stuttgart: Kohlhammer, 1998), 132-33.

[77] Debbie Hunn, "Who Are 'They' in John 8:33?" *CBQ* 66 (2004): 387-99; also, Hahn, *Theologie des Neuen Testaments*, 1:698.

[78] Cornelis Bennema, "The Identity and Composition of οἱ Ἰουδαῖοι in the Gospel of John," *TynBul* 60 (2009): 239-63.

[79] Augenstein, "Jesus und das Gesetz im Johannesevangelium," 165. Beutler lists Bultmann, Simon Schoon, and Jean Zumstein along the line of this interpretation. Johannes Beutler, *Judaism and the Jews in the Gospel of John* (Rome: Pontificio Istituto Biblico, 2006), 149.

[80] N.L. Calvert, "Abraham," *DJG*, 3-4. For a lengthy survey of the intertestamental Jewish literature on Abraham's monotheistic faith as a Jewish model, see Nancy Calvert-Koyzis, *Paul, Monotheism and the People of God: The Significance of Abraham Traditions for Early Judaism and Christianity* (London: T & T Clark, 2004), 6-84.

32:1.[81] Thus, the confused reaction of the Jewish listeners seems to be an attempt to set Jesus up in a trap since the immortality of souls was not an uncommon concept in the time of Jesus.[82]

Nonetheless, the challenge of the Jews boils down to the order to which Jesus belongs. It can be paraphrased as following, "our heroic ancestors belong to the terrestrial order. Are you, Jesus, claiming otherwise?"[83] Their question is exactly the same as the Samaritan woman's inquiry with the same negative expectation indicated by a negative particle μή and these two verses demonstrate a typical example of Johannine ironies:

μὴ σὺ μείζων εἶ τοῦ πατρὸς ἡμῶν 'Αβραάμ (8:53)

μὴ σὺ μείζων εἶ τοῦ πατρὸς ἡμῶν 'Ιακώβ (4:12)

The comparison of Jesus' status with that of the Jewish arch-forefather, however, is appropriate and effective since Abraham possessed a high status in ancient Judaism.[84] Sirach, for instance, records that no one in ancient times had the glory equal to Abraham's: "Abraham was the great father of a multitude of nations, and no one has been found like him in glory" (*Sirach* 44:19). Another important element pertinent to the present reference to the forefather is the ancient Jewish belief in the eternal duration of souls via resurrection. Although the state of soul after death in early Judaism is known to be multi-faceted and a systematic inquiry of such theme is notoriously elusive due to the Greek influence of the soul mortality belief, the expressions of the eternal duration of souls are commonly found in early Jewish literature.[85] For example, Josephus indirectly attests to the

---

[81] Ernest G. Clarke, *Targum Pseudo-Jonathan: Deuteronomy* (Collegeville: Liturgical, 1997), 88. Further, Wengst (*Das Johannesevangelium*, 1:356) lists more sources that contain the idiom; *4 Esdra* 6:26; *BerR* 9:5; *WaR* 18:1; *PesR Hosafa* 1:1. Also the Wisdom of Solomon and 4 Maccabees are permeated with the concept of the enduring state of souls.

[82] Ludger Schenke, *Johannes: Kommentar* (Düsseldorf: Patmos, 1998), 178. The Jews at the time of Jesus seem to have had a considerable degree of common belief on certain aspects of the after-life, especially, on the states of the just and the wicked. Émile Puech, "Jesus and Resurrection Faith in Light of Jewish Texts," in *Jesus and Archaeology*, ed. James H. Charlesworth (Grand Rapids: Eerdmans, 2006), 639-59.

[83] Theobald, "Abraham—(Isaak—) Jacob," 305.

[84] For the summaries of Abraham's status in OT and early Judaism, see Dietzfelbinger, *Das Evangelium nach Johannes*, 261-62; James E. Bowley, "The Compositions of Abraham," in *Tracing the Threads: Studies in the Vitality of Jewish Pseudepigrapha*, ed. J.C. Reeves (Atlanta: Scholars, 1994), 215-38; H.G.M. Williamson, "Abraham in Exile," in *Perspectives on Our Father Abraham: Essays in Honor of Marvin R. Wilson*, ed. Steven A. Hunt (Grand Rapids: Eerdmans, 2010), 68-80; Christiane Noisette, "Abraham ou le chemin de la foi," *Théophilyon* 16 (2011): 149-69. Bowley finds that the ancient portraits of Abraham conform to two models: the righteous and faithful patriarch or the expert astrologer.

[85] Richard Bauckham, "Life, Death, and the Afterlife in Second Temple Judaism," in *Life in the Face of Death: The Resurrection Message of the New Testament*, ed. Richard N.

widespread belief in the eternal existence of souls in the first-century Palestine:

"They [Sadducees] also take away the belief of the immortal duration of the soul, and the punishments and rewards in Hades." (Josephus *Jewish War* 2.165b)

"But the doctrine of the Sadducees is this: That soul dies with the bodies. . . . but this doctrine is received but by a few." (Josephus *Antiquities* 18.16-17)

Thus, the more recent generation of scholars tends to recognize the presence of a widespread belief in the eternal endurance of souls in Jewish culture and the soul immortality after death in Greek thoughts.[86] For the former, one can refer to Mark 12:24-27, and for the latter Philo and 4 Maccabees (of the first century A.D.)

Longenecker (Grand Rapids: Eerdmans, 1998), 80-95: C.D. Elledge, "Future Resurrection of the Dead in Early Judaism: Social Dynamics, Contested Evidence," *CurBR* 9 (2011): 394-421. I have incurred a debt of gratitude to my doctoral supervisor, John B. Polhill, who advised me to adopt more refined terms on this point. The Jewish concept, "the eternal duration of soul," differs from the Greek soul immortality idea in that the former is enabled via resurrection. The Pharisaic documents from the Qumran (especially 4Q521) also attest to the belief in eternal life through resurrection. Émile Puech, "Les Esséniens croyaient-ils à la résurrection?" in *Qoumrân et les manuscrits de la mer Morte: Un cinquantenaire*, ed. Ernest-Marie Laperrousaz (Paris: Cerf, 1997), 409-40; Hogeterp, *Expectations of the End*, 277-81, 325-26, 330; Sabine and Kluas Bieberstein, "Auferweckt gemäss der Schrift: Das Ringen um Gottes Gerechtigkeit und die Hoffnung auf Auferweckung der Toten," *BK* 64 (2009): 70-77.

[86] Günther Stemberger, *Der Leib der Auferstehung: Studien zur Anthropologie und Eschatologie des palästinischen Judentums im neutestamentlichen Zeitalter (ca. 170 v. Chr.-100 n. Chr.)* (Rome: Biblical Institute, 1972); idem, *Jewish Contemporaries of Jesus: Pharisees, Sadducees, Essenes* (Minneapolis: Fortress, 1995), 68-73; Steve Mason, *Flavius Josephus on the Pharisees: A Composition-Critical Study* (Leiden: Brill, 1991), 132-69, 293-99; Emile Puech, *La croyance des Esséniens en la vie future: Immortalité, résurrection, vie éternelle?: histoire d'une croyance dans le judaïsme ancien*, 2 vols (Paris: Lecoffre, 1993); Anthony J. Saldarini, *Pharisees, Scribes and Sadducees in Palestinian Society: A Sociological Approach* (Grand Rapids: Eerdmans, 2001), 121; Jacob Neusner and Alan J. Avery-Peck, eds., *George W. E. Nickelsburg in Perspective: An Ongoing Dialogue of Learning* (Leiden: Brill, 2003), 2:315-41; George W.E. Nickelsburg, *Resurrection, Immortality, and Eternal Life in Intertestamental Judaism* (Cambridge: Harvard University Press, 2006); C.D. Elledge, *Life after Death in Early Judaism: The Evidence of Josephus* (Tübingen: Mohr Siebeck, 2006), esp. 53-80; James H. Charlesworth et al, eds., *Resurrection: The Origin and Future of a Biblical Doctrine* (London: T & T Clark, 2006); Bernd Janowski, "Der Gott Israels und die Toten: Eine religions und theologiegeschichtliche Skizze," in *JHWH und die Götter der Völker: Symposium zum 80. Geburtstag von Klaus Koch*, ed. Martin Rösel & Friedhelm Hartenstein (Neukirchen-Vluyn: Neukirchener, 2009), 99-138. For the widespread influence of Pharisaism in the Hasmonean period, see Lester L. Grabbe, "Israel from the Rise of Hellenism to 70 CE," in *The Oxford Handbook of Biblical Studies*, ed. J.W. Rogerson and Judith M. Lieu (Oxford: OUP, 2006), 292-93. On the contrary, for a view that sees the competing religious movements without dominance, see Judith M. Lieu, "Movements," in *The Oxford Handbook of Biblical Studies*, ed. J.W. Rogerson and Judith M. Lieu (Oxford: OUP, 2006), 372-81.

clearly attest to such a belief.[87] In particular, the three patriarchs, Abraham, Isaac, and Jacob, represent ideal figures who attained immortality by means of the overcoming of fleshly desires, practice of virtues, and martyrdom as witnessed in the following:

> But as many as attend to religion with a whole heart, these alone are able to control the passions of the flesh, since they believe that they, like our patriarchs Abraham and Isaac and Jacob, do not die to God, but live to God. (*4 Macc* 7:18-19)

> For the nature of mankind is mortal, but that of virtues is immortal; and it is more reasonable that the name of the everlasting God should be conjoined with what is immortal than with what is mortal, since what is immortal is akin to what is imperishable, but death is hostile to it. (Philo *Abr.* 55)

The Fourth Maccabees also notes the enduring life of Abraham through his martyrdom:

> They knew also that those who die for the sake of God live to God, as do Abraham and Isaac and Jacob and all the patriarchs. (*4 Macc* 16:25)[88]

Accordingly, at first glance, Abraham and Jesus share a common ground that they are related to the eternal endurance of souls (that is, "the eternal life" in the Johannine language) and/or its analogous concept, the soul immortality.[89]

However, on a closer reading, a contrasting element between the two figures is observed in view of the Jewish belief in Abraham.[90] That is, for the forefather, the enjoying of eternal life was dependent upon his virtuous deeds, i.e., the

---

[87] See F. Gerald Downing, "The Resurrection of the Dead: Jesus and Philo," *JSNT* 15 (1982): 42-50; Fred W. Burnett, "Philo on Immortality: A Thematic Study of Philo's Concept of Palingenesia," *CBQ* 46 (1984): 447-70; Alan F. Segal, "Some Observations about Mysticism and the Spread of Notions of Life after Death in Hebrew Thought," *SBLSP* 35 (1996): 385-99.

[88] The near-sacrifice experience of Abraham and Isaac is seen united here. A number of early Jewish traditions praise their unwavering resolution even in the face of loss and death, which brings out God's favorable disposition toward the nation of Israel. David A. de Silva, *4 Maccabees: Introduction and Commentary on the Greek Text in Codex Sinaiticus* (Leiden: Brill, 2006), 236-37.

[89] The mode of the enduring existence of souls does not affect the comparative analysis of Abraham and Jesus since the present inquiry concerns on whom their eternal existence is dependent.

[90] However, the incomplete nature of this comparison should be noted. The extant sources do not allow us to recover the comprehensive picture of the early Jewish beliefs (especially, in the time of Jesus within the Pharisaic circle) in the soul after life. The Pharisaic doctrine on the issue is only partially known primarily through the witness of Josephus. Thus, the result of this comparison could be a reflection of the difference between the Hellenistic and Semitic conceptual frameworks, rather than a broader category, "early Judaism," and the Gospel of John. For a more detailed discussion on the Pharisaic beliefs on the resurrection of souls, see Claudia Setzer, *Resurrection of the Body in Early Judaism and Early Christianity: Doctrine, Community, and Self-Definition* (Leiden: Brill, 2004), 21-36.

obedience of Torah and martyrdom. On the other hand, the eternal life bestowed by Jesus hinges upon the condition of keeping his own word, i.e., the words of Jesus. This prerequisite indicates a self-divine revelation on the part of Jesus, evoking "biblical language for obeying God's law and word."[91] This startling assertion is unmistakably further clarified in vv. 56 through 58, which induced Jews' attempt to hurl stones at Jesus in v. 59.

Abraham's Witness of the Pre-Existent Jesus

In vv. 56 and 58, Jesus makes a distinctive messianic statement, elucidating his pre-existence to which Abraham bears testimony. Especially, v. 56 has rendered a perennial riddle to Johannine exegetes.[92] The word used to depict Abraham's witness of Jesus is ἠγαλλιάσατο, an aorist tense and middle voice of ἀγαλλιάω in the present text. Some exegetes posit that this expression is reminiscent of Abraham's laugh in Genesis 17:17 and 18:2-13 where the angels disclosed the birth of Isaac.[93] These commentators point to some ancient Jewish writings, such as, *Jubillies* 15:17 (of the second century B.C.), *Targum Onkelos* on Genesis (of the second to third centuries A.D.), and Philo (*De mutatione nominum* 154-75).[94] In these texts, Abraham is presumed to have encountered God and received an eschatological revelation (cf., "τὴν ἡμέραν τὴν ἐμήν, my day" in v. 56 echoes the eschatological language of the Old Testament). This group of writings tends to manifest a shift of emphasis which stresses the virtue of Abraham, especially his faith in the face of the divine promise concerning the birth of Isaac. Especially,

---

[91] Keener, *The Gospel of John*, 1:765. It must be also noted that the Jews misunderstood Jesus in that they took him to mean that one will never die physically if he keeps the word of Jesus (as the Greek mythology envisages). This never-dying promise stands in stark contrast with Abraham, who enjoyed the eternal life upon resurrection at the *eschaton* in Jewish beliefs. However, it does not seem to be what Jesus meant by "not tasting death."

[92] For a convenient summary of the history of research on the text, see Linwood Urban and Patrick Henry, "'Before Abraham Was I Am': Does Philo Explain John 8:56-58?" *SPhilo* 6 (1979-1980): 157-95.

[93] Lindars, *The Gospel of John*, 335; Schnackenburg, *The Gospel according to St. John*, 2:221; Ernst Haenchen, *John: A Commentary on the Gospel of John*, ed. Robert W. Funk and Ulrich Busse, Hermeneia (Philadelphia: Fortress, 1984), 2:29; Hanson, *The Prophetic Gospel*, 126-28; Theobald, "Abraham—(Isaak—) Jacob," 305; Michael Labahn, "Jesus und die Autorität der Schrift im Johannesevangelium: Überlegungen zu einem spannungsreichen Verhältnis," in *Israel und seine Heilstraditionen im Johannesevangelium: Festgabe für Johannes Beutler SJ zum 70. Geburtstag*, ed. Michael Labahn, Klaus Scholtissek, and Angelika Strotmann (Paderborn: Schöningh, 2004), 197-98; Michaels, *The Gospel of John*, 531-32.

[94] For the influence of Jubilees on the present text, see Pierre Grelot, "Jean 8:56 et Jubilés 16:16-29," *RevQ* 13 (1988): 621-28; Mark J. Edwards, "'Not Yet Fifty Years Old': John 8:57," *NTS* 40 (1994): 449-54; of Philo, Urban and Henry, "'Before Abraham Was I Am'"; of Isaianic background, Edwin D. Freed, "Who or What was before Abraham in John 8:58," *JSNT* 17 (1983): 52-59; Brunson, *Psalm 118 in the Gospel of John*, 295-307; and recently of Ps 118, ibid., 302-16.

for example, *Targum Onkelos* changes the verb of the original Hebrew text into one that renders a positive nuance with the result being an emphasis on Abraham's faith.[95] Philo, in addition, attests to the tendency to sanctify this patriarch as well: "And immediately afterward he says, 'Abraham believed in the Lord, and it was counted to him for righteousness'" (Philo *Mut.* 177). However, it is comparatively clear that, in the Old Testament contexts, the laughter of Abraham serves the same function as that of Sarah in that they reflect a misapprehension of the divine prophecy.[96]

In addition to these texts, another group of ancient Jewish texts entertains the idea of Abraham taking a journey into the heavenly realm, including some of pseudepigraphical books and early rabbinic midrashim.[97]

> And you (God) loved him (Abraham) and to him only you revealed the end of the times, secretly by night. (*4 Ezra* 3:14)[98]
>
> After these things, I showed it (the new Jerusalem) to my servant Abraham in the night between the portions of the victims." (*2 Bar* 4:4)[99]
>
> And he said to him, "Is it not regarding this people that I spoke to Abraham in a vision, . . . when I lifted him above the firmament and showed him the arrangements of all the stars . . . and on account of his blood I chose them . . . I will reveal everything I am doing to Abraham." (*L.A.B.* [*Pseudo-Philo*] 18:5)[100]

These witnesses all date to around the first century A.D. Another early Jewish literature from the same period, *the Apocalypse of Abraham* offers an even more elaborate account of Abrahamic visions.[101] Chs. 1 through 8 report Abraham's rejection of idolatry and his request to know the living God. The rest of the book (chs. 9-32) recounts his celestial expedition in which he receives visions concerning the end times.[102]

The implications of these early Jewish texts are adduced in some of the Johannine commentaries as following. If the first group is taken in view as the conceptual background of the present text, then, two possibilities are conceivable. Abraham may have eye-witnessed the pre-existent Son in his previous earthly

---

[95] Aberbach and Grossfeld, *Targum Onkelos to Genesis*, 104. The official targum to the Pentateuch, *Targum Onkelos* is dated between the 1st through the 4th centuries A.D.

[96] So is in Philo *Legum Allegoriae* III.218.

[97] Rabbinic literature on this issue, see *Gen. Rab.* 44:12 (Freedman, *Genesis*, 367-68); and *Ber. R.* 44:21.

[98] *OTP*, 1:528. This writing dates to the early first century A.D.

[99] *OTP*, 1:622. This writing dates to the early second century A.D.

[100] *OTP*, 2:325. This writing dates between the second century B.C. and the late first century A.D.

[101] The document is considered to be originally written in Hebrew, but the extant manuscripts have survived only in Slavonic and date back to the first to second centuries A.D. R. Rubinkiewicz, "Apocalypse of Abraham," in *OTP* 1:681-82.

[102] *Apo. Ab.* 9-32 (*OTP*, 1:693-705).

ministry prior to the incarnation. Some Old Testament exegetes view "the Lord" or "His angels" as implicit references to the pre-New Testament appearances of Christ. Or, the forefather may have comprehended the implications of the unfolding of the redemptive history inherent in the birth and life of his son, Isaac that will be realized in the later messianic figure.[103] When the second group of Jewish writings is taken into account, John suggests Abraham's eye-witness of the pre-existent Son in his heavenly abode.[104]

Nonetheless, similar to the passages examined earlier in this study, the dearth of explicit textual evidence precludes any firm conclusion on whether or to what extent the present text directly refers to certain contemporary and/or later Jewish traditions on Abraham's reception of visions. No matter which view reflects more directly the original reading of the fourth evangelist, the concept of Abraham's knowledge of the end time, or more specifically, his encounter with God was probably not too foreign to the first *sitz-im-leben* audience (who were presumably familiar with the common concurrent Jewish traditions about the patriarch) of this narrative, but it was his specific witness of the pre-existent Jesus that perplexed the hearers in v. 56.

Temporal Priority of Jesus over Abraham

Abraham's witness of the pre-existent Christ in v. 56 leads to a more revealing christological statement in v. 58 in terms of the chronological priority of Jesus over Abraham.[105] The temporal priority is a typical Johannine expression, which the Synoptic Gospels do not attest to.[106] The Greek text of v. 58 has drawn a good deal of attention from commentators due to the presence of the so-called "*ego eimi*" construction: "before Abraham was I am (πρὶν Ἀβραὰμ γενέσθαι ἐγὼ εἰμί)." Although it is somewhat common to relate all the occurrences of Johannine

---

[103] Labahn, "Jesus und die Autorität der Schrift im Johannesevangelium," 198.

[104] Martin Hengel, "The Old Testament in the Fourth Gospel," in *The Gospels and the Scriptures of Israel*, ed. Craig A. Evans and W. Richard Stegner (Sheffield: Sheffield, 1994), 387. Menken also opts for the latter view at the absence of explicit reference to earthly activities of Jesus in John (with an exception in the prologue where the Son's participation in the creation is recorded). As convincing as his argument is, his case seems to be based too much on the silence of the evangelist. M.J.J. Menken, "Observations on the Significance of the Old Testament in the Fourth Gospel," in *Theology and Christology in the Fourth Gospel: Essays by the Members of the SNTS Johannine Writings Seminar*, ed. Gilbert van Belle, Jan G. van der Watt, and P.J. Maritz (Leuven: Leuven University, 2005), 166-69.

[105] For the importance of the temporal priority for Johannine Christology, see Labahn, "Jesus und die Autorität der Schrift im Johannesevangelium," 188-98. For the textual integrity of this pericope, see Léonard Ramaroson, "Paraboles évangéliques et autres textes néotestamentaires 'à double ao a triple pointe,'" *ScEs* 49 (1997): 181-82.

[106] For the idiom similarly applied to John the Baptist earlier, see John 1:15, 30. Marinus de Jonge, "John the Baptist and Elijah in the Fourth Gospel," in *The Conversation Continues: Studies in Paul & John in Honor of J. Louis Martyn*, ed. Robert T. Fortna and Beverly R. Gaventa (Nashville: Abingdon, 1990), 303.

"I-am" sayings with a deifying nomenclature, the present usage lacks sufficient analogous ancient parallels so that it makes a special pleading in this case.[107] However, its predicate clause (i.e., "before Abraham was") warrants a theistic reading, namely, prolonging the current existence of Jesus at least by two millennia. In this respect, commentators detect an allusion to the Old Testament divine descriptions, particularly, Exodus 3:14 and Isaiah 43:10.[108] While one may not agree with the conceptual background and exact nature of this I-am saying, it is quite obvious from the reaction of Jews in v. 59 that the hearers of Jesus took it as an offense of blasphemy (in v. 59), which infringement in ancient Jewish culture was often dealt with stoning to death.

> One who blasphemes the name of the LORD shall be put to death; the whole congregation shall stone the blasphemer. Aliens as well as citizens, when they blaspheme the Name, shall be put to death. (Lev 24:16, NRSV)

> He that blasphemed God, let him be stoned, and let him hang upon a tree all that day, and then let him be buried in an ignominious and obscure manner. (Jos *Ant.* 4.202)

The hostile reaction of the Jews in v. 59 disproves their self-claim of being "the children of Abraham" because, in stark contrast to their ill-reception, the forefather took delight in witnessing to Jesus.[109] Hakola provides an insightful observation of the present text under examination.

> The Jews' appeal to Abraham is rejected in two different ways: first, it is said that their relationship to Abraham is wrong, and then it is said that Abraham has only a subsidiary role to play in the divine drama as a witness of Jesus. What Jesus says of Abraham is close to what he has earlier said of Moses. Both Abraham and Moses are portrayed as witnesses of Jesus.[110]

Summary

In the present text (John 8:51-59), a clash between two groups of individuals is observed. The group of Jews brings forth Abraham as their ideal progenitor from whom their physical lineage originated and from whom they also inherited their

---

[107] Daniel B. Wallace, *Greek Grammar beyond the Basics: An Exegetical Syntax of the New Testament* (Grand Rapids: Zondervan, 1996), 515, 530-31.

[108] For the former, see Odeberg, *The Fourth Gospel*, 308-10; for the latter, John L. Ronning, "Targum of Isaiah and the Johannine Literature," *WTJ* 69 (2007): 254-55; Keener (*The Gospel of John*, 1:770-2) cites Ethelbert Stauffer, *Jesus and His Story*, trans. Richard Winston and Clara Winston (New York: Knopf, 1960), 176-78; Philip B. Harner, *The "I Am" of the Fourth Gospel: A Study in Johannine Usage and Thought* (Philadelphia: Fortress, 1970), 15-17; David M. Ball, *"I Am" in John's Gospel: Literary Function, Background, and Theological Implications* (Sheffield: Sheffield, 1996), 195-98; Richard Bauckham, *God Crucified: Monotheism and Christology in the New Testament* (Grand Rapids: Eerdmans, 1998), 55; Köstenberger, "John," 459; for both, Wengst, *Das Johannesevangelium*, 1:360.

[109] Dietzfelbinger, *Das Evangelium nach Johannes*, 1:269.

[110] Raimo Hakola, *Identity Matters: John, the Jews and Jewishness* (Leiden: Brill, 2005), 194.

status (as Abraham was free, the Jews conceived to have been free in v. 33). On the other hand, to Jesus, the forefather functions merely as a witness to the pre-existent divine characteristics of Jesus. In other words, the validity of Abraham stands as long as it verifies the divine nature of Jesus in terms of his pre-existence. To this point, Labahn and Theobald add as following concerning the present pericope:

> The Holy Scriptures and Abraham are certainly recognized as an identity-creating authority. However, they are arranged in a structure in which the pre-existent Son is the decisive criterion.[111]

> Although Abraham is not employed for the believers of Jesus as a progenitor and identity figure, he is nevertheless a witness of Christ.[112]

Furthermore, it is not the Jewish arch-forefather but Jesus who is truly superior since his revelation comes directly from the Father (8:16-19, 26, 29, 38, 42) and he can impart redemption from sin (8:32-36, 51).

Conclusion

In this chapter, three passages in John (1:51; 4:10-14; 8:51-58) have been investigated that contain explicit references to or allusions to the Jewish patriarchs, namely, Abraham and Jacob. An exegetical examination of these passages reveals a consistent characterization of the two personages and they serve the same function of confirming the messianic identity of Jesus. Some conclusions can be drawn from the preceding assessment of these texts in view of the surrounding literary contexts and related questions raised earlier in the first chapter. First, the messianic witness function of Abraham and Jacob fits nicely in the overall narrative flow of the chapters which surround the texts under discussion. As the focus of chs. 1 through 8 is directed at Jesus with particular reference to his messianic identity, the two prominent Jewish patriarchs consistently play the supportive role to corroborate the Johannine Christology.

Second, although the Jewish forefathers were conceived as ideal and identity figures in the second temple Judaism, just as the Jews and Samaritans regarded them with admiration in John, they remain satisfied as mere witnesses for Christ in the present texts. On the one hand, their introduction to the discourses provides a contact point, with which the onset of the new redemptive history through Jesus stands in continuity, namely, with the outworking of the old redemptive history, most remarkably in their foreshadowing of the divine characteristics of the Messiah. Just as the salvific outworking was unraveled through Jacob in the Old Testament, so will it be through Jesus in John. The patriarchs, however, are presented as the point of comparison/contrast since they demonstrate the enormous magnitude of the radical unfolding of the new redemptive program. This

---

[111] Labahn, "Jesus und die Autorität der Schrift im Johannesevangelium," 197.
[112] Theobald, "Abraham—(Isaak—) Jacob," 305.

surpassing nature of the new redemptive history is reflected upon the divine nature of Messiah and the gift that is bestowed upon through him.

Lastly, the observations inferred from the second point call into question the congruity of John's Gospel with ancient Judaism. Dissimilar to the non-canonical Jewish writings of the intertestamental period, the fourth Gospel does not promote the virtuous characteristics of Jacob and Abraham (although it does not rigorously disavow them at the same time). The fourth evangelist also does not conceive the forefathers as the spiritual progenitors since they cannot offer what this new redemptive program avails to believers through the Messiah. To this point, Johnson's judgment is helpful:

> Much of the literature which sees the Fourth Gospel as being dependent on rabbinic traditions needs to be seriously questioned. The use of the Jacob traditions in the Fourth Gospel presupposes that the reader has some sort of access to the Jacob Narrative (either oral or written). But it does not presuppose a knowledge of the traditions of early Judaism and especially of the rabbinic traditions found in the targumim and midrashim. The intertextuality involved in interpreting the Jacob Narrative in the Fourth Gospel is quite restricted. It seems reasonable that any hints elsewhere in the Gospel to Jewish traditions may be more reflections of the historical situation being described than part of the intention of the Evangelist. In the passages studied in this dissertation it has been shown that there is no hint that rabbinic traditions are in view beyond what can be gathered from the biblical text itself.[113]

---

[113] Johnson, "Our Father Jacob," 251-52.

CHAPTER 3

Elijah

²⁰ καὶ ὡμολόγησεν καὶ οὐκ ἠρνήσατο, καὶ ὡμολόγησεν ὅτι ἐγὼ οὐκ εἰμὶ ὁ χριστός. ²¹ καὶ ἠρώτησαν αὐτόν·τί οὖν; σὺ Ἠλίας εἶ; καὶ λέγει· οὐκ εἰμί. ὁ προφήτης εἶ σύ; καὶ ἀπεκρίθη·οὔ. ²² εἶπαν οὖν αὐτῷ·τίς εἶ; ἵνα ἀπόκρισιν δῶμεν τοῖς πέμψασιν ἡμᾶς·τί λέγεις περὶ σεαυτοῦ; ²³ ἔφη·
 ἐγὼ φωνὴ βοῶντος ἐν τῇ ἐρήμῳ·
 εὐθύνατε τὴν ὁδὸν κυρίου,
καθὼς εἶπεν Ἠσαΐας ὁ προφήτης. (John 1:20-23, NA²⁸)

²⁰ He confessed and did not deny it, but confessed, "I am not the Messiah." ²¹ And they asked him, "What then? Are you Elijah?" He said, "I am not." "Are you the prophet?" He answered, "No." ²² Then they said to him, "Who are you? Let us have an answer for those who sent us. What do you say about yourself?" ²³ He said,
 "I am the voice of one crying out in the wilderness,
 'Make straight the way of the Lord,'"
as the prophet Isaiah said. (John 1:20-23, NRSV)

Introduction

Unlike Abraham and Jacob, a significant number of early Jewish documents portray Elijah, David, and Moses as distinctly eschatological redemptive figures. As such, it is necessary to treat their messianic images in the period in a separate section. As far as Elijah the Tishbite (1 Kgs 17:1) is concerned, he exerted a prominent influence in early Judaism and in the New Testament. The dimension of the eschatological prophet, in particular, emerged as a more conspicuous one out of various characteristics and hopes related to Elijah such as a miracle worker or his translation into heaven:

> Elijah appears as the only figure whose personal eschatological return was expected in the Old Testament . . . he is the only eschatological *redivivus* figure of the Old Testament.[1]

Of all the Old Testament messianic prefigurations, Elijah is the only Jewish eschatological redeemer figure with whom the epithet *redivivus* is often associated. Some scholars object to this nomenclature since he never tasted death but

---

[1] Géza G. Xeravits, *King, Priest, Prophet: Positive Eschatological Protagonists of the Qumran Library* (Leiden: Brill, 2003), 184.

only was translated into heaven alive.² This point is valid because the term literally denotes the dead being brought back to life. Joynes, thus, suggests "Elijah *reditus*" instead, but her suggestion has not found a wide acceptance yet.³ As such, the term Elijah *redivivus* will be used in this study because of its popular usage. Another justification for the use of such a term is because we mean, by the terminology, a figurative conception of a prophetic figure who works "in the spirit and power of Elijah" (Luke 1:17), not the physical return of the Tishbite.⁴

This expectation in the return of the prophet is conspicuously addressed in the New Testament, especially, in the Gospels. At this juncture, it is necessary to probe into that particular expression of Elijah *redivivus* in second temple Judaism so as to understand the possible reception of such an early Jewish conceptual trait in John. That enquiry entails a number of questions. How Elijah was perceived by Jews in the intertestamental period, especially with reference to messianic hopes; how the messianic expectations regarding the prophet were received in the New Testament and, particularly, in the Gospel of John; and, finally, whether or not the Fourth Gospel presents Elijah as a messianic prefigure. In order to shed light on these issues, this chapter begins with the perception of Elijah in the second temple period.

Elijah in Second Temple Judaism

The Jewish traditions related with Elijah *redivivus* can be classified into three broad categories: eschatological expectation primarily in terms of his reconciliation ministry (as described in the MT, LXX, and Sirach); the apocalyptic return of the prophet with the result of the militant subjugation of the unrighteous; and settling legal disputes. The witnesses of the third category are mostly attested in rabbinical writings, which variously date from the end of the first century A.D. onward. Examples of the third category are the following:

> It is [families of] this sort that Elijah will come to declare unclean and to declare clean, to put out and to draw near. (*m. Eduy.* 8:7)
>
> Let it lie there until Elijah comes (*m. B. Mes.* 1:8); Utensils of gold and of glass he should not touch them until Elijah comes. (*m. B. Mes.* 2:8)
>
> But leave the whole sum until Elijah comes [and no one will be paid off]. (*m. B. Mes.* 3:4)

---

² Markus Öhler, *Elia im Neuen Testament: Untersuchungen zur Bedeutung des alttestamentlichen Propheten im frühen Christentum* (Berlin: Walter de Gruyter, 1997), 3.
³ Christian E. Joynes, "A Question of Identity: 'Who Do People Say That I Am?': Elijah, John the Baptist and Jesus in Mark's Gospel," in *Understanding, Studying and Reading: New Testament Essays in Honour of John Ashton*, ed. Christopher Rowland and Crispin H.T. Fletcher-Louis (Sheffield: Sheffield, 1998), 16.
⁴ Walter C. Kaiser, *The Uses of the Old Testament in the New* (Chicago: Moody, 1985), 77-88.

And the rest of the money [received for the sale of the larger one] is left until Elijah comes. (*m. B. Mes.* 3:5)[5]

They represent late traditions that are probably least reflected in the New Testament, and thus, are hardly pertinent to the present investigation.

Eschatological Reconciliation Ministry

Malachi. It is commonplace to take the point of departure for an examination of the Jewish expectations of Elijah *redivivus* from the very last verses of Malachi, which also bear testimony to an impressive postlude to conclude the entire corpus of the Hebrew canon with the anticipation of the prophet's return:[6]

---

[5] For the use of the Elijah tradition in the rabbinic writings, see Gerd Häfner, *Der verheißene Vorläufer: Redaktionskritische Untersuchung zur Darstellung Johannes des Täufers im Matthäusevangelium* (Stuttgart: Katholisches Bibelwerk, 1994), 337-38; Karin Hedner Zetterholm, "Elijah and the Messiah as Spokesmen of Rabbinic Ideology," in *The Messiah in Early Judaism and Christianity*, ed. Magnus Zetterholm (Minneapolis: Fortress, 2007), 57-78; idem, "Elijah and the Books of Kings in Rabbinic Literature," in *Books of Kings: Sources, Composition, Historiography and Reception*, ed. André Lemaire & Baruch Halpern (Leiden: Brill, 2010), 585-606.

[6] For surveys of the conception of Elijah in the intertestamental period and related issues, see J. Jeremias, "'Ηλ(ε)ιας," *TDNT*, 2:928-34; Horst Seebaß, "Elia I:Altes Testament," *TRE*, 9:498-502; Nico Oswald, "Elia II: Judentum," *TRE*, 9:502-04; Dieter Zeller, "Elija und Elischa im Frühjudentum," *BK* 41 (1986): 154-60; Johannes M. Nützel, "Elija- und Elischa-Traditionen im Neuen Testament," *BK* 41 (1986): 160-71; Eric L. Friedland, "'Elija der Prophet möge bald mit dem Messias kommen': Messianismus in der Pesach-Haggada des fortschrittlichen Judentums," in *Der Messias*, ed. Ernst Dassmann and Günter Stemberger, vol. 8 of *Jahrbuch für Biblische Theologie* (Neukirchen-Vluyn: Neukirchener, 1993), 251-71; Thomas W. Overholt, "Elijah and Elisha in the Context of Israelite Religion," in *Prophets and Paradigms: Essays in Honor of Gene M. Tucker*, ed. Stephen Breck Reid (Sheffield: Sheffield, 1996), 94-111; Hartmut Gese, "Zur Bedeutung Elias für die biblische Theologie," in *Evangelium, Schriftauslegung, Kirche: Festschrift für Peter Stuhlmacher zum 65. Geburtstag*, ed. Jostein Ådna, Scott J. Hafemann, and Otfried Hofius (Göttingen: Vandenhoeck & Ruprecht, 1997), 126-50; Gerold Necker, "Elia II: Judentum," *RGG*, 2:1211-12; Öhler, *Elia im Neuen Testament*, 1-30; idem, "Elija und Elischa," in *Alttestamentliche Gestalten im Neuen Testament: Beiträge zur biblischen Theologie*, ed. Markus Öhler (Darmstadt: Wissenschaftliche Buchgesellschaft, 1999), 185-87; Xeravits, *King, Priest, Prophet*, 184-204; Hermann Lichtenberger, "Elia-Tradition bei vor- bzw. frührabbinischen Wundertätern," in *Biblical Figures in Deuterocanonical and Cognate Literature*, ed. Hermann Lichtenberger and Ulrike Mittmann-Richert (Berlin: Walter de Gruyter, 2009), 547-63; Otto Kaiser, "Der Prophet Elia in Flavius Josephus *Ant.* XVIII und XIX," in *Geschichte Israels und deuteronomistisches Geschichtsdenken: Festschrift zum 70. Geburtstag von Winfried Thiel*, ed. Peter Mommer & Andreas Georg Scherer (Münster: Ugarit, 2010), 152-63; Bart J. Koet, "Elijah as Reconciler of Father and Son: From 1 Kings 16:34 and Malachi 3:22-24 to Ben Sira 48:1-11 and Luke 1:13-17," in *Rewriting Biblical History: Essays on Chronicles and Ben Sira in Honor of Pancratius C. Beentjes*, ed. Jeremy Corley and Harm W.M. van Grol (Berlin: Walter de Gruyter, 2011), 173-90; Jürgen Werlitz,

Lo, I will send you the prophet Elijah before the great and terrible day of the LORD comes. He will turn the hearts of parents to their children and the hearts of children to their parents, so that I will not come and strike the land with a curse. (Mal 4:5-6, NRSV)

Coupled with a previous prophecy concerning the messenger who will "prepare the way before God" in Malachi 3:1, this Elijah *redivivus* theme of Malachi 4:5-6 constitutes an *inclusio* and expresses a tenacious hope of the prophet's return. His return is hoped to restore the bond between the fathers and sons before the wrath of God strikes them.[7]

Sirach. Further elaborations of the eschatological Elijah conception appear in some later Jewish traditions. For instance, the Septuagint broadens the scope of the prophet's reconciliation ministry so as to encompass the relationship between the people with their neighbors, along with the fathers with their sons (καρδίαν ἀνθρώπου πρὸς τὸν πλησίον αὐτοῦ, Mal 3:25, LXX).[8] On the other hand, Sirach, dating to 180 B.C., demonstrates a glimpse of the Jewish hope for the national restoration along with individual reconciliation *vis-à-vis* the return of Elijah:

> At the appointed time, it is written, you [Elijah] are destined to calm the wrath of God before it breaks out in fury, to turn the hearts of parents to their children, and to restore the tribes of Jacob. (Sir 48:10)[9]

Horsley judges this text to be reflective of a popular rabbinic belief in the Persian and Hellenistic periods. His reasoning is based on the fact that the entire book of Sirach is disinterested in eschatological matters. He is probably correct to say that this Elijah *redivivus* text stands out in Sirach, but he certainly overestimates the place of the text in contemporary Judaism based on one appearance. These three passages reviewed above voice more or less a unified hope of reconciliation in the aftermath of Elijah's return, a hope of unity and restoration both at the

---

"Vom feuerigen Propheten zum Versöhner: Ein Überblick über die biblischen Elijatexte mit Schwerpunkt auf dem Alten Testament," *BK* 66 (2011): 192-200.

[7] For different suggestions for the historical settings behind the return of the prophet, see Innocent Himbaza, "La finale de Malachie sur Elie (Ml 3, 23-24): Son influence sur le livre de Malachie et son impact sur la littérature postérieure," in *Un carrefour dans l'histoire de la Bible: Du texte à la théologie au IIe siècle avant J-C*, ed. Innocent Himbaza & Adrian Schenker (Göttingen: Vandenhoeck & Ruprecht, 2007), 21-44; idem, "L'eschatologie de Malachi 3," in *Les prophètes de la Bible et la fin des temps: XXIIIe congrès de l'Association catholique française pour l'étude de la Bible (Lille, 24-27 août 2009)*, ed. Jacques Vermeylen (Paris: Cerf, 2010), 359-66; Elie Assis, "Moses, Elijah and the Messianic Hope: A New Reading of Malachi 3, 22-24," *ZAW* 123 (2011): 207-20.

[8] Another notable change from the Hebrew (MT) to the Greek text (LXX) is that the day of the Lord is "great and glorious" (μεγάλην καὶ ἐπιφανῆ), instead of "great and dreadful" (הַגָּדוֹל וְהַנּוֹרָא).

[9] Richard A. Horsley, "Like One of the Prophets of Old: Two Types of Popular Prophets at the Time of Jesus," *CBQ* 47 (1985): 440.

individual level and at the national level (with the latter being of lesser emphasis).[10]

Apocalyptic Militant Subjugation

Sibylline Oracles and the Coptic *Apocalypse of Elijah*. The second category of the Elijah *redivivus* anticipation often entailed the military subjugation of the unrighteousness. The *Sibylline Oracles*, for example, envisage the return of Elijah that will precipitate the apocalyptic judgment.

> Then the Thesbite, driving a heavenly chariot at full stretch from heaven, will come on earth and then display three signs to the whole world, as life perishes. . . . And then a great river of blazing fire will flow from heaven, and will consume every place, land and great ocean and gleaming sea, lakes and rivers, springs and implacable Hades and the heavenly vault. But the heavenly luminaries will crash together, also into an utterly desolate form. For all the stars will fall together from heaven on the sea. All the souls of men will gnash their teeth, burning in a river, and brimstone and a rush of fire in a fiery plain, and ashes will cover all. (*Sib. Or.* 2:187-204)[11]

The Sibylline Oracles are composed of fourteen oracles and each book dates to various periods between the second century B.C. and the seventh century A.D.[12]

Similarly, the Coptic *Apocalypse of Elijah* announces the return of Elijah and Enoch who will come to slay "the son of lawlessness."

> After these things, Elijah and Enoch will come down. They will lay down the flesh of the world, and they will receive their spiritual flesh. They will pursue the son of lawlessness and kill him since he is not able to speak. On that day, he [the antichrist] will dissolve in their presence like ice which was dissolved by a fire. He will perish like a serpent which has no breath in it. They [Elijah and Enoch] will say to him, "Your time has passed by for you. Now therefore you and those who believe you will perish." They will be cast into the bottom of the abyss and it will be closed for them. (*Apoc. El. [C]* 5:32 35)[13]

---

[10] In addition to the Malachi texts, J.D. Martin detects an echo of Isa 49:6 which speaks of the restoration of the tribes of Jacob and the nation of Israel. James D. Martin, "Ben Sira's Hymn to the Fathers: A Messianic Perspective," in *Crises and Perspectives: Studies in Ancient Near Eastern Polytheism, Biblical Theology, Palestinian Archaeology, and Intertestamental Literature, Papers Read at the Joint British-Dutch Old Testament Conference, Held at Cambridge, U.K., 1985*, ed. Johannes Cornelis de Moor (Leiden: Brill, 1986), 107-23.

[11] *OTP*, 1:349-50. The origin of *the Sibylline Oracles* is presumed to be a mixture of Jewish and Christian with the strong imprints of the latter. John J. Collins, "The Sibylline Oracles," in *Jewish Writings of the Second Temple Period: Apocrypha, Pseudepigrapha, Qumran, Sectarian Writings, Philo, Josephus*, ed. Michael E. Stone (Assen: Van Gorcum, 1984), 377.

[12] For a discussion on the different traditions and manuscripts of this writing, see Jane L. Lightfoot, *The Sibylline Oracles: With Introduction, Translation, and Commentary on the First and Second Books* (Oxford: OUP, 2007), 257-68. For the commentary on the text, see idem, 480-87.

[13] *OTP*, 1:752-53.

The same document contains a longer version of the account of the return of Elijah and Enoch in 4:7-20. The explicit mention of "antichrist" and the similar language of the Book of Revelation suggest a Christian influence on this literature, which dates back to first to fourth centuries A.D.[14] In this apocalyptic expectation of the prophet's return, he is also sometimes associated with Phinehas the zealot (*Tg. Yer. I* Ex 6:18; *Tg. Yer. I* Num 25:12; *L.A.B.* 48; *Liv. Pro.* 21:1). Because of his connection with the Levites, Elijah was sometimes considered a priestly figure as early as the second century B.C.[15] However, some of the documents (esp. *The Sibylline Oracles* and the Coptic *Apocalypse of Elijah*) that contain this strand of thought display traces of a Christian influence and most of them (the rabbinic writings) do not predate the Gospel of John.[16]

The Nag Hammadi Library. The prominence of Elijah is not attested in the Nag Hammadi Library. Since its discovery in upper Egypt in 1945, this collection of early gnostic writings has altered the traditional view of the early Gnosticism. Instead of an aberrant Christian heresy, early Gnosticism probably had more divergent origins and beliefs. Overall, however, the current of the movement demonstrates a relatively tenacious penchant to emphasize a special saving knowledge, *gnosis*, which may have not been compatible with the strong miracle-working image of Elijah. Or, when they depart from the traditional *gnosis*-focused view, these documents manifest a heavy Hellenistic and/or evident Christian influence. Thus, this mixture of ideas raises a question of validity about inquiring into the literary relationship between these documents and the Fourth Gospel. For instance, one of the Nag Hammadi documents akin to early Christianity is "the Treatise on the Resurrection" (aka. The Epistle to Rheginos). In an apologetic with a fictional dialog partner, Rheginos, this document explores on the resurrection of the Savior and that of Christians. In a number of places, an emphasis on understanding and soul rather than physical body is expressed.

> The thought of those who are saved shall not perish. The mind of those who have known him shall not perish. Therefore, we are elected to salvation and redemption since we are predestined from the beginning not to fall into the foolishness of those who are without knowledge, but we shall enter into the wisdom of those who have

---

[14] Richard Bauckham, "Enoch and Elijah in the Coptic Apocalypse of Elijah," in *The Jewish World around the New Testament: Collected Essays I* (Tübingen: Mohr Siebeck, 2008), 27-38.

[15] R. Meyer, "'Elia' und 'Ahab': (Tg. Ps.-Jon. zu Deut. 33,11)," in *Abraham unser Vater: Juden und Christen im Gespräch über die Bibel: Festschrift für Otto Michel zum 60. Geburtstag*, ed. Otto Betz, Martin Hengel, and Peter Schmidt (Leiden: Brill, 1963), 356-68; and Uwe Gleßmer, *Einleitung in die Targume zum Pentateuch* (Tübingen: Mohr Siebeck, 1995), 185-87.

[16] Daniel J. Harrington, "Biblical Text of Pseudo-Philo's Liber Antiquitatum Biblicarum," *CBQ* 33 (1971): 1-17; Robert Hayward, "Phinehas—the Same is Elijah: The Origins of a Rabbinic Tradition," *JJS* 29 (1978): 23; Horsley, "Like One of the Prophets of Old," 439; Bauckham, "Enoch and Elijah in the Coptic Apocalypse of Elijah," 27-38.

> known the Truth. . . . That which is better than the flesh is that which is for it (the) cause of life. . . . What, then, is the resurrection? It is always the disclosure of those who have risen. For if you remember reading in the Gospel that Elijah appeared and Moses with him, do not think the resurrection is an illusion. It is no illusion, but it is truth! Indeed, it is more fitting to say that the world is an illusion, rather than the resurrection which has come into being through our Lord the Savior, Jesus Christ. (*Treat. Res.* 46:23-29; 47:9-10; 48:3-20)[17]

This document contains the only occurrence of Elijah the prophet mentioned by name in the entire corpus of the Nag Hammadi Library. With the late dating, an Hellenistic emphasis on knowledge, underestimation of the physical body, and the apparent dependency on the Christian tradition combined together, it is extremely difficulty to take this writing into serious consideration for a possible literary relationship with the Fourth Gospel.

> The naming of Elijah occurs once in the Epistle to Rheginos. . . . The Elijah *redivivus* of this document seems to suggest that the author was a Christian Gnostic, and this gnostic letter according to Harnack's type is an acute Hellenization of Christianity.[18]

The Qumran Documents. The stark disinterest in Elijah in the Nag Hammadi is explicable. Nonetheless, the dearth of reference to Elijah in the Qumran library is surprising in light of its pervasive eschatological enthusiasm. At this juncture, Collins' assessment of the prophet in Qumran is helpful.

> *Elijah redivivus* was not a distinctively [Qumran] sectarian figure, in the sense that the messiah of Aaron, or the Teacher at the end of days, was. The Elijah-like eschatological prophet had clear scriptural basis and did not require a sectarian perspective. He did not, however, figure as prominently as the Davidic messiah in the literature of the time, and presumably he was not as well established in popular belief.[19]

Only one mention of Elijah by name appears in 4Q558, which is basically an Aramaic citation of Malachi 3:23.[20]

---

[17] James M. Robinson, ed., *The Nag Hammadi Library in English* (Leiden: Brill, 1996), 55-56; Einar Thomassen and Marvin Myer, "The Treatise on Resurrection," in *The Nag Hammadi Scriptures: The International Edition*, ed. Marvin Meyer (New York: Harper Collins, 2007), 53-54; Bentley Layton, *The Gnostic Treatise on Resurrection from Nag Hammadi* (Missoula: Scholars, 1979), 24-27.

[18] Walter Beltz, "Elia redivivus: Ein Beitrag zum Problem der Verbindung von Gnosis und Altem Testament," in *Altes Testament-Frühjudentum-Gnosis: Neue Studien zun "Gnosis und Bibel,"* ed. Karl-Wolfgang Tröger (Gütersloh, Germany: Gütersloher Verlagshaus Mohn, 1980), 138. Cf. J. Robert Douglas, "The Epistle to Rheginos: Christian-Gnostic Teaching on the Resurrection," in *Looking into the Future: Evangelical Studies in Eschatology*, ed. David W. Baker (Grand Rapids: Baker, 2001), 115-23.

[19] John J. Collins, *The Scepter and the Star: The Messiahs of the Dead Sea Scrolls and Other Ancient Literature* (Grand Rapids: Eerdmans, 2010), 141.

[20] 4Q174 is briefly suggested as possibly reflecting the Qumran belief in the end-time figure like Elijah. Julio T. Barrera, "Elijah," *EDSS*, 1:246. For an overview of various issues at stake in the messianic figure of 4Q558, see Xeravits, *King, Priest, Prophet,*

4Q521. Noteworthy allusions to the prophet occur in 4Q521, which resonates the prophet's praying for draught and rain and the reconciliation between the fathers and sons that are paralleled in 1 Kings and Malachi 4:6 (Mal 3:24 of the Masoretic texts).[21]

> [For the heav]ens and the earth will listen to his anointed one . . . . For he will honour the pious upon the throne of an eternal kingdom, freeing prisoners, giving sight to the blind, straightening out the twis[ted]. . . . And the Lord will perform marvelous acts such as have not existed, just as he sa[id,] [for] he will heal the badly wounded and will make the dead live, he will proclaim good news to the poor and . . . he will lead the . . . and enrich the hungry. . . . It is su[re:] The fathers will return towards the sons. (4Q521 2 ii 1, 7-8, 11-13; 2 iii 2)[22]

Additionally, allusions to Isaiah 61:1 are plausible with reference to the preaching of the good news and various beneficiary miraculous acts.[23]

> The spirit of the Lord GOD is upon me,
>   because the LORD has anointed me;
> he has sent me to bring good news to the oppressed,
>   to bind up the brokenhearted,
> to proclaim liberty to the captives,
>   and release to the prisoners. (Isa 61:1, NRSV)

It is of particular interest that both 4Q521 and the Old Testament texts call the prophet "anointed," which term is never applied to Old Testament prophets with the only exception of Elisha (1 Kgs 19:6) and Isaiah ("the spirit of the Lord God is upon me, because the Lord has anointed me," Isa 61:1).[24] Three observations suggest that "the anointed one" (משיחו in the original Qumran script) in the text should be taken as an allusion to the hope of Elijah *redivivus*). First, the obeying of the heavens was recounted in the Old Testament only with reference to Elijah

---

187-88. He concludes that the Elijah *redivivus* of 4Q558 is the result of an extra-Qumranic influence which displays theological affinities with Malachi and Ben Sirach on Elijah the eschatological prophet. Ibid., 188.

[21] Öhler, *Elia im Neuen Testament*, 16-22. The first fragment of 4Q558 reads " . . . evil . . . their . . . who . . . the eighth as an elected one. And see, I . . . to you I will send Eliyah, befo[re . . .] po[w]er, lightning and met[eors . . .] . . . and . . . again . . . ." *DSS*, 2:1114-15.

[22] *DSS*, 2:1044-45. Årstein Justnes, *The Time of Salvation: An Analysis of 4QApocryphon of Daniel ar (4Q246), 4QMessianic Apocalypse (4Q521), and 4QTime of Righteousness (4Q215a)* (Frankfurt: Peter Lang, 2009), 179-280.

[23] Michael Becker, "Die 'messianische Apokalypse' 4Q521 und der Interpretationsrahmen der Taten Jesu," in *Apokalyptik und Qumran*, ed. Michael Becker & Jörg Frey (Paderborn: Bonifatius, 2007), 237-310.

[24] John J Collins, "Jesus, Messianism and the Dead Sea Scrolls," in *Qumran— Messianism: Studies on the Messianic Expectations in the Dead Sea Scrolls*, ed. James H. Charlesworth, Hermann Lichtenberger, and Gerbern S. Oegema (Tübingen: Mohr Siebeck, 1998), 113.

(1 Kgs 17:1-18:46).[25] Second, only Elijah and Elisha are related to raising the dead in the Old Testament narratives (1 Kgs 17; 2 Kgs 4) and the subsequent Jewish traditions:

> You [Elijah] raised a corpse from death and from Hades, by the word of the Most High. (Sir 48:5)

> The resurrection of the dead comes through Elijah. (*m. Sotah* 9, end)

> Everything that the Holy One will do, he has already anticipated by the hands of the righteous in this world, the resurrection of the dead by Elijah and Ezekiel. (*Pesiq. Rab Kah.* 76a)[26]

Finally, the phrase, "the turning of the fathers to their sons," is a comparably clear echo of the language in Malachi 4:6.

> He will turn the hearts of parents to their children and the hearts of children to their parents, so that I will not come and strike the land with a curse. (Mal 4:6, NRSV)

> At the appointed time, it is written, you [Elijah] are destined to calm the wrath of God before it breaks out in fury, to turn the hearts of parents to their children . . . . (Sir 48:10)[27]

וְהֵשִׁיב לַב־אָבוֹת עַל־בָּנִים וְלֵב בָּנִים עַל־אֲבוֹתָם (Mal 3:24a, BHS[5])

באים אבות על בנים (4Q521 2 iii 2b)

---

[25] Also, "By the word of the Lord he [Elijah] shut up the heavens and also three times brought down fire" (Sir 48:3).

[26] This text is cited in Collins, *The Scepter and the Star*, 134-35. Puech also reconstructs the Hebrew text of Sir 48:11 to read, "Blessed is he who sees you [Elijah] before he dies, for you [Elijah] give life and he will live." Émile Puech, "Ben Sira 48:11 et la Résurrection," in *Of Scribes and Scrolls: Studies on the Hebrew Bible, Intertestamental Judaism and Christian Origins Presented to John Strugnell on the Occasion of His Sixtieth Birthday*, ed. Harold Attridge, John J. Collins, and Thomas H. Tobin (Lanham: University Press of America, 1990), 81-89, cited in Collins, *The Scepter and the Star*, 135.

[27] For similar judgments that identify the divine agent of this passage as Elijah *redivivus*, see John Strugnell, "Moses-Pseudepigrapha at Qumran: 4Q375, 4Q376, and Similar Works," in *Archaeology and History in the Dead Sea Scrolls: The New York University Conference in Memory of Yigael Yadin*, ed. Lawrence H. Schiffman (Sheffield: JSOT, 1990), 234; Collins, "Jesus, Messianism and the Dead Sea Scrolls," 112-16; Johannes Zimmermann, *Messianische Texte aus Qumran: Königliche, priesterliche und prophetische Messiasvorstellungen in den Schriftfunden von Qumran* (Tübingen: Mohr Siebeck, 1998), 332-42; Xeravits, *King, Priest, Prophet*, 188-90; John C. Poirier, "The Endtime Return of Elijah and Moses at Qumran," *DSD* 10 (2003): 227-28; Michael Becker, "4Q521 und die Gesalbten," *RevQ* 18 (1997): 73-96. The last scholar opposes Puech's multiple referent interpretation. Cf. Émile Puech, "Une apocalypse messianique (4Q521)," *RevQ* 15 (1992): 475-522; idem, "Some Remarks on 4Q246 and 4Q521 and Qumran Messianism," in *Provo International Conference on the Dead Sea Scrolls: Technological Innovations, New Texts, and Reformulated Issues*, ed. Donald W. Parry and Eugene C. Ulrich (Leiden: Brill, 1999), 554-64.

The literal translation of the Malachi passage would be something like "he will bring the heart of the fathers to the sons" and the Qumran text is something like "the fathers will return towards the sons."[28] The agents of the events are different (the former being God and the latter being the prophet), but they share the basic idea of reconciliation and the father-son phrase.

However, what is questionable with this passage is that this series of thoughts is extremely thin in view of the entire corpus of the sect's massive collection of documents, so much so that this particular document is believed not to have originated from within the community, but to have been imported from outside.[29] It is logical, therefore, not to take this text too seriously into account for the Qumranic expectation of the apocalyptic prophet's return. Horsley is in tune with the general sentiment of scholarship, therefore, which is skeptical about the widespread expectation of such an eschatological prophet before the time of Jesus.

> There appears to be very little textual attestation of any concept of an eschatological prophet in Jewish society during the early period of Roman domination. . . . there was some expectation of the return of Elijah, but that expectations of an eschatological prophet or of the coming of a prophet like Moses, if present in the minds of some, were not important factors in Jewish literature at the time of Jesus.[30]

No matter what the provenance of the belief was, however, the hope of the eschatological Elijah (that is, Elijah *redivivus*) is not unattested, although not predominant either, in second temple Judaism prior to and contemporaneous with the shaping of John's Gospel.

Scribal Expectation of Elijah's Return

One of the most intriguing questions, and also one pertinent for the present inquiry, has been debated as to whether there was an expectation of Elijah's coming as a messianic forerunner in the intertestamental period and more specifically in the rabbinic traditions. This question is directly related to the disci-

---

[28] The translation of the Qumran passage is from *DSS*, 2:1045. The translation of the Hebrew text is mine.

[29] Collins, *The Scepter and the Star*, 131-41. In addition, the lack of typical Qumran vocabularies reinforces such a judgment. Idem, "The Works of the Messiah," *DSD* 1 (1994): 106; idem, *Apocalypticism in the Dead Sea Scrolls* (New York: Routledge, 1997), 89, 128-29; Devorah Dimant, "The Qumran Manuscripts: Contents and Significance," in *Time to Prepare the Way in the Wilderness*, ed. Devorah Dimant and Lawrence H. Schiffman (Leiden: Brill, 1995), 48; idem, *Pseudo-Prophetic Texts*, part 4 of *Qumran Cave 4, XXI: Parabiblical Texts* (Oxford: Clarendon, 2001), 13. Contra, Émile Puech, *Qumrân grotte 4, XVIII: Textes hébreux (4Q521-4Q528, 4Q576-4Q579)*, DJD 25 (Oxford: Clarendon, 1998), 25, 36-38; Poirier, "The Endtime Return of Elijah and Moses at Qumran," 221-42. The latter construes that Elijah constitutes the dominant messianic paradigm in the Qumran community along with Moses. However, his argument appears to rest too much on extra-Qumranic textual evidence.

[30] Horsley, "Like One of the Prophets of Old," 443.

ples' question posed to Jesus: "And the disciples asked him, 'Why, then, do the scribes say that Elijah must come first?'" (Matthew 17:10, also, Mark 9:11) Morris Faierstein argued, in contrast to the scholarly consensus at the time of his writing, that all the Jewish texts previously alleged to conceive of Elijah's return as a messianic forerunner postdate Jesus' time (often under Christian influence) and that there are no clear literary examples which correlate Elijah with the Messiah in the Jewish eschatological texts.[31] In opposition, Dale Allison called for a more nuanced reading of the Jewish eschatological texts that describe Elijah as the harbinger of the *eschaton*, because the day of the Lord in Jewish conceptual patterns, he contended, implies the return of Messiah (for his case, Allison refers to 1QS 9:1; *T. Levi* 18:1-9; *T. Jud.* 24:1-6).[32] In defense of Faierstein, Joseph Fitzmyer responded that the Messianic texts adduced by Allison do not explicitly connect the Day of the Lord with the coming of the Messiah.[33] Markus Öhler, who has conducted one of the most recent and comprehensive investigations on Elijah with reference to his conception in the second temple period, also sides with Faierstein and Fitzmyer.[34] This brief review indicates a good portion of the current scholarship that perceive the synoptic accounts of certain scribes' expectation of Elijah's return as messianic forerunner as reflective of a marginal current of rabbinic interpretations or the result of the synoptic redactions.

The implication of these particular scholars' argument (those of Faierstein, Fitzmyer, and Öhler) is that we cannot cast the picture of Elijah depicted in the Synoptic Gospels onto that of the Fourth Gospel. Much confusion over the role of Elijah in John can be cleared up when we take the Johannine portrayal of Elijah on its own right, independent of the Synoptics. Another point that needs to be taken into consideration is that a great deal of the early Jewish tradition on Elijah does not share much congruity with John's Gospel. There are questions about whether the category of the apocalyptic prophet was influenced by the Christian apocalyptic traditions such as the Revelation of John and whether the category of the legal judge represents later rabbinic developments. Thus, it would be exegetically safe to delimit the scope of the pertinent early Jewish Elijah traditions to Malachi (the MT and LXX), Sirach, and 4Q521 for this present research into the eschatological prophet conception in John's Gospel.[35]

---

[31] Morris M. Faierstein, "Why Do the Scribes Say That Elijah Must Come First," *JBL* 100 (1981): 75-86. His examination covers a wide range of early Jewish literature, such as, the Old Testament, the Apocrypha, the Pseudepigrapha, the Qumran scrolls, Philo, and the rabbinic literature.

[32] Dale C. Allison, Jr., "Elijah Must Come First," *JBL* 103 (1984): 256-58.

[33] Joseph A. Fitzmyer, "More about Elijah Coming First," *JBL* 104 (1985): 295-96.

[34] Öhler, *Elia im Neuen Testament*, 12-30; idem, "The Expectation of Elijah and the Presence of the Kingdom of God," *JBL* 118 (1999): 461-76. Also, Horsley ("Like One of the Prophets of Old," 443) and Xeravits (*King, Priest, Prophet*, 184-90) share this judgment.

[35] Öhler, *Elia im Neuen Testament*, 12.

Elijah in the Synoptic Gospels

The preceding survey on Elijah in the intertestamental period reveals his predominant influence in that period as expressed in three distinct hopes.[36] The prophet continued to occupy an important place in the Pseudepigrapha, and his distinction is carried more strongly over in the New Testament period.[37] Among all the ancient Jewish heroic figures, he is most frequently mentioned in the New Testament (29-30 times) after Moses (80), Abraham (73), and David (59).[38]

In the Synoptic Gospels a somewhat unified picture emerges concerning the prophet. That is, the expectation of his return and his subsequent role is envisaged *vis-à-vis* John the Baptist.[39] Matthew and Mark concur on the identification of the Baptist as Elijah on the lips of Jesus.[40] In Mark, it is recognized that John's coming as Elijah *redivivus* is in terms commensurate with the prediction of the Scripture:

> But I tell you that Elijah has come, and they did to him whatever they pleased, as it is written about him. (Mark 9:13, NRSV)[41]

The Matthean parallel appears to be attuned with this Markan tradition:

> but I tell you that Elijah has already come, and they did not recognize him. (Matt 17:12a, NRSV)

Earlier in the same Gospel, Jesus unmistakably identifies the Baptist with the prophet: "He is Elijah who is to come" (Matt 11:14).[42] On the other hand, the

---

[36] "No biblical figure influenced later Judaism more than Elijah." Jeremias, *TDNT*, 2:928; similarly, Gese, "Zur Bedeutung Elias für die biblische Theologie," 127.

[37] Öhler, *Elia im Neuen Testament*, 12.

[38] Jeremias, *TDNT*, 2:934.

[39] D.L. Bock, "Elijah and Elisha," *DJG*, 204-05. Michael Tilly surveyed the image of the prophet as perceived in Palestinian Judaism at the time of John the Baptist. According to his comparative analysis of the Synoptic portrayals and contemporary Jewish understanding, the fellow Jews would have understood John the Baptist as a prophet based on his appearance and the content of his preaching. Michael Tilly, *Johannes der Täufer und die Biographie der Propheten: Die synoptische Täuferüberlieferung und das jüdische Prophetenbild zur Zeit des Täufers* (Stuttgart: Kohlhammer, 1994). For another comparative survey of John the Baptist in light of the contemporary prophetic tradition, see Joan E. Taylor, *The Immerser: John the Baptist within Second Temple Judaism* (Grand Rapids: Eerdmans, 1997), 261-316.

[40] A.M. Okorie, "Jesus and the Eschatological *Elijah*," *Scriptura* 73 (2000): 189-92.

[41] The misunderstanding of the bystanders at Jesus' crucifixion seems to be a rhetorical device to prepare readers for the confession of the centurion on the messianic identity of Jesus. Mark F. Whitters, "Why Did the Bystanders Think Jesus Called upon Elijah before He Died (Mark 15:34-36)?: The Markan Position," *HTR* 95 (2002): 119-24.

[42] "Matthew develops John's role in terms of his relation to the Kingdom of Heaven and his identity as Elijah." Walter Wink, *John the Baptist in the Gospel Tradition* (Cambridge: CUP, 1968), 28. For another study that positively identifies John the Baptist with Elijah and his high authority in Matthew, see Hubert Frankemölle, "Johannes der

Lukan rendering of the connection between the two figures is more oblique, characterizing John as only possessing the qualities attached to the prophet:

> With the spirit and power of Elijah he will go before him, to turn the hearts of parents to their children, and the disobedient to the wisdom of the righteous, to make ready a people prepared for the Lord. (Luke 1:17)[43]

Elijah in John's Gospel

An examination of the role of Elijah in John, however, sets a Johannine exegete in a quandary. The reason is partly because the Gospel seems to lack any explicit references or allusions to the prophet; and no synoptic parallels that affirm the association of the prophet with the Baptist are found. Furthermore, more strikingly, John the Baptist, whom the Synoptic Gospels unanimously portray as Elijah *redivivus*, blatantly renounces his contemporaries' inquiry on whether or not he is Elijah or the prophet, presumably an eschatological figure, in John 1:21.

> And they asked him, "What then? Are you Elijah?" He said, "I am not." "Are you the prophet?" He answered, "No." (John 1:21, NRSV)

As such, Walter Wink's statement appears to be warranted.

> The [fourth] evangelist . . . sharply contradicts the earlier tradition [of the Synoptics] that John was Elijah. For him the idea of a forerunner is anathema.[44]

Some explanations, therefore, have been offered to remedy the seeming inconsistency. Before turning our attention to such attempts, it is worthwhile to mention a group of scholars who maintain that it is Jesus, not John, who reflects the role of Elijah *redivivus* in the Fourth Gospel.[45]

Täufer und Jesus im Matthäusevangelium: Jesus als Nachfolger des Täufers," *NTS* 42 (1996): 196-218.

[43] Kaiser, *The Uses of the Old Testament in the New*, 77-88. Cf. R.J. Miller, who, mistakenly in my estimation, argues that Luke identifies Elijah with John the Baptist and Jesus interchangeably. Robert J. Miller, "Elijah, John, and Jesus in the Gospel of Luke," *NTS* 34 (1988): 611-22. For another treatment of Luke on John the Baptist as Elijah, see Christophe Pichon, "Un parallèle entre Jésus, Jean-Baptiste et Élie: Présupposés méthodologiques," *RevScRel* 82 (2008): 497-516.

[44] Wink, *John the Baptist in the Gospel Tradition*, 89.

[45] Studies that understand the Johannine Jesus as the eschatological Elijah to a large extent have not appeared in recent years. For the past examples of such an approach, see Reginald H. Fuller, *The Foundations of New Testament Christology* (New York: Scribner, 1965), 46-48, 67, 125-29, 167-73; Oscar Cullmann, *The Christology of the New Testament* (Philadelphia: Westminster, 1963), 13-50; Ferdinand Hahn, *The Titles of Jesus in Christology: Their History in Early Christianity* (London: Lutterworth, 1969), 352-406; J. Louis Martyn, "We Have Found Elijah," in *Jews, Greeks, and Christians: Essays in Honor of William David Davies*, ed. R. Hamerton-Kelly and R. Scroggs (Leiden: Brill, 1976), 181-219; repr. in *The Gospel of John in Christian History* (New York: Paulist, 1979), 9-54. The only recent exception is Henricus

Jesus as Elijah

Cullmann, Schnackenburg, and Robinson. In a conclusion to a section which deals with the concept of the eschatological prophet in the New Testament, Oscar Cullmann defines the presence and use of the idea of Jesus as Elijah in John:

> The synoptic writers did not express their personal faith in Jesus by means of this conception [the eschatological Elijah, or Elijah *redivivus*]. On the other hand, it does seem to have had a certain meaning for the writer of the Fourth Gospel. His particular emphasis of the fact that the Baptist rejected for himself the title of the Prophet, the returned Elijah, suggests that the writer of John wants to reserve this title for Jesus—along with other Christological designations and concepts . . . .[46]

Cullmann's conclusion is based on his observation of John the Baptist's denial of being Elijah. Likewise, Schnackenburg also notes that

> when John the Baptist denies that he is "the prophet" or an eschatological figure of salvation like Elijah (1:21, 25), this indirectly reinforces the idea that Jesus is this "prophet" or "Elijah."[47]

In support of this view, Cullmann further points to the early chapters of Acts (esp. 3:22; 7:37) which, he believes, preserve a tradition of Elijah *redivivus* Christology.[48] Similarly, J.A.T. Robinson detects an element of Elijah-like Christology in Acts 3, where Peter calls for repentance on the basis of identifying Jesus with the one promised by a series of prophets. This prophet is expected to properly restore everything to God's rule, and, to Robinson, this restoration theme evokes Elijah *redivivus* motif (Mal 3).[49]

> According to this very primitive Christology (Acts 3:12-26) [an earlier belief that understood Jesus as a prophetic figure], Jesus is quite explicitly the Prophet like Moses (as he is also in Stephen's speech in Acts 7:37). It should hardly therefore come as a shock to find that he *is equally evidently Elijah in all but name*. . . . Jesus was indeed to

---

Pidyarto Gunawan, "Jesus and the New Elijah: An Attempt to the Question of John 1:21," *SCS* 9 (2010): 29-53.

[46] Cullmann, *The Christology of the New Testament*, 37. Cullmann also represents pre-critical scholarship on Jewish messianism via a prophetic figure. "Jesus appears not only as *a* prophet but as *the* Prophet, the final Prophet who should 'fulfill' all prophecy at the end of time. We shall see that the expectation of such a prophet with a very definite task to perform at the end of time was widespread in Judaism at the time of Jesus." Cullmann, *The Christology of the New Testament*, 13 (italics original). However, R. Horsley simply refutes this view. "But there is very little evidence for any Jewish expectation of an eschatological prophet prior to the early Christian communities' interpretation of Jesus (and John the Baptist) and the emergence of rabbinic Judaism following the crisis created by the Roman devastation of Jewish Palestine in A.D. 70." Horsley, "Like One of the Prophets of Old," 437.

[47] Rudolf Schnackenburg, *Jesus in the Gospels: A Biblical Christology* (Louisville: Westminster/John Knox, 1995), 271.

[48] Cullmann, *The Christology of the New Testament*, 38.

[49] See especially v. 21: "Who must remain in heaven until the time of universal restoration that God announced long ago through his holy prophets."

be the Christ. But he was Elijah first.[50]

These observation, however, raise a serious skepticism concerning the identification of Jesus with Elijah as proposed by Cullmann, Schnackenburg, and Robinson. That is, they commit the fallacy of superimposing the Elijah eschatology on the texts that display more the traits of the Mosaic eschatological prophet (cf. Deut 18:15).[51] Their confusion is somewhat understandable in view of some early Jewish texts that fuse the two figures closely in their eschatological expressions. However, ill-defined criteria and their application in studies such as this create unnecessary confusion over the presence of certain personages in the texts. Tracking down the traits of early Jewish traditions with more refined care allows us to have a clearer picture of Jesus as Horsley suggests:

> In the few and scattered textual references [to Elijah *redivivus* and a prophet like Moses] that are available, their particular forms or images do not appear to be mixed or conflated; hence they can be discussed separately.[52]

Moreover, it is particularly problematic when their judgments are largely based on arguments from silence. We cannot assume the Elijah *redivivus* Christology because a text does not deny such to be the case. It is comparably evident that the texts adduced to support their views infer a Mosaic eschatological prophetic idea rather than that of Elijah. In addition, these scholars fail to prove how such Elijah

---

[50] J.A.T. Robinson, "Elijah, John and Jesus: An Essay in Detection," *NTS* 4 (1958): 277. For a critique of Cullmann and Robinson on this issue, see John Knox, "'Prophet' in New Testament Christology," in *Lux in lumine: Essays to Honor W. Norman Pittenger*, ed. R.A. Norris, Jr. (New York: Seabury, 1966), 23-34. J. Polhill lists one more exegete who holds the Elijah Christology in Acts 3. Otto Bauernfeind, *Kommentar und Studien zur Apostelgeschichte* (Tübingen: Mohr Siebeck, 1980), 65-69; idem, "Tradition und Komposition in dem Apokatastasisspruch Apostelgeschichte 3:20f.," in *Abraham unser Vater: Juden und Christen im Gespräch über die Bibel. Festschrift für Otto Michel zum 60. Geburtstag*, ed. Otto Betz, Martin Hengel, and Peter Schmidt (Leiden: Brill, 1963), 13-23. One more article can be added along the same line of argument. Robert Macina, "Jean le Baptiste était-il Élie: Examen de la tradition néotestamentaire," *POC* 34 (1984): 209-32. Polhill also lists two scholars who are opposed to this Elijah-Christology in the Acts passage: Donald L. Jones, "The Title Christos in Luke-Acts," *CBQ* 32 (1970): 69-76; C.F.D. Moule, "Christology of Acts," in *Studies in Luke-Acts: Essays Presented in Honor of Paul Schubert*, ed. Leander E. Keck, Paul Schubert, and J. Louis Martyn (Nashville: Abingdon, 1966), 168-69. Cf. John B. Polhill, *Acts* (Nashville: Broadman, 1992), 134-35, esp. n. 23.

[51] Johann Maier, "Schriftrezeption im jüdischen Umfeld des Johannesevangeliums," in *Israel und seine Heilstraditionen im Johannessevangelium: Festgabe für Johannes Beutler SJ zum 70. Geburtstag*, ed. Michael Labahn, Klaus Scholtissek, and Angelika Strotmann (Paderborn: Schöningh, 2004), 58-59. Two influential studies that identify "prophet" with a prophet like Moses of Deut 18:18 are Wayne A. Meeks, *The Prophet-King: Moses Traditions and the Johannine Christology* (Leiden: Brill, 1967); Marie-Émile Boismard, *Moses or Jesus: An Essay in Johannine Christology*, trans. B. T. Viviano (Minneapolis: Fortress; Leuven: Peeters, 1993).

[52] Horsley, "Like One of the Prophets of Old," 438.

Christological motif of Acts can be imported into the Gospel of John with legitimate exegetical warrant.

J. Louis Martyn. In distinction to his predecessors, J. Louis Martyn put forward a more rigorous and nuanced study of Elijah Christology in John.[53] He traced the presence of the Elijah-like Christology in the pre-Johannine traditions through a convoluted source reconstruction. His contention is that the earlier "Signs Source" conceived of Christology in terms of Elijah *redivivus* while such tradition was suppressed in the later redactional layers. An example of the latter is most explicitly attested in John 3:13 in the form of anti-Elijah polemic ("no one has ascended into heaven except the one who descended from heaven, the Son of Man"). On the other hand, the traits of an Elijah-Christology are found in several allusions to Elijah's miracles and references to his second coming: the former in the pericopae of the changing of water into wine (2:1-11), the healing of the official's son (4:46-54), the feeding of the multitude (6:1-14), the healing of the blind (9:1-7), and raising of Lazarus (11:1-44). Therefore, his reconstruction of the Johannine sources leads him to postulate that the original source of John 1:43-49 (the testimony of Nathanael) actually contained a phrase, "we have found Elijah," instead of "we have found the Messiah" (John 1:41).

A reader of Martyn's essay as glaring as it sounds, however, becomes mystified as to whether such a complex reconstruction of multiple source layers can be undertaken with as high a degree of certainty as Martyn asserts. Marinus de Jonge's assessment of Martyn's theory is illuminating:

> It is one thing to say that the Fourth Gospel presupposes earlier written and oral traditions . . . , but it is quite another matter to claim that we are still able to determine beyond reasonable doubt what the source employed in 1:19-51 contained.[54]

His view of Moses in John's Gospel, however, seems to be largely contingent upon his hypothetical reconstruction of the history of the so-called Johannine community. If his theory of the community does not stand up to scrutiny, his view of Moses also breaks down.

Martyn proposes that, in its first phase, the Johannine community remained actively involved within orthodox Jewish synagogues with an outspoken conviction that Jesus is the long-awaited eschatological messiah (Martyn posits that the signs source reflects such a phase). Later on, the community had to detach itself from mainstream Judaism because of the irreconcilable theological differences. The problem with Martyn's thesis, however, is that no extant literary evidence unambiguously supports his proposal (i.e., "signs source" or proto-Johannine Gospel with his contended phrase "we have found Elijah"). His

---

[53] Martyn, "We Have Found Elijah." 9-54.
[54] Marinus de Jonge, "John the Baptist and Elijah in the Fourth Gospel," in *The Conversation Continues: Studies in Paul & John in Honor of J. Louis Martyn*, ed. Robert T. Fortna and Beverly R. Gaventa (Nashville: Abingdon, 1990), 302.

reconstruction could be only a product of creative imagination, and the alleged background history of the Johannine community seems to be merely a mirror-reading.[55] As such, his multi-redactional interpretation of the Mosaic portrayal in John cannot be decisive, but suggestive at best.

From this brief sketch of three representative exegetes who perceive Jesus to be the eschatological Elijah in John, it becomes evident that their interpretations invite much criticism. The vulnerability of their conclusions becomes visible especially when one takes into account the way in which the fourth evangelist presents the Jewish Scripture and the Old Testament characters consistently as messianic witnesses and not as messianic prefigures.

---

[55] For recent criticisms of Martyn's reconstruction of the development history of the Johannine community as reflected in the Johannine literature and early rabbinic literature, see Peter Schäfer, "Die sogannante Synode von Jabne," in *Studien zur Geschichte und Theologie des rabbinischen Judentums* (Leiden: Brill, 1978), 45-55; Reuven Kimelman, "Birkat ha-minim and the Lack of Evidence for an Anti-Christian Jewish Prayer in Late Antiquity," in *Jewish and Christian Self-Definition*, ed. E.P. Sanders, Albert I. Baumgarten, and Alan Mendelson (Philadelphia: Fortress, 1981), 2:226-44; Gary M. Burge, "How Much of the Johannine Community Can We Find in the 4th Gospel?: Critical Analysis of R. Brown and J.L. Martyn" (Evangelical Theological Society Papers, 1982); Steven T. Katz, "Issues in the Separation of Judaism and Christianity after 70 CE: A Reconsideration," *JBL* 103 (1984): 43-76; Richard Bauckham, "The Audience of the Fourth Gospel," in *Jesus in Johannine Tradition*, ed. Robert T. Fortna und Tom Thatcher (Louisville: Westminster/John Knox, 2001), 101-06; Daniel Boyarin, "Justin Martyr Invents Judaism," *CH* 70 (2001): 427-61; Tobias Hägerland, "John's Gospel: A Two-Level Drama?" *JSNT* 25 (2003): 309-22; Robert Kysar, "The Expulsion from the Synagogue: The Tale of a Theory," in *Voyages with John: Charting the Fourth Gospel* (Waco: Baylor University Press, 2005), 237-46; idem, "The Whence and Whither of the Johannine Community," in *Life in Abundance: Studies of John's Gospel in Tribute to Raymond E. Brown, S.S.*, ed. John R. Donahue (Collegeville: Liturgical, 2005), 65-81; Timothy J.M. Ling, *The Judaean Poor and the Fourth Gospel* (Cambridge: CUP, 2006); Peter M. Phillips, *The Prologue of the Fourth Gospel: A Sequential Reading* (London: T & T Clark, 2006), 58-59; Edward W. Klink, III, *The Sheep of the Fold: The Audience and Origin of the Gospel of John* (Cambridge: CUP, 2007); Michael Bird, "Sectarian Gospels for Sectarian Christians?: The Non-Canonical Gospels and Bauckham's *The Gospels for All Christians*," in *The Audience of the Gospels: The Origin and Function of the Gospels in Early Christianity*, ed. Edward W. Klink, III (London: T & T Clark, 2010), 27-48. In addition, the presence and use of the signs source is widely and critically questioned in recent Johannine scholarship. For the critiques, see Wolfgang J. Bittner, *Jesu Zeichen im Johannesevangelium: Die Messias-Erkenntnis im Johannesevangelium vor ihrem jüdischen Hintergrund* (Tübingen: Mohr Siebeck, 1987), 2-14; Daniel Marguerat, "La 'source des signes' existe-t-elle?: Réception des récits de miracle dans l'évangile de Jean," in *Communauté johannique et son histoire: La trajectoire de l'évangile de Jean aux deux premier siècles*, ed. Johannes Beutler and Jean-Daniel Kaestli (Geneva: Labor et Fides, 1990), 69-93; Gilbert van Bell, *The Signs Source in the Fourth Gospel: Historical Survey and Critical Evaluation of the Semeia Hypothesis* (Louvain: Peeters, 1994); John Ashton, "The Signs Source," in *Studying John: Approaches to the Fourth Gospel* (Oxford: OUP, 1998), 90-113.

Excursus 3: John Meier's Eschatological Prophet Paradigm

Probably it is John P. Meier who has advanced the most elaborate argument for Jesus as the eschatological Elijah-like prophet. He has so far published a series of four books on the very topic and is planning on writing one more book in the series. "And yet the massive amount of the Gospel record dedicated to Jesus' miracle working, his itinerant prophetic ministry, his eschatological message, and even his narrative parables, which belong more to the prophetic than to the sapiential mode of speaking, argues that the Elijah-like eschatological prophet is probably the best single model for the historical Jesus, however it must be supplemented by elements from the legal and sapiential traditions of Israel. The Elijah-like prophet is not the total explanation of the historical Jesus, but it is, in my view, the dominant pattern."[56] His thesis is generally valid in that Jesus is depicted as a prophetic figure, but it manifests a grave exegetical oversight in two respects. First, he ignores the accounts of the Synoptic Gospels that explicitly identify John the Baptist, not Jesus, as the Elijah-like figure. Second, his reconstruction of the historical Jesus is largely dependent on the Synoptic Gospels. The Gospel of John, as will be demonstrated later in this chapter, does not care to employ the conventional Jewish expectations of the Elijah *redivivus* figure. Furthermore, since this Gospel was received as a part of the Christian canon it should be taken seriously into account in the reconstruction of the "historical Jesus." By implication, it could be inferred that the image of Jesus as an Elijah figure was not a major concern for the disciples and early Christians.[57]

John the Baptist as Elijah

Marinus de Jonge. In contrast to the scholars noted above, some explanations have been offered so as to make better sense of the blatant denial of John the Baptist which runs directly counter to the testimonies of the Synoptic accounts concerning his identity as Elijah *redivivus*. Marinus de Jonge, for instance, drew a clue from the testimonies of an early church father, Justin Martyr (*Apology* 35:1; *Dialogue with Trypho* 8:4) who reports that, in the time of Jesus, there was a popular belief of Elijah anointing the Messiah.[58] Until the anointing by the

---

[56] John P. Meier, "From Elijah-like Prophet to Royal Davidic Messiah," in *Jesus: A Colloquium in the Holy Land*, ed. Doris Donnelly (London: Continuum, 2001), 46. Also, idem, "The Present State of the 'Third Quest' for the Historical Jesus: Loss and Gain," *Bib* 80 (1999): 483.

[57] For his books on this topic, see idem, *A Marginal Jew: Rethinking the Historical Jesus*, 4 vols (New York: Doubleday, 1991-2009); but for his virtually exclusive dependence on the Synoptic Gospels, see especially John P. Meier, *Mentor, Message, and Miracles*, vol. 2 of *A Marginal Jew: Rethinking the Historical Jesus* (New York: Doubleday, 1994), 19-1038; idem, *Companions and Competitors*, vol. 3 of *A Marginal Jew: Rethinking the Historical Jesus* (New York: Doubleday, 2001), 19-285.

[58] *Dialogue with Trypho* is an early Christian apologetic written by an apostolic father, Justin Martyr. Larry R. Helyer, *Exploring Jewish Literature of the Second Temple Period: A Guide for New Testament Students* (Downers Grove: InterVarsity, 2002), 492-94. For the theological commonality between this document and John's Gospel, see Jorg Christian Salzmann, "Jüdische Messiasvorstellungen in Justins Dialog mit Trypho und im Johannesevangelium," *ZNW* 100 (2009): 247-68.

prophet, the messiah is unknown and powerless.[59] Polhill suggests a similar solution:

> The Fourth Gospel's refusal to depict John as Elijah, thus differing from Matthew and Mark, may be due to the view that Elijah would anoint the Messiah, a status which the fourth evangelist does not wish to grant the Baptist in his polemic directed at the disciples of John.[60]

The text of Justin the Martyr reads as following regarding the Johannine account of the Baptist's denial of his identity as Elijah *redivivus*:

> But if the Messiah has been born and exists anywhere, He is not known, nor is He conscious of His own existence, nor has He any power until Elias comes to anoint Him and to make Him manifest to all. But you [Christians] have believed this foolish rumor, and you have invented for yourselves a Christ for whom you blindly give up your lives. (Justin *Dialogue with Trypho* 8:4)[61]

This tradition can certainly lead one to posit the dependence of the messiah on his forerunner and such tension could be what the fourth evangelist was trying to avoid. There is another Johannine text that could be cited as a trace of reminiscence to such a tradition:

> John answered them, "I baptize with water. Among you stands one whom you do not know, the one who is coming after me." (John 1:26-27a, NRSV)

Etienne Trocmé. Another scholarly attempt explains the John-Elijah question with a later tension between the Johannine community and the so-called "party of the Baptist." It is argued that some later church fathers hint at the posthumous sanctification of John the Baptist by his disciples. The advocates of this view usually substantiate their position on two grounds. First, Acts 18:24-19:7 speaks of Apollos and a group of Christian believers who were baptized only in the baptism of John. From this text, Trocmé, for instance, presumes a continuing presence of the Johannine followers in the Transjordan area.[62] A more explicit

---

[59] Marinus de Jonge, "Jewish Expectations about the 'Messiah' according to the Fourth Gospel," *NTS* 19 (1973): 246-70; repr., in *Jesus, Stranger from Heaven and Son of God: Jesus Christ and the Christians in Johannine Perspective* (Missoula: SBL, 1977), 77-116; idem, "John the Baptist and Elijah in the Fourth Gospel," 299-309.

[60] Polhill, "John 1-4," 457, n. 10.

[61] *Saint Justin Martyr*, trans. Thomas B. Falls (New York: Christian Heritage, 1948), 161.

[62] Etienne Trocmé, "Jean-Baptiste dans le Quatrième Évangile," *RHPR* 60 (1980): 129-51; Wilhelm Baldensperger, *Der Prolog des vierten Evangeliums: Sein polemisch-apologetischer Zweck* (Tübingen: Mohr Siebeck, 1898). Both are reviewed in Raymond E. Brown, *An Introduction to the Gospel of John*, ed. Francis J. Moloney (New York: Doubleday, 2003), 153-57; Wink, *John the Baptist in the Gospel Tradition*, 149. Cf. Lichtenberger construes a presence of the followers of the Baptist in Rome in the late first century A.D. Hermann Lichtenberger, "Täufergemeinden und frühchristliche Täuferpolemik im letzten Drittel des 1. Jahrhunderts," *ZTK* 84 (1987): 36-57, cited in Polhill, *Acts*, 399.

reference to the remaining group of the Baptist sect is, however, found in a late second-to-fourth-centuries testimony of the Pseudo-Clementines, especially *Recognitions* 1.54.8; 1.60.1-11 and *Homilies* 2.23.[63] The Latin version of *Recognitions* reveals that a group of John's followers led by Simon believed the Baptist to be the Messiah (although the Syriac version of *Recog.* 1.54.8, the older tradition, does not record this belief).

Table 3. Comparison of the Syriac and Latin versions of Ps.-Clem. *Recog.* on John the Baptist[64]

Translations of the Syriac version	Translations of the Latin version
"Now the pure disciples of John separated themselves greatly from the people and spoke to their teacher as if he was concealed [or: said that their teacher was, as it were, concealed]" (Ps.-Clem. *Recog.* 1.54.8).	"Some of the disciples of John who imagined they were great separated themselves from the people and proclaimed their master as the Christ" (Ps.-Clem. *Recog.* 1.54.8).
"One of the disciples of John approaches and boasted regarding John, 'He is the Christ, and not Jesus, just as Jesus himself spoke concerning him, namely, that he is greater than any prophet who had ever been. If he is thus greater than Moses, it is clear that he is also greater than Jesus for Jesus arose just as did Moses. Therefore, it is right that John, who is greater than these, is the Christ'" (Ps.-Clem. *Recog.* 1.60.1-2).	"And behold, one of John's disciples asserted that John was Christ, and not Jesus. 'This is so much the case,' he said, 'that even Jesus himself proclaimed that John is greater than all humans and prophets. If therefore,' he said, 'he is greater than all, he should doubtless be considered greater than both Moses and Jesus himself. Now if he is greater than all, he is Christ'" (Ps.-Clem. *Recog.* 1.60.1-2).

There appeared a certain John the Baptist, who according to the disposition of the syzygies was at the same time the forerunner of our Lord Jesus. And as the Lord had twelve apostles according to the number of the solar months, so also there gathered about John thirty eminent persons according to the reckoning of the lunar month . . . (Ps.-Clem. *Hom.* 2.23).[65]

---

[63] For helpful anthologies to Pseudo-Clementines, see Frédéric Manns, "Les pseudo-clémentines (Homélies et Reconnaissances): Etat de la question," *SBFLA* 53 (2003): 157-84; Frédéric Amsler, ed., *Nouvelles intrigues pseudo-clémentines: Actes du deuxième colloque international sur la littérature apocryphe chrétienne, Lausanne - Genève, 30 août - 2 septembre 2006* (Prahins: Éditions du Zèbre, 2008); Jan N. Bremmer, ed., *The Pseudo-Clementines* (Leuven: Peeters, 2010).

[64] F. Stanley Jones, *An Ancient Jewish Christian Source on the History of Christianity: Pseudo-Clementine Recognitions 1.27-71* (Atlanta: Scholars, 1995), 88 & 94.

[65] *NTA* (1963), 2:547.

It has been argued that the early church fathers (i.e., Irenaeus and Justin) identified the founding father of Gnosticism, Simon Magus, as a follower of John the Baptist and as the patriarch of all kinds of early Christian heresies. This view was first proposed by Ernst Haenchen and further argued and elaborated by Gerd Lüdemann.[66] As such, some exegetes believe that the fourth evangelist was refuting the budding Gnostic movement by downplaying John the Baptist at that particular point in the Gospel of John. In contrast, a major weakness of this view is that it is based on a conjectured historical reconstruction. A large number of biblical exegetes are hesitant to identify Simon in Acts with the founder of Gnosticism.[67] In addition, we cannot be decisive of the competition that allegedly existed between the so-called Simonians and nascent Christianity, let alone the late date of the Pseudo-Clementines poses a problem.[68]

John the Baptist Not as Elijah

Markus Öhler. In contrast to the views that articulate the Baptist as Elijah *redivivus*, Markus Öhler sets forth his reservations in a four-fold argument.[69] First, in view of the magnitude of the trouble that the alleged tension would have caused to the early church, the Synoptic Gospels are surprisingly silent, and seek to remedy the alleged traditions. Second, contrary to the suggestion of Trocmé and others, the "hidden" language in John 1:26 represents a typical Johannine expression. Accordingly, it is difficult to attribute that verse to something other

---

[66] Ernst Haenchen, "Gab es eine vorchristliche Gnosis," *ZTK* 49 (1952): 316-49; Gerd Lüdemann, *Untersuchungen zur simonianischen Gnosis* (Göttingen: Vandenhoeck und Ruprecht, 1975); idem, "The Acts of the Apostles and the Beginnings of Simonian Gnosis," *NTS* 33 (1987): 420-26; idem, *The Acts of the Apostles: What Really Happened in the Earliest Days of the Church* (Amherst: Prometheus, 2005), 118-20. For the research history, see Kurt Rudolph, "Simon-Magus oder Gnosticus: Zum Stand der Debatte," *TRu* 42 (1977): 279-359; Robert McL Wilson, "Simon and Gnostic Origins," in *Actes des Apôtres: Traditions, rédaction, théologie*, ed. Jacob Kremer (Louvain: Leuven University Press, 1979), 485-91; Niclas Förster, *Marcus Magus: Kult, Lehre und Gemeindeleben einer valentinianischen Gnostikergruppe: Sammlung der Quellen und Kommentar* (Tübingen: Mohr Siebeck, 1999), 7-53; Stephen Haar, *Simon Magus: The First Gnostic?* (Berlin: Walter de Gruyter, 2003); David R. Cartlidge, "The Fall and Rise of Simon Magus," *BRev* 21 (2005): 24-36.

[67] Karlmann Beyschlag, *Simon Magus und die christliche Gnosis* (Tübingen: Mohr, 1974); Wayne A. Meeks, "Simon Magus in Recent Research," *RSR* 3 (1977): 137-42; Roland Bergmeir, "Die Gestalt des Simon Magus in Apg 8 und in der simonianischen Gnosis: Aporien einer Gesamtdeutung," *ZNW* 77 (1986): 267-75; Jarl Fossum, "Samaritan Sects and Movements," in *Samaritans*, ed. Alan D. Crown (Tübingen: Mohr Siebeck, 1989), 357-89; Polhill, *Acts*, 216 (where Bergmeir and others are cited); Martin Hengel, "Judaism and Hellenism Revisited," in *Hellenism in the Land of Israel*, ed. John J. Collins and Gregory E. Sterling (Notre Dame: University of Notre Dame Press, 2001), 16.

[68] Christoph Markschies, *Gnosis: An Introduction*, trans. John Bowden (London: T & T Clark, 2003), 73-83.

[69] Öhler, *Elia im Neuen Testament*, 94-97.

than a Johannine redactional trait as Trocmé posits it to belong to a pre-Johannine tradition.[70] Third, Justin's use of an independent Jewish tradition is unlikely in view of Justin's verbatim quotation in 88.7. The citation resembles the wording of the Fourth Gospel so closely, that the literary dependence should be reckoned from the Gospel onto Justin (although it could be an indirect one). On this point, Hengel also construes this resemblance as hardly a coincidence: "This triple agreements of the two texts can hardly be a mere coincidence."[71]

οὐκ εἰμὶ ὁ Χριστός ἀλλὰ φωνὴ βοῶντος ἥξει γὰρ ὁ ἰσχυρότερός μου. (*Dialogus cum Tryphone* 88.7)[72]

οὐκ εἰμὶ ὁ χριστός . . .   *φωνὴ βοῶντος*. (John 1:20-23, NA[28])

Finally, it is hard to imagine that the fourth evangelist decidedly went against the popular current of belief in John the Baptist as Elijah, the messianic forerunner, as witnessed in the Synoptic Gospels. It is rather easier to assume that the fourth evangelist was simply unaware of the pre-Markan tradition, in which the Baptist was seen as a harbinger of the messianic age. The research of Faierstein and Öhler himself confirms that such pre-Markan tradition may well have been of only marginal influence if present at all. These observations make a compelling case since the fourth evangelist does not manifest recourse to the passages of Malachi and Sirach that represent arguably the closest examples of the so-called "Jewish hope of Elijah's return as the messianic forerunner."[73]

---

[70] Also, Martin Stowasser, *Johannes der Täufer im Vierten Evangelium: Eine Untersuchung zu seiner Bedeutung für die johanneische Gemeinde* (Klosterneuburg: Österreichisches Katholisches Bibelwerk, 1992), 93.

[71] Martin Hengel, *Die johanneische Frage: Ein Lösungsversuch* (Tübingen: Mohr Siebeck, 1993), 64. For a further example of scholarship that sees Justin's dependence on John, see John W. Pryor, "Justin Martyr and the Fourth Gospel," *SecCent* 9 (1992): 153-69. However, there are also scholars who are skeptical about the direct literary dependence between John and Justin Martyr. Michael Mees, *Die frühe Rezeptionsgeschichte des Johannesevangeliums: Am Beispiel von Textüberlieferung und Väterexegese*, ed. Georg Scheuermann and Andreas-P. Alkofer (Würzburg: Echter, 1994), 200-10; Titus Nagel, *Die Rezeption des Johannesevangeliums im 2. Jahrhundert: Studien zur vorirenäischen Aneignung und Auslegung des vierten Evangeliums in christlicher und christlich-gnostischer Literatur* (Leipzig: Evangelische Verlagsanstalt, 2000), 94-116; Günter Reim, *Jochanan: Erweiterte Studien zum alttestamentlichen Hintergrund des Johannesevangeliums* (Erlangen: Ev.-Luth. Mission, 1995), 487-534; Johann Maier, "Schriftrezeption im jüdischen Umfeld des Johannesevangeliums," in *Israel und seine Heilstraditionen im Johannessevangelium: Festgabe für Johannes Beutler SJ zum 70. Geburtstag*, ed. Michael Labahn, Klaus Scholtissek, and Angelika Strotmann (Paderborn: Schöningh, 2004), 86.

[72] Iustini Martyris *Dialogus cum Tryphone*, ed. M. Marcovich (Berlin: Walter de Gruyter, 1997), 224.

[73] Whereas John cites only Isa 40:3 for the identity of John the Baptist, Mark associates the Isaian text with Mal 3:1. Cf. Jan Lambrecht, "John the Baptist and Jesus in Mark 1:1-15: Markan Redaction of Q?" *NTS* 38 (1992): 357-84; Santiago Guijarro Oporto,

High view of John the Baptist. In addition to the reservations of Öhler, some other aspects can be noted in contrast to the views articulated by Trocmé, de Jonge, and others. First, the high esteem reserved for John the Baptist in the Gospel does not tally with their views. The divine origin of the Baptist is only matched by that of Jesus. The divine provenance of the Baptist as witnessed in John 1:6 and 3:28b depicts an analogous picture with the Johannine missionary Christology.

> There was a man sent from God, whose name was John (1:6); I am not the Messiah, but I have been sent ahead of him. (3:28b)

The passive voice of the latter text clearly demonstrates the divine initiative of his mission. Also, the authority of John's ministry as Christological witness amounts to that of the Scripture as the Baptist reveals Jesus to Israel.[74]

> I myself did not know him; but I came baptizing with water for this reason, that he might be revealed to Israel. (John 1:31, NRSV)

> He who has the bride is the bridegroom. The friend of the bridegroom, who stands and hears him, rejoices greatly at the bridegroom's voice. For this reason my joy has been fulfilled. (John 3:29, NRSV)

Therefore, Menken finds a conspicuous functional resemblance between the Old Testament scriptures and John the Baptist. At the same, the narrative plot of both entities remain as witnesses for the Christological identity of Jesus. It is, therefore, difficulty to presume a coincidental nature at this juncture.

> We can fruitfully compare the functions of which the evangelist ascribes to the scriptural text and to John the Baptist. There is a striking similarity between these two functions; at the same time, the evangelist's view of the Baptist is more elaborated at the textual level of his gospel than his view of the Scripture . . . the role of John the Baptist is almost completely reduced to that of a witness on behalf of Jesus . . . . In this respect, his [John the Baptist] role agrees with that of the OT: the positive, theological meaning of both John the Baptist and the OT within the Fourth Gospel is that they testify to Jesus.[75]

Moreover, the fourth evangelist's high view of John is further illuminated in his references to the Baptist's possession of the unique revelations that are not attested in the Synoptic Gospels. Such concepts as, Jesus the Lamb of God, the preexistent Son, God's chosen one, and the bridegroom of Israel (1:29-34; 3:39)

"Why Does the Gospel of Mark Begin as It Does?" *BTB* 33 (2003): 28-38. For another exegete who does not see the Baptist as an eschatological figure, but a precursor, see Jean-Marie Sevrin, "Le commencement du quatrième évangile: Prologue et prelude," in *La Bible en récits*, ed. Daniel Marguerat (Genève: Labor et Fides, 2005), 343.

[74] Brown, *An Introduction to the Gospel of John*, 156.

[75] M.J.J. Menken, "Observations on the Significance of the Old Testament in the Fourth Gospel," in *Theology and Christology in the Fourth Gospel: Essays by the Members of the SNTS Johannine Writings Seminar*, ed. G. van Belle, J.G. van der Watt, and P. Maritz (Leuven: Leuven University, 2005), 164.

are made known through him.

Anachronism and the textual testimony. The traditions that allegedly point to the tension between Jesus and John the Baptist (i.e., Justin and pseudo-Clement) are late and the number of such witnesses is quite meager, especially in light of the extent of the crises it would have entailed. The extant literary evidence, therefore, precludes any firm conclusion that the fourth evangelist was portraying John the Baptist over against such traditions as Elijah's anointing the Messiah or the Johannine community's conflict with the full-blown Baptist party. Finally, if we assume the competent editorial and/or writing ability of the fourth evangelist (whoever was responsible for the final shape of the present Gospel), the most important clue for the identity of John the Baptist should be his own self-revealing statement which the evangelist believed to be important enough to preserve in the present text and placed it in quotation marks: "What then? Are you Elijah?" He said, "I am not."

Narrative Function of John the Baptist in the Fourth Gospel

Although John the Baptist is not related to Elijah in the Fourth Gospel, his role is quite interesting. His profile nicely fits with the characteristic that is reserved for the Old Testament characters in terms of the witness motif.[76] John the Baptist appears in the four major sections throughout the Gospel: (1) 1:6-8, 15, 19-36; (2) 3:23-30; (3) 5:33-36; (4) 10:40-42. Each time he is mentioned, the length and importance of him are reduced.[77] He is extensively addressed only in the first chapter, whereas, in chs. 3, 5, and 10, he is mentioned only in passing references. Thus, it is worthwhile to focus an inquiry into his narrative function to the first chapter, especially John 1:19-34, due to the concentrated attention devoted to the Baptist in the discourse. However, the fourth evangelist's view of the Baptist as reflected in chs. 3, 5, and 10 will be taken into account when deemed necessary.

Witness

Virtually all scholarly assessments of John the Baptist agree on his witness narrative function. In comparison to the Synoptic Gospels, almost all of his personal details are extremely reduced in the Johannine accounts: his provenance, appearance, identity, and activity. As such, he remains as a mere witness.[78] Furthermore, some observations characterize his narrative function as identical as that of the scripture and the Old Testament heroic figures, that is, the theme of witness.

---

[76] Michael Theobald, *Die Fleischwerdung des Logos: Studien zum Verhältnis des Johannesprologs zum Corpus des Evangeliums und zu 1 Joh* (Münster: Aschendorff, 1988), 148.

[77] T.F. Glasson, "John the Baptist in the Fourth Gospel," *ExpTim* 67 (1956): 245-46.

[78] Cornelis Bennema, "The Character of John in the Fourth Gospel," *JETS* 52 (2009): 271-84.

Five major observations can be adduced from John 1:19-34, as well as from 3:23-30, 5:33-36, and 10:40-42. First, the formal analysis demonstrates a marked interest in the witness theme in three respects. The *hina* clause of John 1:7 indicates the sole purpose of John's commission, that is, to bear witness to the light.[79]

οὗτος ἦλθεν εἰς μαρτυρίαν ἵνα μαρτυρήσῃ περὶ τοῦ φωτός, ἵνα πάντες πιστεύσωσιν δι' αὐτοῦ. (John 1:7, NA[28])

He came as a witness to testify to the light, so that all might believe through him. (John 1:7, NRSV)

In addition, the present pericope is structurally delimited with an *inclusio*, which is marked by the testimony of John the Baptist ("Καὶ αὕτη ἐστὶν ἡ μαρτυρία τοῦ Ἰωάννου": v. 19a; "κἀγὼ ἑώρακα καὶ μεμαρτύρηκα": v. 34a), and which also accounts for the first two days or the inauguration of John the Baptist's ministry.

Table 4 The Witness Function of John the Baptist in John 1[80]

> The indirect witness of John concerning Jesus (1:19-28)
>
> The direct witness of John concerning Jesus (1:29-34)

Finally, this section is replete with the recurrent keyword "μαρτυρία" and a conceptually related term "ὁμολογέω" (vv. 19, 20, 32, 34). Although some exegetes identify John the Baptist with Elijah in the present text, John's solemn denial militates against such a view. The reason for rejecting the association of the Baptist with Elijah, which is clearly indicated in the Synoptics, seems to be due to the evangelist's intention to limit the role of the Baptist specifically and exclusively to that of a witness (esp. 1:7, 15).[81] Concurring with this judgment, Wengst comment on this verse as following: "The intention related to this text is probably to define him entirely and exclusively as the role of the witness."[82]

---

[79] Klaus Wengst, *Das Johannesevangelium* (Stuttgart: Kohlhammer, 2000), 1:62; Ulrich B. Müller, *Johannes der Täufer: Jüdischer Prophet und Wegbereiter Jesu* (Leipzig: Evangelische Verlagsanstalt, 2002), 168-69; Hartwig Thyen, *Das Johannesevangelium* (Tübingen: Mohr Siebeck, 2005), 76. For a study that sees John the Baptist as Jesus' betrothal witness, see Mary L. Coloe, "Witness and Friend: Symbolism Associated with John the Baptist," in *Imagery in the Gospel of John: Terms, Forms, Themes, and Theology of Johannine Figurative Language*, ed. Jörg Frey, Jan G. van der Watt, and Ruben Zimmermann (Tübingen: Mohr Siebeck, 2006), 326-30.

[80] This structural analysis is indebted to Thyen, *Das Johannesevangelium*, 111-28, and Wengst, *Das Johannesevangelium*, 1:86-93.

[81] Morna D. Hooker, "John the Baptist and the Johannine Prologue," *NTS* 16 (1969-1970): 358.

[82] Wengst, *Das Johannesevangelium*, 1:88. "As in the rest of the Gospel, John here [in the Johannine prologue] functions primarily or solely as a witness to Jesus—a theme in the Fourth Gospel that extends far beyond whatever significance the author attaches to

John's explicit self-identification, "the voice crying in the wilderness," in John 1:23b is virtually a verbatim quotation from Isaiah 40:3:[83]

ἐγὼ φωνὴ βοῶντος ἐν τῇ ἐρήμῳ· εὐθύνατε τὴν ὁδὸν κυρίου. (John 1:23b, NA[28])

φωνὴ βοῶντος ἐν τῇ ἐρήμῳ Ἑτοιμάσατε τὴν ὁδὸν κυρίου. (Isa 40:3a, LXX)

קוֹל קוֹרֵא בַּמִּדְבָּר פַּנּוּ דֶּרֶךְ יְהוָה (Isa 40:3a, BHS[5])

However, an interesting shift is observed in the Greek translation of the Hebrew predicate for the voice. The semantic force of the Hebrew participle (קוֹרֵא, "proclaiming") carries a strong prophetic overtone while its Greek counterpart (βοῶντος, "crying out") does not bear such a connotation.[84] This use of the identical verb probably points to the Johannine recourse to the Greek text of the Old Testament. Menken convincingly points out two reasons which show the dependence of John on the Septuagint rather than on the Hebrew text.[85] First, the verb of the adjectival participle is βοάω (to cry out), a Johannine *hapax legomenon*, which Menken construes to be an indication of John's dependence on the Septuagint. Second, the Hebrew verb, פַּנּוּ (the piel form of פָּנָה) means "to make clear" not "make straight" as described in the Johannine and the Greek Isiaian texts (εὐθύνατε and ἑτοιμάσατε).[86] Furthermore, the use of Isaiah 40:3 in John reveals a degree of affinity with the Qumran community (perhaps indirectly) as it is quite frequently attested in the literary collection of the sect. Accordingly, a number of scholars postulate that the very text defined the identity of the community.[87]

---

its particular application to the Baptist." Craig S. Keener, *The Gospel of John: A Commentary* (Peabody: Hendrickson, 2003), 1:391.

[83] The mode of John's witness is via "crying out" (κέκραγεν). Although formally it is in the perfect tense, the sense is in the present. *BDF*, 176 (§ 341); Wengst, *Das Johannesevangelium*, 1:76.

[84] *BDAG* (p. 180) renders the meaning of βοάωας to "use one's voice at high volume, *call, shout, cry out*" or to "roar." The *qal* participle of קרא means to "call someone, shout, proclaim, announce." Especially, the latter connotation seems to be in mind. Louis Jonker, "קרא," *NIDOTTE*, 3:972; *HALOT*, 2:1129.

[85] M.J.J. Menken, "'I Am the Voice of One Crying in the Wilderness...' (John 1:23)," in *Old Testament Quotations in the Fourth Gospel: Studies in Textual Form* (Kampen: Kok, 1996), 22-25.

[86] *BDAG* (p. 406) renders εὐθύνωτο mean "to straighten, make straight." ἑτοιμάζω means to "prepare" (*BDAG*, 400; *Liddell and Scott*, 703).

[87] George J. Brooke, "Isaiah 40:3 and the Wilderness Community," in *New Qumran Texts and Studies: Proceedings of the First Meeting of the International Organization for Qumran Studies, Paris 1992*, ed. George J. Brooke and Florentino García Martínez, (Leiden: Brill, 1994), 117-32; James H. Charlesworth, "Intertextuality: Isaiah 40:3 and the Serek ha-Yahad," in *Quest for Context and Meaning: Studies in Biblical Intertextuality in Honor of James A. Sander*, ed. Craig A. Evans and Shmaryah Talmon (Leiden: Brill, 1997), 197-224.

Divine Provenance

Second, the divine provenance of the Baptist is recognized in that he is sent from God (1:6).[88]

> There was a man *sent from God*, whose name was John. (John 1:6, NRSV)
>
> But *he who sent me* to baptize with water said to me (John 1:33b, NRSV)

This divine commission also evokes the calling of the Old Testament prophets, and is matched only by the missionary Christology (3:17, 34; 5:38) and that of the paraclete (14:26; 15:26) in John's Gospel:

> Verse six speaks of the Baptist as an envoy from God as the prophets of the Old Testament were sent by God.[89]

However, this divine origin is not stated for self-interest or self-promotion, but rather functions to verify the legitimacy of his testimony. It is God who validates the witness of John (and his eyewitness testimony of the accompanying of the Holy Spirit on Jesus):[90]

> [32] And John testified, "I saw the Spirit descending from heaven like a dove, and it remained on him. [33] I myself did not know him, but the one who sent me to baptize with water said to me, 'He on whom you see the Spirit descend and remain is the one who baptizes with the Holy Spirit.'" (John 1:32-33, NRSV)

On v. 33, Schnackenburg comments that "God himself is behind John's testimony in two ways: he authorizes his office as witness, and he guarantees the content of his testimony."[91]

Analogy with and Comparison to Jesus

Third, John the Baptist provides a point of comparison with Jesus in this discourse (Jn 1:19-34). Before making this point, an objection must be raised, as a point of clarification, against some exegetes who postulate an interpolation of a later historical tension between the Johannine community and the Baptist circle into the text.[92] This reconstruction, however, seems to be susceptible to a mirror

---

[88] A great number of Johannine exegetes posit that vv. 6 and 15 are inserted into an original early Christian hymn. For a lengthy discussion on source criticism of the John the Baptist discourse in the prologue, see Thyen, *Das Johannesevangelium*, 76-79.

[89] Christian Dietzfelbinger, *Das Evangelium nach Johannes* (Zürich: Theologischer, 2001), 1:27; Similarly, Müller, *Johannes der Täufer*, 164.

[90] Müller, *Johannes der Täufer*, 162; Thyen, *Das Johannesevangelium*, 75-76, 80.

[91] Rudolf Schnackenburg, *The Gospel according to St John* (New York: Crossroad, 1982), 1:304.

[92] Lichtenberger, "Täufergemeinden und frühchristliche Täuferpolemik im letzten Drittel des 1. Jahrhunderts," 36-57; Josef Ernst, *Johannes der Täufer: Interpretation, Geschichte, Wirkungsgeschichte* (Berlin: Walter de Gruyter, 1989), 210-11; Stowasser, *Johannes der Täufer im Vierten Evangelium*, 43; Wengst, *Das Johannesevangelium*, 1:61.

reading. Three reasons rule out such a construal. First, the anachronistic nature of their assessment renders fragile the high degree of certainty with which these exegetes reconstruct the specific communities of the Baptist and the evangelist.[93] Second, the extant data are insufficient to construe a coherent community related to the Baptist or to the Fourth Gospel. In this respect, Müller's judgment is helpful.

> The term "Baptist school" is to be avoided because it suggests the system of the rabbinic training house. The same applies to the designations "Baptist sect" or "Johannine sect" because these suggest a community education with high inner-coherence and strong external isolation.[94]

Finally, the textual testimonies of John's Gospel that highly regard the Baptist contradict the historical reconstruction of the tension between the Johannine community and the Baptist sect. On this point, Wink's conclusion is decisive:

> It is methodologically illegitimate . . . to reconstruct the views of John's disciples by reversing every denial and restriction placed on John in the Fourth Gospel. . . . By [this] line of reasoning, John was worshipped as Elijah, prophet, messiah, the Light and the Life of men, a wonderworker, the pre-existent Logos through whom all things were made, indeed, even as the Word made flesh! If such an advanced "John-cult" had in fact antedated the fourth Gospel, John would never have been conferred such an exalted role by the Evangelist.[95]

In addition, it must be also noted that the exponents of such a historical reconstruction depend heavily on the extra-Johannine witnesses (especially those of Acts). Certainly, Acts 19:1-7 seems to reflect the presence of nascent Christians who were under continuous influence of John the Baptist. However, it is one thing to say that the Acts passage reflects such a tension within the early Christian groups but it is an entirely different matter to say that the Fourth Gospel reflects the same historical situation as portrayed in Acts.

As we return back to the comparison between the Baptist and Jesus, although he himself is of a divine origin just as Jesus is, John substantially differs from the one to whom he bears witness. This fundamental difference is expressed in various languages: he is not the light (1:8); nor is he Christ, Elijah, or even the prophet (1:20-21; 3:28). His water baptism is distinguished from the ministry of Jesus, for the latter is accompanied with the Holy Spirit (1:33).[96] He is a friend of the bridegroom, at whose voice he takes joy:

---

[93] Knut Backhaus, *Die "Jüngerkreise" des Täufers Johannes: Eine Studie zu den religionsgeschichtlichen Ursprüngen des Christentums* (Paderborn: Schöningh, 1991), 356, 439; Daniel S. Dapaah, *The Relationship between John the Baptist and Jesus of Nazareth: A Critical Study* (Lanham: University Press of America, 2005), 133-34.

[94] Müller, *Johannes der Täufer*, 187-88.

[95] Wink, *John the Baptist*, 102. Here Wink refers to Bultmann, *Gospel of John*, 17-18.

[96] Müller, *Johannes der Täufer*, 173.

This joy is the point of the comparison, as the final clause shows: the Baptist, who wishes to be no more than the friend of the bridegroom, sees his hopes fulfilled.[97]

His existence is provisional:

> He must increase, but I must decrease. (John 3:30, NRSV)
>
> He was a burning and shining lamp, and you were willing to rejoice for a while in his light. (John 5:35, NRSV)[98]

He is a burning and shining lamp for the time being (5:35) in contrast to Jesus the true and perennial light (1:8-9). His testimony is not a prerequisite for Jesus' messianic qualifications:

> You sent messengers to John, and he testified to the truth. Not that I accept such human testimony. (John 5:34, NRSV).

He performed no sign whereas Jesus did many (10:41). His testimony of Jesus' temporal precedence harkens back to John 1:1-2 where Jesus' pre-existence is equated with that of God.[99]

Mediator

The fourth particular narrative function of John the Baptist in John 1:19-34 stands out as mediation, which is displayed in his witness ministry. Through his testimony, Jesus and the unbelieving world are brought together, and John leads the latter to the spiritually awakening light:

> The next day John again was standing with two of his disciples, and as he watched Jesus walk by, he exclaimed, "Look, here is the Lamb of God!" The two disciples heard him say this, and they followed Jesus. (John 1:35-37, NRSV)
>
> Many came to him, and they were saying, "John performed no sign, but everything that John said about this man was true." And many believed in him there. (John 10:41-42, NRSV)

This mediating function could entitle him the "first Christian" as it is a repeated pattern of the Gospel that one person leads another to the faith in Jesus (Philip with Nathanael, the Samaritan woman with the Samaritan villagers).[100]

Recapitulation of the Old Testament

Finally, the witness function of the Baptist appears to be a recapitulation of the function of the Hebrew Scripture and Old Testament characters as perceived by the fourth evangelist.

---

[97] Schnackenburg, *The Gospel according to St John*, 1:416-17.
[98] Müller, *Johannes der Täufer*, 177.
[99] Edwin Hoskyns, *The Fourth Gospel* (London: Faber, 1947), 151; Keener, *The Gospel of John*, 1:419.
[100] Stowasser, *Johannes der Täufer im Vierten Evangelium*, 53; Müller, *Johannes der Täufer*, 162-63.

> You search the scriptures because you think that in them you have eternal life; and it is they that testify on my behalf. (John 5:39, NRSV)

Just as the Scripture and Old Testament protagonists point to the messianic nature of Jesus, the content of John's witness ministry reveals Jesus as the light and illuminates his Christological qualifications, one of which is pre-existence (1:7-15). This analysis of John's narrative function locates him within the rank of the Old Testament heroic figures notwithstanding his chronological place in the New Testament era. On this point, Brodie's assessment is worth mentioning.

> John appears to be . . . the embodiment of the OT. . . . It is as though, when the incarnation finally arrived, full of covenant love, the OT stood up and cheered.[101]

For the same reason, Köstenberger finds the narrative function of John in line with that of the Old Testament or the Jewish protagonist figures:

> The Baptist serves as the prototypical OT prophetic witness to Jesus and his coming, which makes his testimony an integral part of the salvation history canvassed by the evangelist.[102]

Conclusion

If the observations stated above stand, it is quite plausible that the fourth evangelist did not fully take advantage of the Jewish eschatological expectations of Elijah *redivivus*, partly because they were of only marginal influence in view of the wide spectrum of Jewish messianic hopes, for instance, in comparison with the Davidic or Mosaic messianic hopes.[103] More importantly, however, it is probably because the Jewish views of Elijah *redivivus* do not dovetail with the evangelist's literary schema he reserved for the Scripture and the Old Testament heroic characters, that is, the role of messianic witnesses. Margaret Davies concurs on this judgment:

> The First Gospel offers an apologetic explanation of why Jesus was baptized by John. The Fourth Gospel avoids the difficulty by backgrounding baptism and foregrounding John's role as witness to Jesus. . . . Indeed, his baptismal ministry serves the sole purpose of revealing Jesus to Israel, making explicit what the Synoptics imply. Since he is given this crucial but limited function, he is not identified with Elijah.[104]

---

[101] Thomas L. Brodie, *The Gospel according to John: A Literary and Theological Commentary* (New York: OUP, 1993), 143.

[102] Andreas Köstenberger, *John* (Grand Rapids: Baker, 2004), 45.

[103] In contrast, Gese positively evaluates the connection of the two Testaments in terms of Elijah. "The New Testament stands in comparison with the picture of Elijah which is developed in the Old Testament through Sir 48. The profound truth and important meaning of his picture impressively testify the unity between the Old and New Testaments in this case." Gese, "Zur Bedeutung Elias für die biblische Theologie," 150.

[104] Margaret Davies, *Rhetoric and Reference in the Fourth Gospel* (Sheffield: JSOT, 1992), 316. Contrary to Blomberg's judgment, it seems fairly obvious in the subsequent context that the inquirers were concerned with the association of the Baptist with

In other words, it is the Synoptic Gospels that picked up a relatively marginal current on the eschatological hopes at the time, and re-read and redefined the eschatological texts of Elijah into Christian messianism (that is to assume that there were such early rabbinic beliefs from the statements of Mark 9:11 *par*).

Concerning the inquiry on the narrative role of Elijah in John, the answer must be given in the negative since the Johannine protagonists that would most likely meet the expectations of Elijah *redivivus*, such as Jesus and John the Baptist, are not cast as such. On the contrary, John the Baptist, who is consistently portrayed as Elijah *redivivus* in the Synoptics, is characterized exclusively as a messianic witness instead throughout the Fourth Gospel, so that he is placed almost in the equal standing as that of the Old Testament protagonist characters. He does not baptize Jesus but only witnesses the Spirit descending as a dove and remaining on Jesus. He does not even compare himself with Jesus ("the one who is stronger than I," Mark 1:7 *par*) but only acknowledges the temporal priority of Christ (John 1:15).[105] These observations enable us to conclude that the fourth evangelist Christianized the Baptist in his own way to suit his Christological emphasis (just as the Synoptics Christianized the Elijah *redivivus* traditions to their literary end), and stressed the witness function of the Baptist just as he brought forth the same function performed by the Scripture and the Old Testament heroic figures. This characterization of John as messianic witness is quite impressive since the fourth evangelist did not take advantage of the eschatological prophet traditions concerning Elijah (i.e., Malachi and Sirach) that were readily available, as much to John as to the Synoptic evangelists. Although it is to some degree an argument from silence that the evangelist did not opt for such traditions, it still speaks loudly of his tenacious penchant to describe John the Baptist solely as a messianic witness, and to neglect the role of Elijah expected at the *eschaton* throughout his Gospel.

---

the prophet, especially of his authority, not of the prophet's physical re-appearance. Cf. "But none of these texts (the synoptic accounts of John as Elijah) implies that John was the literal Elijah returned from heaven, which may be precisely what John is denying in the Fourth Gospel." Craig L. Blomberg, *The Historical Reliability of John's Gospel: Issues and Commentary* (Downers Grove: InterVarsity, 2001), 76.

[105] The Christological temporal priority, which is a typical Johannine characteristic, is equally applied to John the Baptist just as it is to Abraham. Michael Labahn, "Jesus und die Autorität der Schrift im Johannesevangelium: Überlegungen zu einem spannungsreichen Verhältnis," in *Israel und seine Heilstraditionen im Johannes-evangelium: Festgabe für Johannes Beutler SJ zum 70. Geburtstag*, ed. Michael Labahn, Klaus Scholtissek, and Angelika Strotmann (Paderborn: Schöningh, 2004), 188-98.

CHAPTER 4

David

Introduction

"A man after God's own heart," David, is one of the most favorite Biblical characters cherished by both Jews and Christians around the world. Rooted in the Old Testament, his popularity continued to play out a significant role in intertestamental Judaism and in the New Testament. His role as a messianic prefiguration, in particular, has drawn a great deal of attention in biblical scholarship, and recently even in the field of Johannine studies. It is this question that the present chapter will seek to address. That is, we will explore whether the fourth evangelist presents David as a messianic prefiguration. In order to gain a proper understanding on that question, this chapter will begin with an inquiry on the perceptions of David in the Old Testament and in early Judaism with special attention to the messianic expectations. Then, the latter part of this chapter will be devoted to the question set forth in the beginning, namely, the messianic prefigurative role of David in John.

David in the Old Testament and the Second Temple Period

The Old Testament writings and subsequent Jewish traditions portray David the son of Jesse from a variety of angles.[1] These various perceptions can be classi-

---

[1] For convenient surveys on the images of David in the Old Testament and in early Judaism, see Tae-Soo Im, *Das Davidbild in den Chronikbüchern: David als Idealbild des theokratischen Messianismus für den Chronisten* (Frankfurt: Peter Lang, 1985); Robert P. Gordon, "David," *NIDOTTE*, 4:505-12; Egbert Ballhorn, "'Um deines Knechtes David willen' (Ps 132:10): Die Gestalt Davids im Psalter," *BN* 76 (1995): 16-31; Craig A. Evans, "David in the Dead Sea Scrolls," in *The Scrolls and the Scriptures: Qumran Fifty Years After*, ed. Stanley E. Porter and Craig A. Evans (Sheffield: Sheffield, 1997), 183-97; Louis H. Feldman, "David," in *Josephus's Interpretation of the Bible* (Berkeley: University of California Press, 1998), 537-69; Jacques Bernard, "David et le péché original chez les Tannaïm," in *Figures de David à travers la Bible: XVIIe congrès de l'ACFEB (Lille, 1er-5 septembre 1997)*, ed. Louis Derousseaux and Jacques Vermeylen (Paris: Cerf, 1999), 277-314; Claude Coulot, "David à Qumrân," in *Figures de David à travers la Bible: XVIIe congrès de l'ACFEB (Lille, 1er-5 septembre 1997)*, ed. Louis Derousseaux and Jacques Vermeylen (Paris: Cerf, 1999), 315-44; Walter Dietrich, "David I: Biblisch 1, Altes Testament," *RGG*, 2:593-96; Martin Jacobs, "David III: Judentum 1, Antike," *RGG*, 2:598-99; Peter Höffken, "Zur Rolle der Davidsverheissung bei Josephus Flavius," *ZAW* 114 (2002):

fied under three headings: an ideal ruler, an exemplary Jew, and a messianic prefiguration.

Ideal Ruler

The earlier Jewish traditions, that is, historical narratives (i.e., the books of Chronicles and Samuel), generally present him in the first category rather than in the image of a warrior.[2] Similarly, the early rabbinic literature does not emphasize his earlier career as a warrior. When his military victories are mentioned, they function to highlight the divine intervention for the weak and righteous over the strong and impious.[3] David is first and foremost the king of Israel. Therefore, it is natural to understand him in this category.

However, related to his kingship in part, another portrayal of this heroic Jewish figure stems from some early Jewish traditions that identify him as the author of the book of Psalms. Although only little more than half of the Psalms are explicitly attributed to David as the writer, some Jewish interpretive traditions (i.e., the Qumran and later rabbinic literature) embrace the Davidic authorship of the entire corpus of the Psalter (i.e., *b. Pesah.* 117a; *m. Tehar.* 1:6, 24:3; *b. Ber.* 3a).[4] For example, the Babylonian Talmud speaks of him as the general editor of the Psalms (*b. Bat.* 14b-15a).

A third view, which could be also somewhat related to this current of thought, is the understanding of David as a prophet. Acts 2:30 bears witness to the recognition of him as such:

577-93; Kenneth Pomykala, "Images of David in Early Judaism," in *Ancient Versions and Traditions*, vol. 1 of *Of Scribes and Sages: Early Jewish Interpretation and Transmission of Scripture*, ed. Craig A. Evans (London: T & T Clark, 2004), 33-46; Rolf Rendtorff, *Canonical Hebrew Bible: A Theology of the Old Testament* (Leiden: Deo, 2005), 560-74; Yuzuru Miura, *David in Luke-Acts: His Portrayal in the Light of Early Judaism* (Tübingen: Mohr Siebeck, 2007), 14-138; Pancratius C. Beentjes, "Portrayals of David in Deuterocanonical and Cognate Literature," in *Biblical Figures in Deuterocanonical and Cognate Literature*, ed. Hermann Lichtenberger and Ulrike Mittmann-Richert (Berlin: Walter de Gruyter, 2009), 165-82; Stefan C. Reif, "The Figure of David in Early Jewish Prayer," in *Biblical Figures in Deuterocanonical and Cognate Literature*, ed. Hermann Lichtenberger and Ulrike Mittmann-Richert (Berlin: Walter de Gruyter, 2009), 509-46; A. Graeme Auld and Erik Eynikel, eds., *For and against David: Story and History in the Books of Samuel* (Leuven: Peeters, 2010); Anthony Petterson, "The Shape of the Davidic Hope across the Book of the Twelve," *JSOT* 35 (2010): 225-46.

[2] Lawrence A. Sinclair, "David I: Altes Testament," *TRE* 8:382-83.

[3] Jouette M. Bassler, "A Man for All Seasons: David in Rabbinic and New Testament Literature," *Int* 40 (1986): 157.

[4] Brevard S. Childs, "Psalm Titles and Midrashic Exegesis," *JSS* 16 (1971): 137-50; George J. Brooke, "The Psalms in Early Jewish Literature in the Light of the Dead Sea Scrolls," in *The Psalms in the New Testament*, ed. Steve Moyise and Maarten J.J. Menken (London: T & T Clark, 2004), 9-10.

> [30] Since he [David] was a prophet, he knew that God had sworn with an oath to him that he would put one of his descendants on his throne. [31] Foreseeing this, David spoke of the resurrection of the Messiah, saying,
> "He was not abandoned to Hades,
> nor did his flesh experience corruption." (Acts 2:30-31, NRSV)

V. 31 of this text seems to be a clear allusion to Psalm 16:10: "For you do not give me up to Sheol, or let your faithful one see the Pit."[5] Interestingly, among various strands of the intertestamental Jewish writings, only some of the Qumran writings demonstrate considerations analogous to the Acts passage in that David is seen as a spirit-inspired prophet.[6] The Psalm scrolls retrieved from Qumran Cave 11 contain some non-canonical psalms in addition to thirty-nine canonical psalms. They date to A.D. 30-50. This collection of psalms is unique because it contains a prose in its midst that is attributed to David (hence, it is called "David's composition").[7]

> And David, the son of Jesse, was wise, and a light like the light of the sun, and literate, and discerning and perfect in all his ways before God and men. And the Lord gave him a discerning spirit. And he wrote 3,600 psalms; and songs to sing before the altar over the whole-burnt perpetual offering every day, for all the days of the year, 364; and for the offering of the Sabbaths, 52 songs; and for the offering of the New Moons and for all the Solemn Assemblies and for the Days of Atonement, 30 songs. And all the songs that he composed were 446, and songs for making music over the stricken, 4. And the total was 4,050. All these he composed through prophecy which was given him from before the Most High. (11QPs^{a}DavComp Col. xxvii, 2-11)[8]

It has been debated whether or not the origin of this section belongs to the Qumran community. Scholars are increasingly beginning to recognize the unique vocabularies and concepts that are characteristics of Qumran's Psalm scrolls. It is not only this section, but the entire collection of 11Q is now generally accepted as having originated from within and maintained by the Qumran

---

[5] A colleague, Lars Kierspel, deserves credit for directing me to this scriptural reference.

[6] For the Qumran influence on the Acts passage, see Joseph A. Fitzmyer, "David, 'Being Therefore a Prophet' (Acts 2:30)," *CBQ* 34 (1972): 332-39; Craig A. Evans, "David in the Dead Sea Scrolls," in *The Scrolls and the Scriptures: Qumran Fifty Years After*, ed. Stanley E. Porter and Craig A. Evans (Sheffield: Sheffield, 1997), 183-97. For the Psalter influence, see James L. Kugel, "David the Prophet," in *Poetry and Prophecy: The Beginnings of a Literary Tradition* (Ithaca: Cornell University Press, 1990), 45-55. For the influence of 1 Sam 7:12-13, see John B. Polhill, *Acts*, NAC, vol. 26 (Nashville: Broadman, 1992), 114.

[7] For helpful introductions to "David's Composition," see William Hugh Browlee, "Significance of David's Compositions," *RevQ* 5 (1966): 569-74; James C. Vander-Kam, "Studies on 'David's Compositions' (11QPs[a] 27:2-11)," *ErIsr* 26 (1999): 212-20.

[8] James A. Sanders, ed., *The Psalms Scroll of Qumran Cave 11 (11QPs^a)*, DJD 4 (Oxford: Clarendon, 1965), 137. Cf. Peter W. Flint, *The Dead Sea Psalms Scrolls and the Book of Psalms* (Leiden: Brill, 1997), 79, 207-08, 224.

community.⁹

Exemplary Jew

On the other hand, Psalms and some later rabbinic documents focus on his exemplary Jewish characteristics such as his genuine repentance, prayer, and ardent study of Torah.[10] This category seems to have developed partly from the anecdotes surrounding David's affair with Bathsheba and the subsequent contrite supplications recorded in the Psalter to his credit. Although his sin and God's punishment demonstrate the nature of a just world order, his repentance and ensuing divine forgiveness epitomize an encouraging example of the genuine adherence to early Judaism (*m. Tehar.* 40:2; 51:1, 3).[11] In addition, other pseudepigraphical writings underscore his wholehearted devotion to God (Sir 47:3), his merciful character (1 Macc 2:57), and tenacious intercessory prayers (2 Esdr 7:108).[12]

Some later rabbinic traditions also reveal examples of an elevated view about the origin of David: His maternal origin traces back to Miriam. It probably was to remedy the ethnical vulnerability of his maternal lineage, for his great grand-mother Ruth was a foreigner (*b. Ber.* 7b; *b. Sotah* 11b). In addition, even the creation of the world and its well-being are dependent on him (*b. Sanh.* 98b; *b. Sotah* 49a; *m. Tehar.* 25:1).[13]

Davidic Messianic Expectations in the Old Testament

However, more pertinent to the present investigation of his narrative role with reference to Johannine Christology is the last category, that is, the later developments of messianic hopes via a Davidic figure. It is generally accepted that the Synoptic Gospels relate Jesus to David but not John's Gospel. In more congruous terms with the New Testament portrayals of David, especially those of the Synoptics, the last category of intertestamental Jewish beliefs, thus, projected

---

[9] Vered Noam, "The Origin of the List of David's Songs in 'David's Compositions,'" *DSD* 13 (2006): 134-49; Brent A. Strawn, "David as One of the 'Perfect of (the) Way': On the Provenience of David's Compositions (and 11QPs as a Whole?)," *RevQ* 24 (2010): 607-26.

[10] Thoma classifies the rabbinic traditions on David under two subheadings: the actualization of the rabbinic spirit and the exemplary expression of Jewish identity and Jewish confidence. The latter category is further divided into three sub-categories, the last of which concerns the messianic expectations. Clemens Thoma, "David II: Judentum," *TRE* 8:383-87.

[11] For the ideal characters of David, see Bassler, "A Man for All Seasons," 159-61; for his genuine repentance, see Gary N. Knoppers, "Images of David in Early Judaism: David as Repentant Sinner in Chronicles," *Bib* 76 (1995): 449-70.

[12] For David as an ideal person of offering prayer, Klaus Berger, "Die königlichen Messiastraditionen des Neuen Testaments," *NTS* 20 (1973): 1-44.

[13] Thoma, *TRE*, 8:386-87. For a survey of rabbinic literature that defends David's rightful Jewish status, see Bassler, "A Man for All Seasons," 158-59.

him in the image of a royal Messiah.¹⁴ The later prophets articulated more explicitly this salvific anticipation in relation with him.

> Afterward the Israelites shall return and seek the LORD their God, and David their king; they shall come in awe to the LORD and to his goodness in the latter days. (Hos 3:5, NRSV)

> A shoot shall come out from the stump of Jesse,
> and a branch shall grow out of his roots. (Isa 11:1, NRSV)

> But you, O Bethlehem of Ephrathah,
>   who are one of the little clans of Judah,
> from you shall come forth for me
>   one who is to rule in Israel,
> whose origin is from of old,
>   from ancient days. (Mic 5:2, NRSV)

Copious examples of references and allusions to such Davidic messianic hopes are interspersed throughout the prophetic books of the Old Testament (Isa 55:3; Jer 33:15, 21-22, 25-26; Ezek 34:23-24, 37:24-25; Hos 1:11; Amos 9:11-15; Hag 2:23).

Daniel Block, thus, argues that the provenance of these later Davidic messianic hopes can be traced back to the earlier historical narrative accounts. Four such passages in particular can be identified as the roots of the royal Davidic messianism for the later Old Testament writings according to Block: (1) Yahweh's promise that "kings would come from Abraham" (Gen 17:6, 16; 35:11); (2)

---

¹⁴ For surveys on the Davidic messianic images in the second temple period, see F. Furman Kearley, "Davidic and Messianic Expectations in the Dead Sea Scrolls," in *Last Things: Essays Presented by His Students to Dr. W.B. West, Jr., upon the Occasion of His Sixty-Fifth Birthday*, ed. Jack P. Lewis (Austin: Sweet, 1972), 74-95; Bassler, "A Man for All Seasons," 156-62; John Bowman, "David, Jesus Son of David and Son of Man," *AbrN* 27 (1989): 1-22; Cleon L. Rogers, Jr., "The Promises to David in Early Judaism," *BSac* 150 (1993): 285-302; Yehezkel Kaufmann, "The Messianic Idea: The Real and the Hidden Son-of-David," *JBQ* 22 (1994): 141-50; Kenneth Pomykala, *The Davidic Dynasty Tradition in Early Judaism: Its History and Significance for Messianism* (Atlanta: Scholars, 1995), 127-229; Rex Mason, "The Messiah in the Postexilic Old Testament Literature," in *King and Messiah in Israel and the Ancient Near East: Proceedings of the Oxford Old Testament Seminar*, ed. John Day (Sheffield: Sheffield, 1998), 338-64; Michael E. Fuller, "The Davidic Messiah in Early Jewish Literature," in *Spirit and the Mind: Essays in Informed Pentecostalism to Honor Dr. Donald N. Bowdle Presented on His 65th Birthday*, ed. Terry L. Cross and Emerson B. Powery (Lanham: University Press of America, 2000), 65-86; Ernst-Joachim Waschke, *Der Gesalbte: Studien zur alttestamentlichen Theologie* (Berlin: Walter de Gruyter, 2001), 74-99; Daniel I. Block, "My Servant David: Ancient Israel's Vision of the Messiah," in *Israel's Messiah in the Bible and the Dead Sea Scrolls*, ed. Richard S. Hess and M. Daniel Carroll R. (Grand Rapids: Baker, 2003), 36-49; John J. Collins, *The Scepter and the Star: Messianism in Light of the Dead Sea Scrolls* (Grand Rapids: Eerdmans, 2010), 52-78.

Jacob's prediction that the scepter would not depart from the tribe of Judah (Gen 49:10); (3) Balaam's oracle that a star and the scepter would rise from Jacob/Israel (Num 24:17); and (4) Moses' charge for the Israelites to put Yahweh's chosen one on the throne instead of a king (Deut 17:14-20). Based upon his construal of a continuous and organic growth of this messianic expectation from the earlier traditions, therefore, he finds more examples of later prophetic developments that evoke the idea of the Davidic Messiah (1 Sam 2:1-10; 2 Sam 5:1-3, 7:19; Pss 2:2, 6-8, 18:50-51, 89:20-21, 27-28; Isa 9:5-7, 11:1; Jer 23:5-6; Ezek 17:22, 34:23-24, 37:22-25; Dan 9:25-26; Hos 3:5; Mic 5:2-5; Zech 3:8, 6:12, 9:9-10, 12:10, 13:7-8).[15]

As impressive as the number of references appear, however, the Davidic messianic idea does not seem to be as obvious as Block argues in those texts. His assessment is problematic at least in two respects.[16] First, all the biblical passages he provides do not carry an eschatological redeemer figure in their original literary and historical contexts. What is envisaged in those texts is the restoration of the Davidic monarchy which subjugates the gentile intrusion and establish a rightful Israelite dynasty, not an eschatological, perpetual, and maybe spiritual messiah in the sense that nascent Christianity conceived.[17] Second, the Davidic expectations promised in those accounts are different from later exilic and post-exilic messianic ideas, which often exegetes of this position suggest to bolster their arguments.[18] It is not those Old Testament passages, but the Jewish traditions from much later periods that confer a messianic overtone on those narratives, so exegetes often fuse those two scriptural traditions.[19] To this point, Collins' judgment is succinct and helpful that the Davidic messianic idea is extremely sparse in the earlier phase of the Hebrew scriptural traditions:

---

[15] Block, "My Servant David," 37-39.

[16] Also, some of the passages he suggests do not carry a royal Davidic messianic overtone. J. Daniel Hays, "If He Looks like a Prophet and Talks like a Prophet, Then He Must Be . . .: A Response to Daniel I. Block," in *Israel's Messiah in the Bible and the Dead Sea Scrolls*, ed. Richard S. Hess and M. Daniel Carroll R. (Grand Rapids: Baker, 2003), 57-70. M. Daniel Carroll R., "New Lenses to Establish Messiah's Identity?: A Response to Daniel I. Block," in *Israel's Messiah in the Bible and the Dead Sea Scrolls*, ed. Richard S. Hess and M. Daniel Carroll R. (Grand Rapids: Baker, 2003), 71-81. For a more detailed treatment on messianism in the Old Testament, see Appendix 1: "Messianism/Christology in John's Gospel."

[17] J.J.M. Roberts, "The Old Testament's Contribution to Messianic Expectations," in *The Messiah: Developments in Earliest Judaism and Christianity*, ed. James H. Charlesworth (Minneapolis: Fortress, 1992), 39-43.

[18] For another example of fusing later Davidic texts with earlier Hebrew textual traditions, see Joshua W. Jipp, "Luke's Scriptural Suffering Messiah: A Search for Precedent, a Search of Identity," *CBQ* 72 (2010): 255-74.

[19] Yehezkel Kaufmann, "The Messianic Idea: The Real and the Hidden Son-of-David," *JBQ* 22 (1994): 141-50; Johannes Tromp, "The Davidic Messiah in Jewish Eschatology of the First Century BCE," in *Restoration: Old Testament, Jewish, and Christian Perspectives*, ed. James M. Scott (Leiden: Brill, 2001), 180-201.

The absence of any messianic hope, in the sense of expectation of a Davidic restoration, in the early apocalypses is striking and undermines some common assumptions about the nature of messianism. . . . But the emergence of messianism in the first century BCE does not warrant any inference about a messianic movement at an earlier time. As we have seen, the evidence suggests that messianism was virtually dormant from the early fifth to the late second century BCE.[20]

Davidic Messianic Expectations in Second Temple Judaism

1 Maccabees and Sirach. In view of the relatively elevated interest in a Davidic Messiah in the Old Testament contended by some exegetes, the paucity of references to such a figure in the intertestamental Jewish literature is surprising. This assessment should be, however, qualified by the fact that there are a number of references to Davidic metaphors in this body of literature, such as root, branch, seed, horn, or shoot of David. Yet an explicit reference to David in terms of "Messiah" is lacking. The entire body of early rabbinic literature is also hesitant to speak of Davidic messianism.[21] Bassler points to several passages from rabbinic literature for the Davidic messianic hope (*b. Sanh.* 98b; *Midr. Ps.* 5.4, 18.27; *b. Meg.* 17b).[22] However, the dating issue of the Talmudic literature poses difficulty for her comparison of the messianic passages in rabbinic literature and the New Testament. The composition of the Babylonian Talmud dates back to the 6th century and the Midrashim on Psalms to the 3rd century respectively.[23] There is

---

[20] Collins, *The Scepter and the Star*, 50-51. Tremper Longman construes that the Old Testament does not provide a clear picture of the Messiah. To him, the New Testament fulfillment of a messianic expectation came as a surprise. The Hebrew passages inferred for messianism by Old Testament scholars do not have an inkling of the messianic significance as other exegetes often propose. In his all honest assessment, the New Testament reading of the Old Testament messianic texts is *sensus plenior*. Tremper Longman, III, "The Messiah: Explorations in the Law and Writings," in *The Messiah in the Old and New Testaments*, ed. Stanley E. Porter (Grand Rapids: Eerdmans, 2007), 30-33.

[21] Thoma, *TRE*, 8:384-85. Munnich's careful study on the comparison between the Greek Old Testament and rabbinic use of the Hebrew Davidic traditions reveals that the early rabbinic traditions are generally reticent about speaking of a Davidic messianic expectation even in their use of the Hebrew messianic texts. Olivier Munnich, "Le messianisme à la lummière des livres prophétiques de la Bible grecque," in *Septuagint and Messianism*, ed. Michael A. Knibb (Leuven: Leuven University Press; Peeters, 2006), 327-55.

[22] Bassler, "A Man for All Seasons," 159.

[23] Günther Stemberger, *Introduction to the Talmud and Midrash* trans. and ed. Markus Bockmuehl (Edinburgh: T & T Clark, 1996), 322-23; Craig A. Evans, *Ancient Texts for New Testament Studies: A Guide to the Background Literature* (Peabody: Hendrickson, 2005), 228-29; Jeffrey L. Rubenstein, "Social and Institutional Settings of Rabbinic Literature," in *The Cambridge Companion to the Talmud and Rabbinic Literature*, ed. Charlotte Elisheva Fonrobert & Martin S. Jaffee (Cambridge: CUP, 2007), 9, 59; David Weiss Halivni, *The Formation of the Babylonian Talmud*, trans. Jeffrey L. Rubenstein (Oxford: OUP, 2013). For a more detailed discussion on the messianism in the Qumran library, see Appendix 1: "Messianism/Christology in John's Gospel."

no explicit mention of a Davidic Messiah in the Apocrypha, only twice in the Pseudepigrapha, and once in the Qumran library. For the first group of writings, 1 Maccabees 2:57 and Sirach 47:22 are sometimes cited to assert the presence of a Davidic messianic figure, but they do not display a clear eschatological overtone:

> David, because he was merciful, inherited the throne of the kingdom forever. (1 Macc 2:57)[24]

> But the Lord will never give up his mercy, or cause any of his works to perish; he will never blot out the descendants of his chosen one, or destroy the family line of him who loved him. So he gave a remnant to Jacob, and to David a root from his own family. (Sir 47:22)[25]

Psalms of Solomon. On the other hand, two documents in the Old Testament Pseudepigrapha make an explicit mention of David in reference to the Messiah (i.e., Psalms of Solomon and 4 Ezra). The Psalms of Solomon is particularly associated with the Davidic messianic expectations of the intertestamental period. This writing contains one of the most detailed messianic expectations that resonates with such a belief of early Christianity. R.B. Wright's introduction to this book is helpful:

> There is more substance to the ideas concerning the Messiah in the Psalms of Solomon than in any other extant Jewish writings. The *Messiah* is here identified as a son of David who will come to establish an everlasting kingdom of God. Although not a supernatural being, both he and the devout over whom he reigns are without sin, and he rules with all the ancient virtues heightened to superlatives: wisdom, justice, mercy, power. He will restore the ancient tribal divisions and with them the ancient ways of righteousness and fidelity. He will bring back the Diaspora of Israel to a purified homeland. The nations likewise will come, to pay homage to Jerusalem and her king.[26]

The Psalms of Solomon, which dates from the mid first-century A.D., explicitly mentions "Messiah" in three different junctures:

> And he will be a righteous king over them, taught by God. There will be no unrighteousness among them in his days, for all shall be holy, and their king shall be the Lord

---

[24] The original Greek text reads as following: Δαυιδ ἐν τῷ ἐλέει αὐτοῦ ἐκληρονόμησεν θρόνον βασιλείας εἰς αἰῶνας. The genitive pronoun αὐτοῦ has generated a good deal of debates. Traditionally, it has been taken as subjective, but more recent exegetes take it as an objective. The first option emphasizes his merit-accumulating behavior, whereas the latter points to the divine mercy promised to him. A grammatical consideration supports the traditional "subjective" reading. Pierre Bordreuil, "Les 'graces de David' et 1 Maccabees 2:57," *VT* 31 (1981): 73-76.

[25] Michael D. Coogan, ed., *The New Oxford Annotated Apocrypha* (Oxford: OUP, 2010), 163, 205. For some kind of Davidic messianism expressed in Sirach 47:22, see Jeremy Corley, "Seeds of Messianism in Hebrew Ben Sira and Greek Sirach," in *Septuagint and Messianism: Colloquium Biblicum Lovaniense LIII, July 27-29, 2004*, ed. Michael A. Knibb (Leuven: Leuven University Press; Peeters, 2006), 303-06.

[26] R.B. Wright, "Psalms of Solomon," in *OTP*, 2:643.

Messiah. (Pss. Sol. 17:32)

> May God cleanse Israel for the day of mercy in blessing, for the appointed day when his Messiah will reign. . . . under the rod of discipline of the Lord Messiah, in the fear of his God, in wisdom of spirit, and of righteousness and of strength. (Pss. Sol. 18:5, 7)[27]

Michael Fuller draws four common characteristics from these texts with regards to messianism: (1) He will be a son of David; (2) the coming of the Messiah will usher the commencement of Israel's restoration; (3) the primary task of the Messiah is the establishment and maintenance of righteousness and holiness; and (4) this Messiah is utterly reliant on God.[28] Yet his evaluation neglects an important aspect common in the narrative contexts surrounding these texts, which is also a recurrent theme of the intertestamental messianism, that is, the militant subjugation of the unrighteousness through this messianic figure.[29]

4 Ezra. Dated to the late first century A.D. for the actual writing of the extant manuscript, Fourth Ezra also mentions an eschatological redeemer, a Davidic successor in the so-called Eagle Vision.[30]

> And as for the lion that you saw rousing up out of the forest and roaring and speaking to the eagle and reproving him for his unrighteousness, and as for all his words that you have heard. This is the Messiah whom the Most High has kept until the end of days, who will arise from the posterity of David, and will come and speak to them; he will denounce them for their ungodliness and for their wickedness, and will cast up before then their contemptuous dealings. For first he will set them before his judgment seat, and when he has reproved them, then he will destroy them. But he will deliver in mercy the remnant of my people, those who have been saved throughout my borders, and he will make them joyful until the end comes, the day of judgment, of which I spoke to you at the beginning. (4 Ezra 12:31-34)[31]

Over against the destruction of the Jerusalem temple (either of the sixth century B.C. or of the first century A.D.), Fourth Ezra envisages the coming of Messiah with a (angelic) cohort to judge the nations and to commence the gathering of the tribes of Israel.[32] In this respect, the general tenor of this text overall seems to

---

[27] Wright, "Psalms of Solomon," 668-69.

[28] Fuller, "The Davidic Messiah in Early Jewish Literature," 71-73; also Wright, "Psalms of Solomon," 643-46; Pomykala, *The Davidic Dynasty Tradition in Early Judaism*, 159-70.

[29] K. Atkinson connects this feature with Qumranic messianic hopes. Kenneth Atkinson, "On the Herodian Origin of Militant Davidic Messianism at Qumran: New Light from Psalm of Solomon 17," *JBL* 118 (1999): 435-60.

[30] Bruce M. Metzger, "The Fourth Book of Ezra," in *OTP*, 1:520.

[31] *OTP*, 1:550.

[32] Fuller, "The Davidic Messiah in Early Jewish Literature," 83-85; Metzger, "The Fourth Book of Ezra," 520-22; Pomykala, *The Davidic Dynasty Tradition in Early Judaism*, 216-29. Stone strongly argues that the main thrust of the text is the military overthrowing of the gentile empire. Michael E. Stone, "The Concept of the Messiah in

David

correspond to that of the Psalm of Solomon messianic texts.

4Q252. A portion of the Qumran commentary on Genesis (4Q252), which is considered as a loose compilation of "rewritten bible" and a commentary on Genesis, explicitly interprets the divine oracle in Genesis 49:10 in terms of a Davidic Messiah, which is absent in the original Genesis.[33]

> The scepter shall [no]t depart from the tribe of Judah. While Israel has the dominion, there [will not] be cut off someone who sits on the throne of David. For "the staff" is the covenant of royalty, [and the thou]sands of Israel are "the standards" . . . . Until the messiah of righteousness comes, the branch of David. For to him and to his descendants has been given the covenant of the kingship of his people for everlasting generations, which he observed [. . .] the Law with the men of the Community, for [. . .] it is the assembly of the men of [. . .] He gives. (4Q252 5.1-7)[34]

However, the compiled nature of the document makes it difficult to designate the main theme of the entire commentary. In addition, the meticulous concern for the chronicles of Jewish historical events pervades the greater portion of the document, so that it is probably unwarranted to ascribe a messianic interest to the entire document (only one out of the entire six fragments expresses an eschatological concern).

On the other hand, an echo of or allusions to a Davidic messiah appears elsewhere in three different Qumran documents (e.g., in terms of "the branch of David" or "the Prince of the Congregation": 4QFlor; 4QpIsa^a; 4Q285).[35] Thus, the Davidic messianic idea was probably indigenous in the community and seems to reflect that strand of thought. Brooke and Fröhlich construe that this

---

IV Ezra," in *Religions in Antiquity: Essays in Memory of Erwin Ramsdell Goodenough*, ed. Jacob Neusner, SHR 14 (Leiden: Brill, 1968), 295-312; idem, *Fourth Ezra: A Commentary on the Book of Fourth Ezra* (Minneapolis: Fortress, 1990), 368-71.

[33] Markus Bockmuehl, "The Dead Sea Scrolls and Ancient Commentary," in *Text, Thought, and Practice in Qumran and Early Christianity*, ed. Daniel R. Schwartz & Ruth A. Clements (Leiden: Brill, 2009) 3-29.

[34] *DSS*, 1:505. The Princeton version reads as following: "A ruler shall [not] depart from the tribe of Judah when there is dominion for Israel; [there will not] be cut off one sitting (on) the throne for David. For 'staff' is the covenant of the kingdom; [and the thous]ands of Israel are 'the standards' until the righteous Messiah comes, the Branch of everlasting generations, who kept [. . .] the Torah with the men of the Community, for [. . .] it is the congregation of the men of [. . .] he gave." Joseph L. Trafton, "Commentary on Genesis A (4Q252=4QcommGenA=4QPBless)," in *Pesharim, Other Commentaries, and Related Documents*, vol. 6B of *The Dead Sea Scrolls: Hebrew, Aramaic, and Greek Texts with English Translations*, ed. James H. Charlesworth (Tübingen: Mohr Siebeck, 2002), 217.

[35] Trafton, "Commentary on Genesis," 206; Pomykala, *The Davidic Dynasty Tradition in Early Judaism*, 171-216; Fuller, "The Davidic Messiah in Early Jewish Literature," 73-83; Lawrence H. Schiffman, "Messianic Figures and Ideas in the Qumran Scrolls," in *Qumran and Jerusalem: Studies in the Dead Sea Scrolls and the History of Judaism* (Grand Rapids: Eerdmans, 2010), 280-83.

section contains a sectarian messianism to some extent, but Bernstein counters their views. Probably Bernstein's estimation is correct that it is to read too much into the text to find an excessive concern for an exclusively community-oriented messianism here.[36] The dearth of references to the Davidic messianic idea in the Qumran library does not allow a reconstruction of tenacious and widespread Davidic messianism. Assessments of two Qumran experts are helpful on this issue. They are hesitant to accept a full-blown eschatological messianism from these texts.

> Qumran usage of the title *Nāśî* [a tribal chief or leader] resists simplification to the model of "Davidic Messianism." . . . In comparison, Qumran description of the *Nāśî* is, at best, quasi- or proto-messianic.[37]

> Those texts that espouse the Davidic messiah tend toward the restorative. [They] do not envisage a Davidic messiah. . . . since there is no Davidic allegiance.[38]

Summary
Three important elements common to these texts are often overlooked in scholarly discussions that contain a direct bearing on the examination of the relation between the Davidic Messiah and the Johannine Christology: first, the messianic activities in these texts involve militant conquest of the unrighteous, who are usually gentiles:

> The prime features are still military, the overthrowing of the great Roman Empire and the description of this activity in legal terms . . . .[39]

Second, the purpose of such messianic activities was in large measure to restore the nation of Israel. Finally, the presence of a Davidic Messiah is an ancillary aspect of the unfolding of the divine redemptive program. John Barton's assessment of this aspect is particularly noteworthy:

---

[36] Cf. George J. Brooke, "The Thematic Content of 4Q252," *JQR* 85 (1994): 33-59; Ida Fröhlich, "The Biblical Narratives in Qumran Exegetical Works (4Q252; 4Q180; The Damascus Document)," in *Qumranstudien: Vorträge und Beiträge der Teilnehmer des Qumranseminars auf dem internationalen Treffen der Society of Biblical Literature, Münster, 25.-26. Juli 1993*, ed. Heinz-Josef Fabry, Armin Lange, and Hermann Lichtenberger (Göttingen: Vandenhoeck & Ruprecht, 1996), 111-24; Moshe J. Bernstein, "4Q252: Method and Context, Genre and Sources," *JQR* 85 (1994): 61-79. For a recent and brief overview of the Qumranic messianic interpretation of some Psalm passages, see Marvin E. Tate, "David as Messianic King," in *Psalms 1-50*, Peter C. Craigie (Nashville: Thomas Nelson, 2004), 460-61.

[37] C.D. Elledge, "The Prince of the Congregation: Qumran 'Messianism' in the Context of *Milḥāmâ*," in *Qumran Studies: New Approaches, New Questions*, ed. Michael Thomas Davis and Brent A. Strawn (Grand Rapids: Eerdmans, 2007), 206. The parenthetical explanation is added.

[38] Schiffman, "Messianic Figures and Ideas in the Qumran Scrolls," 284-85.

[39] Michael E. Stone, *Features of the Eschatology of IV Ezra* (Atlanta: Scholars, 1989), 118.

Belief in the Messiah rests ultimately on the belief that God can be relied on to have the right people in place at the right time to save and deliver Israel, whether through the specific vehicle of a descendant of David or in some other way.[40]

The last point is evidenced in the dearth of references to a Davidic Messiah in the entire body of the intertestamental Jewish literature. Within the vast scope of the entire Jewish intertestamental writings, only three documents (*Pss. Sol.*, 4Q252 from Qumran, and 4 Ezra) make an explicit mention of the Messiah in the personage of David. Thus, the caveat expressed by K. Pomykala is appropriate for the present study:

> The image of David as progenitor of the messiah is attested in only three provenances ... one of the least frequently attested images of David in early Jewish texts ... its status as a relatively minor image of David in early Jewish texts should caution us about seeing a latent allusion to messianism in every reference to David.[41]

A Davidic messianic expectation may have been at work in second temple Judaism, but only a due emphasis needs to be recognized. Furthermore, the late dating of those Davidic messianic texts should also be taken into account. Kaufmann may well be right in his judgment that the Davidic messianic hope is a later development in the aftermath of the disappointing failure of the Hasmonean dynasty, which usurped the Jewish expectations of the Davidic royal lineage.[42]

David in the Synoptic Gospels

In slight contrast to the meager projection of David as a messianic precursor in the early Jewish writings, he frequently emerges in conjunction with Jesus the Messiah in the New Testament, most conspicuously in the Synoptic Gospels, and a great deal of scholarly attention has been drawn to this issue.[43] Both Matthew

---

[40] John Barton, "The Messiah in Old Testament Theology," in *King and Messiah in Israel and the Ancient Near East: Proceedings of the Oxford Old Testament Seminar*, ed. John Day (Sheffield: Sheffield, 1998), 377.

[41] Kenneth Pomykala, "Images of David in Early Judaism," in *Ancient Versions and Traditions*, vol. 1 of *Of Scribes and Sages: Early Jewish Interpretation and Transmission of Scripture*, ed. Craig A. Evans (London: T & T Clark, 2004), 34.

[42] Kaufmann, "The Messianic Idea," 141-50. Similarly, Tromp, "The Davidic Messiah in Jewish Eschatology of the First Century BCE," 180-201.

[43] Non-Gospel occurrences of a Davidic messianic picture include Acts 13:22-23, Rom 1:3-4, and Rev 5:5, 22:16. For studies on the Davidic messianic prefigure in the New Testament, see Eduard Schweizer, "Concept of the Davidic 'Son of God' in Acts and Its Old Testament Background," in *Studies in Luke-Acts: Essays Presented in Honor of Paul Schubert*, ed. Leander E. Keck and J. Louis Martyn (Nashville: Abingdon, 1966), 186-93; F.F. Bruce, "The Davidic Messiah in Luke-Acts," in *Biblical and Near Eastern Studies: Essays in Honor of William Sanford LaSor*, ed. Gary A. Tuttle (Grand Rapids: Eerdmans, 1978), 7-17; Bruce D. Chilton, "Jesus Ben David: Reflections on the Davidssohnfrage," *JSNT* 14 (1982): 88-112; Bassler, "A Man for All Seasons," 163-69; Marinus de Jonge, "Jesus, Son of David and Son of God," in *Intertextuality in Biblical Writings: Essays in Honour of Bas van Iersel*, ed. Sipke Draisma (Kampen:

and Luke trace the genealogy of Jesus through David (Matt 1:6; Luke 3:31), which especially signifies the royal messianic qualification of Jesus.[44] This connection becomes more conspicuously visible in the expression "son of David" in referring to Jesus.[45] Jack D. Kingsbury obscured this point to some extent but recently Novakovic and Paffenroth put this conventional thesis to the forefront, especially, the royal messianic overtone of the title in various healing contexts.[46] Three different groups of contexts could be recognized where that title carries messianic nuances: the healing accounts (Matt 9:27, 12:23, 15:22, 20:31-32; Mark 10:47-48; Luke 18:38-39); the praise of the crowd (Matt 21:9, 15; Mark 11:10); and the disputes with religious leaders (Matt 22:42-43, 45; Mark 12:35; Luke 20:41-44).[47] Accordingly, it can be concluded that the image of a Davidic Messiah quite sporadically pervades the Synoptic Gospels. Upon turning to the Fourth Gospel, however, a reader becomes vexed to find very few, if any, corresponding examples (perhaps three passages could arguably be singled out as

---

Kok, 1989), 95-104; Terence Y. Mullins, "Jesus, the 'Son of David,'" *AUSS* 29 (1991): 117-26; Dennis C. Duling, "Matthew's Plurisignificant 'Son of David' in Social Science Perspective: Kinship, Kingship, Magic, and Miracle," *BTB* 22 (1992): 99-116; Cleon L. Rogers, Jr., "The Davidic Covenant in the New Testament," *BSac* 150 (1993): 458-78; idem, "The Davidic Covenant in the New Testament," *BSac* 151 (1994): 71-84; Donald J. Verseput, "The Davidic Messiah and Matthew's Jewish Christianity," *SBLSP* 34 (1995): 102-16; Mark L. Strauss, *The Davidic Messiah in Luke-Acts: The Promise and Its Fulfillment in Lukan Christology* (Sheffield: Sheffield, 1995); Lidija Novakovic, "Jesus as the Davidic Messiah in Matthew," *HBT* 19 (1997): 148-91; Jean-Marie van Cangh, "'Fils de David' dans les évangiles synoptiques," in *Figures de David à travers la Bible: XVIIe congrès de l'ACFEB (Lille, 1er-5 septembre 1997)*, ed. Louis Desrousseaux and Jacques Vermeylen (Paris: Cerf, 1999), 345-96; Damià Roure, "La figure de David dans l'évangile de Marc: Des traditions juives aux interprétations évangéliques," in *Figures de David à travers la Bible: XVIIe congrès de l'ACFEB (Lille, 1er-5 septembre 1997)*, ed. Louis Desrousseaux and Jacques Vermeylen (Paris: Cerf, 1999), 397-412; Roland Meynet, "Jésus, fils de David dans l'évangile de Luc," in *Figures de David à travers la Bible: XVIIe congrès de l'ACFEB (Lille, 1er-5 septembre 1997)*, ed. Louis Desrousseaux and Jacques Vermeylen (Paris: Cerf, 1999), 413-28; Christopher G. Whitsett, "Son of God, Seed of David: Paul's Messianic Exegesis in Romans 1:3-4," *JBL* 119 (2000): 661-81; Margaret Daly-Denton, "David in the Gospels," *WW* 23 (2003): 421-29; Young S. Chae, *Jesus as the Eschatological Davidic Shepherd: Studies in the Old Testament, Second Temple Judaism, and in the Gospel of Matthew* (Tübingen: Mohr Siebeck, 2006).

[44] Herman C. Waetjen, "Genealogy as the Key to the Gospel according to Matthew," *JBL* 95 (1976): 205-30; Ernst Lerle, "Die Ahnenverzeichnisse Jesu: Versuch einer christologischen Interpretation," *ZNW* 72 (1981): 112-17.

[45] D.R. Bauer, "Son of David," *DJG*, 768-69.

[46] Jack D. Kingsbury, "The Title 'Son of David' in Matthew's Gospel," *JBL* 95 (1976): 591-602; Novakovic, "Jesus as the Davidic Messiah in Matthew," 148-91; Kim Paffenroth, "Jesus as Anointed and Healing Son of David in the Gospel of Matthew," *Bib* 80 (1999): 547-54. Similarly, Bassler ("A Man for All Seasons," 156-69) finds the parallels between David and Jesus, as well as between Solomon and Jesus.

[47] Rogers, "The Davidic Covenant in the New Testament," 460-64.

such: 2:17, 7:42, 12:13). On the contrary, however, Margaret Daly-Denton presumes extensive parallels to the Synoptic passion accounts in John. Her arguments will be addressed in detail in the following section.[48]

Messianic Role of David in John

The research history of John's Gospel itself clearly indicates the difficulty of undertaking an inquiry into a Davidic messianic prefiguration in the Gospel of John. Until Daly-Denton's study, which appeared in the year 2000, there was virtually no single study principally devoted to the issue, and exegetes hardly detected any significant presence of a Davidic messianic motif.[49] Such facts place John in stark contrast to the Synoptic Gospels, which have been the object of a myriad of studies that have addressed the Davidic messianic conceptions. As such, Daly-Denton is justified in her comment that "the 'Davidlikeness' of Jesus is, perhaps, a neglected strand in the multi-hued texture of the Fourth Gospel."[50] A host of Johannine exegetes concur with her judgment. For example, Margaret Davies, Paul Anderson, and Jorg Salzmann note the lack of David/Jesus analogy in John:

> Jesus' life is so unlike that of David . . . that the connexion which the Synoptics make could be misleading;[51]

> John is nearly devoid of Davidic messianic motifs;[52]

> John's Gospel is different from the Synoptics that it does not take an explicit identification of Jesus with the son of David. We hear Son of Man instead of son of David.[53]

Likewise, recently, Andrew Brunson comes to a conclusion concerning the titles usually attributed to the Davidic messianic nature of Jesus as follows:

> Davidic ideology is not prominent throughout the Gospel, and Jesus is not programmatically compared to David, John can more easily re-direct the reader towards other backgrounds. . . . he also does not identify Jesus explicitly with David. . . . The Gospel's relative silence on David supports the suggestion that the title [king of Israel] is

---

[48] See especially, Margaret Daly-Denton, *David in the Fourth Gospel: The Johannine Reception of the Psalms* (Leiden: Brill, 2000), 289-92.

[49] Minor exceptions to this current include the following: T. Francis Glasson, "Davidic Links with the Betrayal of Jesus," *ExpTim* 85 (1974): 118-19; Paul Trudinger, "Davidic Links with the Betrayal of Jesus: Some Further Observations," *ExpTim* 86 (1974-75): 278-79; idem, "Hosanna to the Son of David: St John's Perspective," *DRev* 109 (1991): 297-301.

[50] Daly-Denton, *David in the Fourth Gospel*, 7.

[51] Margaret Davies, *Rhetoric and Reference in the Fourth Gospel* (Sheffield: JSOT, 1992), 212.

[52] Paul N. Anderson, *The Christology of the Fourth Gospel: Its Unity and Disunity in the Light of John 6* (Tübingen: Mohr Siebeck, 1996), 229.

[53] Jorg Christian Salzmann, "Jüdische Messiasvorstellungen in Justins Dialog mit Trypho und im Johannesevangelium," *ZNW* 100 (2009): 251.

not intended primarily to evoke Davidic association.[54]

Daly-Denton

In contrast to the assessment of the majority of Johannine exegetes, Daly-Denton, however, asserts that the Gospel of John is permeated with the portrayal of Jesus in a Davidic image.[55] Her argument is supported by noting a number of parallels in the lives of Jesus and David. First, just as David (in the aftermath of Absalom's conspiracy in 1 Sam 15:23), Jesus begins his journey by crossing the Kidron valley (John 18:1), which is the only New Testament reference:

> And all the people passed by over the Kidron valley, and the king passed over the Kidron valley, and all the people and the king passed on towards the way of the wilderness. (2 Sam 15:23, NRSV)

> When Jesus had spoken these words, he went forth with his disciples across the Kidron valley, where there was a garden, which he and his disciples entered. (John 18:1, NRSV)

Second, as a foreigner, Ittai the Gittite, pledged to follow David at any cost, "so must a servant of Jesus do" implies Jesus to Greek inquirers (Jn 12:20-26):

> As the Lord lives, and as my lord the King lives, in whatever place my lord shall be, whether it be for death or life, there shall your servant be. (1 Sam 15:23, NRSV)

> Whoever serves me must follow me, and where I am there will my servant be also." (John 12:26, NRSV)

Third, just as Caiaphas advised that "one man (Jesus) should die for the people and the whole nation should not perish" (Jn 11:50), so Ahithophel urges Absalom that "you need only seek the life of one man and all the people shall have peace" (2 Sam 17:3). Finally, just as Samuel does not know whom to anoint (1 Sam 16:1-13), so also does John the Baptist not know who the Messiah will be (Jn 1:31). A couple more elements can be listed in support of her argument here.[56] Jesus' body was lavished with a royal burial as it would have befitted the Davidic king par excellence. In addition, Pseudo-Philo designates Samuel as "the light" proceeding before wisdom just as John was a provisional lamp shining until the coming of the true light (Jn 1:8-9; 5:35). "For when the light from which wisdom is to be born will go forth" (*L.A.B.* 51:4).[57] However, the first parallel seems to read too much into the text, and the argumentative force of the latter one, on the other hand, is obscured by the late date of the source. Most scholars place the writing of Pseudo-Philo in the late first century.[58] Collectively,

---

[54] Andrew C. Brunson, *Psalm 118 in the Gospel of John: An Intertextual Study on the New Exodus Pattern in the Theology of John* (Tübingen: Mohr Siebeck, 2003), 227.
[55] Daly-Denton, *David in the Fourth Gospel*, 292-307.
[56] Ibid., 299-301, 304-06.
[57] *OTP*, 2:365.
[58] Evans, *Ancient Texts for New Testament Studies*, 49.

David 143

they mount to a strong parallel messianic linkage, Daly-Denton argues.

> [T]aken individually, any of these similarities between David and Jesus . . . might seem insignificant or even tenuous . . ., the cumulative effect of these recollection of David is a strong impression of his latent presence in the Fourth Gospel.[59]

> [T]he whole point of placing the psalms (Pss 22, 69) on the lips of Jesus is that David is ancestor of the Messiah (the synoptic view) or a prophetic prefiguration of Jesus (the Johannine view). The psalms tell of how David experienced betrayal, torment, isolation, and eventually, the deliverance that gave rise to the praise that characteristically follows his laments. For the first Christians, David's experience prefigures Jesus' life, death, and resurrection.[60]

> The literary persona of David, as it had evolved by the Second Temple period, as the protagonist of narrative traditions, as "author" of the psalms, and as an idealized symbol of hope for the future, provided the Evangelist with a paradigm and a resource for such reinterpretation.[61]

As convincing as the suggested analogies might sound, however, these allusions still appear to be too subtle, so that it is altogether questionable whether the originally intended audience would have immediately detected those connections without difficulty. This possibility seems even less likely in view of the growing awareness of Gospel scholarship regarding the primary communication pattern of the first century Mediterranean world. The orality of the culture necessitates the intended messages be quite obvious, otherwise they stand a meager chance to be understood by the audience.[62] Nevertheless, in addition to the four situational analogies, there are eight passages that explicitly refer to or allude to David that merit close scrutiny. These passages will be discussed with respect to the possibility of presenting Jesus as a Davidic figure, especially in a significant interaction with the arguments set forth by Daly-Denton for the remainder of this chapter.

Jesus as the Replacement of the Temple: John 2:17

> His disciples remembered that it was written, "Zeal for your house will consume me." (John 2:17, NRSV)

> ὁ ζῆλος τοῦ οἴκου σου καταφάγεταί με. (John 2:17b, NA[28])

> ὁ ζῆλος τοῦ οἴκου σου κατέφαγέν με. (Ps 68:10a, LXX)

> כִּי־קִנְאַת בֵּיתְךָ אֲכָלָתְנִי׃ (Ps 69:10a, BHS[5])

The so-called "temple cleansing" pericope in John 2:13-22 contains an almost

---

[59] Daly-Denton, *David in the Fourth Gospel*, 314-15.
[60] Ibid., 315.
[61] Ibid., 428.
[62] For a fuller treatment of this issue, see pp. 52-54 ("Implication of Orality") of this book.

exact verbatim quotation from Psalm 69:9.[63] There are two reasons in particular that might demand the presence of a Davidic prefiguration motif. First, Daly-Denton's point is probably valid that the Psalter quotations would automatically remind the first-century readers of David, especially since Psalm 69 is already placed under the Davidic authorship in the Hebrew canon.[64] This point is reinforced by the fact that this particular chapter of the Psalms is popularly quoted in other parts of the New Testament writings. On this basis, C.H. Dodd postulated the presence of "a testimony collection" that circulated in the early churches: Matthew 27:34 (Ps 69:21); Luke 23:36 (Ps 69:21); John 15:25 (Ps 69:4); John 19:28 (Ps 69:21); Acts 1:20 (Ps 69:25); Romans 11:9-10 (Ps 69:22-23), 15:3 (Ps 69:9b).[65] Second, it is relatively evident in the text that the suffering of David has a close correlation with that of Jesus. Just as David suffered because of his enemies' misunderstanding of his zeal for the temple in Psalm 69, so also does Jesus in the latter half of the Gospel.[66]

However, upon a closer reading of its narrative context, this pericope calls for more than a Davidic prefiguration motif. First, the section ranging from the end of the first chapter to the pericope immediately preceding this text is replete with a recurrent replacement theme. Jacob's encountering of Yahweh is replaced with

---

[63] For an overview of various scholarly assessments of this pericope, see Alexander J.M. Wedderburn, "Jesus' Action in the Temple: A Key or a Puzzle?" *ZNW* 97 (2006): 1-22. The change of tense is probably due to the shift of emphasis from the action itself to the lasting effect of the event. J. Ramsey Michaels, *The Gospel of John* (Grand Rapids: Eerdmans, 2010), 162. For the fulfillment aspect of this Psalm quotation, see Nicolas Farelly, "Lire le Psaume 69 (68) en Jean 2, 13-22," *ÉTR* 86 (2011): 195-207.

[64] Daly-Denton, *David in the Fourth Gospel*, 121. For the authorship of Psalms, see André Lelièvre, "Qui parle dans les Psaumes," *FoiVie* 87 (1988): 3-13; Beate Kowalski, "Die Tempelreinigung Jesu nach Joh 2,13-25," *MTZ* 57 (2006): 194-208; Klaus Seybold, "Dimensionen und Intentionen der Davidisierung der Psalmen: Die Rolle Davids nach den Psalmenüberschriften und nach dem Septuagintapsalm 151," in *Composition of the Book of Psalms*, ed. Erich Zenger (Leuven: Peeters, 2010), 125-40. This pericope is variously called "temple expulsion (*Tempelaustreibung*)," "temple protest," or neutrally "temple action." For scholarly suggestions for these different titles, see Kowalski, "Die Tempelreinigung Jesu nach Joh 2,13-25," 194. For the narrative delimitation of the present text, see ibid., 195-96.

[65] C.H. Dodd, *According to the Scriptures: The Substructure of New Testament Theology* (London: Nisbet, 1952), 58. His postulation is indebted to J. Rendel Harris, *Testimonies*, 2 vols. (Cambridge: CUP, 1916-20).

[66] D.A. Carson, *The Gospel according to John* (Grand Rapids: Eerdmans, 1991), 180; M.J.J. Menken, "'Zeal for Your House Will Consume Me' (John 2:17)," in *Old Testament Quotations in the Fourth Gospel: Studies in Textual Form* (Kampen: Kok, 1996), 44; Daly-Denton, *David in the Fourth Gospel*, 125-31. Richard Hays also finds a subtle 'figural correlation" between Jesus and the psalmist in this text. Richard B. Hays, "Can the Gospels Teach us How to Read the Old Testament?" *ProEccl* 11 (2002): 412-15. But, recently, Bryan argues "zeal" in the text refers to that of Jesus' enemies. Steven M. Bryan, "Consumed by Zeal: John's Use of Psalm 69:9 and the Action in the Temple," *BBR* 21 (2011): 479-94.

the New Testament Christians' meeting with Jesus (Jn 1:51). The old wine (τὸν ἐλάσσω, "inferior wine" in Jn 2:10) is replaced with the new wine, which Jesus provides, and which the banquet master attests to be "the good wine" (Jn 2:10). Immediately after this sign in Cana is placed the present "temple cleansing" anecdote, which is followed by the "new birth speech" to Nicodemus (Jn 3:1-15), and John the Baptist's notion that Jesus must increase and he himself decrease (Jn 3:30). As such, the present paragraph under discussion must be understood in light of the narrative flow of the surrounding texts that repeatedly underscore a replacement or contrast theme.[67] In this respect, J.H. Ulrichsen's assessment of the present text loses sight of the narrative context. Although he only finds the Jewish unbelief theme, John 2:13-22 makes better sense in terms of "replacement" for three reasons. First, the surrounding literary contexts (chs. 1-4) are replete with the replacement theme especially in terms of Jesus as the replacement of the Jewish temple.[68] Second, the first half of the pericope and the latter one are woven together with a keyword "sign" that the cleansing act is best understood as a symbolic referent to the sign of Jesus' resurrection which replaces the physical Jerusalem temple: "But he was speaking of the temple of his body" (John 2:21). Immediately following this temple incident, the fourth evangelist reminds his readers that Jesus' stay in Jerusalem has much to do with signs that are supposed to evoke faith, but only as an initial step toward true faith:

> [23] When he was in Jerusalem during the Passover festival, many believed in his name because they saw the signs that he was doing. [24] But Jesus on his part would not entrust himself to them, because he knew all people. (John 2:23-24, NRSV)

Therefore, the citation of Psalm 69:9 that was occasioned by his temple cleansing act serves as a well-known Johannine double *entendre*, which not only comments on the action he just completed but on his impending tragic destiny.[69]

---

[67] Paul M. Hoskins, *Jesus as the Fulfillment of the Temple in the Gospel of John* (Milton Keynes: Paternoster, 2006), 108-16; Brunson, *Psalm 118 in the Gospel of John*, 147-49; Camillus Umoh, "The Temple in the Fourth Gospel," in *Israel und seine Heilstraditionen im vierten Evangelium: Festgabe für Johannes Beutler SJ zum 70. Geburtstag*, ed. Michael Labahn, Klaus Scholtissek, & Angelika Strotmann (Paderborn: Schöningh, 2004), 323; Christian Grappe, "Du sanctuaire au jardin: Jésus, nouveau et véritable Temple dans le quatrième évangile," in *Studien zu Matthäus und Johannes: Festschrift für Jean Zumstein zu seinem 65. Geburtstag*, ed. Andreas Dettwiler and Uta Poplutz (Zürich: Theologischer, 2009), 285-96.

[68] Hoskins, *Jesus as the Fulfillment of the Temple in the Gospel of John*, 108-46; Benny Thettayil, *In Spirit and Truth: An Exegetical Study of John 4:19-26 and a Theological Investigation of the Replacement Theme in the Fourth Gospel* (Leuven: Peeters, 2007), 382-403; Grappe, "Du sanctuaire au jardin," 285-87.

[69] Martin Stowasser, "Die johanneische Tempelaktion (Joh 2,13-17): Ein Beitrag zum Verhältnis von Johannesevangelium und Synoptikern," in *Im Geist und in der Wahrheit: Studien zum Johannesevangelium und zur Offenbarung des Johannes sowie andere Beiträge, Festschrift für Martin Hasitschka SJ zum 65. Geburtstag*, ed. Konrad

Third, it is difficult not to take into account the catastrophic fall of the Jerusalem temple for the background of this passage.[70]

Thus, Barnabas Lindars' assessment of the Psalm quotation in John 2:17 seems to be on target that the verse is a parenthesis (i.e., a post-Easter interpolation), which interrupts the narrative flow.[71] This point becomes more convincing when coupled with the statement about the disciples' misunderstanding of the temple replacement theme at first:

> After he was raised from the dead, his disciples remembered that he had said this; and they believed the scripture and the word that Jesus had spoken. (John 2:22, NRSV)

Similarly,

> his disciples did not understand these things at first; but when Jesus was glorified, then they remembered that these things had been written of him and had been done to him. (John 12:16, NRSV)

As such, the main theme of this pericope is Jesus' replacement of the Jerusalem temple with his body, a spiritual temple.[72] Accordingly, the key words are

---

Huber & Boris Repschinski (Münster: Aschendorff, 2008), 43; Grappe, "Du sanctuaire au jardin," 287.

[70] Jarl H. Ulrichsen, "Jesus—der neue Tempel?: Ein kritischer Blick auf die Auslegung von Joh 2,13-22," in *Neotestamentica et Philonica: Studies in Honor of Peder Borgen*, ed. David E. Aune, Torrey Seland, and Jarl H. Ulrichsen (Leiden: Brill, 2003), 202-14. For an example of the understanding that sees the temple cleansing pericope as an integral part of a larger narrative unit, see Mark A. Matson, "The Temple Incident: An Integral Element in the Fourth Gospel's Narrative," in *Jesus in Johannine Tradition*, ed. Robert T. Fortna and Tom Thatcher (Louisville: Westminster/John Knox, 2001), 145-53.

[71] Barnabas Lindars, *The Gospel of John* (London: Marshall, Morgan & Scott, 1972), 140. For this point, Lindars cites Jürgen Roloff, "Der johanneische 'Lieblingsjünger' und der Lehrer der Gerechtigkeit," *NTS* 15 (1968-1969): 129-51. This insertion of parentheses is a typical Johannine literary device observed in John 11:13, 12:16-33, 13:7, 18:32, 20:9). See also Udo Schnelle, "Die Tempelreinigung und die Christologie des Johannesevangeliums," *NTS* 42 (1996): 362, n. 7. For a discussion of Johannine fulfillment formulae, see Gilbert van Belle, "Les parenthèses johanniques: Un Premier Bilan," in *Four Gospels 1992: Festschrift Frans Neirynck*, ed. Frans van Segbroeck et al (Louvain: Peeters, 1992), 3:1901-33.

[72] Although Busse seems to overstate somewhat his case by finding too many correlations, his observation is in general on target that Jesus realizes the Old Testament symbolic images related to the Jerusalem temple in John 2:13-22. Ulrich Busse, "Die Tempelmetaphorik als ein Beispiel von implizitem Rekurs auf die biblische Tradition im Johannesevangelium," in *The Scripture in the Gospels*, ed. Christopher M. Tuckett (Louvain: Leuven University Press, 1997), 395-428. Also, Hays, "Can the Gospels Teach us How to Read the Old Testament?," 412-13; William Loader, "Jesus and the Law in John," in *Theology and Christology in the Fourth Gospel: Essays by the Members of the SNTS Johannine Writings Seminar*, ed. Gilbert van Belle, Jan G. van der Watt, and P. Maritz (Leuven: Leuven University, 2005), 140-41. It is probably the resurrected body of Jesus that is to be identified as the new temple. Ulrich Busse, *Das*

"temple" (vv. 17, 19, 20, 21) and its cognates "house" (v. 16), not "consume" or "zeal" in the psalm citation. That is precisely why the evangelist placed the Psalm quotation at this point instead of leaving it after the resurrection.[73] This Johannine text also does not dwell on elaborating Jesus' suffering as a consequence of this temple-cleansing act as Matthew (26:61) and Mark (11:18; 14:58) point it out as a cause of Jesus' arrest.

> Thereby, the scene experiences a surprising and fundamental change compared to the Synoptic representations. No longer the fate of the temple cult or its operation, but the fate of Jesus, occurs at the center of the narrative.[74]

This proportional aspect militates against the reading of this text as a prefiguration of David's righteous suffering in Psalm 69.[75] This narrative plot explains why John does not here refer to the well-known Old Testament righteous suffering traditions (i.e., Isaiah 56:7 and Jeremiah 7:11 do not speak of a "righteous suffering" tradition in their original literary contexts), as Matthew 21:13 and Mark 11:17 do. To some extent, this argument runs in danger of postulating a literary relationship between the Synoptics and John. At least some degree of indirect influence, however, should be reckoned, because the synoptic Gospels draw on the same temple cleansing incident tradition as John does.[76] The fourth evangelist, therefore, seems to focus on the new temple theme, and does not divert the attention of his readers to ancillary elements.[77] This temple replacement theme in ch. 2, then, stands in continuity with John 1:51, in which Jesus is

---

Johannesevangelium: Bildlichkeit, Diskurs und Ritual mit einer Bibliographie über den Zeitraum 1986-1998 (Leuven: Leuven University Press; Peeters, 2002), 340. Also, for a brief summary of the Johannine replacement (of Jewish feasts) theme, see Frank Thielman, "Grace in Place of Grace: Jesus Christ and the Mosaic Law in John's Gospel," in *The Law and the New Testament: The Question of Continuity* (New York: Crossroad, 1999), 96-104.

[73] Lindars, *The Gospel of John*, 140; A.T. Hanson, *The Prophetic Gospel: A Study of John and the Old Testament* (Edinburgh: T & T Clark, 1991), 43.

[74] Johanna Rahner, *Er aber sprach vom Tempel seines Leibes: Jesus von Nazaret als Ort der Offenbarung Gottes im vierten Evangelium* (Bodenheim an Rhein, Germany: Philo, 1998), 262, n. 4.

[75] In this respect, the exegetical value of Richard Hays' reading is diminished as he recognizes the replacement theme in the text, but then quickly moves onto the righteous suffering and vindication of the nation of Israel. Hays, "Can the Gospels Teach us How to Read the Old Testament?" 412-15.

[76] For the recent attempts to account for the relationship between the Synoptics and the Fourth Gospel, see Michael Labahn and Manfred Lang, "Johannes und die Synoptiker: Positionen und Impulse seit 1990," in *Kontexte des Johannesevangeliums: Das vierte Evangelium in religions und traditionsgeschichtlicher Perspektive*, ed., Jörg Frey & Udo Schnelle (Tübingen: Mohr Siebeck, 2004), 443-515; Stefan Schreiber, "Kannte Johannes die Synoptiker?: Zur aktuellen Diskussion," *VF* 51 (2006): 7-24; Stowasser, "Die johanneische Tempelaktion," 41-60.

[77] Hanson, *The Prophetic Gospel*, 45; Christian Dietzfelbinger, *Das Evangelium nach Johannes* (Zürich: Theologischer, 2001), 1:76-77.

articulated as the new Bethel. Hanson says, "I finally suggest that the transition from 1.51 to 2.17 is the transition from Christ as the place of God's presence to Christ as the house of God."[78]

Finally, this citation from Psalms (as well as the following catena) serves to manifest that Jesus' replacement of the Jerusalem temple is in accordance with the testimony or more precisely witness of the Scriptures. This scriptural reference serves as a proleptic prophecy to the Post-Easter faith of Christ's suffering.[79] This interpretation stands in line with the fourth evangelist's change from the past tenses of its sources (the perfect tense of the MT and aorist of the LXX) to the future tense.[80] All these observations, however, do not preclude the possibility that one might find a Davidic motif or the judgment theme that is more popularly claimed for the synoptic parallel accounts.[81] What the literary contexts suggest is, however, that such a motif, if present at all, should be kept at a secondary level next to the replacement theme, probably even on the level of a prophet motif, as some commentators have noted.[82]

Jesus as a Davidic Posterity?: John 7:42

οὐχ ἡ γραφὴ εἶπεν ὅτι ἐκ τοῦ σπέρματος Δαυὶδ καὶ ἀπὸ Βηθλέεμ τῆς κώμης ὅπου ἦν Δαυὶδ ἔρχεται ὁ χριστός. (John 7:42, NA[28])

Has not the scripture said that the Messiah is descended from David and comes from Bethlehem, the village where David lived? (John 7:42, NRSV)

This passage seems to share a common tradition with Matthew 2:5-6 where Jewish scholars were readily able to locate the birthplace of the anticipated Messiah based on Micah 5:2.[83] A couple of questions have been raised con-

---

[78] Hanson, *The Prophetic Gospel*, 44.
[79] Umoh, "The Temple in the Fourth Gospel," 323. Thus, the assessment of Evans is rather a little off the track. He thinks that the function of the citation is analogical but it seems to be more prophetic. See Craig A. Evans, "Old Testament in the Gospels," *DJG*, 588. "This scripture serves the function of the witness to Christ as post-Easter representation of Christ in the scripture of Israel." Kowalski, "Die Tempelreinigung Jesu nach Joh 2,13-25," 199. Also, for the witness function of this scriptureal citation, see Andreas Obermann, *Die christologische Erfüllung der Schrift im Johannesevangelium: Eine Untersuchung zur johanneischen Hermeneutik anhand der Schriftzitate* (Tübingen: Mohr Siebeck, 1996), 123.
[80] Kowalski, "Die Tempelreinigung Jesu nach Joh 2,13-25," 198.
[81] Wedderburn, "Jesus' Action in the Temple," 20-22.
[82] R. Brown identifies Jesus' action with that of a prophet. Raymond Brown, *The Gospel according to John* (New York: Doubleday, 1966), 1:121. Francis J. Moloney, on the other hand, points to Phineas, Elijah, or Mattathias. Francis J. Moloney, *The Gospel of John* (Wilmington: Liturgical, 1998), 77.
[83] Johan Lust, "Mic 5,1-3 in Qumran and in the New Testament, and Messianism in the Septuagint," in *Scriptures in the Gospels*, ed. Christopher M. Tuckett, (Louvain: Leuven University Press; Peeters, 1997), 82-87; Hans F. Fuhs, "Alttestamentliche Wurzeln des Messiasanspruchs Jesu," *ThGl* 98 (2008): 326-40.

cerning this passage. First, it is peculiar that the question is left unanswered. Accordingly, Bultmann concludes that "the evangelist knows nothing or wants to know nothing of the birth in Bethlehem."[84] Similarly, Wengst also construes that the fourth evangelist was not aware of such a tradition: "It is in my opinion probable that John did not know the tradition of the Davidic origin of Jesus and his birth in Bethlehem."[85] Their judgment, however, ignores the level of civilization in the first century Mediterranean world. Recent assessment of archaeological and literary discoveries of that period render unlikely their presupposition that the alleged Johannine community or the fourth evangelist were extremely isolated from the rest of early Christendom.[86]

Another problem is that there is no clear indication in early rabbinic literature for Bethlehem as Messiah's birth place, although the town was often closely associated with David.[87] Different suggestions have been put forth. The Matthean passage (2:5-6) is a New Testament example of rabbinic midrash or a redemptive historical reading of the Old Testament.[88] On the other hand, based on the supposed earlier oral tradition of *Targum Jonathan to the Prophets*, Schnackenburg and Becker posit that the expectation of messianic birth in Bethlehem was a common current at the time of Jesus.[89] *Targum of the Minor*

---

[84] Rudolf Bultmann, *The Gospel of John: A Commentary*, trans. George R. Beasley-Murray (Louisville: Westminster, 1971), 306 n. 6.

[85] Klaus Wengst, *Das Johannesevangelium* (Stuttgart: Kohlhammer, 2000), 1:296. On the other hand, Christoph Burger construes that the fourth evangelist did not consider Jesus as a Davidic descendant although he might have known the tradition which traced Jesus' lineage to David. Christoph Burger, *Jesus als Davidssohn: Eine traditionsgeschichtliche Untersuchung* (Göttingen: Vandenhoeck & Ruprecht, 1970), 153-58.

[86] Michael B. Thompson, "The Holy Internet: Communication between Churches in the First Christian Generation," in *The Gospels for All Christians: Rethinking the Gospel Audiences*, ed. Richard Bauckham (Grand Rapids: Eerdmans, 1998), 49-70; Loveday Alexander, "Ancient Book Production and the Circulation of the Gospels," in *The Gospels for All Christians: Rethinking the Gospel Audiences*, ed. Richard Bauckham (Grand Rapids: Eerdmans, 1998), 71-112.

[87] Str-B, 1:83; Burger, *Jesus*, 155-56; Raymond E. Brown, *The Birth of the Messiah: A Commentary on the Infancy Narratives in the Gospels of Matthew and Luke* (New York: Doubleday, 1993), 513-16.

[88] For the former, see Moisés Silva, "Ned B Stonehouse and Redaction Criticism, pt 2: The History of the Synoptic Tradition," *WTJ* 40 (1978): 281-303. For the latter, A.J. Petrotta argues that the Matthean interpretation goes beyond what the Old Testament warrants and that it is only comprehensible in light of the redemptive history in Christ. Anthony J. Petrotta, "A Closer Look at Matt 2:6 and Its Old Testament Sources," *JETS* 28 (1985): 47-52.

[89] Rudolf Schnackenburg, *Das Johannesevangelium* (Freiburg: Herder, 1985), 2:219; Jürgen Becker, *Das Evangelium nach Johannes* (Würzburg: Echter, 1991), 1:329, n. 20; both cited in Christoph Heil, "Jesus aus Nazaret oder Betlehem?: Historische Tradition und ironischer Stil im Johannesevangelium," in *Im Geist und in der Wahrheit: Studien zum Johannesevangelium und zur Offenbarung des Johannes sowie*

Prophets (a part of *Targum Jonathan to the Prophets*) arose after A.D. 70 in Palestine and was subject to a written edition around the 3rd to 4th centuries in Babylon.[90] Or, it may be the case that the Matthean Gospel account reflects a minor rabbinic tradition that has not survived to this day. On the basis of a messianic anticipation thrown into this text, which is couched in terms of a Davidic posterity, however, some have argued for a Davidic messianic motif spoken out loudly in this text. At first glance, it seems warranted; but, a closer examination that takes into account of the narrative flow requires a different reading.

The section which contains the inquiry of Davidic ancestry is preceded by a repeated theme of unbelief or misunderstanding. Not only in this section, but throughout the Gospel, "misunderstanding" is an important Johannine literary device. It drives the narrative flow to move forward, and at the same time it stimulates the Johannine main characters to deepen their faith in Christ.

> Such a narrative-strategic use falls on the fact that the misunderstanding itself 'collaborates' concretely to the deepening of the Christological theme. Misunderstanding is, therefore, a strong expression of performance for its Christologically intended statement within the Fourth Gospel.[91]

In ch. 5, the Jews do not understand the healing authority of Jesus, which provides an occasion to manifest his equality with God (Jn 5:15-29). The entire ch. 6 is marked by the misunderstanding of the Jews over the true meaning of the feeding of the five thousand miracle account (6:1-15), and even that of Jesus' own disciples with reference to Jesus' authority over nature (6:16-21) and the bread of life discourse (6:22-59). This theme of misunderstanding or more precisely of unbelief continues in ch. 7, during the feast of Tabernacles, on the part of the crowd, the Pharisees, and the high priest. In the following chs., 8 through 12, the stubborn unbelief of the Jews is recurring (8:13, 19, 22, 27, 33, 41, 43, 46, 48, 52-53, 59; 9:28-29, 40-41; 10:19-21, 24, 31, 39; 11:12-13, 16; 12:16, 34-35, 37, 39).[92] Thus, the questioning (or accusing) of Jesus' Davidic origin in v. 42

---

andere Beiträge: Festschrift für Martin Hasitschka SJ zum 65. Geburtstag, ed. Konrad Huber & Boris Repschinski (Münster: Aschendorff, 2008), 116-19.

[90] Kevin J. Cathcart and Robert P. Gordon, *The Targum of the Minor Prophets: Translated, with a Critical Introduction, Apparatus, and Notes* (Wilmington: Michael Glazier, 1989), 16-18; Robert P. Gordon, *Studies in the Targum to the Twelve Prophets: From Nahum to Malachi* (Leiden: Brill, 1994), 150.

[91] Johanna Rahner, "Missverstehen um zu verstehen: Zur Funktion der Missverständnisse im Johannesevangelium," *BZ* 43 (1999): 212-19 (217).

[92] Some examples of exception and contrast to this misunderstand and unbelief are as following: "As he was saying these things, many believed in him" (8:30); "He said, 'Lord, I believe.' And he worshiped him" (9:38); "And many believed in him there" (10:42); "Many of the Jews therefore, who had come with Mary and had seen what Jesus did, believed in him" (11:45); "Nevertheless many, even of the authorities, believed in him. But because of the Pharisees they did not confess it, for fear that they would be put out of the synagogue" (12:42).

should be seen in line with this persistent misunderstanding or unbelief *leitmotif*. That is why the Jews rhetorically assert that a prophet or Christ cannot come from Galilee:

> When they heard these words, some in the crowd said, "This is really the prophet." Others said, "This is the Messiah." But some asked, "Surely the Messiah does not come from Galilee, does he?" (John 7:40-41, NRSV)[93]

> They replied, "Surely you are not also from Galilee, are you? Search and you will see that no prophet is to arise from Galilee." (John 7:52, NRSV)[94]

While the unbelief motif permeates chs. 5 through 12, another prominent theme emerges in this section, namely, that of Jesus' heavenly origin.[95] This concept is often expressed in the language of father/son (5:19-29; 6:32-40), flesh/spirit (6:63), light/darkness (8:12), above/below (8:23), and God/Satan (8:44-47). What this heavenly origin entails is that Jesus does not need a human witness (John 2:24-25; 5:34, 36-37, 39, 41; 8:14-20) because it is God who bears witness to him. This is why the question concerning Jesus' Davidic origin is left without an answer in v. 42. The lack of an answer is not to dismiss the Davidic lineage of Jesus, but it is to indicate that Jesus' messianic identity does not rest on human testimonies or qualifications. In other words, the earthly royal lineage does not add to buttress his status as Messiah.

> What did the evangelist himself think about Jesus' ancestry and origin? His theology is not concerned with the human antecedents or earthly homeland of Jesus, but only with his heavenly origin. In this respect, he has no desire to establish the legitimacy of his Christ by the criteria of Jewish messianic expectation. . . . [John] is suggesting the same answer as Jesus gave in v. 28: you know Jesus, yet you do not really know him; to be Son of David and born in Bethlehem is not what matters.[96]

---

[93] There is a precedence, however, that a Hebrew prophet came from Galilee, i.e., Jonah (2 Kings 14:25). Becker, *Das Evangelium nach Johannes*, 1:330, n. 20; Hartwig Thyen, *Das Johannesevangelium* (Tübingen: Mohr Siebeck, 2005), 415-18, n. 60. The Pharisees probably had in mind the prophet-like-Moses.

[94] John mentions Nicodemus three times throughout the Gospel. This text contains his second appearance. He is described as moving closer to Christ each time he is mentioned. His neutral or perhaps friendly remark here functions to provoke a charge from the Pharisees. A contrast is drawn in this text between the increasing faith of Nicodemus and the stark unbelief of the Jews. Peter Dschulnigg, "Nikodemus im Johannesevangelium," *SNTSU* 24 (1999): 103-18.

[95] George R. Beasley-Murray, *John* (Nashville: Thomas Nelson, 1999), 118-19.

[96] Rudolf Schnackenburg, *The Gospel according to St John* (New York: Crossroad, 1982), 2:158-59; Bassler, "A Man for All Seasons," 166; C.K. Barrett, *The Gospel according to St. John: An Introduction with Commentary and Notes on the Greek Text* (Philadelphia: Westminster, 1978), 330-31; D. Moody Smith, *John* (Nashville: Abingdon, 1999), 175-76; Wengst, *Das Johannesevangelium*, 1:308-09; Michaels, *The Gospel of John*, 470-71. Similarly, "Beweis, daß Jesus der Christus ist, kann nur er selbst sein . . . er als der vom Vater Gesendete, in dem der Vater für die Menschen anschaubar und erfahrbar wird. Man kann es zugespitzt so sagen: Gerade als der, der

Jesus as Davidic King of Israel?: John 12:13

¹³ ἔλαβον τὰ βαΐα τῶν φοινίκων καὶ ἐξῆλθον εἰς ὑπάντησιν αὐτῷ καὶ ἐκραύγαζον·
ὡσαννά·
εὐλογημένος ὁ ἐρχόμενος ἐν ὀνόματι κυρίου,
[καὶ] ὁ βασιλεὺς τοῦ Ἰσραήλ.
¹⁴ εὑρὼν δὲ ὁ Ἰησοῦς ὀνάριον ἐκάθισεν ἐπ᾽ αὐτό, καθώς ἐστιν γεγραμμένον·
¹⁵ μὴ φοβοῦ, θυγάτηρ Σιών·
ἰδοὺ ὁ βασιλεύς σου ἔρχεται,
καθήμενος ἐπὶ πῶλον ὄνου.
¹⁶ ταῦτα οὐκ ἔγνωσαν αὐτοῦ οἱ μαθηταὶ τὸ πρῶτον, ἀλλ᾽ ὅτε ἐδοξάσθη Ἰησοῦς τότε ἐμνήσθησαν ὅτι ταῦτα ἦν ἐπ᾽ αὐτῷ γεγραμμένα καὶ ταῦτα ἐποίησαν αὐτῷ. (John 12:13-16, NA[28])

¹³ So they took branches of palm trees and went out to meet him, shouting,
"Hosanna!
Blessed is the one who comes in the name of the Lord—
the King of Israel!"
¹⁴ Jesus found a young donkey and sat on it; as it is written:
¹⁵ "Do not be afraid, daughter of Zion.
Look, your king is coming,
sitting on a donkey's colt!"
¹⁶ His disciples did not understand these things at first; but when Jesus was glorified, then they remembered that these things had been written of him and had been done to him. (John 12:13-16, NRSV)

In John, the epithet "King" is mentioned in four different contexts with reference to Jesus: Nathanael's confession (Jn 1:49); the crowd's attempt to crown Jesus following the miraculous feeding of five thousand (6:15); the triumphant entry (12:13-16) and in the passion narratives (chs. 18-19). In three of these instances, the Davidic association is too subtle or Jesus refuses to accept such a designation. Nonetheless, the pilgrim's hail of Jesus in 12:13-16 seems to evoke fairly obviously the Davidic royal messianic image. In addition, Jesus and the evangelist appear to sanction such praise.[97]

Although various questions arise from this text, the main question pertinent to the present investigation is the exact nature of the crowd's acclamation. Some preliminary inquiries, however, need to be discussed. First, H. Koester asserted that this acclamation (i.e., "Hosanna"), being a popular early Christian liturgical

---

nach traditionellen Maßstäben nicht der Messias sein kann, ist er der Messias, so wie er laut V. 25-29 als der ganz und gar Bekannte der gänzlich Unbekannte ist." Dietzfelbinger, *Das Evangelium nach Johannes*, 1:228.

[97] Daly-Denton, *David in the Fourth Gospel*, 45-46, 176-87. However, John Ashton, *Understanding the Fourth Gospel* (Oxford: Clarendon, 1991), 262, notes the absence of the title "Son of David" in the Fourth Gospel as a negative factor to be taken into consideration before assuming that "King of Israel" is a messianic title in John.

phrase, is a later interpolation.⁹⁸ On the contrary, given the dominant scholarly acceptance of the independence between the Synoptic Gospels and John, it is difficult to explain the coincidental insertion by later redactors. Matthew, Mark, and John (Matt 21:9, 15; Mark 11:9, 10; John 12:13) equally contain the idiosyncratic Greek transliteration (ὡσαννά) of the Hebrew word (הוֹשִׁיעָה נָּא, Ps 118:25, BHS⁵).⁹⁹ Phonetically, the Greek pronunciation (hosanna) departs slightly from that of the Hebrew word (hosia-na). The Septuagint does not use this Greek word and the only later attestation is found in *Didache* 10:6 which is dated to a late first or early second century A.D.¹⁰⁰

> May grace come and may this world pass away. Hosanna to the God of David. If any man is holy, let him come; if any man is not, let him repent. Marana-tha. Amen.¹⁰¹

Thus, the insertion of the word is presumed to have originated from an earlier tradition(s) on the account of the criteria of multiple attestation.¹⁰²

The second question has to do with a claim that the hail of the crowd was a normal expression of welcome for any festal pilgrim.¹⁰³ This contention seems justified in view of the Roman authority's seemingly tacit allowance of the commotion. If the acclamation had a political or royal messianic overtone, it is hard to conceive that the Roman authority did not stop it. Nonetheless, what concerns our investigation the most is how the evangelist colors the historical

---

⁹⁸ Helmut Koester, *Synoptische Überlieferung bei den apostolischen Vätern* (Berlin: Akademie, 1957), 196-98, cited in J.F. Coakley, "Jesus' Messianic Entry into Jerusalem (John 12:12-19 par.)," *JTS* 46 (1995): 473.

⁹⁹ Fitzmyer argued for an Aramaic provenance of the Greek transliteration. Joseph A. Fitzmyer, "Aramaic Evidence Affecting the Interpretation of Hosanna in the New Testament," in *Tradition and Interpretation in the New Testament: Essays in Honor of E. Earle Ellis for His 60th Birthday*, ed. Gerald F. Hawthorne and Otto Betz (Grand Rapids: Eerdmans, 1987), 110-18. However, it is unlikely since the use of the alleged Aramaic root word, ישע, is extremely rare in ancient literature. Coakley, "Jesus' Messianic Entry into Jerusalem," 474, n. 48. For a convenient survey of its usage throughout the Old Testament, the intertestamental period, and the New Testament, see Klaus Seybold, "Der Hilfe - und Huldigungsruf: Hosianna," in *Der Segen und andere liturgische Worte aus der hebräischen Bibel* (Zürich: Theologischer, 2004), 97-103.

¹⁰⁰ Jonathan A. Draper, "The Apostolic Fathers: The Didache," *ExpTime* 117 (2006): 177–81.

¹⁰¹ *I Clement, II Clement, Ignatius, Polycarp, Didache*, vol. 1 of *The Apostolic Fathers*, ed. & trans. Bart D. Ehrman (Cambridge: Harvard University Press, 2003), 432-33.

¹⁰² For the criteria of multiple attestation, see John P. Meier, *Origins of the Problem and the Person*, vol. 1 of *A Marginal Jew: Rethinking the Historical Jesus* (New York: Doubleday, 1991), 174–75; Stanley E. Porter, *The Criteria for Authenticity in Historical-Jesus Research: Previous Discussion and New Proposals* (Sheffield: Sheffield, 2000), 82-89; Tom Holmén, "Seven Theses on the So-called Criteria of Authenticity of Historical Jesus Research," *RCT* 33 (2008): 367-71.

¹⁰³ Coakley, "Jesus' Messianic Entry into Jerusalem," 464-65.

event as recorded in the present text. It is relatively clear from the surrounding contexts that the acclamation of the crowd has a direct bearing on the passion of Jesus as a qualification of the Johannine Messiah, which is indicated by two subsequent quotations from Scripture (Ps 118:25-26; Zech 9:9).[104]

> [25] Save us, we beseech you, O LORD!
> O LORD, we beseech you, give us success!
> [26] Blessed is the one who comes in the name of the LORD.
> We bless you from the house of the LORD. (Ps 118:25-26, NRSV)
>
> Rejoice greatly, O daughter Zion!
> Shout aloud, O daughter Jerusalem!
> Lo, your king comes to you;
> triumphant and victorious is he,
> humble and riding on a donkey,
> on a colt, the foal of a donkey. (Zech 9:9, NRSV)[105]

The significance of the so-called "triumphant entry" as a messianic qualification is marked by the surrounding narratives. The present pericope of John 12:12-16 is placed between the paragraphs that address the resurrection of Lazarus, which is one of the main causes for Jesus' crucifixion and perhaps a proto-type of Jesus' resurrection. These "Lazarus" passages are further surrounded by texts that allude to the sacrificial death of Jesus. A chiastic structure can be drawn from the narrative context of this passage as following:

Table 5 Chiastic Structure surrounding the Triumphant Entry

> The preparation of Jesus' death: 12:1-8
> Lazarus: 12:9-11
> Welcoming Jesus: 12:12-16
> Lazarus: 12:17-19
> A kernel of wheat: 12:20-33

In this respect, the messianic image of Jesus in the present text does not correspond to the conventional intertestamental hopes expected of the Davidic Mes-

---

[104] In this respect, Coakley's assessment misses the target. Although the scriptural fulfillment formulae in John 12:13-15 (Ps 18:25-26; Zech 9:9) probably did not ring a bell with the crowd as Coakley rightly notes, they had a significant import to the intended reader of John in contrast to Coakley's assumption. This significance is recognized via the disciples' post-Easter reminiscence: "His disciples did not understand these things at first; but when Jesus was glorified, then they remembered that these things had been written of him and had been done to him" (Jn 12:16).

[105] For the variegated use of Zechariah 9-14 in the New Testament, see Sandra Hübenthal, *Transformation und Aktualisierung: Zur Rezeption von Sach 9-14 im Neuen Testament* (Stuttgart: Katholisches Bibelwerk, 2006); for a representation of the entire Book of Zechariah as a hope of Davidic figure, see Anthony R. Petterson, *Behold Your King: The Hope for the House of David in the Book of Zechariah* (London: T & T Clark, 2009).

siah, who would display the majestic and glorious working of Yahweh in his militant subjugation of the ungodly.[106] This sacrificial aspect of the messianic qualification, thus, militates against the view that perceives a strong Davidic royal messianic overtone in the text.[107]

> It is not concerning David in his role of majesty, pomp and power as "king" only that John understands Jesus as a successor to David. It is precisely in references to moments of deep humility in David's life story.[108]

In addition, the riding of a donkey is not to carry an image of "a humble, peaceable king," rather it functions to indicate that such an act accords well with the scriptural testimony.[109]

Another view proposed by Wayne Meeks connects the raising of Lazarus with an act of the king of Israel and does not take into account the misunderstanding of the crowd.[110] However, it is exactly that which the fourth evangelist refutes.[111] Against the hope of Jews, Jesus entered the great city, not to assume a political and nationalistic leader as a Davidic figure, but to offer himself up as a sacrifice (see the kernel of wheat speech in the immediately following pericope, esp. 12:24-27) and as a humble servant (see the foot-washing anecdote in the next chapter of John 13). Moreover, it is difficult to see the miracle-working nature as a constituent of a Davidic Messiah contra Meeks' supposition. The wonder-working savior is cast at least not in the immediate literary contexts of Psalm 118 and the book of Zechariah.

Passion as a Messianic Qualification

Towards the latter half of the fourth Gospel, the Old Testament is closely tied with the fulfillment motif in the suffering of Jesus. So much so that it constitutes one of Obermann's theses that the passion of Jesus is the "explicit" fulfillment

---

[106] John J. Collins, *The Scepter and the Star: The Messiahs of the Dead Sea Scrolls and Other Ancient Literature* (Grand Rapids: Eerdmans, 2010), 77-78.

[107] Hans Kvalbein, "The Kingdom of God and the Kingship of Christ in the Fourth Gospel," in *Neotestamentica et Philonica: Studies in Honor of Peder Borgen*, ed. David E. Aune, Torrey Seland, and Jarl H. Ulrichsen (Leiden: Brill, 2003), 230-32.

[108] Paul Trudinger, "Hosanna to the Son of David: St John's Perspective," *DRev* 109 (1991): 297.

[109] Coakley, "Jesus' Messianic Entry into Jerusalem," 461-62, who, for this point, also cites J.D.M. Derrett, "Law in the New Testament: The Palm Sunday Colt," *NovT* 13 (1971): 255.

[110] Wayne A. Meeks, *The Prophet-King: Moses Traditions and the Johannine Christology* (Leiden: Brill, 1967), 87.

[111] M.J.J. Menken, "'Do Not Fear, Daughter Zion . . .' (John 12:15)," in *Old Testament Quotations in the Fourth Gospel: Studies in Textual Form* (Kampen: Kok, 1996), 86-87. In this respect, A. Brunson's Yahwistic reading of the text ignores the adjacent context. See Brunson, *Psalm 118 in the Gospel of John*, 180-239.

whereas the preceding ministry of Jesus is the "implicit" fulfillment.[112] Some exegetes find an obduracy motif in the passion fulfillment passages.[113] However, the stubbornness and obduracy on the part of Jews seem to be a contingent effect to accomplish the divine salvific program in these texts. Only Matthew, among the Synoptics, follows similar fulfillment patterns.[114] Like Matthew, John introduces the Old Testament material with the fulfillment formulae (i.e., with an introductory remark, πληρόω); but unlike the first evangelist, he does not hesitate to put the formula in the mouth of Jesus (13:18; 15:25; 19:28; 20:9; cf. 5:45-46). Moreover, John uses the formula to introduce reflections based on words of Jesus spoken earlier:

> This was to fulfill the word that he had spoken, "I did not lose a single one of those whom you gave me." (John 18:9, NRSV)
>
> This was to fulfill what Jesus had said when he indicated the kind of death he was to die. (John 18:32, NRSV)[115]

---

[112] Obermann, *Die christologische Erfüllung der Schrift im Johannesevangelium*, 348-50. Similarly, Craig A. Evans, "On the Quotation Formulas in the Fourth Gospel," *BZ* 26 (1982): 79-83; Joel Marcus, "The Old Testament and the Death of Jesus: The Role of Scripture in the Gospel Passion Narratives," in *The Death of Jesus in Early Christianity*, ed. John T. Carroll and Joel B. Green (Peabody: Hendrickson, 1995), 229-33; Wolfgang Kraus, "Die Vollendung der Schrift nach Joh 19,28: Überlegungen zum Umgang mit der Schrift im Johannesevangelium," in *The Scriptures in the Gospels*, ed. Christopher M. Tuckett (Leuven: Leuven University Press, 1997), 630.

[113] Craig A. Evans, "Obduracy and Lord's Servant: Some Observations on the Use of the Old Testament in the Fourth Gospel," in *Early Jewish and Christian Exegesis: Studies in Memory of William Hugh Brownlee*, ed. Craig A. Evans and William F. Stinespring (Atlanta: Scholars, 1987), 221-36; D.A. Carson, "John and Johannine Epistles," in *It Is Written: Scripture Citing Scripture: Essays in Honour of Barnabas Lindars*, ed. D.A. Carson and H.G.M. Williamson (Cambridge: CUP, 1988), 248. Bultmann and Käsemann downplayed the death of Jesus in John but more recent studies are increasingly becoming aware of its importance. John Dennis, "Jesus' Death in John's Gospel: A Survey of Research from Bultmann to the Present with Special Reference to the Johannine Hyper-Texts," *CurBS* 4 (2006): 331-64.

[114] John J. O'Rourke, "Explicit Old Testament Citations in the Gospels," *StudMonR* 7 (1964): 433.

[115] The hermeneutical dynamics of these fulfillment formulae are an object of scholarly debates. For a broad range of typological interpretation, see Richard N. Longenecker, "'Who is the Prophet Talking about?': Some Reflections on the New Testament's Use of the Old," *Them* 13 (1987): 4-8; Gregory K. Beale, "Positive Answer to the Question Did Jesus and His Followers Preach the Right Doctrine from the Wrong Texts?" in *The Right Doctrine from the Wrong Texts? Essays on the Use of the Old Testament in the New* (Grand Rapids: Baker, 1994), 396-97; M.J.J. Menken, "Observations on the Significance of the Old Testament in the Fourth Gospel," *Neot* 33 (1999): 137-39. For example, "From their Christocentric and so new revelational perspective they laid stress on 'fulfillment'—with fulfillment being understood to include everything from direct prediction precisely enacted on through typological correspondences in history." Longenecker, "'Who is the Prophet Talking About?'" 379. For those who approach

It is clear that the fourth evangelist explains Jesus' passion in terms of "fulfillment." This theme is set forth in ch. 12 and continues to play out through the following chapters. Ever since C.H. Dodd's initial proposal, the bi-partite nature of the Fourth Gospel is commonly accepted with chs. 1-11 as the book of signs and with chs. 13-20 as the book of the passion.[116] With such a division in view, ch. 12 is a transitional section that ushers in a new phase.[117] On this ground, it can be argued that the first half of John spells out the greatness of Jesus as confirmed by prominent Old Testament figures, while the latter part justifies how the greatness of Jesus is consistent with the Jewish rejection of him as Messiah, because it is already foreshadowed in the Old Testament and by the main protagonists of the Scriptures.[118] D.M. Smith suggests a plausible historical explanation that makes sense of this progression of logic. He argues that any missionary tractate designed to convince Jews would run into difficulties if a satisfactory explanation of Jesus' rejection and death was not offered. Contrary to a Hellenistic setting where the proclamation of the resurrection itself would be an adequate explanation, there would have to be some specific explanation for this rejection. There are two significant questions to be resolved for Jews. First, how could the messiah be crucified? Second, how could Jews reject their messiah? Smith asserts that the rejection of Jews was unthinkable and it is attested by the constant New Testament reference to Christ's crucifixion as a "stumbling block" to the Jews (e.g., 1 Cor 1:23). This fulfillment scheme of the Johannine passion

---

these formulae in terms of a traditional historical-grammatical interpretation, see R.T. France, *Jesus and the Old Testament: His Application of Old Testament Passages to Himself and His Mission* (Vancouver: Regent College Publishing, 1982), 38-40, David L. Baker, *Two Testaments, One Bible: A Study of the Theological Relationship between the Old and New Testaments* (Downers Grove: InterVarsity, 1991), 190.

[116] First proposed by C.H. Dodd, *The Interpretation of the Fourth Gospel* (Cambridge: CUP, 1954), 289. Followed by Brown with different phrases (book of signs and book of glory which mixes Dodd's and Bultmann's proposal for the structure of the Gospel). Brown, *The Gospel According to John*, 1:cxxxviii-ix. Beasley-Murray basically accepts such a division but proposes to see the whole Gospel as a book of signs, since he sees the purpose of the Gospel as being stated in 21:24-25. Beasley-Murray, *John*, xc.

[117] D.M. Smith made a plausible case for viewing 12:37-40 as a "primitive transition" linking the seemingly contradictory Christologies explicated in the two divisions of the Gospel of John: D. Moody Smith, "Setting and Shape of a Johannine Narrative Source," *JBL* 95 (1976): 239. Smith's view is influenced by B. Lindars who believed that John is here closer to the original understanding and usage of the Old Testament quotations used by early Christians to explain the death of Jesus than is Matthew. Barnabas Lindars, *New Testament Apologetic: The Doctrinal Significance of the Old Testament Quotations* (Philadelphia: Westminster, 1961), 271-72.

[118] Anton Dauer, *Die Passionsgeschichte im Johannesevangelium: Eine traditions-geschichtliche und theologische Untersuchung zu Joh. 18, 1-19, 30* (München: Kösel, 1972), 304; Evans, "Obduracy and the Lord's Servant," 228; idem, "Old Testament in the Gospels," *DJG*, 587.

narratives affords satisfactory answers to those problems.[119] Thus, John 12:37-41, which quotes Isaiah 6:10, could be understood as a high point of John's apologetic for the passion of Christ.[120]

> [37] Although he had performed so many signs in their presence, they did not believe in him. [38] This was to fulfill the word spoken by the prophet Isaiah:
> "Lord, who has believed our message,
> and to whom has the arm of the Lord been revealed?"
> [39] And so they could not believe, because Isaiah also said,
> [40] "He has blinded their eyes
> and hardened their heart,
> so that they might not look with their eyes,
> and understand with their heart and turn—
> and I would heal them."
> [41] Isaiah said this because he saw his glory and spoke about him. (John 12:37-41, NRSV)

From 12:39-41 onward, John forcefully explicates that the rejection of the Messiah accords with God's redemptive program as it is so prophesied in the Old Testament.[121] This is not, however, to say that the Passion was simply to comply with the prophecies, since Jesus existed before the Old Testament figures and through whom the divine revelation was delivered to Israel. The function of these fulfillment accounts is to show that Jesus fulfills the goal or purpose of the Jewish scriptures.[122] Thus, the fourth evangelist calls forth Isaiah not as a prophet

---

[119] Smith, "Setting and Shape of a Johannine Narrative Source," 236-41. Cf. Rudolf Bultmann, *Theology of the New Testament* (London: SCM, 1955), 1: 44-46. W. Rebell and E. Stegemann further identify the function of the concentrated recourse to the Scripture in John; that is, to "fight for tradition (*Kampf um Tradition*)" in order for the fourth evangelist to win fellow Jews because the tradition had an authenticating strength (*Legitimationskraft*). Walter Rebell, *Gemeinde als Gegenwelt: Zur soziologischen und didaktischen Funktion des Johannesevangeliums* (Frankfurt: Lang, 1987), 109; Ekkehard Stegemann, "Die Tragödie der Nähe: Zu den judenfeindlichen Aussagen des Johannesevangeliums," *Kul* 4 (1989): 119.

[120] C.K. Barrett, "The Old Testament in the Fourth Gospel," *JTS* 48 (1947): 169. Some exegetes consider the function of the psalm citations in the Gospel passion narratives as polemic. U.P. McCaffrey, "Psalm Quotations in the Passion Narratives of the Gospels," in *Relationship between the Old and New Testament: Proceedings of the Sixteenth Annual Meeting of the New Testament Society of South Africa, Held at the University of Potchefstroom for Christian Higher Education from the 1st to the 3rd of July 1980*, ed. Nuwe-Testamentiese Werkgemeenskap van Suid-Afrika (Bloemfontein, South Africa: New Testament Society of South Africa, 1981), 74; Brown, *The Gospel according to John*, 913. However, the non-apologetic nature of the Johannine psalm citations is expressed in Wilhelm Rothfuchs, *Die Erfüllungszitate des Matthäus-Evangeliums: Eine biblisch-theologische Untersuchung* (Stuttgart: Kohlhammer 1969), 170-72.

[121] Hamid-Khani, *Revelation and Concealment of Christ*, 258-330.

[122] "These passages [i.e., the Matthean fulfillment texts] are not saying that the Law and the Prophets are just predictions of future events, nor is it saying that Jesus simply

who foresees and predicts the future coming of Messiah but as a witness who bears testimony to the conversation between Yahweh God and the preexistent Christ.[123]

Interesting is a high concentration of the catenae from the Psalms in these Passion narratives that contain five out of the eighteen quotations which include a fulfillment formulae (see Appendix 6: "Explicit Old Testament Materials in John"). On these grounds, thus, Daly-Denton posits that the fourth evangelist portrays the passion of Jesus in terms of the Davidic trials image.[124]

Judas' betrayal as foreshadowed in David: John 13:18. In the end of the foot-washing account in John 13, Jesus covertly reveals his betrayer as foreshadowed in the life of David:

περὶ πάντων ὑμῶν λέγω· ἐγὼ οἶδα τίνας ἐξελεξάμην· ἀλλ' ἵνα ἡ γραφὴ πληρωθῇ· ὁ τρώγων μου τὸν ἄρτον ἐπῆρεν ἐπ' ἐμὲ τὴν πτέρναν αὐτοῦ. (John 13:18, NA[28])

"I am not speaking of all of you; I know whom I have chosen. But it is to fulfill the scripture, 'The one who ate my bread has lifted his heel against me.'" (John 13:18, NRSV)

Even my bosom friend in whom I trusted,
who ate of my bread, has lifted the heel against me. (Ps 41:9, NRSV)

καὶ γὰρ ὁ ἄνθρωπος τῆς εἰρήνης μου, ἐφ' ὃν ἤλπισα, ὁ ἐσθίων ἄρτους μου, ἐμεγάλυνεν ἐπ' ἐμὲ πτερνισμόν. (Psalm 40:10, LXX)

גַּם־אִישׁ שְׁלוֹמִי ׀ אֲשֶׁר־בָּטַחְתִּי בוֹ אוֹכֵל לַחְמִי הִגְדִּיל עָלַי עָקֵב׃ (Ps 41:10, BHS[5])

This Johannine text contains the only occurrence of Psalm 41:9 in the entire corpus of the New Testament. Unlike other Old Testament quotations in John, the text form of this verse indicates a closer proximity to the Hebrew scriptural traditions than those of the Septuagint.[125] The Hebrew text literally reads "the one who ate my bread raised up the heel against me." On the other hand, the LXX text can be read as following: "the one who eats my loaves raised up treachery against me." Such gesture as lifting up of heels is regarded as obscene in the Middle East even today.[126] Late rabbinic traditions attribute the original Hebrew

---

fulfills the parts of the Law and the Prophets which happen to be predictions. It means Jesus is the true purpose and goal of the OT." Dan McCartney and Peter Enns, "Matthew and Hosea: A Response to John Sailhamer," *WTJ* 63 (2001): 104.

[123] Günter Reim, "Wie der Evangelist Johannes gemäss Joh 12,37 ff: Jesaja 6 gelesen hat," *ZNW* 92 (2001): 33-46.

[124] Daly-Denton, *David in the Fourth Gospel*, 189-242.

[125] Menken believes that the present quotation is John's own translation from the Hebrew text. M.J.J. Menken, "'He Who Eats My Bread, Has Raised His Heel against Me' (John 13:18)," in *Old Testament Quotations in the Fourth Gospel: Studies in Textual Form* (Kampen: Kok, 1996), 123-38. Similarly, Wengst, *Das Johannesevangelium*, 2:99, n. 43.

[126] Michaels, *The Gospel of John*, 740, n. 93.

text to the incidents related with Ahithophel's betrayal against David in 2 Samuel 15-17 (*b. Sanh.* 106b; *Tg. Ps.* 55; *Num. R.* 18.17; *m. Abot* 6.3).[127] At first glance, therefore, it seems that the quotation serves to establish a David-Jesus typology.[128]

However, a narrative contextual reading points to another direction. The immediately preceding paragraph recounts the servant-hood of Jesus in a foot-washing account (Jn 13:1-17).[129] The following section narrates the new commandment of the master, Jesus' charge to love one another (Jn 13:34-35). Furthermore, the introduction to the fulfillment formula states that the quotation is to assist the disciples to have faith in Christ even at the face of the imminent betrayal:

> I tell you this now, before it occurs, so that when it does occur, you may believe that I am he. (John 13:19, NRSV)

That is, the betrayal did not take Jesus by surprise, but, in his omniscience, he willingly obeyed the course of action as prescribed by God. Söding's comment on this aspect is particularly helpful:

> Throughout the Passion narratives, John emphasizes the sovereignty of Jesus. He knows his fate (13:1f), he gives out a long farewell speech (John 14-16) and is in an intense intercessory prayer (John 17) for his disciples before his time of death. Before Pilate, he uses the necessity of the defense process forced upon him an opportunity for a final revelation of his mission, being uncompromising, and with the greatest claim to the highest intensity: 'I am a king' (18:37).[130]

Accordingly, the omniscience and willingness on the part of Jesus qualify the glory language and offset the shocking betrayal by a close pupil:

---

[127] *Babylonian Talmud*, of which *Sanhedrin* is a part, dates to the second through fifth centuries A.D. Evans, *Ancient Texts for New Testament Studies*, 228. The *Targum of Psalms* belongs to the body of Targums, which, at the earliest, dates to the fifth century A.D. Paul V.M. Flesher and Bruce Chilton, *The Targums: A Critical Introduction* (Waco: Baylor University Press, 2011), 235-36, 252-54. *Numbers Rabbah* is a late homiletic midrash dating to the eleventh century A.D. H.L. Strack and G. Stemberger, *Introduction to the Talmud and Midrash*, trans. Markus Bockmuehl (Minneapolis: Fortress, 1992), 337-39. These rabbinic occurrences are identified in Nicholas J. Zola, "'The One Who Eats My Bread Has Lifted His Heel against Me': Psalm 41:10 in 1QHa 13.25-26 and John 13:18," *PRSt* 37 (2010): 417.

[128] Daly-Denton, *David in the Fourth Gospel*, 191-201.

[129] For the theological and hermeneutical importance of this pericope for the ensuing Johannine narratives, see Christoph Demke, "Das Evangelium der Dialoge: Hermeneutische und methodologische Beobachtungen zur Interpretation des Johannesevangeliums," *ZTK* 97 (2000): 164-82.

[130] Thomas Söding, "Kreuzerhöhung: Zur Deutung des Todes Jesu nach Johannes," *ZTK* 103 (2006): 7-8. For the tradition history of this motive, see Stefan Schreiber, *Gesalbter und König: Titel und Konzeptionen der königlichen Gesalbtenerwartung in frühjüdischen und urchristlichen Schriften* (Berlin: Walter de Gruyter, 2000), 453f, cited in Söding, "Kreuzerhöhung," 8, n. 16.

³¹ When he had gone out, Jesus said, "Now the Son of Man has been glorified, and God has been glorified in him. ³² If God has been glorified in him, God will also glorify him in himself and will glorify him at once. (John 13:31-32, NRSV)[131]

On this point, Zumstein succinctly summarizes the power, authority, and omniscience of Christ in the Fourth Gospel and the passion narratives in particular:

> The concept of power proves to be one of the key categories of the Johannine Christology. . . . In the first twelve chapters of the Gospel, the Johannine Christ is indeed presented as the one who has all authority and power over the cosmos and human beings. The motifs of narratives that support this judgment are as follows. The power of the Johannine Christ at the first noticeable level is of knowledge.[132] Omniscience of the Son is equal with that of the Father and he knows the heart of human beings.[133] This power is then manifested in sovereign freedom that Christ demonstrated. . . . he is the undisputed master of his destiny.[134] Moreover, the signs say he accomplished his unquestionable authority over creation. Finally, the pronouncement discourse presents him as an eschatological agent who was commissioned by God and who was given all power. . . . Indeed, if the Johannine Christ is omniscient, omniscience does not remove the hostility of human beings, but on the contrary leads to face the cross. The knowledge of the hour is nothing other than the knowledge of the hour of the cross. . . . The last sign, which is also the greatest, the resurrection of Lazarus, is the very act that triggers the Passion. The greatest sign triggers the greatest hostility. The eschatological offer of life leads to the death of the revelator [Christ]. . . . So we are faced with a paradox. On the one hand, the Johannine Christ is the holder of all power and authority, but this power does not fit into the world order, nor does it impose according to the criteria of the world. All manifested sovereignty leads to the cross. The dramatic structure of the Gospel that makes a story oriented toward the cross conclusively supports this thesis.[135]

Therefore, the point of citing Psalm 41:9 seems to underscore the divine characteristics of Jesus. If the Davidic analogy is intended at all, it is certainly kept on a secondary level.[136]

---

[131] Wengst, *Das Johannesevangelium*, 2:99; Dietzfelbinger, *Das Evangelium nach Johannes*, 2:15.

[132] Omniscience is a characteristic feature of the Johannine portrait of Christ. This narrative feature allows to highlight the omnipotence and freedom of revelator *vis-à-vis* the world. On this note, Zumstein refers to Rudolf Bultmann, *Theologie des Neuen Testaments* (Tübingen: Mohr Siebeck, 1984), 395-96.

[133] Jn 2:24-25; 10:30; 17:11, 12.

[134] Jn 8:59; 10:39.

[135] Jean Zumstein, "Le lavement des pieds (Jean 13,1-20): Un exemple de la conception johannique du pouvoir," *RTP* 132 (2000): 345-47. Zumstein lists three prolepses that signals the direction of the story. In the first twelve chapters, the prolepses of time (ἡ ὥρα), elevation (ὑψόω) and glorification (δοξάζω) are clearly oriented toward the cross. Ibid., 347, n. 9. Also, idem, "L'interprétation johannique de la mort du Christ," in *Four Gospels 1992: Festschrift Frans Neirynck*, ed. Frans van Segbroeck and Christopher M. Tuckett (Louvain: Peeters, 1992), 3:2121-23.

[136] Zumstein, "Le lavement des pieds," 347-49. *Pace* Carson, *The Gospel according to John*, 470-71.

Irony of Jewish persecution: John 15:25. In the midst of the so-called "farewell discourse," Jesus provides his disciples with the new commandment to love one another and warns them also of impending persecution.[137] It is in this context that Jesus brings forth the groundlessness of Jewish persecution, which "fulfills" Scripture:

> It was to fulfill the word that is written in their law, "They hated me without a cause." (John 15:25, NRSV)

> ἀλλ' ἵνα πληρωθῇ ὁ λόγος ὁ ἐν τῷ νόμῳ αὐτῶν γεγραμμένος ὅτι *ἐμίσησάν με δωρεάν*. (John 15:25, NA[28])

It can be argued that this citation reinforces the alleged recurrent theme of David as a proto-type of Jesus. Ps 35:19 or Ps 69:4 are in view as possible sources of this reference:

> Do not let my treacherous enemies rejoice over me,
>   or those who hate me without cause wink the eye. (Ps 35:19, NRSV)

> More in number than the hairs of my head
>   are those who hate me without cause;
> many are those who would destroy me,
>   my enemies who accuse me falsely.
> What I did not steal
>   must I now restore? (Ps 69:4, NRSV)

The textual form of this psalm quotation is closer to the LXX than the MT as usual.[138] The tenor of this verse is that just as the world hated the psalmist, David, without reason, so will the disciples of Jesus be persecuted groundlessly:[139] "If the world hates you, be aware that it hated me before it hated you" (John 15:18, NRSV).

However, a closer reading of the narrative flow requires us to focus on a more prominent theme of the pericope. In vv. 1 through 17 of John 15, Jesus speaks of bearing the fruit of love in the imagery of grapevine and friend.[140] This special

---

[137] For the intertextual dynamics of this text with the Hebrew scriptures, see Hanna Stettler, "Die Gebote Jesu im Johannesevangelium (14,15.21; 15,10)," *Bib* 92 (2011): 554-79. Stettler finds a three-fold allusion to the new covenant texts in Jeremiah 31:31-34 and Ezekiel 36:26-27 and the eschatological prophet like Moses in Deuteronomy 18:15-19.

[138] M.J.J. Menken, "'They Hated Me without Reason' (John 15:25)," in *Old Testament Quotations in the Fourth Gospel: Studies in Textual Form* (Kampen: Kok, 1996), 139-46.

[139] Daly-Denton, *David in the Fourth Gospel*, 201-08.

[140] For a history of research of this pericope, see Fernando F. Segovia, "The Theology and Provenance of John 15:1-17," *JBL* 101 (1982): 115-28; Michel Gourgues, "La vigne du Père (Jn 15,1-17) ou le rassemblement des enfants de Dieu," in *Communion et réunion: Mélanges Jean-Marie Roger Tillard*, ed. Gillian Rosemary Evans, Michel Gourgues, and Jean-Marie-Roger Tillard (Louvain: Leuven University Press; Peeters, 1995), 265-81.

relationship with Jesus and the ensuing fruit-bearing result in the reception of persecution from the world (or Jews). It is in this context that a quotation from the Psalter is inserted in the present text. This citation serves two functions in particular. First the excerpt from the Psalm underscores the irony that the law, to which Jews adhere so staunchly, condemns their rebellion against the law in persecuting Jesus and his followers. As a consequence, they unwittingly fulfill their own scriptures.[141] At the same time, they have no excuse for their transgression since they witnessed the signs and heard the words of Jesus:

> If I had not come and spoken to them, they would not have sin; but now they have no excuse for their sin. . . . If I had not done among them the works that no one else did, they would not have sin. But now they have seen and hated both me and my Father. (John 15:22, 24, NRSV)

Second, the quotation serves as a pre-warning that points forward the impending persecution:

> I have said these things to you to keep you from stumbling. (John 16:1, NRSV)

Just as in John 13:18, rather than providing a palpable David-Jesus typology, the quotation from the Psalter in John 15:25 reveals a divine characteristic of Jesus, namely, his foreknowledge which prompted Him to warn His followers of the upcoming trials.

Allocation of Jesus' clothes: John 19:24. Like the Synoptic Gospels (Matt 27:35; Mark 15:24; Luke 23:34), John records the division of Jesus' clothes by the Roman soldiers. Yet it is only John who brings out the Scripture to depict this scene in terms of "fulfillment." In addition, it should be noted that the quote from the Psalm is unmistakable because of the introductory formula, although the wording is slightly different from its original source.[142]

> ^{24} So they said to one another, "Let us not tear it, but cast lots for it to see who will get it." This was to fulfill what the scripture says,
> "They divided my clothes among themselves,
>   and for my clothing they cast lots." (John 19:24, NRSV)

They divide my clothes among themselves,
    and for my clothing they cast lots." (Ps 22:18, NRSV)

εἶπαν οὖν πρὸς ἀλλήλους· μὴ σχίσωμεν αὐτόν, ἀλλὰ λάχωμεν περὶ αὐτοῦ τίνος ἔσται· ἵνα ἡ γραφὴ πληρωθῇ [ἡ λέγουσα]·
    διεμερίσαντο τὰ ἱμάτιά μου ἑαυτοῖς
    καὶ ἐπὶ τὸν ἱματισμόν μου ἔβαλον κλῆρον.
Οἱ μὲν οὖν στρατιῶται ταῦτα ἐποίησαν. (John 19:24, NA^{28})

---

[141] Carson, *The Gospel according to John*, 527.

[142] Menken posits that the quotation of the verse is a direct excerpt from the LXX. M.J.J. Menken, "The Use of the Septuagint in Three Quotations in John: Jn 10,34; 12,38; 19,24," in *Scriptures in the Gospels*, ed. Christopher M. Tuckett (Louvain: Leuven University Press, 1997), 367-93.

יְחַלְּקוּ בְגָדַי לָהֶם וְעַל־לְבוּשִׁי יַפִּילוּ גוֹרָל: (Ps 22:19, BHS⁵)

Two observations stand out with regards to the interest of this study. First, some have argued that the un-torn inner garment symbolizes the unity of and the everlasting promise given to the Davidic kingdom, a precedent of the Johannine community or the early church.[143] For example,

> In biblical lore, prophetic garment-tearing symbolizes the loss of the kingship (Saul) or the division of the kingdom with concomitant diminishment of the king's sovereignty (Ahijah). Set against this background, the Johannine insistence that Jesus' tunic was not torn is a declaration that, in spite of the utter despoliation that he willingly suffered, Jesus' royal status remained intact and undiminished. "The hour" thus emerges as the definitive moment when the 2 Sam 7 promise to David of everlasting kingship is realized.[144]

Some early exegetes, based on some Talmudic literature and Josephus, also posited that the unity of the undergarment signifies the priesthood of Jesus.[145] A growing number of recent exegetes refute these views.[146] This interpretation runs into difficulty not only for its allegorical hermeneutics but also for its ignorance of the narrative context that the garment is taken away from Jesus. Second, some commentators observe that the catena from Psalm 22:18 functions to bring forth the aspect of Jesus' death as a righteous sufferer foreshadowed in David's life.[147] In this respect, Schnackenburg's interpretation seems more cogent to the narrative flow that the giving up of his garments implicates his total sacrifice.[148]

The second observation, however, is still feasible in view of the recurrent quotations from the book of Psalms in the passion narratives, because the Psalter was closely associated with David in early Judaism. In contrast, it must be noted,

---

[143] For example, R. Alan Culpepper, "The Theology of the Johannine Passion Narrative: John 19:16b-30," *Neot* 31 (1997): 27-28.

[144] Daly-Denton, *David in the Fourth Gospel*, 208-19 (218).

[145] Helen K. Bond, "Discarding the Seamless Robe: The High Priesthood of Jesus in John's Gospel," in *Israel's God and Rebecca's Children: Christology and Community in Early Judaism and Christianity*, ed. David B. Capes et al (Waco: Baylor University Press, 2007), 183-94, 414-18.

[146] Ignace de la Potterie, "La tunique 'non divisée' de Jésus, symbole de l'unité messianique," in *New Testament Age: Essays in Honor of Bo Reicke*, ed. William C. Weinrich (Macon: Mercer University Press, 1984), 1:133; Elizabeth G. Pemberton, "The Seamless Garment: A Note on John 19:23-24," *ABR* 54 (2006): 50-55. For a discussion on the research history of the views, see Wengst, *Das Johannesevangelium*, 2:255-56. Dietzfelbinger discards both theories in view of the narrative context. Dietzfelbinger, *Das Evangelium nach Johannes*, 2:300.

[147] Carson, *The Gospel according to John*, 612-13; Andreas Köstenberger, *John* (Grand Rapids: Baker, 2004), 547.

[148] Bultmann, *The Gospel of John*, 671, n. 2; Schnackenburg, *The Gospel according to St. John*, 3:274; Garland, "Fulfillment Quotations in John's Account of the Crucifixion," 238; Beasley-Murray, *John*, 347-48; Dietzfelbinger, *Das Evangelium nach Johannes*, 2:300.

however, that such a connection is largely overshadowed by the theme of the divine sovereignty in this Johannine text.[149] The psalmic catena is probably better understood in terms of the cohesion of Jesus' crucifixion with the divine redemptive program, rather than Jesus' fulfilling the qualification expected of a Davidic Messiah. In this respect, Keener's comment is illuminating.

> John's most central implication at this point, however, is the fulfillment of Scripture. His οὖν at the end of v. 24 ("this is why the soldiers did these things") reinforces the point: the soldiers may have acted according to custom and may have acted according to evil desires, but they ultimately were unwittingly fulfilling God's unbreakable word.[150]

David Garland also detects the divine sovereignty as an overarching theme in this account:

> On the one hand, [for the Jews] the specific fulfillment of Scripture reveals that Jesus' death does not disqualify him, but rather validates him as Messiah. On the other hand, [for Christians] the Evangelist also unfurls the soteriological significance of that death and shows how, in this crucifixion, God overrules the actions of humans to achieve salvation.[151]

Jesus' thirst: John 19:28. Some suggest that the last word of Jesus in John 19:28 indicates his thirst to be in union with God, as the Psalms often portray David to be.[152]

> After this, when Jesus knew that all was now finished, he said (in order to fulfill the scripture), "I am thirsty." (John 19:28, NRSV)

> Μετὰ τοῦτο εἰδὼς ὁ Ἰησοῦς ὅτι ἤδη πάντα τετέλεσται, ἵνα τελειωθῇ ἡ γραφή, λέγει· διψῶ. (John 19:28, NA[28])

The following poetic expressions paint a sentimentally moving picture of his dire spiritual hunger, especially over against the backdrop of Palestine's dry landscapes.

> As a deer longs for flowing streams,
> so my soul longs for you, O God. (Ps 42:1, NRSV)

---

[149] Carson, *The Gospel according to John*, 612.
[150] Craig S. Keener, *The Gospel of John: A Commentary* (Peabody: Hendrickson, 2003), 2:1140.
[151] David E. Garland, "The Fulfillment Quotations in John's Account of the Crucifixion," in *Perspectives on John: Method and Interpretation in the Fourth Gospel*, ed. Robert B. Sloan and Mikeal C. Parsons (Lewiston: Edwin Mellen, 1993), 232. Garland concludes the two-fold functions (apologetic and soteriological) of the four catenae from the Psalms in the Johannine passion narratives.
[152] Daly-Denton, *David in the Fourth Gospel*, 219-29. Dauer considers the participle εἰδὼς to hold together the passion pericope (13:1-19:29) as an *inclusio*. Dauer, *Die Passionsgeschichte im Johannesevangelium*, 202.

> O God, you are my God, I seek you,
>   my soul thirsts for you;
>   my flesh faints for you,
>   as in a dry and weary land where there is no water. (Ps 63:1, NRSV)

On the contrary, however, the fourth evangelist forcefully and meticulously endeavors to bring forth the point that every turn of events involved in Jesus' passion complies with the will of God as recorded in the Old Testament Scripture. Even a common phenomenon, which can happen to an average man hanged on a tree, serves to fulfill the Scripture prophesied of the Messiah. This declaration of thirst and the subsequent drinking of vinegar could refer to the cup of sacrifice alluded to earlier in John 18:11, or to the flowing of the living water promised in John 7:28.[153] Yet the focus of attention should still be given to the motif of the fulfillment of Scripture.[154] The New Revised Standard Version places the purpose phrase "in order to fulfill the scripture" within parentheses, indicating that it may not have been in the original writing. It is because Papyrus 66 (the third century) and codex Alexandrinus (the fifth century) do not contain that phrase. However, the textual attestation for its inclusion in the original reading is also quite early and strong, although the textual reading without the phrase outnumbers. This purpose phrase is found in the following manuscripts: ℵ (codex Sinaiticus, the fourth century), D^s (codex Bezae, the fifth century), Θ (codex Koridethi, the ninth century), $f^{1.13}$ and others.[155] A highly significant aspect for the textual assessment of these readings is that the reading of codex Sinaiticus is often considered more important than any other manuscripts in New Testament textual criticism. In addition, the textual witnesses in favor of this reading are represented by both the Alexandrian and Western text types.[156] On this textual assessment, thus, the UBS fourth edition differs from the Nestle-Aland twenty-eighth edition that it includes the phrase without parentheses or any textual notes.[157]

It has been noted that the fulfillment theme is an overarching motif that drives

---

[153] "When Jesus says, 'I thirst,' therefore, he not only points to the fulfillment of scripture and the fulfillment of his offer of living water to those who would come to him; he also figuratively announces his own death." Culpepper, "The Theology of the Johannine Passion Narratives," 32. Also Barrett sees the implication for the promise of the living water in the flowing of Jesus' water and blood. C.K. Barrett, *The Gospel according to St. John: An Introduction with Commentary and Notes on the Greek Text* (Philadelphia: Westminster, 1978), 534.

[154] Dietzfelbinger, *Das Evangelium nach Johannes*, 2:304.

[155] NA^{28}, 313.

[156] For a helpful survey for New Testament textual criticism, see Bruce M. Metzger and Bart D. Ehrman, *The Text of the New Testament: Its Transmission, Corruption, and Restoration* (Oxford: OUP, 2005); Paul D. Wegner, *A Student's Guide to Textual Criticism of the Bible: Its History, Methods & Results* (Downers Grove: InterVarsity, 2006), 207-301.

[157] UBS^4, 398.

home the culmination of the redemptive plan in the sacrificial death of Jesus Christ. On the same token, however, an equal theological emphasis is due to the aspect of Jesus' active engagement in that divine salvific program. Even to the very last moment, it is Jesus who moves forward through the path of sacrifice incumbent upon him as the Messiah. That is, he is not a reluctant participant of the cross event.[158] That point sheds light to the following remark:

> When Jesus had received the wine, he said, "it is finished." Then, he bowed his head and gave up his spirit. (John 19:30, NRSV)[159]

Christ's last outcry, "it is finished," should be seen as an expression of relief and satisfaction that he has accomplished all that he was expected and he hoped to do. The fulfillment formulae observed so far, including the one found in John 19:28, indicate that Jesus, in his suffering and death, willingly fulfilled the qualifications required of the Messiah in minute details as expected in Scripture. To this point, Brown's comment is pertinent:

> We may suppose that Jesus really is thirsty; but he is thirsty only by his own volition, because of his own awareness that there is a prophecy to be realized.[160]

Kraus even describes this cross event in stronger terms, "accomplishment" or "completion" rather than more popular "fulfillment":

> [E]ven in the deepest humiliation and the greatest agony Jesus is the sovereign and has the perfection of God's will, which is recorded in the Scriptures in view. V. 30 then states that with the drinking of vinegar wine everything is done (τετέλεσται) now. With this τετέλεσται in v. 30, one aspect is certain that the revelation of God reached its goal through Jesus on the cross now. . . . the verse also speaks of completion of the scriptures. . . Just as Jesus completed his father's work, the scripture itself is brought to perfection by him.[161]

Not breaking of the legs: John 19:36-37. The last reference to the book of Psalms appears in John 19:36 where the failure to break Jesus' legs is referred to as "fulfilling the Scripture." John, then, goes on to mention Zechariah 12:10, in order to show how the death of Jesus tallies with the picture of the Messiah as prescribed in the Old Testament. These two citations or allusions to the Old Testament are tied with one another by the introductory formula, "these things

---

[158] Dietzfelbinger, *Das Evangelium nach Johannes*, 2:305.

[159] For a study that theologically and historically explores the last words of Jesus in a nuanced way, see Michael Theobald, "Der Tod Jesu im Spiegel seiner 'letzten Worte' vom Kreuz," *TQ* 190 (2010): 1-30.

[160] Brown, *The Gospel according to John*, 2:928. Also, "The thirst of Jesus represents his complete obedience to the Father's will, drinking to the dregs the cup of death; and by it, salvation, living water, is poured out for human kind. To use another Johannine image, from the bitter wine vinegar comes the good wine that has been kept until now." Garland, "Fulfillment Quotations in John's Account of the Crucifixion," 244.

[161] Kraus, "Die Vollendung der Schrift nach Joh 19,28," 632-33.

occurred so that the Scripture might be fulfilled (ἐγένετο γὰρ ταῦτα ἵνα ἡ γραφὴ πληρωθῇ):

> ³³ But when they came to Jesus and saw that he was already dead, they did not break his legs. ³⁴ Instead, one of the soldiers pierced his side with a spear, and at once blood and water came out. ³⁵ (He who saw this has testified so that you also may believe. His testimony is true, and he knows that he tells the truth.) ³⁶ These things occurred so that the scripture might be fulfilled, "None of his bones shall be broken." ³⁷ And again another passage of scripture says, "They will look on the one whom they have pierced." (John 19:33-37, NRSV)

However, the exact provenance of the allusion for the first reference is difficult to ascertain because the wording differs slightly from the alleged Old Testament texts. Usually, Exodus 12:46, Numbers 9:12, and Psalm 34:20 are suggested. Two passages from the Pentateuch refer to a commandment not to break a Paschal lamb's leg bones. The first example is found in Exodus 12:46:

> It shall be eaten in one house; you shall not take any of the animal outside the house, and you shall not break any of its bones. (Ex 12:46, NRSV)

The second example is mentioned in Numbers 9:12:

> They shall leave none of it until morning, nor break a bone of it; according to all the statute for the passover they shall keep it. (Num 9:12, NRSV)

The last passage appears in Psalm 34:20:

> He keeps all their bones; not one of them will be broken. (Ps 34:20, NRSV)

There are three possibilities. If the first two passages are assumed to be the origin, then, the fourth evangelist associates Jesus with the Paschal lamb, whose bones should be kept intact according to the Levitical regulations.[162] On the other hand, if the Psalm text is opted for, the picture is of Jesus who is cast as a righteous sufferer, as was David when Yahweh protected him from Abimelech.[163] Finally, a growing number of exegetes mediate the tension between the two options by positing a confluence of the two traditions on the present Johannine text.[164] Some

---

[162] J.M. Ford, "'Mingled Blood' from the Side of Jesus (John XIX.34)," *NTS* 15 (1969): 337-38.

[163] Dodd, *The Interpretation of the Fourth Gospel*, 233; idem, *The Historical Tradition in the Fourth Gospel* (Cambridge: CUP, 1963), 131; Edwin D. Freed, *Old Testament Quotations in the Gospel of John* (Leiden: Brill, 1965), 110.

[164] C.K. Barrett, "The Old Testament in the Fourth Gospel," *JTS* 48 (1947): 157; idem, *The Gospel according to St. John*, 558; Bultmann, *The Gospel of John*, 677-79; Lindars, *New Testament Apologetic*, 96; Schnackenburg, *The Gospel according to St. John*, 3:291-92; A.T. Hanson, *The Prophetic Gospel: A Study of John and the Old Testament* (Edinburgh: T & T Clark, 1991), 222; Bruce G. Schuchard, *Scripture within Scripture: The Interrelationship of Form and Function in the Explicit Old Testament Citations in the Gospel of John* (Atlanta: Scholars, 1992), 133-40; M.J.J. Menken, "'Not a Bone of Him Shall be Broken' (John 19:36)," in *Old Testament Quotations in*

from this group argue that the Psalm quotation attributes a characteristic of David to Jesus, that is, he is a royal Messiah because of the Psalm's association with David.[165] For instance, Daly-Denton unfolds her logic for this contention as follows:

> It is the contention of this study that the exegetical warrant for regarding a psalm quotation such as ὀστοῦν οὐ συντριβήσεται as spoken about Jesus the Messiah is to be found in the supposed Davidic authorship of the Psalter. According to the midrashic logic which this warrant permits, Jesus is to be recognized by his Davidic-likeness (not, John would say, by linear descent from David) as the king in whose name King David prophetically composed this psalm. Thus John's psalm citation portrays Jesus not as "righteous," but as royal.[166]

However, her argument and those of other exegetes along this line lose sight of the citation in view of the narrative contexts both of John and of the Psalm (let alone it seems unlikely that the original hearers immediately captured "the midrashic logic" of John). In Psalm 34, one verse of which is alluded to in the Johannine text, the psalmist speaks of God's redemption of a righteous sufferer (i.e., David) in the midst of trials. The gory portrayal of John 19:33-37, which recounts the piercing of Jesus' side that leads to the depletion of the inner bodily fluid, precludes, thus, a royal enthronement interpretation of the Psalm citation. The primary sense in which Psalm 34 is quoted is probably, as John plainly states, to show that the death of Jesus, even the manner in which he died, does not contradict the will of God but rather fulfills it.[167]

Piercing of the side: John 19:37. A more explicit allusion to David and particularly to his kingship is the last Old Testament citation found in John; he quotes Zechariah 12:10 with reference to the piercing of Jesus' side.[168]

---

the Fourth Gospel: Studies in Textual Form (Kampen: Kok, 1996), 147-66; Daly-Denton, David in the Fourth Gospel, 229-42.

[165] Martin Hengel, The Atonement: The Origins of the Doctrine in the New Testament (London: SCM, 1981), 41; Donald Juel, Messianic Exegesis: Christological Interpretation of the Old Testament in Early Christianity (Philadelphia: Fortress, 1988), 103.

[166] Daly-Denton, David in the Fourth Gospel, 239. Also, "as cited in John 19:36, it underlines the Johannine conception of Jesus' death as his triumphant royal enthronement." Ibid., 241.

[167] Garland, "Fulfillment Quotations in John's Account of the Crucifixion," 247-48.

[168] Menken posits that the citation from Zechariah derived from an early Christian translation of the Hebrew text, i.e., testimonium. M.J.J. Menken, "'They Shall Look on Him Whom They Have Pierced' (John 19:37)," in Old Testament Quotations in the Fourth Gospel: Studies in Textual Form (Kampen: Kok, 1996), 167-85; Arnold Stiglmair, "Der Durchbohrte: Ein Versuch zu Sach 12," ZKT 116 (1994): 451-56; Michaels, The Gospel of John, 976, n. 132. Recently, the Qumranic influence has been suggested. More precisely, the Greek Minor Prophets Scrolls discovered at the Cave of Horror in Nahal Hever in 1952 and 1961, hence 8QHevXIIgr. The date of this writing is between 50 B.C. and 50 A.D. William Randolph Bynum, The Fourth Gospel and the

And again another passage of scripture says, "They will look on the one whom they have pierced." (John 19:37, NRSV)

καὶ πάλιν ἑτέρα γραφὴ λέγει· ὄψονται εἰς ὃν ἐξεκέντησαν. (John 19:37, NA[28])

And I will pour out a spirit of compassion and supplication on the house of David and the inhabitants of Jerusalem, so that, when they look on the one whom they have pierced, they shall mourn for him, as one mourns for an only child, and weep bitterly over him, as one weeps over a firstborn. (Zech 12:10, NRSV)

καὶ ἐκχεῶ ἐπὶ τὸν οἶκον Δαυιδ καὶ ἐπὶ τοὺς κατοικοῦντας Ιερουσαλημ πνεῦμα χάριτος καὶ οἰκτιρμοῦ, καὶ ἐπιβλέψονται πρός με ἀνθ᾽ ὧν κατωρχήσαντο καὶ κόψονται ἐπ᾽ αὐτὸν κοπετὸν ὡς ἐπ᾽ ἀγαπητὸν καὶ ὀδυνηθήσονται ὀδύνην ὡς ἐπὶ πρωτοτόκῳ. (Zech 12:10, LXX)

וְשָׁפַכְתִּי עַל־בֵּית דָּוִיד וְעַל׀ יוֹשֵׁב יְרוּשָׁלַ͏ִם רוּחַ חֵן וְתַחֲנוּנִים וְהִבִּיטוּ אֵלַי אֵת אֲשֶׁר־דָּקָרוּ וְסָפְדוּ עָלָיו כְּמִסְפֵּד עַל־הַיָּחִיד וְהָמֵר עָלָיו כְּהָמֵר עַל־הַבְּכוֹר׃ (Zech 12:10, BHS[5])

Because of the phrase, "house of David," in Zechariah, some argue for the presence of the kingly characteristics in relation to the piercing of Jesus' side. A closer examination of the original context and that of John, however, militates against such a construal. Scholarly interpretations of Zechariah 12:10 are decisively divided on a number of issues (such as whether or not the subject of the violent act is the house of David) but one element enjoys a near-unanimous agreement, that is, David (or the house of David) is not identified with the one who is pierced, as it is related thus to Jesus in John.[169] Furthermore, the general message of Zechariah 12 is that Yahweh will transform the hearts of people of Israel, and the house of David will be a recipient of this blessing.[170] In view of the narrative contexts of both passages, thus, the following assessment of Daly-Denton concerning the implication of the Zechariah quotation does not stand under close scrutiny:

> The two sources complement each other: the paschal lamb reference points to the sacrificial efficacy of Jesus' death, the testimony of David pointing to the vindication of Jesus, not merely as "righteous," but as royal. . . . This royal portrayal of Jesus facilitates the recognition of the pierced one (Zech 12:10) as the one in whom κύριος εἰς βασιλέα ἐπὶ πᾶσαν τὴν γῆν (Zech 14:9).[171]

Contrary to Daly-Denton, the one pierced in Zechariah is someone other than

---

Scriptures: Illuminating the Form and Meaning of Scriptural Citation in John 19:37, NovTSup 144 (Leiden: Brill, 2012). Cf. Emanuel Tov, *The Greek Minor Prophets scroll from Naḥal Ḥever (8ḤevXII gr): The Seiyal Collection I*, DJD 8 (Oxford: Clarendon; OUP, 1990). For the rabbinic literary influence, see Frédéric Manns, "Zacharie 12,10 relu en Jean 19,37," *SBFLA* 56 (2006): 304-06.

[169] For interpretive issues and options of Zech 12:10, see Carol L. and Eric M. Meyers, *Zechariah 9-14: A New Translation with Introduction and Commentary* (New York: Doubleday, 1993), 333-59; Menken, "'They Shall Look on Him Whom They Have Pierced' (John 19:37)," 178-85.

[170] Manns, "Zacharie 12,10 relu en Jean 19,37," 302-03; Söding, "Kreuzerhöhung," 15.

[171] Daly-Denton, *David in the Fourth Gospel*, 240.

David, probably Yahweh or a prophetic figure who could be argued for a type of Jesus in this Johannine text.[172] In addition, the Lord, who will become Lord over the earth in Zechariah 14:9, is also, not David, as Daly-Denton maintains, but Yahweh. Thus, John seems to correlate Jesus with Yahweh (or a prophetic figure) and David (i.e., his house) with the New Testament believers (with particular emphasis on the eye-witness theme) in his use of the Zechariah texts.[173] If the fourth evangelist wishes to speak of a certain nature of Jesus by means of the citations from the Psalm and Zechariah, it is of his divinity, not his relation to David as some consider him to be expressed as a messianic precursor in this text. However, even such a high Christology of Jesus is not brought to the fore of the narratives in the passion accounts.

Conclusion

The Jewish writings in the second temple period envisaged David as an ideal figure such as a capable ruler, a genuine Jew, and even a messianic figure. Some New Testament writings such as the Synoptic Gospels and the Revelation display affinity with the motif of his image as a royal messianic prefiguration. In contrast to such a prefiguration motif, however, the fourth evangelist does not present Jesus from that angle, but rather seems to be in terms more congruous with the perception of him as a righteous sufferer.

The frequency of quotations from the book of Psalms should be noted at least on the sub-conscious level, if not on the surface as indicating this aspect. The reason is because the texts explicitly cited from the Psalter serve to expose that Jesus possesses messianic qualifications, especially his divine characteristics, such as omniscience and an unremitting willingness to comply with the Father's will. This aspect points to the authenticity of Jesus as Messiah as it is prescribed in the supreme authority of Judaism. Second, the texts cited from Scripture function to indicate that his death conforms to the divine redemptive program as foreshadowed in Scripture, and that evidently the cross event was not a precarious venture that inadvertently happened.

Finally, concerning the question posed at the beginning of this chapter, as to whether or not there is a messianic correspondence between David and Jesus, these observations aforementioned answer in the negative. The royal messianic image of David, which was most often envisaged in the contexts of the intertestamental Jewish eschatological hopes, does not fit the messianic picture that the Fourth Gospel provides. If the correlation must be pressed hard, it is

---

[172] Manns, "Zacharie 12,10 relu en Jean 19,37," 308.

[173] The house of David is a typological thesis to the New Testament believers. Menken, "'They Shall Look on Him Whom They Have Pierced' (John 19:37)," 178-85. For a prominent witness function of the citation, see Dietzfelbinger, *Das Evangelium nach Johannes*, 2:310-11. For an apologetic charge to believe in Jesus by the vivid description of his death, see Ludger Schenke, *Johannes: Kommentar* (Düsseldorf: Patmos, 1998), 363; Wengst, *Das Johannesevangelium*, 2:265.

found rather in the witness function of David for the messianic qualification of Jesus. In his numerous trials, the ideal Jewish figure offers analogies to the righteous suffering of Jesus, and in doing so David, perhaps unconsciously, foreshadows the characteristics of Messiah. Moreover, the house of David bears witness to the prefiguration of Jesus, i.e., the pierced Yahweh, just as the disciples of Jesus eye-witness the death of Jesus (as the citation from Zech 12:10 points out). This aspect is what most straightforwardly comes into the fore of the Johannine narratives in their use of the Old Testament passages that are related to David.

CHAPTER 5

Moses

Introduction

Of all the major Old Testament characters, Moses, "the man of God" (Deut 33:1; Josh 14:6; 1 Chr 23:14; Ezra 3:2; Ps 90:1; 1 Esdr 5:49; 4Q378 26 2; 4Q381 24 4), is most frequently addressed in the study of John's Gospel. Therein, not only his importance is often noted, but it is contended with much vigor that he is portrayed as a messianic prefiguration in the Gospel. Beginning with T.F. Glasson, a host of exegetes have understood the Johannine portrayal of Jesus in terms of a new Moses.[1] Or, at least, an earlier redactional trait of the Fourth Gospel is reflective of such a view, according to Wayne Meeks and J.L. Martyn.[2] This typological interpretation has been applied to other parts of the New Testament writings.[3] In a similar vein, a group of scholars draws attention to some early

---

[1] T. Francis Glasson, *Moses in the Fourth Gospel* (London: SCM, 1963); Marie-Émile Boismard, *Moïse ou Jésus: Essai de christologie Johannique* (Leuven: Peeters; Leuven University Press, 1988); Bertold Klappert, "'Mose hat von mir geschrieben': Leitlinien einer Christologie im Kontext des Judentums Joh 5,39-47," in *Hebräische Bibel und ihre zweifache Nachgeschichte: Festschrift für Rolf Rendtorff zum 65. Geburtstag*, ed. Erhard Blum, Christian Macholz, and Ekkhard W. Stegemann (Neukirchen-Vluyn: Neukirchener, 1990), 619-40; Siegfried Kreuzer, "'Wo ich hingehe, dahin könnt ihr nicht kommen': Joh 7,34; 8:21; 13,33 als Teil der Mosetypologie im Johannesevangelium," in *Die Kirche als historische und eschatologische Grösse: Festschrift für Kurt Niederwimmer zum 65. Geburtstag*, ed. W. Pratscher and G. Sauer (Frankfurt: Peter Lang, 1994), 63-76; Paul Trudinger, "A Prophet Like Me (Deut 18:5): Jesus and Moses in St Johns Gospel, Once Again," *DRev* 113 (1995): 193-95; Klaus Scholtissek, "'Die unauflösbare Schrift' (Joh 10,35): Zur Auslegung und Theologie der Schrift Israels im Johannesevangelium,'" in *Johannesevangelium—Mitte oder Rand des Kanons?: Neue Standortbestimmungen*, ed. Thomas Söding (Freiburg: Herder, 2003), 146-77; Sukmin Cho, *Jesus as Prophet in the Fourth Gospel* (Sheffield: Sheffield Phoenix, 2006).

[2] Wayne A. Meeks, *The Prophet-King: Moses Traditions and the Johannine Christology* (Leiden: Brill, 1967); J. Louis Martyn, "From the Expectation of the Prophet-Messiah like Moses . . . ," in *History and Theology in the Fourth Gospel*, 3rd ed. (Louisville: Westminster John Knox, 2003), 101-23; idem, ". . . To the Presence of the Son of Man," in *History and Theology in the Fourth Gospel* (Louisville: Westminster John Knox, 2003), 124-43.

[3] For the Gospel of Matthew, see François Refoulé, "Jésus, nouveau Moïse, ou Pierre, nouveau Grand Prêtre? (Mt 17,1-9; Mc 9,2-10)," *RTL* 24 (1993): 145-62; Dale C. Al-

strands of Jewish eschatological conceptions (particularly to the early rabbinic and Samaritan traditions) that allegedly exerted influence on Johannine Christology. On the opposite side stands another group of scholars which does not find a typological reading of the Moses texts to be pervasive in John. For example, Dieter Sänger finds no explicit trait of thought concerning Moses in terms of correspondence or typology not only in John but in the entire purview of the New Testament writings. Rather, the concepts of "intensification" and a "qualitative improvement" best depict the images of Moses in the New Testament.[4]

With such a divergence of scholarly assessment in view, this chapter seeks to explore the narrative function of Moses with regards to the Johannine Christology and in light of his messianic prefigurative references in the Old Testament and in the intertestamental Jewish literature. The first half of this chapter will address a sufficient number of selected passages from the Old Testament and early Jewish writings (especially those of the Palestinian provenance) that are particularly germane to the present investigation.

A word of caveat is in order at the outset. A large number of biblical scholars are skeptical about the benefit of comparing early gnostic writings with the Fourth Gospel. The main reason lies in the paucity of influence from early Judaism onto early Gnosticism. Thus, an inquiry into its literary dependence with John does not seem exegetically promising. For instance, a highly important early Jewish figure, Moses, is virtually absent in the entire early Gnostic documents: "This brief survey of references and/or attitudes to Moses in Gnostic writings suggests that any Jewish influence on Gnosticism may have been at most rather superficial."[5]

Upon grasping the Mosaic images in the Old Testament and in early Judaism, the second half of this chapter will deal with John's depiction of Moses and his narrative function with special reference to the christological conception in the Gospel. In conclusion, the possible link between early Judaism and Johannine Christology via Moses and his Christological contribution to the Gospel will be

---

lison, Jr., *The New Moses: A Matthean Typology* (Minneapolis: Fortress, 1993). For Luke-Acts, see David P. Moessner, "Paul and the Pattern of the Prophet like Moses in Acts," *SBLSP* 22 (1983): 203-12; J. Severino Croatto, "Jesus, Prophet like Elijah, and Prophet-Teacher like Moses in Luke-Acts," *JBL* 124 (2005): 451-65. For Hebrews, see Mary R. D'Angelo, *Moses in the Letter to the Hebrews* (Missoula: Scholars, 1979). For overviews of the research history, see John Lierman, *The New Testament Moses: Christian Perceptions of Moses and Israel in the Setting of Jewish Religion* (Tübingen: Mohr Siebeck, 2004), 10-29.

[4] Dieter Sänger, "'Von mir hat er geschrieben' (Joh 5,46): Zur Funktion and Bedeutung Mose im Neuen Testament," *KD* 41 (1995): 112-35.

[5] Christopher Tuckett, "Moses in Gnostic Writings," in *Moses in Biblical and Extra-Biblical Traditions*, ed. Axel Graupner and Michael Wolter (Berlin: Walter de Gruyter, 2007), 227-40 (p. 238 for the citation). Cf., Matthieu Smyths, "La figure de Moïse dans les sources gnostiques," in *Interprétations de Moïse: Égypte, Judée, Grèce et Rome*, ed. Philippe Borgeaud, Thomas Römer, and Youri Volokhine (Leiden: Brill, 2010), 247-67.

assessed.

Mosaic Images in the Old Testament and in Early Judaism

The Old Testament and Early Judaism mention a large number of persons. Yet none is more prominent than Moses. For example, Philo describes Moses as the "greatest and most perfect man" (*Mos.* 1:1).[6] His standing and multi-hued character have far reaching implications for understanding the Christian Bible. He is variously portrayed as the cult founder, a prophet, a priestly and kingly figure, the law-giver, and an example of Jewish royalty.[7] Some scholars have

---

[6] *Philo*, trans. F.H. Colson (Cambridge: Harvard University Press, 1935), 6:276-77; Sänger, "Von mir hat er geschrieben' (Joh 5,46)," 112.

[7] Lierman, *The New Testament Moses*, 32-257. Lierman even detects a strand of Jewish thought that associates Moses with baptism (ibid., 175-208). For more convenient surveys on the issues related to the perceptions of Moses in the Old Testament, see Erich Zenger, "Mose/Moselied/Mosesegen/Moseschriften I: Altes Testament," *TRE*, 23:330-41; M.A. Taylor and J.E. Harvey, "Moses," *NIDOTTE*, 4:949-60; Carl S. Ehrlich, "Moses, Torah, and Judaism," in *Rivers of Paradise: Moses, Buddha, Confucius, Jesus, and Muhammad as Religious Founders*, ed. David Noel Freedman and Michael J. McClymond (Grand Rapids: Eerdmans, 2001), 11-119; E. Otto, "Mose I: Altes Testament," *RGG*, 5:1534-38; Rolf Rendtorff, *Canonical Hebrew Bible: A Theology of the Old Testament* (Leiden: Deo, 2005), 545-59; for those of early Jewish literature, see J. Jeremias, "Μωϋσῆς," *TDNT*, 4:849-64; G. Oberhänsli-Widmer, "Mose/Moselied/Mosesegen/Moseschriften III: Apokalyptische und jüdisch-hellenistische Literatur," *TRE*, 23:347-57; Stan Harstine, *Moses as a Character in the Fourth Gospel: A Study of Ancient Reading Techniques* (Sheffield: Sheffield, 2002), 96-129; Meindert Dijkstra, "Moses, the man of God," in *Interpretation of Exodus: Studies in Honor of Cornelis Houtman*, ed. Riemer Roukema (Leuven: Peeters, 2006), 17-36; Axel Graupner and Michael Wolter, eds, *Moses in Biblical and Extra-Biblical Traditions* (Berlin: Walter de Gruyter, 2007); Christophe Nihan, "'Un Prophète Comme Moïse' (Deutéronome 18,15): Genèse Et Relectures D'une construction Deutéronomiste," in *La Construction de la Figure de Moïse*, ed. Thomas Römer (Paris: Gabalda, 2007), 43-76; George J. Brooke, "Moses in the Dead Sea Scrolls: Looking at Mount Nebo from Qumran," in *La construction de la figure de Moïse*, ed. Thomas Römer (Paris: Gabalda, 2007), 209-21; Thomas Römer, "Moses outside the Torah and the Construction of a Diaspora Identity," *JHS* 8 (2008): 1-12, idem, "Moïse: Un héros royal entre échec et divinisation," in *Interprétations de Moïse: Égypte, Judée, Grèce et Rome*, ed. Philippe Borgeaud, Thomas Römer, and Youri Volokhine (Leiden: Brill, 2010), 187-98. For the Mosaic portrait in early Greco-Egyptian and early rabbinic traditions, see M. Niehoff, "Mose III, 1: Antike Judentum," *RGG*, 5:1539-42; Claudio Zamagni, "Eusèbe de Césarée et les traditions extra-canoniques sur Moïse en Ethiopie," in *La Construction de la Figure de Moïse*, ed. Thomas Römer (Paris: Gabalda, 2007), 145-56; Thomas Römer, "Les guerres de Moïse," in *La Construction de la Figure de Moïse*, ed. Thomas Römer (Paris: Gabalda, 2007), 169-94; Philippe Borgeaud, Thomas Römer, and Youri Volokhine, eds., *Interprétations de Moïse: Égypte, Judée, Grèce et Rome* (Leiden: Brill, 2010); Klaus Wengst, "Der jüdische Mose: Die Gestalt des Mose im rabbinischen Judentum," *BK* 66 (2011): 19-24.

traced the various traditions of Jewish key figures (such as, prophetic, priestly, and scribal) to Moses. That is, Moses is the first in the prophet tradition. For example, the image of Elijah as the suffering prophet is in line with the suffering of Moses in the wilderness. On the other hand, the priestly succession also stems from Moses through his spiritual subordinate, Aaron. Furthermore, the book of Deuteronomy is considered as the Mosaic interpretation of the Sinai Torah. As such, Moses stands as the first in the line of the scribal tradition.[8] Of these images, however, four characteristics stand out, and they are particularly pertinent to the present discussion as they concern Johannine Christology. A considerable number of investigations into the historic Moses were advanced categorically such as a cult founder, legislator, prophet, charismatic leader, priest, etc., rather than biographically, due to the skeptical form critical influence of Wellhausen.[9] Zenger notes the danger of overgeneralization inherent in this type of systematic categorization.[10] For the convenience of presentation, however, the present study proceeds in line with this type of survey with such a caution in mind. The following preliminary survey will focus on his images in early Judaism as a figure of authority, a prophet, and a king. It is also noteworthy that some scholars contend that some of the early Jewish ascension and enthronement narratives confer a certain degree of divinity to Moses. Since such deification bears a direct bearing on this study, a close scrutiny of those texts will be included in the remainder of this section. Finally, an examination will be undertaken concerning some early Jewish texts that depict Moses as an eschatological redeemer figure, which could have readily developed into a Johannine Mosaic Christology.

Moses as Authority Figure with Particular Emphasis on Law-Giving and Legitimatizing

The Old Testament. This category of perception largely stems from Moses' reception and transmission of the Sinai revelation as recorded in Exodus 24 and the concomitant reinforcement of the Sinaitic covenant in the lives of Israelites as witnessed in the Book of Deuteronomy. The reception of oracles is a particular mark of a prophet in the Old Testament. It is, in Moses' case, most conspicuously evidenced in the Sinai event. As such, the issues related to the Sinai event should be treated under the category of a prophet. The Sinai event should be seen in terms of the messenger function, that is, the delivery of a divine oracle, which is the dominating aspect of the Old Testament prophets.[11] The enormous magnitude of the Torah reception, nevertheless, merits a separate treatment.

---

[8] Otto, *RGG*, 5:1537-38.
[9] Rudolf Smend, "Methoden der Moseforschung," in *Gesammelte Studien*, vol. 2 of *Zur ältesten Geschichte Israels* (Munich: Kaiser, 1987), 90; Zenger, *TRE*, 23:331.
[10] Ibid.
[11] James F. Ross, "The Prophet as Yahweh's Messenger (1962)," in *Prophecy in Israel: Search for an Identity*, ed. David L. Peterson (Philadelphia: Fortress, 1987), 112-21.

His role in the process of imparting the Law granted him a long-lasting status of authority. Another particular reason, for which his authority stands out, is due to the unparalleled degree of directness with which he received the divine revelation. The books of Exodus, Numbers, and Deuteronomy testify to the intimacy Moses enjoyed in his encounter with Yahweh. That is, unlike any of the other Old Testament prophets to whom God revealed himself in visions and dreams, God conversed with Moses "face to face."

> Thus the LORD used to speak to Moses face to face, as one speaks to a friend. (Ex 33:11a, NRSV)

> [6] And he said, "Hear my words:
> When there are prophets among you,
> I the LORD make myself known to them in visions;
> I speak to them in dreams.
> [7] Not so with my servant Moses;
> he is entrusted with all my house
> [8] With him I speak face to face—clearly, not in riddles;
> and he beholds the form of the LORD.
> Why then were you not afraid to speak against my servant Moses?" (Num 12:6-8, NRSV)

> Never since has there arisen a prophet in Israel like Moses, whom the LORD knew face to face. (Deut 34:10, NRSV)

The expression for "face-to-face" in the Numbers passage literally means "mouth to mouth" (פֶּה אֶל־פֶּה) but the New Revised Standard Version idiomatically translates "face to face."[12] The Exodus and Deuteronomy passages literally read "face to face" (פָּנִים אֶל־פָּנִים). An important qualification should be noted concerning the expression "face to face." In light of the surrounding literary contexts, the phrase does not imply that Moses directly beheld God, but it signifies his intimate relation or the directness of his encounter with Yahweh (i.e., without mediation). In other places, the Pentateuch clearly indicates that the prophet could not have observed the face of Yahweh (Exod 33:20-23) and he only beheld the "form or likeness (תְּמוּנָת)" of Yahweh (Num 12:8). Jeffrey Tigay's summation on this idiom is helpful in this respect:

> The point of the text is that Moses had the most direct contact with God of any prophet, and hence had the clearest knowledge of Him and His will.[13]

---

[12] J.A. Thompson and Elmer A. Martens, "פה," *NIDOTTE*, 3:583.

[13] Jeffrey H. Tigay, *Deuteronomy: The Traditional Hebrew Text with the New JPS Translation* (Philadelphia: Jewish Publication Society, 1996), 340. Some other reasonable suggestions for a better understanding of the phrase are "one on one," Richard D. Nelson, *Deuteronomy: A Commentary* (Louisville: Westminster/John Knox, 2002), 394; "an idiom of intimacy," John I. Durham, *Exodus* (Waco: Word, 1987), 443; "in person," "directly," or "without mediation," Duane L. Christensen, *Deuteronomy 21:10-34:12* (Nashville: Thomas Nelson, 2002), 873. For a discussion on the later rabbinic interpretations in a similar vein, see Anthony T. Hanson, "The Word on Sinai

Indeed, a direct observance of Yahweh is an extremely rare occurance throughout the entire Hebrew Scriptures. Apart from Moses, only the Book of Ezekiel makes reference to one of such phrases, "face-to-face."

> And I will bring you into the wilderness of the peoples, and there I will enter into judgment with you face to face. (Ezek 20:35, NRSV)

Nonetheless, even here the emphasis lies not in the intimate relationship but in the directness of encounter with which the divine wrath will be poured upon some Israelites.[14]

It is, not only the directness of his reception, but the content of his oracle that distinctly sets apart the authority of Moses from other major Old Testament figures. The commanding nature of the Sinai covenant and its lasting impact on every aspect of the life and thought of Israelites (with which he is frequently associated) equally confer upon him the superlatively authoritative standing in the Old Testament and the following early Jewish traditions. McBride summarizes this trait of tradition as follows:

> Significantly this [Ex 24:12 where Moses receives the Torah] is the first occurrence of the term "the Torah" in its general sense in the Mosaic portrait. What was first spoken through Moses to the people is now given a permanent existence and conveyed to Moses in a form called "the Torah and commandment," so that through his service it would guide the covenant people throughout their future history. The use of the singular forms means the text refers to more than a series of particular stipulations. Rather, "the Torah" refers to a very comprehensive authority of guidance that was given to Moses. "The commandment" is the mandate found in and derived from the Torah in a continuing fashion. The substance of the Torah is not only content but authority and function intended to preserve the covenanted people in the covenant.[15]

---

and at Bethel," in *The Prophetic Gospel: A Study of John and the Old Testament* (Edinburgh: T & T Clark, 1991), 21-24. Jacob Milgrom argues that the expressions imply a prophet's intercession with God for Israelites and the image is that of a royal trusted servant seeing the king (2 Kings 25:19). Jacob Milgrom, *Numbers: The Traditional Hebrew Text with the New JPS Translation Commentary* (Philadelphia: Jewish Publication Society, 1990), 96. However, his imagery seems suggestive at best. Joosten attributes these seemingly contradicting testimonies to different redactional layers as reflected in the Septuagintal traditions. Jan Joosten, "To See God: Conflicting Exegetical Tendencies in the Septuagint," in *Die Septuaginta: Texte, Kontexte, Lebenswelten, internationale Fachtagung veranstaltet von Septuaginta Deutsch (LXX.D), Wuppertal 20.-23. Juli 2006*, ed. Martin Karrer and Wolfgang Kraus (Tübingen: Mohr Siebeck, 2008), 287-99.

[14] Daniel I. Block, *The Book of Ezekiel: Chapters 1-24* (Grand Rapids: Eerdmans, 1997), 651.

[15] S. Dean McBride, Jr., "Transcendent Authority: The Role of Moses in Old Testament Traditions," *Int* 44 (1990): 238. Thomas Dozeman, however, detects the transitional nature of the Mosaic role in Exodus 34:29-35. He posits that the masking and unveiling indicate the theocentric idealization of Moses at the expense of his personality, so that it is not Moses but Yahweh who is present in Moses' presence. Thomas B. Dozeman, "Masking Moses and Mosaic Authority in Torah," *JBL* 119 (2000): 21-45. However

The frequent reference to Moses in conjunction with the Torah further testifies to his prominent place occupied in the minds of Israelites. Although his name does not appear as frequently in the rest of the Old Testament as in the Pentateuch, the historical narratives often recognize the integral part Moses played at the Sinai event.[16] During his reformation, King Josiah, for instance, charges his people to comply with the Levitical regulations that were given through Moses. The Hebrew text renders a vivid illustration of Moses' role by means of the expression that the law was given into the hands of Moses:

לַעֲשׂוֹת כִּדְבַר־יְהוָה בְּיַד־מֹשֶׁה: (2 Chr 35:6b, BHS[5])

Act according to the word of Yahweh [given] *in the hand of Moses*. (2 Chr 35:6b)[17]

Similarly, Ezra also records that a group of priests rebuilt the altar of God "as prescribed in the law of Moses" and identifies him as the man of God (similarly, Josh 14:6; 1 Chr 23:14; Ps 90:1; 1 Esd 5:49):[18]

> Then Jeshua son of Jozadak, with his fellow priests, and Zerubbabel son of Shealtiel with his kin set out to build the altar of the God of Israel, to offer burnt offerings on it, as prescribed in the law of Moses, the man of God. (Ezra 3:2, NRSV)

The last phrase of this verse is particularly significant for the post-Exilic understanding of Moses:

כַּכָּתוּב בְּתוֹרַת מֹשֶׁה אִישׁ־הָאֱלֹהִים: (Ezra 3:2c, BHS[5])

As prescribed in the law of Moses the man of God. (Ezra 3:2c, NRSV)

Sirach, the Assumption of Moses, and 1 Esdras. The Hebrew scriptures' emphasis on Moses as the mediator of the Torah continues to be found in the

---

interesting the argument goes, his suggestion appears to hang too much weight on a few passages, and his psycho-sociological reading does not take into account properly the preeminent emphasis on Moses unfolded in the following pericopae.

[16] "In the light of his vast importance in that literature and time, it is quite surprising that Moses as topic and name is mentioned so infrequently in the rest of the Old Testament. If it appears from this that the Mosaic presence is absent from the record in the other books, then appearances are deceiving. The above illustrations insist that by the charisma and tradition transmitted through him, he is present wherever spirit and Torah work together to bring Israel to God and God to Israel." McBride, "Transcendent Authority," 239. For the important place Moses plays out in the giving of the Torah in the Old Testament traditions, see Ansgar Mönikes, *Tora ohne Mose: Zur Vorgeschichte der Mose-Tora* (Berlin: Philo, 2004).

[17] Translation is mine. The italics are added for emphasis and brackets are added for clarification.

[18] Some other examples of identifying the Torah with Moses include the following passages: 1 Kgs 2:3; 8:9; 14:6; 18:6, 12; 2 Kgs 21:8; 23:25; 1 Chr 6:49; 15:15; 22:13; 2 Chr 8:13; 23:18; 25:4; 30:16; 33:8; 34:14; 35:6, 12; Ezra 6:18; 7:6; Neh 1:7, 8; 8:1, 14; 9:14; 10:29; Dan 9:11, 13; Mal 4:4. Cf., Dijkstra, "Moses, the man of God," 17-36.

Apocrypha and Pseudepigrapha (Tob 1:8; Bar 2:2, 28; Sus 1:3, 62; 2 Macc 7:30; 1 Esdr 1:6, 11; 5:49; 7:9; 8:3; 9:39).[19] In addition, the privileged nature of his reception of the divine revelation is also recognized in this group of Jewish writings *vis-à-vis* the "face-to-face" phrase (Sir 45:5) and the pre-appointment language (*As. Mos.* 1:14):

> By his words he performed swift miracles; the Lord glorified him in the presence of kings. He gave him commandments for his people, and revealed to him his glory. For his faithfulness and meekness he consecrated him, choosing him out of all humankind. He allowed him to hear his voice, and led him into the dark cloud, and gave him the commandments face to face, the law of life and knowledge, so that he might teach Jacob the covenant, and Israel his decrees. (Sir 45:3-5)[20]

> Therefore, he has devised and invented me, I who have been prepared from the beginning of the world to be the mediator of his covenant. (*Ass. Mos.* 1:14)

> And having testified, he also called on heaven and earth to be witnesses, lest we should transgress his commandments, which he had mediated to us. (*Ass. Mos.* 3:12)[21]

Related to this emphasis on the authority of Moses is an interesting note from Scott Hafemann who writes that 1 Esdras shifts the emphasis from Moses' instrumental function in the transmission of the Torah in 2 Chronicles to his being the object (or the final destination) of the impartation.[22] 1 Esdras is basically a Greek translation of the Book of Ezra with an addition of the last two chapters of the Second Chronicles at the beginning of this Apocryphal writing. Its dating is difficult to ascertain but it can be placed around 150 B.C.[23]

---

[19] On the other hand, the depiction of the Hellenistic apologists conforms to the Greek ideals that Moses is a great civilizer, philosopher, inventor, ideal king embodying the offices of legislator, high priest, prophet, and a "divine man." Daniel K. Falk, "Moses," *EDSS*, 1:576-77.

[20] Michael D. Coogan, ed., *The New Oxford Annotated Apocrypha* (Oxford: OUP, 2010), 159-60.

[21] Johannes Tromp, *The Assumption of Moses: A Critical Edition with Commentary* (Leiden: Brill, 1993), 6-7, 10-11. For a study that understands "the heavenly messenger" in chs. 10, 11, and 12 of *Assumption of Moses* as Moses the mediator and intercessor, see Jan Willem van Henten, "Moses as Heavenly Messenger in Assumptio Mosis 10:2 and Qumran Passages," *JJS* 54 (2003): 216-21. The writing of Assumption of Moses is usually dated in the first quarter of the first century A.D. Tromp, *The Assumption of Moses*, 116-17. This pseudepigraphic writing is missing the Mosaic ascension account, which is also called "Testament of Moses."

[22] Scott H. Hafemann, "Moses in the Apocrypha and Pseudepigrapha: A Survey," *JSP* 7 (1990): 80-81.

[23] Jacob M. Myers, *I and II Esdras: Introduction, Translation and Commentary*, AB 42 (Garden City: Doubleday, 1974), 8-15. For another helpful introduction to 1 Esdras, see Michael Bird, *1 Esdras: Introduction and Commentary on the Greek Text in Codex Vaticanus* (Leiden: Brill, 2012).

Table 6 Comparison of 1 Esdras, Ezra, and 2 Chronicles

MT	LXX	Summary
2 Chr 35	1 Esdr 1:1-33	King Josiah
2 Chr 36	1 Esdr 1:34-58	The last kings of Judah
Ezra 1	1 Esdr 2:1-14	Cyrus' edict to rebuild the temple
Ezra 4:7-14	1 Esdr 2:15-30a	Proleptic reminiscence of Artaxerxes' reign

Slaughter the passover lamb, sanctify yourselves, and on behalf of your kindred make preparations, acting according to the word of the LORD by (literally, "in the hand of") Moses. (2 Chr 35:6, NRSV)

καὶ θύσατε τὸ φασεχ καὶ τὰ ἅγια ἑτοιμάσατε τοῖς ἀδελφοῖς ὑμῶν τοῦ ποιῆσαι κατὰ τὸν λόγον κυρίου διὰ χειρὸς Μωυσῆ. (2 Chr 35:6, LXX)

[A]nd kill the passover lamb and prepare the sacrifices for your kindred, and keep the passover according to the commandment of the Lord that was given to Moses. (1 Esdr 1:6, NRSV)

θύσατε τὸ πασχα καὶ τὰς θυσίας ἑτοιμάσατε τοῖς ἀδελφοῖς ὑμῶν καὶ ποιήσατε τὸ πασχα κατὰ τὸ πρόσταγμα τοῦ κυρίου τὸ δοθὲν τῷ Μωυσῆ. (1 Esdr 1:6, LXX)

The Hebrew idiom, "in the hand of (בְּיַד) Moses," as found in 2 Chronicles is replaced with "to Moses" (τῷ Μωυσῆ) in 1 Esdras.[24] Hafemann's observation could be tenable in two respects. First, the similarity in wording in both texts is so close that the Esdras passage is likely to have reread the Chronicles with the intention as suggested by Hafemann. Second, the expression, the Torah *given* to Moses, is surely a peculiar form since it does not appear anywhere else in the Old Testament. Common expressions for the law in relation to Moses are "the law of Moses" (1 Kgs 2:3; 2 Kgs 14:6; 2 Chr 23:18; 30:16; Ezra 3:2; 7:6; Neh 8:1; Dan 9:11, 13) and "the law given through (or by) Moses" (2 Chr 33:8; 34:14; Neh 8:14; 10:29).[25] However, the two texts under discussion cannot be examined in isolation from the rest of the Hebrew canon and the intertestamental writings, which reflect the Jewish interpretive currents of the period. The popular expressions that depict the conferral of the law, "the law of Moses" and "the law given through Moses" mentioned above logically presuppose that Yahweh passed the Torah onto Moses in the first place. Therefore, "the law given to Moses" or "in the hands of Moses" could be understood as common-sensical extensions of the phrases that were previously in popular use.

---

[24] For ב as an indication of "the agency or instrument," see *BDB*, 391.

[25] Such expressions also abound in the Apocrypha: "the law of Moses" (Tob 1:8; 7:13; Bar 2:2; Sus 1:3, 62; 1 Esdr 8:1, 9:39); "the law given through Moses" (2 Macc 7:30). Similarly, 1QS 1:2-3. James H. Charlesworth, ed., *Rule of the Community and Related Documents*, vol. 1 of *The Dead Sea Scrolls: Hebrew, Aramaic, and Greek Texts with English Translations* (Tübingen: Mohr Siebeck; Louisville: Westminster/John Knox, 1994), 7.

Another important factor concerning the law and Moses is that some texts structure the language in such a way that Moses is identified as the one who gave the Torah to the Israelites.

> [44] This is the law that Moses set before the Israelites. [45] These are the decrees and the statutes and ordinances that Moses spoke to the Israelites when they had come out of Egypt. (Deut 4:44-45, NRSV)

> All this is the book of the covenant of the Most High God,
> the law that Moses commanded us
> as an inheritance for the congregations of Jacob. (Sir 24:23, NRSV)

These texts demand the idea that Yahweh first gave the Torah to Moses, and he in turn delivered it to the nation of Israel. It is highly unfeasible to construe that Moses initially created and imparted the Torah. Contrary to Hafemann's assertion, therefore, the logical inference of the passing on of the Torah suggests that the Esdras passage may be a reflection of the common understanding among Jews in the time of its writing, instead of an intentional shift from the preposition of instrument to that of locative, in order to superimpose a "relecture" of the Chronicles passage.[26]

4 Maccabees. Two other passages that refer to the authoritative position of Moses are also worthy of inquiry. The Catholics and Protestants generally do not accept the Fourth Maccabees as canonical, but the Orthodox Church has embraced it into the canonical order. Nevertheless, it displays heavy Hellenization in its overall expression. The main body of this literature promotes reason over passion. The immortality of soul is maintained, but resurrection is never mentioned. Although its origin seems to be early Jewish, the dense Hellenistic overpainting is fairly visible throughout the text. The dating of this writing seems to be between the early first to early second centuries A.D.[27] Interesting is a verse in this book which appears to equate the authority of the Torah with that of Moses:

> [W]e are obviously putting our forebears to shame unless we should practice ready obedience to the law and to Moses our counselor. (4 Macc 9:2)

However, the issue of Hellenistic coloring reduces the relevance of the document for the present discussion because the Hebrew scriptural traditions seem to be clear about the incomparable supreme authority of Yahweh over all his chosen

---

[26] For a survey of various degrees of Moses' involvement in the transmission of the Torah, see Lierman, *The New Testament Moses*, 127-28. For a notion of the precarious nature of establishing the role of Moses in the transmission of the Torah based on the selected texts, see H.G.M. Williamson, "History," in *It is Written: Scripture Citing Scripture, Essays in Honour of Barnabas Lindars*, ed. D.A. Carson and H.G.M. Williamson (Cambridge: CUP, 1988), 25.

[27] David A. deSilva, *4 Maccabees: Introduction and Commentary on the Greek Text in Codex Sinaiticus* (Leiden: Brill, 2006), xiv-xvii.

people including even the prophet *par excellence* Moses.[28] Some of the examples of Hellenistic influence are as follows:

> The subject that I am about to discuss is most philosophical, that is, whether devout reason is sovereign over the emotions. So it is right for me to advise you to pay earnest attention to philosophy. (4 Macc 1:1, NRSV)

> I could prove to you from many and various examples that reason is dominant over the emotions. (4 Macc 1:7, NRSV)[29]

2 Maccabees. Another example of early Jewish testimony to the Mosaic authority is attested to in Second Maccabees which probably dates between the second century B.C. to the early second century A.D.[30] Its seventh chapter recounts the transmission of the law through Moses.[31]

> "The Lord God is watching over us and in truth has compassion on us, as Moses declared in his song that bore witness against the people to their faces, when he said, 'And he will have compassion on his servants.'" (2 Macc 7:6, NRSV)

> While she was still speaking, the young man said, "What are you waiting for? I will not obey the king's command, but I obey the command of the law that was given to our ancestors through Moses." (2 Macc 7:30, NRSV)

Second Maccabees contains the narratives of Jewish persecutions wreaked by Antiochus IV and the ensuing Jewish revolt.[32] Until chs. 6 and 7, Antiochus IV is

---

[28] H. Anderson, "4 Maccabees," in *OTP*, 2:533-37; Jan Willem van Henten, *The Maccabean Martyrs as Saviours of the Jewish People: A Study of 2 and 4 Maccabees* (Leiden: Brill, 1997), 73-91. For another example of the elevation of Moses in terms of his virtues as the grounds for the divine selection, see Sir 45:3-5: "By his words he performed swift miracles; the Lord glorified him in the presence of kings. He gave him commandments for his people, and revealed to him his glory. For his faithfulness and meekness he consecrated him, choosing him out of all humankind. He allowed him to hear his voice, and led him into the dark cloud, and gave him the commandments face to face, the law of life and knowledge, so that he might teach Jacob the covenant, and Israel his decrees."

[29] Cf., Robert J.V. Hiebert, "The Greek Pentateuch and 4 Maccabees," in *Scripture in Transition: Essays on Septuagint, Hebrew Bible, and Dead Sea Scrolls in Honour of Raija Sollamo*, ed. Anssi Voitila and Jutta Jokiranta (Leiden: Brill, 2008), 239-54.

[30] For the second century B.C., see Robert Doran, *2 Maccabees: A Critical Commentary*, Hermeneia (Minneapolis: Fortress, 2012), 14-15; for the second century A.D., see David A. deSilva, *Introducing the Apocrypha: Message, Context, and Significance* (Grand Rapids: Baker, 2002), 268-70.

[31] Daniel R. Schwartz, *2 Maccabees* (Berlin: Walter de Gruyter, 2008), 302-03.

[32] For the descriptions of the historical circumstance in this period, see Niels Hyldahl, "The Maccabean Rebellion and the Question of 'Hellenization,'" in *Religion and Religious Practice in the Seleucid Kingdom*, ed. Per Bilde, SHC 1 (Aarhus: Aarhus University Press, 1990), 188-203; Leonard J. Greenspoon, "Between Alexander and Antioch: Jews and Judaism in the Hellenistic Period," in *Oxford History of the Biblical World*, ed. Michael D. Coogan (Oxford: Oxford University Press, 1998), 420-65; David Volgger, "1 Makk 1: Der Konflikt zwischen Hellenen und Juden—Die Mak-

depicted as an agent to carry out the divine wrath poured upon Israel for her unfaithfulness. It is, however, this very persecution that turned the wrath of God into the divine redemptive intervention on behalf of Jews as narrated from ch. 7 onwards. In the course of this turmoil, Moses is remembered as one who encourages others to be faithful to the Torah even to the point of martyrdom.[33] The phrase "Moses declared in his song" in the Second Maccabees 7:6 harkens back to Deuteronomy 32:36 in the form of verbatim citation from the Greek Deuteronomy.[34] The song of Moses in Deuteronomy 32 was relatively widespread in early Judaism.[35]

Table 7 Comparison of Deuteronomy and 2 Maccabees on Mosaic loyalty to the Law[36]

> ὅτι κρινεῖ κύριος τὸν λαὸν αὐτοῦ καὶ *ἐπὶ τοῖς δούλοις αὐτοῦ παρακληθήσεται*, εἶδεν γὰρ παραλελυμένους αὐτοὺς καὶ ἐκλελοιπότας ἐν ἐπαγωγῇ καὶ παρειμένους. (Deut 32:36, LXX)
>
> Indeed the LORD *will* vindicate his people,
>   *have compassion on his servants*,
>   when he sees that their power is gone,
>   neither bond nor free remaining. (Deut 32:36, NRSV)

---

kabäische Reichspropaganda," *Anton* 73 (1998): 459-81; James C. VanderKam, *An Introduction to Early Judaism* (Grand Rapids: Eerdmans, 2001), 16-23; Daniel R. Schwartz, "Antiochus IV Epiphanes in Jerusalem," in *Historical Perspectives: From the Hasmoneans to Bar Kokhba in Light of the Dead Sea Scrolls, Proceedings of the Fourth International Symposium of the Orion Center for the Study of the Dead Sea Scrolls and Associated Literature, 27-31 January, 1999*, ed. David M. Goodblatt, Avital Pinnick, and Daniel R. Schwartz (Leiden: Brill, 2001), 45-56.

[33] For the importance of martyrdom in 2 Maccabees, see Bertram Herr, "Ist Gott blutrünstig?: Die Theologie der Stellvertretungen im Zweiten Makkabäerbuch," *MTZ* 60 (2009): 377-89; Barbara Schmitz, "Geschaffen aus dem Nichts? Die Funktion der Rede von der Schöpfung im Zweiten Makkabäerbuch," in *Theologies of Creation in Early Judaism and Ancient Christianity: In Honour of Hans Klein*, ed. Tobias Nicklas and Korinna Zamfir (Berlin: Walter de Gruyter, 2010), 61-79.

[34] Peter Katz, "Text of 2 Maccabees Reconsidered," *ZNW* 51 (1960): 14; Hafemann, "Moses in the Apocrypha and Pseudepigrapha," 84-85; George W.E. Nickelsburg, *Jewish Literature between the Bible and the Mishnah: A Historical and Literary Introduction* (Minneapolis: Fortress, 2005), 107-08.

[35] For studies that illuminate the use of the song in other writings of the second temple period, especially over against catastrophic historical contexts, see Alfred E. Krause, "Historical Selectivity: Prophetic Prerogative or Typological Imperative?" in *Israel's Apostasy and Restoration: Essays in Honor of Roland K. Harrison*, ed. Avraham Gileadi (Grand Rapids, MI: Baker, 1988), 175-212; John M. Wiebe, "The Form, Setting and Meaning of the Song of Moses," *StudBibTh* 17 (1989): 119-63; Ronald Bergey, "The Song of Moses (Deuteronomy 32.1-43) and Isaianic Prophecies: A Case of Early Intertextuality?" *JSOT* 28 (2003): 33-54.

[36] Italics are added for emphasis.

> Ὁ κύριος ὁ θεὸς ἐφορᾷ καὶ ταῖς ἀληθείαις ἐφ' ἡμῖν παρακαλεῖται, καθάπερ διὰ τῆς κατὰ πρόσωπον ἀντιμαρτυρούσης ᾠδῆς διεσάφησεν Μωυσῆς λέγων Καὶ *ἐπὶ τοῖς δούλοις αὐτοῦ παρακληθήσεται.* (2 Macc 7:6, LXX)
>
> "The Lord God is watching over us and in truth has compassion on us, as Moses declared in his song that bore witness against the people to their faces, when he said, 'And *he will have compassion on his servants.*'" (2 Macc 7:6, NRSV)

In a series of persecutions geared to cause forsaking of Jewish religious practices, a number of Jews went through awful tortures. It is in the midst of this tribulation that the present text recounts a story of a mother with seven sons (2 Macc 7:1-6). This family is forced to eat swine flesh. Upon their defiance, the first son's tongue and his four limbs are cut off. Ultimately, he was scalped and was fried to death. While watching this horrible incident, the mother and the six brothers remember the divine promise promulgated in the lips of Moses that Yahweh will comfort his faithful and take vengeance upon the heathens.[37] By this citation, they also recognize themselves to be the ones in whom the divine promise of Deut 32:36 has been fulfilled.[38] What this explicit reference to Moses seems to hint at is that he is recognized not only as the transmitter (2 Macc 7:30) but as the defender of the Torah at all costs (2 Macc 7:6).[39]

Qumran. In contrast to the various portrayals in other Jewish writings of the intertestamental period (both the Palestinian and Diaspora settings), the Qumran library demonstrates more or less a consistent view of Moses in three distinct terms: as an authoritative figure, a prophetic intercessor, and possibly an eschatological figure.[40] So does Xeravits assesses the Qumranic view of Moses:

> The Qumranic picture of Moses is quite uniform. Compositions from the Qumran library describe Moses as an authoritative figure. His authority derives from his legislative role.[41]

Virtually no reference is made concerning Moses as king regardless of some

---

[37] R. Doran takes this account to be a literary interpolation so as to increase the dramatic effect of the document. Robert Doran, "The Second Book of Maccabees," in *1 & 2 Maccabees, Introduction to Hebrew Poetry, Job, Psalms*, vol. 4 of *NIB*, ed. Leander E. Keck (Nashville: Abingdon, 1996), 240. His reason is based only on the presence of the parallel folktales in other Jewish writings that speak of a mother with seven sons who bravely encounter a trial.

[38] Jonathan A. Goldstein, *II Maccabees: A New Translation with Introduction and Commentary* (Garden City: Doubleday, 1983), 304; Werner Dommershausen, *1 Makkabäer, 2 Makkabäer* (Würzburg: Echter, 1995), 138.

[39] For further elaborations of Moses as the authority figure in early Judaism, see Hafemann, "Moses in the Apocrypha and Pseudepigrapha," 80-88; Lierman, *The New Testament Moses*, 128-39.

[40] Géza G. Xeravits, "Moses *Redivivus* in Qumran?" *QC* 11 (2003): 91-105.

[41] Xeravits, "Moses *Redivivus* in Qumran?" 92.

counter-arguments, and his priestly role of atonement is mentioned only in passing in 4Q504 2 ix-x.[42] It is not that the Qumran conceptual current is far removed from those reflected in other writings of early Judaism. Rather, the Dead Sea Scrolls constitute so important a part of early Judaism that they deserve a separate treatment concerning Mosaic images in the intertestamental period. This section will concern only the first category, that of authority.[43]

That his authority is evidently acknowledged in the community of Qumran is observed in the juxtaposition of Moses with the Torah, which implies several ideas. First, Moses plays an identity marker role for the divine stipulations. In other words, when such an association is mentioned, it is the particular divine revelation given through Moses that is being referred to in the discourse. Such association is expressed in the following phrases: "the Torah of Moses," "the laws commanded to Moses," or "God spoke to Moses" (4Q174 2 ii 3, 4Q175 1 i, 4Q252 1 iv 2, 4Q270 11 i 20, 4Q377 2 ii 2), "by the hand of Moses" (which echoes 2 Chr 35:6; 1QS i 3, 4Q504 1 v 14), "God spoke through/by Moses" (1Q22 1 i, 1QM 10 vi, 1QHa 17 xii, 4Q255 1 iii, 4Q259 1 iii 6, 4Q266 18 v 1-2, 4Q267 2 v-vi), "Moses said" (4Q266 3 ii 19, 4Q267 2 ix), and "as it is written in the book of Moses" (4Q398 1 v, 4Q397 4 x, 4Q174).

Second, stemming from this first point is the conception that the authority of the Torah is in turn transferred to Moses. The identification of Moses' authority with that of the Torah is attested in several respects. For example, in addition to the first five books of the Hebrew Scriptures, the Qumran community attributed Mosaic authorship to a dozen more books.

> The sheer number of these writings testifies to the overwhelming importance of Moses as the legitimator of religious ideas in Second Temple times. If the Bible did not say what you thought it should, what you were convinced God would have said through Moses but somehow neglected to say, then you took reed in hand and, as it were, wrote for Moses.[44]

Moreover, towards the end of the rule section of the Damascus Document, the one who wishes to join the sect is repeatedly instructed to take an oath to "return

---

[42] Falk, *EDSS*, 1:576-77; James R. Davila, *Liturgical Works* (Grand Rapids: Eerdmans, 2000), 255-56; André Caquot, "Trois textes religieux de la Grotte 4," *RHPR* 84 (2004): 129-47.

[43] For a detailed discussion on Qumran's view of Moses as the authoritative figure, see James E. Bowley, "Moses in the Dead Sea Scrolls: Living in the Shadow of God's Anointed," in *The Bible at Qumran: Text, Shape, and Interpretation*, ed. Peter W. Flint (Grand Rapids: Eerdmans, 2001), 159-70.

[44] Michael O. Wise, Martin G. Abegg, and Edward M. Cook, *The Dead Sea Scrolls: A New Translation* (San Francisco: HarperSanFrancisco, 2005), 427. The writings the Qumran community attributed to Moses as the author are Jubilees, the Words of Moses, rewritten Bible texts, the Test of a True Prophet, the Temple Scroll, the Apocryphon of Moses, and possibly the Discourse on the Exodus and Conquest.

to the Torah of Moses."[45] The Damascus Document was first discovered in the Cairo Geniza in the late 19th century. Then, it was called the Zadokite Fragments. Later on, the earlier editions have been retrieved from the Qumran Cave IV, which have been published only recently.[46] This text manifests a keen interest in eschatological hope of the restoration of a Davidic monarchy.[47] Along with this end-time concern, this document narrates detailed stipulations for the community rules that are based upon the Torah. In this context, Moses is quite often mentioned.

> But when he has imposed upon himself to return to the law of Moses with all his heart and all his soul. (4Q266 17 i 3 [CD 15:12])

> [W]ith Israel, the covenant to rev[ert to] the law of Moses with the whole heart and [with] the who[le]. (CD 15:9)

> [T]he law of Moses, for in it all is defined. . . . And the exact interpretation of their ages about the blindness . . . to the law of Moses, the angel Mastema will turn aside from following him, should he keep his words. (4Q271 2 ii 3-4 [CD16:2, 5])

The Damascus Document is believed to represent the most important Qumran view of the history of Israel, which was judged to be a protracted manifestation of repreated rebellion and transgression against Yahweh. It is only with the founding of the Qumran community that the nation took a decisive turn in history to a positive direction, for the law of God is finally being observed within and by

---

[45] "This statement indicates that formally the *Yaḥad* (community) viewed the Torah of Moses as the ultimate source of all Qumranic halakah and indeed of all things necessary for proper living." Bowley, "Moses in the Dead Sea Scrolls," 161. The parentheses are added for clarification. For the meaning of *Yaḥad*, see Arie van der Kooij, "The Yahad—What Is in a Name?" *DSD* 18 (2011): 109-28. The Damascus Document appears to have originated from the Qumran community from around 100 B.C. Nickelsburg, *Jewish Literature between the Bible and the Mishnah*, 122-23. For a comprehensive introduction to the Damascus Document, see Charlotte Hempel, *The Damascus Texts* (Sheffield: Sheffield, 2000). Also, the members are called "the returnees to the Torah" and "the doers of Torah" (4Q171 2 ii-iii, xiv, xxii). John M. Allegro, *Qumran Cave 4: 4Q158-4Q186* (Oxford: Clarendon, 1968), 43-44. For the ultimate authority of the Mosaic law in the Qumran community, see Geza Vermes, "The Qumran Interpretation of Scripture in Its Historical Setting," *LUOSA* 6 (1966-68): 87.

[46] Joseph M. Baumgarten, *Qumrân Cave 4. XIII: The Damascus Document (4Q266-273)* (Oxford: Clarendon, 1996). For the implication of the later Zadokite documents upon the earlier Damascus Document in the Qumran library, see Lawrence H. Schiffman, "From the Cairo Genizah to Qumran: The influence of the Zadokite Fragments on the Study of the Qumran Scrolls," in *Dead Sea Scrolls: Texts and Context*, ed. Charlotte Hempel (Leiden: Brill, 2010), 451-66.

[47] Albert Hogeterp, "Eschatological Identities in the Damascus Document," in *Defining Identities: We, You, and the Other in the Dead Sea Scrolls, Proceedings of the Fifth Meeting of the IOQS in Gröningen*, ed. Florentino García Martínez and Mladen Popović (Leiden: Brill, 2008), 111-30. For a helpful survey of the Damascus Document, see David Hamidovic, *L'écrit de Damas: Le manifeste esséníen* (Louvain: Peeters, 2011).

the community. It is in this important context that Moses is brought to the front who, through the law, calls on Israelites to join or remain in the sect for salvation.[48]

Not only is the means of entering the community predicated by Moses, but the identity of the members is also defined by the tenacious determination to observe the rules set forth through and/or by him.[49] Third, the Damascus Document also spells out the benefit of joining the band, that is, the departing of an evil angel, Mastema (lit., "obstruction"), from new members.

> They shall muster him with the oath of the covenant which Moses made with Israel, the covena[nt] to re[turn t]o the Torah of Moses with all (his) heart [and with all] (his) soul .... But when he takes upon himself to return to the Torah of Moses ... a man shall take upon himself (an oath) to return to the Torah of Moses ... and on the day when a man takes upon himself (an oath) to return to the Torah of Moses, the angel of Mastema shall turn aside from after him, if he fulfills his words. (*CD* 15 viii-16 v [=4Q271 2 ii 6])[50]

Conversely, however, any deliberate or negligent breach of the Torah of Moses is punishable by expulsion from the community.[51]

Finally, some scholars posit that the Qumran community understood themselves as preserving the authoritative interpretation of Moses as it is reflected in 4Q266 3 ii (=*CD* V 17-VI 7).[52]

[For former]ly [stood Moses and Aaron by the hand of] the Prince of L[ights, and]

---

[48] Hermann Lichtenberger, "Geschichte und Heilsgeschichte in der Damaskusschrift," in *Heil und Geschichte: Die Geschichtsbezogenheit des Heils und das Problem der Heilsgeschichte in der biblischen Tradition und in der theologischen Deutung*, ed. Jörg Frey, Stefan Krauter, Hermann Lichtenberger (Tübingen: Mohr Siebeck, 2009), 175-84.

[49] 1QS 5 vii-x (*CD* 15 viii-ix); *DSS*, 1:80-81.

[50] James H. Charlesworth, ed., *Damascus Document, War Scroll, and Related Documents*, vol. 2 of *The Dead Sea Scrolls: Hebrew, Aramaic, and Greek Texts with English Translations* [Tübingen: Mohr Siebeck; Louisville: Westminster/John Knox, 1995], 39; 4Q270 6 ii 6, Joseph M. Baumgarten, ed., *Qumran Cave 4. XIII: The Damascus Document (4Q266-273)* (Oxford: Clarendon, 1996), 179.

[51] 4Q377 2 ii; 4Q266 18 v 14-16. J. Duncan M. Derrett, "The Reprobate's Peace: 4QDa (4Q266) (18 v 14-16)," in *Legal Texts and Legal Issues: Proceedings of the Second Meeting of the International Organization for Qumran Studies, Cambridge, 1995, Published in Honour of Joseph M. Baumgarten*, ed. Moshe Bernstein, Florentino García Martínez, and John Kampen (Leiden: Brill, 1997), 245-49.

[52] "Dans ce contexte palestinien ... il apparaît que le Mohoqqéq, Interprète de la Torah, docteur supreme de la Communauté et chef de son exode ... est vraiment représenté comme un 'nouveau Moïse.'" Geza Vermes, "La Figure de Moïse au tournant des deux Testaments," in *Moïse: L'homme de l'alliance*, ed. Henri Cazelles (Paris: Desclée, 1955), 81-82. Also, Naftali Wieder, "The 'Law-Interpreter' of the Sect of the Dead Sea Scrolls: The Second Moses," *JJS* 4 (1953): 172. Coupled with the witness of 4QMMT, Bowley suggests that the authoritative interpretation of the Qumran community is equated with the status of Moses. Bowley, "Moses in the Dead Sea Scrolls," 165-66.

[Belial raised up] Jannes and his [brother in his] plotting when he wrought evil [against Israel in the begin]ing *vacat*. [And at the time of the destruction] of the l[and], trespassers [arose] and led Is[rael] astray [and the l]and [became desolate,] for they spoke defiantly against the commandments of God (given) thro[ug]h Moses, *vacat* and also against the anointed holy ones. And they prophesied falsely so as to cause [Isra]el to turn away from God. And God recalled the covenant with the fir[st o]nes, and he raised up men of understanding [from Aa]ron and wise men from Israel, and [he] caused them to [hea]r. And [they d]ug the well of which Moses said, "the well was dug by the princes and excavated by the nobles of [the people], with a ruler" *vacat*. The "well" is the Law, [and those who "dig" it] are the penitent of Israel who departed from the land of Ju[dah and sojourned in the dwel]lings [of Damascus], God [called them] all "princes" for they all [sought him, and their glory was not rejected] by anyone's mouth. *vacat* [And the "ruler" is the Interpreter of the L]aw, [of whom Isaiah said, "He takes out"].[53]

In this allegorically interpretive account, "the interpreter of the Law," which some exegetes identify with Moses, is said to have retained the binding authority until the appearance of the "one who shall teach righteousness at the End of Days" (*CD* 6 xi).[54]

Three caveats, nonetheless, are in order concerning the "Interpreter of the Law" text. First, it could be an important indication that the explicit reference to Moses is missing in another version of the similar account (4Q266 3 ii 1-15), with the implication being that he is mentioned only peripherally in this text. Second, the equation of Moses with the "Interpreter of the Law" appears to distort the natural reading of the text concerning the role of Moses. He appears only as the medium by which the law was transmitted to the community, and the text does not seem to explicitly identify him with "the Interpreter of the Law."[55] Finally, the "Interpreter of the Law" is mentioned three other times in the Qumran library. These three other references seem to refer to three different characters, with one in 4Q174 3 x-xii in terms of David and another in terms of a priest or a prophet. 4Q174 3 x-xii seems to clearly indicate a Davidic figure in reference to the "Interpreter of the Law." The two other occurrences are from 4Q177 2 v (the text of which is too fragmentary to be certain about the identity of the figure) and *CD* 7 ix-8 ii. Scholars are divided over the identity of the figure in the latter text.[56] These differing characterizations signify that the epithet was

---

[53] For the similar text that is missing the explicit reference to Moses, see *CD* V 17-VI 7 (= 4Q266 3 ii 1-15), Baumgarten, *Qumran Cave 4. XIII*, 97-98; Charlesworth, *Damascus Document, War Scroll, and Related Documents*, 22-23.

[54] Charlesworth, *Damascus Document, War Scroll, and Related Documents*, 22-23.

[55] Another point can be noted along this line of argument although it is an indirect one. Other Qumran documents, 4QPatriarchal Blessings (4Q252) and 4QFlorilegium (4Q174), juxtapose "the Interpreter of the Law" with a Davidic figure, not with that of Moses. Daniel R. Schwartz, "The Messianic Departure from Judah (4Q Patriarchal Blessings)," *TZ* 37 (1981): 257-66.

[56] For an argument for the prophetic figure, see Florentino García Martínez, "Messianic Hopes in the Qumran Writings," in *The People of the Dead Sea Scrolls: Their Writ-*

meaningful in terms of his function (e.g., an end-time redeemer) and not so much in his analogy to a specific historical figure. In view of these three observations, therefore, discernment should be exercised so as not to overestimate the authoritative place of Moses as based on the "Interpreter of the Law" texts.[57]

Lastly, a stunning instruction illuminates the status of Moses, in that the community forbids pronouncing the Torah of Moses, just as the divine names, because the law contains the spelled out names of Yahweh.

> [He will not sw]ear by Aleph and Lamed ('el = God) nor by Aleph and Daleth ('adonai = the Lord), but by the oath of the youths, by the curses of the covenant. (blank) Neither should one mention the law of Moses, for in it is the full enunciation of the name. (*CD*-A XV 1-2 [4Q266 8 i-ii])[58]

It is not Moses but the names of Yahweh that were included in the book of the Torah that forbad the Qumranites from uttering "the law of Moses." Again, Moses seems to be an anciliary element in this prohibitive stipulation.

As briefly discussed so far, Moses enjoyed an incomparable status as an authority figure in various strands of the Old Testament and the intertestamental Jewish writings. However, there seems to have been a growing tendency to elevate his status as he was remembered in the later post-biblical traditions.

Excursus 4: The Letter of Aristeas and Moses

> A Jewish pseudepigraphical writing, the Letter of Aristeas (or the Letter to Philocrates) is a second century B.C. Hellenistic document.[59] It provides one of the most detailed accounts of the genesis of the Septuagint. The awe-inspiring story begins with the Egyptian King, probably Ptolemy II, who, struck by the majesty of the Hebrew Jewish canon, arranged and furnished its translation into Greek.[60] The details of this account include a number of supernatural and mystifying anecdotes. For instance, each 72 Jewish scholars translated in their own chamber, and after 72 days, they found out their translations match exactly. Hence, the importance of the Torah is highly emphasized in this document. Moses, at the same time, was revered like no other. However, Hafe-

---

ings, Beliefs, and Practices, ed. Florentino Garcia Martinez and Julio Trebolle Barrera (Leiden: Brill, 1995), 182-84. For an argument for the priestly figure, see Michael A. Knibb, "Interpreter of the Law," *EDSS*, 1:384. For an overview of the debate surrounding this title, see Hempel, *The Damascus Texts*, 75-77.

[57] Richard Bauckham, "Jewish Messianism according to the Gospel of John," in *Challenging Perspectives in the Gospel of John* (Tübingen: Mohr Siebeck, 2006), 214-15. Especially, see footnote 26 on p. 214.

[58] *DSS*, 1:562-63; Wise, Abegg, and Cook, *The Dead Sea Scrolls*, 68.

[59] The majority of scholarship will date it to the second century B.C., but for a minor voice which dates it to the third century B.C., see Uriel Rappaport, "The Letter of Aristeas again," *JSP* 21 (2012): 285-303.

[60] Raija Sollamo, "The Letter of Aristeas and the Origin of the Septuagint," in *X Congress of the International Organization for Septuagint and Cognate Studies, Oslo, 1998*, ed. Bernard A. Taylor (Atlanta: Society of Biblical Literature, 2001), 329-42; Dries de Crom, "The Letter of Aristeas and the Authority of the Septuagint," *JSP* 17 (2008): 141-60.

mann's assessment concerning the place of Moses in this writing seems to be a little too far-fetched. "The incredible authority is vested in Moses. Moses does not derive his status from the law; the law derives its status from Moses!"[61] He cites a number of places in the letter of Aristeas, vv. 4-5, 31, 147-53, 161, 168, 171, 240, and 313, for this point. Although its heavy Hellenistic coloring (namely, an emphasis on human virtues) overshadows the sovereign nature in the transmission of the Torah, the document still holds, to a considerable degree, to a belief in the providence of God in granting the wisdom to Moses. For example, "in his [Moses'] wisdom the legislator . . . endowed by God for the knowledge of universal truths surrounded us with unbroken palisades and iron walls to prevent our mixing with any of the other people in any matter, being thus kept pure in body and soul, preserved from false beliefs, and worshiping the only God omnipotent over all creation . . . . [The king] commanded this man, and said to the next, 'How can one avoid doing anything contrary to the Law?' To this he replied, 'By realizing that God has given to legislators the purpose of saving men's lives, you would follow them'" (*Let. Aris.* vv. 139, 240).[62] Moreover, the designation, "the legislators," in the plural form does not always refer to Moses in the document as Hafemann suggests. Starting with Victor Tcherikover, the majority of scholars maintain that the document reflects the Jewish contentment with the Hellenistic elements that were compatible with Palestinian Judaism. Although often described in positive terms, however, such adaptation reveals the compromised nature of the letter, most starkly observed in its identification of Yahweh with Zeus (see *Let. Aris.* v. 16).[63]

Moses as Prophet with Particular Emphasis on Intercession and Miracle-Working

The Old Testament. Without a doubt, Moses is depicted as the prophet *par excellence* in the Hebrew scriptural traditions.[64] The reason is not because he is so frequently dubbed as such, but because the series of events surrounding his calling and subsequent ministry set forth the pattern of a prophet's life followed by other Hebrew prophets.[65] Some qualities corollary to his life and ministry as a

---

[61] Hafemann, "Moses in the Apocrypha and Pseudepigrapha," 87-88.

[62] *OTP*, 2:22, 28.

[63] *OTP*, 2:13. For the positive acceptance of Hellenism in the letter, see Victor Tcherikover, "Ideology of the Letter of Aristeas," *HTR* 2 (1958): 59-86; Naomi Janowitz, "Translating Cult: The Letter of Aristeas and Hellenistic Judaism," *SBLSP* 22 (1983): 347-57; Jonathan Goldstein, "Jewish Acceptance and Rejection of Hellenism," in *Semites, Iranians, Greeks, and Romans: Studies in Their Interactions* (Atlanta: Scholars, 1990), 27; John J. Collins, *Between Athens and Jerusalem: Jewish Identity in the Hellenistic Diaspora* (Grand Rapids: Eerdmans, 2000), 97-102, 191-94.

[64] Michael Widmer, *Moses, God, and the Dynamics of Intercessory Prayer: A Study of Exodus 32-34 and Numbers 13-14* (Tübingen: Mohr Siebeck, 2004), 72-75; Rendtorff, *The Canonical Hebrew Bible*, 550-52; Ernst-Joachim Waschke, "Mose und David: Ein überlieferungs- und redaktionsgeschichtliches Desiderat?" in *Auf dem Weg zur Endgestalt von Genesis bis II Regum: Festschrift Hans-Christoph Schmitt zum 65. Geburtstag*, ed. Martin Beck and Ulrike Schorn (Berlin: Walter de Gruyter, 2006), 217-30.

[65] For Moses as the arche-typical prophet, see Henry McKeating, "Ezekiel the 'Prophet Like Moses,'" *JSOT* 61 (1994): 97-109; Martin O'Kane, "Isaiah: A Prophet in the

prophet can be discussed in two sub-categories: his performing of miracles and his intercessory role.

First, the signs and wonders that Moses performed entitle him to be called the greatest prophet. Some later Old Testament traditions remember the miracles wrought against Egypt as the grandiose manifestation of the divine power, and, thus, he is symbolically portrayed as the protector of the covenant people of Yahweh:

> By a prophet the LORD brought Israel up from Egypt,
>   and by a prophet he was guarded. (Hos 12:13, NRSV)

Furthermore, the Deuteronomist defies comparison of the number and magnitude of his miracles with those of other prophets:

> [11] He was unequaled for all the signs and wonders that the LORD sent him to perform in the land of Egypt, against Pharaoh and all his servants and his entire land, [12] and for all the mighty deeds and all the terrifying displays of power that Moses performed in the sight of all Israel. (Deut 34:11-12, NRSV)

As such, McConville even detects the analogy of Moses with Yahweh in this text (i.e., it is Moses who performed the miracles):

> And remarkably, the language typically used of Yahweh himself in Deuteronomy to describe the defeat of Pharaoh and the powerful feats of the exodus from Egypt (4:34) is now used of Moses.[66]

However, this notion gravely overlooks the explicit reference to God as the source of Moses' miracles in v. 11 and his reluctance to follow the divine initiative especially at the inauguration of his mission to Pharaoh (Exod 4:1-17).

Turning now to the intercessory function of a prophet's ministry, Moses ex-

---

Footsteps of Moses," *JSOT* 69 (1996): 29-51; William Johnstone, "The Portrayal of Moses as Deuteronomic Archetypal Prophet in Exodus and Its Revisal," in *Elusive Prophet: The Prophet as a Historical Person, Literary Character and Anonymous Artist*, ed. Johannes C. de Moor (Leiden: Brill, 2001), 159-74; Brian Britt, "Prophetic Concealment in a Biblical Type Scene," *CBQ* 64 (2002): 37-58. For the prophetic characteristics of Moses' calling and ministry, see Wolfgang Richter, *Die sogenannten vorprophetischen Berufungsberichte: Eine literaturwissenschaftliche Studie zu 1 Sam 9,1-10,16, Ex 3f. und Ri 6,11b-17* (Göttingen: Vandenhoeck & Ruprecht, 1970), 139 (Andeutung der Not, Auftrag, Einwand, Zusicherung des Beistandes, and Zeichen), whose characterization of Moses as the arch-prophet is taken up by Scott J. Hafemann, *Paul, Moses and the History of Israel: The Letter/Spirit Contrast and the Argument from Scripture in 2 Corinthians 3* (Tübingen: Mohr Siebeck, 1995), 47-62 (theophany, divine commission, identification of an obstacle to the performance of the commission, and divine provision for overcoming the obstacle).

[66] J. Gordon McConville, *Deuteronomy* (Downers Grove: InterVarsity, 2002), 478. Similarly, Stephen L. Herring, "Moses as Divine Substitute in Exodus," *CTR* 9 (2012): 53-68.

ceeds other intercessory prophets as well.⁶⁷ His intercession begins with calling upon Yahweh for the deliverance of Pharaoh and Egyptian officials. His prayer on behalf of the fellow Israelites continues to appear in a large part of the Pentateuch (Exod 32, Num 11, 14, 21, 32, Deut 9).

> Moses said to Pharaoh, "Kindly tell me when I am to pray for you and for your officials and for your people, that the frogs may be removed from you and your houses and be left only in the Nile." (Exod 8:9, NRSV)

> The people came to Moses and said, "We have sinned by speaking against the LORD and against you; pray to the LORD to take away the serpents from us." So Moses prayed for the people. (Num 21:7, NRSV)

> "The LORD was so angry with Aaron that he was ready to destroy him, but I interceded also on behalf of Aaron at that same time." (Deut 9:20, NRSV)

Although he failed to have his request answered, his intercessory ministry reaches its climax in Exodus 32:30-32 where he risks his own existence on behalf of the rebellious Israelites.

> On the next day Moses said to the people, "You have sinned a great sin. But now I will go up to the LORD; perhaps I can make atonement for your sin." So Moses returned to the LORD and said, "Alas, this people has sinned a great sin; they have made for themselves gods of gold. But now, if you will only forgive their sin—but if not, blot me out of the book that you have written." (Exod 32:30-32, NRSV)⁶⁸

Sirach, 2 Maccabees, the Wisdom of Solomon. In early Jewish writings, Moses is also remembered for the signs and wonders wrought through him:

> "By his words he performed swift miracles; the Lord glorified him in the presence of kings." (Sir 45:3a, NRSV)⁶⁹

> Just as Moses prayed to the Lord, and fire came down from heaven and consumed the

---

⁶⁷ It is debated whether this particular ministry was a constitutive quality for a prophet. Contrary to the assessment of the previous scholarship (F. Hesse, A.S. Herbert, H.G. Reventlow, J. Jeremias, and A.B. Rhodes), Samuel Balentine argued that the intercessory ministry is not a mark of Jewish prophets. Only four figures manifest a considerable degree of intercessory ministry: Abraham, Moses, Samuel, and Jeremiah. Sameul E. Balentine, "The Prophet as Intercessor: A Reassessment," *JBL* 103 (1984): 161-73. On the contrary, however, Widmer notes frequent references to the intercessory ministry of the Hebrew prophets and non prophetic figures. Widmer, *Moses, God, and the Dynamics of Intercessory Prayer*, 80-85.

⁶⁸ For a detailed treatment of Moses as an intercessor as depicted in the Pentateuch, see Robert Martin-Achard, "Moïse, figure du médiateur selon l'Ancien Testament," *CRTP* 11 (1984): 107-28; Wesley J. Fuerst, "Moses as Intercessor," in *Scripture and Prayer: A Celebration for Carroll Stuhlmueller*, ed. Carolyn Osiek and Donald Senior (Wilmington: Michael Glazier, 1988), 5-19; Widmer, *Moses, God, and the Dynamics of Intercessory Prayer*, 89-349; Vincent Sénéchal, *Retribution et intercession dans le Deutéronome* (Berlin: Walter de Gruyter, 2009), 364-82.

⁶⁹ Coogan, *The New Oxford Annotated Apocrypha*, 159.

sacrifices, so also Solomon prayed, and the fire came down and consumed the whole burnt offerings. (2 Macc 2:10, NRSV)[70]

The Wisdom of Solomon also relates the miraculous Exodus events in chs. 11 through 19, which are preceded by the title of Moses, the "holy prophet":

> She [Wisdom] prospered their works by the hand of a holy prophet. (*Wis. Sol.* 11:1)[71]

The Assumption of Moses. Furthermore, his intercession is recounted frequently in the Assumption of Moses. Known also as the Testament of Moses, this text narrates the secret revelations that Moses passed onto Joshua before his assumption in twelve chapters. The extant manuscript of the writing dates to the sixth century A.D. written in Latin, but it is clearly a translation of the first or second century Greek text or even of a Semitic origin.[72] Thus, a substantial glimpse into the Mosaic images in the intertestamental period can be obtained from this document.[73] At the end of a historical retrospect, Moses reveals sort of an eschatological prophecy, in which he mentions his intense intercessory ministry that God has appointed him.

> Or who will pray for them, not omitting one single day, so that I can lead them into the land of the Amorites? . . . For their (number) was a hundred thousand, but now they have grown into this multitude here, only because of your prayers, lord Moses. . . . If the enemies will sin against their Lord once more, there is no longer an advocate for them, who will supplicate to the Lord for them, as Moses was, the great messenger, who bent his knees on earth every hour of the day and of the night, praying; and who could look at him who rules the entire world with mercy and justice, reminding him of the covenant with the fathers, and placating the Lord. . . . The Lord has appointed me for them and for their sins that I should pray and supplicate for them. (*Ass. Mos.* 11:11, 14, 17, 12:6)[74]

Another interesting note about Moses in the Assumption of Moses also deserves a separate treatment.

---

[70] Coogan, *The New Oxford Annotated Apocrypha*, 245. Second Maccabees 2:10, which Hafemann deals with under the category of "authority" ("Moses in the Apocrypha and Pseudepigrapha," 82-84), seems to better fit the intercession category.

[71] Coogan, *The New Oxford Annotated Apocrypha*, 83. Cf. Meeks, *The Prophet-King*, 154.

[72] J. Priest, "Testament of Moses," in *OTP*, 1:920-21.

[73] John Muddiman, "The Assumption of Moses and the Epistle of Jude," in *Moses in Biblical and Extra-Biblical Traditions*, ed. Axel Graupner and Michael Wolter (Berlin: Walter de Gruyter, 2007), 169.

[74] Tromp, *The Assumption of Moses*, 22-23, 24-25. Also, "I answered and said, 'How then do we find that first Abraham prayed for the people of Sodom, and Moses for our ancestors who sinned in the desert.'" (4 Esdr 7:106) Meeks reckons that the passage cited above speaks of Moses' enduring intercessory prayer, but such a reading does not seem warranted. Meeks, *The Prophet-King*, 160. For a more detailed discussion on the early Jewish depiction of Moses as a prophet, see Lierman, *The New Testament Moses*, 34-45.

And then his kingdom will appear in his entire creation. And then the devil will come to an end, and sadness will be carried away together with him. Then the hands of *the messenger*, when he will be in heaven, will be filled, and he will then avenge them against their enemies. (*Ass. Mos.* 10:1-2)[75]

In an eschatological context, the messenger is depicted as a divine agent/mediator who executes the divine wrath upon the ungodly. The key question is the identity of the "messenger (*nuntius*)" in v. 2. Since the word seems to have been translated from the Greek synonym ἄγγελος, and is usually associated with the archangel Michael, some scholars suggested that it refers to a messianic angelic being as an interesting parallel passage is also observed in 11QMelchizedek, which speaks of an eschatological Mosaic figure.[76]

> [18] And the messenger i[s] the anointed of the spir[it] as Dan[iel] said [about him: *Dan 9:25* "until an anointed, a prince, it is seven weeks." And the messenger of] [19] good who announ[ces salvation] is the one about whom it is written that [. . .]. (11Q13 [11QMelch] 13 xviii-xix)[77]

Three observations strongly suggest that the referent of the word is Moses. First, the lack of any reference to an angelic figure as an eschatological divine agent elsewhere in the document corroborates such a conclusion.[78] In addition, the word "*nuntius*" usually refers to a human agent in other Latin writings that are similar to the Assumption of Moses.[79] Second, in the same book, Moses is denoted as arbiter in 1:14 and *magnus nuntius* in 11:17 (a Greek equivalent would be μεριστής ["mediator"]). In the following chapter, he is also called *nuntius*. Finally, the literary context of this document, i.e., a testament of Moses to Joshua, suggests that Moses could be the object of this narrative. As such, the messenger in the pericope seems to connote a Moses *redivivus* figure, an agent of divine judgment.[80] The composite picture of Moses from this book (particularly 10:2, 11:16-17, and 12:6) is that he is a chief intercessor and mediator for Israel.

Qumran. Much as in the Hebrew scriptures and early Jewish literature, Moses is also considered as the prophet *par excellence* in the Qumran documents.[81] The

---

[75] Tromp, *The Assumption of Moses*, 18-19. Italics are added for emphasis.
[76] Florentino García Martínez, "Las tradiciones sobre Melquisedec en los manuscitos de Qumrán," *Bib* 81 (2000): 70-80; Eric F. Mason, "The Identification of MLKY SDQ in 11QMelchizedek: A Survey of Recent Scholarship," *QC* 17 (2009): 51-61.
[77] *DSS*, 2:1208-09.
[78] For a Davidic messianic reading of this messenger, see Paul A. Rainbow, "Melchizedek as a Messiah at Qumran," *BBR* 7 (1997): 179-94.
[79] Johannes Tromp, "Taxo, the Messenger of the Lord," *JSJ* 21 (1990): 202-05.
[80] Crispin H. Fletcher-Louis, "4Q374: A Discourse on the Sinai Tradition: The Deification of Moses and Early Christology," *DSD* 3 (1996): 246; Henten, "Moses as Heavenly Messenger in Assumptio Mosis 10:2 and Qumran Passages," 218-21.
[81] Meeks, *Prophet-King*, 173; James E. Bowley, "Prophets and Prophecy at Qumran," in *Dead Sea Scrolls after Fifty Years: A Comprehensive Assessment*, ed. Peter W. Flint

Jewish traditions on Moses can be broken down into two broad categories: first, he is seen in the images as depicted in the Hebrew scriptures as the law-giver, an intercessor, a receiver of revelations concerning the end-times, and, second, as an ideal human figure so portrayed in Greek apologetical writings (Aristobulus, Artapanus, Philo, and Josephus) in terms of the great civilizer, philosopher, inventor, the ideal king, and a divine man.[82] This section will concern Moses' role as the miracle-worker and intercessor seen in the Qumran library.

It is, nevertheless, somewhat perplexing to observe that virtually no Qumran document elaborates on or explicitly mentions Moses as a miracle-worker. Charlesworth's concordance lists no juxtaposition of Moses with the noun, "sign" (אוֹת)," which, however, occurs about a hundred times in the Qumran library without reference to him.[83] The complete lack of a general entry to semantic synonyms to אוֹת, such as, miracle or wonders, in *Encyclopedia of the Dead Sea Scrolls* is also highly indicative of the community's disinterest in the miracle-working aspect of the prophet.[84] In the Qumran literature, the word "sign" is generally mentioned as an indicator of true prophets or divine prophecy.[85] Nonetheless, this lack of interest in Moses as a miracle-worker may well explain the similar indifference in the prophet Elijah who could be above all recalled as *the* miracle worker in the Hebrew biblical tradition but not in the Qumran texts (see the Qumran expectation of Elijah, pp. 110-113 of this book). Hence it is possible to postulate on the basis of the two observations mentioned above that the Qumran community was not overtly preoccupied with the miracle-working aspect of the prophets. This orientation may be due to the community's belief that, although the eschaton is expected to arrive soon, it had not come to pass yet. Therefore, the signs were not as important as the inspired interpretation. Despite the minor interest in the miracle-working aspect, Moses is still portrayed as the yardstick by which a true prophet is measured. Such a notion is expressed particularly in three documents: the Temple Scroll (11Q19), 4Q175 (4QTestimonia), and the Apocryphon of Moses (4Q375-76; 1Q22; 1Q29). These writings will be further examined in detail later under the subheading of "Moses as the eschatological prophet."

---

and James C. VanderKam (Leiden: Brill, 1999), 2:361; Xeravits, *King, Priest, Prophet*, 176. For the summarizing epithet of Moses as "God's servant and Messiah," see Bowley, "Moses in the Dead Sea Scrolls," 181.

[82] Falk, *EDSS*, 1:576-77.

[83] James H. Charlesworth, *Graphic Concordance to the Dead Sea Scrolls* (Tübingen: Mohr Siebeck; Louisville: Westminster/John Knox, 1991), 10-11.

[84] Lawrence H. Schiffman and James C. VanderKam, eds., *Encyclopedia of the Dead Sea Scrolls*, 2 vols. (Oxford: OUP, 2000).

[85] Otto A. Piper, "The 'Book of Mysteries' (Qumran I 27): A Study in Eschatology," *JR* 38 (1958): 96; Alfred R.C. Leaney, *The Rule of Qumran and Its Meaning: Introduction, Translation, and Commentary* (London: SCM, 1966), 147; Eduard Lohse, *Die Texte aus Qumran: Hebräisch und deutsch mit masoretischer Punktation* (München: Kösel, 1986), 157; Paul A. Kruger, "אוֹת," *NIDOTTE*, 1:333.

Turning to the image of Moses as an intercessor, a number of passages can be mentioned. In an allusion to the golden calf episode of Exodus 32, 4Q504 (4QWords of Luminaries) mentions that, on account of Moses' atonement, God took pity on the Israelites:

> You [God] became angry with them to destroy them; but you took pity on them in your love for them, and on account of your covenant—for Moses atoned for their sin—and so that they would know your great power and your abundant kindness for everlasting generations. (4Q504 1 ii 8-11)[86]

4Q374 (4QDiscourse on the Exodus/Conquest Tradition), in passing, mentions Moses as "a mediator for your people" (לעמך מליץ):

> "[...] your ... blank [...] [...] a mediator for your people [...] [...] clouds, and above [...] [...] ... [...]. (4Q374 7 ii)[87]

2Q21 (2QApocryphon of Moses) also recounts the intercession of Moses:

> [... Nadab and] Ab[i]hu, Elea[zar and Ithamar ...] [... in order to do] you justice in truth, and in order to reprove with faith[ful]ness [...] blank [...] [And Moses went outsi]de the camp and pleaded with YHWH and bowed do[wn before ...] [And he said: YHWH Go]d, how can I look at you, and how can I li[ft] my face [towards you ...] [...] one nation by your d[e]eds [...]. (2Q21)[88]

In analogous terms with the Old Testament, 4Q368 also documents the effectiveness of Moses' intercession, resulting from his direct encounter with Yahweh (e.g., face to face):

> [...] ... [...] [... and he spoke wi]th Moses [these] words [... Exod 33:11-13 and YHWH spoke to Moses face] to face as [one man speaks to another. And Moses said to YHWH: "Se]e [y]ou are telling [me: Lead up this people. But you have not made known to me] whom you will send with me. [You have said. I know you by name. And also: You have found favour] in [my] ey[es]. But now, if [I have really found favour in your eyes, make then your way known to me] so [that]. (4Q368 1)[89]

---

[86] *DSS*, 2:12-13; Maurice Baillet, *Qumrân Grotte 4 III (4Q482-4Q520)*, DJD 7 (Oxford: Clarendon, 1982), 139-41. The Deuteronomy text is not crystal-clear, but seems to speak of the unabated divine wrath even in the face of Moses' intercession. For a helpful introduction and notes for this Qumran document, see Caquot, "Trois textes religieux de la Grotte 4," 129-47.

[87] *DSS*, 2:740-41. C. Newsom finds a close parallel with Exod 20:18-20. However, the Hebrew Old Testament does not apply the term, "mediator (מליץ)," to Moses. Carol A. Newsom, "4Q374: A Discourse on the Exodus/Conquest Tradition," in *Qumrân Cave 4 XIV: Parabiblical Texts*, part 2, ed. M. Broshi (Oxford: Clarendon, 1995), 107. Fletcher-Louis conceives of a deified identity of Moses in this Qumranic parallel to the Sinai event. Crispin H. Fletcher-Louis, "4Q374: A Discourse on the Sinai Tradition: The Deification of Moses and Early Christology," *DSD* 3 (1996): 236-52.

[88] *DSS*, 1:214-17.

[89] *DSS*, 2:726-27. For helpful textual notes on this text, see Howard Jacobson, "4Q368 fg. 3," *RevQ* 21 (2003): 117-18.

However, one of the more interesting accounts is the notion of Moses' heavenly intercession as recorded in several ascension narratives. With a series of catenae from Deuteronomy (1:3, 9-18; 6:10-11; 11:15; 17; 27:9-19; 28:15), 1Q22 (1QWords of Moses) 1-3 depicts Moses as one who establishes a covenant between God and Israel and charges obedience to the decrees.[90] The first half of the fourth (which is the last) column presents an account of a heavenly council:

> In the congregation of the gods [and in the council of the ho]ly ones, and in their [. . ., in favour of the sons of Isra]el and on behalf of the la[nd. And] ta[ke] from [its blood and] pour (it) on the earth [. . .] . . . [. . .] . . . [and atone]ment [shall be made] for them by it [. . . And] Moses [spoke saying:] Observe. (1Q22 4 i-iii)[91]

The extensive presence of lacunae in this text allows one only to posit some type of connection between Moses and the atonement.[92]

On the other hand, the ambiguous role of Moses in 1Q22 receives illumination in view of 4Q378, which contains a similar heavenly council account.[93]

> [. . .] and who kno[ws] the knowledge of the Most High and *m*[. . .]
> [. . .]*h* man of God made known to us according to *o*[. . .]
> [. . .] and the congregation of the Most High gave ear to the voice of M[oses . . .]
> [. . .] his *m*[. . .] and *b*[. . .] God Most Hig[h . . .]
> [. . .] great signs and he restrained his wrath
> [. . .]*yš* acts of [ki]ndness and until its ages remember
> [. . .]*ot* unto *lm*[. . .]
> vacat
> [. . .]*ó*[ ]*oo*[   ]*kh*[. . .]. (4Q378 [4QApocryphon of Joshua] 26)[94]

---

[90] *DSS*, 1:58-63.

[91] Ibid., 1:62-63. The composition of the heavenly council consists of divine beings (אלים). For a survey on the meaning of this word, see S.B. Parker, "Sons of (the) God(s)," *DDD*, 794-800.

[92] Henten's assessment that this pericope presents Moses as an intercessor seems to be at best suggestive. Henten, "Moses as Heavenly Messenger in *Assumptio Mosis* 10:2 and Qumran Passages," 224.

[93] The Apocryphon of Joshua enjoyed a fairly wide reception at the turn of the era in Palestine. Emanuel Tov, "The Rewritten Book of Joshua as Found at Qumran and Masada," in *Biblical Perspectives: Early Use and Interpretation of the Bible in Light of the Dead Sea Scrolls, Proceedings of the First International Symposium of the Orion Center for the Study of the Dead Sea Scrolls and Associated Literature, 12-14 May 1996*, ed. Michael E. Stone and Esther G. Chazon (Leiden: Brill, 1998), 233-56.

[94] Carol A. Newsom, "4Q378 and 4Q379: An Apocryphon of Joshua," in *Qumranstudien: Vorträge und Beiträge der Teilnehmer des Qumranseminars auf dem internationalen Treffen der Society of Biblical Literature, Münster, 25.-26. Juli 1993*, ed. Heinz-Josef Fabry, Armin Lange, and Hermann Lichtenberger (Göttingen: Vandenhoeck & Ruprecht, 1996), 56-57. The translation of García Martínez and Tigchelaar is as follows: "[. . .] having the knowledge of the Most High and [seeing] the vision [of Shaddai . . .] the man of God an[no]unced us, according [. . .] and the assembly of Elyon; they pa[i]d attention to the voice of Mo[ses . . .] . . . [. . .] God Most

It is clear from the text that Moses appealed to the celestial assembly and his intercession placated the divine wrath. In this respect, some scholars juxtapose this text with 4Q427 7 and 4Q491 11-12, in order to further identify the deified nature of the enthroned Moses:

> [My] office is among the gods! (4Q427 [4Qhodayot^a] 7 i 11)[95]

> For I have sat on a [throne] in the heavens. (4Q491 [4QWar Scroll] 11 i 13).[96]

Nevertheless, the identification of the character in 4Q491 is under severe debate (i.e., "the Teacher of Righteousness," Moses, and Melchizedek).[97] Furthermore,

---

Hig[h . . .] great signs; and in anger he restrained [. . .] [. . . m]an of the [pi]ous ones and until its ages remember [. . .] eternal, to [. . .]." *DSS*, 2:748-49.

[95] This Qumran document may have originated from outside the community. Eric Miller, "The Self-Glorification Hymn Reexamined," *Hen* 31 (2009): 307-24.

[96] The entire text of 4Q491 11 is worthwhile to cite here. It illustrates the potential connection of this text with 4Q378: "[. . .] has done awesome things marvelously [. . .] [. . . in the streng]th of his power the just exult, and the holy ones rejoice in [. . .] in justice [. . .] he established [I]srael from eternity; his truth and the mysteries of his wisdom in al[l generations . . .] might [. . .] . . . [. . .] and the council of the poor for an eternal congregation. [. . .] the perfect ones of [. . . et]ernal; a mighty throne in the congregation of the gods above which none of the kings of the East shall sit, and their nobles no[t . . .] silence (?) [. . .] my glory is in {comparable} and besides me no-one is exalted, nor comes to me, for I reside in [. . .], in the heavens, and there is no [. . .] . . . I am counted among the gods and my dwelling is in the holy congregation; [my] des[ire] is not according to the flesh, [but] all that is precious to me is in (the) glory (of) [. . .] the holy [dwel]ling. [W]ho has been considered despicable on my account? And who is comparable to me in my glory? Who, like the sailors, will come back and tell? . . . Who bea[rs all] sorrows like me? And who [suffe]rs evil like me? There is no-one. I have been instructed, and there is no teaching comparable [to my teaching . . .] And who will attack me when [I] op[en my mouth]? And who can endure the flow of my lips? And who will confront me and retain comparison with my judgment? [. . . friend of the king, companion of the holy ones . . . incomparable, f]or among the gods is [my] posi[tion, and] my glory is with the sons of the king. To me (belongs) [pure] gold, and to me, the gold of Ophir [. . .] [. . . exult,] just ones, in the God of [. . .] in the holy dwelling, sing for h[im . . .] [. . . p]roclaim during the meditation jubilation [. . .] in eternal happiness; and there is no . . . [. . .] to establish the horn of [his] Messi[ah . . .] [. . .] to make known his power with strength [. . .]." *DSS*, 2:980-81.

[97] For the identification of this figure with Moses, see Meeks, *The Prophet-King*, 170; Collins, *The Scepter and the Star*, 148; Henten, "Moses as Heavenly Messenger," 224-25; with "the Teacher of Righteousness," see Esther Eshel, "4Q471B: A Self-Glorification Hymn," *RevQ* 17 (1996): 175-203; idem, "The Identification of the 'Speaker' of the Self-Glorification Hymn," in *Provo International Conference on the Dead Sea Scrolls: Technological Innovations, New Texts, and Reformulated Issues*, ed. Donald W. Parry and Eugene C. Ulrich (Leiden: Brill, 1999), 619-35; Martin G. Abegg, Jr., "Who Ascended to Heaven?: 4Q491, 4Q427, and the Teacher of Righteousness," in *Eschatology, Messianism, and the Dead Sea Scrolls*, ed. Craig A. Evans and Peter W. Flint (Grand Rapids: Eerdmans, 1997), 61-73; with a Davidic figure (Melchizedek-like), see J.C. O'Neill, "'Who Is Comparable to Me in My Glory?':

when the figurative genre of the text is taken into consideration, it is not entirely certain whether the person is related to the historical figure (of the past, present, or future) or the text is simply intended to justify the existence of the community via symbolic language.[98] What the foregoing observations point out is that Moses was held in high regard, and some post-biblical Jewish sources entertain the elevated status of Moses via ascension narratives. Nevertheless, what is open to dispute is the extent to which these writings intend to promote the super-human or quasi-divine characteristics of Moses.

Moses as Royal Figure

The Old Testament. In the ancient world, royal and priestly roles were often closely interrelated. At other times, the primary function of the royal office was to enact and implement the law. In this respect, some scholars propose that the Pentateuchal depiction of Moses as the mediator of the divine law confers on him a royal office based on adjacent ancient Near Eastern traditions.[99] Although the connection between kingship and priesthood in early Jewish tradition is beyond the scope of this research, a close examination of a selective number of passages related to the kingship of Moses has merit for substantiating the thesis of this study.

Two Old Testament passages are usually referred to with reference to the royal office of Moses. The first passage is from Exodus 4:20 in which Moses is said to carry with him "the staff (מַטֵּה) of God" as he embarked on the journey back to Egypt:

> So Moses took his wife and his sons, put them on a donkey and went back to the land of Egypt; and Moses carried the staff of God in his hand. (Exod 4:20, NRSV)

Some exegetes suggest that "the staff of God" connotes Moses' royal standing.[100] Their judgment is based on two observations. The word refers to the scepter of a ruler mentioned elsewhere in the Old Testament (Ezek 19:11, 14; Ps 110:2) and a later rabbinic interpretation understood the staff as a royal scepter. For instance, a Midrash on Psalm 21:2 reads as follows:

> Yet Moses was allowed to take the scepter of the Holy One, blessed be He, for it is said

---

4Q491 Fragment 11 (4Q191C) and the New Testament," *NovT* 42 (2000): 27-28; Igor R. Tantlevskij, "Melchizedek Redivivus in Qumran: Some Peculiarities of Messianic Ideas and Elements of Mysticism in the Dead Sea Scrolls," *QC* 12 (2004): 3-80.

[98] Abegg, "Who Ascended to Heaven?," 72-73; Michael K. Knibb, "Teacher of Righteousness," *EDSS*, 2:920-21.

[99] Especially some Babylonian traditions. Otto, *RGG*, 5:1537; Römer, "Moïse," 192-93.

[100] Meeks, *The Prophet-King*, 188; Lierman, *The New Testament Moses*, 79-80. This Exodus text took on another religious development in the form of Moses worship in the mediterranean world. Philippe Borgeaud, "Quelques remarques sur Typhon, Seth, Moïse et son âne, dans la perspective d'un dialogue réactif transculturel," in *Interprétations de Möise: Égypte, Judée, Grèce et Rome*, ed. Philippe Borgeaud, Thomas Römer, and Youri Volokhine (Leiden: Brill, 2010), 173-85.

Moses took the scepter of God in his hand.[101]

However, their view appears to be problematic. The royal usage of מַטֶּה (*maṭṭeh*) and its cognate words in the Old Testament is extremely rare. Only three out of two hundred fifty-three occurrences of this word and its cognates refer to an explicit royal connotation. Those three royal usages appear only in Ezekiel 19 and Psalm 110. Out of those two hundred fifty instances, fifty-plus times, the word, מַטֶּה (*maṭṭeh*) and its synonym, שֵׁבֶט (*šēbeṭ*), originally referring to parts of a tree, are translated as "tribe." In contrast to its synonym, שֵׁבֶט (which usually involved an authority figure such as a father, a king, or God), מַטֶּה is usually associated with a shepherd's staff or lower authoritative figures such as a priest, prince, or tribal leader rather than with God or king.[102] Furthermore, not only is it anachronistic to read the midrashic passage back into the Exodus (for the same reason, that of Ezekiel and Psalm into the Exodus),[103] but the Exodus passage in its literary context requires little royal reading of Moses' undertaking of the journey or his staff.[104] Although some scholars point to the reading of the Greek Old Testament, which qualifies the staff as "from God (τὴν ῥάβδον τὴν παρὰ τοῦ θεοῦ)," the divine provenance of the rod does not necessarily suggest the kingship of the recipient as much as it does the divine instrumentality of the carrier.[105]

Deuteronomy 33:4-5 is the other passage that is often adduced to promote the royal standing of Moses:

> [4] Moses charged us with the law, as a possession for the assembly of Jacob. [5] There arose a king in Jeshurun, when the leaders of the people assembled—the united tribes of Israel. (Deut 33:4-5, NRSV)

The thirty-third chapter of Deuteronomy, which is often called the "blessing of

---

[101] William G. Braude, trans., *The Midrash on Psalms* (New Haven: Yale University Press, 1959), 293.

[102] *TDOT*, an older lexicon, finds a relatively wide use of the word in the royal sense, but newer dictionaries on the contrary, such as *NIDOTTE* and *HALOT*, find minimal instances (for *HALOT* none). Cf. H. Simian-Yofre, "מַטֶּה" *TDOT*, 8:241-49; David Fouts, "מַטֶּה," *NIDOTTE*, 2:924; idem, "שֵׁבֶט," *NIDOTTE*, 4:27; *HALOT*, 1:573, 2:1990.

[103] The Midrash document at best dates back to the third through thirteenth centuries. Braude, *The Midrash on Psalms*, xi, xxxi; Günther Stemberger, *Introduction to the Talmud and Midrash* trans. and ed. Markus Bockmuehl (Edinburgh: T & T Clark, 1996), 322-23.

[104] Fouts takes *maṭṭeh* of Moses as a shepherd's staff. Fouts, *NIDOTTE*, 924. In addition, the meaning of the word מַטֶּה in Ps 110:2 is subject to debate. Ibid., 925; Mitchell Dahood, *Psalms III: 101-150* (Garden City: Doubleday, 1970), 115; Bruce K. Waltke, "Micah," in *Obadiah, Jonah, Micah, Nahum, and Habakkuk*, vol. 2 of *The Minor Prophets*, ed. Thomas E. McComiskey (Grand Rapids: Baker, 1993), 757.

[105] Schneider also takes ῥάβδος (*rhabdos*) of Moses in Exod 20:4 as a mere rod. G. Schneider, "ῥάβδος," *TDNT*, 6:967.

Moses," contains Moses' last testament to the Israelites. Structurally, vv. 1 through 5 and 26 through 29 constitute an *inclusio*. The former recounts the blessings of Yahweh granted upon Israel and the latter reminds Israelites of their privileged status as God's chosen people. Verses 6 through 25 speak of prophecies concerning the twelve tribes. The first three Hebrew words in v. 5 can be literally translated as "there arose a king in Jeshurun" or "he became a king in Jeshurun" (וַיְהִי בִישֻׁרוּן מֶלֶךְ).[106] Because the referent of the waw consecutive is not clearly designated, Moses, the subject of the previous sentence, is often pointed out as the implied subject in v. 5.[107]

There are some exegetes who find a messianic expectation latent in this text. For instance, Lierman brings forward certain later rabbinic interpretation of the text in terms of Mosaic kingship.[108] These traditions, nevertheless, do not constitute definitive evidence due to their late date of composition. In addition, other exegetes point to the change of the waw-consecutive into the future tense in the LXX as a hint at an expectation of Moses *redivivus*' arrival as a kingly figure.[109] In contrast, however, it is equally important to note that the LXX changes מֶלֶךְ into ἄρχων, which indicates merely a human ruler and not a king. In using a much diminished expression, the LXX seems to have sought to convey a coming of a leader rather than a royal figure.[110] The Revised Standard Version clarifies the subject of v. 5 to be Yahweh, but the New Revised Standard Version changes it to an improper pronoun: hence, "there arose a king." A possibility is left open for Moses to be the referent of Jeshurun in the New Revised Standard Version.

The messianic reading of this text encounters exegetical difficulties at least on two accounts. First, the immediately preceeding context manifests a progression of thought with the emphasis on the kingship of Yahweh.

He said: The LORD came from Sinai, and dawned from Seir upon us; he shone forth

---

[106] "יְשֻׁרוּן" occurs only four times in the Old Testament and it is usually considered as a euphemism for Israel and/or Jacob. M. J. Mulder, "יְשֻׁרוּן," *TDOT*, 6:472-77. Seebass identifies *Jeshurun* as the tribe of Simeon. Horst Seebass, "Die Stämmeliste von Dtn. XXXIII," *VT* 27 (1977): 158-69.

[107] J.R. Porter, *Moses and Monarchy: A Study in the Biblical Tradition of Moses* (Oxford: Blackwell, 1963), 14, n. 35; Lierman, *The New Testament Moses*, 80-81.

[108] Ibid., 81-82.

[109] Odo Camponovo, *Königtum, Königsherrschaft und Reich Gottes in den frühjüdischen Schriften* (Freiburg: Universitätsverlag Freiburg; Göttingen: Vandenhoeck & Ruprecht, 1995), 387; John W. Wevers, *Notes on the Greek Text of Deuteronomy* (Atlanta: Scholars, 1995), 541; Lierman, *The New Testament Moses*, 82-83; William Horbury, "Monarchy and Messianism in the Greek Pentateuch," in *The Septuagint and Messianism: Colloquium Biblicum Lovaniense LIII, July 27-29, 2004*, ed. M.A. Knibb, (Leuven: Leuven University Press; Peeters, 2006), 79-128.

[110] John J. Collins, "Messianism and Exegetical Tradition: The Evidence of the LXX Pentateuch," in *The Septuagint and Messianism: Colloquium Biblicum Lovaniense LIII, July 27-29, 2004*, ed. M.A. Knibb (Leuven: Leuven University Press; Peeters, 2006), 129-49.

from Mount Paran. With him were myriads of holy ones; at his right, a host of his own. Indeed, O favorite among peoples, all his holy ones were in your charge; they marched at your heels, accepted direction from you. (Deut 33:2-3, NRSV)

Coupled with vv. 26 through 29, which also praise Yahweh for his majesty, the royal language of vv. 2 and 3 suggests the subject of king in v. 5 to be Yahweh.[111] In this regard, v. 5 can be seen as standing in parallel with v. 26:

> There arose a king in Jeshurun, when the leaders of the people assembled—the united tribes of Israel. (Deut 33:5, NRSV)

> There is none like God, O Jeshurun, who rides through the heavens to your help, majestic through the skies. (Deut 33:26, NRSV)

The presence of God side by side with Jeshurun in v. 26 renders it highly reasonable to take "king" in v. 5 as Yahweh.

Furthermore, although Moses can be said to have played a partial role of a king, the general tenor of Deuteronomy prevents conferring him a full-fledged title as such. In his comment on the text under discussion, D.L. Christensen precisely sums up the ancient Israelites' attitude towards the kingship ideology.

> In giving the Torah, Moses functions as a prophet; but he also takes on much of the functions of "a king" in his capacity as leader in ancient Israel. At the same time, it is important to note that Moses never takes upon himself the name or the position of royalty. . . . They [Israelites] made God their king. At least that is what it was at the outset, in the teaching of Moses. . . . The principle that God alone is in reality king in Israel means that God's official spokesperson, the prophet like Moses, must share political authority alongside the designated king, who was originally known as a נָגִיד, "leader" in the sense of being a permanent warlord, rather than a מֶלֶךְ, "king."[112]

At the least, it could be said that some Deuteronomy texts seem to allow room for the establishment of kingship in Israel.[113] Nonetheless, the power of king in

---

[111] Nelson notes the concentric structure of ch. 33, which is held together by proper names, Yahweh in vv. 2 and 29, Jacob in vv. 4 and 28, and Jeshurun in vv. 5 and 26. Nelson, *Deuteronomy*, 387. The majority of Deuteronomy commentators take the referent of the king to be Yahweh. Peter C. Craigie, *The Book of Deuteronomy* (Grand Rapids: Eerdmans, 1976), 393-94; S.R. Driver, *A Critical and Exegetical Commentary on Deuteronomy* (Edinburgh: T & T Clark, 1978), 394; Patrick D. Miller, *Deuteronomy* (Louisville: John Knox, 1990), 238-40; Eugene H. Merrill, *Deuteronomy*, (Nashville: Broadman and Holman, 1994), 435; Ronald E. Clements, "The Book of Deuteronomy: Introduction, Commentary, and Reflections," in *The Book of Numbers, the Book of Deuteronomy, Introduction to Narrative Literature, the Book of Joshua, the Book of Judges, the Book of Ruth, the First and Second Books of Samuel*, vol. 2 of *The New Interpreter's Bible*, ed. Leander E. Keck (Nashville: Abingdon, 1998), 534.

[112] Christensen, *Deuteronomy 21:10-34:12*, 838. Also, similarly, S. Dean McBride, Jr., "Polity of the Covenant People: The Book of Deuteronomy," in *A Song of Power and the Power of Song: Essays on the Book of Deuteronomy*, ed. Duane L. Christensen (Winona Lake: Eisenbrauns, 1993), 62-77.

[113] Udo Rüterswörden, *Von der politischen Gemeinschaft zur Gemeinde: Studien zu Dt 16, 18-18, 22* (Frankfurt: Athenäum, 1987), 90-91.

ancient Israel is substantially limited in comparison with the surrounding Near Eastern empires. The restrictions of the Deuteronomistic circumscription include the following: the source of power being Yahweh; no power to grant land; no inherent right to make an executive decision; appointed by people, and no military figure.[114] As such, the royal office of Moses constitutes an extremely thin conceptual trajectory in the Hebrew Bible:

> Deuteronomy evidently intends somehow to circumscribe or restrict the powers of the king. The king as presented here differs enormously from that of the usual ancient Near Eastern concept of the king as the chief executive in all aspects of the nation's life.[115]

James Watts also notes the fundamental incongruity between the Ancient Near Eastern kings and those of Israel. That is, the Jewish kings never gave a law, whereas the former group was often marked by the proclamation of laws.

> Deuteronomy characterizes Moses less in royal terms than as prophet and teacher/scribe, characterizations that the book's position in the larger Pentateuch both amplifies and restricts.[116]

Finally, remarks are in order concerning the methodology employed by Lierman and other exegetes in favor of the messianic king motif. Caveats can be expressed in two respects. First, they impose foreign materials onto the Old Testament texts so as to corroborate the presence of the "prophet-king" imagery. A great deal of ancient Near Eastern literature and extra-biblical sources have been adduced to argue on their behalf. However, they draw too little attention to the exegesis of the actual Old Testament passages. Too often, the aforementioned extra-biblical (virtually always much later) sources are brought forth to support their thesis. For example, Lierman spends about four pages (pp. 79-81 and 84-86) in a discussion of the Old Testament passages which allegedly speak of Moses as a royal figure. Then, he goes on to examine the extra-biblical sources for the rest of the chapter (pp. 79-123).[117] Even worse, Wayne Meeks reserves no section for a discussion of the "prophet-king" concept found in the Old Testament, for Moses or any other prophets.[118] This disproportional imbalance leaves a reader wondering whether there really is a strand of thought in terms of a

---

[114] J. Gordon McConville, "King and Messiah in Deuteronomy and the Deuteronomistic History," in *King and Messiah in Israel and the Ancient Near East: Proceedings of the Oxford Old Testament Seminar*, ed. John Day (Sheffield: Sheffield, 1998), 276; Norbert Lohfink, "Distribution of the Functions of Power: The Laws concerning Public Offices in Deuteronomy 16:18-18:22," in *A Song of Power and the Power of Song: Essays on the Book of Deuteronomy*, ed. Duane L. Christensen (Winona Lake: Eisenbrauns, 1993), 345.

[115] McConville, "King and Messiah in Deuteronomy and the Deuteronomistic History," 276-78.

[116] James W. Watts, "The Legal Characterization of Moses in the Rhetoric of the Pentateuch," *JBL* 117 (1998): 416-18.

[117] Lierman, *The New Testament Moses*, 79-123.

[118] Meeks, *The Prophet-King*.

Mosaic king-prophet in the Old Testament in the first place or if it simply results from a much later re-reading of the text. Furthermore, Lierman and others refer to only three verses (Exod 4:20; Deut 18:15; 33:5) out of the entire books of Exodus, Leviticus, Numbers, and Deuteronomy, which they believe speak of Moses' kingship.[119] Such a dearth of references is surprising as one would expect that such an important theme as the kingship of Moses (especially in view of his prominence in the Pentateuch) would appear more often in the major bulk of the Hebrew Scripture.

Another exegetical fallacy of Lierman and others is their employment of ill-defined terms. For instance, Lierman brings up David and Saul to propose that the prophetic office and that of the king were conceived as overlapping in the Old Testament traditions.[120] As true as they are in the cases of David and Saul, it is a totally different matter to claim that the same holds true of Moses, who lived in the pre-Monarchy period. Lierman quotes K. Berger who states that prophets can play a royal function.[121] Nevertheless, it is fallacious to generalize isolated instances. Saul, in particular, was mockingly dubbed as a prophet (1 Sam 10:10-11; 19:23-24). In addition, although David and Saul may have played both kingly and prophetic functions at times, it would be more accurate to admit that the overlapping of the roles took place on only a few occasions and that they were seen primarily as kings, especially in the case of Saul. Certainly, it is only the two examples that Lierman is able to provide from a long line of the Israelite monarchical tradition. That case seems to lack conclusive evidences.

God language of Moses in Exodus, Sirach, and Philo. In metaphorical language, Exodus 4:16 seems to depict Yahweh as conferring a divine status to Moses: "I give you, a god, to Pharaoh." This is recounted in Exodus 7:1:[122]

---

[119] Although Lierman finds a kingship motif in Deut 18:15 (Lierman, *The New Testament Moses*, 82-89), McConville detects an important demarcation between king and prophet from the text. Yahweh chooses king and priest through public ceremony performed by people. On the other hand, a prophet is chosen privately as the need arises. Thus, it is necessary to have means to confirm the true prophethood, which is explicated in vv. 16-17. That is whenever prophecy comes true then a prophet could be regarded as a true messenger of God. McConville, *Deuteronomy*, 302.

[120] Lierman, *The New Testament Moses*, 84-85.

[121] "Propheten können in der Tat auch also solche königliche Funktion haben." Klaus Berger, "Die königlichen Messiastraditionen des Neuen Testaments," *NTS* 20 (1974): 26, quoted in Lierman, *The New Testament Moses*, 84, n. 22.

[122] Durham, *Exodus*, 85. Some scholars speculate the divinization of Moses in the text as a result of the tension between the priestly source and prophetic source which were incorporated into the Pentateuch. For a summary of scholarly debates on the issue, see Brevard S. Childs, *The Book of Exodus: A Critical, Theological Commentary* (Louisville: Westminster, 1973), 113-14; Jean Louis Ska, "La sortie d'Egypte (Ex 7-14) dans le récit sacerdotal (Pg) et la tradition prophétique," *Bib* 60 (1979): 191-215; Werner H. Schmidt, "Die Intention der beiden Plagenerzählungen (Exodus 7-10) in ihrem Kontext," in *Studies in the Book of Exodus: Redaction, Reception, Interpretation*, ed. Marc Vervenne (Leuven: Leuven University Press; Peeters, 1996), 225-43; William H.C.

And the LORD said unto Moses, "See, I have made thee a god to Pharaoh." (Exod 7:1a, KJV)

(Exod 7:1, BHS⁵) וַיֹּאמֶר יְהוָה אֶל־מֹשֶׁה רְאֵה נְתַתִּיךָ אֱלֹהִים לְפַרְעֹה׃

Although the language of these texts is intriguing, it does not seem to be intended to focus on the ontological transformation of Moses. The point of such a stark metaphor to indicate God's sovereignty over a series of ensuing events. In the course of time, Moses was to play as a divine instrument so as to facilitate the outworking of the divine redemptive plan. John Durham articulates so well the functionality of the "god-language" with reference to Moses in terms of divine sovereignty.

> Thus a question of Moses is once again an opening for an assertion of Yahweh that makes clear that Moses (and this time, Aaron as well) is but an instrument of God's activity.... That Moses is to be a god to Pharaoh will be Yahweh's doing, not his.... The assertion that Moses is to be made a god (אלהים) to Pharaoh, and that Aaron will function as his prophet (נביא, "spokesman") is to be understood as a credit to Yahweh and not to Moses or to Aaron.... Yahweh makes it clear that both Moses (and in this passage also Aaron) and Pharaoh are to be instruments in the proof of his Presence.[123]

Three observations in particular reinforce this judgment. First, the linguistic inability of Moses does not add up to his alleged divine status.[124] Second, that Yahweh is the subject of conferring the supposed divine quality to Moses is as significant as his hardening of Pharaoh. In other words, Moses is no more special, especially in view of his hesitation to carry out the divine commission, than Pharaoh in what would unfold as divine instruments. Finally, the following context repeatedly highlights the role of Yahweh as the sole conductor who is responsible for orchestrating the subsequent divine miracles.[125] Accordingly, the

---

Propp, *Exodus 1-18: A New Translation with Introduction and Commentary* (New York: Doubleday, 1998), 284-86; Randall C. Bailey, "'And They Shall Know That I Am YHWH!': The P Recasting of the Plague Narratives in Exodus 7-11," in *Liberating Biblical Study: Scholarship, Art, and Action in Honor of the Center and Library for the Bible and Social Justice*, ed. Laurel Dykstra (Eugene: Cascade, 2011), 35-49.

[123] Durham, *Exodus*, 86-87. Childs also notes the function, not the ontological statement, by means of the "god language." Childs, *The Book of Exodus*, 118. Terence Fretheim takes this god-language as divine self-effacement. However, the subsequent divine miracles in the literary context speak against such an assessment because the subject of the signs is expressively designated as Yahweh. Cf. Terence E. Fretheim, *Exodus* (Louisville: Westminster/John Knox, 1991), 90-91.

[124] Propp, *Exodus 1-18*, 282.

[125] Yahweh as the primary conductor and Moses and Pharaoh as protagonists of this plague narratives, see Michaela Bauks, "Das Dämonische im Menschen: Einige Anmerkungen zur priesterschriftlichen Theologie (Ex 7-14)," in *Dämonen: Die Dämonologie der israelitisch-jüdischen und frühchristlichen Literatur im Kontext ihrer Umwelt*, ed. Armin Lange, Hermann Lichtenberger, and Diethard Römheld (Tübingen: Mohr Siebeck, 2003), 239-53; William A. Ford, *God, Pharaoh and Moses: Ex-*

aforementioned observations foster the conclusion that the god-language in Exodus 4:16 and 7:1 does not promote the idea of a deified Moses. In addition, a later interpretive tradition consolidates the non-deification reading of the text. For instance, an interesting allusion to Exodus 4:16 and 7:1 is attested to in Sirach 45:1-5 (in the context of praising the Jewish forefathers) in which Moses was said to have been made "equal in glory to the holy ones":

> And was beloved by God and people, Moses, whose memory is blessed. He made him equal in glory to the holy ones, and made him great, to the terror of his enemies. By his words he performed swift miracles; the Lord glorified him in the presence of kings. He gave him commandments for his people, and revealed to him his glory. (Sir 45:1-3, NRSV)
>
> ¹ Καὶ ἐξήγαγεν ἐξ αὐτοῦ ἄνδρα ἐλέους εὑρίσκοντα χάριν ἐν ὀφθαλμοῖς πάσης σαρκὸς ἠγαπημένον ὑπὸ θεοῦ καὶ ἀνθρώπων Μωυσῆν, οὗ τὸ μνημόσυνον ἐν εὐλογίαις, ² ὡμοίωσεν αὐτὸν δόξῃ ἁγίων καὶ ἐμεγάλυνεν αὐτὸν ἐν φόβοις ἐχθρῶν, ³ ἐν λόγοις αὐτοῦ σημεῖα κατέπαυσεν, ἐδόξασεν αὐτὸν κατὰ πρόσωπον βασιλέων, ἐνετείλατο αὐτῷ πρὸς λαὸν αὐτοῦ καὶ ἔδειξεν αὐτῷ τῆς δόξης αὐτοῦ. (Sir 45:1-3, LXX)

Instead of Yahweh, Sirach explicitly compares the status of Moses with that of angels in his reference to "holy ones (ἁγίων)."[126] The deification of Moses in this Sirach passage has been asserted on the basis of its connection with 4Q374, which, some exegetes argue, contains a reference to Moses's deification upon ascension into heaven.[127] Nonetheless, the texts of Deuteronomy, Sirach, and the Qumran library seem to implicate an analogical sense. That is, Moses is likened to Yahweh or angels in reference to certain divine nature. It is evident that the prophet shares some divine qualifications or attributes, but the exact nature of the shared attributes is uncertain at the same time.[128] Philo's comment on the deification of Moses (on Exod 7:1) probably is an important indicator, for highly Hellenized Jewish thinkers, such as Philo himself, understood the divine entitlement of Moses not as ontological (i.e., "not in reality") but as functional and

---

plaining the Lord's Actions in the Exodus Plague Narratives (Milton Keynes: Paternoster, 2006).

[126] John G. Snaith, *Ecclesiasticus or the Wisdom of Jesus Son of Sirach* (Cambridge: CUP, 1974), 220-21; Alexander A. Di Lella and Patrich W. Skehan, *The Wisdom of Ben Sira* (New York: Doubleday, 1987), 511; Larry W. Hurtado, *One God, One Lord: Early Christian Devotion and Ancient Jewish Monotheism* (London: T & T Clark, 1998), 56-57.

[127] Fletcher-Louis, "4Q374," 243; idem, "Some Reflections on Angelomorphic Humanity Texts among the Dead Sea Scrolls," *DSD* 7 (2000): 298; Henten, "Moses as Heavenly Messenger in *Assumptio Mosis* 10:2 and Qumran Passages," 226-27; Lierman, *The New Testament Moses*, 244.

[128] This uncertainty is in part due to the extremely fragmentary nature in the case of 4Q374. James R. Davila, "Heavenly Ascents in the Dead Sea Scrolls," in *The Dead Sea Scrolls after Fifty Years: A Comprehensive Assessment*, ed. Peter W. Flint and James C. VanderKam (Leiden: Brill, 1998), 2:472-73.

representational (i.e., "conceived as such in opinion").[129]

Wayne Meeks points to Philo's *De vita Mosis* (*On the Life of Moses*) 1:158-59 where Moses is "named god and king of the whole nation" and is taken into the divine realm.[130] His analysis, however, fails to consider adequately the context, in which the providence of God is the cause of Moses' exaltation. Moses may enjoy an elevated status, but it is so only under the divine provision.

> For, since God judged him worthy to appear as a partner of His own possessions, He gave into his hands the whole world as a portion well fitted for His heir. . . . Perhaps, too, since he was destined to be a legislator, the providence of God which afterwards appointed him without his knowledge to that work, caused him long before that day to be the reasonable and living impersonation of law. (*Mos.* 1:155c, 162a)

Due to the highly symbolic or figurative conception of the text, a more explicit and literal description mentioned above should be taken more seriously into account. The foregoing observation of these intertestamental Jewish texts suggests that the "divine language" in these texts seems to point to Moses' exalted and privileged status as an agent of Yahweh.[131] A siginificant aspect to consider concerning a deified status of Moses is his last scene on earth. Deuteronomy 34:5 records that Moses died as decreed by Yahweh (עַל־פִּי יְהוָה, *lit.* "at the mouth of Yahweh"). The implication is that it was God who buried Moses, which runs counter to some other early Jewish beliefs that Moses did not die and ascended

---

[129] *Det.* 160-62 (Philo III); *Prob.* 43-44 (Philo IX); Carl R. Holladay, *Theios Aner in Hellenistic-Judaism: A Critique of the Use of This Category in New Testament Christology* (Missoula: Scholars, 1977), 126; David T. Runia, "God and Man in Philo of Alexandria," *JTS* 39 (1988): 63; Ian W. Scott, "Is Philo's Moses a Divine Man?" *SPhiloA* 14 (2002): 106-08.

[130] Wayne A. Meeks, "The Divine Agent and His Counterfeit in Philo and the Fourth Gospel," in *Aspects of Religious Propaganda in Judaism and Early Christianity*, ed. Elisabeth Schüssler Fiorenza (Notre Dame: University of Notre Dame Press, 1976), 45-49. For an overview of Philonic description of Moses in his *De vita Mosis*, see Louis H. Feldman, "Philo's View of Moses' Birth and Upbringing," *CBQ* 64 (2002): 258-81.

[131] For skepticism against a Mosaic messianic idea on this Sirach passage, see Frederic Raurell, "Ecli 45,1-5: La 'doxa de Moisès,'" *RCT* 17 (1992): 1-42; Heinz-Josef Fabry, "Die Messianologie der Weisheitsliteratur in der Septuaginta," in *The Septuagint and Messianism: Colloquium Biblicum Lovaniense LIII, July 27-29, 2004*, ed. Michael A. Knibb (Leuven: Leuven University Press; Peeters, 2006), 263-89. But, for those who argue for at least a latent messianism in this text, see Markus Witte, "'Mose, sein Andenken sei zum Segen' (Sir 45:1): Das Mosebild des Sirachbuchs," *BN* 107/108 (2001): 161-86; Jeremy Corley, "Seeds of Messianism in Hebrew Ben Sira and Greek Sirach," in *Septuagint and Messianism: Colloquium Biblicum Lovaniense LIII, July 27-29, 2004*, ed. Michael A. Knibb (Leuven: Leuven University Press; Peeters, 2006), 301-12.

into heaven.¹³²

The *Exagoge* of Ezekiel. The Exagoge of Ezekiel the Tragedian, usually dated back to the second century B.C., is a composition of Greek drama centered on Moses in parallel accounts with Exodus 1-15.¹³³ In lines sixty-eight through eighty-nine, Ezekiel the tragedian relates the enthronement vision of Moses, in which a "man (φῶς)" hands over to Moses the crown, scepter, and throne. Φῶς is a Homeric poetic form of ἀνήρ, and represents God in the context. The emphasis, however, should be placed on his keeping authority as emblematic of royal power, rather than on anthropomorphic theology.¹³⁴

> On Sinai's peak I saw what seemed a throne so great in size it touched the clouds of heaven. Upon it sat a man of noble men, becrowned, and with a scepter in one hand while with the other he did beckon me. I made approach and stood before the throne. He handed o'er the scepter and he bade me mount the throne, and gave to me the crown; then he himself withdrew from off the throne. I gazed upon the whole earth round about; things under it, and high above the skies. Then at my feet a multitude of stars fell down, and I their number reckoned up. They passed by me like armed ranks of men. Then I in terror wakened from the dream. (Ezek. Trag. 68-82)¹³⁵

A scholarly debate has arisen concerning the implication of Moses' enthronement. This controversy can be divided into three categories: the deification of Moses, the appointment of Moses as divine agent, and the polemic against the elevated Moses traditions.¹³⁶ The advocates of the first view often point to three

---

¹³² Römer, "Moïse," 197. Cf. Samuel E. Loewenstamm, *From Babylon to Canaan: Studies in the Bible and Its Oriental Background* (Jerusalem: Hebrew University, 1992), 136-66.

¹³³ R.G. Robertson, "Ezekiel the Tragedian," in *OTP*, 2:803-04. There is a minor opinion that the document dates back to the late first century A.D. Rick van de Water, "Moses' Exaltation: Pre-Christian?" *JSP* 21 (2000): 59-69. But, it was recently refuted by William Horbury, "The Gifts of God in Ezekiel the Tragedian," in *Messianism among Jews and Christians: Twelve Biblical and Historical Studies* (London: T & T Clark, 2003), 66-68. The provenance is generally thought to be Alexandria. Nina L. Collins, "Ezekiel, the Author of the Exagoge: His Calendar and Home," *JSJ* 22 (1991): 201-11.

¹³⁴ Erich S. Gruen, *Heritage and Hellenism: The Reinvention of Jewish Tradition* (Berkeley: University of California Press, 1998), 132, n. 91.

¹³⁵ Robertson, "Ezekiel the Tragedian," 2:811-12. Cf. Carl R. Holladay, "Ezekiel the Tragedian," in *Poets: The Epic Poets Theodotus and Philo and Ezekiel the Tragedian*, vol. 2 of *Fragments from Hellenistic Jewish Authors* (Atlanta: Scholars, 1989), 362-67, 436-41.

¹³⁶ For the first, see Meeks, *The Prophet-King*, 148-49; idem, "Moses as God and King," 359; Pieter W. van der Horst, "Moses' Throne Vision in Ezekiel the Dramatist," *JJS* 34 (1983): 25; idem, "Some Notes on the Exagoge of Ezekiel," in *Essays on the Jewish World of Early Christianity* (Fribourg: Universitätsverlag; Göttingen: Vandenhoeck & Ruprecht, 1990), 72-93; Charles A. Gieschen, *Angelomorphic Christology: Antecedents and Early Evidence* (Leiden: Brill, 1998), 163-65; Lierman, *The New Testament Moses*, 90-94; Andrei A. Orlov, "The Heavenly Counterpart of Moses in the Book of

observations as indicators of Moses' deification. First, the divine man not only hands over the scepter and crown but yields his throne to Moses. Thus, Moses seems to assume the standing of the divine man. Second, the ability of Moses to count the stars (in line seventy-nine) finds the only parallel with that of God in Psalm 147:4 and Isaiah 40:26:

> He determines the number of the stars; he gives to all of them their names. (Ps 147:4, NRSV)

> Lift up your eyes on high and see: Who created these? He who brings out their host and numbers them, calling them all by name; because he is great in strength, mighty in power, not one is missing. (Isa 40:26, NRSV)

Likewise, the Metatron, probably an angel in this text, names all the stars:

> This teaches us that the Holy One [Metatron], blessed be he, has given to every single star a name. (3 Enoch 46:12; *OPT*, 1:299)

Finally, in the same verse (line seventy-nine), the stars, which are common symbols of angels, are depicted to worship Moses.[137] However, as Bauckham elucidates, the point of the vision must not be placed on the deification of Moses but on his role as ruler and prophet over Israel. The dream appears to have been employed as an illustration for the divine instrumental function of Moses. In the process, he undoubtedly manifests a degree of divine quality.[138] An interesting

---

Jubilees," in *Enoch and the Mosaic Torah: The Evidence of Jubilees*, ed. Gabriele Boccaccini and Giovanni Ibba (Grand Rapids: Eerdmans, 2009), 131-44. For the second, see Martin Hengel, "'Sit at My Right Hand!': The Enthronement of Christ at the Right Hand of God and Psalm 110:1," in *Studies in Early Christology* (Edinburgh: T & T Clark, 1995), 190-91; Hurtado, *One God, One Lord*, 57-59, 152 n. 40; Gruen, *Heritage and Hellenism*, 132-34; Richard Bauckham, "The Throne of God and the Worship of Jesus," in *The Jewish Roots of Christological Monotheism: Papers from the St. Andrews Conference on the Historical Origin of the Worship of Jesus*, ed. Carey C. Newman, James R. Davila, and Gladys S. Lewis (Leiden: Brill, 1999), 55-57. For the last, see Howard Jacobson, "Mysticism and Apocalyptic in Ezekiel's Exagoge," *ICS* 6 (1981): 272-78. A minor, and the fourth view, would be that of Holladay who sees little connection between the text and Jewish traditions. Holladay, "Ezekiel the Tragedian," 437-38.

[137] Hurtado, *One God, One Lord*, 59.

[138] Some scholars have engaged in a debate concerning the implication of this text for Jewish monotheism. The confusion arises from extending certain divine qualities into assuming the divine status equal to that of Yahweh. Certain figures and angelic beings no doubt shared some form of divine qualities. Regardless of some common divine qualities, however, there seems to be a definite borderline between these figures and God so that Yahweh deserves the unique degree of worship. In that sense, Judaism of the first century could be called monotheistic, especially in the context of the Hebrew scriptures. E.P. Sanders, *Judaism: Practice and Belief, 63 BCE-66 CE* (Philadelphia: Trinity, 1992), 242-47; N.T. Wright, *The New Testament and the People of God* (Minneapolis: Fortress, 1992), 248-59; Richard Bauckham, *God Crucified: Monotheism and Christology in the New Testament* (Grand Rapids: Eerdmans, 1998), 1-24; Maurice Casey, "Monotheism, Worship and Christological Developments in the

Old Testament parallel is Joseph's dream recorded in Genesis 37:9-10. Worshiping of stars in this case is not to be interpreted as deification of Joseph. Likewise, the focus of the Exagoge of Ezekiel texts is not on his ontological transformation, but rather on functionality.[139]

The Sibylline Oracle. A text from the Sibylline Oracle, written in Alexandria and dated to the turn of the first century A.D., is commonly cited to indicate the royal standing of Moses as believed in the intertestamental period.[140]

Pauline Churches," in *Jewish Roots of Christological Monotheism: Papers from the St. Andrews Conference on the Historical Origins of the Worship of Jesus*, ed. Carey C. Newman, James R. Davila, and Gladys S. Lewis (Leiden: Brill, 1999), 214-18; Larry W. Hurtado, "First-Century Jewish Monotheism," *JSNT* 71 (1998): 3-26; idem, *Lord Jesus Christ: Devotion to Jesus in Earliest Christianity* (Grand Rapids: Eerdmans, 2003), 29-48; idem, *How on Earth Did Jesus Become a God?: Historical Questions about Earliest Devotion to Jesus* (Grand Rapids: Eerdmans, 2005), 111-33; Stephen A. Geller, "The God of the Covenant," in *One God or Many?: Concepts of Divinity in the Ancient World*, ed. Barbara N. Porter (Chebeague: Casco Bay Assyriological Institute, 2000), 273-319; James D.G. Dunn, *The Partings of the Ways: Between Christianity and Judaism and Their Significance for the Character of Christianity* (London: SCM, 2006), 26-29. For some of the more prominent arguments advanced for the presence of multi-theism within first century Judaism, see Peter Hayman, "Monotheism—Misused Word in Jewish Studies?" *JJS* 42 (1991): 1-15; Michael Mach, "Concepts of Jewish Monotheism in the Hellenistic Period," in *The Jewish Roots of Christological Monotheism: Papers from the St. Andrews Conference on the Historical Origins of the Worship of Jesus*, ed. Carey C. Newman, James R. Davila, and Gladys S. Lewis (Leiden: Brill, 1999), 21-42; Adela Yarbro-Collins, "The Worship of Jesus and the Imperial Cult," in *The Jewish Roots of Christological Monotheism: Papers from the St. Andrews Conference on the Historical Origin of the Worship of Jesus*, ed. Carey C. Newman, James R. Davila, and Gladys S. Lewis (Leiden: Brill, 1999), 235-39; William Horbury, "Jewish and Christian Monotheism in the Herodian Age," in *Early Jewish and Christian Monotheism*, ed. Loren T. Stuckenbruck and Wendy E.S. North (London: T & T Clark, 2004), 16-44; Chiara Peri, "The Construction of Biblical Monotheism: An Unfinished Task," *SJOT* 19 (2005): 135-42.

[139] Bauckham, "The Throne of God and the Worship of Jesus," 56-57. Even, later Mediterranean contemporaries did not develop this text into such a direction that identified Moses as a divine being. Sabrina Inowlocki-Meister, "Le Moïse des auteurs juifs hellénistiques et sa réappropriation dans la littérature apologétique chrétienne: Le cas de Clément d'Alexandrie," in *Interprétations de Möise: Égypte, Judée, Grèce et Rome*, ed. Philippe Borgeaud, Thomas Römer, and Youri Volokhine (Leiden: Brill, 2010), 103-31.

[140] John J. Collins, *The Sibylline Oracles of Egyptian Judaism* (Missoula: Society of Biblical Literature, 1974), 180, n. 108; idem, "The Sibylline Oracles," in *OTP*, 1:430-32; idem, "The Sibylline Oracles," in *Jewish Writings of the Second Temple Period: Apocrypha, Pseudepigrapha, Qumran, Sectarian Writings, Philo, Josephus*, ed. Michael E. Stone (Assen: Van Gorcum, 1984), 373-74. For helpful surveys, see Helmut Merkel, *Sibyllinen* (Gütersloh: Gütersloher, 1998); Jean-Michel Roeslli, "Oracles sibyllins," in *Écrits apocryphes chrétiens II*, ed. Pierre Geoltrain and Jean-Daniel Kaestle (Paris: Gallimard, 2005), 1045-83.

Then when the people of twelve tribes, bidden by the Immortal, leave the fruitful plain of destruction and God himself, the prince, gives a law to men, then a great, great-spirited king will rule the Hebrews, one who has a name from sandy Egypt, a man falsely thought to have Thebes as his homeland. (*Sib. Or.* 11:35-40)[141]

Contrary to Lierman's contention that the anonymity of Moses in the text is an indication of the popular belief of his kingship over Israel, the point of this account seems to be on his leadership in the Exodus event, not so much on his royal standing in the historical context.[142]

Philo. Philo provides an important window through which the first century Jewish exegetical traditions are glimpsed. His understanding and interpretation of Jewish scriptures is expressed under the Greek philosophical traits that were roughly contemporaneous with the New Testament writings.[143] In his exegesis of the Old Testament, he often refers to Moses as king and goes on to elaborate on his royal calling as uniquely appointed by God. For example, in a piece of writing that addresses the law (*De Praemiis et Poenis*, "On Rewards and Punishments"), Philo reveals an eschatological belief, a topic he scarecely deals with in his writings, in terms that could be described as a Mosaic eschatological redeemer figure.[144]

> For he [Moses] did not become king in the ordinary way by the aid of troops and weapons or of the might of ships and infantry and cavalry. It was God who appointed him by the free judgment of his subjects, God who created in them the willingness to choose him as their sovereign. Of him alone we read that without the gifts of speech or possessions or money he was made a king, he who eschewed the blind wealth and embraced that which has eyes to see, and, as we may say without reserve, held that all he owned was to have God for his heritage. (*Praem.* 54)[145]

In the last verse of the first book of *De vita Mosis* ("the Life of Moses"), Philo identifies the purpose of his writing in its entirety to portray Moses as king:

> We have now told the story of Moses' actions in his capacity of king (τὰ κατὰ τὴν βασιλείαν ... πεπραγμένα). We must next deal with all that he achieved by his powers

---

[141] Collins, "The Sibylline Oracles," in *OTP*, 1:434-35.
[142] Lierman, *The New Testament Moses*, 103.
[143] For helpful anthologies on Philo for the study of the New Testament, see Roland Deines and Karl-Wilhelm Niebuhr, eds., *Philo und das Neue Testament: Wechselseitige Wahrnehmungen, 1. Internationales Symposium zum Corpus Judaeo-Hellenisticum 1.—4. Mai 2003* (Tübingen: Mohr Siebeck, 2004); Kenneth Schenck, *A Brief Guide to Philo* (Louisville: Westminster/John Knox, 2005); Adam Kamesar, ed., *The Cambridge Companion to Philo* (Cambridge: CUP, 2009); Beatrice Wyss, "Philon und die Philologen," *BN* 148 (2011): 67-83.
[144] For the eschatology of Philo, see Schenck, *A Brief Guide to Philo*, 107; Cristina Termini, "Philo's Thought within the Context of Middle Judaism," in *The Cambridge Companion to Philo*, ed. Adam Kamesar (Cambridge: CUP, 2009), 106-09.
[145] *Philo VIII*, trans. F.H. Colson (Cambridge: Harvard University Press, 1935), 342-43. Parentheses are added for clarification.

as high priest and legislator, powers which he possessed as the most fitting accompaniments of kingship (βασιλείᾳ). (*Mos.* 1:334; *Philo VI*, 448-49)[146]

In the immediately following verses (*Mos.* 2:1-2), Philo further clarifies that the various virtues of Moses, i.e., a chief priest, law-giver, and philosopher, are integral characteristics of his royal status:

> The former treatise dealt with the birth and nurture of Moses; also with his education and career as a ruler, in which capacity his conduct was not merely blameless but highly praiseworthy . . . For it has been said, not without good reason, that states can only make progress in well-being if either kings are philosophers or philosophers are kings. But Moses will be found to have displayed, and more than displayed, combined in his single person, not only these two faculties—the kingly and the philosophical—but also three others, one of which is concerned with law-giving, the second with the high priest's office, and the last with prophecy. (*Mos.* 2:1-2; *Philo VI*, 450-51)

Furthermore, Moses is called "the truly perfect ruler (τῷ τελειοτάτῳ ἡγεμόνι)," "archetype (ἀρχέτυπον)," and "model (παράδειγμα)" of all future rulers:

> We said above that there are four adjuncts to the truly perfect ruler. He must have kingship, the faculty of legislation, priesthood and prophecy. (*Mos.* 2:187a; *Philo VI*, 540-41)

> Thus all future rulers would find a law to guide them right by looking to Moses as their archetype and model, and one would grudge to give good advice to their successors, but all would train and school their souls with admonitions and exhortations. (*Virt.* 70b; *Philo VIII*, 204-07)

From the aforementioned texts, it becomes evident that Moses is pictured almost as a super-human figure who occupied a royal office. Despite this royal depiction, however, Philo rejects straightforwardly Moses being a divine entity. What this term describes is his superior place of influence and leadership, and not as a ruler of a dynasty even less than a divine being.[147] This feature is highly telling in the face of the Hellenistic tendency which often defied a large number of Greek protagonists such as Roman emperors.[148]

---

[146] Erwin R. Goodenough, *By Light, Light: The Mystic Gospel of Hellenistic Judaism* (New Haven: Yale University Press, 1935), 181; Lierman, *The New Testament Moses*, 104. For an observation of the influence of *Exagoge* upon *De vita Mosis*, see Pierluigi Lanfranchi, "Reminiscences of Ezekiel's *Exagoge* in Philo's *De vita Mosis*," in *Moses in Biblical and Extra-Biblical Traditions*, ed. Axel Graupner and Michael Wolter (Berlin: Walter de Gruyter, 2007), 143-50.

[147] Louis H. Feldman, *Philo's Portrayal of Moses in the Context of Ancient Judaism* (Notre Dame: University of Notre Dame Press, 2007), 283-84.

[148] For the Philonic tendency of deifying the earthly ruler under the influence of Egyptian and Hellenistic politics and philosophies in relation to his depiction of Moses in terms of kingship, see Joachim Kügler, "Spuren ägyptisch-hellenistischer Königstheologie bei Philo von Alexandria," in *Ägypten und der östliche Mittelmeerraum im 1. Jahrtausend v. Chr.: Akten des interdisziplinären Symposions am Institut für Ägyptologie der Universität München 25.-27.10.1996*, ed. Manfred Görg and Günther Hölbl (Wiesbaden: Harrassowitz, 2000), 231-49.

Josephus and Qumran. Josephus and the Qumran library stand in contrast to the Philonic picture of Moses as a royal figure. Both literary collections are generally reticent about his kingship. In the case of Josephus, Lierman supposes that the theocracy might explain the lack of royal portrayal of Moses:

> Our lawgiver, however, was attracted by none of these forms of polity, but gave to his constitution the form of what—if a forced expression be permitted—may be termed a "theocracy," placing all sovereignty and authority in the hands of God. (*Ag. Ap.* 2:165)[149]

In the case of Qumran, the same reason probably accounts for the lack of highlighting his royal office.[150]

Moses as Eschatological Prophet

Deuteronomy 18:15. Some exegetes have pointed out that early Jewish belief in Moses *redivivus* is an important clue to understanding the New Testament Christology. This eschatological hope derives from Deuteronomy 18:15, in which a prophet-like Moses is alleged to return:[151]

> The LORD your God will raise up for you a prophet like me from among your own people; you shall heed such a prophet. (Deut 18:15, NRSV)

נָבִיא מִקִּרְבְּךָ מֵאַחֶיךָ כָּמֹנִי יָקִים לְךָ יְהוָה אֱלֹהֶיךָ אֵלָיו תִּשְׁמָעוּן (Deut 18:15, MT)

προφήτην ἐκ τῶν ἀδελφῶν σου ὡς ἐμὲ ἀναστήσει σοι κύριος ὁ θεός σου, αὐτοῦ ἀκούσεσθε. (Deut 18:15, LXX)

It is argued at times that this trajectory of thought continues to be at work in the later Jewish prophetic traditions, for instance, in Jeremiah 1:4-10.[152] Such ex-

---

[149] *Josephus I*, trans. H. St. J. Thackeray (Cambridge: Harvard University Press, 1926), 358-59. For helpful overviews on Moses in Josephus, see Renée Bloch, "Moïse chez Flavius Josèphe: Un exemple juif de littérature héroïque," in *Interprétations de Moïse: Égypte, Judée, Grèce et Rome*, ed. Philippe Borgeaud, Thomas Römer, and Youri Volokhine (Leiden: Brill, 2010), 85-102; idem, *Moses und der Mythos: Die Auseinandersetzung mit der griechischen Mythologie bei jüdisch-hellenistischen Autoren* (Leiden: Brill, 2011). For a possible literary comparison between Josephus portrayal of Moses and Jesus, see Marie-Odile Gruson, "Flavius Josèphe: Miracles de Jésus et de Moïse," *MScRel* 65 (2008): 51-62; Philippe Borgeaud, "Quelques remarques sur Typhon, Seth, Moïse et son âne, dans la perspective d'un dialogue réactif transculturel," in *Interprétations de Moïse: Égypte, Judée, Grèce et Rome*, ed. Philippe Borgeaud, Thomas Römer, and Youri Volokhine (Leiden: Brill, 2010), 173-85.

[150] Meeks, *The Prophet-King*, 175.

[151] Also, similarly, "I will raise up for them a prophet like you from among their own people; I will put my words in the mouth of the prophet, who shall speak to them everything that I command" (Deut 18:18, NRSV).

[152] Sebastian Grätz, "'Einen Propheten wie mich wird dir, der Herr, dein Gott erwecken': Der Berufungsbericht Jeremias und seine Rückbindung an das Amt des Mose," in *Moses in Biblical and Extra-Biblical Traditions*, ed. Axel Graupner (Berlin: Walter de Gruyter, 2007), 61-77. However, for discrepancies within the Old Testament traditions

pectation, nevertheless, is surprisingly scant in intertestamental Jewish writings. 1 Maccabees 14:41 is almost the only apocryphal reference that can be adduced for this thread of hope, which vaguely speaks of some type of an end-time prophetic figure:

> The Jews and their priests have resolved that Simon should be their leader and high priest forever, until a trustworthy prophet should arise. (1 Macc 14:41)

A small number of scholars, such as Marc Philonenko, take this statement to be reflective of the hope of the Mosaic eschatological prophet.[153] At a closer examination of its literary context, however, 1 Maccabees 14:41-49 seems to speak of a composite picture of a priestly and political eschatological figure in stead of a prophetic one. Accordingly, a greater number of exegetes link this text with the Jewish expectation of the restoration of Davidic dynasty.[154] In addition, this type of thought elsewhere in the early Jewish literature is rather meager. In light of this context, therefore, Collins is justified when he associates this text with the early Jewish eschatological hopes in terms of either David or Elijah.[155]

This dearth of hope in Moses *redivivus* is also explicable within the Old Testament context itself, in which Deuteronomy 18:15 was originally addressed. That is, the verse is located in the midst of a series of divine stipulations on how to choose public offices such as, kings, judges, and priests (Deut 16:18-18:22). At the end of these instructions comes the declaration of Yahweh that he would send to Israel a Moses-like prophet to whom they need to heed and by whom they should be able to discern false prophets. Accordingly, the crux of this narrative appears to be the envisioning of legitimate prophets, not a forecasting of the historical Moses or of anyone with his identity. Driver's comment on this Deuteronomy text is helpful in that respect:

---

on this expectation, see Reinhard Achenbach, "'A Prophet Like Moses' (Deuteronomy 18:15)—'No Prophet Like Moses' (Deuteronomy 34:10): Some Observations on the Relation between the Pentateuch and the Latter Prophets," in *Pentateuch: International Perspectives on Current Research*, ed. Thomas B. Dozeman, Konrad Schmid, and Baruch J. Schwartz (Tübingen: Mohr Siebeck, 2011), 435-58.

[153] Marc Philonenko, "'Jusqu'à ce que se lève un prophète digne de confiance' (1 Maccabées 14,41)," in *Messiah and Christos: Studies in the Jewish Origins of Christianity, Presented to David Flusser on the Occasion of His Seventy-Fifth Birthday*, ed. Ithamar Gruenwald, Shaul Shaked, and Gedaliahu A.G. Stroumsa (Tübingen: Mohr Siebeck, 1992), 95-98.

[154] Herbert Donner, "Der verlässliche Prophet: Betrachtungen zu I Makk 14,41ff und zu Ps 110," in *Prophetie und geschichtliche Wirklichkeit im alten Israel: Festschrift für Siegfried Herrmann zum 65. Geburtstag*, ed. Rüdiger Liwak and Siegfried Wagner (Stuttgart: Kohlhammer, 1991), 89-98. Cf., Arie van der Kooij, "The Septuagint of Psalms and the First Book of Maccabees," in *The Old Greek Psalter: Studies in Honour of Albert Pietersma*, ed. Robert J.V. Hiebert, Claude E. Cox, and Peter J. Gentry (Sheffield: Sheffield, 2001), 229-47.

[155] Collins, *The Scepter and the Star*, 55, 129.

> The "prophet" contemplated is not a simple individual, belonging to a distant future, but Moses' representative for the time being, whose office it would be to supply Israel, whenever in its history occasion should arise, with needful guidance and advice; in other words . . . the reference is not to an individual but to a prophetical order.[156]

Similarly, "the 'raising up' of the prophet need not mean a single act, or a single individual, therefore. It rather envisages a succession of prophets, as and when the Lord deems it right."[157] This contextual reading of a succession of prophets is further strengthened in view of the emphasis of the context, that is, not on the appointment of the prophet, but on the human obeisance to the divine oracle which would be delivered through the prophet.[158]

> For Moses to say that the prophet to come will be "like me" refers to the role of Moses played as God's messenger, not to his person; for 34:10 makes clear that "there has not arisen a prophet since in Israel like Moses, whom YHWH knew face to face."[159]

Finally, the fact that the later Jewish traditions (Apocrypha, Pseudepigrapha, and early rabbinic literature) did not interpret Deuteronomy 18:15 eschatologically speaks in favor of the true prophethood reading. It is highly instructive that the entire corpus of the Old Testament Pseudepigrapha does not take up Deuteronomy 18:15 in reference to an eschatological figure. A host of scholars (such as, Howard Teeple, W.D. Davies, and Joachim Jeremias) confirm this judgment.[160]

---

[156] Driver, *A Critical and Exegetical Commentary on Deuteronomy*, 229.

[157] McConville, *Deuteronomy*, 303. Also, Craigie, *The Book of Deuteronomy*, 262; Christensen, *Deuteronomy 1:1-21:9, Revised*, 405.

[158] Nelson, *Deuteronomy*, 235.

[159] Christensen, *Deuteronomy 1:1-21:9, Revised*, 409. In this respect, the Deuteronomy text plays out as the defining category for the identity of Israel. Robert L. Cohn, "The Second Coming of Moses: Deuteronomy and the Construction of Israelite Identity," in *Comity and Grace of Method: Essays in Honor of Edmund F. Perry*, ed. Thomas Ryba, George D. Bond, and Herman W. Tull (Evanston: Northwestern University Press, 2004), 133-46.

[160] Cf. Renée Bloch, "Quelques aspects de la Figure de Moïse dans la Tradition Rabbinque," in *Moïse, l'homme de l'alliance*, ed. Henri Cazelles (Tournai: Desclée, 1955), 161; Raymond E. Brown, "The Messianism of Qumrân," *CBQ* 19 (1957): 59-60, n. 35; Steve Delamarter, *A Scripture Index to Charlesworth's the Old Testament Pseudepigrapha* (Sheffield: Sheffield, 2002); Meeks, *The Prophet-King*, 146-64; Allison, *The New Moses*, 75-76. Meeks does not refer to a single text from Philo, Josephus, Apocrypha, or Pseudepigrapha that identifies Moses as an eschatological "prophet-king." Meeks, *The Prophet-King*, 100-64. Scott Hafemann also does not touch on the eschatological depiction of Moses in Apocrypha and Pseudepigrapha. Hafemann, "Moses in the Apocrypha and Pseudepigrapha." Finally, J.J. Collins' treatment of intertestamental messianic hopes also does not address the Moses-like eschatological prophet in connection with Deut 18:15. John J. Collins, *The Scepter and the Star: The Messiahs of the Dead Sea Scrolls and Other Ancient Literature* (Grand Rapids: Eerdmans, 2010). Although an argument from silence, this accumulated evidence constitutes a convincing case in view of this relatively wide-ranging research into the secondary literature on the issue.

Richard Horsley, for instance, perceptively articulates the textual testimony on the issue.

> We find very little evidence that the expectation of a prophet like Moses (whether linked with or separate from Deut 18:15-18) played an important role during the time of Jesus. The text on which such an expectation might have been based, Deut 18:15-18, originally did not have an eschatological orientation, but referred to the regular succession, or perhaps rather the periodic appearance, of prophets as spokespersons for God.... Moreover, it is difficult to find textual references to an eschatological prophet like Moses in biblical or post-biblical Jewish literature whether before or after the time of Jesus, except in the Qumran scrolls.[161]

Rabbinic tradition. In distinction to the apparent Hebrew scriptural context and the silence of Apocrypha and Pseudepigrapha on the Mosaic eschatological prophetic expectations, nonetheless, some exegetes, such as, Jeremias, Teeple, Meeks, and Lierman, point to certain rabbinic sources as an indicator for the presence of such a belief.[162] Nonetheless, their analysis of the rabbinic view of Moses, especially in conjunction with the Gospel of John, should be called into question. Some recent New Testament scholarship generally encourages one to take into account early rabbinic literature so as to illuminate the possible correlation between Jewish religious/cultural elements and early Christianity.[163] No

---

[161] Richard A. Horsley, "Like One of the Prophets of Old: Two Types of Popular Prophets at the Time of Jesus," *CBQ* 47 (1985): 441. Similarly, Howard M. Teeple, *The Mosaic Eschatological Prophet* (Philadelphia: Society of Biblical Literature, 1957), 47; W.D. Davies, *The Setting of the Sermon on the Mount* (Cambridge: CUP, 1964), 118. Also, in a survey of early rabbinic literature, Jeremias reaches the same conclusion that there is no pre-Christian witness of the returning eschatological Moses tradition. "Nowhere, however, in the older literature do we find the idea that the returning Moses will be the Messiah [in the sense of an eschatological figure]." Jeremias, *TDNT*, 4:857. For a possible exception, see "The Testament of Benjamin" 9:2 (*OTP* 1:827, n. b). This is suggested by Lars Kierspel.

[162] Ibid., 857-64; Teeple, *The Mosaic Eschatological Prophet*, 43-68; Meeks, *The Prophet-King*, 168-70, 211-13, 246-53; idem, "Moses as God and King," 356-59; Gerbern S. Oegema, *The Anointed and His People: Messianic Expectations from the Maccabees to Bar Kochba* (Sheffield: Sheffield, 1998), 259-86; Lierman, *The New Testament Moses*, 84-90. However, their contention is somewhat eclipsed since a recent comparative examination of the so-called messianic later prophetic texts as understood in the Septuagint and the rabbinic literature yields little evidence of a Mosaic eschatological messianism especially in the latter body of literature. Olivier Munnich, "Le messianisme à la lummière des livres prophétiques de la Bible grecque," in *Septuagint and Messianism*, ed. Michael A. Knibb (Leuven: Leuven University Press; Peeters, 2006), 354-55.

[163] For examples, Mikeal C. Parsons, "The Critical Use of the Rabbinic Literature in New Testament Studies," *PRSt* 12 (1985): 85-102; John C. Thomas, "The Fourth Gospel and Rabbinic Judaism," *ZNW* 82 (1991): 159-82; H. Maccoby, "Rabbinic Literature: Talmud," *DNTB*, 897-902; Bruce D. Chilton, "Rabbinic Literature: Targumim," *DNTB*, 907-09; William Horbury, "Rabbinic Literature in New Testament Interpretation," in *Herodian Judaism and New Testament Study* (Tübingen: Mohr Seibeck,

serious student would deny that the New Testament writings and the Gospel of John in particular must have come into contact with some traits of Pharisaism or emerging rabbinic traditions. As a consequence, there must have been a certain form of mutual influence at work.

Nevertheless, a responsible inquiry into the influence of rabbinic literature on the New Testament is susceptible to dispute at least for two reasons. First, the late date of the composition of the rabbinic literature leaves one to wonder the direction of influence. Those parallels seem to demonstrate rather Christian influence on the rabbinic writings or, at best, some common Jewish traditions rooted in the Old Testament tradition that were current at the time of nascent Christianity. For instance, Meeks cites extensively from Midrash Rabbah (of the Soncino collection), which dates to A.D. 450-1100 for its composition. Most writings in this collection attribute the authors to the rabbis from as early as the Amoraic period which ranges from A.D. 220-500. These alleged authors postdate the final composition of John, at least, by a century.[164] Although Epstein points to the ancient records of early midrashic activities, we do not have a concrete piece of textual evidence for "midrash" in the form analogous to the Soncino collection.[165] An earlier rabbinic body of literature, Mishnah, is not helpful for the present analogical investigation of messianism/Christology, since it is primarily concerned with the legal system.[166] Second, the compiled nature of the body of rabbinic literature also hampers the legitimacy of such comparative investigations because it is virtually impossible to discern which part of certain rabbinic literature traces back to the earlier oral traditions that were hypothetically in the air at the time of the New Testament.[167] Therefore, the extant early rabbinic

---

2006), 221-35; Anne-Françoise Loiseau, "Traditions évangéliques et herméneutique juive: Le serpent d'airain de Jean ne repose-t-il pas sur une guématrie?" *ETL* 83 (2007): 155-63; Frédéric Manns, "'Pour que l'Ecriture s'accomplît': Vers une rétroversion araméenne," *EstB* 66 (2008): 429-44; Christian Grappe, "Les deux anges de Jean 20,12: Signes de la présence mystérieuse du Logos (à la lumière du targum d'Ex 25,22)?" *RHPR* 89 (2009): 169-77; Paul V.M. Flesher and Bruce Chilton, *The Targums: A Criticial Introduction* (Waco: Baylor University Press, 2011), 423-36.

[164] Craig A. Evans, *Ancient Texts for New Testament Studies: A Guide to the Background Literature* (Peabody: Hendrickson, 2005), 224, 238.

[165] I. Epstein, "Foreword," in *Genesis*, vol. 1 of *Midrash Rabbah*, trans. H. Greedman and Maurice Simon (London: Soncino, 1951), x-xiii.

[166] Jacob Neusner, *Messiah in Context* (Philadelphia: Fortress, 1984), 18-19.

[167] These two cautions are expressed in the following studies: Joseph A. Fitzmyer, "Review of Matthew Black, *An Aramaic Approach to the Gospels and Acts*," *CBQ* 30 (1968): 417-28; idem, "Review of Martin McNamara, *The New Testament and the Palestinian Targum to the Pentateuch*," *TS* 29 (1968): 322-28; Anthony D. York, "Dating of Targumic Literature," *JSJ* 5 (1974): 49; Jacob Neusner, "One Theme, Two Settings: The Messiah in the Literature of the Synagogue and in the Rabbis' Canon of Late Antiquity," *BTB* 14 (1984): 110-21; idem, *Messiah in Context*, 19; Horsley, "Like One of the Prophets of Old," 442; Günter Stemberger, "Pesachhaggada und Abendmahlsberichte des Neuen Testaments," *Kairos* 29 (1987): 147-58; Philip Al-

materials should only serve as an aid to illustrate the common Jewish cultural/religious matrix of first century Palestine which intertestamental Judaism and nascent Christianity shared in common (cf. "Appendix 7: The Use of the Rabbinic Materials for the New Testament").[168]

Samaritan tradition. In addition to rabbinic literature, other scholars have attempted to find early Jewish conceptual traits of the Mosaic eschatological prophet tied to Deuteronomy 18:15 within early Samaritan traditions.[169] The

---

exander, "Jewish Aramaic Translations of Hebrew Scriptures," in *Mikra: Text, Translation, Reading and Interpretation of the Hebrew Bible in Ancient Judaism and Early Christianity*, ed. M. Jan Mulder (Assen: Van Gorcum, 1988), 238; Anthony J. Saldarini, "Rabbinic Literature and the NT," *ABD*, 5:602-04; James H. Charlesworth, "From Messianology to Christology: Problems and Prospects," in *The Messiah: Developments in Earliest Judaism and Christianity: The First Princeton Symposium on Judaism and Christian Origins*, ed. James H. Charlesworth (Minneapolis: Fortress, 1992), 15-16; Stephen A. Kaufman, "Dating the Language of the Palestinian Targums and Their Use in the Study of First Century CE Texts," in *The Aramaic Bible: Targums in Their Historical Context*, ed. D.R.G. Beattie and M.J. McNamara (Sheffield: JSOT, 1994), 118-41; Johann Maier, "Schriftrezeption im jüdischen Umfeld des Johannes evangeliums," in *Israel und seine Heilstraditionen im Johannessevangelium: Festgabe für Johannes Beutler SJ zum 70. Geburtstag*, ed. Michael Labahn, Klaus Scholtissek, and Angelika Strotmann (Paderborn: Schöningh, 2004), 87-88; Burton L. Visotzky, "Midrash, Christian Exegesis, and Hellenistic Hermeneutics," in *Current Trends in the Study of Midrash*, ed. Carol Bakhos (Leiden: Brill, 2006), 112-17. For studies that point to the compilation nature of the Targumic collections geographically and chronologically distant from their possible Palestinian provenance, see Edward M. Cook, "New Perspective on the Language of Onqelos and Jonathan," in *The Aramaic Bible: Targums in Their Historical Context*, ed. D.R.G. Beattie and M.J. McNamara (Sheffield: JSOT, 1994), 142-56; Chilton, *DNTB*, 906.

[168] Idem, *DJG*, 659; Catherine Hezser, "Diaspora and Rabbinic Judaism," in *The Oxford Handbook of Biblical Studies*, ed. J.W. Rogerson and Judith M. Lieu (Oxford: OUP, 2006), 128-29.

[169] Convenient recent overviews on the Samaritan religion and literature can be found in the following studies: Alan D. Crown, ed., *The Samaritans* (Tübingen: Mohr Siebeck, 1989); idem, *Samaritan Scribes and Manuscripts* (Tübingen: Mohr Siebeck, 2001); idem, Reinhard Pummer, and Abraham Tal, eds., *A Companion to Samaritan Studies* (Tübingen: Mohr Siebeck, 1993); Robert T. Anderson, "Samaritans," *ABD*, 5:940-47; idem, "Samaritan Literature," *DNTB*, 1052-56; Richard J. Coggins, "Issues in Samaritanism," in *Where We Stand: Issues and Debates in Ancient Judaism*, Part 3, vol. 1 of *Judaism in Late Antiquity*, ed. Alan J. Every-Peck and Jacob Neusner (Leiden: Brill, 1999), 63-77; Ingrid Hjelm, *The Samaritans and Early Judaism: A Literary Analysis* (Sheffield: Sheffield, 2000); Robert T. Anderson and Terry Giles, *The Keepers: An Introduction to the History and Culture of the Samaritans* (Peabody: Hendrickson, 2002); idem, *Traditions Kept: The Literature of the Samaritans* (Peabody: Hendrickson, 2005); H.G.M. Williamson and C.A. Evans, "Samaritans," *DNTB*, 1059-61; Benny Thettayil, *In Spirit and Truth: An Exegetical Study of John 4:19-26 and a Theological Investigation of the Replacement Theme in the Fourth Gospel* (Leuven: Peeters, 2007), 182-93; Menahem Mor and Friedrich V. Reiterer, eds, *Samaritans:*

specific Samaritan literature cited to indicate such an interpretive tradition is Memar Marqah. This composite body of documents claims its author to be Marqah (=Marcus), a renowned Samaritan religious leader who lived in the third to fourth centuries. Regardless of its alleged authorship, the writing of the extant manuscripts is variously located in the fourteenth through nineteenth centuries.[170]

Despite the late date of the extant manuscripts, however, some scholars argue that early Samaritan eschatological hope, which was recorded later in the Samaritan writing, is reflected in the Gospel of John with particular reference to Christology.[171] For example, Ferdinand Dexinger, one of the more vocal advocates of this view, has extensively put forward his case that Memar Marqah reflects Jewish understanding of the Mosaic eschatological prophet prior to and current in the time of early Christianity.[172] He points to Memar Marqah's inter-

---

Past and Present, Current Studies (Berlin: Walter de Gruyter, 2010); Gary N. Knoppers, *Jews and Samaritans: The Origins and History of Their Early Relations* (Oxford: OUP, 2013). Just as recent scholarship stresses the diversity within early Judaism, the same is often emphasized with early Samaritanism. However, usually three beliefs are recognized as central to Samaritans in the time of the New Testament: One God, Moses the prophet, and the law and Gerazim as the place of worship. Scholars are less certain about the date and influential extent of two other creeds: the Day of Judgment and the return of Moses as Taheb. Williamson and Evans, "Samaritans," 1059.

[170] Zeev Ben-Hayyim detects two major phases of the writing of the Memar Marqah: the first from the fourteenth to sixteenth centuries and the second from the eighteenth to nineteenth centuries. Abraham Tal, "Samaritan Literature," in *The Samaritans*, ed. Alan D. Crown (Tübingen: Mohr Siebeck, 1989), 463. Ben-Hayyim is the editor/translator of the most recent critical edition of Memar Marqah.

[171] John Bowman, "The Fourth Gospel and the Samaritans," *BJRL* 40 (1958): 298-308; Nicolas Séd, "Le Mēmar samaritain: Le Sēfēr Yesīrā et les trente-deux sentiers de la Sagesse," *RHR* 170 (1966): 159-84; Edwin D. Freed, "Samaritan Influence in the Gospel of John," *CBQ* 30 (1968): 580-87; idem, "Did John Write His Gospel Partly to Win Samaritan Converts?" *NovT* 12 (1970): 241-56; George Wesley Buchanan, "Samaritan Origin of the Gospel of John," in *Religions in Antiquity: Essays in Memory of Erwin Ramsdell Goodenough*, ed. Jacob Neusner (Leiden: Brill, 1968), 149-75; Meeks, *The Prophet-King*, 246-54; Charles H.H. Scobie, "Origins and Development of Samaritan Christianity," *NTS* 19 (1973): 390-414; Boismard, *Moses or Jesus*, 3, 30-32, 40-41; John McHugh, "'In Him Was Life,'" in *Jews and Christians: The Parting of the Ways A.D. 70 to 135, the Second Durham-Tübingen Research Symposium on Earliest Christianity and Judaism (Durham, September, 1989)*, ed. James D.G. Dunn (Grand Rapids: Eerdmans, 1999), 130-34; Lierman, *The New Testament Moses*, 88-89. Purvis partly revised this view that the congruity and incongruity with Moses coexist. James D. Purvis, "Fourth Gospel and the Samaritans," *NovT* 17 (1975): 161-98.

[172] For his arguments, see Ferdinand Dexinger, "Die frühesten samaritanischen Belege der Taheb-Vorstellung," *Kairos* 26 (1984): 224-52; idem, "Der 'Prophet wie Mose' in Qumran und bei den Samaritanern," in *Mélanges bibliques et orientaux en l'honneur de M. Mathias Delcor*, ed. André Caquot, Simon Légasse, and Michel Tardieu (Kevelaer: Butzon und Bercker, 1985), 97-111; idem, "Der Taheb: Ein 'messianischer'

pretation of Deuteronomy 18:18 in terms of the Mosaic eschatological prophet (whom some medieval Samaritans call תהב, "Taheb," lit. meaning "restorer" or "one who returns"), and argues that "this expectation traces back to Judaism from the second century B.C. on."[173]

In order to substantiate his case, Dexinger advances two prerequisite theses: First, the traditionally held Jewish-Samaritan hostility was marginal and was developed in a large scale only after the third century A.D. The implication is that Samaritanism was an integral part of early Judaism, as some Samaritan interpretive traits seem to be at play in some Qumran writings. Second, although the extant manuscripts of Memar Marqah originated from the medieval period, the eschatological conceptions, especially with reference to the Mosaic prophet, reflect the beliefs of the intertestamental period.

Excursus 5: The Schism between Jews and Samaritans

One of the curious debates in New Testament scholarship revolves around the context and date of rupture between Jews and Samaritans. Some New Testament texts shed a glimpse into this deterioration of relationship between the two biblical ethnic groups, for example, in the dialogue of Jesus and the Samaritan woman: "The Samaritan woman said to him, 'How is it that you, a Jew, ask a drink of me, a woman of Samaria?' (Jews do not share things in common with Samaritans)."[174] There is, however, exteremly scant textual evidence of anti-Samaritanism in the intertestamental Jewish literature including the apocrypha and Pseudepigrapha. For instance, Pummer examined a large sweep of early Jewish literature where Samaritans are mentioned with significance: Jubilees 30; 49:16-21; Judith 9:2-4, 4:4, 5:16; Testament of Levi; Theodotus' *on the Jews*; and 2 Maccabees 5:23, 6:12. His conclusion is that these texts present little anti-Samaritan polemic. Even when there seems to be such a sentiment, there are textual-critical problems and those of authenticity. Furthermore, none of these texts are indicative of a sudden schism between the two groups.[175] On the other hand, Alan Crown analyzed the so-called proto-Samaritan texts of Qumran. These

---

Heilsbringer der Samaritaner," *Kairos* 27 (1985): 1-172; idem, "Die Taheb-Vorstellung als politische Utopie," *Numen* 37 (1990): 1-21; idem, "Josephus Ant 18,85-87 und der samaritanische Taheb," in *Proceedings of the First International Congress of the Société d'Études Samaritaines, Tel-Aviv, April 11-13, 1988*, ed. Abraham Tal and Moshe Florentin (Tel-Aviv: Chaim Rosenberg School for Jewish Studies, Tel-Aviv University, 1991), 49-59; idem, "Die Moses-Terminologie in Tibåt Mårqe: Einige Beobachtungen," in *Frankfurter Judaistische Beiträge*, vol. 25, ed. Margarete Schlüter (Frankfurt: Gesellschaft zur Förderung judaistischer Studien, 1998), 51-62; idem, "Reflections on the Relationship between Qumran and Samaritan Messianology,"in *Qumran-Messianism: Studies on the Messianic Expectations in the Dead Sea Scrolls*, ed. James H. Charlesworth, Hermann Lichtenberger, and Gerbern S. Oegema (Tübingen: Mohr Siebeck, 1998), 83-99.

[173] "Die Taheb-Vorstellung wurzelt in der spezifischen Interpretation von Dtn 18,18, die ab dem 2.Jh.v.Chr. im Judentum belegbar ist." Dexinger, "Der Taheb," 25. For a further definition of Taheb, see Dexinger, "Der Taheb," 37.

[174] John 4:9, NRSV.

[175] Reinhard Pummer, "Antisamaritanische Polemik in jüdischen Schriften aus der intertestamentarischen Zeit," *BZ* 26 (1982): 224-42.

texts, according to him, manifest a remarkable affinity with Samaritanism as opposed to other early Palestinian scriptural traditions, i.e., the Masoretic and the Septuagint traditions. Therefore, he comes to a conclusion that the hostility between Judaeans and Samaritans fully developed not before the third century A.D.[176] In this case, the statements of Josephus (*J.W.* 2.232-33; *Ant.* 20.118-38) and the New Testament (John 4:3-4; Luke 9:52) that record the enmity between the these groups must reflect only a trace of minor regional sentiment of the time.

Notwithstanding their complicated arguments, the view of Dexinger and others has been seriously called into question especially in three respects. First, the degree or plausibility of integral nature of Samaritanism within early Judaism does not seem to be substantial. The relation between Jews and Samaritans was ambivalent at a number of theological fronts. Although Samaritans and Jews shared in common the adherence to the Mosaic writings, they were sharply divided over other important issues, such as, the acceptance of the Prophets and Writings, the centrality of the Jerusalem temple, and the idea of the resurrection of the body.[177] Second, as John MacDonald maintains, the direction of influence is to be construed from John onto Memar Marqah. Since there are remarkable parallels present between these two bodies of literature (not only some eschatological expressions, but especially the likening of Moses to "Christ" in wordings similar to those of John), it is difficult to deny some type of literary and/or oral dependence. A fair assessment of the correlation between them would be the Samaritan reception of the Johannine tradition in view of the dates of the extant manuscripts of both bodies of documents and the obscure characterization of "Christ" in Jewish literature prior to the Christian era.[178] Third, even if the early

---

[176] Judith E. Sanderson, *An Exodus Scroll from Qumran: 4QpaleoExodum and the Samaritan Tradition* (Atlanta: Scholars, 1986), 317-20; Alan D. Crown, "Redating the Schism between the Judaeans and the Samaritans," *JQR* 82 (1991): 17-50; Ingrid Hjelm, *The Samaritans and Early Judaism: A Literary Analysis* (Sheffield: Sheffield, 2000), 52-102. The works of E. Nodet also in some measure contribute to the integral nature of Samaritanism within early Judaism. However, both of these views are called into question by the recent monograph of Hjelm, *The Samaritans and Early Judaism*, 52-75. For Nodet's view on the importance of the Samaritan tradition within the intertestamental and early Judaism, see Etienne Nodet, *A Search for the Origins of Judaism: From Joshua to the Mishnah* (Sheffield: Sheffield, 1997), 122-201. On the other hand, a recent monograph on the origin of Samaritanism estimates the break much earlier, that is, slightly prior to the coming of Christ. Jean-Daniel Macchi, *Les Samaritains: Histoire d'une légende, Israël et la province de Samarie* (Geneva: Labor et Fides, 1994).

[177] Pieter W. van der Horst, "Anti-Samaritan Propaganda in Early Judaism," in *Jews and Christians in Their Graeco-Roman Context: Selected Essays on Early Judaism, Samaritanism, Hellenism, and Christianity* (Tübingen: Mohr Siebeck, 2006), 134-50.

[178] John MacDonald, *The Text*, vol. 1 of *Memar Marqah: The Teaching of Marqah* (Berlin: A. Töpelmann, 1963), xx; idem, *The Theology of the Samaritans* (London: SCM, 1964), 150-61, 420-46; Anderson and Giles, *The Keepers*, 119-20. Anderson and Giles also record the scholarly suggestions of the New Testament influence (especially of

dating (i.e., the third century A.D. onward) of some parts of the documents may be supposed for the sake of argument, the recent philological examinations of the Aramaic language used in Memar Marqah usually detect much later (i.e., medieval period) editorial layers.[179] Coupled with this presence of much later linguistic traits as well as the lack of a systematic understanding of the first century Palestinian Aramaic linguistic framework, the composite nature severely hampers the value of this literature for the present discussion.[180]

Qumran tradition. As mentioned before, the hope of the eschatological prophet like Moses based on Deuteronomy 18:18 appears sparse in early Judaism. The same is true with the Qumran community. Such a judgment probably should be qualified with an observation that the Deuteronomy text is often cited but not often with eschatological overtones. For the most part, Moses stands as an identity figure for true prophets in a context where he is frequently brought up in order to be contrasted with false prophets. Accordingly, the emphasis often lies on the recognition of false prophets and not so much on the hope of the coming prophet like Moses. Discouraged by such a state of reality, Boismard sums up the

---

Mark and John) on Memar Marqah. Anderson and Giles, *Tradition Kept*, 274-75, 221-30.

[179] The different editorial phases of the documents are surmised in Abraham Tal, "The Samaritan Targum of the Pentateuch," in *Mikra: Text, Translation, Reading and Interpretation of the Hebrew Bible in Ancient Judaism and Early Christianity*, ed. Martin Jan Mulder (Assen: Van Gorcum; Philadelphia: Fortress, 1988), 189-90; idem, "Samaritan Literature," 462-65; and Anderson and Giles, *Tradition Kept*, 267-68. The earliest Aramaic linguistic stratum seems to belong to the fourth century A.D. Tal, "Samaritan Literature," 465. The theological development of the eschatological prophet concept toward the medieval period is documented in Anderson and Giles, *The Keepers*, 123-25.

[180] These skeptical assessments are expressed in the following: Margaret Pamment, "Is There Convincing Evidence of Samaritan Influence on the Fourth Gospel," *ZNW* 73 (1982): 221-30; Horsley, "Like One of the Prophets of Old," 442; Charlesworth, "From Messianology to Christology: Problems and Prospects," 14; Oegema, *The Anointed and His People*, 246-47; Maier, "Schriftrezeption im jüdischen Umfeld des Johannesevangeliums," 81. John MacDonald also conceived of the Samaritan influence on the Johannine Mosaic Christology but later changed his position to the opposite side, that is, the Johannine influence on the Samaritan literature. For the former view, see John MacDonald, "Samaritan Doctrine of Moses," *SJT* 13 (1960): 149-62, esp. 160-61. For the latter expression, see idem, *The Text*, xx; idem, *The Theology of the Samaritans*, 150-61, 420-46. Also, although Boismard finds the two expressions, "the king of Israel" and "son of Joseph" to be particular marks of Samaritanism, the former epithet is too generic a term to indicate the exclusive Samaritan influence and the latter seems to point to Jesus' immediate father in the literary context. The presence of his hometown (Nazareth) renders it unlikely that his association with Joseph refers to one of the arch-patriarchs. In John 1:45, Jesus is referred to as Ἰησοῦν υἱὸν τοῦ Ἰωσὴφ τὸν ἀπὸ Ναζαρέτ, literally translated as "Jesus, who is son of Joseph and is from Nazareth." For Boismard's argument on this reading, see Boismard, *Moses or Jesus*, 30-36, 66-67.

virtual absence of Mosaic expectation in Qumran, writing that

> We know that the Qumran sectarians awaited two messiahs, one a warrior, the other a priest, and that their coming would be preceded by a prophet; but nothing indicates that this indeterminate prophet should be identified with the prophet like Moses of Deut 18:18-19.[181]

There are only three documents that are usually cited as referring to the eschatological prophet of Deuteronomy 18:15. These writings as well as 11Q13=11QMelch (which has recently been brought up as containing a Mosaic eschatological hope) will be evaluated. An examination of these writings will manifest the lack of an eschatological concern via Moses in Qumran.

Of the three Qumran passages often referred to in conjunction with Deuteronomy 18 (the Temple Scroll=11Q19 54:8-18 and 60:21; 61:1-5; 4Q175=4QTestimonia; and the so-called Apocryphon of Moses=4Q375-76; 1Q22; 1Q29), the Temple Scroll and the Apocryphon of Moses display virtually no concern for the end time.[182] Although they extensively quote from Deuteronomy 18 where the rising of a Moses-like prophet is promised, the context of the entire corpus or the immediate context militates against an eschatological reading of the text.[183] Rather, in view of the primary purpose of the documents (the Deuteronomic legal codes), the catenae in this text should be viewed as the provision for discerning future false prophets.[184]

---

[181] Boismard, *Moses or Jesus*, 3.

[182] For the texts and translations, see Elisha Qimron, *The Temple Scroll: A Critical Edition with Extensive Reconstructions* (Beer Sheva: Ben-Gurion University of the Negev Press; Jerusalem: Israel Exploration Society, 1996); John Strugnell, "Moses-Pseudepigrapha at Qumran: 4Q375, 4Q376, and Similar Works," in *Archaeology and History in the Dead Sea Scrolls: The New York University Conference in Memory of Yigael Yadin*, ed. Lawrence H. Schiffman (Sheffield: JSOT, 1990), 221-56; idem, "Apocryphon of Moses," in *Parabiblical Texts*, part 2 of *Qumran Cave 4, XIV*, ed. Joseph A. Fitzmyer and James A. Vanderkam (Oxford: Clarendon, 1995), 111-36; Élie Latour, "Une proposition de reconstruction de l'Apocryphe de Moïse (1Q29, 4Q375, 4Q376, 4Q408)," *RevQ* 88 (2006): 575-91.

[183] No significant study so far has been produced that reads the catenae or these texts in terms of full-fledged eschatology. A minor exception to this current is Lawrence H. Schiffman, "The Temple Scroll: A Utopian Plan for Second Temple Times," in *The Temple of Jerusalem: From Moses to the Messiah in Honor of Professor Louis H. Feldman*, ed. Steven Fine and Louis H. Feldman (Leiden: Brill, 2011), 45-56. His study, however, envisages only a generic eschatological hope of the Qumran community as reflected in the Temple Scroll.

[184] The primary concern of the entire Temple Scroll is to readdress the Deuteronomic law codes, including the provisions for the building of the Temple. Johann Maier, *The Temple Scroll: An Introduction, Translation & Commentary* (Sheffield: JSOT, 1985), 3-7; Sidnie White Crawford, *The Temple Scroll and Related Texts* (Sheffield: Sheffield, 2000), 17-19; Simone Paganini, "Von Ezechiel zur Tempelrolle: Der Tempel als Realität und Vision," in *Qumran und die Archäologie: Texte und Kontexte*, ed. Jörg

In contrast to the first two documents discussed above, 4Q175 is more controversial as to whether or not it speaks of the Mosaic eschatological prophet. This document is comprised of three blocks of catenae from the Old Testament and ends with an application of these texts with view to either the present or a future situation. The fragment begins with a quotation of two passages from Deuteronomy (5:28-29, 18:18-19), virtually word-for-word from the Masoretic text and the Samaritan Pentateuch. This section records the prediction of a new Moses.[185]

> And Yahweh spoke to Moses, saying "I have heard the sound of the words of this people which they spoke to you. They have well (said) all that they have spoken. Would that they were of such heart to fear me and to keep all of my ordinances always that it may be well with them and with their children forever. I will raise up a prophet for them from among their own kindred like you and I will put my words in his mouth, and he will speak to them all that I command him. If there is someone who does not heed my words which the prophet speaks in my name, I myself will call him to account." (4Q175 1-8)[186]

In the form of a citation from Numbers 24:15-17, the second section reinterprets the Old Testament text to indicate the coming of eschatological figures, such as the Star of Jacob (a Davidic messiah) and the Scepter of Israel (a priestly messiah, elsewhere dubbed as messiah of Aaron).[187]

> And he uttered his verse and said, "Oracle of Balaam, son of Beor, and oracle of the man whose eye is true; oracle of one who hears the words of God, and knows (the) knowledge of the Most High; who beholds (the) vision of Shadday, in a trance but with eye unveiled; what I see (is) not yet; what I behold (is) not soon. A star comes forth

---

Frey, Carsten Claussen, and Nadine Kessler (Tübingen: Mohr Siebeck, 2011), 399-419.

[185] The judgment of Xeravits on this text is slightly off the mark. He remarks that "the *Testimonia* connects Moses to an eschatological personage, the future prophet, as in several currents of early Judaism. It must, however, be mentioned that this prophet in the Testimonia is not identified with Moses, who only serves as a *typos* for the figure to come." Xeravits, *King, Priest, Prophet*, 176. His assessment is correct as far as Moses in the text plays as a type of the future prophet. However, he does not seem to grasp the point of the citation that such a concept is meant in the original Deuteronomy context as well. In other words, both Deut 18:15 and the first section of 4Q175 conceive of the same eschatological prophet who is "like" Moses in some measure.

[186] Frank Moore Cross, "Testimonia (4Q175 = 4QTestimonia = 4QTestim)," in *Pesharim, Other Commentaries, and Related Documents*, vol. 6B of *The Dead Sea Scrolls: Hebrew, Aramaic, and Greek Texts with English Translations*, ed. James H. Charlesworth (Tübingen: Mohr Siebeck; Louisville: Westminster/John Knox, 2002), 312-13.

[187] These figures often occur together (1QS 9 xi; CD 12 xxiii) or apart (4QpPsalms^a 3 xv) in the Qumran library. John J. Collins, "The Nature of Messianism in the Light of the Dead Sea Scrolls," in *The Dead Sea Scrolls in Their Historical Context*, ed. Timothy H. Lim (Edinburgh: T & T Clark, 2000), 208-17; Craig A. Evans, "Messiahs," *EDSS*, 537-42; David C. Mitchell, "The Fourth Deliverer: A Josephite Messiah in 4QTestimonia," *Bib* 86 (2005): 545-53.

from Jacob, and a scepter arises from Israel; and it smashes through the brows of Moab, and it demolishes all the sons of Seth." (4Q175 9-13)[188]

Afterwards, the last citation follows from Deuteronomy 33:8-11, which is originally Moses' blessing of Levi. In this section, the tribe of Levi is praised for its steadfast adherence to the covenant of Yahweh. Then, this section probably envisages the Teacher of Righteousness by its emphasis on the teaching aspect of the Levites as well as the priestly function.[189]

> And of Levi he said, "Give to Levi your Thummim, and your Urim to your faithful one whom you tried at Massah, and (with whom) you contested at the Waters of Meribah; who said to his father and to his mother, 'I do not know you'; and his brothers he disregards, and his children he does not know. For he has kept your command and guards your covenant. And they will teach your judgments to Jacob, your law to Israel. They shall place incense in your nostril(s), and the whole offering on your altar. Bless, O Yahweh, his substance, and favor the work of his hands. Smite the loins of his foes, and as for his enemies, let them not rise again. (4Q175 14-20)[190]

Finally, the document addresses "the cursed man" and his two sons, "the weapons of violence." These antagonists are portrayed as fulfilling the curse of Joshua (i.e., premature death on their parts) with reference to the rebuilding of Jericho (Joshua 6:26), following their building program of Jerusalem in line 30 of this text.

> When Joshua finished praising and giving thanks with his praises, then he said, "Cursed be the man who will rebuild this city. With his firstborn he shall lay its foundation, and with his younger son he shall set up its gates. Behold a cursed man, (a man of) Belial shall arise, to become a [fo]wler's sna[re] to his people, and terror to all his neighbors; and he shall arise [and ... shall a]ris[e ... to be]come, the two of them, weapons of violence. And they shall again build [this city and cons]truct its wall and towers to make a wicked fortress [and great wickedness] in Israel, and its horrors in Ephraim and in Judah. [... And they] shall produce pollution in the land and great strife among the children of [Jacob; and they shall pour out blo]od like water on the rampart of Daughter Zion, and in the district of [. . .] (*vacat*) Jerusalem. (4Q175 21-30)[191]

The antagonists in the final section have sparked debate over their identities and the characteristic of the document, namely, whether it reflects eschatology or past events.[192] The detailed description of the antagonists, however, has led some

---

[188] Cross, "Testimonia," 314-15.

[189] Ibid., 309.

[190] Ibid., 316-17.

[191] Cross, "Testimonia," 318-19. This text is often called the "Psalms of Joshua," which is partially preserved in 4Q379 (4QPsalms of Joshua).

[192] Two of the more popular identifications of the antagonists are (1) Simon and his two sons who fortified Jericho in 135 B.C. (2) and John Hyrcanus I (135-105 B.C.) and his sons who also rebuild Jericho. The former view is espoused by Frank Moore Cross, *The Ancient Library of Qumran* (Sheffield: Sheffield, 1995), 111-15; idem, "Testimonia," 309-10; Jonathan G. Campbell, "4QTestimonia (4Q175)," in *The Exegetical*

to conclude that the main concern of the document was to address the contemporary problem, that is, the apostasy or deviant practice of the Torah, rather than eschatology.[193]

Table 8. Contents of 4Q175

Lines	Citations	Contents
1-8	Deut 5:28-29; 18:18-19	Coming of a prophet like Moses
9-13	Num 24:15-17	The oracle of Balaam
14-20	Deut 33:8-11	Moses' blessing of Levi
21-30	Josh 6:26	The Apocryphon (Psalms) of Joshua

Notwithstanding the possibility of adressing present or past concerns, taken at face value, all three catenae seem to relate to future events *vis-à-vis* the popular eschatological figures.[194] Relevant to the present study is the degree in which the Mosaic eschatological prophet is invoked. As is the case in its original Deuteronomic context, the focus in this Qumran text seems to lie on Moses as an ideal prophetic figure by which false prophets are to be discerned. That is, the primary function of the citation is to provide criteria for recognizing the present or future antagonists, rather than to forecast a coming of an eschatological redeemer figure like Moses. The reason that the Deuteronomy text is cited, therefore, seems incidental. That is, it is not because the cited text contains a reference to the prophet, but because it was one of the more popular eschatological texts readily available at the time.

As briefly discussed thus far, the Qumran community did not pervasively and

---

Texts (London: T & T Clark, 2004), 97. The latter view is maintained by Otto Betz, "Donnersöhne, Menschenfischer und der Davidische Messias," *RQ* 3 (1961): 42, n. 4; Jean Starcky, "Les Maîtres de Justice et la chronologie de Qumrân," in *Qumrân: Sa piété, sa théologie et son milieu*, ed. M. Delcor (Louvain: Louvain University Press, 1978), 253; Hanan Eshel, "The Historical Background of the Pesher Interpreting Joshua's Curse on the Rebuilder of Jericho," *RQ* 15 (1991-92): 409-20; Armin Lange, "The Essene Position on Magic and Divination," in *Legal Texts and Legal Issues: Proceedings of the Second Meeting of the International Organization for Qumran Studies Cambridge 1995, Published in Honour of Joseph M. Baumgarten*, ed. Moshe Bernstein, Florentino García Martínez, and John Kampen (Leiden: Brill, 1997), 429-30; Wise, Abegg, and Cook, *The Dead Sea Scrolls*, 258-59.

[193] For instance, John Lübbe, "A Reinterpretation of 4Q Testimonia," *RevQ* 12 (1986): 187-97.

[194] Jozef Tadeusz Milik, "Lettre de Siméon Bar Kokheba," *RB* 60 (1953): 290; Brown, "The Messianism of Qumrân," 53, 83; Joseph A. Fitzmyer, "'4QTestimonia' and the New Testament," in *Essays on the Semitic Background of the New Testament* (London: G. Chapman, 1971), 83-84; Xeravits, *King, Priest, Prophet*, 57-58.

enthusiastically anticipate a Mosaic eschatological prophet.[195] Géza Xeravits, however, recently suggested that 11Q13 (=11QMelchizedek) is an exception to this current of thought.

> Based on Deut. 18:15, the Community expected the arrival of an eschatological prophet like Moses. The figure of Moses only occurs once as an eschatological, *redivivus* figure, as the anointed prophet of 11QMelch. He will emerge as herald of the heavenly Melchizedek, as one who will comfort God's afflicted people in the time of the eschatological battle.[196]

11QMelch is a Qumran sectarian writing, dated back to the middle of the first century B.C.[197] Of the thirteen fragments, only the second and third ones preserve recoverable readings. The others are too fragmentary to make out their original readings. An intense eschatological document, this Qumranic writing speaks of two end-time figures, a heavenly Melchizedek and his messenger, "the anointed of the spirit." For the author of this Qumran document, Melchizedek is the agent who brings about the eschaton, atoning the sins of the righteous and executing judgment upon the wicked. What calls for special attention is that not only were these actions usually reserved for God, but divine names such as *el, elohim*, and *Yahweh* are applied to Melchizedek. Scholarly opinions are divided over the identity of this Melchizedek, ranging from an angelic being and a human super hero.[198] What is relevant to the present discussion is, nonetheless, the description

---

[195] For an ambiguous and meager presence of the eschatological and messianic expectations in the Qumran scrolls, see Lawrence H. Schiffman, "Messianic Figures and Ideas in the Qumran Scrolls," in *Qumran and Jerusalem: Studies in the Dead Sea Scrolls and the History of Judaism* (Grand Rapids: Eerdmans, 2010), 270-85.

[196] Xeravits, *King, Priest, Prophet*, 183; idem, "Moses Redivivus in Qumran?" *QC* 11 (2003): 105-05.

[197] J.J.M. Roberts, "Melchizedek (11Q13 = 11QMelch)," in *Pesharim, Other Commentaries, and Related Documents*, vol. 6B of *The Dead Sea Scrolls: Hebrew, Aramaic, and Greek Texts with English Translations*, ed. James H. Charlesworth (Tübingen: Mohr Siebeck; Louisville: Westminster/John Knox, 2002), 264.

[198] For the former view, see Adam S. van der Woude, "Melchisedek als himmlische Erlösergestalt in den neugefundenen eschatologischen Midraschim aus Qumran Höhle XI," *OtSt* 14 (1965): 354-73; George J. Brooke, "Melchizedek (11QMelch)," *ABD*, 4:687-88; Florentino García Martínez, Eibert J.C. Tigchelaar, and Adam S. van der Woude, "11QMelchizedek," in *Qumran Cave 11, II: 11Q2-18, 11Q20-31* (Oxford: Clarendon, 1998), 222; Eric F. Mason, "The Identification of MLKY SDQ in 11QMelchizedek: A Survey of Recent Scholarship," *QC* 17 (2009): 51-61; Heinz-Josef Fabry and Ulrich Dahmen, "Melchisedek in Bibel und Qumran," in *"Ich werde meinen Bund mit euch niemals brechen!" (Ri 2,1): Festschrift für Walter Groß zum 70. Geburtstag*, ed. Erasmus Gaß (Freiburg: Herder, 2011), 377-98. For the latter view, see Jean Carmignac, "Le document de Qumran sur Melchisédeq," *RevQ* 7 (1970): 343-78; Anders Hultgård, "The Ideal 'Levite,' the Davidic Messiah, and the Saviour Priest in the Testaments of the Twelve Patriarchs," in *Ideal Figures in Ancient Judaism: Profiles and Paradigms*, ed. John J. Collins and George W.E. Nickelsburg (Chico, CA: Scholars, 1980), 93; David Flusser, "Melchizedek and the Son of Man,"

of "the messenger" of Melchizedek, dubbed also as "the anointed of the spirit" whose message people should heed. Of direct relevance for this discussion are lines 18 and 19 of 11QMelch:

> And "the messenger" i[s] the anointed of the spir[it about] whom Dan[iel] said, ["Until (the coming) of an anointed one, a leader, (there shall be) seven weeks." And "the messenger of] good (news) who announc[es salvation"] is the one concerning whom it is wr[it]ten that [. . .].[199]

Xeravits argues that the descriptions of this second figure fit the profile of the Mosaic eschatological prophet at several points. First, the "messenger" is clearly depicted as a prophetic figure in the text. Second, in the Qumran writings, it is only Moses who bears the title מבשר ("messenger") and is described as a prophet at the same time, as evidenced in 4Q377.[200] In addition, the presence of the name of Moses, which is the only legible word in the first fragment, further convinces him.

Notwithstanding that his conjecture is somewhat intriguing, however, his argument calls for some reservation. For one, the presence of the word "Moses" in fragment one is too fragmentary to be of any use. Second, the non-sectarian provenance of 4Q377 clouds the argumentative force of its comparison with 11Q13 which is of sectarian origin. Furthermore, the instances of Moses' identification with "messenger" and "anointed" are too infrequent within the entire corpus of the Qumran library. Finally, even if the presence of the Mosaic eschatological prophet is acknowledged in 11Q13, it is strikingly meager in view of its potential importance within the Qumran community and the wider Jewish thought world of the Palestinian origin.[201]

---

in *Judaism and the Origins of Christianity* (Jerusalem: Magnes, 1988), 186-92; Paul A. Rainbow, "Melchizedek as a Messiah at Qumran," *BBR* 7 (1997): 179-94; Igor R. Tantlevskij, "Melchizedek Redivivus in Qumran: Some Peculiarities of Messianic Ideas and Elements of Mysticism in the Dead Sea Scrolls," *QC* 12 (2004): 3-80.

[199] Roberts, "Melchizedek," 268-69.

[200] 4Q377 portrays Moses as the messenger *par excellence* and God's anointed. Xeravits, *King, Priest, Prophet*, 177-81; Henten, "Moses as Heavenly Messenger in *Assumptio Mosis* 10:2 and Qumran Passages," 216-27; Brooke, "Moses in the Dead Sea Scrolls," 214-15. *Pace*, see Wido von Deursen, "Who Is Standing on the Mountain?: The Portrait of Moses in 4Q377," in *Moses in Biblical and Extra-Biblical Traditions*, ed. Axel Graupner and Michael Wolter (Berlin: Walter de Gruyter, 2007), 99-113; Heinz-Josef Fabry, "Mose, der 'Gesalbte JHWHs': Messianische Aspekte der Mose-Interpretation in Qumran," in *Moses in Biblical and Extra-Biblical Traditions*, ed. Axel Graupner and Michael Wolter (Berlin: Walter de Gruyter, 2007), 129-42.

[201] Similarly, at the end of his preliminary research into the role of Moses in early Judaism, Dale Allison states that "the outcome of this discussion is that the expectation of an eschatological prophet like Moses, founded upon Deut. 18:15 and 18, was not little known, or just the esoteric property of the Qumran community and Jewish-Christian churches. It was instead very much in the air in first-century Palestine and helped to instigate several short-lived revolutionary movements." However, most of the evidence he adduces postdates the time of Jesus. Furthermore, his analysis is too brief or

Summary

Some summarizing remarks can be drawn from the foregoing observations that are pertinent to the following discussion. First, of all the Old Testament protagonists surveyed (i.e., Jacob, Abraham, Elijah, and David), Moses enjoyed a higher estimation than others, which derived from his involvement in the Sinai event and his life and ministry in the subsequent events. His prominent status is readily observed in the large number of early Jewish writings that also take on his pseudonym. Second, the post-biblical Jewish traditions tend to elevate the status of Moses in various terms. The early Jewish ascension narratives, for instance, portray Moses as a semi-deified being especially in the ascension narratives of the Diaspora settings. Josephus, on the other hand, painted a royal image out of the Pentateuch narratives. Finally, in view of the preeminence of Moses, the expectation of the eschatological prophet like Moses (or an end-time redeemer figure *vis-à-vis* Moses) is surprisingly sparse in intertestamental Judaism. This feature is particularly remarcable in the Qumran writings because of their prominent eschatological tenor.[202] With the possible exception of a few instances (i.e., 11Q13), the Old Testament and intertestamental Jewish literature that are chronologically prior to or contemporary of the time of Jesus and of Palestinian provenance in particular are extremely reticent about the coming of Moses *redivivus*.

Moses in the New Testament

The insurmountable importance of Moses in the New Testament becomes immediately noticeable by the fact that he is mentioned more frequently in the New Testament than any other Old Testament protagonists (80 times in total, cf. 40 of Elijah and 59 of David).[203] These frequent references seem understandable in view of his importance in the Jewish history. On the other hand, however, it is surprising that scholars have paid only sporadic attention to the narrative role of Moses in the New Testament. This relatively sparse interest is partially justified by the significance the New Testament writers attribute to him.[204] For the sake of brevity, the role of Moses in the New Testament can be broken down into functional categories. Hubert Frankemölle, for example, divides the functions of

---

plagued by heavy dependence on the secondary literature. Allison, *The New Moses*, 75-84.

[202] Fabry, "Mose, der 'Gesalbte JHWHs'," 129-42.

[203] Jeremias, *TDNT*, 4:864; G. Fitzer, "Μωϋσῆς," *EDNT*, 2:451.

[204] Stefan Schapdick, "Autorität ohne Inhalt: Zum Mosebild des Johannesevangeliums," *ZNW* 97 (2006): 177. Schapdick (ibid.) mentions only two major substantial contributions on this topic, one by Kastner and the other by Saito. Josef M. Kastner, "Moses im Neuen Testament: Eine Untersuchung der Mosestraditionen in den neutestamentlichen Schriften" (Th.D. diss., Ludwig-Maximilians Universität, 1967); Tadashi Saito, *Die Mosevorstellungen im Neuen Testament* (Bern: Peter Lang, 1977).

Moses in terms of the mediator of the Torah, a prophet, and a type of Jesus.[205] However, the scope of his analysis encompasses passages from only Matthew and 2 Corinthians. In contrast, the purview of Hays' examination is more comprehensive. According to Hays, Moses functions in various ways to clarify the writers' Christology, cast light onto the Mosaic Scripture, and advance the church's self-understanding within the entirety of the NT writings.[206]

Moses in the Gospel of John

In the past, some scholars have inquired into the role of Moses in the Gospel of John with an eye primarily to the historical situation of the so-called Johannine community. This historical reconstruction was undertaken by means of form critical analyses which sought to identify different layers of editorial hands. Influenced largely by J.L Martyn's theory, these scholars attempted to explain how the discourses concerning Moses reveal an ambivalent attitude within the alleged community. For instance, some have proposed that the Johannine sect tried to break away from mainstream Judaism and, at the same time, had to maintain their loyalty to Moses in an effort to demonstrate the authenticity of its belief in Jesus as the Christ as forshadowed in the writings of Moses.[207] Others maintained that an earlier layer reflects the Samaritan-oriented mission of the Johannine community, while a later layer reveals the distancing of the community from the Jews.[208] These types of studies represent an attempt to account for

---

[205] Hubert Frankemölle, "Mose in Deutungen des Neuen Testaments," *KuI* 9 (1994): 70-86.

[206] David M. Hays, "Moses through New Testament Spectacles," *Int* 44 (1990): 240-52. In addition to these roles, Fitzer detects distancing of Moses in John and the Pauline epistles. Fitzer, *EDNT*, 2:452. For further introductions to the role of Moses in the New Testament, see Saito, *Die Mosevorstellungen im Neuen Testament*; Dieter Sänger, "Mose/Moselied/Mosesegen/Moseschriften II," *TRE*, 23:342-46; idem, "'Von mir hat er geschrieben' (Joh 5,46)," 112-23, 127-32; Florence M. Gilman, "Moses: New Testament," *ABD*, 4:918-20; Wolfgang Kraus, "Moses II: Neues Testament," *RGG*, 5:1538-39. For a survey of the past scholarship on Moses, see Harstine, *Moses as a Character in the Fourth Gospel*, 3-39; Lierman, *The New Testament Moses*, 10-29.

[207] Christian Dietzfelbinger, *Das Evangelium nach Johannes* (Zürich: Theologischer, 2001), 1:291. For Martyn's works on this point, see J. Louis Martyn, "Glimpses into the History of the Johannine Community," in *The Gospel of John in Christian History: Essays for Interpreters* (New York: Paulist, 1979), 90-121; reprinted in *History and Theology in the Fourth Gospel* (Louisville: Westminster/John Knox, 2003), 145-67 and other essays included in the latter anthology.

[208] For examples of this approach, see Walter Rebell, *Gemeinde als Gegenwelt: Zur soziologischen und didaktischen Funktion des Johannesevangeliums* (Frankfurt: Peter Lang, 1987); Ekkehard Stegemann, "Die Tragödie der Nähe: Zu den judenfeindlichen Aussagen des Johannesevangeliums," *KuI* 4 (1989): 114-22; Klaus Wengst, *Bedrängte Gemeinde und verherrlichter Christus: Ein Versuch über das Johannesevangelium*, 4th ed. (München: Chr. Kaiser, 1992), 75-104; Christian Dietzfelbinger, "Der ungeliebte Bruder: Der Herrenbruder Jakobus im Johannesevangelium," *ZTK* 89 (1992): 394-99.

the seemingly stereo-typical depiction of Moses in John, where Moses seems to be portrayed at some points as a messianic prefiguration, while at other times Jesus supersedes and replaces the prophet *par excellence*.[209]

In the face of increased scholarly emphasis on the integrity of the present literary form, however, more recent studies tend to focus on the consistent depiction of Moses and, more pertinently to this research, on the typological correspondence between Moses and Jesus in particular.[210] While interacting with these exegetical contributions, the following section will closely examine the narrative function of the four Moses pericopae in John with a special reference to his Christological understanding. Of course, one can arguably find more passages that supposedly evoke a Mosaic Christology. Nevertheless, these texts represent some of the more explicit depictions of Moses (and a number of exegetes argue in the typological prefigurative sense from these texts) so that a contextual examination of these texts will provide a sufficient sketch for the evangelist's presentation of him in relation to Christology.

Law through Moses, Grace through Jesus: John 1:16-17

[16] ὅτι ἐκ τοῦ πληρώματος αὐτοῦ ἡμεῖς πάντες ἐλάβομεν καὶ χάριν ἀντὶ χάριτος· [17] ὅτι ὁ νόμος διὰ Μωϋσέως ἐδόθη, ἡ χάρις καὶ ἡ ἀλήθεια διὰ Ἰησοῦ Χριστοῦ ἐγένετο. (John 1:16-17, NA[28])

> From his fullness we have all received, grace upon grace. The law indeed was given through Moses; grace and truth came through Jesus Christ. (John 1:16-17, NRSV)

The first explicit mention of Moses appears in the latter part of the Johannine prologue, which articulates divine revelation through Jesus.[211] The reference to

---

[209] Meeks, *The Prophet-King*; Boismard, *Moses or Jesus*. For a brief summation of this ambivalence, see Gillman, *ABD*, 4:919; Sänger, *TRE*, 23:343.

[210] Douglas K. Clark, "Signs in Wisdom and John," *CBQ* 45 (1983): 201-09; Klappert, "'Mose hat von mir geschrieben,'" 619-40; Scholtissek, "'Die unauflösbare Schrift' (Joh 10,35)," 146-77; Diana M. Swancutt, "Hungers Assuaged by the Bread from Heaven: 'Eating Jesus' as Isaian Call to Belief, the Confluence of Isaiah 55 and Psalm 78 (77) in John 6:22-71," in *Early Christian Interpretation of the Scriptures of Israel: Investigations and Proposals*, ed. Craig A. Evans and James A. Sanders (Sheffield: Sheffield, 1997), 218-51; John Dennis, "The Presence and Function of Second Exodus-Restoration Imagery in John 6," *SNTSU* 30 (2005): 105-21.

[211] For surveys of various issues surrounding the prologue, see Michael Theobald, "Der Johannesprolog im 20. Jahrhundert," in *Die Fleischwerdung des Logos: Studien zum Verhältnis des Johannesprologs zum Corpus des Evangeliums und zu 1 Joh* (Münster: Aschendorff, 1988), 54-161; John Painter, *The Quest for the Messiah: The History, Literature and Theology of the Johannine Community* (Nashville: Abingdon, 1993), 137-62; Jan G. van der Watt, "The Composition of the Prologue of John's Gospel: The Historical Jesus Introducing Divine Grace," *WTJ* 57 (1995): 311-32; Walther Bindemann, "Der Johannesprolog: Ein Versuch, ihn zu verstehen," *NovT* 37 (1995): 331-54; John Ashton, "The Transformation of Wisdom," in *Studying John: Approaches to the Fourth Gospel* (Oxford: OUP, 1998), 5-35; Stephen Voorwinde, "John's Prologue: Beyond Some Impasses of Twentieth-Century Scholarship," *WTJ*

Moses in this text does not directly speak to his narrative function other than his integral part in the reception of the Torah, which is repeatedly acknowledged in early Jewish writings (including OT) and in this Gospel (John 7:18-24, 8:5). A closer reading, however, reveals the evangelist's general attitude towards the arch-prophet and provides a glimpse into his role in relation to Johannine Christology.[212]

The broader context of the prologue delineates the incarnation of Jesus as the climactic manifestation of the glory of Yahweh (i.e., "full of grace and truth") which is explicitly illustrated in v. 14. Particularly interesting are the linguistic similarities of v. 14 with Exodus 33-34. In addition to the tabernacle language (σκηνόω, lit. "to tabernacle"), the expression "full of grace and truth" (πλήρης χάριτος καὶ ἀληθείας) bears a resemblance to the Hebrew idiom, "full of love and faithfulness" (רַב־חֶסֶד וֶאֱמֶת, Exod 34:6)."[213] It is within this context that the new

---

64 (2002): 15-44; Jean-Marie Sevrin, "Le commencement du quatrième évangile: Prologue et prélude," in *La Bible en récits*, ed. Daniel Marguerat (Genève: Labor et Fides, 2005), 340-49; Günter Kruck, ed., *Der Johannesprolog* (Darmstadt: Wissenschaftliche Buchgesellschaft, 2009); Eoin de Bhaldraithe, "The Johannine Prologue: Structure and Origins," *ABR* 58 (2010): 57-71. Although Hofius detects several layers of redaction, the literary integrity is attested to in the clear progression of thought in the prologue. Sänger, "'Von mir hat er geschrieben' (Joh 5,46)," 124. Otfried Hofius, "Struktur und Gedankengang des Logos-Hymnus in Joh 1:1-18," *ZNW* 78 (1987): 1-25. Hengel also argues for a thorough Jewish background of the Johannine prologue. Martin Hengel, "The Prologue of the Gospel of John as the Gateway to Christological Turth," in *The Gospel of John and Christian Theology*, ed. Richard Bauckham and Carl Mosser (Grand Rapids: Eerdmans, 2008), 265-94. Cf. David A. Reed, "How Semitic Was John?: Rethinking the Hellenistic Background to John 1:1," *AThR* 85 (2003): 709-26.

[212] A number of Johannine exegetes argue for the polemical motive behind the reference to Moses in order to defend the orthodoxy of the Johannine community. Such an assertion seems to be suggestive at best. Cf. Wengst, *Bedrängte Gemeinde und verherrlichter Christus*, 75-127; Stefan Schapdick, *Auf dem Weg in den Konflikt: Exegetische Studien zum theologischen Profil der Erzählung vom Aufenthalt Jesus in Samarien (Joh 4, 1-42) im Kontext des Johannesevangeliums* (Berlin: Philo, 2000), 441-58.

[213] Lester Jacob Kuyper, "Grace and truth: An Old Testament Description of God, and Its Use in the Johannine Gospel," *Int* 18 (1964): 3-19; Morna D. Hooker, "Johannine Prologue and the Messianic Secret," *NTS* 21 (1974): 53-56; Anthony T. Hanson, "John 1:14-18 and Exodus 34," *NTS* 23 (1976): 90-101; Craig R. Koester, *The Dwelling of God: The Tabernacle in the Old Testament, Intertestamental Jewish Literature, and the Old Testament* (Washington: Catholic Biblical Association of America, 1989), 103-04; Craig A. Evans, *Word and Glory: On the Exegetical and Theological Background of John's Prologue* (Sheffield: Sheffield, 1993), 79-80; Udo Wilckens, *Das Evangelium nach Johannes* (Göttingen: Vandenhoeck & Ruprecht, 1998), 33-34; Erik Aurelius, "Heilsgegenwart im Wort: Dtn 30,11-14," in *Liebe und Gebot: Studien zum Deuteronomium*, ed. Reinhard G. Kratz and Hermann Spieckermann (Göttingen: Vandenhoeck & Ruprecht, 2000), 13-29; Christian Grappe, "Jean 1,14(-18) dans son contexte et à la lumière de la littérature intertestamentaire," *RHPR* 80 (2000): 153-69;

divine revelation is further compared with or contrasted to that of Moses, who is referred to as a metonym for the old covenant, especially the Pentateuch (1:17).[214]

Scholarship is evenly divided over the relation between the Mosaic economy and that of Jesus. A group of Johannine exegetes maintains that the present text signifies the supplementary or accumulating nature of the new salvific revelation through Jesus: hence the "grace and truth" of Jesus came in addition to the law of Moses.[215] Another group favors the supersessionistic reading of the text: the "grace and truth" of Jesus came in replacement of the Mosaic law.[216] Three

---

Klaus Wengst, *Das Johannesevangelium* (Stuttgart: Kohlhammer, 2000), 1:74-76; Hartwig Thyen, *Das Johannesevangelium* (Tübingen: Mohr Siebeck, 2005), 98-100; Joe M. Sprinkle, "Is There Truth in the Law (John 1:17)?: On the Gospel of John's View of the Mosaic Revelation," in *Biblical Law and Its Relevance: A Christian Understanding and Ethical Application for Today of the Mosaic Regulations* (Lanham: University Press of America, 2006), 32-36; J. Ramsey Michaels, *The Gospel of John* (Grand Rapids: Eerdmans, 2010), 82-83.

[214] John 1:45 identifies Moses as the writer of the Pentateuch. Andreas Obermann, *Die christologische Erfüllung der Schrift im Johannesevangelium: Eine Untersuchung zur johanneischen Hermeneutik anhand der Schriftzitate* (Tübingen: Mohr Siebeck, 1996), 60-63.

[215] This supplementary or accumulative sense is read in a few NT translations: Revised Standard Version (1952), New International Version (1984), New Revised Standard Version (1989), New American Standard Bible (1995); New Living Translation, English Standard Version (2001). The commentators favoring this view are: Rudolf Bultmann, *The Gospel of John: A Commentary*, trans. George R. Beasley-Murray (Louisville: Westminster, 1971), 78; Barnabas Lindars, *The Gospel of John* (London: Marshall, Morgan & Scott, 1972), 97; Johannes Schneider, *Das Evangelium nach Johannes* (Berlin: Evangelische Verlagsanstalt, 1976), 62; C.K. Barrett, *The Gospel according to St. John: An Introduction with Commentary and Notes on the Greek Text* (Philadelphia: Westminster, 1978), 168-69; Rudolf Schnackenburg, *The Gospel according to St John* (New York: Crossroad, 1982), 1:275-76; F.F. Bruce, *The Gospel of John* (Grand Rapids: Eerdmans, 1983), 43; Elizabeth Harris, *Prologue and Gospel: The Theology of the Fourth Evangelist* (Sheffield: Sheffield, 1994), 90; Leon Morris, *The Gospel according to John* (Grand Rapids: Eerdmans, 1995), 98; Joachim Gnilka, *Johannesevangelium* (Würzburg: Echter, 1999), 15-16; Jörg Augenstein, "Jesus und das Gesetz im Johannesevangelium," *KuI* 14 (1999): 170-72; Wengst, *Das Johannesevangelium*, 1:78; Christian Blumenthal, "Charis anti charitos (Joh 1,16)," *ZNW* 92 (2001): 290-94; Craig S. Keener, *The Gospel of John: A Commentary* (Peabody: Hendrickson, 2003), 1:421; Eric M.E. Wallace, "The Testimony of Moses: Pentateuchal Traditions and Their Function in the Gospel of John" (Ph.D. diss., Union Theological Seminary and Presbyterian School of Christian Education, 2004), 136-37.

[216] The replacement sense is attested to in fewer Bible versions: New Jerusalem Bible, King James, and New King James Version (1982). The commentators opting for this view include: Raymond E. Brown, *The Gospel according to John* (New York: Doubleday, 1966), 1:15-16; Adolf Schlatter, *Der Evangelist Johannes, wie er spricht, denkt und glaubt: Ein Kommentar zum vierten Evangelium* (Stuttgart: Calwer, 1975), 32; Ruth B. Edwards, "Charin anti charitos (John 1:16): Grace and the Law in the Johannine Prologue," *JSNT* 32 (1988): 3-15; D.A. Carson, *The Gospel according to*

minor alternative readings are possible: that the grace of Christ precedes that of Moses; that the grace of Christ comes in return for the Mosaic covenant; and that the Mosaic economy corresponds to that of Christ. All these interpretations contain some measure of theological truth but they do not seem to fairly represent the plain reading of the text.[217] The following structural, syntactical, and lexical analysis of the text seeks to shed light into the exact nature of this relation of the divine economies of Moses and Jesus.

Structure of the prologue. A number of proposed structural analyses of the prologue can be delimited into two categories: logical progression and chiasmus models (the latter was popularized to a large degree by R. Alan Culpepper).[218] The former model is observed in the studies of C. Dietzfellbinger, K. Wengst, A. T. Lincoln, G. Beasely-Murray, R. Brown, and the latter in S. Voorewinde, J. Stalley, W. Dumbrell, and A. Köstenberger.

Table 9. Various Structural Analyses of the Prologue

Dietzfelbinger[219]
1. The relationship of the Logos to God and to the world (vv. 1-5)
2. Of the witness of the Baptist to the reception of the divine childhood (vv. 6-13)
3. The witness of the believers (vv. 14-18)

John (Grand Rapids: Eerdmans, 1991), 131-34; Jürgen Becker, *Das Evangelium nach Johannes* (Würzburg: Echter, 1991), 66; George R. Beasely-Murray, *John* (Nashville: Nelson, 1999), 15; Francis J. Moloney, *The Gospel of John*, SP 4 (Wilmington: Liturgical, 1998), 40; Wilckens, *Das Evangelium nach Johannes*, 35; Dietzfelbinger, *Das Evangelium nach Johannes*, 1:32; Andreas Köstenberger, *John* (Grand Rapids: Baker, 2004), 46-47; Andrew T. Lincoln, *A Commentary on the Gospel according to St. John* (London: Continuum, 2005), 107-08; Thyen, *Das Johannesevangelium*, 104-05; Peter M. Phillips, *The Prologue of the Fourth Gospel: A Sequential Reading* (London: T & T Clark, 2006), 211-15. Some scholars, however, do not speak for themselves on this issue. See Udo Schnelle, *Das Evangelium nach Johannes* (Leipzig: Evangelische Verlagsanstalt, 1998), 42; Ludger Schenke, *Johannes: Kommentar* (Düsseldorf: Patmos, 1998), 33-34.

[217] For a more detailed discussion of these views, see Edwards, "Charin anti charitos," 3-7. For a redefinition of the two economies, see Sean F. Winter, "The Rhetorical Function of John's Portrayal of the Jewish Law," in *Torah in the New Testament: Papers Delivered at the Manchester-Lausanne Seminar of June 2008*, ed. Michael Tait and Peter Oakes (London: T & T Clark, 2009), 92-94.

[218] R. Alan Culpepper, "The Pivot of John's Prologue," *NTS* 27 (1980): 1-31.

[219] Dietzfelbinger, *Das Evangelium nach Johannes*, 1:22-34.

> Wengst[220]
>
> I. Description of working of the Word, its refusal and reception (vv. 1-13)
>   1. The creation and working of the Word at the beginning (v. 1-4)
>   2. The refusal of the historically working Word (vv. 5, 9-11)
>   Excursus: John the Baptist as witness of the Logos (vv. 6-8)
>   3. The reception of the historically working Word (v. 12-13)
> II. Confession of the Word incarnate and witness for it (vv. 14-18)
>   1. The confession of the believers (v. 14)
>   2. The witness of John (v. 15)
>   3. The common confession and witness of John and the believers (vv. 16-18)

> Lincoln[221]
>
> The Word in relation to God and creation (vv. 1-5)
> The witness of John the Baptist to the Word as Light (vv. 6-8)
> The Word in the world and the two types of responses (vv. 9-13)
> The community's confession about the Word (vv. 14-18)

> Beasley-Murray[222]
>
> 1. The Word of God and creation (vv. 1-5)
> 2. The witness to the Word of God by John the Baptist (vv. 6-8)
> 3. The reactions to the Word of God in the World (vv. 9-13)
> 4. The confession of the Word of God by the church (vv. 14-18)

> Brown[223]
>
> The Word with God (vv. 1-2)
> The Word and creation (vv. 3-5)
>   Parenthesis: John the Baptist's witness to the Light (vv. 6-9)
> The Word in the world (vv. 10-12b)
> The community's share in the Word-become-flesh (vv. 14-16)
>   Parenthesis: the Baptist testifies to the pre-existence of Jesus (v. 15)
>   Editorial expansion of v. 16 (vv. 17-18)

---

[220] Wengst, *Das Johannesevangelium*, 1:47.

[221] Lincoln, *A Commentary on the Gospel according to St. John*, 94-109.

[222] Beasley-Murray, *John*, 10-16.

[223] Brown, *The Gospel according to John*, 1:23-36.

Voorwinde[224]
A. The Word (v. 1)
  B. "With God" (vv. 1-2)
    C. Creation: "Life and light" (vv. 3-5)
      D. The testimony of John (vv. 6-8)
        E. The incarnation: "Light" (vv. 9-10)
          F. Human response: Negative (vv. 10-11)
          F′. Human response: Positive (vv. 12-13)
        E′. The incarnation: "Glory" (v. 14)
      D′. The testimony of John (v. 15)
    C′. New Creation: "Grace and truth" (vv. 14-17)
  B′. "In the bosom of the Father" (v. 18)
A′. "The One and Only God" (v. 18)

Staley[225]
The relationship of the Logos to God/creation/humankind vv. 1-5
  The witness of John (negative) vv. 6-8
    The journey of the Light/Logos (negative) vv. 9-11
      The gift of empowerment (positive) vv. 12-13
    The journey of the Logos (positive) v. 14
  The witness of John (positive) v. 15
The relationship of the Logos to humankind/re-creation/God vv. 16-18

Dumbrell[226]
Jesus' relationship to God (vv. 1-2)
  Jesus' role in the economy of salvation (v. 3)
    Participation of humanity in the salvation revealed in Christ (vv. 4-5)
      The testimony of the forerunner (vv. 6-8)
        The response to the saving presence of Christ negatively (vv. 9-10)
          The centerpiece: the significance of the Incarnation (vv. 11-13)
        The response to the saving presence of Christ positively (v. 14)
      The testimony of the forerunner (v. 15)
    Participation of humanity in the salvation revealed in Christ (v. 16)
  Jesus' role in the economy of salvation (v. 17)
Jesus' relationship to God (v. 18)

---

[224] Voorwinde, "John's Prologue," 27-43.
[225] Jeffrey L. Staley, "The Structure of John's Prologue: Its Implications for the Gospel's Narrative Structure," *CBQ* 48 (1986): 241-64.
[226] William J. Dumbrell, "Law and Grace: The Nature of the Contrast in John 1:17," *EvQ* 58 (1986): 25-37; idem, "Grace and Truth: The Progress of the Argument of the Pro-

> Köstenberger[227]
> A The Word's activity in creation (1:1-5)
>   B John's witness concerning the light (1:6-8)
>   C The incarnation of the Word and the privilege of becoming God's children (1:9-14)
>   B′ John's witness concerning the Word's preeminence (1:15)
> A′ The final revelation brought by Jesus Christ (1:16-18)

Two observations stand out in light of these structural analyses. First, the prologue centers on Jesus, who played an integral role in the creation and through whom the new divine revelation became manifest. More importantly, if the presence of a chiastic structure is accepted, vv. 16 through 17 recapitulate the preexistent Logos idea spelled out in vv. 1 through 2, and further accentuate the culmination of the redemptive plan as unfolded in Jesus. That is, the chiastic structure elucidates the superiority of the new divine economy over the Mosaic covenant. However, it should also be noted that the logical progression models do not necessarily rule out this notion. Nevertheless, the chiasmus more clearly demonstrates the escalating progression of emphasis on Jesus.

Syntax. Some earlier Johannine commentators understood the parallel between Moses and Jesus in v. 17 as an antithesis.[228] Ruth Edwards and Klaus Wengst, for instance, cite Chrysostom, Cyril of Alexandria, Origen, Theophylact, Augustine and Jerome as patristic evidence that opted for this interpretation.[229] Some contemporary exegetes also hold to this view as well.[230] Futhermore, this anti-thesis

---

logue of John's Gospel," in *Doing Theology for the People of God: Studies in Honor of J. I. Packer*, ed. Donald Lewis and Alister McGrath (Downers Grove: InterVarsity, 1996), 105-21. Dumbrell's structural analysis is virtually identical to that of Culpepper, only with the exception of the centerpiece being the theme of "children of God" in Culpepper's. Cf. Culpepper, "The Pivot of John's Prologue," 1-31.

[227] Köstenberger, *John*, 21.

[228] Becker, *Das Evangelium nach Johannes*, 1:101; Rudolf Bultmann, *Das Evangelium des Johannes* (Göttingen: Vandenhoeck & Ruprecht, 1986), 53; Dietzfelbinger, *Das Evangelium nach Johannes*, 1:32; Schnelle, *Das Evangelium nach Johannes*, 42-43; Wilckens, *Das Evangelium nach Johannes*, 35. Some scholars posit the interpolation of vv. 16-18 based on the idiosyncratic nature of grace/law antithesis in John. For example, Painter, *The Quest for the Messiah*, 147-49. However, the structural and syntactical examination of the text displays a cohesive place of vv. 16-18 in the context.

[229] Edwards, "Charin anti charitos," 7; Wengst, *Das Johannesevangelium*, 1:79, n. 75.

[230] Walter Bauer, *Das Johannesevangelium* (Tübingen: Mohr Siebeck, 1933), 124; Markku Kotila, *Umstrittener Zeuge: Studien zur Stellung des Gesetzes in der johanneischen Theologiegeschichte* (Helsinki: Suomalainen Tiedeakatemia, 1988), 142-45; Hans Weder, "Mein hermeneutisches Anliegen im Gegenüber zu Klaus Bergers Hermeneutik des Neuen Testaments," *EvT* 52 (1992): 320; Otfried Hofius, "'Der in des Vaters Schoss ist': Joh 1:18," in *Johannesstudien: Untersuchungen zur Theologie des Vierten Evangeliums*, ed. Otfried Hofius and Hans-Christian Kammler

tension has become a foundation for the supposed historical setting of the Johannine community. For instance, Matthew Gawlick reaches a historical reconstruction based on an analysis of John 1:14-18 as follows:

> Moses' relationship to Jesus is antithetical. Readers are informed of the indisputable priority of Jesus. It is not right to speak of the tension between the Johannine community and the Jews as follows: Moses stands in line with Jesus so that there is a continuity of the redemptive history. More problematic is an attempt to identify Jesus with the previously given category of the Torah because the law is narrow, especially the Torah is described negatively in the whole context of John's gospel. Although there is an element of thesis and anti-thesis, one should not press too hard such a category. It is not the intention of John to discredit Moses in this way. The mention of Moses in John 1:17 is a hermeneutical signal for how Christian believers are to be distinguished from their Jewish brothers. The polemic is not against Moses but againt the Jews, the followers of Moses who placed too high a meaning to him in comparison with Jesus.[231]

Syntactical observations, nevertheless, militate against such a view and lend weight to either the accumulation or replacement sense. The lack of a conjunction or particle between the first and the second halves of v. 17 make it difficult to determine the relationship between the two clauses. A clue, however, is found in the conjunction ὅτι plus the indicative construction (v. 17), which usually functions as a causal subordinate clause in biblical Greek.[232] Therefore, the literal rendition of vv. 16-17 could be as follows:

> From his fullness we have all received grace upon/instead of grace (χάριν ἀντὶ χάριτος) because the law was given through Moses and/but grace and truth came through Jesus Christ.

As such, the two occurrences of χάρις in v. 16 correspond to the Mosaic law and the new divine economy of Jesus in v. 17 respectively. This syntactical observation avails an important hermeneutical point. The Mosaic economy and that of Jesus are equally extensions of the divine grace.[233] The common divine provenance is also attested to in the passive voice ("the law was given [ἐδόθη] through

---

(Tübingen: Siebeck, 1996), 29-30; Sänger, "'Von mir hat er geschrieben' (Joh 5,46)," 124; Schnelle, *Das Evangelium nach Johannes*, 42-43.

[231] Matthias Gawlick, "Mose im Johannesevangelium," *BN* 84 (1996): 32.

[232] For the ὅτι plus indicative construction principally as causal, see Daniel B. Wallace, *Greek Grammar beyond the Basics: An Exegetical Syntax of the New Testament* (Grand Rapids: Zondervan, 1996), 662; *BDF*, 238; Herbert Weir Smyth, *Greek Grammar* Gordon M. Messing (Cambridge: Harvard University Press, 1956), 504.

[233] Johannes Beutler, "Das Hauptgebot im Johannesevangelium," in *Das Gesetz im Neuen Testament*, ed. Johannes Beutler and Karl Kertelge (Freiburg: Herder, 1986), 12; Obermann, *Die christologische Erfüllung der Schrift im Johannesevangelium*, 54-56; Moloney, *The Gospel of John*, 40; Thyen, *Das Johannesevangelium*, 104. Thus, Klappert stresses the category of "correspondence" as the basis of a messianic Christology in this context. Klappert, "'Mose hat von mir geschrieben,'" 619-40.

Moses"), which signifies the divine initiative.[234]

One caveat, nonetheless, is in order regarding an implication of this parallelism, as Wengst asserts, namely, that the two clauses seem to focus on the intermediary role of Moses and Jesus in passing on the divine grace:

> This verse is founded upon the statement that received grace "because the law was given through Moses but grace and truth came through Jesus Christ." Two halves of the verse form a complete parallel. Subjects are placed in the beginning of the each half: the law, and grace and truth. The reports of the mediators also follow in each half: Moses and Jesus Christ. Each predicates are conclusions in the grammatically passive form, and the subject is God as logos. He is the giver of the law through mediating Moses. It is also He who has come through Jesus Christ in His grace and truth. God is a gracious giver through Moses and through Jesus Christ. The confession that received grace overly in v. 16 is founded dually: by the giving of the law through Moses in the first place and then through the presence of the gracious and truthful God in Jesus Christ.[235]

His notion, however, does not seem to take adequately into account the point of the pericope comprising vv. 16-18 in the wider context. First, the entire scope of the prologue disproportionately underscores Jesus as being tantamount to God and being the first divine exposure to men in human form (esp. vv. 1, 14, and 18):

> In the beginning was the Word, and the Word was with God, and the Word was God;

> And the Word became flesh and lived among us, and we have seen his glory, the glory as of a father's only son, full of grace and truth;

> No one has ever seen God. It is God the only Son, who is close to the Father's heart, who has made him known. (John 1:1, 14, 18, NRSV)

Second, Wengst's observation does not pay sufficient attention to the message of the immediate context. The tenor of v. 18 could be seen as a polemic against the popular Jewish traditions about Moses who was believed to behold Yahweh however partially.[236] Accordingly, Jesus is the incarnate self-revelation of God

---

[234] Michael Theobald, *Im Anfang war das Wort: Textlinguistische Studie zum Johannesprolog* (Stuttgart: Katholisches Bibelwerk, 1983), 60-63; Kotila, *Umstrittener Zeuge*, 141, 204; Martin Hengel, "Die Schriftauslegung des 4. Evangeliums auf dem Hintergrund der urchristlichen Exegese," in *"Gesetz" als Thema Biblischer Theologie* (Neukirchen-Vluyn: Neukirchen, 1989), 266; Becker, *Das Evangelium nach Johannes*, 1:101; Hofius, "'Der in des Vaters Schoß ist,'" 30. In this respect, the semantic distinction of Ulrich Luz on "law" and "scripture" breaks down. Luz defines the Johannine use of "law" as a means to attack Jesus whereas "scripture" is what is fulfilled in Jesus. Ulrich Luz, "Das Neue Testament," in *Gesetz*, ed. Rudolf Smend and Ulrich Luz (Stuttgart: Kohlhammer, 1981), 120. In John 1:17, "law" does not connote a negative inference nor stands in antithetical contrast to "grace and truth."

[235] Wengst, *Das Johannesevangelium*, 1:79.

[236] Later rabbinic sources, however, express the encounter of Moses with Yahweh in a circumlocutory manner. Anthony T. Hanson, "The Word on Sinai and at Bethel," in

intervened into human history. Unfolded in this logical progression, thus, vv. 16-18 can be paraphrased as follows:

> In his divine kindness, God has granted one grace on top of/in place of another. The first grace came through Moses and/but the second is revealed in Jesus Christ who is the first palpable manifestation of God himself.

Seen in this context, therefore, the parallelism of Moses and Jesus highlights the progression of the divine redemptive plan rather than the mediatory role of the two figures.

Semantics. The causal understanding of ὅτι at the beginning of v. 17 clarifies the divine provenance of both divine economies. In addition, the causal interpretation of the conjunction further hints at the double reference to χάριτος in v. 16 corresponding to the two following clauses in v. 17. Then, the meaning of the preposition ἀντί which connects the double reference to χάριτος becomes a crucial hermeneutical clue to the relation between the Mosaic and the new salvific plan. As briefly reviewed above, the meaning of the preposition also sharply divides scholarship: one group takes it to mean "upon, in addition to, or on top of" whereas the other favors "in place of." Lexical observations, nonetheless, support the latter view.

First, standard Greek lexicons do not refer to a single instance of the word ἀντί meaning "upon" in ancient Greek literature. *A Greek-English Lexicon of the New Testament and Other Early Christian Literature (BDAG)* renders the original meaning of this word to be locally "opposite," from which developed "various types of correspondence ranging from replacement to equivalence."[237] The five uses of the word are to indicate (1) that "one person or thing is, or is to be, replaced by another," hence "instead of, in place of" (2) that one thing is equivalent to another, such as "for, as, in place of" (3) a process of intervention, "in behalf of, for" (4) the reason for something, "because of, for the purpose of" and (5) result with implication of being a replacement for something, "therefore, so then."[238] *Exegetical Dictionary of the New Testament (EDNT)* and *Theological Dictionary of the New Testament (TDNT)* also do not list a single occurrence or usage of the word meaning "upon" or "after." The range of meaning in these lexicons overlaps with the definition of *BDAG*.[239] With the lack of a semantic

---

The Prophetic Gospel: A Study of John and the Old Testament (Edinburgh: T & T Clark, 1991), 22.

[237] *BDAG*, 87.

[238] Ibid., 87-88.

[239] Friedrich Büchsel, "ἀντί," *TDNT*, 1:372-73; H. Frankemölle, "ἀντί," *EDNT*, 1:108-09. Cf. "in John 1:16 *charin anti charitos* denotes a perpetual and rapid succession of blessings, as though there were no interval between the arrival of one blessing and the receipt of the next. Alternatively, the idea of constant renewal may be less prominent than the notion of the replacement of 'old' grace by 'new' grace." M.J. Harris, "Prepositions and Theology in the Greek New Testament," *NIDNTT*, 3:1179-80.

precedence, therefore, it is natural to translate the preposition ἀντί in its most common usage, "instead of."

Second, the examples of ἀντί usually cited in favor of the sense of accumulation do not stand up to a scrutiny. Some commentators point to Sirach 26:15 where a meek or humble woman is described as χάρις ἐπὶ χάριτι ("charm upon charm," i.e., a double blessing).[240] This example is hardly relevant for the present discussion since the preposition is ἐπί not ἀντί. Keener comments that "the preposition differs . . . but LXX readers might have suspected an allusion; prepositions were losing some force by the Koine period."[241] Keener's logic, however, seems to appeal to a special pleading. Another ancient Greek passage often referred to is from Philo's allegorical commentary on Genesis 4:16-25:

> Διὸ τὰς πρώτας αἰεὶ χάριτας, πρὶν κορεσθέντας ἐξυβρίσαι τοὺς λαχόντας, ἐπισχὼν καὶ ταμιευσάμενος εἰσαῦθις ἑτέρας ἀντ' ἐκείνων καὶ τρίτας ἀντὶ τῶν δευτέρων καὶ αἰεὶ νέας ἀντὶ παλαιοτέρων, τοτὲ μὲν διαφερούσας, τοτὲ δ' αὖ καὶ τὰς αὐτὰς ἐπιδίδωσι. (*De Posteritate Caini* 145a)
>
> Wherefore God ever causes His earliest gifts to cease before their recipients are glutted and wax insolent; and storing them up for the future gives others in their stead, and a third supply to replace (ἀντί) the second, and ever new in place of (ἀντί) earlier boons, sometimes different in kind, sometimes the same. (*De Posteritate Caini* 145a)[242]

As is evident in the text, this usage of the preposition adds up to the replacement view since the idea projected in the text is not "accumulation" but clearly "replacement." That is, God dispenses one gift (or blessing) in place of another so as not to spoil men.[243]

At this juncture, it is worthwhile to consider two points, which exegetes bring up in favor of the superabundance of grace view. Despite the apparent indicators, for instance, some commentators point to the general tenor of the entire Gospel and the immediately preceding verses as an important hermeneutical indicator.[244] Yet, the replacement interpretation of vv. 16-17 does not exclude such an insight. The textual exegesis of vv. 16-18 reveals that these texts principally highlight the difference of dispensations. The profusion of the divine grace is logically de-

---

[240] G.H.C. Macgregor, *The Gospel of John* (New York: Harper, 1928), 20; Bruce, *The Gospel of John*, 43, 65, n. 29; Schnackenburg, *The Gospel according to St John*, 1:275-76; Morris, *The Gospel according to John*, 98; Keener, *The Gospel of John*, 1:421.

[241] Ibid., n. 546.

[242] *Philo* trans. F.H. Colson and G.H. Whitaker (Cambridge: Harvard University Press, 1926), 2:412-15. Ruth Edwards translates the passage as follows: "Therefore God, having always held back his first gifts, before those who received them became glutted and insolent, and having husbanded them, distributes others instead of them and a third supply instead of (ἀντί) the second, and continually new gifts instead of (ἀντί) older ones, sometimes different, sometimes the same." Edwards, "Charin anti charitos," 5.

[243] Ibid., 6.

[244] Herman N. Ridderbos, *The Gospel of John: A Theological Commentary* (Grand Rapids: Eerdmans, 1997), 56; Keener, *The Gospel of John*, 1:421.

duced from the shift of these dispensations and particularly from the superlatively rich provision of the new covenant.

In addition to the semantic argument for the accumulation view, some scholars draw attention to the possible Old Testament imagery in the first clause of v. 18: "No one has seen God (Θεὸν οὐδεὶς ἑώρακεν πώποτε)." A.T. Hanson maintains that since Exodus 33:12-34:8 clearly indicates Moses observing Yahweh, it is difficult to postulate that the fourth evangelist is negating such a popular Jewish tradition.[245] Furthermore, John 12:41 also notes the vision of the prophet Isaiah, in which he witnessed the "glory" of Jesus:[246] "Isaiah said this because he saw his glory and spoke about him" (John 12:41, NRSV). Hanson does not mention Abraham's witness which also makes this conjecture more plausible (John 8:56-58).[247] Thus, the idea of witnessing God or, more precisely, the pre-existent Logos is not foreign to John. Consequently, it follows that it was the pre-existent Logos, not Yahweh, that Moses witnessed in the theology of John.[248] In this logic, the latter part of v. 18 explains the first half. Likewise, vv. 16-17 expound on the continuity and abundance of the divine redemptive plan under the Mosaic and the new economies, both through the Logos.

Hanson's interpretation, nonetheless, ignores the wording of John 1:18, which stresses the contrastive nature of God's invisibility and the Son's premier disclosure to human history in the new covenant (this recurring theme of God coming into the world for the first time in this manner is reiterated in vv. 10-11 and 14-15). The accentuation is not on Moses' witness of the pre-existent Christ, which could be secondarily inferred. This text neither directly excludes the possibility of Moses' witnessing the pre-existent Logos in view of the theopha-

---

[245] Hanson, "John 1.14-18 and Exodus 34," 102-04. However, Hofius finds this Logos concept rooted in another part of the Old Testament, Proverbs. Hofius, "'Der in des Vaters Schoss ist,'" 24-32. On the other hand, the possibility of the non Jewish (Hellenistic) influence on the prologue has been explored in Angelika Strotmann, "Relative oder absolute Präexistenz?: Zur Diskussion über die Präexistenz der frühjüdischen Weisheitsgestalt im Kontext von Joh 1,1-18," in *Israel und seine Heilstraditionen im Johannesevangelium: Festgabe für Johannes Beutler SJ zum 70. Geburtstag*, ed. Michael Labahn, Klaus Scholtissek, and Angelika Strotmann (Paderborn: Schöningh, 2004), 91-106; Jutta Leonhardt-Balzer, "Der Logos und die Schöpfung: Streiflichter bei Philo (Op 20-25) und im Johannesprolog (Joh 1,1-18)," in *Kontexte des Johannesevangeliums: Das vierte Evangelium in religions- und traditionsgeschichtlicher Perspektive*, ed. Jörg Frey and Udo Schnelle (Tübingen: Mohr Siebeck, 2004), 295-320.

[246] Catrin H. Williams, "Seeing the Glory: The Reception of Isaiah's Call-Vision in Jn 12.41," in *Judaism, Jewish Identities and the Gospel Tradition: Essays in Honour of Maurice Casey*, ed. James G. Crossley (London: Equinox, 2010), 253-80.

[247] Hanson, "John 1.14-18 and Exodus 34," 86-88. Cf. Pierre Grelot, "Jean 8:56 et Jubilés 16:16-29," *RevQ* 13 (1988): 621-28.

[248] Also Hans Hübner, *Hebräerbrief, Evangelien und Offenbarung, Epilegomena*, vol. 3 of *Biblische Theologie des Neuen Testaments* (Göttingen: Vandenhoeck & Ruprecht, 1995), 158.

nies of Isaiah and Abraham in the Gospel, nor does it positively promote such a notion. Differently put, the point of v. 18 is that, in contrast to the Mosaic dispensation (in which "no one has seen God"), the new salvific economy has made God accessible like never before, thus upholding the close unity between God and the Son and the unique theophany through the latter at the same time. Therefore, it is probably not the primary intention of the evangelist that this text communicates Moses' witness of the pre-existent Logos.[249] Similarly, John 6:46 reiterates the superiority of the new revelation that is based on the direct encounter with Yahweh: "Not that anyone has seen the Father except the one who is from God; he has seen the Father." In this respect, even the possible polemic against Moses (or the Gnostic redeemer figure for the same reason) is relegated onto an ancillary level. William Loader's comment on this text is succinctly illuminating:

> [John] 1,18 discredits all alternative claims to see God. This includes claims made about Moses. But while this may seem to be disparaging of Moses, it stands beside the more positive claim that the Law was given, ἐδόθη, through Moses. . . . Something positive is being said [about the Mosaic covenant] but it is set in contrast with something much greater for which the vocabulary of fullness is used. . . . This gift [given to Moses] from God is now surpassed by a great gift from God.[250]

Summary. In summary, the observations noted so far spell out the positive role of Moses on the one hand. As a representative of the old covenant, he foreshadows the gracious nature of the new salvific plan as unfolded through Christ the Messiah. For this reason, the oversimplistic antithetical understanding of John 1:16-17 fails to take into account this continuity. On the other hand, however, as its superseded status indicates, the common denominator between the two divine economies recedes to the background as the superiority of the new *Heilsgeschichte* is brought to the foreground of the narrative. Standing in the background, Moses still points to the abounding grace and the preeminence of the new divine disclosure. The bread discourse of John 6:32 could serve as a helpful analogy. As Yahweh gave bread to the Israelite ancestors through Moses,

---

[249] Michael Theobald, *Die Fleischwerdung des Logos: Studien zum Verhältnis des Johannesprologs zum Corpus des Evangeliums und zu 1 Joh* (Münster: Aschendorff, 1988), 259-62. Robert takes God's "making him known (ἐξηγήσατο)" as a double meaning of "narrating" and "guiding" of Christ to the Father. René Robert, "La double intention du mot final du prologue johannique," *RThom* 87 (1987): 435-41. Her double entendre interpretation is refuted by de la Potterie who opts for the meaning of the verb solely as "opening up the way." Ignace de la Potterie, "'C'est lui qui a ouvert la voie': La finale du prologue johannique," *Bib* 69 (1988): 340-70. A rejoinder follows. René Robert, "Le mot final du prologue johannique: A propos d'un article recent," *RThom* 89 (1989): 279-88.

[250] William Loader, "Jesus and the Law in John," in *Theology and Christology in the Fourth Gospel: Essays by the Members of the SNTS Johannine Writings Seminar*, ed. Gilbert van Belle, Jan G. van der Watt, and P.J. Maritz (Leuven: Leuven University, 2005), 138.

he now imparts the living bread, Christ, to New Testament believers. Moses' role in the distribution of Manna bears witness to the gracious nature and continuity of the old and new redemptive plans rather than provide a backdrop for messianic typology. Labahn offers a gist of John 1:17 in terms of the relationship between Moses and Jesus as follows:

> John 1:17 is enigmatic in its brevity but it illuminates in its terminology the understanding and conceptions that are found elsewhere in the gospel of John. John 6:32 offers an important analogy. Moses gave Manna to the fathers, but God gave the bread of life, Jesus. As Moses' giving of Manna is a type, a shadow of life-giving, so is Moses' giving of the law a type of giving grace and truth through Jesus. What Moses gives, the law, read over against the historical Jesus, corresponds to the unique witness function of Moses. Moses' giving receives authority as long as his witness is for Jesus.[251]

Although only in an indirect allusion, the witness function of Moses via the law in John 1:16-18 initiates a recurring witness motif followed by that of John the Baptist (v. 15) in the Johannine prologue.[252] To represent Moses in witness terms means a redefinition of the conventional belief in him, i.e., an authority figure. Schapdick's summary statement on the role of Moses is penetrating to the point of this text which highlights the unique place and function of the new redemptive plan through Christ.

> The law is not understood as the divine revelation but as a guide to this revelation. The law is given to Moses to testify to the eschatological divine revelation, Jesus. From there, it (the law) is correctly recognized that the divine gift of grace of the law is not discarded through the truth of Jesus Christ. . . . Its (the law's) soteriological relevance is redefined. It acts as a witness for the salvation in Jesus Christ. A reading of the law without a relation to Christ does not produce any kind of redemption by itself.[253]

Serpent of Moses: John 3:14

> Καὶ καθὼς Μωϋσῆς ὕψωσεν τὸν ὄφιν ἐν τῇ ἐρήμῳ, οὕτως ὑψωθῆναι δεῖ τὸν υἱὸν τοῦ ἀνθρώπου. (John 3:14, NA[28])

> And just as Moses lifted up the serpent in the wilderness, so must the Son of Man be lifted up. (John 3:14, NRSV)

---

[251] Michael Labahn, "Jesus und die Autorität der Schrift im Johannesevangelium: Überlegungen zu einem spannungsreichen Verhältnis," in *Israel und seine Heilstraditionen im Johannessevangelium: Festgabe für Johannes Beutler SJ zum 70. Geburtstag*, ed. Michael Labahn, Klaus Scholtissek, and Angelika Strotmann (Paderborn: Schöningh, 2004), 193.

[252] Martin Hengel, "The Old Testament in the Fourth Gospel," in *The Gospels and the Scriptures of Israel*, ed. Craig A. Evans and W. Richard Stegner (Sheffield: Sheffield, 1994), 387-88. In this light, it makes sense that the Peshitta version supplies the adversative conjunction *dn* between grace and truth in v. 17. Cf. Tjitze Baarda, "John 1,17b: The Origin of a Peshitta Reading," *ETL* 77 (2001): 153-62.

[253] Schapdick describes this redefinition as "the switching of content." Schapdick, "Autorität ohne Inhalt," 186, n. 35.

Context. The present text is located within the pericope of Jesus' conversation with Nicodemus (John 3:1-21). This occasion provides an entry for the first extended discourse into the crucifixion on the part of Jesus. The narrative was prompted by Nicodemus' acknowledgement of Jesus' divinely commissioned nature (v. 2), then it moves onto the "born-again" speech, "the earthly things" (τὰ ἐπίγεια, vv. 3-12).[254] Exegetes have debated over the referents of the "earthly" and "heavenly" things. D.A. Carson convincingly puts out a case for this distinction. Because the new birth takes place on earth, it is the earthly things while the glorification of Jesus occurs in the heavenly realm. In addition, it is natural to take "the earthly things" mentioned in v. 12 as referring back to the previous context (vv. 3-9) which speaks of the new birth (being born again).[255]

At the disbelief of the Jewish teacher Jesus laments because, unless one is born again and/or from above, he has no part in the kingdom of God (v. 3). Furthermore, because of the disbelief or inability to understand "the earthly things," Jesus is somewhat hesitant to divulge his knowledge about "the heavenly things (τὰ ἐπουράνια, v. 12)" so much so that the revelation is given only briefly in two respects. First, he is the only qualified revealer of the heavenly realm because he is the only one who has descended from and ascended to the heaven (v. 13). This fact also implies that he is the only one who has really seen and heard about the "heavenly things" (v. 11). The qualification of Jesus being the only valid witness (vv. 11, 13-14) leads to a glimpse into the "heavenly things." That is, God's intention is to save the world by lifting up his only Son. This "lifting up" relates not only to the crucifixion of Jesus but also to his enthronement in heaven. Even more, this exaltation also involves the judgment of the world:

> Those who believe in him are not condemned; but those who do not believe are condemned already, because they have not believed in the name of the only Son of God. And this is the judgment, that the light has come into the world, and people loved darkness rather than light because their deeds were evil. (John 3:18-19, NRSV)

In John 12:31-32, this aspect of "lifting up" (i.e., crucifixion) is set forth in terms of the judgment of the prince of the world.[256] Therefore, the analogy of Jesus'

---

[254] For a detailed and careful philological examination of this text, see Michael Theobald, *Herrenworte im Johannesevangelium* (Freiburg: Herder, 2002), 201-23.

[255] Carson, *The Gospel according to John*, 199; Schnackenburg, *The Gospel according to St John*, 1:377; Morris, *The Gospel according to John*, 197; Gawlick, "Mose im Johannesevangelium," 33; Köstenberger, *John*, 126; Lincoln, *The Gospel according to Saint John*, 152.

[256] George R. Beasley-Murray, "John 12,31-34: The Eschatological Significance of the Lifting up of the Son of Man," in *Studien zum Text und zur Ethik des Neuen Testaments: Festschrift zum 80. Geburtstag von Heinrich Greeven*, ed. Wolfgang Schrage (Berlin: Walter de Gruyter, 1986), 70-81; idem, "The Lifting up of the Son of Man," in *Gospel of Life: Theology in the Fourth Gospel* (Peabody: Hendrickson, 1991), 50-52; Rick R. Marrs, "John 3:14-15: The Raised Serpent in the Wilderness, the Johannine Use of an Old Testament Account," in *Johannine Studies: Essays in Honor of Frank*

crucifixion to Moses' lifting of a bronze serpent in v. 14 serves two purposes: the qualification of Jesus' witness for "the heavenly things" and his mission to realize the divine redemptive plan, "the heavenly things" (vv. 15-21) in the saving and judgment of the world.[257]

T.F. Glasson. Of the four major typological studies on Moses in John, only T.F. Glasson provides an elaborate typlogical exegesis of this text (*Moses in the Fourth Gospel*, 33-39).[258] He takes notice of some interesting parallels between John 3:14 and the Sinai theophany event in Numbers 21. He does not explicitly maintain that these parallels manifest the Mosaic typology in the section in which the text is discussed. Nonetheless, in view of his remark in the introduction that seeing Jesus as a second Moses is an important hermeneutical key, it seems to be fair to presume that he argues for the presence of a Mosaic messianic typology in the text:

> In recent years increasing attention has been paid to the importance (for the understanding of the New Testament generally) of seeing the Messianic hope in terms of a new Exodus and of recognizing the Messiah as a second Moses. In the following pages it is hoped to show that this approach is one of the keys to the understanding of the Fourth Gospel.[259]

Pack (Malibu: Pepperdine University Press, 1989), 141-47; Jean Zumstein, "L'interprétation johannique de la mort du Christ," in *Four Gospels 1992: Festschrift Frans Neirynck*, ed. Frans van Segbroeck and Christopher M. Tuckett (Louvain: Peeters, 1992), 3:2130; John T. Carroll and Joel B. Green, *The Death of Jesus in Early Christianity* (Peabody: Hendrickson, 1995), 101-03; Christian Dietzfelbinger, "Sühnetod im Johannesevangelium?" in *Evangelium—Schriftauslegung —Kirche: Festschrift für Peter Stuhlmacher zum 65. Geburtstag*, ed. Jostein Ådna, Scott J. Hafemann, and Otfried Hofius (Göttingen: Vandenhoeck & Ruprecht, 1997), 76; Thomas Söding, "Kreuzerhöhung: Zur Deutung des Todes Jesu nach Johannes," *ZTK* 103 (2006): 18-19. This is especially true with John 5:27 in view: Benjamin E. Reynolds, "The Use of the Son of Man Idiom in the Gospel of John," in *"Who Is This Son of Man?": The Latest Scholarship on a Puzzling Expression of the Historical Jesus*, ed. Larry W. Hurtado and Paul L. Owen (London: T & T Clark, 2011), 108-10, 115-16. Cf. "And he has given him authority to execute judgment, because he is the Son of Man." (John 5:27)

[257] The ascension of the "Son of Man" is described in the perfect tense in v. 13 (ἀναβέβηκεν). This tense may indicate a theological reflection of the early church into the first life setting.

[258] The three other studies are Meeks, *the Prophet-King*; Boismard, *Moses or Jesus*; and J. Louis Martyn, *History and Theology in the Fourth Gospel* (Louisville: Westminster/John Knox, 2003). In addition, Duncan Derrett offers also somewhat typological observations related to this text. J. Duncan M. Derrett, "The Bronze Serpent," *EstB* 49 (1991): 322-27. For a possibility of this text sharing a rabbinical hermeneutical tradition, *gezerah shawah*, see, Anne-Françoise Loiseau, "Traditions évangéliques et herméneutique juive: Le serpent d'airain de Jean ne repose-t-il pas sur une guématrie?" *ETL* 83 (2007): 155-63.

[259] Glasson, *Moses in the Fourth Gospel*, 10 (parenthesis original).

As such, his study will be taken into account as a dialogue partner to further an exegetical consideration of this Moses-related text.

Glasson observes a four-fold parallelism that underscores the analogy between Moses and Jesus. First, "looking" is an important theme both in Numbers and John. Although the actual phrase "seeing" or "looking" is lacking in John 3:14 and in its immediate context, the motif emerges in connection with Jesus' crucifixion in John 6:40 and 19:37.[260] Second, "lifting up" is applied both to the brazen serpent and to Jesus. In addition, the fourth evangelist uses the verb for "lifting" as a double *entendre* in reference both to the crucifixion and glorification (i.e., the ascension). In order to substantiate this semantic connection, Loiseau has conducted a lengthy and elaborate examination of the Numbers texts together with other early rabbinic literature. Loiseau traces some Aramaic equivalent usages of this Hebrew word, נֵס (pole, on which the brazen serpent was hung). Pseudo-Jonathan translates this Hebrew term into אל אתר תלי ("on a high place"). The Aramaic word תלי means both "raise" and "hang." Therefore, the first-century Jews familiar with this tradition would have been immediately reminded of Jesus' crucifixion reminiscent of the brazen serpent event recorded in Numbers 21.[261] Third, the term "lift up (ὑψόω)" in John 3:14 can be associated with the word "standard" (נֵס) in Numbers 21:8:

וַיֹּאמֶר יְהוָה אֶל־מֹשֶׁה עֲשֵׂה לְךָ שָׂרָף וְשִׂים אֹתוֹ עַל־נֵס: (Num 21:8a, BHS⁵)

καὶ εἶπεν κύριος πρὸς Μωυσῆν Ποίησον σεαυτῷ ὄφιν καὶ θὲς αὐτὸν ἐπὶ σημείου. (Num 21:8a, LXX)

Then the LORD said to Moses, "Make a fiery *serpent*, and set it on a standard (נֵס)." (Num 21:8a, NASB)

This correlation is also attested to in some passages of Isaiah, in which the expression "lifted up [נשׂא]" is repeatedly linked with a standard [נֵס]" (cf. Isa 5:26, 11:12, 13:2, 18:3, 62:10).[262] Therefore, although the Hebrew text of Numbers does not contain the word "lift up (נשׂא)," the readers of John familiar with the Hebrew tradition must have been reminded of the close connection between the word "lift up (נשׂא)" and the "standard or banner (נֵס)."[263] Finally, the Greek text of Numbers 21:8 refers to the bronze serpent as "σημεῖον," a "banner." However, Glasson suggests that σημεῖον in the Greek Old Testament could have evoked the Johannine miracle language. That is, that Jesus hung upon the cross is both a banner under which all believers should rally around, and a sign, in the sense of

---

[260] Glasson, *Moses in the Fourth Gospel*, 34-35. Also, Derrett, "The Bronze Serpent," 322-23; Söding, "Kreuzerhöhung," 14-15.

[261] Glasson, *Moses in the Fourth Gospel*, 35. Also, G. Lüdemann, "ὑψόω," *EDNT*, 3:410; Loiseau, "Traditions évangéliques et herméneutique juive," 155-56 ; Michèle Morgen, "Le Fils de l'homme élevé en vue de la vie éternelle (Jn 3, 14-15 éclairé par diverses traditions juives)," *RevScRel* 68 (1994): 12.

[262] Glasson, *Moses in the Fourth Gospel*, 36.

[263] Ibid., 36-37.

miracle or wonder, by which a believer reaches a saving knowledge.²⁶⁴

Critique of Glasson. In response to Glasson, a rejection of a Mosaic typology in the present text is necessary for several reasons. First, the connection between John and Numbers via the "seeing" motif is not as explicit as Glasson suggests. Although the following "belief" language (vv. 15-18) might logically require "looking at" Jesus as a prerequisite step of faith, the emphasis of the present Johannine context is on God and Jesus, and not on a believer's regeneration or the necessary procedure for securing salvation. As briefly discussed above, the gist of John 3:1-21, and especially vv. 12-21, is about "the heavenly things (τὰ ἐπουράνια)." The heavenly affairs, i.e., salvation history, are revealed in human history through the "lifting up" (the crucifixion and the exaltation) of the son of man. The "seeing" motif remains only as a peripheral aspect in this new *Heilsgeschichte*.

Second, the association of "lifting up" with "banner" and "sign" could be problematic for two reasons. For one, those two Hebrew words are not semantically related even in their wider contextual usages.²⁶⁵ In addition, reading "lifting up" as a banner, which calls for all believers to gather around according to Hanson, seems to be imposing one's preconception upon this text. Such an interpretation certainly is not impossible, but it sounds like an excessive reading into the text.

Third, the mention of Jesus being the only one to journey back from and forth to heaven excludes a Mosaic typology. In contrast to somewhat widespread Jewish beliefs (this tradition was discussed above on the Assumption of Moses, the Exagoge of Ezekiel, and Philo), John unmistakably denies the possibility of Moses' ascension to heaven. Thus, he is counted out from the rank analogous to Jesus; Moses is no peer of Christ.²⁶⁶

Finally and most importantly, the role of Moses played out in the texts of John and Numbers does not demand a typological reading. In both John and Numbers,

---

²⁶⁴ Glasson, *Moses in the Fourth Gospel*, 38.

²⁶⁵ Elmer A. Martens, "נס," *NIDOTTE*, 3:110-11; Victor Hamilton, "נשׂא," *NIDOTTE*, 3:160-63.

²⁶⁶ For reviews of early Jewish beliefs on the ascension of Moses, see Meeks, *The Prophet-King*, 205-11; Peder Borgen, "The Son of Man Saying in John 3.13-14," in *Logos was the True Light and Other Essays on the Gospel of John* (Trondheim: Tapir, 1983), 133-48; Andreu Grau, "Les ascension en la literature intertestamentària," *ScrBi* 11 (2011): 101-12. A sociological reading of the exclusiveness of Jesus' ascension suggests a polemic against docetism (since the cross event is rooted in a concrete historical event). This point, aside from being a mirror reading, is hardly pertinent to the present discussion but noted here. Jörg Frey, "'Wie Mose die Schlange in der Wüste erhöht hat . . .': Zur frühjüdischen Deutung der Schlange und ihrer christologischen Rezeption in Joh 3,14f," in *Schriftauslegung im antiken Judentum und im Urchristentum*, ed. Martin Hengel and Hermut Löhr (Tübingen: Mohr Siebeck, 1994), 202.

Moses participates in the divine redemptive program as a mere facilitator (with God being the active agent), whereas Jesus is the object or the content of the salvation history in John. In Numbers, Moses was merely to comply with the divine commandment to lift up the brazen serpent which is actually a type of Jesus in the Johannine text.[267] Execept for Jesus, no one ascended into heaven on his own. Enoch, Moses, and Elijah were taken up by God, and not on their own.[268] Therefore, Jesus is not a second Moses although there are elements of typology in the salvation history unfolded in this Johannine narrative.

> There is no Moses typlogy in John 3:14ff. . . . Christ is not characterized as a second Moses in John 3:14ff, especially, this is in conflict with John 3:13. The reason is that there is a polemical undertone stricken in the passage, exept for the Son of Man there is no one who ascended into the heaven. In relation to Moses in particular, however, there was a widespread belief in early Judaism (that Moses ascended into heaven). Thus, the typological correspondence between Moses and Christ set aside, the deeds of Moses, which are completed in godly order, typologically prefigure the Christological salvific events. . . . John explicitly distinguishes Moses from Jesus through the Sophia-and-logos theology.[269]

Furthermore, the redemption brought forth through Moses was only provisional, while that of Jesus takes on an eternal consequence (John 3:15-16). The active agent of salvation history remains the same, but the gift is drastically changed.[270] Such a stark contrast and the different roles played out by Jesus and Moses in this analogical examination exclude the possibility of Moses becoming a messianic prefiguration.

Summary. The foregoing observations reveal the fourth evangelist's unique understanding of Moses not in terms of a messianic prefiguration but as a mere facilitator and spectator of the divine redemptive program.[271] The salvation history of which he was a part bears witness to the gracious and supernatural nature of "the heavenly things." Nevertheless, the contrast is so stark between the old and new *Heilsgeschichten* that a typology between the two is hardly appropriate. At this juncture, Meek's estimation of the text under review is on target.

---

[267] Söding, "Kreuzerhöhung," 14.

[268] Günter Reim, *Jochanan: Erweiterte Studien zum alttestamentlichen Hintergrund des Johannesevangeliums* (Erlangen: Der Ev.-Luth. Mission, 1995), 135; Gawlick, "Mose im Johannesevangelium," 33; Wengst, *Das Johannesevangelium*, 1:135; Schapdick, "Autorität ohne Inhalt," 188.

[269] Sänger, "'Von mir hat er geschrieben' (Joh 5,46)," 126-27.

[270] Dietzfelbinger, *Das Evangelium nach Johannes*, 1:290; Schapdick, "Autorität ohne Inhalt," 188-89.

[271] Andreas Lindemann, "Mose und Jesus Christus: Zum Verständnis des Gesetzes im Johannesevangelium," in *Das Urchristentum in seiner literarischen Geschichte: Festschrift für Jürgen Becker zum 65. Geburtstag*, ed. Ulrich Mell and Ulrich B. Müller (Berlin: Walter de Gruyter, 1999), 314.

The most striking aspect of the Johannine description of Jesus' ascension, however, is paralleled neither in the Gnostic myths nor in the Moses legends. This is the central paradox that Jesus' "being lifted up," his "glorification," takes place in and through his death on the cross. . . . The Johannine paradox is the exclusive product of Christian interpretation of the passion tradition. Comparison of the legends of Moses' ascension with the Johannine theme of the exaltation of the Son of Man thus leads to negative results. The notion of Jesus' paradoxical enthronement is not dependent on the Moses traditions for its fundamental structure.[272]

Witness and Accusation of Moses: John 1:45, 5:37-39, 45-46

εὑρίσκει Φίλιππος τὸν Ναθαναὴλ καὶ λέγει αὐτῷ· ὃν ἔγραψεν Μωϋσῆς ἐν τῷ νόμῳ καὶ οἱ προφῆται εὑρήκαμεν, Ἰησοῦν υἱὸν τοῦ Ἰωσὴφ τὸν ἀπὸ Ναζαρέτ. (John 1:45, NA[28])

Philip found Nathanael and said to him, "We have found him about whom Moses in the law and also the prophets wrote, Jesus son of Joseph from Nazareth." (John 1:45, NRSV)

[37] καὶ ὁ πέμψας με πατὴρ ἐκεῖνος μεμαρτύρηκεν περὶ ἐμοῦ. οὔτε φωνὴν αὐτοῦ πώποτε ἀκηκόατε οὔτε εἶδος αὐτοῦ ἑωράκατε, [38] καὶ τὸν λόγον αὐτοῦ οὐκ ἔχετε ἐν ὑμῖν μένοντα, ὅτι ὃν ἀπέστειλεν ἐκεῖνος, τούτῳ ὑμεῖς οὐ πιστεύετε. [39] ἐραυνᾶτε τὰς γραφάς, ὅτι ὑμεῖς δοκεῖτε ἐν αὐταῖς ζωὴν αἰώνιον ἔχειν· καὶ ἐκεῖναί εἰσιν αἱ μαρτυροῦσαι περὶ ἐμοῦ . . . [45] Μὴ δοκεῖτε ὅτι ἐγὼ κατηγορήσω ὑμῶν πρὸς τὸν πατέρα· ἔστιν ὁ κατηγορῶν ὑμῶν Μωϋσῆς, εἰς ὃν ὑμεῖς ἠλπίκατε. [46] εἰ γὰρ ἐπιστεύετε Μωϋσεῖ, ἐπιστεύετε ἂν ἐμοί· περὶ γὰρ ἐμοῦ ἐκεῖνος ἔγραψεν. (John 5:37-39, 45-46, NA[28])

[37] And the Father who sent me has himself testified on my behalf. You have never heard his voice or seen his form, [38] and you do not have his word abiding in you, because you do not believe him whom he has sent. [39] You search the scriptures because you think that in them you have eternal life; and it is they that testify on my behalf . . . [45] Do not think that I will accuse you before the Father; your accuser is Moses, on whom you have set your hope. [46] If you believed Moses, you would believe me, for he wrote about me. (John 5:37-39, 45-46, NRSV)

A number of Johannine exegetes recognize the key role of the present text (John 5:39-46) for John's hermeneutics of the Scripture. They variously call this text a "Schlüsseltext" or "Kompendium."[273] Furthermore, a small number of scholars recognize even the prominence of "correspondence between Moses and Jesus" in this text.[274] For instance, the systematic defiance of Israelites and the Jews and the redemptive acts of Moses and Jesus are noted as providing points of con-

---

[272] Meeks, *The Prophet-King*, 297.
[273] "Schlüsseltext" for the understanding of the Johannine hermeneutics. Obermann, *Die christologische Erfüllung der Schrift im Johannesevangelium*, 371; Wolfgang Kraus, "Johannes und das Alte Testament: Überlegungen zum Umgang mit der Schrift im Johannesevangelium im Horizont Biblischer Theologie," *ZNW* 88 (1997): 4. "Kompendium" of the Johannine hermeneutics of the Scripture. Scholtissek, "'Die unauflösbare Schrift' (Joh 10,35)," 167.
[274] Klappert, "'Mose hat von mir geschrieben,'" 619-40; Scholtissek, "'Die unauflösbare Schrift' (Joh 10,35)," 146-77.

tact.[275] In contrast, a greater number of exegetes find the witness function more prominent for "scripture" and Moses. With these divergent opinions in view, this section will seek to ascertain the narrative function of Moses in relation to Christology in this controversy narrative.

Controversial context. John 5:31-47 is located after the healing account of the lame man (5:1-9).[276] Since the healing ministry took place on the Sabbath, certain Jews leveled criticism against Jesus in the temple (5:10-18).[277] In response to their charge, Jesus states the grounds for the legitimacy of his work on the Sabbath. That is, Jesus is equal to God, as most conspicuously attested to in his authority over life and death (5:19-29).[278] Therefore, he stands above the Sabbath rule and is exempt from its directives:[279]

> But Jesus answered them, "my Father is still working, and I also am working." For this reason the Jews were seeking all the more to kill him, because he was not only breaking the sabbath, but was also calling God his own Father, thereby making himself equal to God. Jesus said to them, "very truly, I tell you, the Son can do nothing on his

---

[275] Klappert, "'Mose hat von mir geschrieben,'" 621-22.

[276] For overviews on Jesus' healing account at Bethesda in John 5, see R. Alan Culpepper, "Un exemple de commentaire fondé sur la critique narrative: Jean 5,1-18," in *La Communauté johannique et son histoire: La trajectoire de l'evangile de Jean aux deux premiers siècles*, ed. Jean-Daniel Kaestli, Poffet Jean-Michel, and Jean Zumstein, (Geneva: Labor et Fides, 1990), 135-51; Andreas Dettwiler, "Umstrittene Ethik: Überlegungen zu Joh 15,1-17," in *Johannes-Studien: Interdisziplinäre Zugänge zum Johannes-Evangelium, Freundesgabe der Theologischen Fakultät der Universität Neuchâtel für Jean Zumstein*, ed. Martin Rose (Zurich: Theologischer, 1991), 175-89; Michael Labahn, "Eine Spurensuche anhand von Joh 5.1-18: Bemerkungen zu Wachstum und Wandel der Heilung eines Lahmen," *NTS* 44 (1998): 159-79; Rainer Metzner, "Der Geheilte von Johannes 5: Repräsentant des Unglaubens," *ZNW* 90 (1999): 177-93; Steven M. Bryan, "Power in the Pool: The Healing of the Man at Bethesda and Jesus' Violation of the Sabbath (Jn. 5:1-18)," *TynBul* 54 (2003): 7-22; Christian Cebulj, "Texte, Teiche, Theorien: Zum Stellenwert archäologischer Befunde für die Exegese von Joh 5," in *Texte–Fakten–Artefakte: Beiträge zur Bedeutung der Archäologie für die neutestamentliche Forschung*, ed. Max Küchler and Karl M. Schmidt (Göttingen: Vandenhoeck & Ruprecht, 2006), 143-59; Urban C. von Wahlde, "The Pool(s) of Bethesda and the Healing in John 5: A Reappraisal of Research and of the Johannine Text," *RB* 116 (2009): 111-36; Esther Straub, "Alles ist durch ihn geworden: Die Erschaffung des Lebens in der Sabbatheilung Joh 5,1-18," in *Studien zu Matthäus und Johannes: Festschrift für Jean Zumstein zu seinem 65. Geburtstag*, ed. Andreas Dettwiler and Uta Poplutz (Zürich: Theologischer, 2009), 157-67.

[277] For various suggestions on the nature of this Sabbath controversy, see Jörg Augenstein, "Jesus und das Gesetz im Johannesevangelium," *KuI* 14 (1999): 166-67, 177, esp. n. 46.

[278] Michael Mees, "Jesu Selbstzeugnis nach Joh 5,19-30 in frühchristlicher Sicht," *ETL* 62 (1986): 102-17.

[279] Raimo Hakola, *Identity Matters: John, the Jews and Jewishness*, NovTSup 118 (Leiden: Brill, 2005), 113-29.

own, but only what he sees the Father doing; for whatever the Father does, the Son does likewise." (John 5:17-19, NRSV)

"Indeed, just as the Father raises the dead and gives them life, so also the Son gives life to whomever he wishes." (John 5:21, NRSV)

"So that all may honor the Son just as they honor the Father. Anyone who does not honor the Son does not honor the Father who sent him." (John 5:23, NRSV)

Moreover, Jesus appeals to a series of four witnesses in defense of his mission, which includes his healing ministry (5:31-38). The first witness is John the Baptist, but his witness is partial and incomplete. The second witness is God the Father, who provides a witness of the ultimate credential. Jesus does not need a witness from men such as John the Baptist, but his witness was given in order for the benefit of Jesus' audience, his antagonists in particular:

Not that I accept such human testimony, but I say these things so that you may be saved . . . I do not accept glory from human beings. (John 5:34, 41, NRSV)

The witness of these third party individuals justifies the identity and mission of Christ. In contrast to the common belief among the Jews who held Moses to be authoritative and the source of information for life, this Jewish protagonist functions only to bear witness in favor of Jesus.[280] Ironically, this witness function of Moses, in turn, indicts the Jews for their unwillingness to accept the God-commissioned purpose of his writings, the witness function of the scriptures (5:39-47).

A series of witnesses. Contrary to their perception, "the Jews" (5:10, 16, 18) do not enjoy an intimate communion with Yahweh. These Jewish opponents repeatedly rest on recourse to their lineage to Abraham and Moses, implying their privileged position to possess the divine revelation and subsequently the close association with Yahweh through their ancestors of faith:

Then they reviled him, saying, "you are his disciple, but we are disciples of Moses. We know that God has spoken to Moses, but as for this man, we do not know where he comes from." (John 9:28-29, NRSV)[281]

On the contrary, John articulates the outworking of the salvific event (which is variously described as possessing eternal life, and the indwelling of or believing in the Word incarnate) exclusively in terms of Christ. This unique and definitive standing of Jesus is further corroborated through a series of four witnesses in John 5: John the Baptist (vv. 33-35), Jesus (v. 36, 10:25), God the Father (vv.

---

[280] Wolfgang Kraus, "Die Vollendung der Schrift nach Joh 19,28: Überlegungen zum Umgang mit der Schrift im Johannesevangelium," in *The Scriptures in the Gospels*, ed. Christopher M. Tuckett (Leuven: Leuven University Press, 1997), 629; Augenstein, "Jesus und das Gesetz im Johannesevangelium," 170; Schnelle, *Das Evangelium nach Johannes*, 113.

[281] For Abraham, see 8:33, 39, 53.

37-39a), and "the scripture and Moses" (vv. 39b-47).[282] Particularly pertinent to the present chapter is v. 46, where Moses is recognized as the author of "scripture" and is also called in as a witness for Christ.[283] Structurally, the witnesses of Jesus and God are bracketed by the witnesses of the Baptist and Moses. However, the witnesses of God and Jesus are greater than those of John the Baptist and Moses (vv. 36, 39).

Table 10. Four witnesses on behalf of Christ's mission and identity

| John the Baptist (vv. 33-35) |
| Jesus (v. 36) |
| God (vv. 37-39a) |
| The scripture and Moses (vv. 39b-47) |

An allusion to the Sinai account. A large number of exegetes recognize the presence of an allusion to Moses in vv. 37-38, especially in his encounter with Yahweh on Mount Sinai (i.e., Exod 19:9, 33:12-34:35, Num 7:89, 23:6-8, Deut 5):

> And the Father who sent me has himself testified on my behalf. You have never heard his voice or seen his form, and you do not have his word abiding in you, because you do not believe him whom he has sent. (John 5:37-38, NRSV)

This allusion implies a typology between Moses and Jesus. Just like the Israelites in the wilderness, the Jews do not experience God because of their disregard to the divine messenger, Jesus. As such, John 5:37-38 insists readers on accepting Jesus just as the Israelites should have received Moses wholeheartedly. Those who are sympathetic with this typological reading refer to the Pentateuchal accounts of Moses and Deuteronomy 18:15-18, in particular, as the conceptual background of this controversy narrative between Jesus and the Jews over the standing of Moses. Under this circumstance, the readers of John who were familiar with the expectation of a Mosaic prophet would have immediately perceived Jesus as an eschatological figure like Moses, these exegetes assert.

Klaus Scholtissek and the majority view. Scholtissek is one of those who explain the present text in line of this logic. Unless one receives the divine messenger, the searching of the scriptures does not bear the fruit of life it promises, according to Scholtissek.[284] Accordingly, belief in Jesus is crucial because it leads to the immanence of the word of God.[285] This view takes the

---

[282] Scholtissek, "'Die unauflösbare Schrift' (Joh 10,35)," 167-68.
[283] Schapdick, "Autorität ohne Inhalt," 190.
[284] Scholtissek, "'Die unauflösbare Schrift' (Joh 10,35)," 168.
[285] Ibid.

conjunction ὅτι in v. 38 as causal:

ὅτι ὃν ἀπέστειλεν ἐκεῖνος, τούτῳ ὑμεῖς οὐ πιστεύετε. (John 5:38b, NA²⁸)[286]

Thus, vv. 37-38 can be paraphrased as follows:

> Because you do not believe in me (Jesus), as a result, you have not seen or heard God and his word is not abiding in you just like the Israelites in the wilderness had not experienced Yahweh.

An alternative interpretation (the majority view) of this passage in light of the Sinai allusion understands John 5:38b as an explanation for John 5:37b-38a. That is, not experiencing God (which is basically the miscomprehension of the Scripture) explains the Jewish rejection of the divine messenger. This view takes the ὅτι clause as explanatory. As for Carson, this assessment is not subject to debate:[287]

> In the last clause of v. 38, *for you do not believe the one he sent*, the conjunction "for" should therefore be taken as introducing the conclusive evidence in support of the triple indictment, rather than as the cause of the spiritual and moral failure of Jesus' interlocutors.[288]

Thus, the witness of God in the scriptures explains the Jews' rejection of Jesus.

Nevertheless, both views do not adequately take into account the important semantic difference of the terminologies, "word (λόγος, v. 38)" and "scriptures (γραφαί, v. 39)." The Fourth Gospel reserves the Greek word γραφή, exclusively for the Hebrew Old Testament and the Septuagint.[289] On the other hand, λόγος takes on a special meaning. In the prologue, λόγος means "the presence of God in the person of Jesus, not the divine activity in the words of Jesus."[290] In the immediate contexts, the λόγος of Jesus is also closely juxtaposed with "life." The "hearing of λόγος" results in life (5:24). Its semantic cognate, ῥήματά of Jesus are

---

[286] Scholtissek, "'Die unauflösbare Schrift' (Joh 10,35), 168-69.

[287] Both causal and explanatory senses are grammatically possible. Barrett, *The Gospel according to St. John*, 267. The causal use of the ὅτι-clause clearly occurs six times in John (8:45, 15:19, 16:6, 19:42, 20:29). Morris, *The Gospel according to John*, 147, n. 116.

[288] Carson, *The Gospel according to John*, 263. This view is also found in the following: Edwin Hoskyns, *The Fourth Gospel* (London: Faber, 1947), 273; Bultmann, *The Gospel of John*, 266; Johannes Beutler, *Martyria: Traditionsgeschichtliche Untersuchungen zum Zeugnisthema bei Johannes* (Frankfurt: Josef Knecht, 1972), 260-62; Schlatter, *Der Evangelist Johannes*, 157; Meeks, *The Prophet-King*, 300; Morris, *The Gospel according to John*, 291; Borchert, *John 1-11*, 245; Beasley-Murray, *John*, 78; Schnelle, *Das Evangelium nach Johannes*, 112; Köstenberger, *John*, 192-93; Hakola, *Identity Matters*, 149-54, Michaels, *The Gospel of John*, 330.

[289] Wolfgang J. Bittner, *Jesu Zeichen im Johannesevangelium: Die Messias-Erkenntnis im Johannesevangelium vor ihrem jüdischen Hintergrund* (Tübingen: Mohr Siebeck, 1987), 242; Augenstein, "Jesus und das Gesetz im Johannesevangelium," 163.

[290] B. Klappert, "Word," *NIDNTT*, 3:1117.

the spirit and life (6:63). Λόγος and ῥήματά are usually reserved for the word of Jesus (or God), and never used in reference to the writings of Moses (the prologue, 4:41, 50, 6:59-61, 7:40, 10:19). In addition, an important Johannine motif, the internalization of Jesus which is equal to the direct encounter with God or the divine immanence, pervades in the prologue and the rest of the Gospel (1:1-18, 7:37-39, 10:38, 14:9-11, 20, 17:21-23).[291] These two observations suggest that "word (λόγος)" in v. 38 should be understood differently from "scriptures (γραφαί)" in v. 39. Λόγος and γραφή are two entirely different entities.[292] Therein lies the exegetical oversight of a number of Johannine commentators and Scholtissek, as they uncritically equate the two phrases. Jesus, the Word incarnate, is more than the passage to "life." In effect, he is the life (5:26, 6:35, 63, 11:25, 14:6).

In addition to this semantic observation, the Gospel's recurrent emphasis on the superlative revelatory exposure through Jesus mitigates the Sinai allusion view (in addition to the prologue 1:18, also 6:46, "no one has seen the Father except the one who is from God; only he has seen the Father"). The point of vv. 37-38 underscores the witness of God, that which becomes evident in the life of contemporary New Testament believers through the unprecedented indwelling of the "word (λόγος)" of God. Neither this text (5:37-38) nor a wider context emphasizes the witness of the scripture or an allusion to Moses' encounter with Yahweh. This notion also stands in accordance with the tenor of the bread of life discourse in ch. 6 (see the following discussion in the next section).[293] One who rejects Jesus does not enjoy the union with God. *Vice versa*, that immanence through His Son is a witness to God. This "greater witness (τὴν μαρτυρίαν μείζω, v. 36)" theme continues on in v. 39 forward. God's immanent presence is not to be found in "scripture," which only functions to direct to that end (5:39, 6:45). In this way, the scriptures (γραφαί) and Moses bear witness to the coming messiah (John 1:45, 5:46). This way of understanding the role of Moses through his writings is the only valid interpretation of scripture (γραφή). Differently put, a non-Christological hermeneutics of scripture is deficient.[294] It is not in certain passages, but collectively, that the Mosaic writings (γραφαί) point forward to the incomparable messiah, the only *true* way through which God reveals himself completely. In this regard, just like that of John the Baptist, the witness of Moses

---

[291] A distinct Johannine theme is the immant presence of God the Father through His royal Son. Joachim Kügler, "'Meine Königsherrschaft ist nicht von dieser Welt!' (Joh 18,36): Zur Veränderung der Gottesreich-Botschaft im Johannesevangelium," *BK* 62 (2007): 94-97.

[292] C.H. Dodd, *The Interpretation of the Fourth Gospel* (Cambridge: CUP, 1954), 266-67.

[293] J.H.A. Bernard, *Critical and Exegetical Commentary on the Gospel according to St. John* (Edinburgh: T. & T. Clark, 1928), 1: 250-51; Dodd, *The Interpretation of the Fourth Gospel*, 330; Brown, *The Gospel according to John*, 1:227; Barrett, *The Gospel according to St. John*, 266-67.

[294] Obermann, *Die christologische Erfüllung der Schrift im Johannesevangelium*, 61; Schapdick, "Autorität ohne Inhalt," 191.

through his writings (γραφαί, "scriptures") is inferior to the immanent witness of God the Father that comes to men through the indwelling of the Word incarnate in the hearts of believers. As such, there is authority in Moses and in his scripture, but it stands as far as it bears witness to Christ.

Bertold Klappert. Klappert also offers an elaborate exegesis of the present text under discussion along a similar logic as that of Scholtissek. First, the point of departure for his investigation is the miracles and signs of Jesus that invoke the "signs and wonders" performed by Moses as recorded in the exodus accounts. For the Gospel of John, it is a significant indicator that the narrative concerning the healing of the lame man precedes the testimony of Moses in John 5:46-47. The importance of the healing narrative is due to the fact that the account evokes the wonder-working image of Moses. In addition, the feeding of the five-thousand and the bread of life discourses following John 5:46-47 ("the testimony of Moses") reinforce the allusion to Moses, especially the Manna accounts of Exodus. These parallels constitute a Moses-Jesus typology, which is anticipated in Deuteronomy 18:15-18 and confirmed in John 5 and 6.[295]

Second, the miracle accounts of Exodus invite Israelites to believe in Yahweh and in his servant, Moses. Likewise, the Johannine counterparts of the Mosaic miracle accounts (i.e., the signs of Jesus) are reminiscent of the Yahweh experience in the wilderness, and they promote faith in the Johannine divine messenger, Jesus. The faith in Jesus corresponds to the faith in Moses, who is Jesus' eschatological counterpart. As a corollary, not seeing the correspondence between Moses and Jesus is to misunderstand the point of Deuteronomy 18:15-18, the transgression with which Jesus charges the Jews in John 5:46: "if you believed Moses, you would believe me, for he wrote about me."[296] Scholtissek concurs on this point:

> [John] 5:39 speaks of the "opinion of eternal life" in the scriptures. Jesus affirmed this belief by pointing to the testimony of these scriptures just for him and for the indignation of his hearers to come to him (5:39-40): "to have life" is only possible Christologically. The men's search for life (cf. 5:39, 44; 6:24-26), which is, of course, directed to the scriptures, finds its fulfillment only through faith in Jesus, of whom the unfailing Scripture testifies (10:35). Therefore, a critical development for the Johannine biblical theology takes place: The aim of studying the scriptures is "to find the eternal life in him" (5:39; see 1:45, 48). It is also fulfilled only when it is recognized that these scriptures witness for the Son's witness, because only the Father and the Son have "the (eternal) life" in themselves (5:26; cf. 1:4, 5:24, 42). Location and mediator of the "abundant life" (10:10) is Jesus alone, of whom the witness of the scriptures point to (cf. 5:45-47).[297]

---

[295] Klappert, "'Mose hat von mir geschrieben,'" 633-35.
[296] Ibid., 633-37.
[297] Klaus Scholtissek, "Die Brotrede Jesu in Joh 6,1-71: Exegetische Beobachtungen zu ihrem johanneischen Profil," *ZKT* 123 (2001): 39. Parentheses are added for clarification.

Klappert's exegesis of the text is fascinating. Nevertheless, this interpretation results from a gross oversight of the point of the entire Gospel, that is, to proclaim the exclusive and supreme revelatory value of Jesus Christ, the only way through whom the redemption that Jews long hoped for has been finally consummated. The reason for Moses' indictment of the Jews is because they set their hope in a wrong person who metonymically represents the Old Testament and who is supposed to merely point forward to the coming messiah. This indictment of Moses stands in stark contrast to the common Jewish belief; namely, he is their defender.[298] In other words, the guilt of the Jews was more fundamental in nature, that is, they were headed in a wrong direction for "life," not that they were miscomprehending the typological correspondence between Moses and his anti-type. John 5:39 implies that "life" is not to be found in the "scriptures":

> You search the scriptures because you think that in them you have eternal life; and it is they that testify on my behalf. (John 5:39, NRSV)

Furthermore and most importantly, the general tenor of John toward Jesus is that he is far superior to Moses. He is above the Sabbath rule, which was passed down to Jews through Moses (5:1-19, 7:18-24). Moses was not able to provide Manna even for provisional satisfaction (it was Yahweh who provided), but Jesus himself is the bread of life that sustains believers forever (6:1-59). This far-reaching superiority of Christ negates, or at least relegates, the possible typology to a secondary level. The amiable motive for inter-religious dialogue, rather than careful exegesis, seems to be a driving force behind the studies of Scholtissek and Klappert with the result that it seriously distorts a plain reading of the texts.

Marie-Émile Boismard. Finally, another noteworthy study that presents the Johannine Jesus in terms of a Mosaic typology is that of Boismard. He detects such a typology from the conversation between Philip and Nathanael. His view is unfolded in four steps.[299] First, the phrase, "Moses wrote about in the Law and . . . the prophets also wrote," in John 1:45 is an idiosyncratic expression, nowhere else to be found but here within the entire scope of the New Testament writings.

---

[298] Meeks, *The Prophet-King*, 118, 137, 159-61, 174, 200-04. He refers to Philo, Josephus, *As. Mos.*, Pseudo-Philo, Qumran, and rabbinic midrash. Kotila wishes to separate Moses from this text, arguing that the reference to Moses is not to him in person but to the Scripture in its judgment over the Old Testament Israelites. Kotila, *Umstrittener Zeuge*, 26-28. However, his argument loses sight of the future tense of the indictment. The wording of John 5:45-47 is such that it is not Jesus but Moses who shall *accuse* Jews. Carson, *The Gospel according to John*, 265-66; William Loader, *Jesus' Attitude towards the Law: A Study of the Gospels* (Tübingen: Mohr Siebeck, 1997), 463, n. 65.

[299] A thorough and wholly sympathetic review of Boismard is available: Gérard Rochais, "A propos d'un livre de M.-É. Boismard, sur la christologie johannique," *ScEs* 46 (1994): 229-36.

As such, the expression should not be taken as a conventional euphemism for the whole of the Old Testament, but as a reference to the specific scope of the Mosaic writings, namely, the Pentateuch. Second, various reasons suggest that the particular text in mind is Deuteronomy 18:18 for this phraseology. Third, and more specifically, one can detect the evangelist's strong recourse to the Samaritan tradition in the two disciples' recognition of Jesus as a descendant of Joseph the patriarch (not Jesus' legal father) and the King of Israel (i.e., Moses). These two figures were supposed to have enjoyed the highest esteem among the Samaritans in the time of Jesus. From these three steps, Boismard reaches his final conclusion that Jesus is king in imitation of the patriarch Joseph.[300]

Regardless of the painstaking exegetical labor, Boismard's study raises a number of questions. First, it is unclear whether Jesus is associated with Joseph the son of Jacob. The text articulates the provenance of Jesus as "Son of Joseph who is from Nazareth" (Ἰησοῦν υἱὸν τοῦ Ἰωσὴφ τὸν ἀπὸ Ναζαρέτ, 1:45). The juxtaposition of Joseph with Nazareth probably indicates his family and hometown. Elsewhere in the Gospel (6:42), the phrase "son of Joseph" clearly refers to his father, not the patriarch. In the next verse, Nathanael does not take note of Jesus' supposed connection with the patriarch but only of his geographic origin (Nazareth). Both biographical and geographical provenances of Jesus do not appear to impress Nathanael.

Highly puzzling, however, is Nathanael's confession in v. 49, in which Jesus is called "Son of God" (ὁ υἱὸς τοῦ θεοῦ) and "King of Israel" (βασιλεὺς εἶ τοῦ Ἰσραήλ). In the pericope of John 1:35-51 where Jesus calls disciples, his identity is revealed with four different epithets: "rabbi" (v. 38), "Son of God" (ὁ υἱὸς τοῦ θεοῦ) and "King of Israel" (βασιλεὺς εἶ τοῦ Ἰσραήλ) in the mouth of Nathanael (v. 49), and "Son of Man" (v. 51). Langner suggests that these four titles here proleptically function to summarize the upcoming mission and life of Jesus. That is, as a rabbi Jesus provides his teachings; as "Son of God" he was condemned; as King crucified; and as "Son of Man" he was resurrected.[301] As neatly as it sounds, nonetheless, his interpretation seems to be without much textual support. In particular, it is uncertain whether Jesus was resurrected as "Son of Man" because the exact meaning of this epithet is difficulty to define.

More puzzling than the four-fold progression of Jesus' identity is the sequential location of Nathanael's confession within the Gospel, since it appears to be too mature a confession to be placed at such an early stage of the Gospel. Four interpretations, in particular, have been proposed to solve this issue. First, this

---

[300] Boismard, *Moses or Jesus*, 23-41. Another study that associates the Johannine Jesus with Joseph the patriarch is Joachim Kügler, "Der König als Brotspender: Religionsgeschichtliche Überlegungen zu JosAs 4,7; 25,5 und Joh 6,15," *ZNW* 89 (1998): 118-24.

[301] Cordula Langner, "Was für ein König ist Jesus?" in *Israel und seine Heilstraditionen im Johannesevangelium: Festgabe für Johannes Beutler SJ zum 70. Geburtstag*, ed. Michael Labahn, Klaus Scholtissek, and Angelika Strotmann (Paderborn: Ferdinand Schöningh, 2004), 250.

confession is polemically directed at the unbelieving Jews. Therefore, it must be read retrospectively from the end to the beginning of the Gospel (as such, the confession is a redactional insertion).[302] Alternatively, others posit that Nathanael's confessional statement is only provisional in nature, namely, it merely reveals the amazement of the new disciple at Jesus' supernatural knowledge.[303] In this direction, D.A. Carson, for example, partially solves this dilemma by suggesting that the epithet "Son of God" is a functional category, not an ontological one.[304] That is, Jesus shares in the nature of God and he acts as God would (in the sense that we call some fellow Christians "godly men"). Thus, the epithet does not reflect a full-blown messianic confession. This notion sounds plausible, especially in view of Jesus' supernatural knowledge about Nathanael.[305] Additionally, the disciple could have expressed his hope for a mere political liberator by means of the title, "King of Israel." Finally, still some others point to the emphatic function of the confession in relation to the omnipotent supernatural divinity of Jesus (the implication being also the result of a redactional coloring).[306] In the final analysis, nonetheless, the structure and wording of this short pericope requires a certain degree of messianic understanding (in contrast to Wengst and Carson). The titles "Son of God" and "King of Israel" may not be used as technical terms on their own in the present text and in the time of Jesus. Yet coupled with Philip's introduction based on the scriptural witness (i.e., the one whom Moses and the prophets promised in v. 45), however, the double designation seems to be intended to carry some measure of a messianic overtone. Furthermore, "Son of God" is referred to in association with Messiah in John 11:27 and 20:31:

> She said to him, "Yes, Lord, I believe that you are the Messiah, the Son of God, the one coming into the world." (John 11:27, NRSV)

> But these are written so that you may come to believe that Jesus is the Messiah, the Son of God, and that through believing you may have life in his name. (John 20:31, NRSV)

---

[302] Schenke, *Johannes*, 50; Gnilka, *Johannesevangelium*, 21-22.
[303] Wengst, *Das Johannesevangelium*, 1:94-97.
[304] Carson, *The Gospel according to John*, 161-62.
[305] *Contra*, the study of J. J. Collins suggests that the term already took on a messianic significance in Palestine at the time of Jesus. John J. Collins, "The *Son of God* Text from Qumran," in *From Jesus to John: Essays on Jesus and New Testament Christology in Honour of Marinus de Jonge*, ed. Martinus C. de Boer (Sheffield: Sheffield, 1993), 65-82. See 1QSa 2:11-12; 2 Esd 7:28-29.
[306] Ekkehard W. Stegemann and Wolfgang Stegemann, "König Israels, nicht König der Juden?: Jesus als König im Johannesevangelium," in *Messiasvorstellungen bei Juden und Christen*, ed. Ekkehard W. Stegemann (Stuttgart: W. Kohlhammer, 1993), 47; Stefan Schreiber, "Rätsel um den König: Zur religionsgeschichtlichen Herkunft des König-Titels im Johannesevangelium," in *Johannes aenigmaticus: Studien zum Johannesevangelium für Herbert Leroy*, ed. Stefan Schreiber and Alois Stimpfle (Regensburg: Friedrich Pustet, 2000), 58-59.

Messianic or not, the question directly relevant to the present study is whether "King of Israel" bears a Mosaic overtone. The idiom is not a common expression, mentioned only three times, apart from this passage, in the entire New Testament corpus.[307] Both in Matthew 27:42 and Mark 15:32, the crowd mocks Jesus with this title at his crucifixion. In the Johannine triumphal entry account (12:32), Jesus is hailed as "King of Israel." In all these occurrences, if an association with an Old Testament character is to be found, it is David, not Moses. Thus, the extent of Boismard's argument (19 pages) probably (and ironically) speaks against his own view. If John intended a Mosaic messianic overtone with that expression, one wonders why it takes such a lengthy investigation of extra-canonical sources to prove a supposedly important Johannine theme.[308] The extra-biblical materials (later rabbinic and Samaritan sources) to which Boismard has recourse might reveal the kingship of Moses in association with Joseph the patriarch, but the Gospel of John does not (neither Matthew nor Mark for that matter as well) espouse such an association.[309]

Summary. In John 1:45 and 5:36-47 Moses is mentioned and alluded to. Contrary to the arguments of some exegetes, these texts do not paint Moses as a messianic type. His narrative function in these texts is virtually exclusively restricted to that of a witness and not a provider of "life" or a facilitator of the divine immanence. The latter function is strictly reserved for Jesus. The witness function of Moses develops in two ways through his writings (γραφαί, "scripture"). On the one hand, his witness is extended in the service of recognizing the identity of Jesus. That is, his writings do not merely promise an eschatological figure in an abstract manner (especially as Deut 18:15-18 was sometimes understood in the intertestamental literature), but they unambiguously point to Jesus as the promised messiah (1:45, 5:39, 46-47). His role does not proceed beyond this point. His witness does not include "life" itself (the divine immanence) nor does it become internalized in the believers of Christ. This aspect of internalization and being the source of eternal life drastically separates Jesus

---

[307] Morris, *The Gospel according to John*, 147.

[308] Also, it is another important indicator that Glasson and Meeks do not address a Mosaic connotation in John 1:49. Cf. Glasson, *Moses in the Fourth Gospel*; Meeks, *The Prophet-King*.

[309] Schapdick assesses the point of the four descriptions of Jesus mentioned in John 1 as having Christological overtones (which culminates in v. 51 as the presence of God) not as a Mosaic typology. "He is the lamb of God (1:29-36), the messiah, or Christ (1:20, 25, 41, 45), the king of Israel (1:49), the son of man (1:51). The diversity and the diverse backgrounds of all these high titles are less important than his goal to make a single, unified statement about Jesus. It culminates in the picture that the heaven is open upon Jesus in v. 51. In all his life, in all his words and deeds, Jesus of Nazareth is the ultimate place of the presence of God on earth. In 5:45, Moses is presented as a witness of Jesus there together with the prophets, i.e., the prophetic scriptures of the holy scripture." Schapdick, "Autorität ohne Inhalt," 186-87.

from Moses. This distinction, thus, rules out the messianic typological role of Moses. On the other hand, however, his other witness function is also peculiar in contradistinction to the conventional Jewish beliefs that upheld him as their advocate. That is, Moses prosecutes those who distort the purpose of his writings, which is to direct his readers to Jesus the messiah. The two primary roles of Moses, as messianic witness and as prosecutor of Jews, markedly distinguish the Fourth Gospel from its preceding and concurrent currents of Jewish thoughts.

Allusions to the Exodus Events: John 6:14-15, 32-33

[14] Οἱ οὖν ἄνθρωποι ἰδόντες ὃ ἐποίησεν σημεῖον ἔλεγον ὅτι οὗτός ἐστιν ἀληθῶς ὁ προφήτης ὁ ἐρχόμενος εἰς τὸν κόσμον. [15] Ἰησοῦς οὖν γνοὺς ὅτι μέλλουσιν ἔρχεσθαι καὶ ἁρπάζειν αὐτὸν ἵνα ποιήσωσιν βασιλέα, ἀνεχώρησεν πάλιν εἰς τὸ ὄρος αὐτὸς μόνος. (John 6:14-15, NA[28])

[14] When the people saw the sign that he had done, they began to say, "This is indeed the prophet who is to come into the world." [15] When Jesus realized that they were about to come and take him by force to make him king, he withdrew again to the mountain by himself. (John 6:14-15, NRSV)

[32] εἶπεν οὖν αὐτοῖς ὁ Ἰησοῦς· ἀμὴν ἀμὴν λέγω ὑμῖν, οὐ Μωϋσῆς δέδωκεν ὑμῖν τὸν ἄρτον ἐκ τοῦ οὐρανοῦ, ἀλλ' ὁ πατήρ μου δίδωσιν ὑμῖν τὸν ἄρτον ἐκ τοῦ οὐρανοῦ τὸν ἀληθινόν· [33] ὁ γὰρ ἄρτος τοῦ θεοῦ ἐστιν ὁ καταβαίνων ἐκ τοῦ οὐρανοῦ καὶ ζωὴν διδοὺς τῷ κόσμῳ. (John 6:32-33, NRSV)

[32] Then Jesus said to them, "Very truly, I tell you, it was not Moses who gave you the bread from heaven, but it is my Father who gives you the true bread from heaven. [33] For the bread of God is that which comes down from heaven and gives life to the world." (John 6:32-33, NRSV)

The sixth chapter of the Gospel of John has drawn a great deal of scholarly attention.[310] In large measure, the reason lies in the rich allusions to and echoes of

---

[310] As a point of entry, the following studies are helpful for the general understanding of the Johannine appropriation of the Old Testament in the sixth chapter: Martin Rose, "Manna: Das Brot aus dem Himmel," in *Johannes-Studien: Interdisziplinäre Zugänge zum Johannes-Evangelium, Freundesgabe der Theologischen Fakultät der Universität Neuchâtel für Jean Zumstein*, ed. Martin Rose (Zurich: Theologischer, 1991), 75-107; Peder Borgen, "John 6: Tradition, Interpretation and Composition," in *From Jesus to John: Essays on Jesus and New Testament Christology in Honour of Marinus de Jonge*, ed. Martinus C. de Boer (Sheffield: JSOT, 1993), 268-91; Painter, *The Quest for the Messiah*, 253-86; Paul N. Anderson, *The Christology of the Fourth Gospel: Its Unity and Disunity in the Light of John 6* (Tübingen: Mohr Siebeck, 1996); R. Alan Culpepper, ed., *Critical Readings of John 6* (Leiden: Brill, 1997); Johannes Beutler, "Zur Struktur von Johannes 6," in *Studien zu den johanneischen Schriften* (Stuttgart: Katholisches Bibelwerk, 1998), 247-62; Michael Labahn, *Jesus als Lebensspender: Untersuchungen zu einer Geschichte der johanneischen Tradition anhand ihrer Wundergeschichten* (Berlin: Walter de Gruyter, 1999), 265-304; idem, *Offenbarung in Zeichen und Wort: Untersuchungen zur Vorgeschichte von Joh 6,1-25a und seiner Rezeption in der Brotrede* (Tübingen: Mohr Siebeck, 2000); Klaus Scholtissek, *In ihm sein und bleiben: Die Sprache der Immanenz in den Johanneischen Schriften*

the Old Testament anecdotes related to Moses. Usually, the crossing of the Red Sea, the reception of Manna, and the ingathering of the twelve tribes are mentioned as that which evoke the exodus traditions. The following discussion will engage in a dialogue with exegetes who see this chapter as containing a Mosaic typology with reference to the aforementioned Old Testament traditions. Afterwards, the narrative contribution of Moses to the Johannine Christological understanding will be proposed.

Narrative unity. In the aftermath of the rise of canonical and literary criticisms (commonly associated with B.S. Childs and R.A. Culpepper), Johannine exegetes agree upon the importance of the context. In this concurrence, what is also assumed and affirmed simultaneously is the importance of literary unity, in the case of the present discussion, that of chapter 6 within the surrounding narrative units.[311] Based upon this scholarly agreement, this section proceeds with a contextual examination of the preceeding and subsequent chapters. Some recent commentators detect a slight transposition of the narrative units. For instance, Udo Wilckens rearranges the chs. 4 through 9 as follows: 4; 6:1-71; 5:1-47; 7:15-24, 9:1-14, 25-53.[312] Ismo Dunderberg, on the other hand, postulates that ch. 6

(Freiburg: Herder, 2000), 194-209; idem, "Die Brotrede Jesu in Joh 6,1-71," 35-55; Jean Zumstein, "Die Schriftrezeption in der Brotrede (Joh 6)," in *Israel und seine Heilstraditionen im Johannesevangelium: Festgabe für Johannes Beutler SJ zum 70. Geburtstag*, ed. Michael Labahn, Klaus Scholtissek, and Angelika Strotmann (Paderborn: Ferdinand Schöningh, 2004), 123-39; idem, "La réception de l'écriture en Jean 6," in *Analyse narrative et Bible: Deuxième colloque international du RRENAB, Louvain-la-Neuve, avril 2004*, ed. Camille Focant and André Wénin (Leuven: Leuven Univ Press; Peeters, 2005), 147-66; John Dennis, "The Presence and Function of Second Exodus-Restoration Imagery in John 6," *SNTSU* 30 (2005): 105-21; Michael Theobald, "Schriftzitate im 'Lebensbrot'-Dialog Jesu (Joh 6): Ein Paradigma für den Schriftgebrauch des vierten Evangelisten," in *Studien zum Corpus Iohanneum* (Tübingen: Mohr Sieberck, 2010), 309-48; Michel Roberge, "Composition et argumentation en Jean 6,35-58," in *L'intrigue dans le récit biblique: Quatrième colloque international du RRENAB, Université Laval, Québec, 29 mai-1er juin 2008*, ed. Anne Pasquier, Daniel Marguerat, and André Wénin (Leuven: Uitgeverij Peeters, 2010), 265-302.

[311] For the unity of chapter 6 in the literary context, see Ludger Schenke, "Die formale und gedankliche Struktur von Joh 6:26-58," *BZ* 24 (1980): 21-41; idem, "Die literarische Vorgeschichte von Joh 6:26-58," *BZ* 29 (1985): 68-89; Eugen Ruckstuhl, *Die literarische Einheit des Johannesevangeliums: Der gegenwärtige Stand der einschlägigen Forschungen* (Freiburg: Universitätsverlag; Göttingen: Vandenhoeck & Ruprecht, 1987), 220-71; Hartwig Thyen, "Ich bin das Licht der Welt: Das Ich- und Ich-Bin-Sagen Jesu im Johannesevangelium," *JAC* 35 (1992): 32-37; Michael Labahn, "Controversial Revelation in Deed and Word: The Feeding of the Five Thousand and Jesus' Crossing of the Sea as a 'Prelude' to the Johannine Bread of Life Discourse," *IBS* 22 (2000): 146-81; idem, *Offenbarung in Zeichen und Wort*, 277-88.

[312] Wilckens, *Das Evangelium nach Johannes*, 5-6, 91-137.

is a later interpolation in between chs. 5 and 7.³¹³ Not only are such reconstructions without textual-critical attestation, they seem to be suggestive at best and arbitrary from one study to another. A great number of scholars do not embrace the disarrayment and they respect the fourth evangelist's compositional intention as we have its canonical form in our hand.³¹⁴

Thematic link between John 5 and 6. In his recent essay, Klaus Scholtissek perceptively notes the narrative cohesion of ch.6 within the context of chs. 5 through 7.³¹⁵ The following contextual analysis is largely indebted to his study and, accordingly, follows his outline with some modifications. First, the witness theme is at work in both chapters. In John 5:36-47, four witnesses are called in on behalf of the authenticity of Jesus: John the Baptist (34-35), the works of Jesus (5:36), the witness of the Father (5:36-38), the witness of the scriptures (5:39-40, 46-47). Three of these four are invoked again: the "works" of Jesus (6:27-28, 30); the Father's "sealing (ἐσφράγισεν)" of the Son (6:27) and his sending of the true bread, which is reminiscent of the logos in John 5:38 (6:27, 32); and the Jews' misunderstanding of the scripture and Jesus' corrective interpretation (6:31-32). Second, the inaccessibility of God and the unique intermediary function of Jesus are reiterated in 5:37 and 6:46. Third, the controversy over the reception in the name of the Father pervades (1:11-13, 5:43; 6:41, 52, 60-71).³¹⁶ Fourth, related to this "reception motif" is the concomitant immanent presence of God in the believers' heart (5:37-38). The reception of the divine messenger sharply separates the believers from the unbelievers (5:43-44, 6:41, 52). In addition, the themes of "searching" and "finding" permeate chs. 5 and 6 (5:39-40; 6:24-26).³¹⁷ Fifth, after enlisting his disciples in John 1:19-51, two "feast cycles" run through the first half of the Gospel: the first from Cana to Cana (2:1-4:54) and the second from Jerusalem to Jerusalem (5:1-10:39).³¹⁸ These two pericopae are replete with reference to the Jewish calendars and feasts, such as, the Sabbath, the Passover, and the Feast of

---

³¹³ Ismo Dunderberg, *Johannes und die Synoptiker: Studien zu Joh 1-9* (Helsinki: Suomalainen Tiedeakatemia 1994), 131-41.

³¹⁴ Alfons Weiser, *Die Theologie der Evangelien*, vol. 2 of *Theologie des Neuen Testaments* (Stuttgart: W. Kohlhammer, 1993), 172-73; Schnelle, *Das Evangelium nach Johannes*, 13.

³¹⁵ Scholtissek, "Die Brotrede Jesu in Joh 6,1-71," 37-41.

³¹⁶ F. Mußner calls this concept the "semantic axle" of John's Gospel. Franz Mußner, "Die 'semantische Achse' des Johannesevangeliums: Ein Versuch," in *Jesus von Nazareth im Umfeld Israels und der Urkirche: Gesammelte Aufsätze*, ed. Michael Theobald (Tübingen: Mohr Siebeck, 1999), 260-69.

³¹⁷ This searching motif is also attested to in John 1:35-51, 4:23, 7:34-36, 8:21-22, 11:56, 12:21, 13:33, 36, 18:4, 7-8, 20:11-18.

³¹⁸ Michael Labahn, "Between Tradition and Literary Art: The Miracle Tradition in the Fourth Gospel," *Bib* 80 (1999): 192-95.

Tabernacles.[319] One of the more salient characteristics common to these narratives is that only Jesus can fufill human needs.[320] Finally, the elusiveness of Jesus is deeply woven into the fabric of the narratives of John 6 through 7 (6:1, 14-15, 19, 21, 24-26, 7:1-13, 9:1-41, 11:7-16, 54-57).[321] The bread of life speech, which is centered upon ch. 6, is precipitated by the two "signs" discourses (the feeding of the multitude in 6:1-15 and the crossing of the sea in 6:16-21).[322]

> The bread discourse [which occupies the center stage of John 6 in its entirety] is aimed at the faith decision. It exposes unbelief and leads to a crisis, provoking the confession as Peter speaks in verses sixty-eight through sixty-nine on behalf of the twelve disciples.[323]

In conclusion, ch. 6 continues to spell out the missionary Christology of ch. 5 and these two chapters demonstrate a high degree of literary integrity.

Wayne Meeks. Wayne Meeks has, in various ways, blazed a new trail in Johannine scholarship with his contribution, *The Prophet-King*.[324] First, despite some previous attempts, he has presented one of the most elaborate cases for the influence of the Samaritan and early rabbinic sources upon the shaping of John's Gospel. Second, the studies subsequent to his have had to respond, at least in some degree, to his thesis; namely, that the fourth evangelist redefined Jesus' messiahship radically in terms of "prophet-king":

> The following investigation undertakes to clarify the way in which the motifs represented by the two terms "prophet" and "king" in the Fourth Gospel not only are interrelated, but interpret each other.[325]

---

[319] Maarten J.J. Menken, "Die jüdischen Feste im Johannesevangelium," in *Israel und seine Heilstraditionen im Johannesevangelium: Festgabe für Johannes Beutler SJ zum 70. Geburtstag*, ed. Michael Labahn, Klaus Scholtissek, and Angelika Strotmann (Paderborn: Ferdinand Schöningh, 2004), 269-86. "For the Johannine community, what was done in the Jewish celebration of the Passover was but a sign and a shadow of the perfection of the gift of God in the person of Jesus Christ, the true bread from heaven . . . . In Jesus Christ the Passover traditions are enfleshed, not destroyed." Francis J. Moloney, *Signs and Shadows: Reading John 5-12* (Minneapolis: Fortress, 1996), 64.

[320] Johannes Frühwald-König, *Tempel und Kult: Ein Beitrag zur Christologie des Johannesvangeliums* (Regensburg: Pustet, 1998), 227.

[321] Mark W.G. Stibbe, *John as Storyteller: Narrative Criticism and the Fourth Gospel* (Cambridge: CUP, 1992), 83; idem, "The Elusive Christ: A New Reading of the Fourth Gospel," in *Gospel of John as Literature: An Anthology of Twentieth-Century Perspectives*, ed. Mark W.G. Stibbe (Leiden: Brill, 1993), 231-47.

[322] Labahn, "Controversial Revelation in Deed and Word," 146-81; idem, *Offenbarung in Zeichen und Wort*, 277-88. On the two "signs," see Labahn, *Jesus als Lebensspender*, 265-304.

[323] Scholtissek, "Die Brotrede Jesu in Joh 6,1-71," 42.

[324] Meeks, *The Prophet-King*.

[325] Ibid., 1. His Mosaic prophet-king Christology, especially in John 6:14-15, is recognized and taken up in the following as well: Brown, *The Gospel according to John*,

Finally, based upon the allegedly divergent views on this Mosaic Christology (positive at some points but negative at others), he confirmed the then-popular two level drama hypothesis: that is, the tension toward Moses reflects the shift of the Johannine community's historical settings. That the first and third points are subject to dispute does not need to be repeated here.[326] Directly relevant to this study, however, is the question whether John portrays Jesus as a Mosaic prophet-king.

The concept of a Mosaic prophet-king that Meeks constructed is largely dependent upon his interrelated exegesis of John 6:14-15 (people coercing Jesus to be a king), 10:1-39 (the good shepherd discourse), and 18:33-38a (the crucifixion trial scene before Pilate). After noting several texts (1:49, 7:37-52, 12:12-19, 18:28-19:22) that associate Jesus with a king, Meeks goes on to argue that John 6:14-15 reflects a common Jewish hope at the time for a Mosaic prophet-king derived from Deuteronomy 18:15-22.[327]

> When the people saw the sign that he had done, they began to say, "This is indeed the prophet who is to come into the world." When Jesus realized that they were about to come and take him by force to make him king, he withdrew again to the mountain by himself. (John 6:14-15, NRSV)

Such a notion, he maintains, is further confirmed by recurrent allusions to the Exodus events related to Moses in the following discourses in John 6, especially in terms of "signs":[328]

> In any case it is sufficiently evident that the discourse [John 6] sets Jesus' σημεῖον parallel with God's miraculous care of Israel under Moses' leadership. This adds very strong support to the supposition that "the prophet" of verse 14 is the Mosaic eschatological prophet.[329]

Related to this allusion to the Manna event is the theme of "gathering." As gathering of fragments is mentioned in 6:13, John 11:50-52 also mentions the death of Jesus so as to gather the scattered children of God:[330]

> "You do not understand that it is better for you to have one man die for the people than to have the whole nation destroyed." He did not say this on his own, but being high priest that year he prophesied that Jesus was about to die for the nation, and not for the nation only, but to gather into one the dispersed children of God. (John 11:50-52, NRSV)

1:234; Barrett, *The Gospel according to St. John*, 231; Schnackenburg, *The Gospel according to St John*, 2:18; Becker, *Das Evangelium nach Johannes*, 1:193; Wilckens, *Das Evangelium nach Johannes*, 96-97; Wengst, *Das Johannesevangelium*, 1:223.

[326] See Appendix 7: "Use of the Rabbinic Materials for the New Testament Studies" for the first point; see a discussion on J. Louis Martyns' contribution to Johannine theology (pp. 112-13 in ch. 3) for the third point.

[327] Meeks, *The Prophet-King*, 32-87.

[328] Ibid., 87-96.

[329] Ibid., 92-93.

[330] Ibid., 96-98.

In addition, Jesus died a death of a good shepherd as he described one would do (John 10:1-39).[331] Since David was not primarily considered to be a prophet, therefore, the recurrent description of Jesus as a prophet fits with the profile of the eschatological prophet like Moses but in the redefined royal-prophetic terms.[332]

Critique of Meeks. Notwithstanding some interesting parallels that Meeks draws, his observations fail to be persuasive at a number of points. Most significantly, the sixth chapter of John as a whole does not appear to put a great emphasis on a Mosaic typology. Although some allusions are employed, they set a stage to clarify the surpassing nature of the new gift, namely, the bread of life. In other words, the value or narrative function of the Mosaic references is in providing the contrasting and exceeding aspect of the new redemptive history in contrast to the old. When the people requested a sign by which they identified Jesus with Moses, Jesus' reply was in the emphatic negative:[333]

> ἀμὴν ἀμὴν λέγω ὑμῖν, οὐ Μωϋσῆς δέδωκεν ὑμῖν τὸν ἄρτον ἐκ τοῦ οὐρανοῦ. (John 6:32a, NA²⁸)

> Truly truly I say to you, it was *not* Moses who gave you the bread from heaven. (John 6:32a, NRSV)[334]

It is highly indicative that this verse begins with the double amen idiom, and the repudiation of Moses giving bread is followed by the negative adverb οὐ. It was inappropriate for people to look for a sign analogous to that which was brought about through Moses (6:32b). Not only is it God (not Moses) who supplies the bread, but the new bread, in stark contrast to its old counterpart, is perennially unperishing and enlivening (6:48-58). The references to Moses are mentioned only in passing remarks, and Jesus emphatically rejects the people's mundane hope of setting him up as an earthly king as Moses. In light of the proportion of the passages allusive of the Mosaic accounts, the bread of life pericope should take hermeneutical priority over the previous allusions to the exodus events (feeding of the multitude and the crossing of the sea) as recorded in the first half of ch. 6. The latter accounts mainly serve to stimulate the main discourse about Jesus being the source of everlasting life.

Furthermore, another question that can be raised against the argument of

---

[331] "The central function of the king is to be the mediator between the people and the gods, or to be the divine tutelary. He is the shepherd who grazes the people and reflects on the iconography and dress of the divine presence. It is hardly a coincidence that Moses received the call of Yahweh while he was serving the work of shepherd (as well as David)." Römer, "Moïse," 192.

[332] Meeks, *The Prophet-King*, 97-99.

[333] Marinus de Jonge, "Jesus as Prophet and King in the Fourth Gospel," *ETL* 47 (1973): 167.

[334] Italics are added for emphasis.

Meeks is whether the good shepherd discourse and the trial scene necessarily demand a Mosaic typology. The exegetical oversight of Meeks lies in his presupposition that the evangelist must have presented Jesus exclusively in terms of personal figures, instead of abstract images, such as, the Passover lamb, water, and bread. In accordance with John's more explicit analogy to these abstract Jewish symbols, the good shepherd may have to be viewed from a non-personal messianic prefigurative perspective. In addition, Meeks' reason for excluding David from being a good shepherd is arbitrary. He allows a "radical redefinition" for Moses to become a royal-prophet. Yet, David does not enjoy such flexibility. It is unclear why John should not have employed the radical redefining of David as a royal prophet in the inverse way Meeks constructs the Mosaic prophet-king image from various extra-canonical sources.[335]

John Dennis. The last noteworthy study to be reviewed that detects a wide range of exodus typology in John 6 is the one by John Dennis, "The Presence and Function of Second Exodus-Restoration Imagery in John 6."[336] Having surveyed the contemporaneous Jewish expectations of the Mosaic eschatological prophet, he delineates the Johannine depiction of Jesus as a prophet like Moses in three aspects. As Moses parted and crossed the Red Sea, Jesus also provides safe passage for his disciples. As Moses supplied Manna, Jesus makes the bread of life available. Finally, as Moses gathers and leads the twelve tribes of Israel, Jesus draws together the twelve disciples, a symbol of the new Israel.[337] This eschatological ingathering is also signaled in the collecting of the leftover fragments that filled the twelve baskets in John 6:13.[338] With these Mosaic echoes in the background, therefore, Jesus is presented as "the prophet like Moses *par excellence* who is . . . leading a second exodus restoration."[339]

Critique of Dennis. A number of Johannine exegetes have noted the rich echoes

---

[335] It is also indicative of the contemporaneous literature that it was not so enthusiastic to using Moses in the eschatological kingship category. "Apart from Philo, most Jewish writers of the Second Temple period seem, like Josephus and following scriptural practice, to have avoided calling Moses king, but use other terms to describe his leadership." Richard Bauckham, "Jewish Messianism according to the Gospel of John," in *Challenging Perspectives in the Gospel of John*, ed. John Lierman (Tübingen: Mohr Siebeck, 2006), 50.

[336] Dennis, "The Presence and Function of Second Exodus-Restoration Imagery in John 6," 105-21.

[337] Ibid., 109-14.

[338] Ibid., 114-21.

[339] Ibid., 121.

of the Exodus events alluded to in John 6.[340] The question at stake for this study, nevertheless, is not whether this text employs such intertextuality, but whether the allusions and echoes in this text invoke the Mosaic messianic prefiguration motif. More specifically, the question to be addressed is not whether people viewed Jesus as such but whether the evangelist presents him in such a manner. In this respect, it is significant that Jesus refused the desire of the people to appoint him as their alleged "prophet-king" (the kingship of Jesus is no doubt present in John at least in the mind of the crowd, but it is salvation-historically redefined) because his kingship is not tantamount to their interpretation of the Pentateuchal images of Moses, especially that of Deuteronomy 18.[341] The exegetical pitfall of Dennis (and that of Meeks as well as others) is that he uncritically equates these exodus imageries with the Mosaic Christological typology. An exegetical disadvantage of this superficial reading can be spelled out in three ways.

First, he ignores the principal function of the exodus allusions; that is, to invite Jesus to reveal his identity as the source of eternal life. As reviewed above (in critique of Meeks), the three allusions to the exodus events serve as vivid illustrations, over which the unique and superlative nature of the new redemptive history through Jesus Christ can be better comprehended in comparison. In the same vein, the request of the people, who could have found the similarity of Jesus with Moses upon experiencing the feeding of the multitude, prompts an occasion to specifically articulate the identity of Jesus' mission and his relation to God (note that Jesus calls "His Father" the source of Manna in John 6:32). It is surprising that the feeding of the five thousand with a few pieces of staples did not convince the people (designated as "crowd" in 6:2, 5, 22, 24 and "Jews" in 41, 52) of the divinely commissioned nature of Jesus, so they had to ask for another sign (6:30). As such, some exegetes posit that the crowd was asking for a

---

[340] Maarten J.J. Menken, "'He Gave Them Bread from Heaven to Eat' (John 6:31)," in *The Old Testament Quotations in the Fourth Gospel: Studies in Textual Form* (Kampen: Kok, 1996), 47-65; Theobald, "Schriftzitate im 'Lebensbrot'-Dialog Jesu (Joh 6)," 309-48; Andrew C. Brunson, *Psalm 118 in the Gospel of John: An Intertextual Study on the New Exodus Pattern in the Theology of John* (Tübingen: Siebeck, 2003), 153-63; Scholtissek, "Die Brotrede Jesu in Joh 6,1-71," 35-55; Zumstein, "Die Schriftrezeption in der Brotrede (Joh 6)," 123-39; Susan Hylen, *Allusion and Meaning in John 6* (Berlin: Walter de Gruyter, 2005), 119-56.

[341] There is no doubt that Jesus is associated sometimes with kingly and prophetic images. Nonetheless, it is open to question whether the converged concept of the two images is applied to Jesus in John. The Johannine portrayal of Jesus as a king is closely related to the divine salvation history. Reimund Bieringer, "'My Kingship Is Not of This World' (Jn 18:36): The Kingship of Jesus and Politics," in *The Myriad Christ: Plurality and the Quest for Unity in Contemporary Christology*, ed. Terrence Merrigan and Jacques Haers (Leuven: Louvain University Press, 2000), 159-75; Hans Kvalbein, "The Kingdom of God and the Kingship of Christ in the Fourth Gospel," in *Neotestamentica et Philonica: Studies in Honor of Peder Borgen*, ed. David E. Aune, Torrey Seland, and Jarl H. Ulrichsen (Leiden: Brill, 2003), 227-32.

continuous feeding as Moses supplied for forty years.[342] No matter what the exact nature of the demand was, the kind of sign people requested probably had something to do with satisfying their physical hunger. Yet, Jesus (and God) intends to meet the spiritual needs with the true "heavenly bread."[343] Accordingly, those Mosaic allusions serve primarily to set a stage for Christological discourses (i.e., the bread speech).

> The signs in the Fourth Gospel find their most natural background in the events of the exodus, and are most often associated by scholars with the signs of Moses. However, although Moses does figure prominently in John and was inseparably linked to the exodus and events in the wilderness, it is of interest that the great majority of "sign(s)" references from Exodus through Deuteronomy point specifically not to Moses but to God. Thus when Jesus takes the first exodus as a model for much of his ministry, he may be intent not so much on reproducing the signs and works of Moses as on associating his work with that of Yahweh. Consequently, although it is appropriate to speak of Jesus as a second Moses, this is only in a secondary sense. In fact, he surpasses Moses in every sense, not only in signs and works, but also in primacy of identity and the role he plays in the new exodus—and Moses himself is called as a witness to this.[344]

Second, and more importantly, the analogy is set up not between Moses and Jesus but between God and Jesus. It was God, not Moses, who provided the Manna and, so does Jesus. This analogy stands in contrast to the belief of the Johannine Jews that Moses provided the Manna.[345] Jesus is the culmination of the *Heilsgeschichte* which Yahweh inaugurated in the book of Exodus and he is the *Heilsgeschichte* itself. On the other hand, Jesus denies the significance of the part that Moses played in the previous salvation history: "It is not Moses who has given you the bread from heaven" (John 6:32a).[346] Some scholars contend that

---

[342] Becker, *Das Evangelium nach Johannes*, 246; Theobald, "Schriftzitate im 'Lebensbrot'-Dialog Jesu (Joh 6)," 348; Wilckens, *Das Evangelium nach Johannes*, 101.

[343] Schapdick, "Autorität ohne Inhalt," 193-94.

[344] Brunson, *Psalm 118 in the Gospel of John*, 161-62. Also, Gawlick, "Mose im Johannesevangelium," 31-32. Also, Wahlde takes the request as "a literary device intended by the evangelist to emphasize the blindness of the Jews." Urban C. von Wahlde, "Literary Structure and Theological Argument in Three Discourses with the Jews in the Fourth Gospel," *JBL* 103 (1984): 578.

[345] Thyen, *Das Johannesevangelium*, 351. For the possible source of the alleged citation with an introductory formula in John 6:31, "as it is written, 'He gave them bread from heaven to eat,'" see Menken, "'He Gave Them Bread from Heaven to Eat' (John 6:31)," 49-54; Thyen, *Das Johannesevangelium*, 351.

[346] Dodd, *The Interpretation of the Fourth Gospel*, 337; Georg Richter, "Die alttestamentlichen Zitate in der Rede vom Himmelsbrot Joh 6,26-51a," in *Schriftauslegung: Beiträge zur Hermeneutik des Neuen Testaments und im Neuen Testament* (Paderborn: Schöningh, 1972), 222; Christian Dietzfelbinger, "Aspekte des Alten Testaments im Johannesevangelium," in *Geschichte-Tradition-Reflexion III, Frühes Christentum: Festschrift für Martin Hengel zum 70. Geburtstag*, ed. Hermann

this denial is a direct polemic against the contemporary Jewish belief in both the eschatological Moses who will provide daily staples and his deified status.[347] The problem with these proposals is that the evidence adduced in favor of the former view is meager and postdates early Christianity.[348] Furthermore, Moses does not occupy the centerstage of this discourse. The attention devoted to Moses appears to be too slim to establish a typology. The only explicit reference and possible allusion to Moses are found in three verses (14-15, 32) out of the seventy-one verses of John 6! As such, the main thrust of this pericope is that Jesus' mission originated from God, and Moses is located only on the periphery (as clearly seen in John 6:32 where Jesus sets Moses aside from the focus):

> In evoking the works/signs parallels to Moses it was no doubt John's intention to take the reader back to the exodus and portray Jesus as the leader of a new or second exodus. However, the Johannine Jesus associates his ministry principally with the Father, not with Moses.[349]

On the other hand, John, in view of the contemporary Jewish traditions, should be credited as the first interpreter to detect the cause of the wilderness generation's demise from eating Manna.[350]

Finally, the disparity between the exodus events and the bread speech is so great that one wonders whether a messianic typology is an appropriate framework. As for the two kinds of bread, the first bread was perishable and it satisfied only temporarily, whereas the second one secures eternal satisfaction (John 6:31-35).[351] The bread given through Moses was not able to keep the fathers in the wilderness alive but the bread of Jesus sustains life forever (John 6:46-51).[352] Furthermore, another stark contrast is the disparity between old Israel and its counterpart in John's Gospel. It is open to question whether the gathering of the twelve disciples is an intended symbolic fulfillment of the hope for the restora-

---

Lichtenberger (Tübingen: Mohr Siebeck, 1996), 205; Theobald, "Schriftzitate im 'Lebensbrot'-Dialog Jesu (Joh 6)," 351.

[347] For the former view, see Howard M. Teeple, *The Mosaic Eschatological Prophet* (Philadelphia: Society of Biblical Literature, 1957), 68; David Daube, "Earliest Structure of the Gospels," *NTS* 5 (1959): 174-87, esp. 178; Bruce J. Malina, *The Palestinian Manna Tradition: The Manna Tradition in the Palestinian Targums and Its Relationship to the New Testament Writings* (Leiden: Brill, 1968), 88. For the latter, see Menken, "'He Gave Them Bread from Heaven to Eat' (John 6:31)," 56-73.

[348] Menken, "'He Gave Them Bread from Heaven to Eat' (John 6:31)," 56.

[349] Brunson, *Psalm 118 in the Gospel of John*, 162.

[350] Anderson, *The Christology of the Fourth Gospel*, 204; idem, "The *Sitz im Leben* of the Johannine Bread of Life Discourse and Its Evolving Context," in *Critical Readings of John 6*, ed. R. Alan Culpepper (Leiden: Brill, 1997), 35; Hakola, *Identity Matters*, 165-66.

[351] Theobald, "Schriftzitate im 'Lebensbrot'-Dialog Jesu (Joh 6)," 351.

[352] Georg Richter, *Studien zum Johannesevangelium* (Regensburg: Pustet, 1977), 229; Theobald, "Schriftzitate im 'Lebensbrot'-Dialog Jesu (Joh 6)," 362; Hakola, *Identity Matters*, 165.

tion of Israel. Immediately after the "gathering of the twelve baskets," Jesus leaves the crowd behind to cross the Sea of Galilee![353] In addition, the scope of the new redemptive history is significantly expanded to include the gentiles, as evident in the Samaritan mission of John 4 and the inclusion of Hellenists in John 12:20 ff. Lastly, the unflinching nature of the "new Israel" clouds the Mosaic typology since this new family of God remains faithful in contrast to the repeatedly rebellious Israelites in the wilderness.[354] The confession of Peter who representatively speaks for this new group demonstrates the loyalty of this new kind of followers.

> Because of this [the difficulty of Jesus' sayings] many of his disciples turned back and no longer went about with him. So Jesus asked the twelve, "Do you also wish to go away?" Simon Peter answered him, "Lord, to whom can we go? You have the words of eternal life. We have come to believe and know that you are the Holy One of God." (John 6:66-69, NRSV)[355]

Although one of the twelve betrays, this group of disciples is still called "the twelve," which displays the unflinching status of this group in contrast to the twelve tribes of the old.

> The Jews' cry that they have no king but Caesar reveals their true identity and seals their exclusion from the true Israel, in contrast to those who in accepting Jesus affirm that Yahweh is their king. As for the disciples, they are still called the twelve (20:24) even though only eleven are left, underlining their significance as a symbol of the restoration of Israel.[356]

One can make a tenable case for the presence of recurrent exodus themes in John 6, but those imageries scarcely constitute a Mosaic Christological typology. Schapdick offers a summative statement of John 6 in a nutshell:

> John 6:30-33 refers back to the two acts of God as John 3:14, the provisional act of Moses on the one hand, and the gift of life through Jesus on the other. The difference is found in the quality of the soteriological gift: on the one hand, Manna with which Israel sustained their life in a special situation, on the other, the eternal life which is given, without restriction or limitation, to all who believe in Jesus of Nazareth, the one

---

[353] It is not Jesus who gathers but the crowd who follows after Jesus. Sherman E. Johnson, "Notes on the Prophet-King in John," *AThR* 51 (1969): 36.

[354] For the "murmuring" theme coalesced in John, see Marianne Meye Thompson, "Thinking about God: Wisdom and Theology in John 6," in *Critical Readings of John 6*, ed. R. Alan Culpepper (Leiden: Brill, 1997), 234-36; Brunson, *Psalm 118 in the Gospel of John*, 166. Kierspel suggested me the function of Moses as "anti-typology," a foil against which Jesus' messianic identity is outlined. Essentially, I agree that Moses demonstrates what Jesus is not. See Lars Kierspel, "'Dematerializing' Religion: Reading John 2-4 as a Chiasm," *Bib* 89 (2008): 526-54.

[355] Brackets are added for clarification.

[356] Brunson, *Psalm 118 in the Gospel of John*, 166.

God sent. The action of God through Moses in the desert serves as a prefiguration of his last and free act of salvation in Jesus.[357]

Summary. The sixth chapter of John's Gospel is replete with rich allusions and echoes of the exodus events. In contrast to some exegetes who argue for the Mosaic Christology based on these allusions, a more careful reading reveals that the typology is between Jesus and God. The role of Moses provides a background, against which the new redemption is better understood. This narrative function of Moses is in accordance with the similar role played out in John 1:16-17, 45, 3:14, 5:37-39, 56. On the one hand, he provides a point of comparison for the gracious nature and the divine initiative of the two redemptive programs, one by Moses and the other by Jesus. Moses foreshadows the salvific plan inaugurated through Jesus. Nevertheless, the fundamental difference of quality between the two salvation histories relegates Moses to the background, and at the same time it highlights the unprecedented eminence of the new *Heilsgeschichte*.[358] In this respect, Schapdick goes so far as to say that Moses is an "empty religious authority figure":

> The picture of Moses in John's Gospel is, therefore, relatively without content. Ultimately, Moses is presented as a mere symbol of religious authority in Jewish/Judeo-Christian thoughts. This authority is stressed and has taken an exclusive claim. However, it is authority without content because this content, especially the salvation, is exclusively transferred into Christological concentration.[359]

Nonetheless, his Christological witness function is not as prominent in this text as in other texts mentioned above. Two summary statements from two recent studies on the use of the Old Testament in the Fourth Gospel basically accord with this finding:

> John's Jesus is not a "second Moses" in the sense of merely recapitulating or building on the mission of his predecessor. John states quite clearly that Jesus supersedes and

---

[357] Schapdick, "Autorität ohne Inhalt," 194.

[358] In his recent article on John's view of Moses, S. Schapdick reaches a five-fold conclusion. First, the reason for a recurrent recourse to the Mosaic authority is due to the Gospel's Jewish context. The God of Moses is none other than the God of Jesus. Second, in the perspective of John, the function of Moses is essentially that of a witness to the divine revelation through Jesus. Third, the mention of the salvific events associated with Moses undergirds the sovereignty of God who is the Lord over life and death. Fourth, the Torah and its author, Moses, emerge in the conflict settings with the Jewish adversaries of Jesus. The Jewish misunderstanding of the Mosaic writings signifies that the only valid hermeneutics of the Torah comes about through a Christological perspective. Finally, Moses is presented as an authority figure, behind which God stands. However, due to the Christocentric perspective, the content of the Mosaic writings is not a valid criterion to judge the divine revelation through Jesus. Rather, the revelation through Jesus is the valid criterion to measure out the revelatory value of the Mosaic writings. Schapdick, "Autorität ohne Inhalt," 202-206.

[359] Ibid., 202-206.

replaces Moses as the decisive bearer of revelation. . . . The relation of Moses to Jesus is that of forerunner to fulfiller. Jesus is the full flowering of the truth to which Moses, for all his greatness, merely hinted. . . . Moses, like John the Baptist, recedes into the background with the coming of Christ. . . . It is in his use of Moses tradition that the boldness of John's approach becomes evident. He does not depict Jesus as a "new Moses" in the same way as does Matthew, for whom the relationship between Moses and Jesus is that of type to antitype. John's Logos Christology leads to this startling exegetical phenomenon: Moses is not the pattern for Jesus; rather, Jesus is the pattern for Moses.[360]

The Johannine Jesus is, then, superior to Moses in every conceivable way, doing everything that Moses did and a great many things that Moses could never hope to do. Moses, recognizing this, wrote the Law—the foundational document of Jewish faith and practice—to point the Jews to Jesus.[361]

Conclusion

Moses emerges frequently throughout the Gospel of John in the context of controversy with Jesus' antagonists. In contrast to their constant appeal to this Jewish authority figure, the Johannine presentation of Moses is more or less in a uniform fashion. Namely, he is a witness to the Christological identity of Jesus, and he is not portrayed as a messianic prefiguration. Moses is often mentioned because the new salvation history through Jesus stands in continuity with the old one (of which Moses was a part as a divine instrument) in a sense that God is the initiator of the two and his gracious intention continues in both. Moses who metonymically stands for the old covenant, then, provides an ample opportunity to communicate this continuity, as well as the divine provenance and divine nature of Jesus.

A comparative analysis of Moses between John and the contemporary Jewish literature, however, yields an ambivalent attitude. The fourth evangelist takes advantage of the available language and images of Moses in order to advance his Christological understanding of Jesus. In so doing, John's portrayal of Moses is highly distinctive, especially in his disinterest in the authoritative standing of Moses on the one hand. On the other, the positive role of Moses as the mediator of the old covenant is not necessarily denounced, but the denial of his authority and the Johannine presentation of him almost exclusively in terms of witness appear to be a practical demotion in view of his status among the contemporary Jewish traditions. More interestingly, granting him a role of prosecutor against "Jews" is a remarkable reversal of expected roles. All these observations allow one to conclude that the fourth evangelist is a creative theologian and an exegete

---

[360] Paul Miller, "'They Saw His Glory and Spoke of Him': The Gospel of John and the Old Testament," in *Hearing the Old Testament in the New Testament*, ed. Stanley E. Porter (Grand Rapids: Eerdmans, 2006), 143-45.

[361] Tom Thatcher, "Remembering Jesus: John's Negative Christology," in *The Messiah in the Old and New Testaments*, ed. Stanley E. Porter (Grand Rapids: Eerdmans, 2007), 183.

notwithstanding his somewhat extensive appropriation of the Jewish languages and imageries related to Moses that were probably available to him and his readers.

CHAPTER 6

Concluding Reflections

Summary of Foregoing Observations

The main inquires set out at the beginning of this study concerned two questions: (1) the role of the major Old Testament characters in the Gospel of John with particular reference to Christology, and (2) the possible conceptual affinities with the current Jewish religious literature. In order to explore these two areas of inquiry, the first part of each chapter (with the exception of chapter two) examined the early Jewish portrayals of Elijah, David, and Moses with special interest in their messianic expectations as delineated in the intertestamental Jewish documents, such as, the Hebrew Old Testament, the Septuagint, the Apocrypha, the Pseudepigrapha, the Qumran writings, the rabbinic literature, and some early Hellenistic Jewish writings including Josephus and Philo. Then, the latter part of each chapter investigated the narrative function of these Old Testament characters (including Jacob and Abraham in chapter 2) for Johannine Christology.

In chapter 2, three pericopae (1:51; 4:10-14; 8:51-58) were examined with particular interest in allusions to Abraham and Jacob. A contextual exegesis of these passages resulted in a consistent portrayal of the two personages in terms of messianic witnesses of Jesus. Their messianic witness function fits nicely in the overall narrative flow of the chapters which surround the texts under discussion. This supportive role stands in contrast to their images conceived in the second temple period, which manifest the recognition of their virtuous characteristics and the provenance of Jewish heritages as one gains a glance of them in chs. 4 and 8. In spite of this role transformation in terms of witness, nevertheless, the presence of the two Jewish patriarchs provides a contact point. That is, the onset of the new redemptive history through Jesus stands in continuity, namely, with the outworking of the old redemptive history, most remarkably in their foreshadowing of the divine characteristics of the Messiah. Just as the salvific outworking was unraveled through Jacob in the Old Testament, so will it be through Jesus in John. On the other hand, the patriarchs are presented as the point of comparison/contrast since they demonstrate the enormous magnitude of the radical unfolding of the new redemptive program. This surpassing and superseding nature, at the same time, of the new redemptive history is reflected upon the divine nature of Messiah and the gift that is bestowed through him. These different depictions between John and second temple Judaism call into question the congruity of the two bodies of literature.

Chapter 3 revealed the fourth evangelist's disinterest in the Jewish messianic expectations of Elijah *redivivus*. One plausible explanation is due to its marginal influence in view of the wide spectrum of Jewish messianic hopes (compared to the Davidic or Mosaic messianic expectations). A more probable reason, however, seems that the Elijah *redivivus* hope does not tally with the evangelist's literary schema he reserved for the Scripture and the Old Testament heroic figures, that is, the role of messianic witnesses. Both Jesus and John the Baptist are not portrayed as an Elijah-like figure in the Fourth Gospel. In the case of the Baptist, the Johannine Gospel is remarkably distinct from the Synoptics, which consistently present him as Elijah *redivivus*. Rather, he occupies an equal standing with the Scripture and the Old Testament characters, that is, as a messianic witness in John. This observation points to the evangelist's emphasis on the witness theme in relation to Christology.

The image of David as envisaged in second temple Judaism and the Fourth Gospel was addressed in chapter 4. Contrary to the Synoptic Gospels and the Book of Revelation, the Gospel of John does not display affinity with some intertestamental Jewish writings that depict him as a royal messianic prefiguration. If a correspondence must be found, it is not in terms of a kingly figure but rather in terms of a righteous sufferer. Nonetheless, it must be also pointed out that second temple Judaism does not frequently appropriate such a theme as a particular mark of the Messiah. A contextual examination of the Johannine passages that relate to David demonstrates that he bears witness to the messianic characteristics of Jesus, his suffering in particular as a messianic qualification. The testimony of David for Jesus' messianic identity as foreshadowed in Psalms also exhibits the unity of the divine redemptive program in the Old and New Testaments regardless of the fourth evangelist's recasting of the ideal king figure merely as a witness for the coming Messiah.

Chapter 5 dealt with the depiction of Moses in John's Gospel and the intertestamental Jewish literature. In contrast to the constant Jewish appeal to Moses who was conceived as the Jewish authority figure, John presents him as a witness for the Christological identity of Jesus, and not as a messianic prefiguration. By his participation in the salvific events of the Pentateuch, the prophet *par excellence* metonymically communicates the gracious nature of the divine redemptive history, which culminates in Jesus events. Because God is the initiator of the salvation histories which involved both Moses and Jesus, Moses underscores the unity between the two Testaments. However, the role transformation of Moses in terms of a messianic witness results in a radical redefinition of his image to the readers of John. Although the positive role of Moses as the instrumental agent of the divine salvation history is not denounced, the denial of his authoritative standing and recasting of him almost exclusively as a witness to the main character must have been a practical devaluation to John's Jewish readers. More shockingly, his role is drastically reversed as a prosecutor of "Jews" to whom he was the one who shapes their identity and provides all divine sources to live a life of the covenant people of Yahweh. These literary schema allow us to label the fourth evangelist as a creative theologian notwithstanding his somewhat extensive appropriation of the Jewish languages and imageries related to Moses.

Research Results

Three final conclusions can be drawn from the foregoing summary. First, the Jewish hopes and the Johannine picture of Messiah via Jewish heroic figures display a certain degree of disparity. Contrary to some scholarly assessment, the messianic expectations via Jewish heroic figures, such as, Elijah, David, and Moses, were not widespread in the second temple period. In addition, the emphasis of Jewish messianism is not on certain personalities but on Yahweh who will be the initiator of the new era. Even when the intertestamental Jewish messianic figures are conceived to play an important part in the eschatological context, their images do not correlate closely with the messianic portrayals of Jesus in John. In particular, the militant warrior image of these figures does not tally with the Johannine picture of the messiah. Furthermore, the vicarious death and resurrection are distinctive features of the Johannine Messiah in the light of the intertestamental eschatological expectations through Jewish heroic figures.[1]

---

[1] A recent anthology on the Isaianic suffering servant explored the possibility of the organic link between Jewish and Johannine suffering messianic ideas. According to Martin Hengel and Daniel Bailey, for instance, the concept of a vicarious suffering messiah is not absent, although not prominent, in early Jewish literature. The implication of their assertion is that the fourth evangelist employed such a stream of ideas. Their observation could be valid. However, it seems to be entirely another matter to argue that such a trait of thought (however subtle) played a formative influence on Johannine Christology. In contrast to their position, a question arises because the vicarious suffering of a righteous one is not exclusively Jewish. The extremely sparse description of messiah as a righteous sufferer in intertestamental Jewish writings as well as the resurrection of Christ in John speaks against their proposition. Cf. Martin Hengel and Daniel P. Bailey, "The Effective History of Isaiah 53 in the Pre-Christian Period," in *The Suffering Servant: Isaiah 53 in Jewish and Christian Sources*, ed. Bernd Janowski and Peter Stuhlmacher (Grand Rapids: Eerdmans, 2004), 75-146; Peter Stuhlmacher, "Isaiah 53 in the Gospels and Acts," in *The Suffering Servant: Isaiah 53 in Jewish and Christian Sources*, ed. Bernd Janowski and Peter Stuhlmacher (Grand Rapids: Eerdmans, 2004), 159-60. Also, David C. Mitchell, "A Dying and Rising Josephite Messiah in 4Q372," *JSP* 18 (2009): 181-205; Marie-Françoise Baslez, "Écrire l'histoire dans le judaïsme hellénisé et le premier christianisme: Les galleries de figures ancestrales," in *Eukarpa: Études sur la Bible et ses exégètes en hommage à Gilles Dorival*, ed. Mireille Loubet and D. Pralon (Paris: Cerf, 2011), 191-204. See a recent investigation of rabbinic sources that contains a suffering messiah idea. The dating issue, nonetheless, is not adequately addressed. Paul Vaissi, "L'interprétation juive des prophéties messianiques de l'Ancien Testament de l'époque hellénistique aux Talmuds et aux premiers Midrashim," *Transversalités* 96 (2005): 105-38. The suffering servant in Isaiah 53 was variously understood, but a general conception was in terms of the people of Israel in the second temple Judaism. Edouard Robberechts, "Une relecture juive de la figure du Serviteur," *LumVie* 278 (2008): 67. For a more detailed discussion on the suffering of the messiah in early

Second, occurring in various contexts, the Old Testament protagonists (Jacob, Abraham, David, and Moses) conspicuously share one function in common in the Gospel of John. That is, they bear witness to the messianic identity of Jesus, and they are not depicted as messianic prefigurations. Taking into consideration the varied contexts in which these figures emerge in the second temple Jewish literature, this uniform function is remarkable. In addition, this witness function of these figures stands in close proximity with that of "." As reviewed in chapter 1, there are a number of German scholars as well as other exegetes from English speaking scholarship who consider the main narrative contribution of "Scripture" in John in terms of Christological witness. The same holds true with the Old Testament characters. This observation both confirms the judgment of those scholars and indicates the close correlation between the narrative functions of "Scripture" and the Old Testament figures. This messianic witness function, however, is hardly attested in the Hebrew Old Testament and subsequent early Jewish traditions. These observations allow us to conclude that a messianic typology via the Old Testament figures (i.e., David or Moses) is an inadequate framework to approach Johannine Christology.

Finally, the rich Old Testament background in echoes of and allusions to the Old Testament characters in John provides an opportunity to further elaborate on Jesus' divinely commissioned mission and his status as being equal to God. Contrary to some Johannine exegetes, the fourth evangelist does not place an emphasis on the messianic prefigurative role of certain Jewish heroic figures in his presentation of Jesus as Christ, the fulfillment of the promised messiah. Rather, the typology set over against this Old Testament background is not with the Jewish heroic figures but with Yahweh himself in relation to Jesus the messiah.

Implications for Study of John's Gospel

The preceding discussion fosters some implications for the study of John's Gospel, in particular, and more broadly for the New Testament writings in two respects. First, the consistent and homogeneous depiction of the Old Testament figures in terms of a witness function bears testimony in favor of the competent redactional capability of the fourth evangelist who is responsible for the present canonical form of the Gospel of John. This insight leaves a certain measure of hesitation toward a historical reconstruction of form-critical layers as proposed by Wayne Meeks and J.L. Martyn in their reconstruction of the so-called Johannine community. This point also adds up to the importance of the present textual form of the Gospel.

Second, the value of the early Jewish traditions for the study of John needs reconsideration. The Gospel of John is replete with a large number of Jewish expressions and images. Nonetheless, their use in John exhibits a considerable

---

Judaism, see Appendix 1: The Messianism/Christology in the Old Testament and in the Gospel of John.

degree of theological and hermeneutical disparity. Exegetes working on a religious comparative investigation are susceptible to translating these imageries into the theology of John without a careful attention to their respective contexts. The unique and creative theological construction of the fourth evangelist even over against his Jewish matrix deserves due attention. A biblical illustration could be helpful to make this point clearer. In 1 Samuel 12, the prophet Samuel rebuked the Israelites, who, in the face of the Ammonite invasion, wished to appoint one of their own as king over them although Yahweh was their king all along: "No, we want a king to rule over us" (1 Sam 12:12). Likewise, certain Jews of Jesus' time sought to find a messianic figure when Christ was with them all along from the beginning. The same tendency seems to pervade in the contemporary Johannine scholarship. That is, some Johannine exegetes are still looking for the Messiah who is anyone other than the Jesus of John's Gospel. Contrary to the repeated pattern of ignorance, the fourth evangelist lays a painstaking stress on the incomparable eminence of Jesus the messiah who uniquely shares the divine qualities with God as the premier revelation, through whom the unprecedented divine redemptive history is realized. The Christ as the fourth evangelist understood denies any comparison or analogy with the heroic and messianic prefigurations of the Jewish heritage. They are not worthy of such an honor as untying of shoe-string was impermissible for John the Baptist who is a representative of what the Old covenant is supposed to do in the divine redemptive history (that is, to make straight the way of the Lord, i.e., to direct attention to the promised messiah):

> He said,
> "I am the voice of one crying out in the wilderness,
> 'Make straight the way of the Lord,'"
> as the prophet Isaiah said;
>
> "the one who is coming after me; I am not worthy to untie the thong of his sandal" (John 1:23, 27, NRSV).

In this respect, the New Perspective studies especially in terms of the "exile and restoration" paradigm and tradition-historical approaches do not seem to give due emphasis on the explicit purpose of the fourth evangelist let alone the history-of-religions school which has not taken into proper perspective the rich Jewish background that permeates the Gospel of John.

As a side note, it strikes the readers of John that the typology set in terms of the Jewish heroic characters seems to be decidedly avoided by John. That aspect stands in stark contrast to other Jewish themes and images that are abundantly in use to portray the messianic identity and role of Jesus. Such conceptions are light, the temple, living water, bread, and the Passover lamb.

APPENDIX 1

The Messianism/Christology in the Old Testament and in the Fourth Gospel

The exploration of Johannine Christology within Jewish religious dimensions has sparked a heated debate over the provenance of Johannine Christology.[1] Such dissension has been expressed on a number of fronts. For instance, Charlesworth summarizes the scholarly consensus on the difficulty of messianic discussion in the New Testament: (1) the phrase "Messiah" (*ha Mashiach*) does not occur in the Old Testament per se, and it occurs only rarely in early Jewish literature in general, (2) Jewish messianism really arose in a noticeable way only in the first century B.C., due to the disintegration of the Hasmonean dynasty, (3) one cannot claim that in Jesus' day all or the vast majority of Jews were looking for a single messiah figure to rescue them, (4) there was no normative concept of messiah by which possible candidates, such as Jesus, were measured, (5) messianic titles and ideas were fluid and often related to each other, and (6) the first clear evidence for the use of messiah as a technical term for a royal figure in the line of David is found in the Psalms of Solomon 17-18 and the Parable of Enoch, both of which probably date to the first century B.C.[2] In addition, dissimilar to John, messianism is not a dominant motif running throughout the Old Testament and early Judaism. Georg Fohrer construes that messianism is not overall the culmination of the Old Testament theology:

---

[1] For methodological considerations concerning research into Messianism, see James H. Charlesworth, "Introduction: Messianic Ideas in Early Judaism," in *Qumran-Messianism: Studies on the Messianic Expectations in the Dead Sea Scrolls*, ed. James H. Charlesworth, Hermann Lichtenberger, Gerbern S. Oegeman (Tübingen: Mohr Siebeck, 1998), 1-8.

[2] James H. Charlesworth, "From Messianology to Christology: Problems and Prospects," in *The Messiah: Developments in Earliest Judaism and Christianity: The First Princeton Symposium on Judaism and Christian Origins*, ed. James H. Charlesworth (Minneapolis: Fortress, 1992), 3-35. For another survey of the difficulties, see Dietmar Neufeld, "And When That One Comes?: Aspects of Johannine Messianism," in *Eschatology, Messianism, and the Dead Sea Scrolls*, ed. Craig A. Evans and Peter W. Flint (Grand Rapids: Eerdmans, 1997), 120-40.

Es verhält sich nicht so, daß die Messiaserwartung die Krönung der alttestamentlichen Theologie darstellt.[3]

Quantitatively speaking, Daniel Block independently accords with Fohrer's judgment.

> With respect to the nature of the Old Testament itself, given the prevalence of messianic expectation in the intertestamental and early New Testament periods, it would be surprising if those responsible for the structure and arrangement of the canon were not driven to some extent by messianic hope. . . . As a matter of fact, the books that make up the Old Testament are not obviously preoccupied with the messiah. . . . the messianic hope [in the OT] is embedded like a diamond, precious not only because of its intrinsic value, but in the Hebraic sense also because of its rarity. . . . [that the Old Testament is filled with the divine redemptive hope], but to characterize this as an overtly and pervasively messianic hope is to overstate the case. Explicit reference to the messiah in the Pentateuch can be counted on a single hand.[4]

However, Block's notion of "the prevalence of messianic expectation in the intertestamental period" needs further qualification in view of the majority of biblical scholars' estimation of messianism in the period. For instance, Charlesworth is one of a large number of experts on the second temple messianism and his judgment on the prevalence of this trait of idea serves as a fair sampling of the current scholarly sentiment on this issue:

> My answer to this question [did most Jews look for or yearn for the coming of the Messiah?], based on the vast number of early Jewish texts . . . is probably "no." What impresses me is that when "the Messiah" is mentioned his functions and his relations to the End of time . . . is far from obvious. I am convinced that the ancient Jew was often intentionally ambiguous. He comprehended that only God knew who would be the Messiah, and what the Messiah would accomplish. An apparent exception may be the *Psalms of Solomon*, but even in this text . . . the author subordinates the Messiah to God; that is, the Lord of the Messiah is God alone.[5]

An example of such a majority view is attested in an article contributed to the same volume in which Block's article is found. Craig Evans, for example, notes the statistical dearth of references to messianism in the Qumran community (of which a large number of scholars find a close affinity, directly or indirectly, with

---

[3] Georg Fohrer, "Das Alte Testament und das Thema 'Christologie,'" *EvTh* 30 (1970): 285, cited in Heinz-Josef Fabry, "Altes Testament, Frühjudentum und Qumran," in *Der Messias: Perspecktiven des Alten und Neuen Testaments*, ed. Heinz-Josef Fabry and Klaus Scholtissek (Würzburg: Echter, 2002), 11.

[4] Daniel I. Block, "My Servant David: Ancient Israel's Vision of the Messiah," in *Israel's Messiah in the Bible and the Dead Sea Scrolls*, ed. Richard S. Hess and M. Daniel Carroll R. (Grand Rapids: Baker, 2003), 20-22. Brackets are added for clarification.

[5] Charlesworth, "Introduction," 5. Italics are original and brackets are added for clarification.

John's Gospel).[6] Out of all the 870 scrolls recovered from the Qumran caves, 650 are non-biblical. Of these 650, only thirteen scrolls refer to a person who is anointed (messiah is named in six scrolls to be exact) or allude to some messianic symbols (i.e., "prince," "scepter," "son," or "branch of David").[7] Two of the final four conclusions which Evans reaches are especially pertinent to our discussion. That is, the Qumran community was not preoccupied with messianism; and in comparison with contemporary Jewish messianism, Qumran's messian-

---

[6] For advocates of close parallels between the New Testament Christology and the Qumran messianism, see Karl G. Kuhn, "Die in Palästina gefundenen hebräischen Texte und das Neue Testament," *ZTK* 47 (1950): 192-211; Raymond E. Brown, "The Qumran Scrolls and the Johannine Gospel and Epistles," in *The Scrolls and the New Testament*, ed. Krister Stendahl (New York: Harper, 1957), 183-207; James H. Charlesworth, ed., *John and the Dead Sea Scrolls* (New York: Crossroad, 1991); Aage Pilgaard, "The Qumran Scrolls and John's Gospel," in *New Readings in John: Literary and Theological Perspectives: Essays from the Scandinavian Conference on the Fourth Gospel in Århus 1997*, ed. Johannes Nissen and Sigfred Pedersen (Sheffield: Sheffield, 1999), 126-42; Hermann Lichtenberger, "Messiasvorstellungen in Qumran und die neutestamentliche Christologie," *CV* 44 (2002): 139-60. However, an increasing number of scholars have recently offered skeptical responses to a linear relationship between the two. See Howard M. Teeple, "Qumran and the Origin of the Fourth Gospel," *NovT* 4 (1960): 6-25; Richard Bauckham, "Qumran and the Fourth Gospel: Is There a Connection?" in *Scrolls and the Scriptures: Qumran Fifty Years After*, ed. Stanley E. Porter and Craig A. Evans (Sheffield: Sheffield, 1997), 267-79; idem, "The Qumran Community and the Gospel of John," in *Dead Sea Scrolls: Fifty Years after Their Discovery, Proceedings of the Jerusalem Congress, July 20-25, 1997*, ed. Galen Marquis et al. (Jerusalem: Israel Exploration Society, 2000), 105-15; David E. Aune, "Dualism in the Fourth Gospel and the Dead Sea Scrolls: A Reassessment of the Problem," in *Neotestamentica et Philonica: Studies in Honor of Peder Borgen*, ed. David E. Aune, Torrey Seland, and Jarl Henning Ulrichsen (Leiden: Brill, 2003), 281-303. For an expression of mild skepticism, see Jörg Frey, "Different Patterns of Dualistic Thought in the Qumran Library: Reflections on Their Background and History," in *Legal Texts and Legal Issues: Proceedings of the Second Meeting of the International Organization for Qumran Studies Cambridge 1995, Published In Honour of Joseph M. Baumgarten*, ed. Moshe Bernstein, Florentino García Martínez, and John Kampen (Leiden: Brill, 1997), 335.

[7] Craig A. Evans, "The Messiah in the Dead Sea Scrolls," in *Israel's Messiah in the Bible and the Dead Sea Scrolls*, ed. Richard S. Hess and M. Daniel Carroll R. (Grand Rapids: Baker, 2003), 86-88. Some scholars posit that "the Righteous Teacher" was an anticipated messianic figure in the Qumran community. For example, see Philip R. Davies, "The Teacher of Righteousness and the 'End of Days,'" in *Sects and Scrolls: Essays on Qumran and Related Topics* (Atlanta: Scholars, 1996), 89-94. However, the possibility has been generally denied. Michael A. Knibb, "Teacher of Righteousness—A Messianic Title?" in *A Tribute to Geza Vermes: Essays on Jewish and Christian Literature and History*, ed. Philip R. Davies and Richard T. White (Sheffield: JSOT, 1990), 51-65; idem, "Teacher of Righteousness," *EDSS*, 2:921; Géza G. Xeravits, *King, Priest, Prophet: Positive Eschatological Protagonists of the Qumran Library* (Leiden: Brill, 2003), 47-50.

ism is not distinctive in any significant way.[8] Of course, there are those who may not concur with Charlesworth and Evans.[9] These two scholars, nonetheless, represent a large segment of biblical scholarship that does not reckon messianism to be the most predominant motif of the Hebrew bible and the Judaism of the Second Temple period.[10]

Second, even those Hebrew texts which do entertain Jewish messianic ideas do not present us with a concrete and consistent picture, but paint variegated images of Messiah.[11] Block's estimation of the unified and linear Davidic royal messianic hope of the Old Testament represents a significant contemporary revival of E. Schürer, who argued that Second Temple Judaism had more or less a monolithic understanding of Messiah and that it could not accept Jesus'

---

[8] Evans, "The Messiah in the Dead Sea Scrolls," 100. For the Qumran library as a fair representative of Second Temple Judaism in general, see John J. Collins, *The Scepter and the Star: The Messiahs of the Dead Sea Scrolls and Other Ancient Literature* (Grand Rapids: Eerdmans, 2010), 1-19.

[9] For an example of those who see a prevalent messianic idea in the Hebrew bible, see John H. Sailhamer, "The Messiah and the Hebrew Bible," *JETS* 44 (2001): 5-23. For a higher interest in messianism of Qumran, see Bilhah Nitzan, "Eschatological Motives in Qumran Literature: The Messianic Concept," in *Eschatology in the Bible and in Jewish and Christian Tradition*, ed. Henning Graf Reventlow (Sheffield: Sheffield, 1997), 132-51.

[10] For example, see E.P. Sanders, *Judaism, Practice and Belief: 63 BCE—66 CE* (Philadelphia: Trinity, 1992), 295; James D.G. Dunn, *The Parting of the Ways between Judaism and Christianity and Their Significance for the Character of Christianity* (London: SCM, 1991), 26-29; and James H. Charlesworth, "The Messiah in the Pseudepigrapha," *ANRW* 19.1:188-218. Cf. "[M]essianic references in the Pseudepigrapha are sparse. There is no evidence of messianism at the time of the Maccabean revolt, and indeed messianic expectations seem to have been dormant throughout much of the Second Temple period." John J. Collins, "Jesus and the Messiahs of Israel," in *Geschichte—Tradition—Reflection: Festschrift für Martin Hengel zum 70. Geburtstag*, ed. Hubert Cancik, Hermann Lichtenberger, and Peter Schäfer (Tübingen: Siebeck, 1996), 3:287-88. Charlesworth finds only five documents that contain explicit messianic references such as "Messiah," "Anointed One," or "Christ," in the entire corpus of the Old Testament Pseudepigrapha. James H. Charlesworth, "Messianology in the Biblical Pseudepigrapha," in *Qumran-Messianism: Studies on the Messianic Expectations in the Dead Sea Scrolls*, ed. James H. Charlesworth, Hermann Lichtenberger, Gerbern S. Oegeman (Tübingen: Mohr Siebeck, 1998), 29. For another mainstream assessment of the minimal messianic ideas in the Old Testament, see Joachim Becker, *Messianic Expectation in the Old Testament* (Philadelphia: Fortress, 1980).

[11] Loren T. Stuckenbruck, "Messianic Ideas in the Apocalyptic and Related Literature of Early Judaism," in *The Messiah in the Old and New Testaments*, ed. Stanley E. Porter (Grand Rapids: Eerdmans, 2007), 90-116; Lawrence H. Schiffman, "Messianic Figures and Ideas in the Qumran Scrolls," in *Qumran and Jerusalem: Studies in the Dead Sea Scrolls and the History of Judaism* (Grand Rapids: Eerdmans, 2010), 270-85.

self-designation of Davidic messiah primarily because of his death on the cross.[12] Schürer's theory, however, has come under severe criticism since the 1990s, due mainly to the increasing scholarly sensitivity to the inadequate exegetical methods of Schürer and the findings of the Qumran documents. In the face of the variegated images of Messiah, Schürer's theory seems to run against the plain reading of the Jewish messianic texts.[13] In addition, in the face of the recent evaluations of the Qumran messianic documents (which conceive three redeemer figures, a priest, a prophet, and a prince), it is precarious to speak of a "central theme" of the Jewish eschatological expectations, especially in terms of royal messianism.[14] In short, early Judaism envisaged eschatological messianic hopes

---

[12] Emil Schürer, *The History of the Jewish People in the Age of Jesus Christ*, 3 vols., trans. T.A. Burkill et al., rev. and ed. Geza Vermes et al. (Edinburgh: T & T Clark, 1973-1986). For criticisms of Block in the same volume, see J. Daniel Hays, "If He Looks like a Prophet and Talks like a Prophet, Then He Must Be . . .: A Response to Daniel I. Block," in *Israel's Messiah in the Bible and the Dead Sea Scrolls*, ed. Richard S. Hess and M. Daniel Carroll R. (Grand Rapids: Baker, 2003), 57-70; M. Daniel Carroll R., "New Lenses to Establish Messiah's Identity?: A Response to Daniel I. Block," in *Israel's Messiah in the Bible and the Dead Sea Scrolls*, ed. Richard S. Hess and M. Daniel Carroll R. (Grand Rapids: Baker, 2003), 71-81. For earlier attempts to subsume various messianic hopes under that of David, see Geo Widengren, "King and Covenant," *JSS* 2 (1957): 1-32; Antonius H.J. Gunneweg, "Sinaibund und Davidsbund," *VT* 10 (1960): 335-41; Klaus Seybold, *Das Davidische Königtum im Zeugnis der Propheten* (Göttingen: Vandenhoeck & Ruprecht, 1972); Hartmut Gese, "The Messiah," in *Essays on Biblical Theology*, trans. Keith Crim (Minneapolis: Augsburg, 1981), 141-66.

[13] For a research history of this development, see Stefan Schreiber, *Gesalbter und König: Titel und Konzeptionen der königlichen Gesalbtenerwartung in frühjüdischen und urchristlichen Schriften* (Berlin: Walter de Gruyter, 2000), 5-19. Cf. "Christian historians must be honest and admit that the Jesus known to us from the New Testament simply does not fit the profile of the Davidic Messiah which was espoused by many Jews of his time." Charlesworth, "Introduction," 6. Also, John Collins does not see the intertestamental messianic expectation to be a uniform system. According to his evaluation of Jewish messianic texts, the early Jewish messianic expectation was, contrary to Schürer and George F. Moore, not ubiquitous and did not have a consistent form. Collins, *The Scepter and the Star*, 3.

[14] Gary N. Knoppers, "David's Relation to Moses: The Contexts, Content and Conditions of the Davidic Promises," in *King and Messiah in Israel and the Ancient Near East: Proceedings of the Oxford Old Testament Seminar*, ed. John Day (Sheffield: Sheffield, 1998), 91-118; Fabry, "Altes Testament, Frühjudentum und Qumran," 11. The linear development of the Jewish messianic expectations are suggested by Block, Antti Laato, *A Star Is Rising: The Historical Development of the Old Testament Royal Ideology and the Rise of Jewish Messianic Expectations* (Atlanta: Scholars, 1997), 394; Schreiber, *Gesalbter und König*; William Horbury, *Jewish Messianism and the Cult of Christ* (London: SCM, 1998); idem, *Messianism among Jews and Christians: Twelve Biblical and Historical Studies* (London: T & T Clark, 2003). For more diversified views of messianism, see Becker, *Messianic Expectation in the Old Testament*; Jacob Neusner, William S. Green, and Ernest S. Frerichs, eds., *Judaisms and Their Messiahs at the Turn of Christian Era* (Cambridge: CUP, 1987); Marinus de Jonge, *Christology*

in various terms such as in priestly, prophetic, or heavenly messianic figures, along with a royal Davidic figure, which can be said to be the most predominant one. This second aspect of Jewish messianism poses an intriguing question since the Fourth Gospel seems to consistently portray the typical Jewish messianic figures, who were expected to play a *redivivus* messiah, in terms of messianic witnesses rather than messianic prefigurations or types. The most pressing question is, not whether the Old Testament messianic ideas can be subsumed under a royal Davidic expectation (although it is questionable), but how we account for this novel and seemingly contrasting element of messianism as depicted in John.[15] Nevertheless, one caveat is in order with reference to early Jewish messianism. Although the intertestamental messianism was expressed via a range of symbols and figures, the Jews in various times and places held to some common elements of messianism, especially in their understandings of more

---

in Context: The Earliest Christian Response to Jesus (Philadelphia: Westminster, 1988); idem, *Jesus, the Servant-Messiah* (New Haven: Yale University Press, 1991); idem, *God's Final Envoy: Early Christology and Jesus' Own View of His Mission* (Grand Rapids: Eerdmans, 1998); Collins, *The Scepter and the Star*; James H. Charlesworth, ed., *The Messiah: Developments in Earliest Judaism and Christianity* (Minneapolis: Fortress, 1992); idem, Hermann Lichtenberger, and Gerbern S. Oegema, eds., *Qumran-Messianism: Studies on the Messianic Expectations in the Dead Sea Scrolls* (Tübingen: Mohr Siebeck, 1998); John Day, ed., *King and Messiah in Israel and the Ancient Near East: Proceedings of the Oxford Old Testament Seminar* (Sheffield: Sheffield, 1998); Johan Lust, *Messianism and the Septuagint: Collected Essays* (Leuven: Leuven University Press, 2004). For those who see a single, composite Messiah in Qumran, see William S. LaSor, "The Messiahs of Aaron and Israel," *VT* 6 (1956): 425-29; Robert B. Laurin, "Problem of Two Messiahs in the Qumran Scrolls," *RevQ* 4 (1963): 39-52; Emil A. Wcela, "Messiah(s) of Qumrân," *CBQ* 26 (1964): 340-49; Martin G. Abegg, Jr., "The Messiah at Qumran: Are We Still Seeing Double?" *DSD* 2 (1995): 125-44; L.D. Hurst, "Did Qumran Expect Two Messiahs?" *BBR* 9 (1999): 157-80. However, recent biblical scholarship is increasingly acknowledging the faith in multiple messianic figures in the Qumran writings. See Jean Starcky, "Les quatre étapes du messianisme à Qumran," *RB* 70 (1963): 481-505; George J. Brooke, "The Amos-Numbers Midrash (*CD* 7:13b-8:1a) and Messianic Expectation," *ZAW* 92 (1980): 397-404; idem, "The Messiah of Aaron in the Damascus Document," *RevQ* 15 (1991-1992): 215-30; idem, "Kingship and Messianism in the Dead Sea Scrolls," in *King and Messiah in Israel und the Ancient Near East: Proceedings of the Oxford Old Testament Seminar*, ed. John Day (Sheffield: Sheffield, 1998), 434-55; Gerbern S. Oegeman, *The Anointed and His People: Messianic Expectations from the Maccabees to Bar Kochba* (Sheffield: Sheffield, 1998), 86-96, 108-26; Johannes Zimmermann, *Messianische Texte aus Qumran: Königliche, priesterliche und prophetische Messiasvorstellungen in den Schriftfunden von Qumran* (Tübingen: Mohr Siebeck, 1998); Géza G. Xeravits, "The Early History of Qumran's Messianic Expectations," *ETL* 76 (2000): 113-21; and John C. Poirier, "The Endtime Return of Elijah and Moses at Qumran," *DSD* 10 (2003): 221-42.

[15] Martin J. Selman, "Messianic Mysteries," in *The Lord's Anointed: Interpretation of Old Testament Messianic Texts*, ed. Philip E. Satterthwaite, Richard S. Hess, and Gordon J. Wenham (Grand Rapids: Baker, 1995), 281-302.

popular "messianic texts" such as Genesis 49:10, Isaiah 10:34-11:5, and Numbers 24:17 for examples from the Old Testament and 1QSa 2.22-23 for an example from the Qumran literature.[16]

Third, although a composite picture of those various Jewish messianic expectations could be supposedly put together as some scholars such as Block suggest, it departs significantly from John's presentation of messiah. Some notable examples can be listed here. First, contrary to the strenuous emphasis of the Fourth Gospel, the messiahs in Jewish texts usually do not carry a divine connotation, at least not on the level attested to in John.[17] Second, the suffering and death of messiah is not clearly anticipated.[18] For instance, it is not entirely clear whether Isaiah 53, one of the favorite Christian messianic proof texts, speaks of the messiah.[19] Furthermore, the messianic fulfillment formulae in the Gospel of

---

[16] Andrew Chester, "Jewish Messianic Expectations and Mediatorial Figures and Pauline Christology," in *Paulus und das antike Judentum: Tübingen-Durham-Symposium im Gedenken an den 50. Todestag Adolf Schlatters (19. Mai 1938)*, ed. Martin Hengel and Ulrich Heckel (Tübingen: Mohr Siebeck, 1991), 40-43; Collins, *The Scepter and the Star*, 4; Pomykala, *The Davidic Dynasty Tradition in Early Judaism*, 180-216; Richard Bauckham, "The Messianic Interpretation of Isa. 10.34 in the Dead Sea Scrolls, 2 Baruch and the Preaching of John the Baptist," *DSD* 2 (1995): 202-16; Evans, "David in the Dead Sea Scrolls," 194; Ed Condra, *Salvation for the Righteous Revealed: Jesus amid Covenantal and Messianic Expectations in Second Temple Judaism* (Leiden: Brill, 2002), 198-271; Richard Bauckham, "Jewish Messianism according to the Gospel of John," in *Challenging Perspectives in the Gospel of John* (Tübingen: Mohr Siebeck, 2006), 52-58.

[17] This aspect has resulted in the recent debate between Larry Hurtado and Maurice Casey. Maurice Casey, "Lord Jesus Christ: A Response to Professor Hurtado," *JSNT* 27 (2004): 83-96; Larry W. Hurtado, "Devotion to Jesus and Historical Investigation: A Grateful, Clarifying and Critical Response to Professor Casey," *JSNT* 27 (2004): 97-104. For more complete arguments of both, see Maurice Casey, *From Jewish Prophet to Gentile God: The Origins and Development of New Testament Christology* (Louisville: Westminster/John Knox, 1991); idem, *Is John's Gospel True?* (London: Routledge, 1996); Larry W. Hurtado, *One God, One Lord: Early Christian Devotion and Ancient Jewish Monotheism* (London: T & T Clark, 1998); idem, *Lord Jesus Christ: Devotion to Jesus in Earliest Christianity* (Grand Rapids: Eerdmans, 2003). The latter conceives a radical redefinition of messianic ideas in the New Testament. What Moule and Chest label as "evolutionary view," Casey's position is summarized and critiqued in Andrew Chester, *Messiah and Exaltation: Jewish Messianic and Visionary Traditions and New Testament Christology* (Tübingen: Mohr Siebeck, 2007), 14-17, also, see James F. McGrath, *The Only True God: Early Christian Monotheism in Its Jewish Context* (Urbana: University of Illinois Press, 2009), 9.

[18] "For nonbelievers in antiquity, however, the great objection to the recognition of Jesus as Davidic messiah was not his nonmessianic career, but the shameful defeat of his death." Collins, *The Scepter and the Star*, 234.

[19] The texts usually attributed to for this concept do not resonate explicit messianic overtones. Bernd Janowski, "The One God of the Two Testaments: Basic Questions of a Biblical Theology," *ThTo* 57 (2000): 306-08; Hays, "If He Looks like a Prophet and Talks like a Prophet, Then He Must Be . . .," 65-66.

John point to a number of Psalm passages, which of course have David in the historical contexts, and they are certainly not prophetic in nature. Third, in the Old Testament and the intertestamental Jewish literature, the most conspicuous qualification of the messiah was the militant subjugation of the Gentiles, which is unlike the New Testament characterization of the Messiah:

> The concept of a royal messiah was more widespread than any other, and this figure was consistently expected to drive out the Gentiles by force .... The *degree* of messianic expectation probably fluctuated considerably in the first century. There does not, however, appear to have been much variation in the *character* of royal messiah that was expected .... Despite its admitted variety, the evidence of the [Qumran] Scrolls provides a persistent profile of the Davidic/royal messiah. The most striking aspect of this profile is the militancy it involved. It was a primary requirement of the messiah that he overcome the Gentile enemies of Israel. Precisely here lies the anomaly of the messianic claims of Jesus of Nazareth, as Albert Schweitzer already saw. There is little evidence of a militant Jesus in the Gospels.[20]

Lastly, the Jewish messiah is hardly expected to be resurrected and to ascend into heaven:

> Jewish *Religionsgeschichte* presents an additional problem. To be sure, we have accounts of the translation of certain righteous men, and we hear also of isolated instances of resurrection. But that a righteous man via resurrection from the dead was appointed as Messiah, is absolutely without analogy. Neither resurrection nor translation have anything to do with messiahship.[21]

The term, "Christology," therefore, represents an expression that is thoroughly baptized in Christian nomenclature in contradistinction to its Jewish semantic origin, "Messiah":

> Thus, although Christ is the Greek translation of the Semitic Messiah, in John Christology is the Christian transformation of Jewish expectations.[22]

---

[20] Collins, "Jesus and the Messiahs of Israel," 290, 295-96. Italics are original and parentheses are added for clarification.

[21] Hengel, "Jesus, the Messiah of Israel: The Debate about the "Messianic Mission" of Jesus," in *Authenticating the Activities of Jesus*, ed. Bruce Chilton and Criag A. Evans (Leiden: Brill, 1999), 327; idem, "Jesus der Messias Israels," in *Der messianische Anspruch Jesu und die Anfänge der Christologie: Vier Studien*, ed. Martin Hengel and Anna M. Schwemer (Tübingen: Mohr Siebeck, 2001), 45-62.

[22] John Painter, "The Point of John's Christology: Christology, Conflict and Community in John," in *Christology, Controversy and Community: New Testament Essays in Honor of David R. Catchpole*, ed. David G. Horrell and Christopher M. Tuckett (Leiden: Brill, 2000), 250; cf. William Horbury, *Jewish Messianism and the Cult of Christ* (London: SCM, 1998), 112-19.

APPENDIX 2

Religionsgeschichte and the Fourth Gospel

Importance of *Religionsgeschichte*

In the middle of the 19th century, a group of biblical scholars began to explore a new approach to apprehend the genesis of the Bible. Commonly referred to as *religionsgeschichtliche Schule* (history of religions school) or *Religionswissenschaft* (science or study of religion), these scholars in this trend generally emphasize the formative influence of the adjacent cultural and religious milieu for the production of the Bible, and not early Jewish traditions and Judaism.[1] The question of *religionsgeschichte* is of crucial importance for the study of the Fourth Gospel. The reason can be unpacked in two respects. First, the issue demands certain kinds of religious writings be taken into consideration more seriously than others. Second, the significance of such an inquiry directly impinges upon the importance of the Hebrew Old Testament and the following Jewish religious traditions for the final analysis of the entire Gospel. In regard to the former, Mandean and Nag Hammadi documents, instead of the Dead Sea Scrolls and other Jewish literature in the second temple period, should be rigorously taken into account. With the latter aspect in view, the outcome of the study on Jewish elements of the Gospel (such as the role of the Old Testament characters for the present study) is only marginally relevant to grasping the core message of the Gospel since it only reveals the primitive and rudimentary Palestinian traditions buried underneath the later Hellenistic redactional layers

---

[1] For surveys of this approach, see Henning Graf Reventlow, *From the Enlightenment to the Twentieth Century*, vol. 4 of *History of Biblical Interpretation*, trans. Leo G. Purdue (Leiden: Brill, 2011), 335-78; Erhard S. Gerstenberger, "Albert Eichhorn and Hermann Gunkel: The Emergence of a History of Religion School," in *The Nineteenth Century*, vol. 3, part 1 of *Hebrew Bible/Old Testament*, ed. Magne Sæbo (Göttingen: Vandenhoeck & Ruprecht, 2013), 454-71; William Baird, *From C.H. Dodd to Hans Dieter Betz*, vol. 3 of *History of New Testament Research* (Minneapolis: Fortress, 2013), 196-211. For helpful discussions on this approach, see Jörg Frey, "Zum Problem der Aufgabe und Durchführung einer Theologie des Neuen Testaments," in *Aufgabe und Durchführung einer Theologie des Neuen Testaments*, ed. Cilliers Breytenbach and Jörg Frey (Tübingen: Mohr Siebeck, 2007), 3-53; Gerd Lüdemann, "The Relationship of Biblical Studies to the History of Religions School, with Reference to the Scientific Study of Religion," *TJT* 24 (2008): 171-81.

contained in John's Gospel.[2] Therefore, it is of grave importance to set the issue of the history of religions in proper perspective so as to secure both appropriate methods by which to get to the center of John's message and to expect the degree of significance that the conclusion of this kind of study will bring forth for a proper understanding of the Gospel of John.

Bickermann/Hengel Theory

The contributions of Bickermann and Hengel have appropriately noticed the inadequate bifurcation of Hellenistic and Palestinian Judaisms in sharply distinct terms, since the Judaism in the Second Temple period was not immune to the contiguous Hellenistic cultures.[3] Accordingly, the classical nomenclature, i.e., "normative Judaism" or even "Hellenistic Judaism" fell out of favor in scholarly dialogues.[4] Nonetheless, it still seems to be legitimate to speak of the distinctly Jewish elements of Judaism against its surrounding cultures in first-century Palestine, not with reference to the language and customs, but particularly with regards to the Jewish monotheism and its concomitant religious practices. This distinction has been duly noted in the recent archaeological discoveries undertaken in Judea and Galilee. Contrary to the previous generation's assumption, some of the most recent researchers strongly suggest that a large number of the Palestinian Jews between the last century B.C. and the first century A.D. (or at least until the first half of the first century) did not compromise, in a substantial measure, their core religious beliefs and practices, such as, monotheism, ethnic exclusivity, particular ethic, the observance of Sabbath, circumcision, the temple

---

[2] Examples of somewhat overgeneralizing form-critical approach to the Gospel of John can be found in Claus Westermann, *The Gospel of John in the Light of the Old Testament*, trans. Siegfried S. Schatzmann (Peabody: Hendrickson, 1998); and Jaime Clark-Soles, *Scripture Cannot Be Broken: The Social Function of the Use of Scripture in the Fourth Gospel* (Leiden: Brill, 2003). Generally speaking, the former operates on the level of the history of religions perspective and the latter on a socio-political one.

[3] Elias J. Bickermann, *The Jews in the Greek Age* (Cambridge: Harvard University Press, 1988); Martin Hengel, *Judaism and Hellenism: Studies in Their Encounter in Palestine during the Early Hellenistic Period* (Minneapolis: Fortress, 1974); idem, "Judaism and Hellenism Revisited," in *Hellenism in the Land of Israel*, ed. John J. Collins and Gregory E. Sterling (Notre Dame: University of Notre Dame Press, 2001), 6-37.

[4] Shaye J.D. Cohen, *From the Maccabees to the Mishnah* (Louisville: Westminster John Knox, 2006), 29. Also, for recent studies that underscore the multi-cultural aspect of the Palestine in the time of Jesus, see Werner Eck, *Rom und Judaea: Fünf Vorträge zur römischen Herrschaft in Palästina* (Tübingen: Mohr Siebeck, 2007); Jürgen Zangenberg, Harold W. Attridge, and Dale B. Martin, eds. *Religion, Ethnicity, and Identity in Ancient Galilee: A Region in Transition* (Tübingen: Mohr Siebeck, 2007); Kenneth C. Hanson and Douglas E. Oakman, *Palestine in the Time of Jesus: Social Structures and Social Conflicts* (Minneapolis: Fortress, 2008); Christopher Stenschke, "Judea in the First Century AD: A Review of Recent Scholarly Contributions and Their Implications," *EuroJT* 20 (2011): 15-28.

cult, and dietary laws.[5]

Hellenistic (Especially Gnostic) Influence

Broadly speaking, the formative religious backgrounds proposed as the backdrop of the Fourth Gospel can be broken down into two general categories, namely, Hellenistic (i.e., mystery religion, Gnosticism, Mandaism, and Platonism) and Jewish (i.e., the Hebrew, Greek, and Aramaic Jewish scriptures, the Qumran scrolls, the Apocrypha, the Pseudepigrapha, and, with further qualifications, some of the early rabbinic literature). The supposed Hellenistic religious backgrounds theory initially arose from the internal textual dissimilarities between the Fourth Gospel and the Synoptics during the heyday of source criticism, although other philosophical factors are suspected to have contributed to the development of the Gnostic provenance theory. For instance, a number of scholars point to the anti-supernatural impulse of the enlightenment period and F.C. Baur's Hegelian dialectical analysis of the developmental history of the early church.[6] These two tendencies are thought to have given impetus to the view that located John's Gospel in an intermediary stage between Hellenism and Judaism although stemming from a Hellenistic community (so much more Hel-

---

[5] Roland Deines, "The Pharisees between 'Judaisms' and 'Common Judaism,'" in *The Complexities of Second Temple Judaism*, vol. 1 of *Justification and Variegated Nomism*, ed. D.A. Carson, Peter T. O'Brien, and Mark A. Seifrid (Tübingen: Mohr Siebeck, 2001), 453. For more recent and nuanced correctives to Hengel's thesis, see Louis H. Feldman, "Hengel's Judaism and Hellenism in Retrospect," *JBL* 96 (1977): 371-82; Jonathan Goldstein, "Jewish Acceptance and Rejection of Hellenism," in *Semites, Iranians, Greeks, and Romans: Studies in their Interactions* (Atlanta: Scholars, 1990), 1-32; Lester L. Grabbe, *Judaic Religion in the Second Temple Period: Belief and Practice from the Exile to Yavneh* (London: Routledge, 2000); idem, "The Jews and Hellenization: Hengel and His Critics," in *Second Temple Studies III: Studies in Politics, Class and Material Culture*, ed. Philip R. Davies and John M. Halligan (Sheffield: JSOT, 2002), 52-66; E.P. Sanders, "Jesus' Galilee," in *Fair Play: Diversity and Conflicts in Early Christianity, Essays in Honour of Heikki Räisänen*, ed. Ismo Dunderberg, Christopher Tuckett, and Kari Syreeni (Leiden: Brill, 2002), 3-42; Uzi Leibner, *Settlement and History in Hellenistic, Roman, and Byzantine Galilee: An Archaeological Survey of the Eastern Galilee* (Tübingen: Mohr Siebeck, 2009), 331-45; Baird, *From C.H. Dodd to Hans Dieter Betz*, 324-25.

[6] F.C. Baur's historical reconstruction of the development of the early church has been proven to be without an adequate basis in the face of the stunning discovery of the John Rylands papyrus which dates back to 125 A.D. More surprising is the manuscript's Egyptian origin for there must have been a significant block of time for John's original manuscript to be copied and travel to Egypt. All these factors locate the writing of the Fourth Gospel at least at the end of the first century A.D. Cf. Bruce M. Metzger and Bart D. Ehrman, *The Text of the New Testament: Its Transmission, Corruption, and Restoration* (Oxford: OUP, 2005), 55-56. *Contra*, Andreas Schmidt, "Zwei Anmerkungen zu P. Ryl. III 457," *APF* 35 (1989): 11-12.

lenistic than Jewish due to its geographic provenance, i.e., Syria or Antioch).[7] Based on these two assumptions, the history of religions school thought to have uncovered close parallels of the Gospel in Hellenistic documents (especially Egyptian and middle-Eastern Gnostic).[8]

Idiosyncratic terms and concepts appearing in John's Gospel have also led a number of scholars to presume disparate religious backgrounds. Such terms as "logos" and "paraclete" are unique to John's Gospel. In addition, some of the peculiar Johannine concepts include the identification of the revelation with the revealer (Jesus), the I am sayings, the pre-existence of Christ, the descending and ascending of the Son of Man, and the dualistic expressions (above/below, light/darkness, true/false, spirit/flesh, and free/enslaved).[9]

---

[7] Joachim Kügler, "Das Johannesevangelium," in *Einleitung in das Neue Testament*, ed. Martin Ebner and Stefan Schreiber (Stuttgart: Kohlhammer, 2008), 217-18.

[8] For a helpful survey of the history of research, see Jörg Frey, "Auf der Suche nach dem Kontext des vierten Evangeliums: Eine forschungsgeschichtliche Einführung," in *Kontexte des Johannesevangeliums: Das vierte Evangelium in religions- und traditionsgeschichtlicher Perspektive*, ed. Jörg Frey and Udo Schnelle (Tübingen: Mohr Siebeck, 2004), 3-45 (esp. 7-35). For a critical assessment of the history of religions approach to the Johannine Christology, see Larry W. Hurtado, "New Testament Christology: Retrospect and Prospect," *Semeia* 30 (1984): 15-27; Hengel, "Jesus, der Messias Israels," 159-62; Earl E. Ellis, "Background and Christology of John's Gospel," in *Christ and the Future in New Testament History* (Leiden: Brill, 2000), 76. Recently, this provenance theory has become more complicated, acknowledging the Jewish roots in a deeper level yet in a syncretistic manner. Jarl Fossum, for instance, offers a representative view of an increasing scholarly assessment of the relationship between Gnosticism, Christianity, and later rabbinic Judaism. As for him, these three Mediterranean religious strata emerge from the same root, that is, intertestamental Judaism. Jarl Fossum, "The New Religionsgeschichtliche Schule: The Quest for Jewish Christology," *SBLSP* 30 (1991): 638-46. Also, "If the research on Gnosticism in the question of the relationship of Judaism and Gnosis, that is, the Apocalyptic and Gnosis arrives at a clear and affirmative answer, then the diverse Judaism, including Gnosticism, might be sufficient as exclusive religious background in the Johannine community. That means three conclusive remarks: (1) the Johannine Gospel is to be read over against Jewish background substantially more strongly than it was frequently accepted in the former generation; (2) (pre)Gnostic currents should be counted as well; (3) then, these two aspects should be sufficient to stress the theological drift of the Fourth Gospel." Ingo Broer, *Einleitung in das Neue Testament* (Würzburg: Echter, 1998), 1:205. However, for a recent expression of the conventional Hellenistic influence on the New Testament, see Gerd Lüdemann, *Primitive Christianity: A Survey of Recent Studies and Some New Proposals* (London: T & T Clark, 2003); and on the Fourth Gospel in particular, C.K. Barrett, "John and Judaism," in *Anti-Judaism and the Fourth Gospel*, ed. Reimund Bieringer, Didlier Pollefeyt, and Frederique Vandecasteele-Vanneville (Louisville: Westminster, 2001), 231-46.

[9] Hans Conzelmann and Andreas Lindemann, *Arbeitsbuch zum Neuen Testament* (Tübingen: Mohr Siebeck, 2004), 374-76. Particularly, the Johannine dualism has puzzled the Johannine exegetes of its religious backgrounds. On the possible provenance of the thought pattern from Judaism, see Otto Böcher, *Der Johanneische*

A number of scholars have attributed these Johannine phenomena to different religious backgrounds: Jewish Hellenism, Qumran, Pharisaic-Rabbinic Judaism, heretical Judaism, the Hermes myths, and Gnosticism.[10] Among these religious backgrounds, Gnosticism has stirred the fiercest debate as to the extent of its influence on the Gospel. The scholars who adhere to a considerable measure of its influence include Bultmann, Käsemann, L. Schottroff, H. Conzelmann, H. Koester, J. Becker, W. Schmithals, and S. Schulz.[11]

Of course, however, the degree of influence varies between one extreme to another within the group of scholars. For instance, an interesting debate arose

---

Dualismus im Zusammenhang des nachbiblischen Judentums (Gutersloh: Gerd Mohn, 1965); from gnosticism, see Luise Schottroff, *Der Glaubende und feindliche Welt: Beobachtungen zum gnostischen Dualismus und seiner Bedeutung für Paulus und das Johannesevangelium* (S.l.: Neukirchener, 1970). However, Becker presumes that they are only two different expressions of the same concept in different religious paradigms, Jürgen Becker, "Beobachtungen zum Dualismus im Johannesevangelium," *ZNW* 65 (1974): 71-87; idem, "Ich bin die Auferstehung und das Leben: Eine Skizze der johanneischen Christologie," *TZ* 39 (1983): 138-51. For similar skeptical assessments of the connection between John and Qumran, see Howard M. Teeple, "Qumran and the Origin of the Fourth Gospel," *NovT* 4 (1960): 6-25; David E. Aune, "Dualism in the Fourth Gospel and the Dead Sea Scrolls: A Reassessment of the Problem," in *Neotestamentica et Philonica: Studies in Honor of Peder Borgen* (Leiden: Brill, 2003), 281-303. Aune is also opposed to positing the direct dependence between the Qumran scrolls and the Fourth Gospel. He is probably right to doubt such a linear connection between the two but the Gnostic provenance theory has not yet produced a better solution. The Qumran/the Fourth Gospel comparison, however, seems to demonstrate closer conceptual affinities. "In conclusion, there is a curious irony to be observed. It was the publication of Qumran texts which effected a shift in Johannine scholarship towards recognizing the thoroughly Jewish character of Johannine theology. In retrospect this appears to have been a case of drawing the correct conclusion from the wrong evidence. There is no need to appeal to the Qumran texts in order to demonstrate the Jewishness of the Fourth Gospel's light/darkness imagery. This can be done more convincingly by comparison with other Jewish sources already available long before the discovery of the Dead Sea Scrolls." Richard Bauckham, "The Qumran Community and the Gospel of John," in *The Testimony of the Beloved Disciple: Narrative, History, and Theology in the Gospel of John* (Grand Rapids: Baker, 2007), 125-36. See also Géza G. Xeravits, ed., *Dualism in Qumran* (London: T & T Clark, 2010).

[10] Joachim Gnilka, *Johannesevangelium* (Würzburg: Echter, 1999), 8.

[11] Jürgen Becker, *Johannesevangelium* (Würzburg: Echter, 1991), 53-55. For the representative views, see Rudolph Bultmann, "Die Bedeutung der neuerschlossenen mandäischen und manichäischen Quellen für das Verständnis des Johannes-evangeliums," *ZNW* 24 (1925): 100-46, esp. 102-04; Siegfried Schulz, *Das Evangelium nach Johannes* (Göttingen: Vandenhoeck & Ruprecht, 1987), 10-12; and Helmut Koester, "The History-of-Religions School, Gnosis, and Gospel of John," *ST* 40 (1986): 115-36; idem, *History and Literature of Early Christianity*, vol. 2 of *Introduction to the New Testament* (New York: Walter de Gruyter, 2000), 183-86.

between Bultmann and Käsemann.[12] The former, while acknowledging the significant contact with Gnosticism, proposed that the Fourth Gospel overcame the core concepts of this religion through the community's unique Christology. On the other hand, Käsemann argued for the close interrelationship of the Gospel with early Gnosticism, which he viewed as being underway to becoming a full-blown development. Thus, for Käsemann, John's Gospel is extensively a "docetic" document.[13] However, this Gnostic provenance theory has come under heavy criticism, mainly for its anachronistic character and the exegetical inconsistencies inherent in Käsemann and his adherents.[14] Furthermore, some of the

---

[12] Rudolf Bultmann, *Das Evangelium des Johannes* (Göttingen: Vandenhoeck & Ruprecht, 1986); Ernst Käsemann, *The Testament of Jesus: A Study of the Gospel of John in the Light of Chapter 17* (Philadelphia: Fortress, 1968).

[13] Käsemann's position is further elaborated and argued by Schottroff, *Der Galubende und die feindliche Welt*, 228-96.

[14] For instance, recently Schnelle convincingly refuted this view. Udo Schnelle, *Antidocetic Christology in the Gospel of John: An Investigation of the Place of the Fourth Gospel in the Johannine School* (Minneapolis: Fortress, 1992); idem, *Das Evangelium nach Johannes* (Leipzig: Evangelische Verlagsanstalt, 1998), 17-20. Also see Lindemann's cautious assessment of Conzelmann. Conzelmann and Lindemann, *Arbeitsbuch zum Neuen Testament*, 219-22. For other skeptical assessments of the gnostic influence theory, see Carsten Colpe, *Die religionsgeschichtliche Schule: Darstellung und Kritik ihres Bildes vom gnostischen Erlösermythus* (Göttingen: Vandenhoeck & Ruprecht, 1961); Edwin M. Yamauchi, *Gnostic Ethics and Mandaean Origins* (Cambridge: Harvard University Press, 1970); idem, "Gnosticism and early Christianity," in *Hellenization Revisited: Shaping a Christian Response within the Greco-Roman World*, ed. Wendy E. Helleman (Lanham: University Press of America, 1994), 29-61; idem, "The Pre-Christian Gnosticism Reviewed in the Light of the Nag Hammadi Texts," in *Nag Hammadi Library after Fifty Years: Proceedings of the 1995 Society of Biblical Literature Commemoration*, ed. Jon Douglas Turner and Anne Marie McGuire (Leiden: Brill, 1997), 72-88; Urban C. von Wahlde, "The Johannine Literature and Gnosticism: New Light on Their Relationship?" in *From Judaism to Christianity: Tradition and Transition, a Festschrift for Thomas H. Tobin S.J., on the Occasion of His Sixty-Fifth Birthday*, ed. Patricia Walters (Leiden: Brill, 2010), 221-54; Titus Nagel, *Die Rezeption des Johannesevangeliums im 2. Jahrhundert: Studien zur vorirenäischen Aneignung und Auslegung des vierten Evangeliums in christlicher und christlich-gnostischer Literatur* (Leipzig: Evangelische Verlagsanstalt, 2000); idem, "Zur Gnostisierung der johanneischen Tradition: Das 'Geheime Evangelium nach Johannes' (Apokryphon Johannis) als gnostische Zusatzoffernbarung zum vierten Evangelium," in *Kontexte des Johannesevangeliums: Das vierte Evangelium in religions- und traditionsgeschichtlicher Perspektive*, ed. Jörg Frey and Udo Schnelle (Tübingen: Mohr Siebeck, 2004), 675-94, esp. see "Sie [the Apocryphon of John] können nur funktionieren und sind allein dann sinnvoll, wenn das Johannesevangelium die Bezugsgröße bleibt. Das AJ [the Apocryphon of John] will das Johannesevangelium nicht verdrängen, sondern fortführen und ergänzen." Nagel, "Zur Gnostisierung der johanneischen Tradition," 693. Parentheses are added for clarification. For one of the earliest researches into this scholarly prejudice for the second century gnostic influence on John, see William Sanday, *The Criticism of the Fourth Gospel: Eight Lectures on the Morse Foundation, Delivered in the*

newer insights provided with the recent archaeological and literary findings in the Palestine area, that is, Judaea and Galilee, mitigate substantially the persuasive force of the heavy Hellenistic influence theory.

C.H. Dodd

It was prior to the discovery of the Dead Sea Scrolls that a great number of critical Johannine scholars enthusiastically probed into the literature represented by the Hellenistic category for alleged affinities with the Gospel.[15] In line with Bultmann, who was then at the high point of his career, C.H. Dodd marked the watershed point in Johannine studies.[16] It was he who assumed the Bultmannian postulation of *Religionsgeschichte* and rigorously applied it into his *The Interpretation of the Fourth Gospel*.[17] However, regardless of his painstaking effort to locate the Gospel within the wider Hellenistic cultural realms, Dodd's study showed ironically the marked differences of the Hellenistic aspects (especially the Platonic and the Hermetic[18]) from the Jewish characteristics inherent in the

---

Union Seminary, New York, in October and November, 1904 (Oxford: Clarendon, 1905).

[15] For elements of Philonic (Christianized Platonism) and mystery religions in the Gospel, see Alfred F. Loisy, *Le quatrième évangile: Les épitres dites de Jean* (Paris: Émile Nourry, 1921). For other early claims for the thorough Hellenistic influences, see Johannes Weiss, *The History of Primitive Christianity* (New York: Wilson-Erikson, 1937), 624; Edgar J. Goodspeed, *An Introduction to the New Testament* (Chicago: University of Chicago Press, 1937), 314-15; Harold W. Attridge, "Philo and John: Two Riffs on One Logos," *SPhiloA* 17 (2005): 103-17. For a review of other scholars who saw the gnostic origin of the Gospel such as Schottroff, J. Becker, Schenke, Fischer, and Schmithals, see Schnelle, *The History and Theology of the New Testament Writings*, 504-05.

[16] Cf. Rudolf Bultmann, *Das Evangelium des Johannes* (Göttingen: Vandenhoeck & Ruprecht, 1986). The commentary first appeared in 1941.

[17] C.H. Dodd, *The Interpretation of the Fourth Gospel* (Cambridge: CUP, 1954). However, Dodd was already aware of the inadequate proposition of Bultmann's gnostic theory including Mandaism: "It seems that we must conclude that the Mandaean literature has not that direct and outstanding importance for the study of the Fourth Gospel which has been attributed to it by Lidzbarski, Reitzenstein and Bultmann. . . . But alleged parallels drawn from this medieval body of literature have no value for the study of the Fourth Gospel unless they can be supported by earlier evidence" (130).

[18] "Against Dodd it should be said that while there is in Philo's writings extensive use of Greek philosophical ideas that largely have a Middle-Platonic stamp, this is not the case in John." Peder Borgen, "The Gospel of John and Hellenism: Some Observations," in *Exploring the Gospel of John: In Honor of D. Moody Smith*, ed. R. Alan Culpepper and C. Clifton Black (Louisville: Westminster/John Knox, 1996), 99. For more recent hesitations against the alleged affinity between Philo and John, see Roland Deines and Karl-Wilhelm Niebuhr, eds., *Philo und das Neue Testament: Wechselseitige Wahrnehmungen, 1. Internationales Symposium zum Corpus Judaeo-Hellenisticum 1.—4. Mail 2003, Eisenach/Jenaeds* (Tübingen: Siebeck, 2004). Of particular help are the three essays in the volume: Roland Deines and Karl-Wilhelm Niebuhr, "Philo und

Gospel as often recognized in the following Johannine scholarship.

The encroachment of the Semitic on New Testament scholarship—an encroachment that has grown ever stronger—so that it also reflects new beginnings. [Dodd's writings] are a mirror of the transition which has marked our time from a predominantly Hellenistic to a more Semitic approach to the New Testament. In him one world was already dying and another struggling to be born.[19]

Semitic Linguistic Features

The recent discovery of the first century Palestinian documents enabled scholars to engage in philological inquiries into the languages of the Gospels and various contemporary literature in Greek, Hebrew, and Aramaic.[20] One of the noteworthy observations from such queries is that the alleged New Testament "septuagintalism" which a number of New Testament scholars believe to be the most palpable expression of Hellenized Judaism, fails to stand comparative linguistic analysis on a number of points.[21] This estimation reminds us of the long standing fact that the default linguistic mode of first century Palestine was Semitic,

---

das Neue Testament—Das Neue Testament und Philo: Wechselseitige Wahrnehmungen," 3-20; Larry W. Hurtado, "Does Philo Help Explain Christianity?" 73-92; and Gregory E. Sterling, "The Place of Philo of Alexandria in the Study of Christian Origins," 21-52. A precedence of these views is found in David T. Runia, *Philo in Early Christian Literature: A Survey* (Van Gorcum: Assen; Minneapolis, MN: Fortress, 1993), especially 78-83. For a negative evaluation of the Hermetic influence on the Gospel, see Schnackenburg, *The Gospel according to St John*, 1:136-38.

[19] W.D. Davies, "Reflections on Aspects of the Jewish Background of the Gospel of John," in *Exploring the Gospel of John: In Honor of D. Moody Smith*, ed. R. Alan Culpepper and C. Clifton Black (Louisville: Westminster/John Knox, 1996), 43.

[20] For some of the more detailed reports, see Joseph A. Fitzmyer, "Methodology in the Study of the Aramaic Substratum of Jesus' Sayings in the New Testament," in *Jésus aux origins de la Christologie* (Gembloux: Duculot, 1975), 73-102, esp., 101-02; idem, *A Wandering Aramean: Collected Aramaic Essays* (Missoula: Scholars, 1979); idem, "The Aramaic Language and the Study of New Testament," *JBL* 99 (1980): 5-21; idem, "Problems of the Aramaic Background of the New Testament," in *Yahweh/Baal Confrontation and Other Studies in Biblical Literature and Archaeology: Essays in Honour of Emmett Willard Hamrick*, ed. Julia M. O'Brien and Fred L. Horton Jr. (Lewiston: Edwin Mellen, 1995), 80-93; idem, *The Semitic Background of the New Testament* (Grand Rapids: Eerdmans, 1997); Raymond E. Brown, "The Dead Sea Scrolls and the New Testament," in *John and the Dead Sea Scrolls*, ed. J.H. Charlesworth (New York: Crossroad, 1990), 1-8; Max Wilcox, "The Aramaic Background of the New Testament," in *The Aramaic Bible: Targums in Their Historical Context*, ed. D.R.G. Beattie and M.J. McNamara (Sheffield: JSOT, 1994), 362-78; Andreas J. Köstenberger, "Jesus as Rabbi in the Fourth Gospel," *BBR* 8 (1998): 97-128.

[21] Schlatter finds no intentional dependence on the *LXX* in John. Adolf Schlatter, *Die sprache und heimat des vierten Evangelisten* (Gütersloh: Bertelsmann, 1902), 199, n. 2. He also finds explicit Semitisms in a total of eleven verses in John. Ibid. Also, Wilcox, "The Aramaic Background of the New Testament," 367-71.

needless to say that Jesus and his disciples spoke most likely in Aramaic.[22] An example to support this judgment can be found in the prologue to *the Wisdom of Ben Sirach*. In it, it can be surmised that it was only after the grandson of Jesus moved to Egypt (132 B.C.) when the need became apparent to translate the book into the Greek language.[23]

Recent Archaeological Discoveries

In contrast to the previous generation's belief, the more recent archaeological discoveries undertaken in Palestine (Judea and Galilee) reveal that the region was pervasively Jewish, much more heavily characterized by distinct Jewish cultural/religious elements than often surmised in the past.[24] The conclusions of

---

[22] At the same time, however, it should be also noted that the Semitic nature of Jesus' and his disciples' linguistic framework is notoriously difficult to apply to the current Greek New Testament texts. Thus, some of the recent efforts to account for the Semitic linguistic background of the Gospels have received more criticism than welcome acceptance. For instance, C.F. Burney, *The Aramaic Origin of the Fourth Gospel* (Oxford: Clarendon, 1922); Roger Le Déaut, "Targumic Literature and New Testament Interpretation," *BTB* 4 (1974): 243-89; Daniel Patte, *Early Jewish Hermeneutic in Palestine* (Missoula: Scholars, 1975), 65-81; Martin McNamara, *The New Testament and the Palestinian Targum to the Pentateuch* (Rome: Biblica, 1978); Geza Vermes, "Jewish Literature and New Testament Exegesis: Reflections on Methodology," *JJS* 33 (1982): 361-76; Matthew Black, *An Aramaic Approach to the Gospels and Acts* (Peabody: Hendrickson, 1998); Maurice Casey, *Aramaic Sources of Mark's Gospel* (Cambridge: CUP, 1998); idem, *An Aramaic Approach to Q: Sources for the Gospels of Matthew and Luke* (Cambridge: CUP, 2002). For an example of such caution, see the writings of Fitzmyer mentioned in n. 36; Earl Richard, "The Old Testament in Acts: Wilcox's Semitisms in Retrospect," *CBQ* 42 (1980): 330-41. "For all these reasons, attempts to retranslate the Greek Gospels into Jesus' own language are extremely speculative." B.D. Chilton, "Targums," *DJG*, 803.

[23] Benjamin G. Wright, "Wisdom of Iesous Son of Sirach," in *A New English Translation of the Septuagint*, ed. Albert Pietersma and Benjamin G. Wright (Oxford: OUP, 2007), 719-20; Harold C. Washington, "*Ecclesiasticus* (or *the Wisdom of Jesus, Son of Sirach*)," in *The New Oxford Annotated Apocrypha*, ed. Michael D. Coogan (Oxford: OUP, 2010), 101.

[24] Roland Deines, *Jüdische Steingefässe und pharisäische Frömmigkeit: Ein archäologisch-historischer Beitrag zum Verständnis von Joh 2,6 und der jüdischen Reinheitshalacha zur Zeit Jesu* (Tübingen: Mohr Siebeck, 1993); idem, *Die Pharisäer: ihr Verständnis im Spiegel der christlichen und jüdischen Forschung seit Wellhausen und Graetz* (Tübingen: Mohr Siebeck, 1997); Richard A. Horsley, *Galilee: History, Politics, People* (Valley Forge: Trinity, 1995); idem, *Archaeology, History, and Society in Galilee: The Social Context of Jesus and the Rabbis* (Valley Forge: Trinity, 1996); idem, "Jesus and Empire," *USQR* 3-4 (2005): 56-65; Eric M. Meyers, "Recent Archaeology in Palestine: Achievements and Future Goals," in *Cambridge History of Judaism*, ed. W. Horbury, W.D. Davies, and J. Sturdy (Cambridge: CUP, 1999), 3:59-74, 1082-85; Jonathan L. Reed, *Archaeology and the Galilean Jesus: A Re-examination of the Evidence* (Harrisburg: Trinity, 2000); idem, "Stone Vessels and Gospel Texts: Purity and Socio-Economics in John 2," in *Zeichen aus Text und Stein:*

these investigations cover a wide range of Palestinian geography and engage in meticulous examinations of the material retrievals. For instance, the evidences for Greek influence, such as, theater or amphitheater in Jerusalem and Sepphoris in the first century are now refuted (most likely late first or second centuries).[25] Roland Deines' extensive assessment of the stone containers used in first-century Palestine further hints at the Pharisaic/rabbinic ritual practice commonly exercised in the region as briefly recorded in John 2 regarding the wedding in Cana.[26] To offer one more example, Mark Chancey's comprehensive

Studien auf dem Weg zu einger Archäologie des Neuen Testaments, ed. Stefan Alkier and Jürgen Zangenberg (Tübingen: Francke, 2003), 381-401; James F. Strange, "Recent Discoveries at Sepphoris and Their Relevance for Biblical Research," *Neot* 34 (2000): 125-41; Mark A. Chancey, *The Myth of a Gentile Galilee* (Cambridge: CUP, 2002); idem, *Greco-Roman Culture and the Galilee of Jesus* (Cambridge: CUP, 2005); idem and Eric M. Meyers, "How Jewish was Sepphoris in Jesus' Time?" *BAR* 26, no. 4 (July/August 2000): 18-33, 61; Mark A. Chancey and Adam Porter, "The Archaeology of Roman Palestine," *NEA* 64, no. 4 (December 2001): 164-203; Seán Freyne, *Galilee and Gospel: Collected Essays* (Tübingen: Mohr Siebeck, 2000); idem, *Jesus, a Jewish Galilean: A New Reading of the Jesus Story* (London: T & T Clark, 2004); E.P. Sanders, "Jesus in Galilee," in *Jesus: A Colloquium in the Holy Land*, ed. Doris Donnelly (London: Continuum, 2001), 5-26; James H. Charlesworth, "Jesus Research and Near Eastern Archaeology: Reflections on Recent Developments," in *Neotestamentica et Philonica: Studies in Honor of Peder Borgen*, ed. D.E. Aune, T. Seland, and J.H. Ulrichsen (Leiden: Brill, 2003), 37-70; Jens Schröter, "New Horizon in Historical Jesus Research?: Hermeneutical Considerations concerning the So-called 'Third Quest' of the Historical Jesus," in *The New Testament Interpreted: Essays in Honour of Bernard C. Lategan*, ed. Cilliers Breytenbach, Johan C. Thom, and Jeremy Punt (Leiden: Brill, 2006), 71-85; Morten Hørning Jensen, *Herod Antipas in Galilee: The Literary and Archaeological Sources on the Reign of Herod Antipas and Its Socio-Economic Impact on Galilee* (Tübingen: Mohr Siebeck, 2008), 7-8, 126-86. Although this list represents various degrees of opinions, it reflects an increasing awareness of current biblical archaeological scholarship on the Jewish cultural/religious matrix of Palestine in the 1st century A.D. (or at least before the destruction of the Jerusalem temple). For example, Richard Horsley's envisioning Jesus as a nationalistic revolutionary is to read too much into the text. However, his point still stands that the Jesus movement was not meant to embrace the Hellenistic-Roman culture. For a general survey on the Jewish cultural contexts of the Gospel accounts, see Craig A. Evans, "Assessing Progress in the Third Quest of the Historical Jesus," *JSHJ* 4 (2006): 35-43.

[25] Mark A. Chancey, "The Cultural Milieu of Ancient Sepphoris," *NTS* 47 (2001): 127-45; Weiss Zeev and Ehud Netzer, "Hellenistic and Roman Sepphoris," in *Sepphoris in Galilee: Crosscurrents of Culture*, ed. Carol L. Meyers and Zeev Weiss (Raleigh: North Carolina Museum of Art, 1996), 32, 122; Achim Lichtenberger, "Jesus and the Theater in Jerusalem," in *Jesus and Archaeology*, ed. James H. Charlesworth (Grand Rapids: Eerdmans, 2006), 283-99.

[26] Deines, *Jüdische Steingefässe und pharisäische Frömmigkeit*, 247-51, 263-75. Also, John C. Thomas, "The Fourth Gospel and Rabbinic Judaism," *ZNW* 82 (1991): 162-65; E. Regev, "Non-Priestly Purity and Its Religious Aspects according to Historical Sources and Archaeological Findings," in *Purity and Holiness*, ed. M.J.H.M.

evaluation of the material culture bears witness to the distinctly Jewish culture deeply permeating first-century Galilee.[27] These investigations confirm the accounts of the Gospels in that no significant presence of a Gentile population or its cultural/religious activities is referred to in the four canonical Gospels.[28] Accordingly, recent archaeological scholarship has recognized the strong and widespread Jewish cultural presence in first-century Palestine.

> In NT times Jews comprised the vast majority of the Galilean population. The view that the area was at that time half-pagan is a modern scientific myth. Josephus refers repeatedly to the piety of the Galileans and their loyalty to the Torah. NT references to the large numbers of synagogues in Galilee confirm this. These references are supported by archaeological findings.[29]

> What is perhaps most striking about the first century is the minimal extent of Roman military-administrative presence in Judea outside of Caesarea and the degree to which Rome relied upon influential priests and laity to maintain the peace.[30]

> Thus, the argument for a pagan Galilee is poorly supported by the literary evidence and receives no confirmation from the archaeological explorations. . . . Excavations at various sites have uncovered such instruments of the distinctive Jewish way of life as ritual baths (*miqvaot*), stone jars and natively produced ceramic household ware. These finds indicate a concern with ritual purity emanating from Jerusalem and its temple as well as an avoidance of the cultural ethos of the encircling pagan cities.[31]

Conceptual Affinities

Finally, the theological presuppositions of the Gospels and the Jewish Scriptures, in contradistinction to their surrounding cultures, have much in common.[32] For

---

Poorthuis and J. Schwartz (Leiden: Brill, 2000), 232. Partly built upon this work, Deines goes on to broaden the implication of the thesis into the place of Pharisaism, which he assesses to have constituted the major paradigm of early Judaism in the first century A.D., although the demands of their regulations were not equally required throughout the regions. "Bewegung im Volk *für* das Volk, deren Rechtmäßigkeit von weitesten Teilen des Volkes auch *akzeptiert* wurde, wenn auch die Forderungen derselben nicht im gleichen Maße *praktiziert* wurden." Deines, *Die Pharisäer*, 512 (italics original).

[27] Chancey, *The Myth of a Gentile Galilee*.

[28] Coupled with these Jewish characteristics of the Palestine area, the profuse geographical and cultural details affirm the early date and the Palestinian provenance of the Gospel of John. Paul W. Barnett, "Indications of Earliness in the Gospel of John," *RTR* 64 (2005): 61-75; James H. Charlesworth, "The Historical Jesus in the Fourth Gospel: A Paradigm Shift?" *JSHJ* 8 (2010): 3-46.

[29] Rainer D. Riesner, "Galilee," *DJG*, 252.

[30] Chris J. Seeman, "Judea," *DNTB*, 622.

[31] Sean Freyne, "Galilee and Judaea in the First Century," in *Origins to Constantine*, vol. 1 of *The Cambridge History of Christianity*, ed. Margaret M. Mitchell and Frances M. Young (Cambridge: CUP, 2006), 41-42.

[32] For hermeneutical compatibilities of the NT with Qumran, see Raymond E. Brown, "The Dead Sea Scrolls and the New Testament," in *John and the Dead Sea Scrolls*, ed.

an example, it is striking that the Gospels make painstaking efforts to preserve monotheism over against the prevalent polytheistic belief and practice of the pan-Mediterranean world. In addition, other symbols and images present in the Gospels are only comprehensible in view of the conventional Jewish heritages.[33] From the observations mentioned above, therefore, it is reasonable to conclude that the Fourth Gospel and the conventional Jewish cultural variables share a great deal of common ground.

After Dodd

Turning our attention back to Dodd, studies subsequent to him, and especially after the discovery of the Qumran scrolls, have reinforced a conviction that "the Fourth Gospel is now judged to be Jewish, and it is [to be] studied in terms of first-century Palestinian Jewish writings."[34]

James H. Charlesworth (New York: Crossroad, 1990), 1-8; Hengel, "The Scriptures in Second Temple Judaism," 169-72; the conceptual affinities of John with the Old Testament, see Saeed Hamid-Khani, *Revelation and Concealment of Christ: A Theological Inquiry into the Elusive Language of the Fourth Gospel* (Tübingen: Mohr Siebeck, 2000), 123-56; with Qumran, see Raymond E. Brown, "The Qumran Scrolls and the Johannine Gospel and Epistles," in *The Scrolls and the New Testament*, ed. Krister Stendahl (New York: Harper & Brothers, 1957), 183-207; James H. Charlesworth, "A Critical Comparison of the Dualism in 1QS 3:13-4:26 and the 'Dualism' Contained in the Gospel of John," in *John and Qumran*, ed. James H. Charlesworth (London: Geoffrey Chapman, 1972), 76-106; Paul N. Anderson, "John and Qumran: Discovery and Interpretation over Sixty Years," in *John, Qumran, and the Dead Sea Scrolls: Sixty Years of Discovery and Debate*, ed. Mary L. Coloe and Tom Thatcher (Atlanta: Society of Biblical Literature, 2011), 15-23, James H. Charlesworth, "The Fourth Evangelist and the Dead Sea Scrolls: Assessing Trends over Nearly Sixty Years," in *John, Qumran, and the Dead Sea Scrolls: Sixty Years of Discovery and Debate*, ed. Mary L. Coloe and Tom Thatcher (Atlanta: Society of Biblical Literature, 2011), 165-72; with early rabbinic Judaism, see Thomas, "The Fourth Gospel and Rabbinic Judaism," 174-77.

[33] A recent attempt to find extensive parallels of Johannine theological concepts that are deeply steeped in an important Old Testament theme (that of covenant) also seems to make a compelling case. John W. Pryor, *John: Evangelist of the Covenant People: The Narrative and Themes of the Fourth Gospel* (Downers Grove: InterVarsity, 1992).

[34] James H. Charlesworth, "The Dead Sea Scrolls and the Gospel according to John," in *Exploring the Gospel of John: In Honor of D. Moody Smith*, ed. R.A. Culpepper and C.C. Black (Louisville: Westminster/John Knox, 1996), 66. Parentheses are added for clarification. See also Thomas Söding, "'Was kann aus Nazareth schon Gutes kommen?' (Joh 1.46): Die Bedeutung des Judenseins Jesu im Johannesevangelium," *NTS* 46 (2000): 21-41; Vhumani Magezi & Peter Manzanga, "A Study to Establish the Most Plausible Background to the Fourth Gospel (John)," *HTSTS* 66 (2010): 1-7; Frédéric Manns, "A Jewish Approach to the Gospel of John: Part One, a Methodological Problem," *Anton* 87 (2012): 259-79; idem, "Some Jewish Traditions in the FG," *Anton* 87 (2012): 549-608; idem, "Some Jewish Traditions in the FG: Terza parte," *Anton* 87 (2012): 743-83. Also, "the origin of the Johannine Gospel, which Adolf von Harnack called the greatest riddle presented to us by the earliest history of

Such a judgment is justified not because the Fourth Gospel derives its theology from the Qumran traditions but because it reflects common Semitic conceptual currents as attested in the writings of the Qumran community. This hermeneutical penchant is not entirely the latest approach but simply a reaffirmation of the belief shared by a number of scholars at the turn of the past century (such as Dalman, Lightfoot, Westcott, Schlatter, Strack, Billerbeck, and Jeremias).

> [T]he accomplishment of scholars like Billerbeck or Jeremias—and also Schlatter—is that they showed that a thorough knowledge of Judaism . . . is one of the non-negotiable requirements in the field of New Testament study. Over against the history of religions tradition which began with W. Bousset and was continued by Rudolf Bultmann and his pupils, whose historical picture of Judaism was based almost entirely on the sources written in Greek, scholars like Strack and Billerbeck and "Jeremias & co." were among the first who responded to the appeal of the "Wissenschaft des Judentums" which was then beginning to blossom, and they thereby helped New Testament scholarship discover the deficits in its knowledge.[35]

To quote a scholar in this stream of thought, Adolf Schlatter advised that

> you must go into the Jewish Literature . . . the Judaism, with which the New Testament stood in fruitful community and fierce conflict, was that of Palestine, of the Pharisees, which you must become acquainted with from its own witness.[36]

To quote another Tübinger, Betz also underscores the value of the Jewish literature for the study of the New and Old Testaments (hence the history of traditions approach).

> I see the methodology that justified in the earliest the unity of the Bible as the tradition-historical analysis. It is important to follow the scripture of the Old Testament and its interpretation: at first, post-biblical Judaism, whether it be Palestine or Hellenistic, then in the New Testament itself and last in rabbinic literatures which is written only after the times of the New Testament but go back to the New Testament times in their oral stages. For such a reason, the legitimacy and limitation of the form-critical method is in order.[37]

Christianity, appears to me to be a riddle of our own making, since every page of this Gospel reveals its conceptual origin. The Johannine world of ideas never departs from its Jewish, Old Testament orbit. It is to this context that the Gospel is inseparably fastened for any meaningful explication of its literary milieu, style, imagery, language and theology." Hamid-Khani, *Revelation and Concealment of Christ*, 156.

[35] Martin Hengel and Roland Deines, "E.P. Sanders' 'Common Judaism,' Jesus, and the Pharisees: Review Article of *Jewish Law from Jesus to the Mishnah* and *Judaism: Practice and Belief* by E.P. Sanders for Hartmut Gese on the Occasion of His 65th Birthday with Gratitude," *JTS* 46 (1995): 69.

[36] Adolf Schlatter, *Rückblick auf meine Lebensarbeit* (Stuttgart: Calwer, 1977), 120.

[37] Otto Betz, "Das Johannesevangelium und das Alte Testament," in *Wie verstehen wir das Neue Testament?* (Wuppertal: Aussaat, 1981), 14-20, here especially 17 for the citation. Here it should be noted that Betz uses the terminologies with different definitions. By him, "the history of tradition approach" refers to a method that takes into

This favorite disposition toward Judaism for the Gospels is, of course, not unanimously espoused by any means within Johannine scholarship on both sides of the Atlantic Ocean.[38] Nonetheless, an increasing number of scholars seem to be leaning sympathetically toward such a perspective. A number of reasons for which the alleged Gnostic influence on John is disavowed could be summarized:[39] John's assumption of his readers' knowledge of certain Jewish symbolisms, festivals (chs. 6, 7, and 10), and Palestinian topographies; the seeming proximity to midrashic interpretive traits (chs. 5 and 6); numerous Semitic flavors of the Gospel; and the anachronistic linking of the Gospel (whose earliest manuscript p^{52} dating at A.D. 125[40]) with the extant Gnostic documents (which variously date from third to seventh centuries A.D.).[41]

---

account the intertestamental literature whereas "the form historical method" designates the extreme history of religions assumptions, such as maintained by Bultmann in the formation of the New Testament writings.

[38] So a pupil of Bultmann says as follows: "Rudolf Bultmann proposed the hypothesis that John used a (non-Christian) Gnostic discourse source for their composition. Although this hypothesis has been widely criticized—and the assumption of the use of a non-Christian source is highly problematic—Bultmann may well have been correct with his notion that the Johannine discourses are indebted to a debate with Gnostic materials and were formulated in the context of that debate. The discovery of the Nag Hammadi Library has made a number of writings accessible that assist in the reconstruction of the evolution of such discourses. . . . The Gospel of John is . . . an important witness for the early development of a Gnostic understanding of the tradition of Jesus' sayings and a spiritualized interpretation of the sacraments." Koester, *History and Literature of Early Christianity*, 183-86.

[39] Gary M. Burge, "Interpreting the Gospel of John," in *Interpreting the New Testament: Essays on Methods and Issues*, ed. David Alan Black and David S. Dockery (Nashville: Broadman & Holman, 2001), 361-64.

[40] For the early second century dating of P^{52}, see Jack Finegan, *Encountering New Testament Manuscripts: A Working Introduction to Textual Criticism* (Grand Rapids: Eerdmans, 1974), 85-90; Victor Salmon, *The Fourth Gospel: A History of the Textual Tradition of the Original Greek Gospel*, trans. M.J. O'Connell (Collegeville: Liturgical, 1976); Conzelmann and Lindemann, *Arbeitsbuch zum Neuen Testament*, 373; Brent Nongbri, "The Use and Abuse of P^{52}: Papyrological Pitfalls in the Dating of the Fourth Gospel," *HTR* 98 (2005): 23-48; Udo Schnelle, *Einleitung in das Neue Testament* (Göttingen: Vandenhoeck & Ruprecht, 2011), 541, n. 120. However, Nongbri is somewhat cautious as to the definite dating of P^{52}. Nongbri, "The Use and Abuse of P^{52}," 46.

[41] The completion of the Mandean literature took place in the seventh and the eighth centuries A.D. Essential elements were present in the third and fourth centuries A.D., and the earliest components of the Mandean hymns could go back as far as the middle of the second century A.D. "In the twentieth century scholars came to doubt this portrait (the gnostic influence on NT) as idealistic and inaccurate. . . . If John was written to combat early Gnosticism, why did the Gnostics of the second century find this Gospel so attractive? . . . Scholars have come to recognize that making sharp distinction between 'orthodoxy' and 'heresy' in the first two or three centuries of Christianity tends to be anachronistic and misleading. . . . The major issue that scholars have de-

For these reasons and others, Schnelle maintains that

[i]n the most recent research, however, the older thesis [that of Schlatter] that John is to be understood exclusively against the background of the Judaism of the period has recovered a great deal of influence.[42]

---

bated is whether or not Gnosticism, in its earliest forms, contributed to NT theology, particularly Christology, in any significant way. Specifically, attention has focused on the question of whether or not there existed a myth of a descending and ascending redeemer and whether or not if such a myth existed, it existed early enough to have influenced NT Christology. A few scholars answer these questions in the affirmative. Most, it would appear, have grave reservations. Edwin Yamauchi has reviewed all of the proposed evidence and finds little that suggests that Gnosticism existed prior to Christian origins. Charles Talbert finds no reason to believe that Christianity derived its Christology of a descending/ascending heavenly savior from anything other than its Jewish roots. . . . the recent assertions of Gesine Robinson and Jack Sanders that the Prologue of the Fourth Gospel has more in common with the mythology of a gnostic work like the *Trimorphic Protennoia* than it has with anything else are wholly unjustified. Pheme Perkins is much closer to the truth when she concludes that the gnostic writings of Nag Hammadi 'developed their picture of the Savior from traditions quite different from those which underlie NT christological assertions.' Martin Hengel adds: 'In reality there is no gnostic redeemer myth in the sources which can be demonstrated chronologically to be pre-Christian. The basic problem with the views of Robinson and Sanders is that those gnostic writings that bear the closest affinities with John contain allusions to, and sometimes explicit quotations of, the writings of the NT. A.D. Nock was right when he commented: 'Certainly it is an unsound proceeding to take Manichaean and other texts [viz. Mandaean and Coptic gnostic texts], full of echoes of the New Testament, and reconstruct from them something supposedly lying back of the New Testament.'" Craig A. Evans, *Ancient Texts for New Testament Studies: A Guide to the Background Literature* (Peabody: Hendrickson, 2005), 279-86. Parentheses are added for clarification and italics are original. Also recently, the alleged link between John and the gnostic movements has been challenged from a historical standpoint. "Surely one of the most striking results of this investigation . . . for other studies have been at least tending towards the same conclusion, is that the major use of the Fourth Gospel among heterodox or gnostic groups up until the Valentinians Ptolemy, Heracleon, and Theodotus, is best described as critical or adversarial. This exposes and should correct the tendency of earlier scholarship to assume that any Johannine borrowings or allusions in gnostic literature are evidence of gnostic/Johannine affinity, or of a common family history. . . The offence of this Gospel among heterodox writers seems to have centered upon two factors of the Gospel . . . : (1) first and foremost on its Christology, including its presentation of the full incarnation of the Logos God . . . , and (2) its assumption of a special and permanent authority joined to the witness of those who were Jesus' original disciples." Charles E. Hill, *The Johannine Corpus in the Early Church* (Oxford: OUP, 2004), 466. Similarly, Rudolf Schnackenburg, "The Gnostic Myth of the Redeemer and the Johannine Christology," in *The Gospel according to St John* (New York: Crossroad, 1982), 1:544-48.

[42] Schnelle, *Antidocetic Christology in the Gospel of John*, 25 (brackets added). "The location of the Gospel of John in its context in the history of religion may no more be explained in terms of a single factor than can its context in the history of traditions. It is rooted in the Old Testament and in the wisdom literature of *Hellenistic Judaism*, while

In view of such a paradigmatic shift of perspective in Johannine scholarship, it follows naturally that an investigation of the Gospel, particularly its use of the Old Testament, in light of its Palestinian Jewish backdrop rather than its Hellenistic counterpart in the first-and-second century Mediterranean religious movements, is expected to yield much more constructive hermeneutical insights into proper appreciation of the Gospel.[43] Hence

> none of the major treatments of New Testament [C]hristology [so far] were able to make use of this data [from Gnostic materials].[44]

Discretion, however, over the judgment of a close correlation between early Judaism and the Fourth Gospel is in order because the Gospel did not grow naturally from Judaism. It was the Christ-event, not the mother religion, that shaped the theology of the fourth evangelist and eventually set it apart from her. The degree of the influence of early Judaism, therefore, should be taken into account with a measure of discernment in the study of the Fourth Gospel.

---

at the same time having indications of a certain proximity to the thought world of Qumran and the Testaments of the Twelve Patriarchs, while individual elements have parallels in Hellenistic philosophy and later gnostic texts, but not in a way that lines of direct dependence may be constructed." Schnelle, *The History and Theology of the New Testament Writings*, 509.

[43] All other Hellenistic influences aside, a "pre-Christian" Gnostic influence is still an object of inquiry for the Johannine *Religionsgeschichte*. Against this stance, see a descriptive summation of some fundamental differences between John and Gnosticism by Herbert Kohler, *Kreuz und Menschwerdung im Johannine Gospel: Ein exegetisch-hermeneutischer Versuch zur johanneischen Kreuzestheologie* (Zürich: Theologischer, 1987), 142-58.

[44] Hurtado, "New Testament Christology," 17. Parentheses are added for clarification. Cf. Devon H. Wiens, "Mystery Concepts in Primitive Christianity and in Its Environment," *ANRW* 23.2:1248-84.

APPENDIX 3

The Old Testament in the Fourth Gospel

Significance of the Old Testament

Biblical scholars have often pointed out a number of idiosyncratic characteristics of the fourth Gospel from the Synoptics. This aspect is also true of the materials and manner in which the Old Testament is employed in the Gospel.[1] In fact, John quotes the Scriptures far less than any of the Synoptic Gospels. Usually, nineteen quotations are attributed to the Old Testament in John. However, when allusions are taken in view, it is difficult to count an exact number of the Old Testament materials because of the paraphrastic nature of the evangelist's use of Scripture.[2] Therefore, some have considered John's use of the Scriptures to be minimalistic and inaccurate in nature. For instance, Bultmann posited that the evangelist's recourse to the Scriptures is scanty.[3] Käsemann also wrote that John

---

[1] C.H. Toy, *Quotations in the New Testament* (New York: Scribner's, 1884), xxxv. For a summary of the history of research on the use of the Old Testament in John, see Andreas Obermann, *Die christologische Erfüllung der Schrift im Johannesevangelium: Eine Untersuchung zur johanneischen Hermeneutik anhand der Schriftzitate* (Tübingen: Mohr Siebeck, 1996), 1-36. For recent helpful treatments of the entire Gospel on this issue, see Anthony T. Hanson, *The Prophetic Gospel: A Study of John and the Old Testament* (Edinburgh: T & T Clark, 1991); Günter Reim, *Jochanan: Erweiterte Studien zum alttestamentlichen Hintergrund des Johannesevangeliums* (Erlangen: Der Ev.-Luth. Mission, 1995); Wolfgang Kraus, "Johannes und das Alte Testament: Überlegungen zum Umgang mit der Schrift im Johannesevangelium im Horizont Biblischer Theologie," (1997): 1-23; Paul Miller, "'They Saw His Glory and Spoke of Him': The Gospel of John and the Old Testament," in *Hearing the Old Testament in the New Testament*, ed. Stanley E. Porter (Grand Rapids: Eerdmans, 2006), 127-51; Andreas Köstenberger, "John," in *Commentary on the New Testament Use of the Old Testament*, ed. G.K. Beale and D.A. Carson (Grand Rapids: Baker, 2007), 415-512; Martin Vahrenhorst, "Johannes und die Tora: Überlegungen zur Bedeutung der Tora im Johannesevangelium," *KD* 54 (2008): 14-36.

[2] Scroggie, who attributes 63 OT references to Mark, 129 to Matthew, 90 to Luke, and 124 to John. W. Graham Scroggie, *A Guide to the Gospels* (London: Pickering & Inglis, 1948), 190, 270, 363, 426.

[3] Rudolf Bultmann, *Theology of the New Testament* (London: SCM, 1955), 2:5.

did not despise the use of the Old Testament even though he can get along without it in large sections and he always puts it in the shadow of his traditions about Jesus.[4]

Reim maintained that John's knowledge or use of the Old Testament is both fragmentary and secondary in that John did not have the Scriptures in front of him, but rather depended on oral traditions (wisdom and rabbinic).[5]

Recently, the landscape of biblical scholarship on this issue has indeed changed. Johannine scholars have increasingly noted the important place of the Old Testament for proper appreciation of John's Gospel. R. Morgan, for example, underscores the qualitative weight of the Jewish Scriptures, especially as attested in the quotation formulae of the Fourth Gospel.

> [T]he author [John] makes sure that the Old Testament is present at every crucial moment in the Gospel. This explains the significance of the Johannine quotations from the Old Testament. Their significance does not lie in the frequency of their occurrence, but rather in their presence at every vital moment in the Messiah's life. It is striking that every crisis in this moving drama of redemption, the Old Testament is there.[6]

Likewise Freed acknowledges the careful construction of the Scriptures intimately embedded in the plot of the Gospel by stating that "in no other writer are the O.T. quotations so carefully woven into the context and the whole plan of composition as in Jn."[7] In addition, an impressive array of recent Johannine commentators concurs on this judgment: "John reflects even more clearly than the Synoptic Gospels the great currents of Old Testament thought." [8] Schnackenburg even goes on to assert that the Old Testament is the ground for the Johannine theology:

---

[4] Ernst Käsemann, *The Testament of Jesus: A Study of the Gospel of John in the Light of Chapter 17* (Philadelphia: Fortress, 1968), 37. Parentheses are added for clarification.

[5] Reim, *Jochanan*, 96, 109, 161-62, and 183. *Contra*, Hanson, *The Prophetic Gospels*, 21-233. However, Reim departed from Bultmann who attributed the Johannine prologue to Gnosticism. Reim is one of the earliest scholars who hold that the Johannine prologue reflects the Jewish wisdom tradition. Günter Reim, *Studien zum alttestamentlichen Hintergrund des Johannesevangeliums* (Cambridge: CUP, 1974), 188.

[6] Richard Morgan, "Fulfillment in the Fourth Gospel: The Old Testament Foundations," *Int* 11 (1957): 156-57. Parentheses are added for clarification.

[7] Edwin D. Freed, *Old Testament Quotations in the Gospel of John* (Leiden: Brill, 1965), 129. Similarly, the Old Testament Scripture "makes the Gospel of John work." Judith Lieu, "Narrative Analysis and Scripture in John," in *The Old Testament in the New Testament: Essays in Honour of J.L North*, ed. Steve Moyise (Sheffield: Sheffield, 2000), 144.

[8] Raymond E. Brown, *The Gospel according to John (i-xii)* (New York: Doubleday, 1966), ix. "There is virtually no dispute over the pervasive Semitic influence on the style of the Fourth Gospel." Rudolf Bultmann, *The Gospel of John: A Commentary* (Philadelphia: Westminster, 1971), 3.

Thus many thoughts and images of the O.T., mostly taken further in theological meditation and development, come together in John and are made to serve Johannine theology. This Gospel would be unthinkable without the O.T. basis which supports it.[9]

From these observations, thus, it becomes obvious that the most distinctive Jewish element, namely, the Old Testament, stands in close affinity with the fourth evangelist, providing a necessary background for a proper understanding of the Gospel:

> The use of the scripture through metaphor and subtle allusions in the fourth Gospel is essentially broader and deeper than the explicit citations and punctual references are assumed.[10]

Another piece of evidence for the importance of the Old Testament is attested in the fulfillment themes. Towards the latter half of the fourth Gospel, the Old Testament is closely tied with the fulfillment motif in Jesus' passion.[11] Only

---

[9] Rudolf Schnackenburg, *The Gospel according to St. John* (New York: Herder and Herder, 1968), 1:124. Beasley-Murray concurs with Schnackenburg. George R. Beasley-Murray, *John* (Nashville: Nelson, 1999), lix. "John's use of the OT . . . apparently demonstrates a thorough knowledge of the Jewish Bible." Craig S. Keener, *The Gospel of John: A Commentary* (Peabody: Hendrickson, 2003), 1:172-73. "At the very outset, John's account is based on OT theology. . . . The Jewish milieu of John's Gospel and the firm grounding of its theology in OT antecedents are also borne out by the various component parts of the Gospel's christological teaching." Andreas J. Köstenberger, *John* (Grand Rapids: Baker, 2004), 13. However, this view is not entirely new; see the earlier exegetes' comments. "The Fourth Gospel is saturated with the thoughts, imagery, and language of the Old Testament." Alfred Plummer, *The Gospel according to St. John* (Cambridge: CUP, 1880), 42. "Without the basis of the Old Testament, the Gospel of St. John is an insoluble riddle." B.F. Westcott, *The Gospel according to St. John* (London: John Murray, 1894), lxix.

[10] Jörg Frey, "'Wie Mose die Schlange in der Wüste erhöht hat . . .': Zur frühjüdischen Deutung der Schlange und ihrer christologischen Rezeption in Joh 3,14f," in *Schriftauslegung im antiken Judentum und im Urchristentum*, ed. Martin Hengel and Hermut Löhr (Tübingen: Mohr Siebeck, 1994), 205.

[11] These fulfillment formulae constitute grounds for Obermann's thesis that the passion of Jesus is the "explicit" fulfillment and the preceding ministry is the "implicit" fulfillment of "scripture." Obermann, *Die christologische Erfüllung der Schrift im Johannesevangelium*, 348-50. Similarly, Craig A. Evans, "On the Quotation Formulas in the Fourth Gospel," *BZ* 26 (1982): 79-83; Joel Marcus, "The Old Testament and the Death of Jesus: The Role of Scripture in the Gospel Passion Narratives," in *The Death of Jesus in Early Christianity*, ed. John T. Carroll and Joel B. Green (Peabody: Hendrickson, 1995), 229-33. Others observe an obduracy motif in the passion fulfillment texts. Craig A. Evans, "Obduracy and Lord's Servant: Some Observations on the Use of the Old Testament in the Fourth Gospel," in *Early Jewish and Christian Exegesis: Studies in Memory of William Hugh Brownlee*, ed. Craig A. Evans and William F. Stinespring (Atlanta: Scholars, 1987), 221-36; D.A. Carson, "John and Johannine Epistles," in *It is Written: Scripture Citing Scripture: Essays in Honour of Barnabas Lindars*, ed. D.A. Carson and H.G.M. Williamson (Cambridge: CUP, 1988), 248.

Matthew, among the Synoptics, follows a similar pattern.[12] Like Matthew, John introduces the Old Testament material with πληρόω; but unlike the first evangelist, he does not hesitate to put the formula on the mouth of Jesus (13:18; 15:25; 19:28; 20:9; cf. 5:45-46).

> This was to fulfill the word that he had spoken, "I did not lose a single one of those whom you gave me." (John 18:9, NRSV)

> (This was to fulfill what Jesus had said when he indicated the kind of death he was to die). (John 18:32, NRSV)

Fulfillment Motif in the Passion Narratives

It is conspicuous that the fourth evangelist explicates the passion of Christ in terms of "fulfillment." This theme of fulfillment is markedly set forth in ch. 12 and continues to play out throughout the remaining portion of the Gospel. A number of exegetes have suggested that the Gospel of John is comprised of two main divisions (chs. 1-11: the book of signs; and 13-20: the book of the passion).[13] If such a division is accepted, ch. 12 is a transitional section that commences a new phase.[14] On this ground, an argument can be advanced that the first half of John spells out the greatness of Jesus as confirmed by prominent Old Testament figures, while the latter part justifies how this greatness of Jesus is consistent with the Jewish rejection of him as Messiah, which is already prophesied and foreshadowed in the ancient Jewish scriptures. Smith points out that any missionary tractate designed to convince Jews would run into difficulties if a satisfactory explanation for Jesus' rejection and death was not offered. These two questions need to be resolved for any Jew if the gospel has to get across. That is, first, how could the Messiah be crucified? Second, how could Jews reject their

---

However, the obduracy on the part of Jews seems to be a contingent effect to accomplish the divine salvific program.

[12] O'Rourke, "Explicit Old Testament Citations in the Gospels," 433.

[13] It was first proposed by Dodd (*The Interpretation of the Fourth Gospel*, 289) and followed by Brown with a different phrase (book of signs and book of glory, Brown, *The Gospel According to John*, 1:cxxxviii-ix). Beasley-Murray basically accepts such division but proposes to see the whole Gospel as a book of signs since he sees the purpose of the Gospel as being stated in 21:24-25. Beasley-Murray, *John*, xc. Also, see the following for a helpful concentric structural analysis of the Fourth Gospel. C. Koch and K. Huber, "Konzentrisches Erzählkonzept im Johannesevangelium: Skizze eines Strukturierungsvorschlags," *ProtoBib* 12 (2003): 129-42.

[14] D. Moody Smith made a plausible case for viewing 12:37-40 as a "primitive transition" linking the seemingly contradictory Christologies explicated in the two divisions of the Gospel of John: D. Moody Smith, "Setting and Shape of a Johannine Narrative Source," *JBL* 95 (1976): 239. Smith's view is influenced by B. Lindars who believes that John is here closer to the original understanding and usage of the Old Testament quotations used by early Christians to explain the death of Jesus than is Matthew. Barnabas Lindars, *New Testament Apologetic: The Doctrinal Significance of the Old Testament Quotations* (Philadelphia: Westminster, 1961), 271-72.

own Messiah?[15]

Accordingly, quoting from Isaiah 6:10, John 12:39-41 provides the starting point of John's apologetic on behalf of Jesus' passion as reflected in the latter half of John's Gospel.[16] From 12:39-41 on, the fourth evangelist forcefully explicates that the rejection of the Messiah accords with the divine redemptive program as it foreshadowed in the Old Testament.[17] This is not to say, nonetheless, that the suffering of Christ was to comply with the Old Testament prophecies, since the Christ has a temporal priority over the Old Testament heroic figures.[18]

---

[15] Smith, "Setting and Shape of a Johannine Narrative Source," 236-41. Smith asserts that the rejection of Jews was unthinkable and it is attested by the constant New Testament reference to Christ's crucifixion as a "stumbling block" to the Jews (e.g., 1 Cor 1:23). Cf. Bultmann, *Theology of the New Testament*, 1: 44-46. Carson presumes that the designated audience of the Fourth Gospel is Diaspora Jews and proselytes. D.A. Carson, *The Gospel according to John* (Grand Rapids: Eerdmans, 1991), 90-95. W. Rebell and E. Stegemann further identify the function of the concentrated recourse to the Scripture in John; that is, to "fight for tradition (Kampf um Tradition)" in order for the fourth evangelist to win fellow Jews because the tradition had an authenticating strength (Legitimationskraft). Walter Rebell, *Gemeinde als Gegenwelt: Zur soziologischen und didaktischen Funktion des Johannesevangeliums* (Frankfurt: Lang, 1987), 109; Ekkerhard W. Stegemann, "Die Tragödie der Nähe: Zu den judenfeindlichen Aussagen des Johannesevangeliums," *KuI* 4 (1989): 119.

[16] C.K. Barrett, "The Old Testament in the Fourth Gospel," *JTS* 48 (1947): 169.

[17] Hamid-Khani, *Revelation and Concealment of Christ*, 258-330.

[18] In this respect, the following statement is helpful. "These passages [i.e., the Matthean fulfillment texts] are not saying that the Law and the Prophets are just predictions of future events, nor is it saying that Jesus simply fulfills the parts of the Law and the Prophets which happen to be predictions. It means Jesus is the true purpose and goal of the OT." Dan McCartney and Peter Enns, "Matthew and Hosea: A Response to John Sailhamer," *WTJ* 63 (2001): 104. Parentheses are added for clarification.

APPENDIX 4

The Internal Well of Living Water in John 7.38

And let the one who believes in me drink. As the scripture has said, "out of the believer's heart shall flow rivers of living water." (John 7:38, NRSV)

ὁ πιστεύων εἰς ἐμέ, καθὼς εἶπεν ἡ γραφή, ποταμοὶ ἐκ τῆς κοιλίας αὐτοῦ ῥεύσουσιν ὕδατος ζῶντος. (John 7:38, NA[28])

This verse has led to an amalgam of scholarly confusion due to three peculiar features:[1] first, the verse is structurally an anacoluthon which has prompted some scholars to debate as to the subject of the sentence.[2] Second, no exact scripture citation is found in the Old Testament as the text claims ("as the scripture said"). Finally, elusive is the Jewish exegetical source of the concept "the internalized well."[3]

---

[1] For summaries of issues surrounding this verse, see Karl H. Kuhn, "St John 7:37-8," *NTS* 4 (1957): 63-65; Juan B. Cortés, "Yet Another Look at Jn 7:37-38," *CBQ* 29 (1967): 75-86; Joel Marcus, "Rivers of Living Water from Jesus' Belly (John 7:38)," *JBL* 117 (1998): 328-30; Michael A. Daise, "'If Anyone Thirsts, Let That One Come to Me And Drink': The Literary Texture of John 7:37b-38a," *JBL* 122 (2003): 687-99; Benny Thettayil, *In Spirit and Truth: An Exegetical Study of John 4:19-26 and a Theological Investigation of the Replacement Theme in the Fourth Gospel* (Leuven: Peeters, 2007), 403-12.

[2] *BDF*, 244 (§§466, [4]); George D. Kilpatrick, "Punctuation of John 7:37-38," *JTS* 11 (1960): 340-42; Gordon D. Fee, "Once More—John 7:37-39," *ExpTim* 89 (1978): 116-18.

[3] Concerning the second and third questions, see Johannes Baptist Bauer, "Drei Cruces: Joh 7:38 und Spr 18:4," *BZ* 9 (1965): 84-91; Bruce H. Grigsby, "'If Any Man Thirsts': Observations on the Rabbinic Background of John 7:37-39," *Bib* 67 (1986): 101-08; Daniel Bodi, "Der altorientalische Hintergrund des Themas der 'Ströme lebendigen Wassers' in Joh 7,38," in *Johannes-Studien: Interdisziplinäre Zugänge zum Johannes-Evangelium, Freundesgabe der Theologischen Fakultät der Universität Neuchâtel für Jean Zumstein*, ed. Martin Rose (Zürich: Theologischer, 1991), 137-58; Glenn Balfour, "The Jewishness of John's Use of the Scriptures in John 6:31 and 7:37-38," *TynBul* 46 (1995): 357-80; M.J.J. Menken, "The Origin of the Old Testament Quotation in John 7:38," *NovT* 38 (1996): 159-74; Henry M. Knapp, "The Messianic Water Which Gives Life to the World," *HBT* 19 (1997): 109-21; Craig R. Koester, *Symbolism in the Fourth Gospel: Meaning, Mystery, Community* (Minneapolis: Fortress, 2003), 193-94.

Contrary to some exegetes who perceive Jesus as the source of living water in this verse, it is syntactically natural to see the water flowing from within the heart of the believer. In addition, the same concept expressed in John 4:14 reinforces this option.[4] It is surprising that the concept of an internalized well within human beings is unattested in the previous or contemporary Jewish literature. This expression thus evidently evokes Jesus' discourse with the Samaritan woman. Two parallel features in both texts warrant such a conclusion: the subject of the granting the water is Jesus and the presence of the unprecedented concept "internalized well." These two Johannine pericopae constitute an unmistakable statement which marks a radical paradigm shift in redemptive history. Especially noteworthy is the characteristic of the indwelling ministry of the Holy Spirit since it is unheard of in the previous and concurrent Jewish traditions.[5] At the end, this prediction of the shift in salvation history serves to attest to the messianic identity of Jesus just as the previous miraculous signs rendered the same service.[6]

---

[4] Barnabas Lindars, *The Gospel of John* (London: Marshall, Morgan & Scott, 1972), 300-01; C.K. Barrett, *The Gospel according to the St. John: An Introduction with Commentary and Notes on the Greek Text* (Philadelphia: Westminster, 1978), 326-27; Herman N. Ridderbos, *The Gospel of John, : A Theological Commentary* (Grand Rapids: Eerdmans, 1997), 273; D.A. Carson, *The Gospel according to John* (Grand Rapids: Eerdmans, 1991), 323-25; Andreas Köstenberger, *John* (Grand Rapids: Baker, 2004), 10-11. For those who see Jesus as the subject of the verse, see Raymond E. Brown, *The Gospel according to John* (New York: Doubleday, 1966), 1:320; George R. Beasley-Murray, *John* (Nashville: Nelson, 1999), 115; Rudolf Schnackenburg, *The Gospel according to St. John* (New York: Crossroad, 1982), 2:154; Menken, "The Origin of the Old Testament Quotation in John 7:38," 165-66; Craig S. Keener, *The Gospel of John: A Commentary* (Peabody: Hendrickson, 2003), 1:728-30. A minor opinion to be noted is Thettayil who perceives the source of the living water as Jerusalem, the place of the temple. Thettayil, *In Spirit and Truth*, 409-13.

[5] Although opting for the provenance of the internalized well both in Jesus and the believers, Baffes rightly underscores the emphatic shift in the salvation history in this text. Melanie Baffes, "Christology and Discipleship in John," *BTB* 41 (2011): 144-50.

[6] After witnessing a number of signs (turning water into wine, 2:1-12; the healing of royal official's son, 4:43-54; and of the lame man, 5:1-47; the feeding of the multitude, 6:1-71), many in the crowd confessed, "When the Messiah comes, will he do more signs than this man has done?" (7:31).

APPENDIX 5

Explicit Old Testament Materials in John[1]

Table 11. Direct Quotations with Introductory Formulae

1:23	He said, "I am the voice of one crying out in the wilderness, 'Make straight the way of the Lord,'" as the prophet Isaiah said.	Isa 40:3	A voice cries out: "In the wilderness prepare the way of the LORD, make straight in the desert a highway for our God.
2:17	His disciples remembered that it was written, "Zeal for your house will consume me."	Ps 69:9	It is zeal for your house that has consumed me; the insults of those who insult you have fallen on me.
6:31	Our ancestors ate the manna in the wilderness; as it is written, 'He gave them bread from heaven to eat.'"	Ps 78:24	he rained down on them manna to eat, and gave them the grain of heaven.
6:45	It is written in the prophets, 'And they shall all be taught by God.' Everyone who has heard and learned from the Father comes to me.	Isa 54:13	All your children shall be taught by the LORD, and great shall be the prosperity of your children.
10:34	Jesus answered, "Is it not written in your law, 'I said, you are gods'?	Ps 82:6	I say, "You are gods, children of the Most High, all of you

---

[1] For a convenient survey of the Old Testament materials in John's Gospel, see Andreas Köstenberger, "John," in *Commentary on the New Testament Use of the Old Testament*, ed. G.K. Beale and D.A. Carson (Grand Rapids: Baker, 2007), 415-21.

12:14 -15	Jesus found a young donkey and sat on it; as it is written: "Do not be afraid, daughter of Zion. Look, your king is coming, sitting on a donkey's colt!"	Ps 62:11; Zech 9:9; cf. Isa 35:4; 40:9	Once God has spoken; twice have I heard this: that power belongs to God; Rejoice greatly, O daughter Zion! Shout aloud, O daughter Jerusalem! Lo, your king comes to you; triumphant and victorious is he, humble and riding on a donkey, on a colt, the foal of a donkey; Say to those who are of a fearful heart, "Be strong, do not fear! Here is your God. He will come with vengeance, with terrible recompense. He will come and save you."; Get you up to a high mountain, O Zion, herald of good tidings; lift up your voice with strength, O Jerusalem, herald of good tidings, lift it up, do not fear; say to the cities of Judah, "Here is your God!"
12:38	This was to fulfill the word spoken by the prophet Isaiah: "Lord, who has believed our message, and to whom has the arm of the Lord been revealed?"	Isa 53:1	Who has believed what we have heard? And to whom has the arm of the LORD been revealed?
12:39 -41	And so they could not believe, because Isaiah also said, "He has blinded their eyes and hardened their heart, so that they might not look with their eyes, and understand with their heart and turn— and I would heal them." Isaiah said this because he saw his glory and spoke about him.	Isa 6:10	Make the mind of this people dull, and stop their ears, and shut their eyes, so that they may not look with their eyes, and listen with their ears, and comprehend with their minds, and turn and be healed."

13:18	I am not speaking of all of you; I know whom I have chosen. But it is to fulfill the scripture, 'The one who ate my bread has lifted his heel against me.'	Ps 41:9	Even my bosom friend in whom I trusted, who ate of my bread, has lifted the heel against me.
15:25	It was to fulfill the word that is written in their law, 'They hated me without a cause.'	Ps 35:19; 69:5	Do not let my treacherous enemies rejoice over me, or those who hate me without cause wink the eye; O God, you know my folly; the wrongs I have done are not hidden from you.
19:24	So they said to one another, "Let us not tear it, but cast lots for it to see who will get it." This was to fulfill what the scripture says, "They divided my clothes among themselves, and for my clothing they cast lots."	Ps 22:18	They divide my clothes among themselves, and for my clothing they cast lots.
19:28	After this, when Jesus knew that all was now finished, he said (in order to fulfill the scripture), "I am thirsty."	Ps 22:15	my mouth is dried up like a potsherd, and my tongue sticks to my jaws; you lay me in the dust of death.
19:36	These things occurred so that the scripture might be fulfilled, "None of his bones shall be broken."	Ex 12:46; Num 9:12; Ps 34:20	It shall be eaten in one house; you shall not take any of the animal outside the house, and you shall not break any of its bones (Ex 12:46); They shall leave none of it until morning, nor break a bone of it; according to all the statute for the passover they shall keep it (Num 9:12); He keeps all their bones; not one of them will be broken (Ps 34:20).

19:37	And again another passage of scripture says, "They will look on the one whom they have pierced."	Zech 12:10	And I will pour out a spirit of compassion and supplication on the house of David and the inhabitants of Jerusalem, so that, when they look on the one whom they have pierced, they shall mourn for him, as one mourns for an only child, and weep bitterly over him, as one weeps over a firstborn.

Table 12. Direct Quotations without Introductory Formulae

1:51	And he said to him, "Very truly, I tell you, you will see heaven opened and the angels of God ascending and descending upon the Son of Man."	Gen 28:12	And he dreamed that there was a ladder set up on the earth, the top of it reaching to heaven; and the angels of God were ascending and descending on it.
12:13	So they took branches of palm trees and went out to meet him, shouting, "Hosanna! Blessed is the one who comes in the name of the Lord— the King of Israel!"	Ps 118:25-26	Save us, we beseech you, O LORD! O LORD, we beseech you, give us success! Blessed is the one who comes in the name of the LORD. We bless you from the house of the LORD.

Table 13. Introductory Formulae without Explicit Quotations

7:38	and let the one who believes in me drink. As the scripture has said, 'Out of the believer's heart shall flow rivers of living water.'"
7:42	"Has not the scripture said that the Messiah is descended from David and comes from Bethlehem, the village where David lived?"
17:12	While I was with them, I protected them in your name that you have given me. I guarded them, and not one of them was lost except the one destined to be lost, so that the scripture might be fulfilled.

Table 14. OT Allusions Discussed in the Present Study

1:45	Philip found Nathanael and said to him, "We have found him about whom Moses in the law and also the prophets wrote, Jesus son of Joseph from Nazareth."
3:10	Jesus answered him, "Are you a teacher of Israel, and yet you do not understand these things?
5:39	"You search the scriptures because you think that in them you have eternal life; and it is they that testify on my behalf.
5:45-47	Do not think that I will accuse you before the Father; your accuser is Moses, on whom you have set your hope. If you believed Moses, you would believe me, for he wrote about me. But if you do not believe what he wrote, how will you believe what I say?"
20:9	for as yet they did not understand the scripture, that he must rise from the dead.

APPENDIX 6

Important Sources on the Study of the Old Testament and the Early Jewish Literature in the Gospel of John

The Hebrew Old Testament
Rudolf Kittel et al., *Biblia Hebraica Stuttgartensia*, 5th rev. ed. (Stuttgart: Deutsche Bibelgesellschaft, 1997).
George V. Wigram, *The Englishman's Hebrew Concordance of the Old Testament: Coded with the Numbering System from Strong's Exhaustive Concordance of the Bible* (Peabody, MA: Hendrickson, 1996).
John R. Kohlenberger and James A. Swanson, *The Hebrew English Concordance to the Old Testament: With the New International Version* (Grand Rapids, MI: Zondervan, 1998).
Victor H. Matthews and Don C. Benjamin, *Old Testament Parallels: Laws and Stories from the Ancient Near East*, 3rd ed. (New York: Paulist, 2007).

The Greek Old Testament
Alfred Rahlfs, ed., *Septuaginta: Vetus Testamentum graecum auctoritate Academiae Scientarum Gottingensis editum*, SSSGA (Göttingen: Vandenhoeck & Ruprecht, 1931-).
—— and Robert Hanhart, eds, *Septuaginta: Id est Vetus Testamentum graece iuxta LXX Interpretes* (Stuttgart: Deutsche Bibelgesellschaft, 2006).
Jennifer Dines, *The Septuagint*, UBIW (London: T & T Clark, 2004).
Edwin Hatch and Henry A. Redpath, *A Concordance to the Septuagint: And the Other Greek Versions of the Old Testament (Including the Apocryphal Books)*, 2nd ed. (Grand Rapids, MI: Baker, 1998).
Martin Hengel, *The Septuagint as Christian Scripture: Its Prehistory and the Problem of Its Canon* (Grand Rapids, MI: Baker, 2004).
M.A. Knibb, ed., *The Septuagint and Messianism: Colloquium Biblicum Lovaniense Liii, July 27-29, 2004*, BETL (Louvain: Peeters, 2006).
Wolfgang Kraus and R. Glenn Wooden, eds., *Septuagint Research: Issues and Challenges in the Study of the Greek Jewish Scriptures*, SCSS (Atlanta: The Society of Biblical Literature, 2006).
Natalio Fernández Marcos, *The Septuagint in Context: Introduction to the Greek Version of the Bible*, trans. Wilfred G.E. Watson (Atlanta: The Society of Biblical Literature, 2009).

Takamitsu Muraoka, *A Greek English Lexicon of the Septuagint* (Louvain: Peeters, 2009).
— *Hebrew/Aramaic Index to the Septuagint: Keyed to the Hatch-Redpath Concordance* (Grand Rapids, MI: Baker, 1998).
R. Timothy McLay, *The Use of the Septuagint in New Testament Research* (Grand Rapids, MI: Eerdmans, 2003).
Albert Pietersma and Benjamin G. Wright, eds., *A New English Translation of the Septuagint* (Oxford: Oxford University Press, 2007).
Moisés Silva and Karen H. Jobes, *Invitation to the Septuagint* (Grand Rapids, MI: Baker, 2005).
The Septuagint Commentary Series (Leiden: Brill, 2005-).
The SBC Commentary on the Septuagint (Atlanta: the Society of Biblical Literature, n.d.).

The Greek New Testament

Barbara Aland et al., eds., *Novum Testamentum Graece*, 28th ed. (Stuttgart: Deutsche Bibelgesellschaft, 2012).
Kurt Aland, *Synopsis Quattuor Evangeliorum: Locis parallelis evangeliorum apocryphorum et patrum adhibitis*, 15th ed. (Stuttgart: Deutsche Bibelgesellschaft, 1996).
W.J. Elliott, and D.C. Parker, eds., *The Papyri*, vol. 1 of *The New Testament in Greek IV: The Gospel according to St. John*, NTTS 20 (Leiden: Brill, 1995).
John R. Kohlenberger, Edward W. Goodrick, and James A. Swanson, *The Exhaustive Concordance to the Greek New Testament* (Grand Rapids, MI: Zondervan, 1995).
I. Howard Marshall, *Moulton and Geden Concordance to the Greek New Testament*, 6th ed. (London: T & T Clark, 2002).
U.B. Schmid, W.J. Elliott, and D.C. Parker, eds., *The Majuscules*, vol. 2 of *The New Testament in Greek IV: The Gospel according to St. John*, NTTSD 37 (Leiden: Brill, 2007).

The Old Testament Apocrypha

Michael D. Coogan, Marc Z. Brettler, and Pheme Perkins, eds., *The New Oxford Annotated Apocrypha*, 4th ed. (Oxford: Oxford University Press, 2010).
David A. deSilva, *Introducing the Apocrypha: Message, Context, and Significance* (Grand Rapids, MI: Baker, 2002).
Daniel Harrington, S.J., *Invitation to the Apocrypha* (Grand Rapids, MI: Eerdmans, 1999).
Bruce M. Metzger, *A Concordance to the Apocrypha/Deuterocanonical Books of the Revised Standard Version* (Grand Rapids, MI: Eerdmans, 1983).
Sever J. Voicu, ed., *Apocrypha*, ACCS (Downers Grove, IL: IVP, 2010).

The Old Testament Pseudepigrapha

Richard Bauckham, James Davila, and Alex Panayotov, eds., *Old Testament*

Pseudepigrapha: More Noncanonical Scriptures (Grand Rapids, MI: Eerdmans, 2013).
James H. Charlesworth, *The Old Testament Pseudepigrapha*, 2 vols., ABRL (New York: Doubleday, 1983-85).
— *The Old Testament Pseudepigrapha and the New Testament: Prolegomena for the Study of Christian Origins* (Valley Forge, PA: Trinity, 1998).
James R. Davila, *The Provenance of the Pseudepigrapha: Jewish, Christian, or Other?* SJSJ 105 (Leiden: Brill, 2005).
Lorenzo DiTommaso, *A Bibliography of Pseudepigrapha Research 1850-1999*, JSPSup 39 (Sheffield: Sheffield, 2001).
Steve Delamater, *A Scripture Index to Charlesworth's the Old Testament Pseudepigrapha* (Sheffield: Sheffield, 2002).

The Qumran literature

Companion to the Qumran Scrolls (London: T & T Clark, 2000-)
The Discoveries in the Judaean Desert, 40 vols. (Oxford: Clarendon, 1955-).
Eerdmans Commentary on the Dead Sea Scrolls (Grand Rapids, MI: Eerdmans, 2001-)
The Princeton Theological Seminary Dead Sea Scrolls Project (Tübingen: Mohr Siebeck; Louisville: Westminster/John Knox, 1991-).
Martin G. Abegg, Jr., James E. Bowley, and Edward M. Cook, *The Dead Sea Scrolls Concordance*, 3 vols. (Leiden: Brill, 2003-).
James H. Charlesworth, *Graphic Concordance to the Dead Sea Scrolls*, PTSDSSP (Tübingen: Mohr Siebeck; Louisville: Westminster/John Knox, 1991).
— and Frank Moore Cross, eds., *The Dead Sea Scrolls: Hebrew, Aramaic, and Greek Texts with English Translations*, PTSDSSP (Tübingen: Mohr Siebeck; Louisville: Westminster/John Knox, 1994-).
Ruth A. Clements and Nadav Sharon, *The Orion Center Bibliography of the Dead Sea Scrolls and Associated Literature (2000-2006)*, STDJ 71 (Leiden: Brill, 2007).
Joseph A. Fitzmyer, *A Guide to the Dead Sea Scrolls and Related Literature*, SDSSRL (Grand Rapids, MI: Eerdmans, 2008).
Timothy Lim & John J. Collins, eds., *The Oxford Handbook of the Dead Sea Scrolls* (Oxford: Oxford University Press, 2010).
Florentino García Martínez and Eibert J. C. Tigchelaar, eds., *The Dead Sea Scrolls: Study Edition*, 2 vols. (Leiden: Brill, 1996-97).
Florentino García Martínez and Donald W. Parry, *A Bibliography of the Finds in the Desert of Judah 1970-1995*, STDJ 19 (Leiden: Brill, 1996).
Donald W. Parry and Emanuel Tov, eds., *The Dead Sea Scrolls Reader*, 6 vols. (Leiden: Brill, 2004-05).
Emanuel Tov, *The Texts from the Judaean Desert: Indices and an Introduction to the Discoveries in the Judaean Desert Series*, DJD 39 (Oxford: Clarendon, 2002).

Michael O. Wise, Martin G. Abegg, and Edward M. Cook, *The Dead Sea Scrolls: A New Translation*, rev. ed. (San Francisco: HarperSanFrancisco, 2005).

David L. Washburn, *A Catalog of Biblical Passages in the Dead Sea Scrolls*, TxCrSt 2 (Leiden: Brill, 2002).

Early rabbinic literature

Isidore Epstein, ed., *The Babylonian Talmud*, 35 vols. (London: Soncino, 1935-48).

Paul V.M. Flesher and Bruce Chilton, *The Targums: A Critical Introduction* (Waco, TX: Baylor University Press, 2011).

Jacob Neusner, *Introduction to Rabbinic Literature*, AYBRL (New Haven, CT: Doubleday, 1994).

— trans., *The Mishnah: A New Translation* (New Haven, CT: Yale University Press, 1988).

— *The Talmud of the Land of Israel*, 35 vols. (Chicago: University of Chicago Press, 1982-1994).

Herman L. Strack and Paul Billerbeck, *Das Evangelium nach Markus, Lukas und Johannes und die Apostelgeschichte erläutert aus Talmud und Midrasch*, 3rd ed., vol. 2 of *Kommentar zum Neuen Testament aus Talmud und Midrasch* (München: Beck, 1924).

Reimund Bieringer, *The New Testament and Rabbinic Literature*, JSJSup 136 (Leiden: Brill, 2010).

Charlotte E. Fonrobert and Martin S. Jaffee, eds., *The Cambridge Companion to the Talmud and Rabbinic Literature*, CCR (Cambridge: Cambridge University Press, 2007).

Martin McNamara, ed., The Aramaic Bible (Collegeville, MN: Liturgical, 1987-).

Hugo Odeberg, *The Fourth Gospel: Interpreted in Its Relation to Contemporaneous Religious Currents in Palestine and the Hellenistic-Oriental World* (Chicago: Argonaut, 1929; repr., Amsterdam: B. R. Grüner, 1968).

Günther Stemberger, *Introduction to the Talmud and Midrash*, 2nd ed., trans. and ed. Markus Bockmuehl (Edinburgh: T & T Clark, 1996).

The Samaritan Pentateuch

Robert T. Anderson and Terry Giles. *The Samaritan Pentateuch: An Introduction to Its Origin, History, and Significance for Biblical Studies*, RBS 72 (Atlanta: The Society of Biblical Literature, 2012).

Alan D. Crown, ed., *Samaritan Scribes and Manuscripts*, TSAJ 80 (Tübingen: Mohr Siebeck, 2001).

— *The Samaritans* (Tübingen: Mohr Siebeck, 1989).

— and Reinhard Pummer, *A Bibliography of the Samaritans: Revised, Expanded and Annotated.*, 3rd ed., ATLABS 51 (Lanham, MD: Scarecrow, 2005).

— and Abraham Tal, ed., *A Companion to Samaritan Studies* (Tübingen: Mohr Siebeck, 1993).
Gary N. Knopper, *Jews and Samaritans: The Origins and History of Their Early Relations* (Oxford: Oxford University Press, 2013).
Reinhard Pummer, Early *Christian Authors on Samaritans & Samaritanism: Texts, Translations & Commentary*, TSAJ 92 (Tübingen: Mohr Siebeck, 2002).
Abraham Tal, ed., *The Samaritan Pentateuch: Edited according to MS 6(C) of the Shekem Synagogue* (Tel Aviv: Tel Aviv University Press, 1994).
Benyamim Tsedaka and Sharon Sullivan, eds., *The Israelite Samaritan Version of the Torah: First English Translation Compared with the Masorectic Version* (Grand Rapids, MI: Eerdmans, 2013).

Hellenistic writings
Peder Borgen, Kåre Fuglseth, and Roald Skarsten, *The Philo Index: A Complete Greek Word Index to the Writings of Philo of Alexandria* (Grand Rapids, MI: Eerdmans, 1999).
Josephus trans. H. St. J. Thackery et al., 10 vols., LCL (Cambridge, MA: Harvard University Press, 1926-65).
Marvin W. Meyer, ed., *The Nag Hammadi Scripture: The Revised and Updated Translation of the Sacred Gnostic Texts* (New York: HarperOne, 2007).
Philo trans. F.H. Colson and G.H. Whitaker, 12 vols., LCL (Cambridge, MA: Harvard University Press, 1929-62).
Adam Kamesar, ed., *The Cambridge Companion to Philo* (Cambridge, MA: Cambridge University Press, 2009).
Karl H. Rengstorf, *The Complete Concordance to Flavius Josephus: Study Edition*, 2 vols. (Leiden: Brill, 2002).
James M. Robinson, ed., *The Coptic Gnostic Library: A Complete Edition of the Nag Hammadi Codices*, 5 vols. (Leiden: Brill, 2000).
David T. Runia, *Philo in Early Christian Literature: A Survey*, CRINT 3/3 (Van Gorcum: Assen; Minneapolis, MN: Fortress, 1993).
Kenneth Schenck, *A Brief Guide to Philo* (Louisville, KY: Westminster/John Knox, 2005).
Udo Schnelle, Michael Labahn, and Manfred Lang, *Texte zum Johannesevangelium*, vol. I/2 of *Neuer Wettstein: Texte zum Neuen Testament aus Griechentum und Hellenismus* (Berlin: Walter de Gruyter, 2001).

Miscellaneous secondary sources
John J. Collins. *The Apocalyptic Imagination: An Introduction to Jewish Apocalyptic Literature*, 2nd ed. (Grand Rapids, MI: Eerdmans, 1998).
— and Daniel Harlow, eds., *The Eerdmans Dictionary of Early Judaism* (Grand Rapids, MI: Eerdmans, 2010).
Craig A. Evans, *Ancient Texts for New Testament Studies: A Guide to the*

Background Literature (Peabody, MA: Hendrickson, 2005).
Larry R. Helyer, *Exploring Jewish Literature of the Second Temple Period: A Guide for New Testament Students* (Downers Grove, IL: InterVarsity, 2005).
Hans-Josef Klauk, *The Religious Context of Early Christianity: A Guide to Graeco-Roman Religions* (Minneapolis, MN: Fortress, 2003).
George W.E. Nickelsburg, *Jewish Literature between the Bible and the Mishnah: A Historical and Literary Introduction*, 2nd ed. (Minneapolis, MN: Fortress, 2005).
Kenton L. Sparks, *Ancient Texts for the Study of the Hebrew Bible: A Guide to the Background Literature* (Grand Rapids, MI: Baker, 2005).
Michael E. Stone, ed., *Jewish Writings of the Second Temple Period: Apocrypha, Pseudepigrapha, Qumran Sectarian Writings, Philo, Josephus*, CRINT 2/3 (Minneapolis, MN: Fortress, 1984).
The New Testament Gospels in Their Judaic Contexts (Leiden: Brill, 2009-).

APPENDIX 7

The Use of Rabbinic Materials in New Testament Studies

The use of early rabbinic literature for New Testament studies is increasingly recognized as problematic due to its dating issue and the composite nature which involved an extended period of redactional reworking.[1] Although McNamara suggests an early dating of the Palestinian Targum because the body of literature is supposed to reflect the earliest rabbinic traditions, the philological examination and the extant manuscripts place this group of writings later than the first century A.D.[2] Most scholars date the extant earliest manuscripts (Targum

---

[1] These hermeneutical reservations are expressed in the following. Joseph A. Fitzmyer, "Review of Matthew Black, *An Aramaic Approach to the Gospels and Acts*," *CBQ* 30 (1968): 417-28; idem, "Review of Martin McNamara, *The New Testament and the Palestinian Targum to the Pentateuch*," *TS* 29 (1968): 322-28; Anthony D. York, "Dating of Targumic Literature," *JSJ* 5 (1974): 49; Jacob Neusner, "One Theme, Two Settings: The Messiah in the Literature of the Synagogue and in the Rabbis' Canon of Late Antiquity," *BTB* 14 (1984): 110-21; idem, *Messiah in Context* (Philadelphia: Fortress, 1984), 19; Günter Stemberger, "Pesachhaggada und Abendmahlsberichte des Neuen Testaments," *Kairos* 29 (1987): 147-58; Philip Alexander, "Jewish Aramaic Translations of Hebrew Scriptures," in *Mikra: Text, Translation, Reading and Interpretation of the Hebrew Bible in Ancient Judaism and Early Christianity*, ed. M. Jan Mulder (Assen: Van Gorcum, 1988), 238; Anthony J. Saldarini, "Rabbinic Literature and the NT," *ABD*, 5:602-604; James H. Charlesworth, "From Messianology to Christology: Problems and Prospects," in *The Messiah: Developments in Earliest Judaism and Christianity: The First Princeton Symposium on Judaism and Christian Origins*, ed. James H. Charlesworth (Minneapolis: Fortress, 1992), 15-16; Stephen A. Kaufman, "Dating the Language of the Palestinian Targums and Their Use in the Study of First Century CE Texts," in *The Aramaic Bible: Targums in Their Historical Context*, ed. D.R.G. Beattie and M.J. McNamara (Sheffield: JSOT, 1994), 118-41; Johann Maier, "Schriftrezeption im jüdischen Umfeld des Johannesevangeliums," in *Israel und seine Heilstraditionen im Johannesevangelium: Festgabe für Johannes Beutler SJ zum 70. Geburtstag*, ed. Michael Labahn, Klaus Scholtissek, and Angelika Strotmann (Paderborn: Schöningh, 2004), 87-88; Burton L. Visotzky, "Midrash, Christian Exegesis, and Hellenistic Hermeneutics," in *Current Trends in the Study of Midrash* (Leiden: Brill, 2006), 112-17.

[2] Cf. Martin McNamara, *The New Testament and the Palestinian Targum to the Pentateuch* (Rome: Biblica, 1978). For an example of studies on the Johannine appropriation of the rabbinic exegetical traditions, see John L. Ronning, "Targum of Isaiah and

Onqelos and Targum Neofiti I on the Pentateuch) to the late third century and others far later (mostly the seventh to eleventh centuries for Targum Pseudo-Jonathan, the Cairo Geniza, and Targum Jonathan). The advocates for the rabbinic influence on the New Testament bring up two evidences on their behalf. First, they point to some parts of Targum Jonathan which seem to reflect a national eschatological concern probably current right after the destruction of Jerusalem in A.D. 70-200. Second, three Qumran writings (4QtgLev, 4QtgJob, and 11QtgJob) resemble the midrashic style of early rabbinic exegesis.

However, it must be stressed that no one denies some type of rabbinic interpretative practice probably existed in the first century but the composite nature of the literature renders it extremely difficult to utilize it in a critical way for the investigation of any literary dependence. In addition, the three Qumran fragments contain so literal a rendering of the Hebrew scriptures that their categorization into Targum appears to be a special pleading.[3] E.P. Sanders offers a three-fold caution against the use of the early rabbinic materials for New Testament studies. First, although most scholars accept a general continuity between Pharisaism of the first century and the early rabbinic ideas of the second century onward, it is not entirely certain as to the conceptual coherence between the former and individual rabbis of a later period. This partial disparity requires a discerning use. Second, the long period of the editorial activity significantly reduces one's confidence in the rabbinic sources' claim to the early provenance. There is virtually no way to be certain of which part originated from the earliest trait of thought (i.e., second century A.D.). A common mistake scholars make in this regard can be mentioned. D. Daube found a reference to "Moses' seat" in a post-biblical rabbinic writing.[4] The term is found nowhere else in the body of the early rabbinic literature but only in Matthew 23:2. Thus, he postulates that the rabbinic document reflects the conceptual currents of the first century. However, his logic manifests the fallacy of generalization. The term may have derived from the first century tradition, but it is a gross overgeneralization to posit that the entire document that contains the term reflects the Judaism of Jesus' time in its entirety. Third, the rabbinic materials' diversity of views hinders the validity of a comparative study because one can often find a contrasting viewpoint from

---

the Johannine Literature," *WTJ* 69 (2007): 247-78. For an example of positive attitude toward the relation between the early rabbinic literature and the New Testament, see Gundrun Holtz, "Rabbinische Literatur und Neues Testament: Alte Schwierigkeiten und neue Möglichkeiten," *ZNW* 100 (2009): 173-98. For a later dating of the body of the rabbinic literature, see also, Craig A. Evans, *Ancient Texts for New Testament Studies: A Guide to the Background Literature* (Peabody: Hendrickson, 2005), 185-215; Philip S. Alexander, "Targum, Targumim," *ABD*, 6:320-31; Gary G. Porton, "Midrash," *ABD*, 4:818-22; and B. D. Chilton, "Targums," *DJG*, 801-02; idem, "Rabbinic Literature: Targumim," *DNTB*, 904-05.

[3] Chilton, *DJG*, 800.

[4] David Daube, *The New Testament and Rabbinic Judaism* (Peabody: Hendrickson, 1990-94), 246.

another rabbi.⁵ A fourth reservation can be added to this list. That is, it is possible that a common (oral) Jewish tradition may account for the parallel shared by the New Testament and rabbinic sources.⁶ As such, the main contribution of inquiries into the rabbinic literature for New Testament studies should remain as an aid to clarify the Jewish cultural/religious milieu of the first century Palestine.⁷

---

⁵ E.P. Sanders, *Paul and Palestinian Judaism: A Comparison of Patterns of Religion* (Philadelphia: Fortress, 1977), 60-61.

⁶ Geza Vermes, "Jewish Literature and New Testament Exegesis: Reflections on Methodology," *JJS* 33 (1982): 273; Grant R. Osborne, *The Hermeneutical Spiral: A Comprehensive Introduction to biblical Interpretation* (Downers Grove: InterVarsity, 2006), 171.

⁷ Bruce D. Chilton, "Rabbinic Traditions and Writings," *DJG*, 659; C. Hezser, "Diaspora and Rabbinic Judaism," in *The Oxford Handbook of Biblical Studies*, ed. J.W. Rogerson and Judith M. Lieu (Oxford: OUP, 2006), 128-29. In a similar vein, Witmer finds no significant exegetical parallels between the hermeneutics of the Fourth Gospel and that of the Qumran. Stephen E. Witmer, "Approaches to Scripture in the Fourth Gospel and the Qumran Pesharim." *NovT* 48 (2006): 313-28. For a detailed review of up-to-date review of early Jewish literature, see David W. Chapman & Andreas J. Köstenberger, "Jewish Intertestamental and Early Rabbinic Literature: An Annotated Bibliographic Resource Updated (Part 1)," *JETS* 55 (2012): 235-72.

Bibliography

Primary Sources

I Clement, II Clement, Ignatius, Polycarp, Didache, vol. 1 of *The Apostolic Fathers*. Edited and translated by Bart D. Ehrman. Loeb Classical Library. Cambridge: Harvard University Press, 2003.

Abegg, Martin G., Jr., James E. Bowley, and Edward M. Cook, eds. *The Dead Sea Scrolls Concordance*. 3 vols. Leiden: Brill, 2003-2009.

Aberbach, Moses, and Bernard Grossfeld, eds. *Targum Onkelos to Genesis: A Critical Analysis together with an English Translation of the Text*. New York: Ktav, 1982.

Aland, Kurt et al, eds. *Novum Testamentum Graece*. 28th ed. Stuttgart: Deutsche Bibelgesellschaft, 2012.

Allegro, John M. *Qumrân Cave 4: 4Q158-4Q186*. Discoveries in the Judaean Desert 5. Oxford: Clarendon, 1968.

Baillet, Maurice. *Qumrân Grotte 4 III (4Q482-4Q520)*. Discoveries in the Judaean Desert 7. Oxford: Clarendon, 1982.

Baumgarten, Joseph M. *Qumrân Cave 4. XIII: The Damascus Document (4Q266-273)*. Discoveries in the Judaean Desert 18. Oxford: Clarendon, 1996.

Charlesworth, James H., ed. *Damascus Document, War Scroll, and Related Documents*. Vol. 2 of *The Dead Sea Scrolls: Hebrew, Aramaic, and Greek Texts with English Translations*. The Princeton Theological Seminary Dead Sea Scrolls Project. Tübingen: Mohr Siebeck; Louisville: Westminster/John Knox, 1995.

— *The Old Testament Pseudepigrapha*. 2 vols. The Anchor Bible Reference Library. New York: Doubleday, 1983-85.

— *Rule of the Community and Related Documents*. Vol. 1 of *The Dead Sea Scrolls: Hebrew, Aramaic, and Greek Texts with English Translations*. The Princeton Theological Seminary Dead Sea Scrolls Project. Tübingen: Mohr Siebeck; Louisville: Westminster/John Knox, 1994.

— and Frank Moore Cross. *The Dead Sea Scrolls: Hebrew, Aramaic, and Greek Texts with English Translations*. The Princeton Theological Seminary Dead Sea Scrolls Project. Tübingen: Mohr Siebeck; Louisville: Westminster/John Knox, 1994- .

Clark, Ernest G., ed. and trans. *Targum Pseudo-Jonathan: Deuteronomy*. The Aramaic Bible 5B. Collegeville: Liturgical, 1997.

— *Targum Pseudo-Jonathan of the Pentateuch: Text and Concordance*. Hoboken: Ktav, 1984.

Coogan, Michael D., Marc Z. Brettler, and Pheme Perkins, eds. *The New Oxford Annotated Apocrypha*. 4th ed. Oxford: Oxford University Press, 2010.

Danby, Herbert. *The Mishnah: Translated from the Hebrew with Introduction and Brief Explanatory Notes*. London: Oxford University Press, 1933.

Dimant, Devorah. *Pseudo-Prophetic Texts*. Part 4 of *Qumran Cave 4, XXI: Parabiblical Texts*. Discoveries in the Judaean Desert 30. Oxford: Clarendon, 2001.

Elliger, Karl, and Willhelm Rudolph, eds. *Biblia Hebraica Stuttgartensia*. 5th rev. ed. Stuttgart: Deutsche Bibelgesellschaft, 1997.

Elliott, W.J., and D.C. Parker, eds. *The Papyri*. Vol. 1 of *The New Testament in Greek IV: The Gospel according to St. John*. New Testament Tools and Studies 20. Leiden: Brill,

1995.
Epstein, Isidore, ed. *The Babylonian Talmud*. 35 vols. London: Soncino, 1935-48.
Flint, Peter W. *The Dead Sea Psalms Scrolls and the Book of Psalms*. Studies on the Texts of the Desert of Judah 17. Leiden: Brill, 1997.
Freedman, H., trans. *Genesis: Midrash Rabbah*. 2 vols. London: Soncino, 1951.
Hennecke, Edgar, and Wilhelm Schneemelcher, eds. *New Testament Apocrypha*. 2 vols. Translated by R. McL. Wilson. Philadelphia: Westminster, 1963.
Iustini Martyris *Dialogus cum Tryphone*. Edited by Miroslav Marcovich. Patristische Texte und Studien 47. Berlin: Walter de Gruyter, 1997.
Josephus. Translated by H. St. J. Thackery. 10 vols. Loeb Classical Library. Cambridge: Harvard University Press, 1926-65.
Martínez, Florentino García, and Eibert J.C. Tigchelaar, eds. *The Dead Sea Scrolls: Study Edition*. 2 vols. Leiden: Brill, 1996-97.
McNamara, Martin, ed. *Targum Neofiti 1: Genesis*. The Aramaic Bible 1A. Collegeville: Liturgical, 1992.
Meyer, Marvin W., ed. *The Nag Hammadi Scripture: The Revised and Updated Translation of the Sacred Gnostic Texts*. New York: HarperOne, 2007.
Midrash Rabbah: Genesis II. Translated by H. Freedman. London: Soncino, 1951.
Neusner, Jacob, trans. *The Mishnah: A New Translation*. New Haven: Yale University Press, 1988.
Parry, Donald W., and Emanuel Tov, eds. *The Dead Sea Scrolls Reader*. 6 vols. Leiden: Brill, 2004-05.
Pietersma, Albert, and Benjamin G. Wright, eds. *A New English Translation of the Septuagint*. Oxford: Oxford University Press, 2007.
Philo. Translated by F.H. Colson and G.H. Whitaker. 12 vols. Loeb Classical Library. Cambridge: Harvard University Press, 1929-62.
Pirkê de Rabbi Eliezer (The Chapters of Rabbi Eliezer the Great) according to the Text of the Manuscript belonging to Abraham Epstein of Vienna. Translated by Gerald Friedlander. New York: Bloch, 1916.
Puech, Emile. *Qumrân grotte 4, XVIII: Textes hébreux (4Q521-4Q528, 4Q576-4Q579)*. Discoveries in the Judaean Desert 25. Oxford: Clarendon, 1998.
Qimron, Elisha. *The Temple Scroll: A Critical Edition with Extensive Reconstructions*. Judean Desert Studies. Beer Sheva: Ben-Gurion University of the Negev Press; Jerusalem: Israel Exploration Society, 1996.
Rahlfs, Alfred, and Robert Hanhart, eds. *Septuaginta: Id est Vetus Testamentum graece iuxta LXX Interpretes*. Rev. ed. Stuttgart: Deutsche Bibelgesellschaft, 2006.
—— *Septuaginta: Vetus Testamentum graecum auctoritate Academiae Scientarum Gottingensis editum*. Septuaginta Societatis Scientiarum Gottingensis auctoritate. Göttingen: Vandenhoeck & Ruprecht, 1931- .
Robinson, James M., ed. *The Coptic Gnostic Library: A Complete Edition of the Nag Hammadi Codices*. 5 vols. Leiden: Brill, 2000.
—— ed., *The Nag Hammadi Library in English*. 4th rev. ed. The Coptic Gnostic Library Project. Leiden: Brill, 1996.
Sanderson, Judith E. *An Exodus Scroll from Qumran: 4QpaleoExodum and the Samaritan Tradition*. Harvard Semitic Studies 30. Atlanta: Scholars, 1986.
Schmid, U.B., W.J. Elliott, and D.C. Parker, eds. *The Majuscules*, Volume Two of *The New Testament in Greek IV: The Gospel according to St. John*. New Testament Tools, Studies and Documents 37. Leiden: Brill, 2007.

Schneemelcher, Wilhelm, ed. *New Testament Apocrypha*. Rev. ed. 2 vols. Translated by R. McL. Wilson. Louisville: Westminster/John Knox, 1991.
Schnelle, Udo, Michael Labahn, and Manfred Lang, eds. *Texte zum Johannesevangelium*. Vol. I/2 of *Neuer Wettstein: Texte zum Neuen Testament aus Griechentum and Hellenismus*. Berlin: Walter de Gruyter, 2001.
Sperber, Alexander. *The Bible in Aramaic: Based on Old Manuscripts and Printed Texts*. 25 vols. Leiden: Brill, 1959-92.
Tsedaka, Benyamim, and Sharon Sullivan, eds. *The Israelite Samaritan Version of the Torah: First English Translation Compared with the Masorectic Version*. Grand Rapids: Eerdmans, 2013.
Tal, Abraham, ed. *The Samaritan Pentateuch: Edited according to MS 6(C) of the Shekem Synagogue*. Tel Aviv: Tel Aviv University Press, 1994.
Tov, Emanuel. *The Greek Minor Prophets scroll from Naḥal Ḥever (8QḤevXII gr): The Seiyal Collection I*. Discoveries in the Judaean Desert 8. Oxford: Clarendon; Oxford University Press, 1990.
—— *The Texts from the Judaean Desert: Indices and an Introduction to the Discoveries in the Judaean Desert Series*. Discoveries in the Judaean Desert 39. Oxford: Clarendon, 2002.
Tromp, Johannes. *The Assumption of Moses: A Critical Edition with Commentary*. Studia in Veteris Testamenti Pseudepigrapha 10. Leiden: Brill, 1993.
Voicu, Sever J., ed. *Apocrypha*. Ancient Christian Commentary on Scripture. Downers Grove: IVP, 2010.
Wevers, John W., ed. *Septuaginta: Vetus Testamentum Graecum*. Göttingen: Vandenhoeck & Ruprecht, 1922- .
Wise, Michael O., Martin G. Abegg, and Edward M. Cook. *The Dead Sea Scrolls: A New Translation*. Rev. ed. San Francisco: HarperSanFrancisco, 2005.

Books

Alkier, Stefan, and Raichard B. Hays, eds. *Die Bibel im Dialog der Schriften: Konzepte intertextueller Bibellektüre*. Neutestamentliche Entwürfe zur Theologie 10. Tübingen: Francke, 2005.
Allison, Dale C., Jr. *The New Moses: A Matthean Typology*. Minneapolis, MN: Fortress, 1993.
Anderson, Paul N. *The Christology of the Fourth Gospel: Its Unity and Disunity in the Light of John 6*. Wissenschaftliche Untersuchungen zum Neuen Testament 2/78. Tübingen: Mohr Siebeck, 1996.
—— Felix Just, and Tom Thatcher, eds. *Aspects of Historicity in the Fourth Gospel*. Vol. 2 of *John, Jesus, and History*. Early Christianity and Its Literature 2. Atlanta: The Society of Biblical Literature, 2009.
Anderson, Robert T., and Terry Giles. *The Samaritan Pentateuch: An Introduction to Its Origin, History, and Significance for Biblical Studies*. Resources for Biblical Studies 72. Atlanta: The Society of Biblical Literature, 2012.
—— *Traditions Kept: The Literature of the Samaritans*. Peabody: Hendrickson, 2005.
Ashton, John. *Studying John: Approaches to the Fourth Gospel*. Oxford: Oxford University Press, 1998.
—— *Understanding the Fourth Gospel*. 2nd ed. Oxford: Oxford University Press, 2007.

Backhaus, Knut. *Die "Jüngerkreise" des Täufers Johannes: Eine Studie zu den religionsgeschichtlichen Ursprüngen des Christentums*. Paderborner theologische Studien 19. Paderborn: Schöningh, 1991.
Baird, William. *From C.H. Dodd to Hans Dieter Betz*. Vol. 3 of *History of New Testament Research*. Minneapolis: Fortress, 2013.
Baker, David L. *Two Testaments, One Bible: The Theological Relationship between the Old and New Testaments*. 3rd ed. Downers Grove: Inter Varsity, 2010.
Balz, Horst R., ed. *Theologische Realenzyklopädie: Abkürzungsverzeichnis*. 36 vols. Berlin: Walter de Gruyter, 1977-2004.
— and Gerhard Schneider, eds. *Exegetical Dictionary of the New Testament*. 3 vols. Grand Rapids: Eerdmans, 1990-93.
Barrett, C.K. *The Gospel of John and Judaism*. Translated by D.M. Smith. Philadelphia: Fortress, 1975.
— *The Gospel according to St. John: An Introduction with Commentary and Notes on the Greek Text*. 2nd ed. Philadelphia: Westminster, 1978.
Barton, John. *Reading the Old Testament: Method in Biblical Study*. Rev. ed. Louisville: Westminster/John Knox, 1996.
Bauckham, Richard. *God Crucified: Monotheism and Christology in the New Testament*. Grand Rapids: Eerdmans, 1998.
— *The Gospels for All Christians: Rethinking the Gospel Audiences*. Grand Rapids: Eerdmans, 1998.
— *Jesus and the God of Israel: God Crucified and Other Studies on the New Testament's Christology of Divine Identity*. Grand Rapids: Eerdmans, 2008.
— *The Jewish World around the New Testament: Collected Essays I*. Wissenschaftliche Untersuchungen zum Neuen Testament 233. Tübingen: Mohr Siebeck, 2008.
— *The Testimony of the Beloved Disciple: Narrative, History, and Theology in the Gospel of John*. Grand Rapids: Baker, 2007.
— and Carl Mosser, eds. *The Gospel of John and Christian Theology*. The St. Andrews Conference on Scripture and Theology. Grand Rapids: Eerdmans, 2008.
Bauckham, Richard, James Davila, and Alex Panayotov, eds. *Old Testament Pseudepigrapha: More Noncanonical Scriptures*. Grand Rapids: Eerdmans, 2013.
Bauer, Walter. *Das Johannesevangelium*. 3rd ed. Handbuch zum Neuen Testament 6. Tübingen: Mohr Siebeck, 1933.
— Frederick William Danker, William F. Arndt, and Frederick W. Gingrich. *A Greek-English Lexicon of the New Testament and Other Early Christian Literature*. 3rd ed. Chicago: The University of Chicago Press, 2000.
Beale, Gregory K., and D.A. Carson, eds. *Commentary on the New Testament Use of the Old Testament*. Grand Rapids: Baker, 2007.
Beasley-Murray, George R. *John*. 2nd ed. Word Biblical Commentary 36. Nashville: Nelson, 1999.
Becker, Jürgen. *Das Evangelium nach Johannes*. 2 vols. 3rd ed. Ökumenischer Taschenbuch Kommentar zum Neuen Testament 4. Würzburg: Echter, 1991.
Becking, Bob, Pieter W. van der Horst, and Karel van der Toorn, eds. *Dictionary of Deities and Demons in the Bible*. 2nd ed. Leiden: Brill, 1999.
Belle, Gilbert van., Jan G. van der Watt, and P.J. Maritz. *Theology and Christology in the Fourth Gospel: Essays by the Members of the SNTS Johannine Writings Seminar*. Bibliotheca ephemeridum theologicarum lovaniensium 184. Leuven: Leuven University Press, 2005.

Bentzen, Aage. *King and Messiah*. 2nd ed. Oxford: Blackwell, 1970.
Berger, Klaus. *Exegese des Neuen Testaments: Neue Wege vom Text zur Auslegung*. 3rd ed. Uni-Taschenbücher 658. Wiesbaden: Quelle und Meyer, 1991.
Bernard, J.H.A. *Critical and Exegetical Commentary on the Gospel according to St. John*. 2 vols. The International Critical Commentary. Edinburgh: T. & T. Clark, 1928.
Betz, Hans D., ed. *Religion in Geschichte und Gegenwart: Handwörterbuch für Theologie und Religionswissenschaft*. 4th ed. 8 vols. Tübingen: Mohr Siebeck, 1998-2007.
Beutler, Johannes. *Judaism and the Jews in the Gospel of John*. Subsidia Biblica 30. Rome: Pontificio Istituto Biblico, 2006.
—— *Martyria: Traditionsgeschichtliche Untersuchungen zum Zeugnisthema bei Johannes*. Frankfurter theologische Studien 10. Frankfurt: Josef Knecht, 1972.
—— *Studien zu den johanneischen Schriften*. Edited by Gerhard Dautzenberg and Norbert Lohfink. Stuttgarter biblische Aufsatzbände 25. Stuttgart: Katholisches Bibelwerk, 1998.
Bieler, Ludwig. *Theios Aner: Das bild des "göttlichen Menschen" in Spätantike und Frühchristentum*. 2 vols. Wien: Oskar Höfels, 1935-36.
Bieringer, Reimund. *The New Testament and Rabbinic Literature*. Supplements to the Journal for the Study of Judaism 136. Leiden: Brill, 2010.
Bittner, Wolfgang J. *Jesu Zeichen im Johannesevangelium: Die Messias-Erkenntnis im Johannesevangelium vor ihrem jüdischen Hintergrund*. Wissenschaftliche Untersuchungen zum Neuen Testament 2/26. Tübingen: Mohr Siebeck, 1987.
Blank, Josef. *Das Evangelium nach Johannes*. Geistliche Schriftlesung 4/1. Düsseldorf: Patmos, 1981.
Blass, Friedrich, Albert DeBrunner, and Robert W. Funk. *A Greek Grammar of the New Testament and Other Early Christian Literature*. Chicago: The University of Chicago Press, 1961.
Bloch, René. *Moses und der Mythos: Die Auseinandersetzung mit der griechischen Mythologie bei jüdisch-hellenistischen Autoren*. Supplements to the Journal for the Study of Judaism 145. Leiden: Brill, 2011.
Böcher, Otto. *Der Johanneische Dualismus im Zusammenhang des nachbiblischen Judentums*. Gutersloh: Gerd Mohn, 1965.
Boismard, Marie-Émile. *Moses or Jesus: An Essay in Johannine Christology*. Translated by B.T. Viviano. Minneapolis: Fortress; Leuven: Peeters, 1993; trans. *Moïse ou Jésus: Essai de christologie Johannique*. Bibliotheca ephemeridum theologicarum lovaniensium 84. Leuven: Peeters; Leuven University Press, 1988.
Borgen, Peder. *Bread from Heaven: An Exegetical Study of the Concept of Manna in the Gospel of John and the Writing of Philo*. Supplement to Novum Testamentum 10. Leiden: Brill, 1965.
—— *Logos Was the True Light and Other Essays on the Gospel of John*. Relieff 9. Trondheim: Tapir, 1983.
—— *Philo, John, and Paul: New Perspectives on Judaism and Early Christianity*. Atlanta: Scholars, 1987.
Borgeaud, Philippe, Thomas Römer, and Youri Volokhine, eds. *Interprétations de Moïse: Égypte, Judée, Grèce et Rome*. Jerusalem Studies in Religion and Culture 10. Leiden: Brill, 2010.
Botterweck, G. Johannes, Helmer Ringgren, and Heinz-Josef Fabry, eds. *Theological Dictionary of the Old Testament*. 14 vols. Grand Rapids: Eerdmans, 1974-2006.

Braude, William G., trans. *The Midrash on Psalms.* Yale Judaica Series 13. New Haven: Yale University Press, 1959.

Broer, Ingo. *Einleitung in das Neue Testament.* 2 vols. Neue Ecter Bibel zum Neuen Testament. Würzburg: Echter, 1998.

Brown, Colin, ed. *The New International Dictionary of New Testament Theology.* 4 vols. Grand Rapids: Zondervan, 1986.

Brown, Francis, S.R. Driver, and Charles A. Briggs, eds. *The Brown, Driver, Briggs Hebrew and English Lexicon: With an Appendix Containing the Biblical Aramaic, Coded with the Numbering System from Strong's Exhaustive Concordance of the Bible.* Peabody: Hendrickson, 1996.

Brown, Raymond E. *The Gospel according to John.* 2 vols. The Anchor Bible 29-29a. New York: Doubleday, 1966-70.

Bruce, F.F. *The Gospel of John.* Grand Rapids: Eerdmans, 1983.

Brunson, Andrew C. *Psalm 118 in the Gospel of John: An Intertextual Study on the New Exodus Pattern in the Theology of John.* Wissenschaftliche Untersuchungen zum Neuen Testament 2/158. Tübingen: Mohr Siebeck, 2003.

Bultmann, Rudolf. *Das Evangelium des Johannes.* 21st ed. Kritisch-exegetischer Kommentar über das Neue Testament 2. Göttingen: Vandenhoeck & Ruprecht, 1986; trans. *The Gospel of John: A Commentary.* Translated by George R. Beasley-Murray. Louisville: Westminster, 1971.

—— *History of the Synoptic Tradition.* New York: Harper & Row, 1963.

—— *Theology of the New Testament.* 2 vols. London: SCM, 1955.

Burger, Christoph. *Jesus als Davidssohn: Eine traditionsgeschichtliche Untersuchung.* Forschungen zur Religion und Literatur des Alten und Neuen Testaments 98. Göttingen: Vandenhoeck & Ruprecht, 1970.

Busse, Ulrich. *Das Johannesevangelium: Bildlichkeit, Diskurs und Ritual mit einer Bibliographie über den Zeitraum 1986-1998.* Bibliotheca ephemeridum theologicarum lovaniensium 162. Leuven: Leuven University Press; Peeters, 2002.

Buttrick, George A., ed. *Interpreter's Dictionary of the Bible.* 4 vols. New York: Abingdon, 1962.

Campbell, Jonathan G. *The Exegetical Texts.* Companion to the Qumran Scrolls 4. London: T & T Clark, 2004.

Camponovo, Odo. *Königtum, Königsherrschaft und Reich Gottes in den frühjüdischen Schriften.* Orbis Biblicus et Orientalis 58. Freiburg: Universitätsverlag Freiburg; Göttingen: Vandenhoeck & Ruprecht, 1995.

Capes, David B. et al, eds. *Israel's God and Rebecca's Children: Christology and Community in Early Judaism and Christianity: Essays in Honor of Larry W. Hurtado and Alan F. Segal.* Waco: Baylor University Press, 2007.

Caron, Gérald. *Qui sont les Juifs de l'Evangile de Jean?* Recherches 35. Quebec: Bellarmin, 1997.

Carrell, Peter R. *Jesus and the Angels: Angelology and the Christology of the Apocalypse of John.* Society for New Testament Studies Monograph Series 95. Cambridge: Cambridge University Press, 1997.

Carson, D.A. *The Gospel according to John.* The Pillar New Testament Commentaries. Grand Rapids: Eerdmans, 1991.

Cathcart, Kevin J., and Robert P. Gordon. *The Targum of the Minor Prophets: Translated, with a Critical Introduction, Apparatus, and Notes.* The Aramaic Bible 14. Wilmington: Michael Glazier, 1989.

Charlesworth, James H., ed. *Jesus and Archaeology*. Grand Rapids: Eerdmans, 2006.
— *The Messiah: Developments in Earliest Judaism and Christianity*. Princeton Symposium on Judaism and Christian Origins 1. Minneapolis: Fortress, 1992.
— *The Old Testament Pseudepigrapha and the New Testament: Prolegomena for the Study of Christian Origins*. Valley Forge: Trinity, 1998.
— Hermann Lichtenberger, and Gerbern S. Oegema, eds. *Qumran-Messianism: Studies on the Messianic Expectations in the Dead Sea Scrolls*. Tübingen: Mohr Siebeck, 1998.
— and Petr Pokorný, eds. *Jesus Research: An International Perspective: The First Princeton-Prague Symposium on Jesus Research, Prague 2005*. Princeton-Prague Symposia Series on the Historical Jesus 1. Grand Rapids: Eerdmans, 2009.
Chester, Andrew. *Messiah and Exaltation: Jewish Messianic and Visionary Traditions and New Testament Christology*. Wissenschaftliche Untersuchungen zum Neuen Testament 207. Tübingen: Mohr Siebeck, 2007.
Childs, Brevard S. *Biblical Theology in Crisis*. Philadelphia: Westminster, 1970.
Chilton, Bruce D. *Targumic Approaches to the Gospels: Essays in the Mutual Definition of Judaism and Christianity*. Studies in Judaism. Lanham: The University Press of America, 1986.
Christensen, Duane L. *Deuteronomy 1:1-21:9, Revised*. Word Biblical Commentary 6A. Nashville: Thomas Nelson, 2001.
— *Deuteronomy 21:10-34:12*. Word Biblical Commentary 6B. Nashville: Thomas Nelson, 2002.
Clements, Ruth A., and Daniel R. Schwartz, eds. *Text, Thought, and Practice in Qumran and Early Christianity: Proceedings of the Ninth International Symposium of the Orion Center for the Study of the Dead Sea Scrolls and Associated Literature, Jointly Sponsored by the Hebrew University Center for the Study of Christianity, 11-13 January, 2004*. Studies on the Texts of the Desert of Judah 84. Leiden: Brill, 2009.
Coats, George W. *Moses: Heroic Man, Man of God*. Journal for the Study of the Old Testament Supplement Series 57. Sheffield: JSOT, 1987.
— *The Moses Tradition*. Journal for the Study of the Old Testament Supplement Series 161. Sheffield: JSOT, 1993.
Collins, John J. *The Apocalyptic Imagination: An Introduction to Jewish Apocalyptic Literature*. 2nd ed. Grand Rapids: Eerdmans, 1998.
— *Beyond the Qumran Community: The Sectarian Movement of the Dead Sea Scrolls*. Grand Rapids: Eerdmans, 2009.
— *Encounters with Biblical Theology*. Minneapolis: Fortress, 2005.
— *The Scepter and the Star: Messianism in Light of the Dead Sea Scrolls*. 2nd ed. Grand Rapids: Eerdmans, 2010.
— *The Sibylline Oracles of Egyptian Judaism*. The Society of Biblical Literature Dissertation Series 13. Missoula: The Society of Biblical Literature, 1974.
— and Daniel Harlow, eds. *The Eerdmans Dictionary of Early Judaism*. Grand Rapids: Eerdmans, 2010.
Coloe, Mary L., and Tom Thatcher, eds. *John, Qumran, and the Dead Sea Scrolls: Sixty Years of Discovery and Debate*. Early Judaism and Its Literature 32. Atlanta: The Society of Biblical Literature, 2011.
Colpe, Carsten. *Die religionsgeschichtliche Schule: Darstellung und Kritik ihres Bildes vom gnostischen Erlösermythus*. Forschungen zur Religion und Literatur des Alten und Neuen Testaments 60. Göttingen: Vandenhoeck & Ruprecht, 1961.

Condra, Ed. *Salvation for the Righteous Revealed: Jesus amid Covenantal and Messianic Expectations in Second Temple Judaism*. Arbeiten zur Geschichte des Antiken Judentums und des Urchristentums 51. Leiden: Brill, 2002.
Conzelmann, Hans, and Andreas Lindemann. *Arbeitsbuch zum Neuen Testament*. 14th ed. Uni-Taschenbücher 52. Tübingen: Mohr Siebeck, 2004.
— *Grundriss der Theologie des Neuen Testaments*. 6th ed. Uni-Taschenbücher 1446. Tübingen: Mohr Siebeck, 1997.
Court, John M., ed. *New Testament Writers and the Old Testament: An Introduction*. London: SPCK, 2002.
Craigie, Peter C. *The Book of Deuteronomy*. The New International Commentary on the Old Testament. Grand Rapids: Eerdmans, 1976.
Crawford, Sidnie White. *The Temple Scroll and Related Texts*. Companion to the Qumran Scrolls 2. Sheffield: Sheffield, 2000.
Cross, Frank Moore. *The Ancient Library of Qumran*. 3rd ed. The Biblical Seminar 30. Sheffield: Sheffield, 1995.
Crossley, James G. *Reading the New Testament: Contemporary Approaches*. Reading Religious Texts Series. New York: Routledge, 2010.
Crown, Alan D., ed. *Samaritan Scribes and Manuscripts*. Texte und Studien zum Antiken Judentum 80. Tübingen: Mohr Siebeck, 2001.
Crown, Alan D., and Abraham Tal., ed. *A Companion to Samaritan Studies*. Tübingen: Mohr Siebeck, 1993.
Cullmann, Oscar. *The Christology of the New Testament*. Rev. ed. Philadelphia: Westminster, 1963.
Culpepper, R. Alan. *Anatomy of the Fourth Gospel: A Study in Literary Design*. Philadelphia: Fortress, 1983.
Dahood, Mitchell. *Psalms: Introduction, Translation, and Notes*. 3 vols. The Anchor Bible 16-17A. Garden City: Doubleday, 1966-70.
Daly-Denton, Margaret. *David in the Fourth Gospel: The Johannine Reception of the Psalms*. Arbeiten zur Geschichte des Antiken Judentums und des Urchristentums 47. Leiden: Brill, 2000
Dauer, Anton. *Die Passionsgeschichte im Johannesevangelium: Eine traditionsgeschichtliche und theologische Untersuchung zu Joh. 18, 1-19, 30*. Studien zum Alten und Neuen Testament 30. München: Kösel, 1972.
Davies, W.D. *The Gospel and the Land: Early Christianity and Jewish Territorial Doctrine*. Sheffield: JSOT, 1994; repr. Berkeley: University of California Press, 1974.
— *The Setting of the Sermon on the Mount*. Cambridge: Cambridge University Press, 1964.
Davila, James R. *Liturgical Works*. The Eerdmans Commentaries on the Dead Sea Scrolls. Grand Rapids: Eerdmans, 2000.
— *The Provenance of the Pseudepigrapha: Jewish, Christian, or Other?* Supplement to the Journal for the Study of Judaism 105. Leiden: Brill, 2005.
Day, John, ed. *King and Messiah in Israel und the Ancient Near East: Proceedings of the Oxford Old Testament Seminar*. Journal for the Study of the Old Testament Supplement Series 270. Sheffield: Sheffield, 1998.
Deines, Roland. *Die Pharisäer: Ihr Verständnis im Spiegel der christlichen und jüdischen Forschung seit Wellhausen und Graetz*. Wissenschaftliche Untersuchungen zum Neuen Testament 101. Tübingen: Mohr Siebeck, 1997.
— *Jüdische Steingefässe und pharisäische Frömmigkeit: Ein archäologisch-historischer*

Beitrag zum Verständnis von Joh 2,6 und der jüdischen Reinheitshalacha zur Zeit Jesu. Wissenschaftliche Untersuchungen zum Neuen Testament 2/52. Tübingen: Mohr Siebeck, 1993.

—— and Karl-Wilhelm Niebuhr, eds. *Philo und das Neue Testament: Wechselseitige Wahrnehmungen, 1. Internationales Symposium zum Corpus Judaeo-Hellenisticum 1.—4. Mai 2003.* Wissenschaftliche Untersuchungen zum Neuen Testament 172. Tübingen: Mohr Siebeck, 2004.

DeSilva, David A. *4 Maccabees: Introduction and Commentary on the Greek Text in Codex Sinaiticus.* The Septuagint Commentary Series. Leiden: Brill, 2006.

—— *Introducing the Apocrypha: Message, Context, and Significance.* Grand Rapids: Baker, 2002.

Dietzfelbinger, Christian. *Das Evangelium nach Johannes.* 2 vols. Zürcher Bibelkommentare zum Neuen Testament 4. Zürich: Theologischer, 2001.

Di Lella, Alexander A., and Patrich W. Skehan. *The Wisdom of Ben Sira.* The Anchor Bible 39. New York: Doubleday, 1987.

Dines, Jennifer. *The Septuagint.* Understanding the Bible and Its World. London: T & T Clark, 2004.

Dodd, C.H. *Historical Tradition in the Fourth Gospel.* Cambridge: Cambridge University Press, 1963.

Dohmen, Christoph, and Thomas Söding, eds. *Eine Bibel, zwei Testamente: Positionen Biblischer Theologie.* Uni-Taschenbücher 1893. Paderborn: Schöningh, 1995.

Dommershausen, Werner. *1 Makkabäer, 2 Makkabäer.* 2nd ed. Die Neue Echter Bibel 12. Würzburg: Echter, 1995.

Doran, Robert. *2 Maccabees: A Critical Commentary.* Hermeneia. Minneapolis: Fortress, 2012.

Driver, S.R. *A Critical and Exegetical Commentary on Deuteronomy.* 3rd ed. The International Critical Commentary. Edinburgh: T & T Clark, 1978.

Dschulnigg, Peter. *Jesus Begegnen: Personen und ihre Bedeutung im Johannesevangelium.* Münster: Lit, 2002.

Dunderberg, Ismo. *Johannes und die Synoptiker: Studien zu Joh 1-9.* Annales Academiae scientiarum fennicae 69. Helsinki: Suomalainen Tiedeakatemia 1994.

Dunn, James D.G. *Jesus Remembered.* Christianity in the Making 1. Grand Rapids: Eerdmans, 2003.

—— *The Partings of the Ways: Between Christianity and Judaism and Their Significance for the Character of Christianity.* 2nd ed. London: SCM, 2006.

—— *Unity and Diversity in the New Testament: An Inquiry into the Character of Earliest Christianity.* 3rd ed. London: SCM, 2006.

Durham, John I. *Exodus.* Word Biblial Commenatry 3. Waco: Word, 1987.

Ebner, Martin, and Stefan Schreiber, eds. *Einleitung in das Neue Testament.* Studienbücher Theologie 6. Stuttgart: Kohlhammer, 2008.

Eck, Werner. *Rom und Judaea: Fünf Vorträge zur römischen Herrschaft in Palästina.* Tria Corda: Jenaer Vorlesungen zu Judentum, Antike und Christentum 2. Tübingen: Mohr Siebeck, 2007.

Efird, James M., ed. *The Use of the Old Testament in the New and Other Essays: Studies in Honor of William Franklin Stinespring.* Durham: Duke University Press, 1972.

Elliott, Mark. *The Survivors of Israel: A Reconsideration of the Theology of Pre-Christian Judaism.* Grand Rapids: Eerdmans, 2000.

Ellis, E. Earle. *The Old Testament in Early Christianity: Canon and Interpretation in the*

Light of Modern Research. Wissenschaftliche Untersuchungen zum Neuen Testament 54. Tübingen: Mohr Siebeck, 1991.

Ernst, Josef. *Johannes der Täufer: Interpretation, Geschichte, Wirkungsgeschichte*. Beihefte zur Zeitschrift für die neutestamentliche Wissenschaft und die Kunde der älteren Kirche 53. Berlin: Walter de Gruyter, 1989.

Evans, Craig A. *Ancient Texts for New Testament Studies: A Guide to the Background Literature*. Peabody: Hendrickson, 2005.

— ed. *From Prophecy to Testament: The Function of the Old Testament in the New*. Peabody: Hendrickson, 2004.

— *The Interpretation of Scripture in Early Judaism and Christianity: Studies in Language and Tradition*. Journal for the Study of the Pseudepigrapha Supplement Series 33. Sheffield: Sheffield, 2000.

— *The Function of Scripture in Early Jewish and Christian Tradition*. Journal for the Study of the New Testament Supplement Series 154. Sheffield: Sheffield, 1998.

— *Word and Glory: On the Exegetical and Theological Background of John's Prologue*. Journal for the Study of the New Testament Supplement Series 89. Sheffield: Sheffield, 1993.

— and J.A. Sanders, eds. *Early Christian Interpretation of the Scriptures of Israel: Investigations and Proposals*. Journal for the Study of the New Testament Supplement Series 148. Sheffield: Sheffield, 1997.

— and Stanley E. Porter, eds. *Dictionary of New Testament Background*. Downers Grove: InterVarsity, 2000.

Evans, Craig A., and W.R. Stegner, eds. *The Gospels and the Scriptures of Israel*. Journal for the Study of the New Testament Supplement Series 104. Sheffield: Sheffield, 1994.

Fabry, Heinz-Josef, and Klaus Scholtissek. *Der Messias: Perspecktiven des Alten und Neuen Testaments*. Die Neue Echter Bibel Themen 5. Würzburg: Echter, 2002.

Feldman, Louis H. *Josephus's Interpretation of the Bible*. Hellenistic Culture and Society 27. Berkeley: The University of California Press, 1998.

— *Philo's Portrayal of Moses in the Context of Ancient Judaism*. Christianity and Judaism in Antiquity 15. Notre Dame: University of Notre Dame Press, 2007.

Fishbane, Michael. *Biblical Interpretation in Ancient Israel*. Oxford: Oxford University Press, 1985.

Fitzmyer, Joseph A. *The One Who Is to Come*. Grand Rapids: Eerdmans, 2007.

Flesher, Paul V.M., and Bruce Chilton. *The Targums: A Critical Introduction*. Waco: Baylor University Press, 2011.

Fonrobert, Charlotte E., and Martin S. Jaffee, eds. *The Cambridge Companion to the Talmud and Rabbinic Literature*. Cambridge Companions to Religion. Cambridge: Cambridge University Press, 2007.

Francke, August H. *Das Alte Testament bei Johannes: Ein Beitrag zur Erklärung und Beurteilung der johanneischen Schriften*. Göttingen: Vandenhoeck & Ruprecht, 1885.

Frankemölle, Hubert. *Studien zum jüdischen Kontext neutestamentlicher Theologien*. Stuttgarter biblische Aufsatzbände 37. Stuttgart: Katholisches Bibelwerk, 2005.

Freed, Edwin D. *Old Testament Quotations in the Gospel of John*. Supplements to Novum Testamentum 11. Leiden: E.J. Brill, 1965.

Freedman, David N., ed. *The Anchor Bible Dictionary*. 6 vols. New York: Doubleday, 1992.

Fretheim, Terence E. *Exodus*. Interpretation. Louisville: John Knox, 1991.

Frey, Jörg, Stefan Krauter, and Hermann Lichtenberger, eds. *Heil Und Geschichte: Die*

Geschichtsbezogenheit Des Heils. Wissenschaftliche Untersuchungen zum Neuen Testament 248. Tübingen: Mohr Siebeck, 2009.

Frey, Jörg, and Udo Schnelle, eds. *Kontexte des Johannesevangeliums: Das vierte Evangelium in religions- und traditionsgeschichtlicher Perspektive*. Wissenschaftliche Untersuchungen zum Neuen Testament 175. Tübingen: Mohr Siebeck, 2004.

Frühwald-König, Johannes. *Tempel und Kult: Ein Beitrag zur Christologie des Johannesvangeliums*. Biblische Untersuchungen 27. Regensburg: Pustet, 1998.

Fuß, Barbara. *"Dies ist die Zeit, von der geschrieben ist . . .": Die expliziten Zitate aus dem Buch Hosea in den Handschriften von Qumran und im Neuen Testament*. Neutestamentliche Abhandlungen NF 37. Münster: Aschendorff, 2000.

Gese, Hartmut. *Essays on Biblical Theology*. Translated by Keith Crim. Minneapolis: Augsburg, 1981.

—— *Vom Sinai zum Zion*. München: Kaiser, 1974.

Glasson, T. Francis. *Moses in the Fourth Gospel*. Studies in Biblical Theology 40. London: SCM, 1963.

Gnilka, Joachim. *Johannesevangelium*. 5th ed. Neue Echter Bibel zum Neuen Testament 4. Würzburg: Echter, 1999.

—— *Theologie des Neuen Testaments*. Herders theologischer Kommentar zum Neuen Testament Supplement 5. Freiburg: Herder, 1994.

Goldstein, Jonathan A. *II Maccabees: A New Translation with Introduction and Commentary*. The Anchor Bible 41A. Garden City: Doubleday, 1983.

Goodenough, Erwin R. *By Light, Light: The Mystic Gospel of Hellenistic Judaism*. New Haven: Yale University Press, 1935.

Gordon, Robert P. *Studies in the Targum to the Twelve Prophets: From Nahum to Malachi*. Supplements to Vetus Testamentum 51. Leiden: Brill, 1994.

Graupner, Axel, and Michael Wolter, eds. *Moses in Biblical and Extra-Biblical Traditions*. Beiheft zur Zeitschrift für die Alttestamentliche Wissenschaft 372. Berlin: Walter de Gruyter, 2007.

Green, Joel B., Scot McKnight, and I. Howard Marshall, eds. *Dictionary of Jesus and the Gospels*. Downers Grove: InterVarsity, 1994.

Grob, Francis. *Faire l'œuvre de Dieu: Christologie et éthique dans l'Evangile de Jean*. Etudes d'histoire et de Philosophie Religieuses 68. Paris: Presses Universitaires de France, 1986.

Gruen, Erich S. *Heritage and Hellenism: The Reinvention of Jewish Tradition*. Hellenistic Culture and Society 30. Berkeley: The University of California Press, 1998.

Gundry, Robert H. *The Old Is Better: New Testament Essays in Support of Traditional Interpretations*. Wissenschaftliche Untersuchungen zum Neuen Testament 178. Tübingen: Mohr Siebeck, 2005.

Haenchen, Ernst. *John: A Commentary on the Gospel of John*. Edited by Robert W. Funk and Ulich Busse. 2 vols. Hermeneia. Philadephia: Fortress, 1984.

Hafemann, Scott J. *Paul, Moses and the History of Israel: The Letter/Spirit Contrast and the Argument from Scripture in 2 Corinthians 3*. Wissenschaftliche Untersuchungen zum Neuen Testament 81. Tübingen: Mohr Siebeck, 1995.

Häfner, Gerd. *Der verheißene Vorläufer: Redaktionskritische Untersuchung zur Darstellung Johannes des Täufers im Matthäusevangelium*. Stuttgarter biblische Beiträge 27. Stuttgart: Katholisches Bibelwerk, 1994.

Hahn, Ferdinand. *Studien zum Neuen Testament*, ed. Jörg Frey and Juliane Schlegel. 2nd

ed. 2 vols. Wissenschaftliche Untersuchungen zum Neuen Testament 191. Tübingen: Mohr Siebeck, 2006.
—— *Theologie des Neuen Testaments*. 3rd ed. 2 vols. Tübingen: Mohr Siebeck, 2011.
Hakola, Raimo. *Identity Matters: John, the Jews and Jewishness*. Supplements to Novum Testamentum 118. Leiden: Brill, 2005.
Hamid-Khani, Saeed. *Revelation and Concealment of Christ: A Theological Inquiry into the Elusive Language of the Fourth Gospel*. Wissenschaftliche Untersuchungen zum Neuen Testament 2/120. Tübingen: Mohr Siebeck, 2000.
Hamidovic, David. *L'écrit de Damas: Le manifeste essénien*. Collection de la Revue des Études juives 51. Louvain: Peeters, 2011.
Hanson, Anthony Tyrrell. *The Living Utterances of God: The New Testament Exegesis of the Old*. London: Barton, Longman and Todd, 1983.
—— *The New Testament Interpretation of Scripture*. London: SPCK, 1980.
—— *The Prophetic Gospel: A Study of John and the Old Testament*. Edinburgh: T & T Clark, 1991.
Harstine, Stan. *Moses as a Character in the Fourth Gospel: A Study of Ancient Reading Techniques*. Journal for the Study of the New Testament Supplement Series 229. Sheffield: Sheffield, 2002.
Haupt, Erich. *Die alttestamentlichen Citate in den vier Evangelien*. London: Williams & Norgate, 1871.
Hawthorne, Gerald F., Ralph P. Martin, and Daniel G. Reid, eds. *Dictionary of Paul and His Letters*. Downers Grove: InterVarsity, 1993.
Hays, Richard B. *Echoes of Scripture in the Letters of Paul*. New Haven: Yale University Press, 1989.
Hengel, Martin. *The Four Gospels and the One Gospel of Jesus Christ: An Investigation of the Collection and Origin of the Canonical Gospels*. Translated by John Bowden. Harrisburg: Trinity, 2000.
—— *Die johanneische Frage: Ein Lösungsversuch*. Wissenschaftliche Untersuchungen zum Neuen Testament 67. Tübingen: Mohr Siebeck, 1993.
—— *Judaica, Hellenistica et Christiana: Kleine Schriften II*. Wissenschaftliche Untersuchungen zum Neuen Testament 109. Tübingen: Mohr Siebeck, 1999.
—— and Hermut Löhr, eds. *Schriftauslegung im antiken Judentum und im Urchristentum*. Wissenschaftliche Untersuchungen zum Neuen Testament 73. Tübingen: Mohr Siebeck, 1994.
Henten, Jan Willem van. *The Maccabean Martyrs as Saviours of the Jewish People: A Study of 2 and 4 Maccabees*. Supplements to the Journal for the Study of Judaism 57. Leiden: Brill, 1997.
Hofius, Otfried. *Johannesstudien: Untersuchungen zur Theologie des Vierten Evangeliums*, ed. Otfried Hofius and Hans-Christian Kammler. Wissenschaftliche Untersuchungen zum Neuen Testament 88. Tübingen: Mohr Siebeck, 1996.
Hogeterp, Albert L. *Expectations of the End: A Comparative Traditio-Historical Study of Eschatological, Apocalyptic and Messianic Ideas in the Dead Sea Scrolls and the New Testament*. Studies on the Texts of the Desert of Judah 83. Leiden: Brill, 2009.
Holladay, Carl R. *Poets: The Epic Poets Theodotus and Philo and Ezekiel the Tragedian*. Vol. 2 of *Fragments from Hellenistic Jewish Authors*. The Society of Biblical Literature Texts and Translations 30. Atlanta: Scholars, 1989.
Holladay, William L. *Jeremiah 1: A Commentary on the Book of the Prophet Jeremiah, Chapters 1-25*. Hermeneia 21/1. Philadelphia: Fortress, 1986.

Horgan, M.P. *Pesharim: Qumran Interpretation of Biblical Books*. Catholic Biblical Quarterly Monograph Series 8. Washington: The Catholic Biblical Association of America, 1979.
Hoskins, Paul M. *Jesus as the Fulfillment of the Temple in the Gospel of John*. Paternoster Biblical Monogrphs. Milton Keynes: Paternoster, 2006.
Hossfeld, F.L., ed. *Wieviel Systematik erlaubt die Schrift?: Auf der Suche nach einer gesamtbiblischen Theologie*. Quaestiones disputatae 185. Freiburg: Herder, 2001.
Huber, Konrad, and Boris Repschinski, eds. *Im Geist und in der Wahrheit: Studien zum Johannesevangelium und zur Offenbarung des Johannes sowie andere Beiträge: Festschrift für Martin Hasitschka SJ zum 65. Geburtstag*. Neutestamentliche Abhandlungen 52. Münster: Aschendorff, 2008.
Hübner, Hans. *Biblische Theologie des Neuen Testaments*. 3 vols. Göttingen: Vandenhoeck & Ruprecht, 1990-95.
— and Antje and Michael Labehn. *Vetus Testamentum in Novo*. 2 vols. Göttingen: Vandenhoeck & Ruprecht, 1997-2002.
Hühn, Eugen H. Th. *Die alttestamentlichen Citate und Reminiscenzen im Neuen Testamente*. Tübingen: Mohr Siebeck, 1900.
Hummelfarb, M. *Ascent to Heaven in Jewish and Christian Apocalypses*. Oxford: Oxford University Press, 1993.
Hurtado, Larry W. *How on Earth Did Jesus Become a God?: Historical Questions about Earliest Devotion to Jesus*. Grand Rapids: Eerdmans, 2005.
Jacobson, Howard. *The Exagoge of Ezekiel*. Cambridge: Cambridge University Press, 1983.
Jenni, Ernst, Wilhelm Hollenberg, and Karl Budde. *Lehrbuch der hebräischen Sprache des Alten Testaments: Neubearbeitung des Hebräischen Schulbuchs*. 2nd ed. Basel: Helbing & Lichtenhahn, 1981.
Jones, Larry P. *The Symbol of Water in the Gospel of John*. Journal for the Study of the New Testament Supplement Series 145. Sheffield: Sheffield, 1997.
Justnes, Årstein. *The Time of Salvation: An Analysis of 4QApocryphon of Daniel ar (4Q246), 4QMessianic Apocalypse (4Q521), and 4QTime of Righteousness (4Q215a)*. Europäische Hochschulschriften 23. Frankfurt: Peter Lang, 2009.
Kaiser, Walter C. *The Uses of the Old Testament in the New*. Chicago: Moody, 1985.
Käsemann, Ernst. *The Testament of Jesus: A Study of the Gospel of John in the Light of Chapter 17*. Philadelphia: Fortress, 1968.
Keener, Craig S. *The Gospel of John: A Commentary*. 2 vols. Peabody: Hendrickson, 2003.
Kierspel, Lars. *The Jews and the World in the Fourth Gospel: Parallelism, Function, Context*. Wissenschaftliche Untersuchungen zum Neuen Testament 2/220. Tübingen: Mohr Siebeck, 2006.
Kim, Seyoon. *The Son of Man as the Son of God*. Wissenschaftliche Untersuchungen zum Neuen Testament 30. Tübingen: Mohr Siebeck, 1983.
Kittel, Gerhard, and Gerhard Friedrich, eds. *Theological Dictionary of the New Testament*. Translated by Geoffrey W. Bromiley. 10 vols. Grand Rapids: Eerdmans, 1964-74.
Klink, Edward W., III., ed. *Audience of the Gospels: The Origin and Function of the Gospels in Early Christianity*. The Library of New Testament Studies. London: T & T Clark, 2010.
Knibb, M.A., ed. *The Septuagint and Messianism: Colloquium Biblicum Lovaniense Liii, July 27-29, 2004*. Bibliotheca ephemeridum theologicarum lovaniensium. Louvain:

Peeters, 2006.

Knöppler, Thomas. *Die theologia crucis des Johannesevangeliums: Das Verständnis des Todes Jesu im Rahmen der johanneischen Inkarnations- und Erhöhungschristologie*. Wissenschaftliche Monographien zum Alten und Neuen Testament 69. Neukirchen-Vluyn: Neukirchener, 1994.

Koehler, Ludwig, and Walter Baumgartner. *The Hebrew and Aramaic Lexicon of the Old Testament: Study Edition*. 2 vols. Leiden: Brill, 2001.

Kohler, Herbert. *Kreuz und Menschwerdung im Johannesevangelium: Ein exegetisch-hermeneutischer Versuch zur johanneischen Kreuzestheologie*. Abhandlungen zur Theologie des Alten und Neuen Testaments 72. Zürich: Theologischer, 1987.

Köstenberger, Andreas. *John*. Baker Exegetical Commentary on the New Testament. Grand Rapids: Baker, 2004.

Kotila, Markku. *Umstrittener Zeuge: Studien zur Stellung des Gesetzes in der johanneischen Theologiegeschichte*. Annales Academiae scientiarum fennicae 48. Helsinki: Suomalainen Tiedeakatemia, 1988.

Kraus, Wolfgang, and R. Glenn Wooden, eds. *Septuagint Research: Issues and Challenges in the Study of the Greek Jewish Scriptures*. Septuagint and Cognate Studies. Atlanta: The Society of Biblical Literature, 2006.

Kruck, Günter, ed. *Der Johannesprolog*. Darmstadt: Wissenschaftliche Buchgesellschaft, 2009.

Kuhn, Hans-Jürgen. *Christologie und Wunder: Untersuchungen zu Joh 1,35-51*. Biblische Untersuchungen 18. Regensburg: Friedrich Pustet, 1988.

Laato, Antti. *Josiah and David Redivivus: The Historical Josiah and the Messianic Expectations of Exilic and Postexilic Times*. Coniectanea biblica Old Testament 33. Stockholm: Almqvist & Wiksell, 1992.

— *A Star Is Rising: The Historical Development of the Old Testament Royal Ideology and the Rise of Jewish Messianic Expectations*. International Studies in Formative Christianity and Judaism 5. Atlanta: Scholars, 1997.

Labahn, Michael. *Jesus als Lebensspender: Untersuchungen zu einer Geschichte der johanneischen Tradition anhand ihrer Wundergeschichten*. Beihefte zur Zeitschrift für die neutestamentliche Wissenschaft und die Kunde der älteren Kirche 98. Berlin: Walter de Gruyter, 1999.

— *Offenbarung in Zeichen und Wort: Untersuchungen zur Vorgeschichte von Joh 6,1-25a und seiner Rezeption in der Brotrede*. Wissenschaftliche Untersuchungen zum Neuen Testament 2/117. Tübingen: Mohr Siebeck, 2000.

— Klaus Scholtissek, and Angelika Strotmann, eds. *Israel und seine Heilstraditionen im Johannessevangelium: Festgabe für Johannes Beutler SJ zum 70. Geburtstag*. Paderborn: Schöningh, 2004.

Levenson, Jon Douglas. *The Hebrew Bible, the Old Testament, and Historical Criticism: Jews and Christians in Biblical Studies*. Louisville: Westminster/John Knox, 1993.

Liddell, Henry G. *An Intermediate Greek-English Lexicon: Founded upon the Seventh Edition of Liddell and Scott's Greek English Lexicon*. Oxford: Clarendon, 1889.

— and Robert Scott. *A Greek-English Lexicon*. Revised by Henry Stuart Jones and Roderick McKenzie. Oxford: Oxford University Press, 1996.

Liebers, Reinhold. *"Wie geschrieben steht": Studien zu einer besonderen Art frühchristlichen Schriftbezuges*. Berlin: Walter de Gruyter, 1993.

Lierman, John. *The New Testament Moses: Christian Perceptions of Moses and Israel in the Setting of Jewish Religion*. Wissenschaftliche Untersuchungen zum Neuen Testament 2/173. Tübingen: Mohr Siebeck, 2004.

Lincoln, Andrew T. *A Commentary on the Gospel according to St. John*. Black's New Testament Commentary 4. London: Continuum, 2005.

— and Angus Paddison, eds. *Christology and Scripture: Interdisciplinary Perspectives*. The Library of New Testament Studies 348. London: T & T Clark, 2007.

Lindars, Barnabas. *The Gospel of John*. The New Century Bible. London: Marshall, Morgan & Scott, 1972.

— *New Testament Apologetic: The Doctrinal Significance of the Old Testament Quotations*. Philadelphia: Westminster, 1961.

Loader, William R.G. *The Christology of the Fourth Gospel: Structure and Issues*. 2nd ed. Beiträge zur biblischen Exegese und Theologie 23. Frankfurt: Peter Lang, 1992.

— *Jesus' Attitude towards the Law: A Study of the Gospels*. Wissenschaftliche Untersuchungen zum Neuen Testament 2/97. Tübingen: Mohr Siebeck, 1997.

Loewenstamm, Samuel E. *From Babylon to Canaan: Studies in the Bible and Its Oriental Background*. Jerusalem: Hebrew University, 1992.

Lohse, Eduard. *Grundriß der neutestamentlichen Theologie*. 5th ed. Theologische Wissenschaft 5. Stuttgart: Kohlhammer, 1998.

— *Die Texte aus Qumran: Hebräisch und deutsch mit masoretischer Punktation*. 4th ed. München: Kösel, 1986.

Loisy, Alfred F. *Le quatrième évangile: Les épitres dites de Jean*. Paris: Émile Nourry, 1921.

Lozada, Francisco, Jr., and Tom Thatcher, eds. *New Currents through John: A Global Perspective*. Atlanta: The Society of Biblical Literature; Leiden: Brill, 2006.

Lucass, Shirley. *The Concept of the Messiah in the Scriptures of Judaism and Christianity*. Library of Second Temple Studies 78. London: T & T Clark, 2011.

Lust, Johan. *Messianism and the Septuagint: Collected Essays*. Bibliotheca ephemeridum theologicarum lovaniensium 178. Leuven: Leuven University Press, 2004.

Macchi, Jean-Daniel. *Les Samaritains: Histoire d'une légende, Israël et la province de Samarie*. Le Monde de la Bible 30. Geneva: Labor et Fides, 1994.

MacDonald, John. *Memar Marqah: The Teaching of Marqah*. 2 vols (the Text and Translation). Beihefte zur Zeitschrift für die alttestamentliche Wissenschaft 84. Berlin: A. Töpelmann, 1963.

— *The Theology of the Samaritans*. The New Testament Library. London: SCM, 1964.

Magne, Sæbø, ed. *From the Beginings to the Middle Ages (Until 1300)*. Vol. 1. of *Hebrew Bible/Old Testament: The History of Its Interpretation*. Göttingen: Vandenhoeck & Ruprecht, 1996.

Maher, Michael, ed. *Targum Pseudo-Jonathan: Genesis*. The Aramaic Bible 1B. Collegeville: Liturgical, 1992.

Maier, Johann. *Die Qumran-Essener: Die Texte vom Toten Meer*. 3 vols. Uni-Taschenbücher 1862, 1863, and 1916. München: E. Reinhardt, 1995-96.

— *The Temple Scroll: An Introduction, Translation & Commentary*. Journal for the Study of the Old Testament Supplement Series 34. Sheffield: JSOT, 1985.

— *Zwischen den Testamenten: Geschichte und Religion in der Zeit des Zweiten Tempels*. Neue Ecter Bibel zum Alten Testament 3. Würzburg: Ecter, 1990.

Marcos, Natalio Fernández. *The Septuagint in Context: Introduction to the Greek Version of the Bible*. Translated by Wilfred G.E. Watson. Atlanta: The Society of Biblical Literature, 2009.

Martyn, J. Louis. *History and Theology in the Fourth Gospel*. 3rd ed. The New Testament Library. Louisville: Westminster/John Knox, 2003.

Mason, Steve. *Flavius Josephus on the Phrarisees: A Composition-Critical Study*. Studia Post-Biblica 39. Leiden: Brill, 1991.

Matthews, Victor H., and Don C. Benjamin. *Old Testament Parallels: Laws and Stories from the Ancient Near East*. 3rd ed. New York: Paulist, 2007.

McConville, J. Gordon. *Deuteronomy*. The Apollos Old Testament Commentary 5. Leicester: Apollos; Downers Grove: InterVarsity, 2002.

McGrath, James F. *The Only True God: Early Christian Monotheism in Its Jewish Context*. Urbana: University of Illinois Press, 2009.

—— *John's Apologetic Christology: Legitimation and Development in Johannine Christology*. Society for New Testament Studies Monograph Series 111. Cambridge: Cambridge University Press, 2001.

McLay, R. Timothy. *The Use of the Septuagint in New Testament Research*. Grand Rapids: Eerdmans, 2003.

McNamara, Martin. *Targum and New Testament: Collected Essays*. Wissenschaftliche Untersuchungen zum Neuen Testament 279. Tübingen: Mohr Siebeck, 2011.

—— *Targum and Testament Revisited: Aramaic Paraphrases of the Hebrew Bible, a Light on the New Testament*. 2nd ed. Grand Rapids: Eerdmans, 2010.

Meeks, Wayne A. *The Prophet-King: Moses Traditions and the Johannine Christology*. Supplements to Novum Testamentum 14. Leiden: Brill, 1967.

Menken, Maarten J.J. *Old Testament Quotations in the Fourth Gospel: Studies in Textual Form*. Kämpen: Kok Pharos, 1996.

Merkel, Helmut. *Sibyllinen*. Jüdische Schriften aus hellenistisch-römischer 5/8. Gütersloh: Gütersloher, 1998.

Metzner, Rainer. *Das Verständnis der Sünde im Johannesevangelium*. Wissenschaftliche Untersuchungen zum Neuen Testament 122. Tübingen: Mohr Siebeck, 2000.

Meyers, Carol L. and Eric M. Meyers. *Zechariah 9-14: A New Translation with Introduction and Commentary*. The Anchor Bible 25C. New York: Doubleday, 1993.

Michaels, J. Ramsey. *The Gospel of John*. The New International Commentary on the New Testament. Grand Rapids: Eerdmans, 2010.

Milgrom, Jacob. *Numbers: The Traditional Hebrew Text with the New JPS Translation Commentary*. The JPS Torah Commentary. Philadelphia: Jewish Publication Society, 1990.

Miller, Patrick D. *Deuteronomy*. Interpretation. Louisville: John Knox, 1990.

Miranda, Juan P. *Der Vater, der mich gesandt hat: Religionsgeschichtlich Untersuchungen zu den johanneischen Sendungsformeln: Zugleich ein Beitrag zur johanneischen Christologie und Ekklesiologie*. Europäische Hochschulschriften 23/7. Bern: Theologischer, 1972.

Mönikes, Ansgar. *Tora ohne Mose: Zur Vorgeschichte der Mose-Tora*. Bonner biblische Beiträge 149. Berlin: Philo, 2004.

Moloney, Francis J. *The Gospel of John*. Sacra Pagina 4. Wilmington: Liturgical, 1998.

—— *Signs and Shadows: Reading John 5-12*. Minneapolis: Fortress, 1996.

Mor, Menahem, and Friedrich V. Reiterer, eds. *Samaritans: Past and Present, Current Studies*. Studia Judaica 53. Berlin: Walter de Gruyter, 2010.

Morris, Leon. *The Gospel according to John*. Rev. ed. The New International Commentary on the New Testament. Grand Rapids: Eerdmans, 1995.

Moyise, Steve, ed. *The Old Testament in the New Testament: Essays in Honour of J.L.*

North. Journal for the Study of the New Testament Supplement Series 189. Sheffield: Sheffield, 2000.

— and Maarten J.J. Menken, eds. *The Psalms in the New Testament*. The New Testament and the Scriptures of Israel. London: T & T Clark, 2004.

Müller, Mogens. *The First Bible of the Church: A Plea for the Septuagint*. Journal for the Study of the Old Testament Series 206. Sheffield: Sheffield, 1996.

— and Hennik Tronier, eds. *The New Testament as Reception*. Journal for the Study of the New Testament Series 230. Sheffield: Sheffield, 2002.

Müller, Ulrich B. *Johannes der Täufer: Jüdischer Prophet und Wegbereiter Jesu*. Biblische Gestalten 6. Leipzig: Evangelische Verlagsanstalt, 2002.

Muraoka, Takamitsu. *A Greek English Lexicon of the Septuagint*. Louvain: Peeters, 2009.

Myers, Jacob M. *I and II Esdras: Introduction, Translation and Commentary*. The Anchor Bible 42. Garden City: Doubleday, 1974.

Nagel, Titus. *Die Rezeption des Johannesevangeliums im 2. Jahrhundert: Studien zur vorirenäischen Aneignung und Auslegung des vierten Evangeliums in christlicher und christlich-gnostischer Literatur*. Arbeiten zur Bibel und ihrer Geschichte 2. Leipzig: Evangelische Verlagsanstalt, 2000.

Nelson, Richard D. *Deuteronomy: A Commentary*. The Old Testament Library. Louisville: Westminster/John Knox, 2002.

Neusner, Jacob. *Genesis Rabbah: The Judaic Commentary to the Book of Genesis*. 3 vols. Brown Judaic Studies 104-06. Atlanta: Scholars, 1985.

— ed. *The Talmud of the Land of Israel*. 35 vols. Chicago: The University of Chicago Press, 1982-1994.

— and Bruce D. Chilton. *Jewish-Christian Debates: God, Kingdom, Messiah*. Minneapolis: Fortress, 1998.

Neyrey, Jerome H. *The Gospel of John*. The New Cambridge Bible Commentary. Cambridge, UK: Cambridge University Press, 2007.

— *The Gospel of John in Cultural and Rhetorical Perspective*. Grand Rapids: Eerdmans, 2009.

Nicholson, Godfrey C. *Death as Departure: The Johannine Descent-Ascent Schema*. SBL Dissertation Series 63. Chico: Scholars, 1983.

Nickelsburg, George W. E. *Jewish Literature between the Bible and the Mishnah: A Historical and Literary Introduction*. 2nd ed. Minneapolis: Fortress, 2005.

Nicol, W. *The Semeia in the Fourth Gospel: Tradition and Redaction*. Novum Testamentum Supplement 32. Leiden: Brill, 1972.

Nodet, Etienne. *A Search for the Origins of Judaism: From Joshua to the Mishnah*. Journal for the Study of the Old Testament Supplement Series 248. Sheffield: Sheffield, 1997.

Obermann, Andreas. *Die christologische Erfüllung der Schrift im Johannesevangelium: Eine Untersuchung zur johanneischen Hermeneutik anhand der Schriftzitate*. Wissenschaftliche Untersuchungen zum Neuen Testament 2/83. Tübingen: Mohr Siebeck, 1996.

Oegeman, Gerbern S. *The Anointed and His People: Messianic Expectations from the Maccabees to Bar Kochba*. Journal for the Study of the Pseudepigrapha Supplement Series 27. Sheffield: Sheffield, 1998.

— and James H. Charlesworth, eds. *The Pseudepigrapha and Christian Origins: Essays from the Studiorum Novi Testamenti Societas*. Jewish and Christian Texts in Contexts and Related Studies 4. London: T & T Clark, 2008.

Öhler, Markus. *Alttestamentliche Gestalten im Neuen Testament: Beiträge zur biblischen Theologie.* Darmstadt: Wissenschaftliche Buchgesellschaft, 1999.

— *Elia im Neuen Testament: Untersuchungen zur Bedeutung des alttestamentlichen Propheten im frühen Christentum.* Beihefte zur Zeitschrift für die neutestamentliche Wissenschaft und die Kunde der älteren Kirche 88. Berlin: Walter de Gruyter, 1997.

Ottillinger, Angelika. *Vorläufer, Vorbild oder Zeuge?: Zum Wandel des Täuferbildes im Johannesevangelium.* Dissertationen theologische Reihe 45. St. Ottilien: EOS, 1991.

Painter, John. *The Quest for the Messiah: The History, Literature und Theology of the Johannine Community.* 2nd ed. London: T & T Clark, 1993.

Pancaro, Severino. *The Law in the Fourth Gospel: The Torah and the Gospel, Moses and Jesus, Judaism and Christianity according to John.* Supplements to Novum testamentum 42. Leiden: Brill, 1975.

Petzke, Gerd. *Die Traditionen über Apollonius von Tyana und das Neue Testament.* Studia ad corpus hellenisticum Novi Testamenti 1. Leiden: Brill, 1970.

Polhill, John B. *Acts.* The New American Commentary 26. Nashville: Broadman, 1992.

Pomykala, Kenneth. *The Davidic Dynasty Tradition in Early Judaism: Its History and Significance for Messianism.* Early Judaism and Its Literature 7. Atlanta: Scholars, 1995.

Porter, Stanley E., ed. *Hearing the Old Testament in the New Testament.* McMaster New Testament Studies. Grand Rapids: Eerdmans, 2006.

— ed. *The Messiah in the Old and New Testaments.* McMaster New Testament Studies. Grand Rapids: Eerdmans, 2007.

Propp, William H. C. *Exodus 1-18: A New Translation with Introduction and Commentary.* The Anchor Bible 2. New York: Doubleday, 1998.

Pummer, Reinhard. Early *Christian Authors on Samaritans & Samaritanism: Texts, Translations & Commentary.* Texts & Studies in Ancient Judaism 92. Tübingen: Mohr Siebeck, 2002.

— *The Samaritans.* Iconography of Religions 23/5. Leiden: Brill, 1987.

Rahner, Johanna. *Er aber sprach vom Tempel seines Leibes: Jesus von Nazaret als Ort der Offenbarung Gottes im vierten Evangelium.* Bonner biblische Beiträge 117. Bodenheim an Rhein: Philo, 1998.

Rebell, Walter. *Gemeinde als Gegenwelt: Zur soziologischen und didaktischen Funktion des Johannesevangeliums.* Beiträge zur biblischen Exegese und Theologie 20. Frankfurt: Peter Lang, 1987.

Reim, Günter. *Jochanan: Erweiterte Studien zum alttestamentlichen Hintergrund des Johannesevangeliums.* Erlangen: Ev.-Luth. Mission, 1995.

— *Studien zum alttestamentlichen Hintergrund des Johannesevangeliums.* Society for the New Testament Studies Monograph Series 22. Cambridge: Cambridge University Press, 1974.

Rendtorff, Rolf. *Canonical Hebrew Bible: A Theology of the Old Testament.* Tools for Biblical Study 7. Leiden: Deo, 2005.

Rengstorf, Karl H. *The Complete Concordance to Flavius Josephus: Study Edition.* 2 vols. Leiden: Brill, 2002.

Richter, Georg. *Studien zum Johannesevangelium.* Ed. Josef Hainz. Biblische Untersuchungen 13. Regensburg: Pustet, 1977.

Richter, Wolfgang. *Die sogenannten vorprophetischen Berufungsberichte: Eine literaturwissenschaftliche Studie zu 1 Sam 9,1-10,16, Ex 3f. und Ri 6,11b-17.* Forschungen zur Religion und Literatur des Alten und Neuen Testaments

101. Göttingen: Vandenhoeck & Ruprecht, 1970.

Römer, Thomas, ed. *La construction de la figure de Moïse*. Supplément à Transeuphratène 13. Paris: Gabalda, 2007.

Rothfuchs, Wilhelm. *Die Erfüllungszitate des Matthaüs-Evangeliums: Eine biblisch-theologische Untersuchung*. Beiträge zur Wissenschaft vom Alten und Neuen Testament 88. Stuttgart: Kohlhammer 1969.

Ruckstuhl, Eugen. *Die literarische Einheit des Johannesevangeliums: Der gegenwärtige Stand der einschlägigen Forschungen*. Novum Testamentum et orbis antiquus 5. Freiburg: Universitätsverlag; Göttingen: Vandenhoeck & Ruprecht, 1987.

—— and Peter Dschulnigg. *Stilkritik und Verfasserfrage im Johannesevangelium: Die Johanneischen Sprachmerkmale auf dem Hintergrund des Neuen Testaments und des zeitgenössischen hellenistischen Schrifttums*. Novum testamentum et orbis antiquus 17. Freiburg: Universitätsverlag, 1991.

Rüterswörden, Udo. *Von der politischen Gemeinschaft zur Gemeinde: Studien zu Dt 16, 18-18, 22*. Bonner biblische Beiträge 65. Frankfurt: Athenäum, 1987.

Sanders, James A., ed. *The Psalms Scroll of Qumran Cave 11 (11QPs^a)*. Discoveries in the Judaean Desert 4. Oxford: Clarendon, 1965.

Schapdick, Stefan. *Auf dem Weg in den Konflikt: Exegetische Studien zum theologischen Profil der Erzählung vom Aufenthalt Jesus in Samarien (Joh 4, 1-42) im Kontext des Johannesevangeliums*. Bonner biblische Beiträge 126. Berlin: Philo, 2000.

Schenke, Ludger. *Johannes: Kommentar*. Düsseldorf: Patmos, 1998.

Schiffman, Lawrence H. *Qumran and Jerusalem: Studies in the Dead Sea Scrolls and the History of Judaism*. Studies in the Dead Sea Scrolls and Related Literature. Grand Rapids: Eermans, 2010.

Schlatter, Adolf. *Der Evangelist Johannes, wie er spricht, denkt und glaubt: Ein Kommentar zum vierten Evangelium*. Stuttgart: Calwer, 1975.

—— *Rückblick auf meine Lebensarbeit*. 2nd ed. Stuttgart: Calwer, 1977.

Schmithals, Walter. *Johannesevangelium und Johannesbriefe: Forschungsgeschichte und Analyse*. Beihefte zur Zeitschrift für die neutestamentliche Wissenschaft und die Kunde der älteren Kirche 64. Berlin: Walter de Gruyter, 1992.

Schnackenburg, Rudolf. *The Gospel according to St John*. 3 vols. Herder's Theological Commentary on the New Testament. New York: Crossroad, 1982; trans. *Das Johannesevangelium*. 4 vols. 4th ed. Herders theologischer Kommentar zum Neuen Testament 4. Freiburg: Herder, 1972-1985.

—— *Jesus in the Gospels: A Biblical Christology*. Louisville: Westminster/John Knox, 1995.

Schneider, Johannes. *Das Evangelium nach Johannes*. 2nd ed. Theologischer Handkommentar zum Neuen Testament. Berlin: Evangelische Verlagsanstalt, 1978.

Schnelle, Udo. *Antidocetic Christology in the Gospel of John: An Investigation of the Place of the Fourth Gospel in the Johannine School*. Minneapolis: Fortress, 1992.

—— *Das Evangelium nach Johannes*. 4th ed. Theologischer Handkommentar zum Neuen Testament 4. Leipzig: Evangelische Verlagsanstalt, 2004.

—— *Einleitung in das Neue Testament*. Uni-Taschenbücher. 7th ed. Göttingen: Vandenhoeck & Ruprecht, 2011.

—— *Theologie des Neuen Testaments*. Göttingen: Vandenhoeck & Ruprecht, 2007.

Scholtissek, Klaus. *In ihm sein und bleiben: Die Sprache der Immanenz in den Johanneischen Schriften*. Herders biblische Studien 21. Freiburg: Herder, 2000.

Schottroff, Luise. *Der Glaubende und die feindliche Welt: Beobachtungen zum gnostischen Dualismus und seiner Bedeutung für Paulus und das Johannesevangelium*. Wissenschaftliche Monographien zum Alten und Neuen Testament 37. Neukirchen: Neukirchener, 1970.

Schräge, Wolfgang. *Ethik des Neuen Testaments*. 2nd ed. Grundrisse zum Neuen Testament 4. Göttingen: Vandenhoeck & Ruprecht, 1989.

Schreiber, Stefan. *Gesalbter und König: Titel und Konzeptionen der königlichen Gesalbtenerwartung in frühjüdischen und urchristlichen Schriften*. Beihefte zur Zeitschrift für die neutestamentliche Wissenschaft und die Kunde der älteren Kirche 105. Berlin: Walter de Gruyter, 2000.

Schuchard, Bruce G. *Scripture within Scripture: The Interrelationship of Form and Function in the Explicit Old Testament Citations in the Gospel of John*. The Society of Biblical Literature Dissertation Series 133. Atlanta: Scholars, 1992.

Schulz, Hans-Joachim. *Die apostolische Herkunft der Evangelien: Zum Ursprung der Evangelienform in der urgemeindlichen Paschafeier*. 3rd ed. Quaestiones disputatae 145. Freiburg: Herder, 1997.

Schulz, Sigfried. *Das Evanglium nach Johannes*. 5th ed. Neue Testament Deutsch 4. Göttingen: Vandenhoeck & Ruprecht, 1987.

Schwartz, Daniel R. *2 Maccabees*. Commentaries on Early Jewish Literature. Berlin: Walter de Gruyter, 2008.

Schweizer, Eduard. *Jesus Christus: Im vielfältigen Zeugnis des Neuen Testaments*. 4th ed. Gütersloher Taschenbücher/Siebenstern 126. Gütersloh: Gütersloher, 1976.

Scobie, Charles H.H. *The Ways of Our God: An Approach to Biblical Theology*. Grand Rapids: Eerdmans, 2003.

Seitz, Christopher R. *The Character of Christian Scripture: The Significance of a Two-Testament Bible*. Studies in Theological Interpretation. Grand Rapids: Baker, 2011.

Sénéchal, Vincent. *Retribution et intercession dans le Deutéronome*. Berlin: Walter de Gruyter, 2009.

Setzer, Claudia. *Resurrection of the Body in Early Judaism and Early Christianity: Doctrine, Community, and Self-Definition*. Leiden: Brill, 2004.

Seybold, Klaus. *Das Davidische Königtum im Zeugnis der Propheten*. Forschungen zur Religion und Literatur des Alten und Neuen Testaments 107. Göttingen: Vandenhoeck & Ruprecht, 1972.

Smalley, Stephen S. *John: Evangelist and Interpreter*. 2nd ed. Downers Grove: IVP, 1998.

Smith, D. Moody. *Johannine Christianity: Essays on Its Setting, Sources, and Theology*. Columbia: University of South Carolina Press, 1984.

—— *John among the Gospels: The Relationship in Twentieth-Century Research*. Minneapolis: Fortress, 1992.

—— *The Theology of the Gospel of John*. New Testament Theology. Cambridge: Cambridge University Press, 1995.

Snaith, John G. *Ecclesiasticus or the Wisdom of Jesus Son of Sirach*. The Cambridge Bible Commentary. Cambridge: Cambridge University Press, 1974.

Spawn, Kevin L. *"As It Is Written" and Other Citation Formulae in the Old Testament: Their Use, Development, Syntax and Significance*. Beihefte zur Zeitschrift für die alttestamentliche Wissenschaft 311. New York: Walter de Gruyter, 2002.

Stanley, Christopher D. *Paul and the Language of Scripture: Citation Technique in the Pauline Epistles and Contemporary Literature*. Society for New Testament Studies Monograph Series 74. Cambridge: Cambridge University press, 1992.

Stone, Michael E. *Features of the Eschatology of IV Ezra*. Harvard Semitic Studies 35. Atlanta: Scholars, 1989.
—— *Fourth Ezra: A Commentary on the Book of Fourth Ezra*. Hermeneia 60/2. Minneapolis: Fortress, 1990.
—— *Jewish Writings of the Second Temple Period: Apocrypha, Pseudepigrapha, Qumran Sectarian Writings, Philo, Josephus*. Compendia rerum iudaicarum ad Novum Testamentum 2/3. Minneapolis: Fortress, 1984.
Stowasser, Martin. *Johannes der Täufer im Vierten Evangelium: Eine Untersuchung zu seiner Bedeutung für die johanneische Gemeinde*. Österreichische biblische Studien 12. Klosterneuburg: Österreichisches katholisches Bibelwerk, 1992.
Strack, H.L., and G. Stemberger. *Introduction to the Talmud and Midrash*. Translated by Markus Bockmuehl. Minneapolis: Fortress, 1992.
Strack, Herman L., and Paul Billerbeck. *Kommentar zum Neuen Testament aus Talmud und Midrasch*. 6 vols. München: C.H. Beck, 1922-1961.
Stuhlmacher, Peter. *Biblische Theologie des Neuen Testaments*. 2 vols. Göttingen: Vandenhoeck & Ruprecht, 1999-2005.
Tait, Michael and Peter Oakes, eds. *The Torah in the New Testament: Papers Delivered at the Manchester-Lausanne Seminar of June 2008*. The Library of New Testament Studies 401. London: T & T Clark, 2009.
Teeple, Howard M. *The Mosaic Eschatological Prophet*. Journal of Biblical Literature Monograph Series 10. Philadelphia: The Society of Biblical Literature, 1957.
Temporini, Hildegard, and Wolfgang Haase, eds. *Aufstieg und Niedergang der römischen Welt*. 37 vols. New York: Walter de Gruyter, 1972-96.
Theobald, Michael. *Die Fleischwerdung des Logos: Studien zum Verhältnis des Johannesprologs zum Corpus des Evangeliums und zu 1 Joh*. Neutestamentliche Abhandlungen (New Series) 20. Münster: Aschendorff, 1988.
—— *Herrenworte im Johannesevangelium*. Herders biblische Studien 34. Freiburg: Herder, 2002.
—— *Im Anfang war das Wort: Textlinguistische Studie zum Johannesprolog*. Stuttgarter Bibelstudien 106. Stuttgart: Katholisches Bibelwerk, 1983.
—— *Studien zum Corpus Iohanneum*. Wissenschaftliche Untersuchungen zum Neuen Testament 267. Tübingen: Mohr Siebeck, 2010.
Thettayil, Benny. *In Spirit and Truth: An Exegetical Study of John 4:19-26 and a Theological Investigation of the Replacement Theme in the Fourth Gospel*. Contributions to Biblical Exegesis and Theology 46. Leuven: Peeters, 2007.
Thielman, Frank. *Theology of the New Testament: A Canonical and Synthetic Approach*. Grand Rapids: Zondervan, 2005.
Thyen, Hartwig. *Das Johannesevangelium*. Handbuch zum Neuen Testament 6. Tübingen: Mohr Siebeck, 2005.
—— *Studien zum Corpus Iohanneum*. Wissenschaftliche Untersuchungen zum Neuen Testament 214. Tübingen: Mohr Siebeck, 2007.
Tigay, Jeffrey H. *Deuteronomy: The Traditional Hebrew Text with the New JPS Translation*. The JPS Torah Commentary. Philadelphia: The Jewish Publication Society, 1996.
Tuckett, Christopher M. *The Scriptures in the Gospels*. Bibliotheca ephemeridum theologicarum lovaniensium 131. Leuven: Leuven University Press, 1997.
Vanderkam, James. *The Dead Sea Scrolls Today*. 2nd ed. Grand Rapids: Eerdmans, 2010.

VanGemeren, Willem A., ed. *New International Dictionary of Old Testament Theology & Exegesis*. 5 vols. Grand Rapids: Zondervan, 1997.
Vermes, Geza. *Jesus in His Jewish Context*. Minneapolis: Fortress, 2003.
Wagner, J. Ross, C. Kavin Rowe, and A. Katherine Grieb, eds. *The Word Leaps the Gap: Essays on Scripture and Theology in Honor of Richard B. Hays*. Grand Rapids: Eerdmans, 2008.
Wansbrough, Henry, ed. *Jesus and the Oral Gospel Tradition*. Journal for the Study of the New Testament Supplement Series 64. Sheffield: JSOT, 1991.
Waschke, Ernst-Joachim. *Der Gesalbte: Studien zur alttestamentlichen Theologie*. Beihefte zur Zeitschrift für die alttestamentliche Wissenschaft 306. Berlin: Walter de Gruyter, 2001.
Webb, Robert L. *John the Baptizer and Prophet: A Socio-Historical Study*. Journal for the Study of the New Testament Supplement Series 62. Sheffield: JSOT, 1991.
Weiser, Alfons. *Die Theologie der Evangelien*. Vol. 2 of *Theologie des Neuen Testaments*. Kohlhammer Studienbücher Theologie 8. Stuttgart: W. Kohlhammer, 1993.
Wengst, Klaus. *Bedrängte Gemeinde und verherrlichter Christus: Ein Versuch über das Johannesevangelium*. 4th ed. Kaiser Taschenbücher 114. München: Chr. Kaiser, 1992.
— *Das Johannesevangelium*. Rev. ed. 2 vols. Theologischer Kommentar zum Neuen Testament 4. Stuttgart: Kohlhammer, 2000-01.
Werner, Dommershausen. *1 Makkabäer, 2 Makkabäer*. 2nd ed. Neue Ecter Bibel 12. Würzburg: Echter, 1995.
Wevers, John W., ed. *Genesis*. Auctoritate Academiae Scientiarum Gottingensis editum 1. Göttingen: Vandenhoeck & Ruprecht, 1974.
— *Notes on the Greek Text of Deuteronomy*. The Society of Biblical Literature Septuagint and Cognate Studies Series 39. Atlanta: Scholars, 1995.
Widmer, Michael. *Moses, God, and the Dynamics of Intercessory Prayer: A Study of Exodus 32-34 and Numbers 13-14*. Forschungen zum Alten Testament 2/8. Tübingen: Mohr Siebeck, 2004.
Wilckens, Udo. *Das Evangelium nach Johannes*. 2nd ed. Das Neue Testament Deutsch 4. Göttingen: Vandenhoeck & Ruprecht, 2000.
Wink, Walter. *John the Baptist in the Gospel Tradition*. Society for New Testament Studies Monograph Series 7. Cambridge: Cambridge University Press, 1968.
Xeravits, Géza G., ed. *Dualism in Qumran*. Library of Second Temple Studies 76. London: T & T Clark, 2010.
— *King, Priest, Prophet: Positive Eschatological Protagonists of the Qumran Library*. Studies on the Texts of the Desert of Judah 47. Leiden: Brill, 2003.
Zumstein, Jean. *Kreative Erinnerung: Relecture und Auslegung im Johannesevangelium*. 2nd ed. Abhandlungen zur Theologie des Alten und Neuen Testaments 84. Zürich: Theologischer, 2004.

Articles

Abegg, Martin G., Jr. "Who Ascended to Heaven?: 4Q491, 4Q427, and the Teacher of Righteousness." In *Eschatology, Messianism, and the Dead Sea Scrolls*, ed. Craig A. Evans and Peter W. Flint, 61-73. Studies in the Dead Sea Scrolls and Related Literature. Grand Rapids, MI: Eerdmans, 1997.

Agua Pérez, Agustín del. "Jewish Procedures of Bible Interpretation in the Gospels: A Proposal for a Systematic Classification." *Estudios bíblicos* 60 (2002): 77-106.

Anderson, H. "4 Maccabees." In *The Old Testament Pseudepigrapha*, ed. James H. Charlesworth, 2:533-64. The Anchor Bible Reference Library. New York: Doubleday, 1985.

Anderson, Paul N. "The *Sitz im Leben* of the Johannine Bread of Life Discourse and Its Evolving Context." In *Critical Readings of John 6*, ed. R. Alan Culpepper, 1-60. Biblical Interpretation Series 22. Leiden: Brill, 1997.

Ashton, John. "Second Thoughts on the Fourth Gospel." In *What We Have Heard from the Beginning: The Past, Present, and Future of Johannine Studies*, ed. Tom Thatcher, 1-18. Waco: Baylor University Press, 2007.

Attridge, Harold W. "Genre Bending in the Fourth Gospel." *Journal of Biblical Literature* 121 (2002): 3-21.

—— "Johannine Christianity." In *Essays on John and Hebrews*, 3-19. Wissenschaftliche Untersuchungen zum Neuen Testament 264. Tübingen: Mohr Siebeck, 2010.

Augenstein, Jörg. "Jesus und das Gesetz im Johannesevangelium." *Kirche und Israel* 14 (1999): 161-79.

Aune, David E. "The Contribution of Howard Merle Teeple to New Testament Scholarship." *Biblical Research* 43 (1998): 70-81.

Aurelius, Erik. "Heilsgegenwart im Wort: Dtn 30,11-14." In *Liebe und Gebot: Studien zum Deuteronomium*, ed. Reinhard G. Kratz and Hermann Spieckermann, 13-29. Forschungen zur Religion und Literatur des Alten und Neuen Testaments 190. Göttingen: Vandenhoeck & Ruprecht, 2000.

Baillet, Maurice. "Le texte samaritain de l'Exode dans les manuscrits de Qumrân." In *Hommages à André Dupont-Sommer*, ed. André Dupont-Sommer, 363-81. Paris: Librarie Adrien-Maisonneuve, 1971.

Balentine, Samuel E. "The Prophet as Intercessor: A Reassessment." *Journal of Biblical Literature* 103 (1984): 161-73.

Barriocana Gómez, José Luis. "Jesús como Nuevo Moisés en el Evangelio de Juan." *Estudios bíblico* 67 (2009): 417-43.

Barr, James. "Childs' *Introduction to the Old Testament as Scripture*." *Journal for the Study of the Old Testament* 16 (1980): 12-23.

Barrett, Charles K. "The Interpretation of the Old Testament in the New." In *The Cambridge History of the Bible, From the Beginnings to Jerome*, ed. P.R. Ackroyd and C.F. Evans, 1: 377-411. Cambridge: Cambridge University Press, 1970.

—— "The Old Testament in the Fourth Gospel." *Journal of Theological Studies* 48 (1947): 155-69.

Barstad, Hans M. "The Understanding of the Prophets in Deuteronomy." *Scandinavian Journal of the Old Testament* 8 (1994): 236-51.

Barth, Gerhard. "Biblische Theologie: Versuch einer vorläufigen Bilanz." *Evangelische Theologie* 58 (1998): 384-99.

Barton, George A. "'A Bone of Him Shall Not Be Broken': John 19:36." *Journal of Biblical Literature* 49 (1930): 13-19.

Barton, John. "Biblical Theology: An Old Testament Perspective." In *The Nature of New Testament Theology: Essays in Honour of Robert Morgan*, ed. Christopher Rowland and Christopher Tuckett, 18-30. Oxford: Blackwell, 2006.

—— "The Messiah in Old Testament Theology." In *King and Messiah in Israel and the Ancient Near East: Proceedings of the Oxford Old Testament Seminar*, ed. John Day,

365-79. Journal for the Study of the Old Testament Supplement Series 270. Sheffield: Sheffield, 1998.

Baslez, Marie-Françoise. "Écrire l'histoire dans le judaïsme hellénisé et le premier christianisme: Les galleries de figures ancestrales." In *Eukarpa: Études sur la Bible et ses exégètes en hommage à Gilles Dorival*, ed. Mireille Loubet and D. Pralon, 191-204. Paris: Cerf, 2011.

Bassler, Jouette M. "A Man for All Seasons: David in Rabbinic and New Testament Literature." *Interpretation* 40 (1986): 156-69.

Bauckham, Richard. "Jewish Messianism according to the Gospel of John." In *Challenging Perspectives in the Gospel of John*, ed. John Lierman, 34-68. Wissenschaftliche Untersuchungen zum Neuen Testament 2/219. Tübingen: Mohr Siebeck, 2006.

——. "The Martyrdom of Enoch and Elijah: Christian or Jewish." *Journal of Biblical Literature* 95 (1976): 447-58.

——. "The Throne of God and the Worship of Jesus." In *The Jewish Roots of Christological Monotheism: Papers from the St. Andrews Conference on the Historical Origin of the Worship of Jesus*, ed. Carey C. Newman, James R. Davila, and Gladys S. Lewis, 43-69. Supplements to the Journal for the Study of Judaism 63. Leiden: Brill, 1999.

Bauer, Johannes Baptist. "Drei Cruces: Joh 7:38 und Spr 18:4." *Biblische Zeitschrift* 9 (1965): 84-91.

Bauks, Michaela. "Das Dämonische im Menschen: Einige Anmerkungen zur priesterschriftlichen Theologie (Ex 7-14)." In *Dämonen: Die Dämonologie der israelitisch-jüdischen und frühchristlichen Literatur im Kontext ihrer Umwelt*, ed. Armin Lange, Hermann Lichtenberger, and Diethard Römheld, 239-53. Tübingen: Mohr Siebeck, 2003.

Beasley-Murray, George R. "John 13-17: The Community of True Life." *Review and Expositor* 85 (1988): 473-84.

——. "The Lifting up of the Son of Man." In *Gospel of Life: Theology in the Fourth Gospel*, 34-58. Peabody: Hendrickson, 1991.

Becker, Jürgen. "Beobachtungen zum Dualismus im Johannesevangelium." *Zeitschrift für die neutestamentliche Wissenschaft und die Kunde der älteren Kirche* 65 (1974): 71-87.

——. "Ich Bin die Auferstehung und das Leben: Eine Skizze der johanneischen Christologie." *Theologische Zeitschrift* 39 (1983): 138-51.

Becker, Michael. "Die 'messianische Apokalypse' 4Q521 und der Interpretationsrahmen der Taten Jesu." In *Apokalyptik und Qumran*, ed. Michael Becker & Jörg Frey, 237-303. Einblicke 10. Paderborn: Bonifatius, 2007.

Belle, Gilbert van. "Christology and Soteriology in the Fourth Gospel: The Conclusion to the Gospel of John Revisited." In *Theology and Christology in the Fourth Gospel: Essays by the Members of the SNTS Johannine Writings Seminar*, ed. Gilbert van Belle, J.G. van der Watt, and P. Maritz, 435-62. Bibliotheca ephemeridum theologicarum lovaniensium 184. Leuven: Leuven University, 2005.

——. "Les parenthèses johanniques: Un Premier Bilan." In *Four Gospels 1992: Festschrift Frans Neirynck*, ed. Frans van Segbroeck et al, 3:1901-33. Bibliotheca ephemeridum theologicarum lovaniensium 100. Louvain: Peeters, 1992.

Beltz, Walter. "Elia redivivus: Ein Beitrag zum Problem der Verbindung von Gnosis und Altem Testament." In *Altes Testament-Frühjudentum-Gnosis: Neue Studien zun "Gnosis und Bibel,"* ed. Karl-Wolfgang Tröger, 137-41. Gütersloh, Germany:

Gütersloher Verlagshaus Mohn, 1980.
Bennema, Cornelis. "A Theory of Character in the Fourth Gospel with Reference to Ancient and Modern Literature." *Biblical Interpretation* 17 (2009): 375-421.
Berges, Ulrich. "Synchronie und Diachronie: Zur Methodenvielfalt in der Exegese." *Bibel und Kirche* 62 (2007): 249-52.
Betz, Otto. "Das Johannesevangelium und das Alte Testament." In *Wie verstehen wir das Neue Testament?* 87-108. Wuppertal: Aussaat, 1981.
—— "Donnersöhne, Menschenfischer und der Davidische Messias." *Revue de Qumran* 3 (1961): 41-70.
Beutler, Johannes. "Das Hauptgebot im Johannesevangelium." In *Das Gesetz im Neuen Testament*, ed. Johannes Beutler and Karl Kertelge, 222-36. Quaestiones disputatae 108. Freiburg: Herder, 1986.
—— "Die Überleitung zu den johanneischen Abschiedsreden (Joh 13,31f.): Ein Beispiel der 'relecture,'" in *Studien zu Matthäus und Johannes: Festschrift für Jean Zumstein zu seinem 65. Geburtstag*, ed. Andreas Dettwiler and Uta Poplutz, 221-31. Abhandlungen zur Theologie des Alten und Neuen Testaments 97. Zürich: Theologischer, 2009.
—— "Joh 6 als christliche 'relecture' des Pascharahmens im Johannesevangelium." In *Neue Studien zu den johanneischen Schriften*, ed. Rudolf Hoppe and Ulrich Berges, 165-85. Bonner biblische Beiträge 167. Göttingen: Vandenhoeck & Ruprecht; Bonn University Press, 2012.
Bindemann, Walther. "Der Johannesprolog: Ein Versuch, ihn zu verstehen." *Novum testamentum* 37 (1995): 331-54.
Black, Matthew. "Christological Use of the Old Testament in the New Testament." *New Testament Studies* 18 (1971): 1-14.
Blanchard, Yves-Marie. "Le fils de l'homme et l'échelle de Jacob: Réflexion sur l'intertextualité scripturaire et relecture de Jean 1,51, à la lumière de la Bible juive." In *Analyse narrative et Bible: Deuxième colloque international du Prenab, Louvain-la-Neuve, Avril 2004*, ed. Camille Focant and André Wénin, 181-95. Bibliotheca ephemeridum theologicarum lovaniensium 191. Leuven: Peeters, 2005.
Bloch, Renée. "Moïse chez Flavius Josèphe: Un exemple juif de littérature héroïque." In *Interprétations de Moïse: Égypte, Judée, Grèce et Rome*, ed. Philippe Borgeaud, Thomas Römer, and Youri Volokhine, 85-102. Jerusalem Studies in Religion and Culture 10. Leiden: Brill, 2010.
—— "Quelques aspects de la Figure de Moïse dans la Tradition Rabbinque." In *Moïse, l'homme de l'alliance*, ed. Henri Cazelles, 93-167. Special Issue of Cahiers Sioniens. Tournai: Desclée, 1955.
Block, Daniel I. "My Servant David: Ancient Israel's Vision of the Messiah." In *Israel's Messiah in the Bible and the Dead Sea Scrolls*, ed. Richard S. Hess and M. Daniel Carroll R., 17-56. Grand Rapids: Baker, 2003.
Blumenthal, Christian. "Charis anti charitos (Joh 1,16)." *Zeitschrift für die neutestamentliche Wissenschaft und die Kunde der älteren Kirche* 92 (2001): 290-94.
Bodi, Daniel. "Der altorientalische Hintergrund des Themas der 'Ströme lebendigen Wassers' in Joh 7,38." In *Johannes-Studien: Interdisziplinäre Zugänge zum Johannes-Evangelium, Freundesgabe der Theologischen Fakultät der Universität Neuchâtel für Jean Zumstein*, ed. Martin Rose, 137-58. Zürich: Theologischer, 1991.
Boer, Martinus D. de. "Narrative Criticism, Historical Criticism, and the Gospel of John." *Journal for the Study of the New Testament* 47 (1992): 35-48. Reprinted in *The*

Johannine Writings: A Sheffield Reader, ed. Stanley E. Porter and Craig A. Evans, 95-108. The Biblical Seminar 32. Sheffield: Sheffield, 1995.

Boismard, Marie-Émile. "Jésus, le prophète par excellence, d'après jean 10, 24-39." In *Neues Testament und Kirche: Für Rudolf Schnackenburg*, ed. Joachim Gnilka, 160-71. Freiburg: Herder, 1974.

Bolyki, János. "Christology in the Gospel of John: A New Approach." In *Testimony and Interpretation: Early Christology in its Judeo-Hellenistic Milieu: Studies in Honour of Petr Pokorný*, ed. Jan Roskovec and Jiří Mrázek, 191-201. Journal for the Study of the New Testament Supplement Series 272. London: T & T Clark, 2004.

Bondi, Richard A. "John 8:39-47: Children of Abraham or of the Devil?" *Journal of Ecumenical Studies* 34 (1997): 473-98.

Borchert, Gerald L. "The Resurrection Perspective in John: An Evangelical Summons." *Review and Expositor* 85 (1988): 501-14.

Bordreuil, Pierre. "Les 'graces de David' et 1 Maccabees 2:57." *Vetus testamentum* 31 (1981): 73-76.

Borgeaud, Philippe. "Quelques remarques sur Typhon, Seth, Moïse et son âne, dans la perspective d'un dialogue réactif transculturel." In *Interprétations de Möise: Égypte, Judée, Grèce et Rome*, ed. Philippe Borgeaud, Thomas Römer, and Youri Volokhine, 173-85. Jerusalem Studies in Religion and Culture 10. Leiden: Brill, 2010.

Borgen, Peder. "The Gospel of John and Hellenism: Some Observations." In *Exploring the Gospel of John: In Honor of D. Moody Smith*, ed. R. Alan Culpepper and C. Clifton Black, 98-123. Louisville: Westminster/John Knox, 1996.

— "Heavenly Ascent in Philo: An Examination of Selected Passages." In *The Pseudepigrapha and Early Biblical Interpretation*, ed. James H. Charlesworth and Craig A. Evans, 246-68. Journal for the Study of the Pseudepigrapha Supplement Series 14. Sheffield: Sheffield, 1993.

— "Observations on the Targumic Character of the Prologue of John" In *Logos was the True Light and Other Essays on the Gospel of John*, 13-20. Trondheim: Tapir, 1983.

— "The Son of Man Saying in John 3:13-14." In *Logos was the True Light and Other Essays on the Gospel of John*, 133-48. Trondheim: Tapir, 1983. Reprinted in *Philo, John and Paul: New Perspectives on Judaism and Early Christianity*, 103-20. Atlanta: Scholars, 1987.

— "The Use of Tradition in John 12:44-50." *New Testament Studies* 26 (1979): 18-35. Reprinted in *Philo, John and Paul: New Perspectives on Judaism and Early Christianity*, 185-204. Atlanta: Scholars, 1987.

Bostock, D. Gerald. "Jesus as the New Elisha." *Expository Times* 92 (1980-81): 39-41.

Bowley, James E. "Moses in the Dead Sea Scrolls: Living in the Shadow of God's Anointed." In *The Bible at Qumran: Text, Shape, and Interpretation*, ed. Peter W. Flint, 159-80. Studies in the Dead Sea Scrolls and Related Literature. Grand Rapids: Eerdmans, 2001.

— "Prophets and Prophecy at Qumran." In *Dead Sea Scrolls after Fifty Years: A Comprehensive Assessment*, ed. Peter W. Flint and James C. VanderKam, 2:354-78. Leiden: Brill, 1999.

Brawley, Robert L. "An Absent Complement and Intertextuality in John 19:28-29." *Journal of Biblical Literature* 112 (1993): 427-43.

Breytenbach, A.P.B. "Moses versus die Messias: 'n Samaritaanse tradisie." *Skrif en Kerk* 19 (1998): 534-43.

Broer, Ingo. "Knowledge of Palestine in the Fourth Gospel?" In *Jesus in Johannine*

Tradition, ed. Robert T. Fortna und Tom Thatcher, 83-90. Louisville: Westminster/John Knox, 2001.

Brooke, George J. "Moses in the Dead Sea Scrolls: Looking at Mount Nebo from Qumran." In *La construction de la figure de Moïse*, ed. Thomas Römer, 209-21. Supplément à Transeuphratène 13. Paris: Gabalda, 2007.

— "The Psalms in Early Jewish Literature in the Light of the Dead Sea Scrolls." In *The Psalms in the New Testament*, ed. Steve Moyise and Maarten J.J. Menken, 5-24. The New Testament and the Scriptures of Israel. London: T & T Clark, 2004.

— "The *Temple Scroll* and the New Testament." In *The Dead Sea Scrolls and the New Testament*, 97-114. Minneapolis: Fortress, 2005.

Brown, Jeannine K. "Creation's Renewal in the Gospel of John." *Catholic Biblical Quarterly* 72 (2010): 275-90.

Brown, Raymond E. "The Messianism of Qumrân." *Catholic Biblical Quarterly* 19 (1957): 53-82.

Brueggemann, Dale A. "Brevard Childs' Canon Criticism: An Example of Post-Critical Naiveté." *Journal of the Evangelical Theological Society* 32 (1989): 311-26.

Brueggemann, Walter. "Biblical Theology Appropriately Postmodern." In *Jews, Christians, and the Theology of the Hebrew Scriptures*, ed. Alice Ogden Bellis and Joel S. Kaminsky, 97-108. SBL Symposium Series 8. Atlanta: The Society of Biblical Literature, 2000.

Bultmann, Rudolph. "Die Bedeutung der neuerschlossenen mandäischen und manichäischen Quellen für das Verständnis des Johannesevangeliums." *Zeitschrift für die Neutestamentliche Wissenschaft und die Kunde der älteren Kirche* 24 (1925): 100-46.

Burns, R.J. "Jesus and the Bronze Serpent." *Bible Today* 28 (1990): 84-89.

Burton, Mack. "Under the Shadow of Moses: Authorship and Authority in Hellenistic Judaism." *The Society of Biblical Literature Seminar Papers* 21 (1982): 299-318.

Busse, Ulrich. "Die Tempelmetaphorik als ein Beispiel von implizitem Rekurs auf die biblische Tradition im Johannesevangelium." In *The Scripture in the Gospels*, ed. C.M. Tuckett, 395-428. Bibliotheca ephemeridum theologicarum lovaiensium 131. Louvain: Leuven University Press, 1997.

Campbell, Jonathan G. "4QTestimonia (4Q175)." In *The Exegetical Texts*, 88-99. Companion to the Qumran Scrolls 4. London: T & T Clark, 2004.

— "11QMelchizedek (11Q13)." In *The Exegetical Texts*, 56-66. Companion to the Qumran Scrolls 4. London: T & T Clark, 2004.

Cangh, Jean-Marie, van. "'Fils de David' dans les évangiles synoptiques." In *Figures de David à travers la Bible: XVIIe congrès de l'ACFEB (Lille, 1er-5 septembre 1997)*, ed. Louis Desrousseaux and Jacques Vermeylen, 345-96. Lectio divina 177. Paris: Cerf, 1999.

Caquot, André. "Trois textes religieux de la Grotte 4." *Revue d'Histoire et de Philosophie Religieuses* 84 (2004): 129-47

Carmignac, Jean. "Le document de Qumran sur Melchisédeq." *Revue de Qumran* 7 (1970): 343-78.

Carroll R., M. Daniel. "New Lenses to Establish Messiah's Identity?: A Response to Daniel I. Block." In *Israel's Messiah in the Bible and the Dead Sea Scrolls*, ed. Richard S. Hess and M. Daniel Carroll R., 71-81. Grand Rapids: Baker, 2003.

Carson, D.A. "John and Johannine Epistles." In *It is Written: Scripture Citing Scripture, Essays in Honour of Barnabas Lindars*, ed. D.A. Carson and H.G.M. Williamson,

245-64. Cambridge: Cambridge University Press, 1988.
Cebulj, Christian. "Texte, Teiche, Theorien: Zum Stellenwert archäologischer Befunde für die Exegese von Joh 5." In *Texte–Fakten–Artefakte: Beiträge zur Bedeutung der Archäologie für die neutestamentliche Forschung*, ed. Max Küchler and Karl M. Schmidt, 143-59. Novum Testamentum et Orbis Antiquus 59. Göttingen: Vandenhoeck & Ruprecht, 2006.
Charlesworth, James H. "Have the Dead Sea Scrolls Revolutionized Our Understanding of the New Testament?" In *Dead Sea Scrolls Fifty Years after Their Discovery: Proceedings of the Jerusalem Congress, July 20-25, 1997*, ed. Lawrence H. Schiffman, Emanuel Tov, James C. VanderKam, and Galen Marquis, 116-32. Jerusalem: Israel Exploration Society, 2000.
— "Introduction: Messianic Ideas in Early Judaism." In *Qumran-Messianism: Studies on the Messianic Expectations in the Dead Sea Scrolls*, ed. James H. Charlesworth, Hermann Lichtenberger, and Gerbern S. Oegema, 1-8. Tübingen: Mohr Siebeck, 1998.
— "Messianology in the Biblical Pseudepigrapha." In *Qumran-Messianism: Studies on the Messianic Expectations in the Dead Sea Scrolls*, ed. James H. Charlesworth, Hermann Lichtenberger, Gerbern S. Oegeman, 21-52. Tübingen: Mohr Siebeck, 1998.
Chester, Andrew. "Jewish Messianic Expectations and Mediatorial Figures and Pauline Christology." In *Paulus und das antike Judentum: Tübingen-Durham-Symposium im Gedenken an den 50. Todestag Adolf Schlatters (19. Mai 1938)*, ed. Martin Hengel and Ulrich Heckel, 17-89. Wissenschaftliche Untersuchungen zum Neuen Testament 58. Tübingen: Mohr Siebeck, 1991.
Childs, Brevard S. "Does the Old Testament Witness to Jesus Christ?" In *Evangelium, Schriftauslegung, Kirche: Festschrift für Peter Stuhlmacher zum 65. Geburtstag*, ed. Jostein Ådna, Scott J. Hafemann, and Otfried Hofius, 57-64. Göttingen: Vandenhoeck & Ruprecht, 1997.
Chinitz, Jacob. "Moses: Intermediary or Teacher?" *Jewish Bible Quarterly* 30 (2002): 196-200.
Chouinard, Larry. "Gospel Christology: A Study of Methodology." In *New Testament Interpretation and Methods: A Sheffield Reader*, ed. Stanley E. Porter and Craig A. Evans. The Biblical Seminar 45. Sheffield: Sheffield, 1997. Reprint, *Journal for the Study of the New Testament* 30 (1987): 21-37.
Ciampa, Roy E. "The History of Redemption." In *Central Themes in Biblical Theology: Mapping Unity in Diversity*, ed. Scott J. Hafemann and Paul R. House, 254-308. Downers Grove: InterVarsity, 2007.
Clements, Ronald E. "The Book of Deuteronomy: Introduction, Commentary, and Reflections." In *The Book of Numbers, the Book of Deuteronomy, Introduction to Narrative Literature, the Book of Joshua, the Book of Judges, the Book of Ruth, the First and Second Books of Samuel*. Vol. 2 of *The New Interpreter's Bible*, ed. Leander E. Keck, 271-538. Nashville: Abingdon, 1998.
Coakley, James F. "Jesus' Messianic Entry into Jerusalem (John 12:12-19 par.)." *Journal of Theological Studies* 46 (1995): 461-82.
Coggins, Richard J. "Issues in Samaritanism." In *Where We Stand: Issues and Debates in Ancient Judaism*, part 3, vol. 1 of *Judaism in Late Antiquity*, ed. Alan J. Every-Peck and Jacob Neusner, 63-77. Handbuch der Orientalistik 40. Leiden: Brill, 1999.
Collins, John J. "Jesus and the Messiahs of Israel." In *Geschichte—Tradition—Reflection: Festschrift für Martin Hengel zum 70. Geburtstag*, vol. 3, ed. Hubert Cancik, Hermann Lichtenberger, and Peter Schäfer, 287-302. Tübingen: Mohr Siebeck, 1996.

— "Jesus, Messianism and the Dead Sea Scrolls." In *Qumran—Messianism: Studies on the Messianic Expectations in the Dead Sea Scrolls*, ed. James H. Charlesworth, Hermann Lichtenberger, and Gerbern S. Oegema, 100-19. Tübingen: Mohr Siebeck, 1998.
— "Jewish Monotheism and Christian Theology." In *Aspects of Monotheism: How God Is One*, ed. Hershel Shanks and Jack Meinhardt, 82-94. Washington: Biblical Archaeology Soceity, 1997.
— "Messianism in the Maccabean Period." In *Judaisms and Their Messiahs at the Turn of the Christian Era*, ed. Jacob Neusner, William S. Green, and Ernest S. Frerichs, 97-107. Cambridge: Cambridge University Press, 1987.
— "Pre-Christian Jewish Messianism: An Overview." In *The Messiah in Early Judaism and Christianity*, ed. Magnus Zetterholm, 1-20. Minneapolis: Fortress, 2007.
— "Pseudepigraphy and Group Formation in Second Temple Judaism." In *Pseudepigraphic Perspectives: The Apocrypha and Pseudepigrapha in Light of the Dead Sea Scrolls, Proceedings of the International Symposium of the Orion Center for the Study of the Dead Sea Scrolls and Associated Literature, 12-14 January, 1997*, ed. Esther G. Chazon, Michael E. Stone, and Avital Pinnick, 43-58. Studies on the Texts of the Desert of Judah 31. Leiden: Brill, 1999.
— "The Sibylline Oracles." In *Jewish Writings of the Second Temple Period: Apocrypha, Pseudepigrapha, Qumran, Sectarian Writings, Philo, Josephus*, ed. Michael E. Stone, 357-81. Compendia rerum iudaicarum ad Novum Testamentum 2/2. Assen: Van Gorcum, 1984.
— "The Sibylline Oracles." In *The Old Testament Pseudepigrapha*. Edited by James H. Charlesworth. The Anchor Bible Reference Library. New York: Doubleday, 1983.
— "The *Son of God* Text from Qumran." In *From Jesus to John: Essays on Jesus and New Testament Christology in Hounour of Marinus de Jonge*, ed. Martinus C. de Boer, 65-82. Journal for the Study of the New Testament Supplement Series 84. Sheffield: Sheffield, 1993.
Colpe, Carsten. "New Testament and Gnostic Christology." In *Religions in Antiquity: Essays in Memory of Erwin Ramsdell Goodenough*, ed. Jacob Neusner, 227-43. Studies in the History of Religions 14. Leiden: Brill, 1968.
Cook, K. "Neutestamentliche Profetenauslegung in vorchristlicher Zeit?: Der Habakuk-Peschär aus Qumran." In *Schriftauslegung in der Schrift: Festschrift für Odil Hannes Steck zu seinem 65. Geburtstag*, ed. Reinhard G. Kratz, Thomas Krüger, and Konrad Schmid, 321-34. Beihefte zur Zeitschrift für die alttestamentliche Wissenschaft 300. Berlin: Walter de Gruyter, 2000.
Cothenet, Edouard. "De Jean-Baptiste au disciple Bien-Aime." *Esprit et Vie* 113, no. 94 (2003): 16-21; n. 95 (2003): 17-24; n. 96 (2003): 10-16.
Cross, Frank Moore. "Testimonia (4Q175 = 4QTestimonia = 4QTestim)." In *Pesharim, Other Commentaries, and Related Documents*, vol. 6B of *The Dead Sea Scrolls: Hebrew, Aramaic, and Greek Texts with English Translations*, ed. James H. Charlesworth, 308-27. The Princeton Theological Seminary Dead Sea Scrolls Project. Tübingen: Mohr Siebeck; Louisville: Westminster/John Knox, 2002.
Crotty, Robert B. "The Suffering Moses of Deutero-Zechariah." *Colloquium* 14 (1982): 43-50.
Culpepper, R. Alan. "The Death of Jesus: An Exegesis of John 19:28-37." *Faith and Mission* 5 (1988): 64-70.
— "The Pivot of John's Prologue." *New Testament Studies* 27 (1980): 1-31.

— "The Theology of the Gospel of John." *Review and Expositor* 85 (1988): 417-32.
— "The Theology of the Johannine Passion Narrative: John 19:16b-30." *Neotestamentica* 31 (1997): 21-37.
— "Un exemple de commentaire fondé sur la critique narrative: Jean 5,1-18." In *La Communauté johannique et son histoire: La trajectoire de l'evangile de Jean aux deux premiers siècles*, ed. Jean-Daniel Kaestli, Poffet Jean-Michel, and Jean Zumstein, 135-51. Geneva: Labor et Fides, 1990.
Cunningham, J. Alexander. "Christology and the Angel of the Lord." *Journal from the Radical Reformation* 6 (1997): 3-15
Daly-Denton, Margaret. "The Psalm in John's Gospel." In *The Psalms in the New Testament*, ed. Steve Moyise and Maarten J.J. Menken, 119-37. The New Testament and The Scriptures of Israel. London: T & T Clark, 2004.
D'Angelo, Mary Rose. "A Critical Note: John 20:17 and Apocalypse of Moses 31." *Journal of Theological Studies* 41 (1990): 529-36.
Daube, David. "Earliest Structure of the Gospels." *New Testament Studies* 5 (1959): 174-87.
Davies, W.D. "Reflections on Aspects of the Jewish Background of the Gospel of John." In *Exploring the Gospel of John: In Honor of D. Moody Smith*, ed. R. Alan Culpepper and C. Clifton Black, 43-64. Louisville: Westminster/John Knox, 1996.
Davila, James R. "Heavenly Ascents in the Dead Sea Scrolls." In *The Dead Sea Scrolls after Fifty Years: A Comprehensive Assessment*, ed. Peter W. Flint and James C. VanderKam, 2:461-85. Leiden: Brill, 1998.
Déaut, Roger, Le. "Targumic Literature and New Testament Interpretation." *Biblical Theology Bulletin* 4 (1974): 243-89.
Deines, Roland. "The Pharisees between 'Judaisms' and 'Common Judaism.'" In *The Complexities of Second Temple Judaism*, vol. 1 of *Justification and Variegated Nomism*, ed. D.A. Carson, Peter T. O'Brien, and Mark A. Seifrid, 443-504. Wissenschaftliche Untersuchungen zum Neuen Testament 2/140. Tübingen: Mohr Siebeck, 2001.
— and Karl-Wilhelm Niebuhr. "Philo und das Neue Testament—Das Neue Testament und Philo: Wechselseitige Wahrnehmungen." In *Philo und das Neue Testament: Wechselseitige Wahrnehmungen, 1. Internationales Symposium zum Corpus Judaeo-Hellenisticum 1.—4. Mail 2003, Eisenach/Jenaeds*, 3-20. Wissenschaftliche Untersuchungen zum Neuen Testament 172. Tübingen: Mohr Siebeck, 2004.
Demke, Christoph. "Das Evangelium der Dialoge: Hermeneutische und methodologische Beobachtungen zur Interpretation des Johannesevangeliums." *Zeitschrift für Theologie und Kirche* 97 (2000): 164-82.
Dennis, John. "Jesus' Death in John's Gospel: A Survey of Research from Bultmann to the Present with Special Reference to the Johannine Hyper-Texts." *Currents in Biblical Research* 4 (2006): 331-64.
— "The Presence and Function of Second Exodus-Restoration Imagery in John 6." *Studien zum Neuen Testament und seiner Umwelt* 30 (2005): 105-21.
Derrett, J. Duncan M. "The Bronze Serpent." *Estudios bíblicos* 49 (1991): 311-29.
— "The Reprobate's Peace: 4QDa (4Q266) (18 v 14-16)." In *Legal Texts and Legal Issues: Proceedings of the Second Meeting of the International Organization for Qumran Studies, Cambridge, 1995, Published in Honour of Joseph M. Baumgarten*, ed. Moshe Bernstein, Florentino García Martínez, and John Kampen, 245-49. Studies on the Texts of the Desert of Judah 23. Leiden: Brill, 1997.

Dettwiler, Andreas. "Umstrittene Ethik: Überlegungen zu Joh 15,1-17." In *Johannes-Studien: Interdisziplinäre Zugänge zum Johannes-Evangelium, Freundesgabe der Theologischen Fakultät der Universität Neuchâtel für Jean Zumstein*, ed. Martin Rose, 175-89. Zurich: Theologischer, 1991.

Dewey, Joanna. "The Gospel of John in Its Oral-Written Media World." In *Jesus in Johannine Tradition*, ed. Robert T. Fortna and Tom Thatcher, 239-52. Louisville: Westminster/John Knox, 2001.

Dexinger, Ferdinand. "Die frühesten samaritanischen Belege der Taheb-Vorstellung." *Kairos* 26 (1984): 224-52.

— "Der 'Prophet wie Mose' in Qumran und bei den Samaritanern." In *Mélanges bibliques et orientaux en l'honneur de M. Mathias Delcor*, ed. André Caquot, Simon Légasse, and Michel Tardieu, 97-111. Alter Orient und Altes Testament 215. Kevelaer: Butzon und Bercker, 1985.

— "Die Moses-Terminologie in Tibât Mårqe: Einige Beobachtungen." In *Frankfurter Judaistische Beiträge*, vol. 25, ed. Margarete Schlüter, 51-62. Frankfurt: Gesellschaft zur Förderung judaistischer Studien, 1998.

— "Josephus Ant 18,85-87 und der samaritanische Taheb." In *Proceedings of the First International Congress of the Société d'Études Samaritaines, Tel-Aviv, April 11-13, 1988*, ed. Abraham Tal and Moshe Florentin, 49-59. Tel-Aviv: Chaim Rosenberg School for Jewish Studies, Tel-Aviv University, 1991.

— "Der Taheb: Ein 'messianischer' Heilsbringer der Samaritaner." *Kairos* 27 (1985): 1-172.

— "Die Taheb-Vorstellung als politische Utopie." *Numen* 37 (1990): 1-21.

Dietzfelbinger, Christian. "Aspekte des Alten Testaments im Johannesevangelium." In *Geschichte-Tradition-Reflexion III, Frühes Christentum: Festschrift für Martin Hengel zum 70. Geburtstag*, ed. Hermann Lichtenberger, 203-18. Tübingen: Mohr Siebeck, 1996.

— "Der ungeliebte Bruder: Der Herrenbruder Jakobus im Johannesevangelium." *Zeitschrift für Theologie und Kirche* 89 (1992): 377-403.

— "Sühnetod im Johannesevangelium?" In *Evangelium—Schriftauslegung—Kirche: Festschrift für Peter Stuhlmacher zum 65. Geburtstag*, ed. Jostein Ådna, Scott J. Hafemann, and Otfried Hofius, 65-76. Göttingen: Vandenhoeck & Ruprecht, 1997.

Dijkstra, Meindert. "Moses, the man of God." In *Interpretation of Exodus: Studies in Honor of Cornelis Houtman*, ed. Riemer Roukema, 17-36. Contributions to Biblical Exegesis & Theology 44. Leuven: Peeters, 2006.

Dimant, Devorah. "New Light from Qumran on the Jewish Pseudepigrapha—4Q390." In *Madrid Qumran Congress: Proceedings of the International Congress on the Dead Sea Scrolls, Madrid, 18-21 March, 1991*, 2 vols., ed. Julio C. Trebolle Barrera and Luis Vegas Montaner, 2:405-48. Studies on the Texts of the Desert of Judah 11. Leiden: Brill, 1992.

Donner, Herbert. "Der verlässliche Prophet: Betrachtungen zu I Makk 14,41ff und zu Ps 110." In *Prophetie und geschichtliche Wirklichkeit im alten Israel: Festschrift für Siegfried Herrmann zum 65. Geburtstag*, ed. Rüdiger Liwak and Siegfried Wagner, 89-98. Stuttgart: Kohlhammer, 1991.

Doran, Robert. "The Second Book of Maccabees." In *1 & 2 Maccabees, Introduction to Hebrew Poetry, Job, Psalms*. Vol. 4 of *The New Interpreter's Bible*, ed. Leander E. Keck, 181-299. Nashville: Abingdon, 1996.

Doutre, Jean. "La narrativité et le langage figuratif de l'évangile de Jean." *Science et*

Esprit 64 (2012): 87-102.
Dozeman, Thomas B. "Masking Moses and Mosaic Authority in Torah." *Journal of Biblical Literature* 119 (2000): 21-45.
— "Moses: Divine Servant and Israelite Hero." *Hebrew Annual Review* 8 (1984): 45-61.
— "Sperma Abraam in John 8 and Related Literature." *Catholic Biblical Quarterly* 42 (1980): 342-58.
Droge, A. J. "'No One Has Ever Seen God': Revisionary Criticism in the Fourth Gospel." In *From Prophecy to Testament: The Function of the Old Testament in the New*, ed. Craig A. Evans, 169-84. Peabody: Hendrickson, 2004.
Dschulnigg, Peter. "Die Berufung der Jünger Joh 1,35-51 im Rahmen des vierten Evangeliums." *Freiburger Zeitschrift für Philosophie und Theologie* 36 (1989): 427-47.
— "Nikodemus im Johannesevangelium." *Studien zum Neuen Testament und seiner Umwelt* 24 (1999): 103-18.
Duhaime, Jean. "Recent Studies on Messianism in the Dead Sea Scrolls." In *Dead Sea Scrolls Fifty Years after Their Discovery: Proceedings of the Jerusalem Congress, July 20-25, 1997*, ed. Lawrence H. Schiffman, Emanuel Tov, James C. VanderKam, and Galen Marquis, 789-99. Jerusalem: Israel Exploration Society, 2000.
Dumbrell, William J. "Grace and Truth: The Progress of the Argument of the Prologue of John's Gospel." In *Doing Theology for the People of God: Studies in Honor of J. I. Packer*, ed. Donald Lewis and Alister McGrath, 105-21. Downers Grove: InterVarsity, 1996.
— "Israel in John's Gospel." In *In the Fullness of Time*, 79-94. Homebush West: Lancer, 1992.
— "Law and Grace: The Nature of the Contrast in John 1:17." *Evangelical Quarterly* 58 (1986): 25-37.
Dunn, James D.G. "Let John Be John: A Gospel for Its Time." In *The Gospel and the Gospels*, ed. Peter Stuhlmacher, 293-322. Grand Rapids: Eerdmans, 1991.
Edgar, S.L. "New Testament and Rabbinic Messianic Interpretation." *New Testament Studies* 5 (1958): 47-54.
Edwards, Ruth B. "Charin anti charitos (John 1:16): Grace and the Law in the Johannine Prologue." *Journal for the Study of the New Testament* 32 (1988): 3-15.
— "The Christological Basis of the Johannine Footwashing." In *Jesus of Nazareth: Essays on the Historical Jesus and New Testament Christology*, ed. Joel B. Green and Max Turner, 367-83. Grand Rapids: Eerdmans, 1994.
Ego, Beate. "Der Diener im Palast des himmlischen Königs: Zur Interpretation einer priesterlichen Tradition im rabbinischen Judentum." In *Königsherrschaft Gottes und himmlischer Kult im Judentum, Urchristentum und in der hellenistischen Welt*, ed. Martin Hengel and Anna Maria Schwemer, 361-83. Wissenschaftliche Untersuchungen zum Neuen Testament 55. Tübingen: Mohr Siebeck, 1991.
Elledge, C.D. "The Prince of the Congregation: Qumran 'Messianism' in the Context of *Milḥāmâ*." In *Qumran Studies: New Approaches, New Questions*, ed. Michael Thomas Davis & Brent A. Strawn, 178-207. Grand Rapids: Eerdmans, 2007.
Ellis, E. Earle. "Foreword." In *Typos: The Typological Interpretation of the Old Testament in the New*, Leonhard Goppelt, ix-xx. Translated by Donald H. Madvig. Grand Rapids: Eerdmans, 1982.
Ellis, Peter F. "Understanding the Concentric Structure of the Fourth Gospel." *St Vladimir's Theological Quarterly* 47 (2003): 131-54.

Epstein, I. "Foreword." In *Genesis*, vol. 1 of *Midrash Rabbah*, trans. H. Greedman and Maurice Simon, ix-xxxiii. London: Soncino, 1951.
Eshel, Hanan. "The Historical Background of the Pesher Interpreting Joshua's Curse on the Rebuilder of Jericho." *Revue de Qumran* 15 (1991-92): 409-20.
Evans, Craig A. "Diarchic Messianism in the Dead Sea Scrolls and the Messianism of Jesus of Nazareth." In *Dead Sea Scrolls Fifty Years after Their Discovery: Proceedings of the Jerusalem Congress, July 20-25, 1997*, ed. Lawrence H. Schiffman, Emanuel Tov, James C. VanderKam, and Galen Marquis, 558-67. Jerusalem: Israel Exploration Society, 2000.
— "The Messiah in the Dead Sea Scrolls." In *Israel's Messiah in the Bible and the Dead Sea Scrolls*, ed. Richard S. Hess and M. Daniel Carroll R., 85-102. Grand Rapids: Baker, 2002.
— "The Old Testament in the New." In *The Face of New Testament Studies: A Survey of Recent Research*, ed. Scot McKnight and Grant R. Osborne, 130-48. Grand Rapids: Baker, 2004.
— "Qumran's Messiah: How Important Is He?" In *Religion in the Dead Sea Scrolls*, ed. John J. Collins and Robert A. Kugler, 135-49. Studies in the Dead Sea Scrolls and Related Literature. Grand Rapids: Eerdmans, 2000.
Fabry, Heinz-Josef. "Altes Testament, Frühjudentum und Qumran." In *Der Messias: Perspecktiven des Alten und Neuen Testaments*, ed. Heinz-Josef Fabry and Klaus Scholtissek, 9-54. Die Neue Echter Bibel Themen 5. Würzburg: Echter, 2002.
— "Die Messianologie der Weisheitsliteratur in der Septuaginta." In *The Septuagint and Messianism: Colloquium Biblicum Lovaniense LIII, July 27-29, 2004*, ed. Michael A. Knibb, 263-89. Bibliotheca ephemeridum theologicarum lovaniensium 195. Leuven: Leuven University Press; Peeters, 2006.
— "Methoden der Schriftauslegung in den Qumranschriften." In *Stimuli: Exegese und Hermeneutik in Antike und Christentum: Festschrift für Ernst Dassmann*, ed. Georg Schöllgen and Clemens Scholten, 18-33. Jahrbuch für Antike und Christentum 23. Münster: Aschendorff, 1996.
— "Mose, der 'Gesalbte JHWHs': Messianische Aspekte der Mose-Interpretation in Qumran." In *Moses in Biblical and Extra-Biblical Traditions*, ed. Axel Graupner and Michael Wolter, 129-42. Beihefte zur Zeitschrift für die alttestamentliche Wissenschaft 372. Berlin: Walter de Gruyter, 2007.
— "Schriftverständnis und Schriftauslegung der Qumran-Essener." In *Bibel in jüdischer und christlicher Tradition: Festschrift für Johann Maier zum 60. Geburtstag*, ed. Helmut Merklein, Karlheinz Müller, and Günter Stemberger, 87-96. Bonner biblische Beiträge 88. Frankfurt: Hain, 1993.
— and Ulrich Dahmen. "Melchisedek in Bibel und Qumran." In *"Ich werde meinen Bund mit euch niemals brechen!" (Ri 2,1): Festschrift für Walter Groß zum 70. Geburtstag*, ed. Erasmus Gaß, 377-98. Herders biblische Studien 62. Freiburg: Herder, 2011.
Farelly, Nicolas. "Lire le Psaume 69 (68) en Jean 2, 13-22." *Études théologiques et religieuses* 86 (2011): 195-207.
Faure, A. "Die alttestamentlichen Zitate im 4. Evangelium und die Quellenscheidungshypothese." *Zeitschrift für die neutestamentliche Wissenschaft* 21 (1922): 99-121.
Fishbane, Michael. "Use, Authority and Interpretation of Mikra at Qumran." In *Mikra: Text, Translation, Reading and Interpretation of the Hebrew Bible in Ancient Judaism and Early Christianity*, ed. M.J. Mulder, 339-77. Compendia rerum iudaicarum ad

Novum Testamentum II/1. Assen; Philadelphia: Fortress, 1988.
Fischer, Georg. "Wie geht das Johannesevangelium mit dem Alten Testament um?" In *Im Geist und in der Wahrheit: Studien zum Johannesevangelium und zur Offenbarung des Johannes sowie andere Beiträge, Festschrift für Martin Hasitschka SJ zum 65. Geburtstag*, ed. Konrad Huber and Boris Repschinski, 3-13. Neutestamentliche Abhandlungen 52. Münster: Aschendorff, 2008.
Fitzmeyer, Joseph A. "'4QTestimonia' and the New Testament." In *Essays on the Semitic Background of the New Testament*, 59-89. London: G. Chapman, 1971.
— "The Role of Daniel 9:25-26 in the Emergence of Messianism." In *The One Who Is to Come*, 56-64. Grand Rapids: Eerdmans, 2007.
— "The Use of Explicit Old Testament Quotations in Qumran Literature and in the New Testament." *New Testament Studies* 7 (1960/1): 297-333.
Flesher, Paul V.M. "The Targumim." In *The Literary and Archaeological Sources*, part 1 of *Judaism in Late Antiquity*, ed. Jacob Neusner, 40-63. Handbook of Oriental Studies 1/16. Leiden: Brill, 1995.
Fletcher-Louis, Crispin H. "4Q374: A Discourse on the Sinai Tradition: The Deification of Moses and Early Christology." *Dead Sea Discoveries* 3 (1996): 236-52.
— "Some Reflections on Angelomorphic Humanity Texts among the Dead Sea Scrolls." *Dead Sea Discoveries* 7 (2000): 292-312.
Fortna, Robert T. "Christology in the Fourth Gospel: Redaction-Critical Perspective." *New Testament Studies* 21 (1975): 489-504.
Fraade, Steven D. "Moses and the Commandments: Can Hermeneutics, History, and Rhetoric Be Disentangled?" In *Idea of Biblical Interpretation: Essays in Honor of James L. Kugel*, ed. Hindy Najman and Judith H. Newman, 399-422. Supplements to the Journal for the Study of Judaism 83. Leiden: Brill, 2004.
Frankemölle, Hubert. "'Biblische' Theologie: Semantisch-historische Anmerkungen und Thesen." In *Studien zum jüdischen Kontext neutestamentlicher Theologien*, 1-22. Stuttgarter biblische Aufsatzbände 37. Stuttgart: Katholisches Bibelwerk, 2005. Reprinted in *Theologie und Glaube* 92 (2002): 157-76.
— "Mose in Deutungen des Neuen Testaments." *Kirche und Israel* 9 (1994): 70-86.
Freedman, David N. "The Formation of the Canon of the Old Testament: The Selection and Identification of the Torah as the Supreme Authority of the Postexilic Community." In *Religion and Law: Biblical-Judaic and Islamic Perspectives*, ed. Edwin B. Firmage, Bernard G. Weiss, and John W. Welch, 315-31. Winona Lake: Eisenbrauns, 1990.
Frey, Jörg. "Auf der Suche nach dem Kontext des vierten Evangeliums: Eine forschungsgechichtliche Einführung." In *Kontexte des Johannesevangeliums: Das vierte Evangelium in religions- und traditionsgeschichtlicher Perspektive*, ed. Jörg Frey and Udo Schnelle, 3-45. Wissenschaftliche Untersuchungen zum Neuen Testament 175. Tübingen: Mohr Siebeck, 2004.
— "Diaspora-Jewish Background oft he Fourth Gospel." *Svensk exegetisk årsbok* 77 (2012): 169-96.
— "Die Bedeutung der Qumranfunde für das Verständnis des Neuen Testaments." In *Qumran-Die Schriftrollen vom Toten Meer: Vorträge des St. Galler Qumran-Symposiums vom 2./3Juli 1999*, ed. Michael Fieger, Konrad Schmid, and Peter Schwagmeier, 129-208. Novum Testamentum et Orbis Antiquus 47. Fribourg: Academic, 2001.
— "Die 'theologia crucifixi' des Johannesevangeliums." In *Kreuzestheologie im Neuen*

Testament, ed. Andreas Dettwiler and Jean Zumstein, 169-238. Wissenschaftliche Untersuchungen zum Neuen Testament 151. Tübingen: Mohr Siebeck, 2002.

— "'Wie Mose die Schlange in der Wüste erhöht hat . . .': Zur frühjüdischen Deutung der Schlange und ihrer christologischen Rezeption in Joh 3,14f." In *Schriftauslegung im antiken Judentum und im Urchristentum*, ed. Martin Hengel and Hermut Löhr, 153-205. Wissenschaftliche Untersuchungen zum Neuen Testament 73. Tübingen: Mohr Siebeck, 1994.

— "Zum Problem der Aufgabe und Durchführung einer Theologie des Neuen Testaments." In *Aufgabe und Durchführung einer Theologie des Neuen Testaments*, ed. Cilliers Breytenbach and Jörg Frey, 3-53. Wissenschaftliche Untersuchungen zum Neuen Testament 205. Tübingen: Mohr Siebeck, 2007.

Fuhs, Hans F. "Alttestamentliche Wurzeln des Messiasanspruchs Jesu." *Theologie und Glaube* 98 (2008): 326-40.

Fuller, Reginald H. "Lower and Higher Christology in the Fourth Gospel." In *The Conversation Continues: Studies in Paul and John in Honor of J. Louis Martyn*, ed. Robert T. Fortna and Beverly R. Gaventa, 357-65. Nashville: Abingdon, 1990.

García Martínez, Florentino. "Las tradiciones sobre Melquisedec en los manuscitos de Qumrán." *Biblica* 81 (2000): 70-80.

Garland, David E. "The Fulfillment Quotations in John's Account of the Crucifixion." In *Perspectives on John: Method and Interpretation in the Fourth Gospel*, ed. Robert B. Sloan and Mikeal C. Parsons, 229-50. NABPR Special Studies Series 11. Lewiston: Edwin Mellen, 1993.

— "John 18-19: Life through Jesus' Death." *Review and Expositor* 85 (1988): 485-500.

Gawlick, Matthias. "Mose im Johannesevangelium." *Biblische Notizen* 84 (1996): 29-35.

Geiger, G. "Aufruf an Rückkehrende: Zum Sinn des Zitats von Ps 78,24b in Joh 6,31." *Biblica* 65 (1984): 449-64.

Gemünden, Petra von. "La figure de Jacob à l'époque hellénistico-romaine: L'exemple de Philon d'Alexandrie." In *Jacob: Commentaire à plusieurs voix de Gen. 25-36, mélanges offerts à Albert de Pury*, ed. Jean-Daniel Macchi, 358-70. Le Monde de la Bible 44. Geneva: Labor et Fides, 2001.

— "Palmensymbolik in Joh 12,13." *Zeitschrift des Deutschen Palästina-Vereins* 114 (1998): 39-70.

Glasson, T. Francis. "John the Baptist in the Fourth Gospel." *Expository Times* 67(1956): 245-46.

Glenny, W. Edward. "Typology: A Summary of the Present Evangelical Discussion." *Journal of the Evangelical Theological Society* 40 (1997): 627-38.

Goodwin, Charles. "How Did John Treat His Sources?" *Journal of Biblical Literature* 73 (1954): 61-75.

Gourgues, Michel. "La vigne du Père (Jn 15,1-17) ou le rassemblement des enfants de Dieu." In *Communion et réunion: Mélanges Jean-Marie Roger Tillard*, ed. Gillian Rosemary Evans, Michel Gourgues, and Jean-Marie-Roger Tillard, 265-81. Bibliotheca ephemeridum theologicarum lovaniensium 121. Louvain: Leuven University Press; Peeters, 1995.

Gosse, Bernard. "Abraham, Isaac et Jacob, Moïse et Josué, Elie et Elisée et l'unification du corpus biblique." *Estudios bíblicos* 58 (2000): 513-26.

Grappe, Christian. "Jean 1,14(-18) dans son contexte et à la lumière de la littérature intertestamentaire." *Revue d'Histoire et de Philosophie Religieuses* 80 (2000): 153-69.

— "Les deux anges de Jean 20,12: Signes de la présence mystérieuse du Logos (à la

lumière du targum d'Ex 25,22)?" *Revue d'histoire et de philosophie religieuses* 89 (2009): 169-77.
Grätz, Sebastian. "'Einen Propheten wie mich wird dir, der Herr, dein Gott erwecken': Der Berufungsbericht Jeremias und seine Rückbindung an das Amt des Mose." In *Moses in Biblical and Extra-Biblical Traditions*, ed. Axel Graupner, 61-77. Beihefte zur Zeitschrift für die Alttestamentliche Wissenschaft 372. Berlin: Walter de Gruyter, 2007.
Grau, Andreu. "Les ascension en la literature intertestamentària." *Scripta biblica* 11 (2011): 101-12.
Gruson, Marie-Odile. "Flavius Josèphe: Miracles de Jésus et de Moïse." *Mélanges de Science Religieuse* 65 (2008): 51-62.
Guijarro Oporto, Santiago. "Why Does the Gospel of Mark Begin as It Does?" *Biblical Theology Bulletin* 33 (2003): 28-38.
Gunneweg, Antonius H.J. "Sinaibund und Davidsbund." *Vetus Testamentum* 10 (1960): 335-41.
Hafemann, Scott H. "Moses in the Apocrypha and Pseudepigrapha: A Survey." *Journal for the Study of the Pseudepigrapha* 7 (1990):79-104.
— "Paul and the Exile of Israel in Galatians 3-4." In *Exile: Old Testament, Jewish, and Christian Conceptions*, ed. James Scott, 329-71. Supplements to the Journal for the Study of Judaism 56. Leiden: Brill, 1997.
— "Paul's Argument from the Old Testament and Christology in 2 Cor 1-9: The Salvation-History/Restoration Structure of Paul's Apologetic." In *Corinthian Correspondence*, ed. Reimund Bieringer, 277-303. Bibliotheca ephemeridum theologicarum lovaniensium 125. Louvain: Leuven University Press, 1996.
Hanson, Anthony T. "The Treatment in the LXX of the Theme of Seeing God." In *Septuagint, Scrolls and Cognate Writings: Papers Presented to the International Symposium on the Septuagint and Its Relations to the Dead Sea Scrolls and Other Writings, (Manchester, 1990)*, ed. George J. Brooke and Barnabas Lindars, 557-68. Septuagint and Cognate Studies Series 33. Atlanta: Scholars, 1992.
Hasel, Gerhard F. "Biblical Theology: Then, Now, and Tomorrow." *Horizons in Biblical Theology* 4 (1982): 61-93.
Hasitschka, Martin. "Die Führer Israels: Mose, Josua und die Richter." In *Alttestamentliche Gestalten im Neuen Testament: Beiträge zur biblischen Theologie*, ed. Markus Öhler, 117-40. Darmstadt: Wissenschaftliche Buchgesellschaft, 1999.
Hay, David. M. "Moses through New Testament Spectacles." *Interpretation* 44 (1990): 240-52.
Hayman, Peter. "Monotheism—A Misused Word in Jewish Studies?" *Journal of Jewish Studies* 42 (1991): 1-15.
Hays, J. Daniel. "If He Looks like a Prophet and Talks like a Prophet, Then He Must Be . . .: A Response to Daniel I. Block." In *Israel's Messiah in the Bible and the Dead Sea Scrolls*, ed. Richard S. Hess and M. Daniel Carroll R., 57-70. Grand Rapids: Baker, 2003.
Hays, Richard B. "Can the Gospels Teach us How to Read the Old Testament?" *Pro Ecclesia* 11 (2002): 402-18.
Heil, Christoph. "Jesus aus Nazaret oder Betlehem?: Historische Tradition und ironischer Stil im Johannesevangelium." In *Im Geist und in der Wahrheit: Studien zum Johannesevangelium und zur Offenbarung des Johannes sowie andere Beiträge: Festschrift für Martin Hasitschka SJ zum 65. Geburtstag*, ed. Konrad Huber &

Boris Repschinski, 109-30. Neutestamentliche Abhandlungen 52. Münster: Aschendorff, 2008.

Hengel, Martin. "Aufgaben der neutestamentlichen Wissenschaft: (Presidential Address, SNTS, Chicago, August 1993)." *New Testament Studies* 40 (1994): 321-57.

— "Jesus, der Messias Israels: Zum Streit über das 'messianische Sendungsbewußtsein' Jesu." In *Messiah and Christos: Studies in the Jewish Origins of Christianity, Presented to David Flusser on the Occasion of His Seventy-Fifth Birthday*, ed. Ithamar Gruenwald, Shaul Shaked, and Gedaliahu G. Stroumsa, 155-76. Tübingen: Mohr Siebeck, 1992.

— "Jesus der Messias Israels." In *Der messianische Anspruch Jesu und die Anfänge der Christologie: Vier Studien*, ed. Martin Hengel and Anna M. Schwemer, 1-80. Wissenschaftliche Untersuchungen zum Neuen Testament 138. Tübingen: Mohr Siebeck, 2001.

— "Jesus, the Messiah of Israel: The Debate about the 'Messianic Mission' of Jesus." In *Authenticating the Activities of Jesus*, ed. Bruce Chilton and Craig A. Evans, 323-50. New Testament Tools and Studies 28/2. Leiden: Brill, 1999.

— "Das Johannesevangelium als Quelle für die Geschichte des antiken Judentums." In *Judaica, Hellenistica, et Christiana: Kleine Schriften II*, ed. Martin Hengel with Jörg Frey and Dorothea Betz, 293-334. Wissenschaftliche Untersuchungen zum Neuen Testament 109. Tübingen: Mohr Siebeck, 1999.

— "The Old Testament in the Fourth Gospel." In *The Gospels and the Scriptures of Israel*, ed. Craig A. Evans and W. Richard Stegner, 380-95. Journal for the Study of the New Testament Supplement Series 104. Sheffield: Sheffield, 1994.

— "Die Schriftauslegung des 4. Evangeliums auf dem Hintergrund der urchristlichen Exegese." In *"Gesetz" als Thema Biblischer Theologie*, ed. Ingo Baldermann and Dwight R. Daniels, 249-88. Jahrbuch für Biblische Theologie 4. Neukirchen-Vluyn: Neukirchen, 1989.

— "'Schriftauslegung' und 'Schriftwerdung' in der Zeit des Zweiten Tempels." In *Schriftauslegung im antiken Judentum und im Urchristentum*, ed. Martin Hengel and Hermut Löhr, 1-71. Wissenschaftliche Untersuchungen zum Neuen Testament 73. Tübingen: Mohr Siebeck, 1994.

— "The Scriptures and Their Interpretation in Second Temple Period." In *The Aramaic Bible: Targums in Their Historical Context*, ed. D.R.G. Beattie and M.J. McNamara, 158-75. Journal for the Study of the Old Testament Supplement Series 166. Sheffield: JSOP, 1994.

— "Tasks of New Testament Scholarship." *Bulletin for Biblical Research* 6 (1996): 67-86.

Henten, Jan Willem van. "Moses as Heavenly Messenger in *Assumptio Mosis* 10:2 and Qumran Passages." *Journal of Jewish Studies* 54 (2003): 216-27.

Herbert, Leroy. "'Kein Bein wird ihm gebrochen werden' (Jo 19,31-37): Zur johanneischen Interpretation des Kreuzes." In *Eschatologie: Bibeltheologische und philosophische Studien zum Verhältnis von Erlösungswelt und Wirklichkeitsbewältigung, Festschrift für Engelbert Neuhäusler zur Emeritierung gewidmet von kollegen, Freunden und Schülern*, ed. Rudolf Kilian, Klemens Funk, and Peter Fassl, 73-81. St. Ottilien: EOS, 1981.

Hieke, Thomas. "Vom Verstehen biblischer Texte: Methodologisch-hermeneutische Erwägungen zum Programm einer 'biblischen Auslegung.'" *Biblische Notizen* 119-120 (2003): 71-89.

Hindley, J. C. "Witness in the Fourth Gospel." *Scottish Journal of Theology* 18 (1965): 319-37.
Hogeterp, Albert. "Eschatological Identities in the Damascus Document." In *Defining Identities: We, You, and the Other in the Dead Sea Scrolls, Proceedings of the Fifth Meeting of the IOQS in Gröningen*, ed. Florentino García Martínez and Mladen Popović, 111-30. Studies on the Texts of the Desert of Judah 70. Leiden: Brill, 2008.
Holladay, Carl H. "Ezekiel the Tragedian." In *Poets: The Epic Poets Theodotus and Philo and Ezekiel the Tragedian*, vol. 2. of *Fragments from Hellenistic Jewish Authors*, 301-529. The Society of Biblical Literature Texts and Translations 30. Atlanta: Scholars, 1989.
— "New Testament Christology: Some Considerations of Method." *Novum testamentum* 25 (1983): 257-78.
Holtz, Gundrun. "Rabbinische Literatur und Neues Testament: Alte Schwierigkeiten und neue Möglichkeiten." *Zeitschrift für die neutestamentliche Wissenschaft und die Kunde der älteren Kirche* 100 (2009): 173-98.
Hooker, Morna D. "Johannine Prologue and the Messianic Secret." *New Testament Studies* 21 (1974): 40-58.
Horbury, William. "Messianism in the Old Testament Apocrypha and Pseudepigrapha." In *King and Messiah in Israel and the Ancient Near East: Proceedings of the Oxford Old Testament Seminar*, ed. John Day, 402-33. Journal for the Study of the Old Testament Supplement Series 270. Sheffield: Sheffield, 1998.
Horsley, Richard A. "Like One of the Prophets of Old: Two Types of Popular Prophets at the Time of Jesus." *Catholic Biblical Quarterly* 47 (1985): 435-63.
Horst, Pieter W. van der. "Moses' Throne Vision in Ezekiel the Dramatist." *Journal of Jewish Studies* 34 (1983): 21-29.
— "Some Notes on the *Exagoge* of Ezekiel." In *Essays on the Jewish World of Early Christianity*, 72-93. Novum Testamentum et Orbis Antiquus 14. Fribourg: Universitätsverlag; Göttingen: Vandenhoeck & Ruprecht, 1990.
Hübner, Hans. "New Testament Interpretation of the Old Testament." In *From the Beginnings to the Middle Ages (Until 1300)*. Vol. 1 of *Hebrew Bible/Old Testament: The History of Its Interpretation*, ed. Magne Sæbø, 332-72. Göttingen: Vandenhoeck & Ruprecht, 1996.
Hugenberger, Gordon P. "Introductory Notes on Typology." In *The Right Doctrine from the Wrong Texts: Essays on the Use of the Old Testament in the New*, ed. G.K. Beale, 331-41. Grand Rapids: Baker, 1994.
— "The Servant of the Lord in the 'Servant Songs' of Isaiah: A Second Moses Figure." In *The Lord's Anointed: Interpretation of the Old Testament Messianic Texts*, ed. Philip E. Satterthwaite, Richard S. Hess, and Gordon Wenham, 105-39. Tyndale House Studies. Grand Rapids: Baker, 1995.
Hunman, Roger J. "The Function and Form of the Explicit Old Testament Quotations in the Gospel of John." *Lutheran Theological Review* 1 (1988/9): 31-54.
Hurtado, Larry W. "Does Philo Help Explain Christianity?" In *Philo und das Neue Testament: Wechselseitige Wahrnehmungen, 1. Internationales Symposium zum Corpus Judaeo-Hellenisticum 1.—4. Mail 2003, Eisenach/Jenaeds*, ed. Roland Deines and Karl-Wilhelm Niebuhr, 73-92. Wissenschaftliche Untersuchungen zum Neuen Testament 172. Tübingen: Mohr Siebeck, 2004.
Inowlocki-Meister, Sabrina. "Le Moïse des auteurs juifs hellénistiques et sa réappropriation dans la littérature apologétique chrétienne: Le cas de Clément

d'Alexandrie." In *Interprétations de Möise: Égypte, Judée, Grèce et Rome*, ed. Philippe Borgeaud, Thomas Römer, and Youri Volokhine, 103-31. Jerusalem Studies in Religion and Culture 10. Leiden: Brill, 2010.

Jacobson, Howard. "4Q368 fg. 3." *Revue de Qumran* 21 (2003): 117-18.

Janowski, Bernd. "Biblical Theology." In *The Oxford Handbook of Biblical Studies*, ed. J.W. Rogerson and Judith M. Lieu, 716-31. Oxford: Oxford University Press, 2006.

— "The One God of the Two Testaments: Basic Questions of a Biblical Theology." *Theology Today* 57 (2000): 297-324.

Jewett, Robert. "New Testament Christology: The Current Dialogue between Systematic Theologians and New Testament Scholars." *Semeia* 30 (1984): 3-12.

Johnson, Sherman E. "Notes on the Prophet-King in John." *Anglican Theological Review* 51 (1969): 35-37.

Jonge, Marinus de. "Christology and Theology in the Context of Early Christian Eschatology, Particularly in the Fourth Gospel." In *Four Gospels 1992: Festschrift Frans Neirynck*, ed. Frans van Segbroeck, 1835-53. Bibliotheca ephemeridum theologicarum lovaniensium 100. Louvain: Leuven University Press; Peeters, 1992.

— "Christology, Controversy and Community in the Gospel of John." In *Christology, Controversy and Community: New Testament Essays in Honor of David R. Catchpole*, ed. David G. Horrell and Christopher M. Tuckett, 209-30. Supplement to Novum Testamentum 99. Leiden: Brill, 2000.

— "The Conflict between Jesus and the Jews and the Radical Christology of the Fourth Gospel." *Perspectives in Religious Studies* 20 (1993): 341-55.

— "Jesus as Prophet and King in the Fourth Gospel." *Ephemeridum theologicarum lovaniensium* 47 (1973): 160-77.

— "Jewish Expectations about the 'Messiah' according to the Fourth Gospel." *New Testament Studies* 19 (1973): 246-70. Reprinted in *Jesus, Stranger from Heaven and Son of God: Jesus Christ and the Christians in Johannine Perspective*, 77-116. Missoula: The Society of Biblical Literature, 1977.

— "John the Baptist and Elijah in the Fourth Gospel." In *The Conversation Continues: Studies in Paul & John in Honor of J. Louis Martyn*, ed. Robert T. Fortna and Beverly R. Gaventa, 299-309. Nashville: Abingdon, 1990.

Joynes, Christine E. "A Question of Identity: 'Who Do People Say That I Am?': Elijah, John the Baptist and Jesus in Mark's Gospel." In *Understanding, Studying and Reading: New Testament Essays in Honour of John Ashton*, ed. Christopher Rowland and Crispin H.T. Fletcher-Louis, 15-29. Journal for the Study of the New Testament Supplement Series 153. Sheffield: Sheffield, 1998.

Katz, Peter. "Text of 2 Maccabees Reconsidered." *Zeitschrift für die neutestamentliche Wissenschaft und die Kunde der älteren Kirche* 51 (1960): 10-30.

Kierspel, Lars. "'Dematerializing' Religion: Reading John 2-4 as a Chiasm." *Biblica* 89 (2008): 526-54.

Kirk, Aan. "Memory Theory: Cultural and Cognitive Approaches." In *Understanding the Social World of the New Testament*, ed. Dietmar Neufeld and Richard E. DeMaris, 57-67. New York: Routledge, 2010.

Kirk, David R. "Heaven Opened: Intertextuality and Meaning in John 1:51." *Tyndale Bulletin* 63 (2012): 237-73.

Klappert, Bertold. "'Mose hat von mir geschrieben': Leitlinien einer Christologie im Kontext des Judentums Joh 5,39-47." In *Hebräische Bibel und ihre zweifache Nachgeschichte: Festschrift für Rolf Rendtorff zum 65. Geburtstag*, ed. Erhard Blum,

Christian Macholz, and Ekkehard W. Stegemann, 619-40. Neukirchen-Vluyn: Neukirchener, 1990.
Klauck, Hans-Josef. "Geschrieben, erfüllt, vollendet: die Schriftzitate in der Johannespassion." In *Israel und seine Heilstraditionen im vierten Evangelium: Festgabe für Johannes Beutler SJ zum 70. Geburtstag*, ed. Michael Labahn, Klaus Scholtissek, and Angelika Strotmann, 140-57. Paderborn: Schöningh, 2004.
Klein, Ralph W. "Aspects of Intertestamental Messianism." *Concordia Theological Monthly* 43 (1972): 507-17; repr. In *The Bible in Its Literary Milieu: Contemporary Essays*, ed. Vincent L. Tollers and John R. Maier, 191-203. Grand Rapids: Eerdmans, 1979.
Knight, Jonathan. "The Origin and Significance of the Angelomorphic Christology in the *Ascension of Isaiah*." *Journal of Theological Studies* 63 (2012): 66-105.
Koakley, J.F. "Jesus' Messianic Entry into Jerusalem (John 12:12-19 par.)." *Journal of Theological Studies* 46 (1995): 461-82.
Koch, C., and K. Huber. "Konzentrisches Erzählkonzept im Johannesevangelium: Skizze eines Strukturierungsvorschlags." *Protokolle zur Bibel* 12 (2003): 129-42.
Koch, Klaus. "Two Testaments—One Bible: New Trends in Biblical Theology." *Bangalore Theogical Forum* 28 (1996): 38-58.
Koskenniemi, Erkki. "Apollonius of Tyana: A Typical Theios Aner?" *Journal of Biblical Literature* 117 (1998): 455-67.
Köstenberger, Andreas J. "Hearing the Old Testament in the New: A Response." In *Hearing the Old Testament in the New Testament*, ed. Stanley E. Porter, 255-94. McMaster New Testament Studies. Grand Rapids: Eerdmans, 2006.
Kowalski, Beate. "Die Tempelreinigung Jesu nach Joh 2,13-25." *Münchener theologische Zeitschrift* 57 (2006): 194-208.
Kraus, Wolfgang. "Die Vollendung der Schrift nach Joh 19,28: Überlegungen zum Umgang mit der Schrift im Johannesevangelium." In *The Scriptures in the Gospels*, ed. Christopher M. Tuckett, 629-36. Bibliotheca ephemeridum theologicarum lovaniensium 131. Leuven: Leuven University Press, 1997.
— "Johannes und das Alte Testament: Überlegungen zum Umgang mit der Schrift im Johannesevangelium im Horizont Biblischer Theologie." *Zeitschrift für die neutestamentliche Wissenschaft* 88 (1997): 1-23.
Kreuzer, Siegfried. "'Wo ich hingehe, dahin könnt ihr nicht kommen': Joh 7,34; 8:21; 13,33 als Teil der Mosetypologie im Johannesevangelium." In *Die Kirche als historische und eschatologische Grösse: Festschrift für Kurt Niederwimmer zum 65. Geburtstag*, ed. Wilhelm Pratscher and Georg Sauer, 63-76. Frankfurt: Peter Lang, 1994.
Küchler, Max. "'Aus seiner Fülle haben wir alle empfangen': Joh 1,16a als literarisches Pendant zum antiken Bildmotiv des überfliessenden Füllhorns." In *Studien zu Matthäus und Johannes: Festschrift für Jean Zumstein zu seinem 65. Geburtstag*, ed. Andreas Dettwiler and Uta Poplutz, 135-55. Abhandlungen zur Theologie des Alten und Neuen Testaments 97. Zürich: Theologischer, 2009.
Kügler, Joachim. "Das Johannesevangelium." In *Einleitung in das Neue Testament*, ed. Martin Ebner and Stefan Schreiber, 208-28. Kohlhammer Studienbücher Theologie 6. Stuttgart: Kohlhammer, 2008.
— "Der König als Brotspender: Religionsgeschichtliche Überlegungen zu JosAs 4,7; 25,5 und Joh 6,15." *Zeitschrift für die Neutestamentliche Wissenschaft* 89 (1998): 118-24.
— "'Meine Königsherrschaft ist nicht von dieser Welt!' (Joh 18,36): Zur Veränderung der

Gottesreich-Botschaft im Johannesevangelium." *Bibel und Kirche* 62 (2007): 94-97.
— "Spuren ägyptisch-hellenistischer Königstheologie bei Philo von Alexandria." In *Ägypten und der östliche Mittelmeerraum im 1. Jahrtausend v. Chr.: Akten des interdisziplinären Symposions am Institut für Ägyptologie der Universität München 25.-27.10.1996*, ed. Manfred Görg and Günther Hölbl, 231-49. Ägypten und Altes Testament 44. Wiesbaden: Harrassowitz, 2000.
Kuhn, Karl G. "Die in Palästina gefundenen hebräischen Texte und das Neue Testament." *Zeitschrift für Theologie und Kirche* 47 (1950): 192-211.
Kvalbein, Hans. "Die Wunder der Endzeit: Beobachtungen zu 4Q521 und Matth 11,5p." *Zeitschrift für die neutestamentliche Wissenschaft und die Kunde der älteren Kirche* 88 (1997): 111-25.
— "The Wonders of the End-Time: Metaphoric Language in 4Q521 and the Interpretation of Matthew 11.5 Par." *Journal for the Study of the Pseudepigrapha* 18 (1998): 87-110.
Labahn, Michael. "Between Tradition and Literary Art: The Miracle Tradition in the Fourth Gospel." *Biblica* 80 (1999): 178-203.
— "Controversial Revelation in Deed and Word: The Feeding of the Five Thousand and Jesus' Crossing of the Sea as a 'Prelude' to the Johannine Bread of Life Discourse." *Irish Biblical Studies* 22 (2000): 146-81.
— "Deuteronomy in John's Gospel." In *Deuteronomy in the New Testament: The New Testament and the Scriptures of Israel*, ed. Maarten J.J. Menken and Steve Moyise, 82-98. The Library of New Testament Studies 358. London: T & T Clark, 2007.
— "Eine Spurensuche anhand von Joh 5.1-18: Bemerkungen zu Wachstum und Wandel der Heilung eines Lahmen." *New Testament Studies* 44 (1998): 159-79.
— "Jesus und die Autorität der Schrift im Johannesevangelium: Überlegungen zu einem spannungsreichen Verhältnis." In *Israel und seine Heilstraditionen im Johannesevangelium: Festgabe für Johannes Beutler SJ zum 70. Geburtstag*, ed. Michael Labahn, Klaus Scholtissek, and Angelika Strotmann, 185-206. Paderborn: Schöningh, 2004.
— and Manfred Lang. "Johannes und die Synoptiker: Positionen und Impulse seit 1990." In *Kontexte des Johannesevangeliums: Das vierte Evangelium in religions und traditionsgeschichtlicher Perspektive*, ed., Jörg Frey & Udo Schnelle, 443-515. Wissenschaftliche Untersuchungen zum Neuen Testament 175. Tübingen: Mohr Siebeck, 2004.
Lanfranchi, Pierluigi. "Reminiscences of Ezekiel's *Exagoge* in Philo's *De vita Mosis*." In *Moses in Biblical and Extra-Biblical Traditions*, ed. Axel Graupner and Michael Wolter, 143-50. Beihefte zur Zeitschrift für die alttestamentliche Wissenschaft 372. Berlin: Walter de Gruyter, 2007.
Lange, Armin. "The Essene Position on Magic and Divination." In *Legal Texts and Legal Issues: Proceedings of the Second Meeting of the International Organization for Qumran Studies Cambridge 1995, Published in Honour of Joseph M. Baumgarten*, ed. Moshe Bernstein, Florentino García Martínez, and John Kampen, 377-435. Studies on the Texts of the Desert of Judah 23. Leiden: Brill, 1997.
Langner, Cordula. "Was für ein König ist Jesus?" In *Israel und seine Heilstraditionen im Johannesevangelium: Festgabe für Johannes Beutler SJ zum 70. Geburtstag*, ed. Michael Labahn, Klaus Scholtissek, and Angelika Strotmann, 247-68. Paderborn: Ferdinand Schöningh, 2004.
La Potterie, Ignace de. "'C'est lui qui a ouvert la voie': La finale du prologue johannique." *Biblica* 69 (1988): 340-70.

— "La tunique 'non divisée' de Jésus, symbole de l'unité messianique." In *New Testament Age: Essays in Honor of Bo Reicke*, 2 vols, ed. William C. Weinrich, 127-38. Macon: Mercer University Press, 1984.

Latour, Élie. "Une proposition de reconstruction de l'Apocryphe de Moïse (1Q29, 4Q375, 4Q376, 4Q408)." *Revue de Qumran* 88 (2006): 575-91.

Lelièvre, André. "Qui parle dans les Psaumes." *Foi et vie* 87 (1988): 3-13.

Leonhardt-Balzer, Jutta. "Der Logos und die Schöpfung: Streiflichter bei Philo (Op 20-25) und im Johannesprolog (Joh 1,1-18)." In *Kontexte des Johannesevangeliums: Das vierte Evangelium in religions- und traditionsgeschichtlicher Perspektive*, ed. Jörg Frey and Udo Schnelle, 295-320. Wissenschaftliche Untersuchungen zum Neuen Testament 175. Tübingen: Mohr Siebeck, 2004.

Lerle, Ernst. "Die Ahnenverzeichnisse Jesu: Versuch einer christologischen Interpretation." *Zeitschrift für die neutestamentliche Wissenschaft und die Kunde der älteren Kirche* 72 (1981): 112-17.

Leske, Adrian M. "Context and Meaning of Zechariah 9:9." *Catholic Biblical Quarterly* 62 (2000): 663-78.

Lewis, Jack P. "The Semitic Background of the Gospel of John." In *Johannine Studies*, 97-110. Malibu, CA: Pepperdine University Press, 1989.

Lichtenberger, Hermann. "Geschichte und Heilsgeschichte in der Damaskusschrift." In *Heil und Geschichte: Die Geschichtsbezogenheit des Heils und das Problem der Heilsgeschichte in der biblischen Tradition und in der theologischen Deutung*, ed. Jörg Frey, Stefan Krauter, Hermann Lichtenberger, 175-84. Wissenschaftliche Untersuchungen zum Neuen Testament 248. Tübingen: Mohr Siebeck, 2009.

— "Messiasvorstellungen in Qumran und die neutestamentliche Christologie." *Communio viatorum* 44 (2002): 139-60.

— "Täufergemeinden und frühchristliche Täuferpolemik im letzten Drittel des 1. Jahrhunderts." *Zeitschrift für Theologie und Kirche* 84 (1987): 36-57.

Lieu, Judith. "Biblical Theology and the Johannine Literature." In *New Directions in Biblical Theology: Papers of the Aarhus Conference, 16-19 September 1992*, ed. Sigfred Pedersen, 93-107. Supplements to Novum Testamentum 76. Leiden: Brill, 1994.

Lindars, Barnabas. "The Son of Man in the Johannine Christology." In *Christ and Spirit in the New Testament: In Honor of Charles Francis Digby Moule*, ed. Barnabas Lindars and Stephen S. Smalley, 43-60. Cambridge: Cambridge University Press, 1973.

Lindemann, Andreas. "Mose und Jesus Christus: Zum Verständnis des Gesetzes im Johannesevangelium." In *Das Urchristentum in seiner literarischen Geschichte: Festschrift für Jürgen Becker zum 65. Geburtstag*, ed. Ulrich Mell and Ulrich B. Müller, 309-34. Beiheft zur Zeitschrift für die neutestamentliche Wissenschaft und die Kunde der älteren Kirche 100. Berlin: Walter de Gruyter, 1999.

Loader, William. "Jesus and the Law in John." In *Theology and Christology in the Fourth Gospel: Essays by the Members of the SNTS Johannine Writings Seminar*, ed. Gilbert van Belle, Jan G. van der Watt, and P.J. Maritz, 135-54. Bibliotheca ephemeridum theologicarum lovaniensium 184. Leuven: Leuven University, 2005.

— "'Your Law'—the Johannine Perspective." In *". . . was ihr auf dem Weg verhandelt habt": Beiträge zur Exegese und Theologie des Neuen Testaments, Festschrift für Ferdinand Hahn zum 75. Geburtstag*, ed. Peter Müller, Christine Gerber, and Thomas Knöppler, 63-74. Neukirchen-Vluyn: Neukirchener, 2001.

Logan, Alastair H.B. "John and the Gnostics: The Significance of the Apocryphon of John for the Debate about the Origins of the Johannine Literature." *Journal for the Study of the New Testament* 43 (1991): 41-69. Reprinted in *The Johannine Writings: A Sheffield Reader*, ed. Stanley E. Porter and Craig A. Evans, 109-37. The Biblical Seminar 32. Sheffield: Sheffield, 1995.

Lohfink, Norbert. "Distribution of the Functions of Power: The Laws concerning Public Offices in Deuteronomy 16:18-18:22." In *A Song of Power and the Power of Song: Essays on the Book of Deuteronomy*, ed. Duane L. Christensen, 336-52. Sources for Biblical and Theological Study 3. Winona Lake: Eisenbrauns, 1993.

Löhr, Hermut. "Isaak, Jakob, Esau, Josef." In *Alttestamentliche Gestalten im Neuen Testament: Beiträge zur biblischen Theologie*, ed. Markus Öhler, 75-96. Darmstadt: Wissenschaftliche Buchgesellschaft, 1999.

Loiseau, Anne-Françoise. "Traditions évangéliques et herméneutique juive: Le serpent d'airain de Jean ne repose-t-il pas sur une guématrie?" *Ephemeridum theologicarum lovaniensium* 83 (2007): 155-63.

Longenecker, Richard N. "Three Ways of Understanding Relations between the Testaments: Historically and Today." In *Tradition and Interpretation in the New Testament: Essays in Honor of E. Earle Ellis for His 60th Birthday*, ed. Gerald F. Hawthorne and Otto Betz, 22-32. Grand Rapids: Eerdmans; Tübingen: Mohr Siebeck, 1987.

——— "'Who is the Prophet Talking About?': Some Reflections on the New Testament's Use of the Old." *Themelios* 13 (1987): 4-8.

Luc, Devillers. "Le prologue du quatrième évangile: Clé de voûte de la littérature johannique." *New Testament Studies* 58 (2012): 317-30.

Lunt, H.G. "Ladder of Jacob." In *The Old Testament Pseudepigrapha*, ed. James H. Charlesworth, 2:401-11. The Anchor Bible Reference Library. New York: Doubleday, 1985.

Lust, Johan. "Mic 5,1-3 in Qumran and in the New Testament, and Messianism in the Septuagint." In *Scriptures in the Gospels*, ed. Christopher M. Tuckett, 65-88. Bibliotheca ephemeridum theologicarum lovaniensium 131. Louvain: Leuven University Press; Peeters, 1997.

Luz, Ulrich. "Das Neue Testament." In *Gesetz*, ed. Rudolf Smend and Ulrich Luz, 58-139. Kohlhammer Taschenbücher 1015. Stuttgart: Kohlhammer, 1981.

——— "Relecture? Reprise!: Ein Gespräch mit Jean Zumstein." In *Studien zu Matthäus und Johannes: Festschrift für Jean Zumstein zu seinem 65. Geburtstag*, ed. Andreas Dettwiler & Uta Poplutz, 233-50. Abhandlungen zur Theologie des Alten und Neuen Testaments 97. Zürich: Theologischer, 2009.

Maier, Johann. "Early Jewish Biblical Interpretation in the Qumran Literature." In *From the Beginnings to the Middle Ages (Until 1300)*. Vol. 1 of *Hebrew Bible—Old Testament: The History of its Interpretation*, ed. M. Saebo, 108-29. Göttingen: Vandenhoeck & Ruprecht, 1996.

——— "Schriftrezeption im jüdischen Umfeld des Johannesevangeliums." In *Israel und seine Heilstraditionen im Johannessevangelium: Festgabe für Johannes Beutler SJ zum 70. Geburtstag*, ed. Michael Labahn, Klaus Scholtissek, and Angelika Strotmann, 54-90. Paderborn: Schöningh, 2004.

Makiello, Phoebe. "Was Moses Considered to Be an Angel by Those at Qumran?" In *Moses in Biblical and Extra-Biblical Traditions*, ed. Axel Graupner and Michael Wolter, 115-27. Beihefte zur Zeitschrift für die alttestamentliche Wissenschaft

372. Berlin: Walter de Gruyter, 2007.
Manns, Frédéric. "'Pour que l'Ecriture s'accomplît': Vers une rétroversion araméenne." *Estudios Bíblicos* 66 (2008): 429-44.
—— "Zacharie 12,10 relu en Jean 19,37." *Studii biblici Franciscani liber annuus* 56 (2006): 301-10.
Marshall, I. Howard. "An Assessment of Recent Developments." In *It is Written: Scripture Citing Scripture: Essays in Honour of Barnabas Lindars*, ed. D.A. Carson and H.G.M. Williamson, 1-24. Cambridge: Cambridge University Press, 1988.
Martin-Achard, Robert. "Israël, peuple sacerdotal." *Cahiers de la revue de théologie et de philosophie* (1984): 129-46.
—— "Moïse, figure du médiateur selon l'Ancien Testament." *Cahiers de la revue de théologie et de philosophie* 11 (1984): 107-28.
Martínez, Florentino García. "Escatologización de los escritos proféticos en Qumrán." *Estudios bíblicos* 44 (1986): 101-16.
—— "Messianic Hopes in the Qumran Writings." In *The People of the Dead Sea Scrolls: Their Writings, Beliefs, and Practices*, ed. Florentino García Martínez and Julio Trebolle Barrera, 159-89. Leiden: Brill, 1995.
—— "Two Messianic Figures in the Qumranic Texts." In *Current Research and Technological Developments on the Dead Sea Scrolls: Conference on the Texts from the Judean Desert, Jerusalem, 30 April, 1995*, ed. Donald W. Parry and Stephen David Ricks, 14-40. Studies on the Texts of the Desert of Judah 20. Leiden: Brill, 1996.
Martínez, Florentino García, Eibert J.C. Tigchelaar, and Adam S. van der Woude. "11QMelchizedek." In *Qumran Cave 11, II: 11Q2-18, 11Q20-31*, 221-41. Discoveries in the Judaean Desert 23. Oxford: Clarendon, 1998.
Martyn, J. Louis. "We Have Found Elijah." In *Jews, Greeks, and Christians: Essays in Honor of William David Davies*, ed. R. Hamerton-Kelly and R. Scroggs, 181-219. Studies in Judaism in Late Antiquity 21. Leiden: Brill, 1976. Reprinted in *The Gospel of John in Christian History*, 9-54. Theological Inquiries. New York: Paulist, 1979.
Mastin, B.A. "Neglected Feature of the Christology of the Fourth Gospel." *New Testament Studies* 22 (1975): 32-51.
McBride, S. Dean, Jr. "Transcendent Authority: The Role of Moses in Old Testament Traditions." *Interpretation* 44 (1990): 229-39.
McConville, J.G. "King and Messiah in Deuteronomy and the Deuteronomistic History." In *King and Messiah in Israel and the Ancient Near East: Proceedings of the Oxford Old Testament Seminar*, ed. John Day, 271-95. Journal for the Study of the Old Testament Supplement Series 270. Sheffield: Sheffield, 1998.
McDonald, Nathan. "Monotheism." In *The World of the New Testament: Cultural, Social, and Historical Contexts*, ed. Joel B. Green and Lee Martin McDonald, 77-84. Grand Rapids: Baker, 2013.
McHugh, John. "'In Him Was Life.'" In *Jews and Christians: The Parting of the Ways A.D. 70 to 135, the Second Durham-Tübingen Research Symposium on Earliest Christianity and Judaism (Durham, September, 1989)*, ed. James D.G. Dunn, 123-58. Grand Rapids: Eerdmans, 1999.
McLay, R. Timothy. "Biblical Texts and the Scriptures for the New Testament Church." In *Hearing the Old Testament in the New Testament*, ed. Stanley E. Porter, 38-58. McMaster New Testament Studies. Grand Rapids: Eerdmans, 2006.
Mealand, David L. "Christology of the Fourth Gospel." *Scottish Journal of Theology* 31 (1978): 449-67.

Meeks, Wayne A. "The Divine Agent and His Counterfeit in Philo and the Fourth Gospel." In *Aspects of Religious Propaganda in Judaism and Early Christianity*, ed. Elisabeth Schüssler Fiorenza, 43-67. University of Notre Dame Center for the Study of Judaism and Christianity in Antiquity 2. Notre Dame: University of Notre Dame Press, 1976.
— "The Man from Heaven in Johannine Sectarianism." *Journal of Biblical Literature* 91 (1972): 44-72.
— "Moses as God and King." In *Religions in Antiquity: Essays in Memory of Erwin Ramsdell Goodenough*, ed. Jacob Neusner, 354-71. Studies in the History of Religions 14. Leiden: Brill, 1968.
Mees, Michael. "Jesu Selbstzeugnis nach Joh 5,19-30 in frühchristlicher Sicht." *Ephemerides theologicae Lovanienses* 62 (1986): 102-17.
— "Simon Magus in Recent Research." *Religious Studies Review* 3 (1977): 130-42.
Menken, Maarten J.J. "Allusions to the Minor Prophets in the Fourth Gospel." *Neotestamentica* 44 (2010): 67-84.
— "The Christology of the Fourth Gospel: A Survey of Recent Research." In *From Jesus to John: Essays on Jesus and New Testament Christology in Honour of Marinus de Jonge*, ed. Martinus C. de Boer, 292-320. Journal for the Study of the New Testament Supplement Series 84. Sheffield: JSOT, 1993.
— "Interpretation of the Old Testament and the Resurrection of Jesus in John's Gospel." In *Resurrection in the New Testament*, ed. Reimund Bieringer, 189-205. Bibliotheca ephemeridum theologicarum lovaniensium 165. Leuven: Leuven University Press, 2002.
— "Die jüdischen Feste im Johannesevangelium." In *Israel und seine Heilstraditionen im Johannesevangelium: Festgabe für Johannes Beutler SJ zum 70. Geburtstag*, ed. Michael Labahn, Klaus Scholtissek, and Angelika Strotmann, 269-86. Paderborn: Ferdinand Schöningh, 2004.
— "The Minor Prophets in John's Gospel." In *The Minor Prophets in the New Testament: The New Testament and the Scriptures of Israel*, ed. M.J.J. Menken & Steve Moyise, 79-96. The Library of New Testament Studies 377. London: T & T Clark, 2009.
— "Observations on the Significance of the Old Testament in the Fourth Gospel." In *Theology and Christology in the Fourth Gospel: Essays by the Members of the SNTS Johannine Writings Seminar*, ed. G. van Belle, J.G. van der Watt, and P. Maritz, 155-76. Bibliotheca ephemeridum theologicarum lovaniensium 184. Leuven: Leuven University, 2005; repr. *Neotestamentica* 33 (1999): 125-43.
— "Old Testament Quotations in the Gospel of John." In *New Testament Writers and the Old Testament: An Introduction*, ed. John M. Court, 29-45. London: SPCK, 2002.
— "The Origin of the Old Testament Quotation in John 7:38." *Novum testamentum* 38 (1996): 160-75.
— "The Provenance and Meaning of the Old Testament Quotation in John 6:31." *Novum testamentum* 30 (1988): 39-56.
— "The Quotations from Zech 9,9 in Mt 21,5 and in Jn 12,15." In *John and the Synoptics*, ed. Adelbert Denaux, 571-78. Bibliotheca ephemeridum theologicarum lovaniensium 101. Leuven: Leuven University Press, 1992.
— "Die Redaktion des Zitates aus Sach 9:9 in Joh 12:15." *Zeitschrift für die neutestamentliche Wissenschaft* 80 (1989): 193-209.
— "The Use of the Septuagint in Three Quotations in John: Jn 10,34; 12,38; 19,24." In *Scriptures in the Gospels*, ed. C.M. Tuckett, 367-93. Bibliotheca ephemeridum theologicarum lovaniensium 131. Louvain: Leuven University Press, 1997.

Merrill, Eugene H. "Royal Priesthood: An Old Testament Messianic Motif." *Bibliotheca Sacra* 150 (1993): 50-61.
Metzger, Bruce M. "The Formulas Introducing Quotations in the N.T. and the Mishna." *Journal of Biblical Literature* 70 (1951): 297-307.
— "The Fourth Book of Ezra." In *The Old Testament Pseudepigrapha*, ed. James H. Charlesworth, 1:517-24. The Anchor Bible Reference Library. New York: Doubleday, 1985.
Metzner, Rainer. "Der Geheilte von Johannes 5: Repräsentant des Unglaubens." *Zeitschrift für die neutestamentliche Wissenschaft* 90 (1999): 177-93.
Meynet, Roland. "Jésus, fils de David dans l'évangile de Luc." In *Figures de David à travers la Bible: XVIIe congrès de l'ACFEB (Lille, 1er-5 septembre 1997)*, ed. Louis Desrousseaux and Jacques Vermeylen, 413-28. Lectio divina 177. Paris: Cerf, 1999.
Michaelis, Wilhelm. "Joh. 1,51, Gen. 28,12 und das Menschensohn-Problem." *Theologisch Literaturzeitung* 85 (1960): 561-78.
Michel, Otto. "Der aufsteigende und herabsteigende Gesandte." In *The New Testament Age: Essays in Honor of Bo Reicke*, ed. William C. Weinrich, 2:335-61. Macon: Mercer University Press, 1984.
Milik, Jozef Tadeusz. "Lettre de Siméon Bar Kokheba." *Revue biblique* 60 (1953): 276-94.
Miller, Merrill P. "The Problem of the Origins of a Messianic Conception of Jesus." In *Redescribing Christian Origins*, ed. Ron Cameron and Merrill P. Miller, 301-35. The Society of Biblical Literature Symposium Series 28. Atlanta: The Society of Biblical Literature, 2004.
Miller, Paul. "'They Saw His Glory and Spoke of Him': The Gospel of John and the Old Testament." In *Hearing the Old Testament in the New Testament*, ed. Stanley E. Porter, 127-51. McMaster New Testament Studies. Grand Rapids: Eerdmans, 2006.
Mitchell, David C. "The Fourth Deliverer: A Josephite Messiah in 4QTestimonia." *Biblica* 86 (2005): 545-53.
Moenikes, Ansgar. "Die Tora des Mose: Beispiel eines kanongeschichtlichen Prozess in der antiken Religionsgeschichte." In *Hairesis: Festschrift für Karl Hoheisel zum 65. Geburtstag*, ed. Manfred Hutter, Wassilios Klein, and Ulrich Vollmer, 19-32. Jahrbuch für Antike und Christentum 34. Münster: Aschendorff, 2002.
Moloney, Francis J. "The Gospel of John: the 'End' of Scripture." *Interpretation* 63(2009): 357-66.
— "Israel, the People and the Jews in the Fourth Gospel." In *Israel und seine Heilstraditionen im Johannessevangelium: Festgabe für Johannes Beutler SJ zum 70. Geburtstag*, ed. Michael Labahn, Klaus Scholtissek, and Angelika Strotmann, 351-64. Paderborn: Schöningh, 2004.
— "Narrative and Discourse at the Feast of Tabernacles: John 7:1-8:59." In *Word, Theology, and Community in John*, ed. John Painter, R. Alan Culpepper, and Fernando F. Segovia, 155-72. St. Louis: Chalice, 2002.
Morgan, Richard. "Fulfillment in the Fourth Gospel: The Old Testament Foundations." *Interpretation* 11 (1957): 155-65.
Morgen, Michèle. "La promesse de Jésus à Nathanaël (Jn 1:51): Éclairée par la hagaddah de Jacob-Israël." *Revue des sciences religieuses* 67 (1993): 3-21.
— "Le Fils de l'homme élevé en vue de la vie éternelle (Jn 3, 14-15 éclairé par diverses traditions juives)." *Revue des sciences religieuses* 68 (1994): 5-17.
Moessner, David P. "Paul and the Pattern of the Prophet like Moses in Acts." *The Society*

of *Biblical Literature Seminar Papers* 22 (1983): 203-12.
Motyer, Stephen. "Two Testaments, One Biblical Theology." In *Between Two Horizons: Spanning New Testament Studies and Systematic Theology*, ed. Joel B. Green and Max Turner, 143-64. Grand Rapids: Eerdmans, 2000.
Moyise, Steve. "Can We Use the New Testament in the Way Which the New Testament Authors Use the Old Testament?" *In die Skriflig* 36 (2002): 643-60.
— "Intertextuality and the Study of the Old Testament in the New Testament." In *The Old Testament in the New Testament: Essays in Honour of J.L. North*, ed. Steve Moyise, 14-41. Journal for the Study of the New Testament Supplement Series 189. Sheffield: Sheffield, 2000.
— "Scripture in the New Testament: Literary and Theological Perspectives." *Neo Testamentica* 42 (2008): 305-26.
Muddiman, John. "The Assumption of Moses and the Epistle of Jude." In *Moses in Biblical and Extra-Biblical Traditions*, ed. Axel Graupner and Michael Wolter, 169-80. Beiheft zur Zeitschrift für die alttestamentliche Wissenschaft 372. Berlin: Walter de Gruyter, 2007.
Muilenburg, James. "Intercession of the Covenant Mediator." In *Words and Meanings: Essays Presented to David Winton Thomas on His Retirement from the Regius Professorship of Hebrew in the University of Cambridge, 1968*, ed. Peter R. Ackroyd and Barnabas Lindars, 159-81. Cambridge: Cambridge University Press, 1968.
Müller, Mogens. "Neutestamentliche Theologie als Biblische Theologie: Einige grundsätzliche Überlegungen." *New Testament Studies* 43(1997): 475-90.
Müller, Ulrich B. "Die Heimat des Johannesevangeliums." *Zeitschrift für die neutestamentliche Wissenschaft und die Kunde der älteren Kirche* 97 (2006): 44-63.
Munnich, Olivier. "Le messianisme à la lummière des livres prophétiques de la Bible grecque." In *Septuagint and Messianism*, ed. Michael A. Knibb, 327-55. Bibliotheca ephemeridum theologicarum lovaniensium 195. Leuven: Leuven University Press; Peeters, 2006.
Muñoa, Phillip. "Raphael, Azariah and Jesus of Nazareth: Tobit's Significance for Early Christology." *Journal for the Study of the Pseudepigrapha* 22 (2012): 3-39.
Mußner, Franz. "Die 'semantische Achse' des Johannesevangeliums: Ein Versuch." In *Jesus von Nazareth im Umfeld Israels und der Urkirche: Gesammelte Aufsätze*, ed. Michael Theobald, 260-69. Wissenschaftliche Untersuchungen zum Neuen Testament 111. Tübingen: Mohr Siebeck, 1999.
Nagel, Titus. "Zur Gnostisierung der johanneischen Tradition: Das 'Geheime Evangelium nach Johannes' (Apokryphon Johannis) als gnostische Zusatzoffernbarung zum vierten Evangelium." In *Kontexte des Johannesevangeliums: Das vierte Evangelium in religions- und traditionsgeschichtlicher Perspektive*, ed. Jörg Frey und Udo Schnelle, 675-94. Wissenschaftliche Untersuchungen zum Neuen Testament 175. Tübingen: Mohr Siebeck, 2004.
Nash, Steven B. "Psalm 2 and the Son of God in the Fourth Gospel." In *Exegetical Studies*, vol. 2 of *Early Christian Literature and Intertextuality*, ed. Craig A. Evans and H. Daniel Zacharias, 85-102. The Library of New Testament Studies 392. London: T & T Clark, 2009.
Neeb, John H.C. "Jacob/Jesus Typology in John 1,51." *Proceedings, Eastern Great Lakes and Midwest Biblical Societies* 12 (1992): 83-89.
Neufeld, Dietmar. "And When That One Comes?: Aspects of Johannine Messianism." In *Eschatology, Messianism, and the Dead Sea Scrolls*, ed. Craig A. Evans and Peter W.

Flint, 120-40. Studies in the Dead Sea Scrolls and Related Literature 1. Grand Rapids: Eerdmans, 1997.
Newsom, Carol A. "4Q374: A Discourse on the Exodus/Conquest Tradition." In *The Dead Sea Scrolls: Forty Years of Research*, ed. Devorah Dimant and Uriel Rappaport, 40-52. Studies on the Texts of the Desert of Judah 10. Leiden: Brill, 1992; repr. *Qumrân Cave 4 XIV: Parabiblical Texts*, part 2, ed. M. Broshi, 99-110. Discoveries in the Judaean Desert 19. Oxford: Clarendon, 1995.
— "4Q378 and 4Q379: An Apocryphon of Joshua." In *Qumranstudien: Vorträge und Beiträge der Teilnehmer des Qumranseminars auf dem internationalen Treffen der The Society of Biblical Literature, Münster, 25.-26. Juli 1993*, ed. Heinz-Josef Fabry, Armin Lange, and Hermann Lichtenberger, 35-85. Schriften des Institutum Judaicum Delitzschianum 4. Göttingen: Vandenhoeck & Ruprecht, 1996.
Neyrey, Jerome H. "The Jacob Allusions in Joh 1:51." *Catholic Biblical Quarterly* 44 (1982): 586-605.
— "Jacob Traditions and the interpretation of John 4:10-26." *Catholic Biblical Quarterly* 41 (1979): 419-37.
Nickelsburg, George W.E. "Abraham the Convert: A Jewish Tradition and Its Use by the Apostle Paul." In *Biblical Figures Outside the Bible*, ed. Michael E. Stone and Theodore A. Bergren, 151-75. Harrisburg: Trinity, 1998.
— "The Bible Rewritten and Expanded." In *Jewish Writings of the Second Temple Period: Apocrypha, Pseudepigrapha, Qumran Sectarian Writings, Philo, Josephus*, ed. Michael E. Stone, 89-156. Compendia rerum iudaicarum ad Novum Testamentum 2/II. Assen: Van Gorcum, 1984.
Niebuhr, Karl-Wilhelm. "Die Werke des eschatologischen Freudenboten: 4Q521 und die Jesusüberlieferung." In *The Scriptures in the Gospels*, ed. Christopher M. Tuckett, 637-46. Bibliotheca ephemeridum theologicarum lovaniensium 131. Leuven: Leuven University Press, 1997.
Nielsen, Jesper Tang. "The Narrative Structure of Glory and Glorification in the Fourth Gospe." *New Testament Studies* 56 (2010): 343-66.
Nihan, Christophe. "'Un Prophète Comme Moïse' (Deutéronome 18,15): Genèse Et Relectures D'une construction Deutéronomiste." In *La Construction de la Figure de Moïse*, ed. Thomas Römer, 43-76. Supplément à Transeuphratène 13. Paris: Gabalda, 2007.
Nilsen, Tina Dykesteen. "The True and the False: The Structure of John 4,16-26." *Biblische Notizen* 128 (2006): 61-64.
North, Wendy E.S. "Monotheism and the Gospel of John: Jesus, Moses, and the Law." In *Early Jewish and Christian Monotheism*, ed. Loren T. Stuckenbruck and Wendy E.S. North, 155-66. Journal for the Study of the New Testament Supplement Series 263. London: T & T Clark, 2004.
Novakovic, Lidija. "4Q521: The Works of the Messiah or the Signs of the Messianic Time?" In *Qumran Studies: New Approaches, New Questions*, ed. Michael Thomas Davis & Brent A. Strawn, 208-31. Grand Rapids: Eerdmans, 2007.
Nwaoru, Emmanuel O. "The Motif 'Food of Life' in Biblical and Extra-Biblical Traditions." *Biblische Notizen* 105 (2000): 16-27.
Oegema, Gerbern S. "Messianic Expectations in the Qumran Writings: Theses on Their Development." In *Qumran-Messianism: Studies on the Messianic Expectations in the Dead Sea Scrolls*, ed. James H. Charlesworth, Hermann Lichtenberger, and Gerbern S. Oegema, 53-82. Tübingen: Mohr Siebeck, 1998.

O'Grady, John F. "Jesus the Revelation of God in the Fourth Gospel." *Biblical Theology Bulletin* 25 (1995): 161-5.
Öhler, Markus. "Elijah und Elischa." In *Alttestamentliche Gestalten im Neuen Testament: Beiträge zur biblischen Theologie*, ed. Markus Öhler, 184-203. Darmstadt: Wissenschaftliche Buchgesellschaft, 1999.
O'Neill, J.C. "The Trinity and the Incarnation as Jewish Doctrines." In *Who did Jesus Think He Was?*, 94-114. Biblical Interpretation Series 11. Leiden: Brill, 1995.
Onuki, Takashi. "Fleischwerdung des Logos und Fehltritt der Sophia—Erwägungen zur johanneischen und gnostischen Lichtsprache." In *". . . was ihr auf dem Weg verhandelt habt": Beiträge zur Exegese und Theologie des Neuen Testaments, Festschrift für Ferdinand Hahn zum 75. Geburtstag*, ed. Peter Müller, Christine Gerber, and Thomas Knöppler, 75-86. Neukirchen-Vluyn: Neukirchener, 2001.
O'Rourke, John J. "Explicit Old Testament Citations in the Gospels." *Studia Montis Regii* 7 (1964): 37-60.
— "John's Fulfillment Texts." *Sciences ecclésiastiques* 19 (1967): 433-43.
O'Toole, Robert F. "The Parallels between Jesus and Moses." *Biblical Theology Bulletin* 20 (1990): 22-29.
Paganini, Simone. "Von Ezechiel zur Tempelrolle: Der Tempel als Realität und Vision." In *Qumran und die Archäologie: Texte und Kontexte*, ed. Jörg Frey, Carsten Claussen, and Nadine Kessler, 399-419. Wissenschaftliche Untersuchungen zum Neuen Testament 278. Tübingen: Mohr Siebeck, 2011.
Painter, John. "C.H. Dodd and the Christology of the Fourth Gospel." *Journal of Theology for Southern Africa* 59 (1987): 42-56.
— "The Enigmatic Johannine Son of Man." In *Four Gospels 1992: Festschrift Frans Neirynck*, ed. F. van Segbroeck, 1869-87. Bibliotheca ephemeridum theologicarum lovaniensium 100. Louvain: Leuven University Press; Peeters, 1992.
— "Inclined to God: The Quest for Eternal Life—Bultmannian Hermeneutics and the Theology of the Fourth Gospel." In *Exploring the Gospel of John: In Honor of D. Moody Smith*, ed. R. Alan Culpepper and C. Clifton Black, 346-68. Louisville: Westminster John Knox, 1996.
— "Monotheism and Dualism: John and Qumran." In *Theology and Christology in the Fourth Gospel: Essays by the Members of the SNTS Johannine Writings Seminar*, ed. G. van Belle, J.G. van der Watt, and P. Maritz, 225-44. Bibliotheca ephemeridum theologicarum lovaniensium 184. Leuven: Leuven University, 2005.
— "The Point of John's Christology: Christology, Conflict and Community in John." In *Christology, Controversy and Community: New Testament Essays in Honor of David R. Catchpole*, ed. David G. Horrell and Christopher M. Tuckett, 231-52. Supplement to Novum Testamentum 99. Leiden: Brill, 2000.
— "Rereading Genesis in the Prologue of John?" In *Neotestamentica et Philonica: Studies in Honor of Peder Borgen*, ed. David E. Aune, Torrey Seland, and Jarl H. Ulrichsen, 179-201. Supplements to Novum Testamentum 106. Leiden: Brill, 2003.
Pamment, Margaret. "Is There Convincing Evidence of Samaritan Influence on the Fourth Gospel." *Zeitschrift für die neutestamentliche Wissenschaft und die Kunde der älteren Kirche* 73 (1982): 221-30.
Pannenberg, Wolfhart. "Problems in a Theology of (Only) the Old Testament." In *Problems in Biblical Theology: Essays in Honor of Rolf Knierim*, ed. Henry T.C. Sun and Keith L. Eades, 275-80. Grand Rapids: Eerdmans, 1997.
Parente, Pascal P. "Ascetical and Mystical Traits of Moses and Elias." *Catholic Biblical*

Quarterly 5 (1943): 183-90.
Pemberton, Elizabeth G. "The Seamless Garment: A Note on John 19:23-24." *Australian Biblical Review* 54 (2006): 50-55.
Perrin, Nicholas. "Exile." In *The World of the New Testament: Cultural, Social, and Historical Contexts*, ed. Joel B. Green and Lee Martin McDonald, 25-37. Grand Rapids: Baker, 2013.
Phillips, Elaine A. "The Singular Prophet and Ideals of Torah: Miriam, Aaron, and Moses in Early Rabbinic Texts." In *Function of Scripture in Early Jewish and Christian Tradition*, ed. Craig A. Evans and James A Sanders, 78-88. Journal for the Study of the New Testament Supplement Series 154. Sheffield: Sheffield, 1998.
Philonenko, Marc. "'Jusqu'à ce que se lève un prophète digne de confiance' (1 Maccabées 14,41)." In *Messiah and Christos: Studies in the Jewish Origins of Christianity, Presented to David Flusser on the Occasion of His Seventy-Fifth Birthday*, ed. Ithamar Gruenwald, Shaul Shaked, and Gedaliahu A.G. Stroumsa, 95-98. Texte und Studien zum antiken Judentum 32. Tübingen: Mohr Siebeck, 1992.
Pichler, Josef. "Abraham." In *Alttestamentliche Gestalten im Neuen Testament: Beiträge zur biblischen Theologie*, ed. Markus Öhler, 54-74. Darmstadt: Wissenschaftliche Buchgesellschaft, 1999.
Piper, Ronald A. "Satan, Demons and the Absence of Exorcisms in the Fourth Gospel." In *Christology, Controversy and Community: New Testament Essays in Honor of David R. Catchpole*, ed. David G. Horrell and Christopher M. Tuckett, Supplements to Novum Testamentum 99, 253-78. Leiden: Brill, 2000.
Poirier, John C. "The Endtime Return of Elijah and Moses at Qumran." *Dead Sea Discoveries* 10 (2003): 221-42.
Polhill, John B. "John 1-4: The Revelation of True Life." *Review and Expositor* 85 (1988): 445-57.
— "Perspectives on the Miracle Stories." *Review and Expositor* 74 (1977): 389-99.
Pomykala, Kenneth. "Images of David in Early Judaism." In *Ancient Versions and Traditions*. Vol. 1 of *Of Scribes and Sages: Early Jewish Interpretation and Transmission of Scripture*, ed. Craig A. Evans, 33-46. Library of Second Temple Studies 50. London: T & T Clark, 2004.
Priest, J. "Testament of Moses." In *The Old Testament Pseudepigrapha*, ed. James H. Charlesworth, 1: 919-34. The Anchor Bible Reference Library. New York: Doubleday, 1985.
Puckett, Gary B. "Elijah Redux." *Trinity Seminary Review* 20 (1998): 99-110.
Puech, Émile. "Ben Sira 48:11 et la Résurrection." In *Of Scribes and Scrolls: Studies on the Hebrew Bible, Intertestamental Judaism and Christian Origins Presented to John Strugnell on the Occasion of His Sixtieth Birthday*, ed. Harold Attridge, John J. Collins, and Thomas H. Tobin, 81-89. Lanham: The University Press of America, 1990.
Pummer, Reinhard. "Antisamaritanische Polemik in jüdischen Schriften aus der intertestamentarischen Zeit." *Biblische Zeitschrift* 26 (1982): 224-42.
Quispel, Gilles. "Nathanael und der Menschensohn (Joh 1 15)." *Zeitschrift für die neutestamentliche Wissenschaft und die Kunde der älteren Kirche* 47 (1956): 281-83.
Rahner, Johanna. "Missverstehen um zu verstehen: Zur Funktion der Missverständnisse im Johannesevangelium." *Biblische Zeitschrift* 43 (1999): 212-19.
Ramón-Díaz, José. "Palestinian Targum and the New Testament." *Novum testamentum* 6 (1963): 75-80.
Raurell, Frederic. "Ecli 45,1-5: La 'doxa de Moisès.'" *Revista Catalana de Teologia* 17

(1992): 1-42.
Refoulé, François. "Jésus, nouveau Moïse, ou Pierre, nouveau Grand Prêtre? (Mt 17,1-9; Mc 9,2-10)." *Revue théologique de Louvain* 24 (1993): 145-62.
Reim, Günter. "Targum und Johannesevangelium." *Biblische Zeitschrift* 27 (1983): 1-13.
— "Wie der Evangelist Johannes gemäss Joh 12,37 ff: Jesaja 6 gelesen hat." *Zeitschrift für die Neutestamentliche Wissenschaft* 92 (2001): 33-46.
Reimer, David J. "Old Testament Christology." In *King and Messiah in Israel und the Ancient Near East: Proceedings of the Oxford Old Testament Seminar*, John Day, ed., 380-400. Journal for the Study of the Old Testament Supplement Series 270. Sheffield: Sheffield, 1998.
Rensberger, David. "The Messiah Who Has Come into the World: The Message of the Gospel of John." In *Jesus in Johannine Tradition*, ed. Robert T. Fortna and Tom Thatcher, 15-24. Louisville: Westminster/John Know, 2001.
Reumann, John H.P. "Profiles, Problems, and Possibilities in Biblical Theology Today Part I." *Kerygma und Dogma* 44 (1998): 61-85.
— "Profiles, Problems, and Possibilities in Biblical Theology Today Part II: New Testament." *Kerygma und Dogma* 44 (1998): 145-69.
Reventlow, Henning Graf. "Response to Klaus Koch: Two Testaments, One Bible: New Trends in Biblical Theology." *Bangalore Theogical Forum* 28 (1996): 59-62.
Richter, Georg. "Die alttestamentlichen Zitate in der Rede vom Himmelsbrot Joh 6,26-51a." In *Schriftauslegung: Beiträge zur Hermeneutik des Neuen Testaments und im Neuen Testament*, 193-279. Paderborn: Schöningh, 1972.
Ridderbos, Herman. "The Christology of the Fourth Gospel: History and Interpretation." In *Saved by Hope: Essays in Honor of Richard C. Oudersluys*, ed. James I. Cook, 15-26. Grand Rapids: Eerdmans, 1978.
Robberechts, Edouard. "Une relecture juive de la figure du Serviteur." *Lumière et Vie* 278 (2008): 67-75.
Roberge, Michel. "Composition et argumentation en Jean 6,35-58." In *L'intrigue dans le récit biblique: Quatrième colloque international du RRENAB, Université Laval, Québec, 29 mai-1er juin 2008*, ed. Anne Pasquier, Daniel Marguerat, and André Wénin, 265-302. Bibliotheca ephemeridum theologicarum lovaniensium 237. Leuven: Uitgeverij Peeters, 2010.
Robert, René. "La double intention du mot final du prologue johannique." *Revue Thomiste* 87 (1987): 435-41.
— "Le mot final du prologue johannique: A propos d'un article recent." *Revue Thomiste* 89 (1989): 279-88.
Roberts, J.J.M. "Melchizedek (11Q13 = 11QMelch)." In *Pesharim, Other Commentaries, and Related Documents*. Vol. 6B of *The Dead Sea Scrolls: Hebrew, Aramaic, and Greek Texts with English Translations*, ed. James H. Charlesworth, 264-73. The Princeton Theological Seminary Dead Sea Scrolls Project. Tübingen: Mohr Siebeck; Louisville: Westminster/John Knox, 2002.
Robertson, R.G. "Ezekiel The Tragedian." In *The Old Testament Pseudepigrapha*, ed. James H. Charlesworth, 803-20. New York: Doubleday, 1985.
Rochais, Gérard. "A propos d'un livre de M.-É. Boismard, sur la christologie johannique." *Science et Esprit* 46 (1994): 229-36.
Roessli, Jean-Michel. "Oracles sibyllins." In *Écrits apocryphes chrétiens II*, ed. Pierre Geoltrain and Jean-Daniel Kaestle, 1045-83. Bibliothèque de la Pléiade 516. Paris: Gallimard, 2005.

Rogers, Cleon L., Jr. "The Davidic Covenant in the New Testament." *Bibliotheca Sacra* 150 (1993): 458-78.

Roloff, Jürgen. "Der johanneische 'Lieblingsjünger' und der Lehrer der Gerechtigkeit." *New Testament Studies* 15 (1968-1969): 129-51.

Romanowsky, J.W. "'When the Son of Man is Lifted Up': The Redemptive Power of the Crucifixion in the Gospel of John." *Horizons* 32 (2005): 100-16.

Römer, Thomas. "Les guerres de Moïse." In *La Construction de la Figure de Moïse*, ed. Thomas Römer, 169-94. Supplément à Transeuphratène 13. Paris: Gabalda, 2007.

— "Moïse: Un héros royal entre échec et divinisation." In *Interprétations de Moïse: Égypte, Judée, Grèce et Rome*, ed. Philippe Borgeaud, Thomas Römer, and Youri Volokhine, 187-98. Jerusalem Studies in Religion and Culture 10. Leiden: Brill, 2010.

— "Moses outside the Torah and the Construction of a Diaspora Identity." *Journal of Hebrew Scriptures* 8 (2008): 1-12.

Rose, Martin. "Manna: Das Brot aus dem Himmel." In *Johannes-Studien: Interdisziplinäre Zugänge zum Johannes-Evangelium, Freundesgabe der Theologischen Fakultät der Universität Neuchâtel für Jean Zumstein*, ed. Martin Rose, 75-107. Publications de la Faculté de Théologie de l'Université de Neuchâtel 6. Zurich: Theologischer, 1991.

Roth, Wolfgang. "Jesus as the Son of Man: The Scriptural Identity of a Johannine Image." In *The Living Text: Essays in Honor of Ernest W. Saunders*, ed. D.E. Groh and R. Jewett, 11-26. Lanham: The University Press of America, 1985.

— "Scriptural Coding in the Fourth Gospel." *Biblical Research* 32 (1987): 6-29.

Roukema, Riemer. "Jesus and the Divine Name in the Gospel of John." In *Revelation of the Name YHWH to Moses: Perspectives from Judaism, the Pagan Graeco-Roman World, and Early Christianity*, ed. Geurt hendrik van Kooten, 207-23. Themes in Biblical Narrative 9. Leiden: Brill, 2006.

Roure, Damià. "La figure de David dans l'évangile de Marc: Des traditions juives aux interprétations évangéliques." In *Figures de David à travers la Bible: XVIIe congrès de l'ACFEB (Lille, 1er-5 septembre 1997)*, ed. Louis Desrousseaux and Jacques Vermeylen, 397-412. Lectio divina 177. Paris: Cerf, 1999.

Rowland, Christopher. "John 1.51, Jewish Apocalyptic and Targumic Tradition." *New Testament Studies* 30 (1984): 498-507.

Ruckstuhl, Eugen. "Johannine Language and Style: The Question of Their Unity." In *L'Évangile de Jean: Sources, rédaction, théologie*, ed. Marinus de Jonge, 125-48. Bibliotheca ephemeridum theologicarum lovaniensium 44. Leuven: Leuven University Press, 1977.

Runia, David T. "God and Man in Philo of Alexandria." *Journal of Theological Studies* 39 (1988): 48-75.

Sabbe, Maurits. "The Johannine Account of the Death of Jesus and Its Synoptic Parallels (Jn 19:16b-42)." *Ephemerides theologicae lovanienses* 70 (1994): 34-64.

Sanders, E.P. "Jesus in Galilee." In *Jesus: A Colloquium in the Holy Land*, ed. Doris Donnelly, 5-26. London: Continuum, 2001.

Sanders, James A. "A New Testament Hermeneutic Fabric: Psalm 118 in the Entrance Narrative." In *Early Jewish and Christian Exegesis: Studies in Memory of William Hugh Brownlee*, ed. Craig A. Evans and William F. Stinespring, 177-90. Atlanta: Scholars, 1987.

Sänger, Dieter. "'Von mir hat er geschrieben' (Joh 5,46): Zur Funktion and Bedeutung

Mose im Neuen Testament." *Kerygma und Dogma* 41 (1995): 112-35.
Schapdick, Stefan. "Autorität ohne Inhalt: Zum Mosebild des Johannesevangeliums." *Zeitschrift für die Neutestamentliche Wissenschaft und die Kunde der älteren Kirche* 97 (2006): 177-206.
— "Religious Authority Re-evaluated: The Character of Moses in the Fourth Gospel." In *Moses in Biblical and Extra-Biblical Traditions*, ed. Axel Graupner and Michael Wolter, 181-210. Beiheft zur Zeitschrift für die alttestamentliche Wissenschaft 372. Berlin: Walter de Gruyter, 2007.
Schencke, H.M. "Jacobs-brunnen-Josephsgrab-Sychar." *Zeitschrift des deutschen Palästina-Vereins* 84 (1968): 159-84.
Schenke, Ludger. "Die formale und gedankliche Struktur von Joh 6:26-58." *Biblische Zeitschrift* 24 (1980): 21-41.
— "Die literarische Vorgeschichte von Joh 6:26-58." *Biblische Zeitschrift* 29 (1985): 68-89.
Schmidt, Andreas. "Zwei Anmerkungen zu P. Ryl. III 457." *Archiv für Papyrusforschung und verwandte Gebiete* 35 (1989): 11-12.
Schmidt, Werner H. "Das Prophetengesetz Dtn 18,9-22 im Kontext erzählender Literatur." In *Deuteronomy and Deuteronomic Literature: Festschrift C.H.W. Brekelmans*, ed. M. Vervenne and J. Lust, 55-69. Bibliotheca ephemeridum theologicarum lovaniensium 133. Louvain: Leuven University Press, 1997.
— "Die Intention der beiden Plagenerzählungen (Exodus 7-10) in ihrem Kontext." In *Studies in the Book of Exodus: Redaction, Reception, Interpretation*, ed. Marc Vervenne, 225-43. Bibliotheca ephemeridum theologicarum lovaniensium 126. Leuven: Leuven University Press; Peeters, 1996.
Schmithals, Walter. "Das Alte Testament im Neuen." In *Paulus, die Evangelien, und das Urchristentum: Beiträge von und zu Walter Schmithals zu Seinem 80. Geburtstag*, ed. Cilliers Breytenbach, 563-614. Arbeiten zur Geschichte des antiken Judentums und des Urchristentums 54. Leiden: Brill, 2004.
Schnackenburg, Rudolf. "'Der Vater, der mich gesandt hat': Zur johanneische Christologie." In *Anfänge der Christologie: Festschrift für Ferdinand Hahn zum 65. Geburtstag*, ed. Ferdinand Hahn, Cilliers Breytenbach, and Henning Paulsen, 275-92. Göttingen: Vandenhoeck & Ruprecht, 1991.
Schnelle, Udo. "Das Johannesevangelium als neue Sinnbildung." In *Theology and Christology in the Fourth Gospel: Essays by the Members of the SNTS Johannine Writings Seminar*, ed. G. van Belle, J.G. van der Watt, and P. Maritz, 291-314. Bibliotheca ephemeridum theologicarum lovaniensium 184. Leuven: Leuven University, 2005.
— "Die Tempelreinigung und die Christologie des Johannesevangeliums." *New Testament Studies* 42 (1996): 359-73.
— "Johannes als Geisttheologe." *Novum testamentum* 40 (1998): 17-31.
— "Trinitarisches Denken im Johannesevangelium." In *Israel und seine Heilstraditionen im Johannesevangelium: Festgabe für Johannes Beutler SJ zum 70. Geburtstag*, ed. Michael Labahn, Klaus Scholtissek, and Angelika Strotmann, 367-86. Paderborn: Schöningh, 2004.
Scholtissek, Klaus. "Die Brotrede Jesu in Joh 6,1-71: Exegetische Beobachtungen zu ihrem johanneischen Profil." *Zeitschrift für katholische Theologie* 123 (2001): 35-55.
— "'Die unauflösbare Schrift' (Joh 10,35): Zur Auslegung und Theologie der Schrift Israels im Johannesevangelium." In *Johannesevangelium—Mitte oder Rand des*

Kanons?: Neue Standortbestimmungen, ed. Thomas Söding, 146-77. Quaestiones disputatae 203. Freiburg: Herder, 2003.

— "'Geschrieben in diesem Buch' (Joh 20,30): Beobachtungen zum kanonischen Anspruch des Johannesevangeliums." In *Israel und seine Heilstraditionen im vierten Evangelium: Festgabe für Johannes Beutler SJ zum 70. Geburtstag*, ed. Michael Labahn, Klauss Scholtissek, and Angelika Strotmann, 207-26. Paderborn: Schöningh, 2004.

— "'Ich und der Vater, wir sind eins' (Joh 10,30): Zum theologischen Potential und zur hermeneutischen Kompetenz der johanneischen Christologie." In *Theology and Christology in the Fourth Gospel: Essays by the Members of the SNTS Johannine Writings Seminar*, ed. Gilbert van Belle, Jan G. van der Watt, and P. Maritz, 315-46. Bibliotheca ephemeridum theologicarum lovaniensium 184. Leuven: Peeters, 2005.

— "Mündiger Glaube: Zur Architektur und Pragmatik johanneischer Begegnungsgeschichten Joh 5 und Joh 9." In *Paulus und Johannes: Exegetische Studien zur paulinischen und johanneischen Theologie und Literatur*, ed. Dieter Sänger and Ulrich Mell, 75-105. Wissenschaftliche Untersuchungen zum Neuen Testament 198. Tübingen: Mohr Siebeck, 2006.

— "Neues Testament." In *Der Messias: Perspecktiven des Alten und Neuen Testaments*, ed. Heinz-Josef Fabry and Klaus Scholtissek, 55-108. Die Neue Echter Bibel Themen 5. Würzburg: Echter, 2002.

— "Relecture und réécreiture: Neue Paradigmen zu Methode und Inhalt der Johannesauslegung aufgewiesen am Prolog 1,1-18 und der ersten Abschiedsrede 13,31-14,41." *Theologie und Philosophie* 75 (2000): 1-29.

Schreiber, Stefan. "Kannte Johannes die Synoptiker?: Zur aktuellen Diskussion." *Verkündigung und Forschung* 51 (2006): 7-24.

— "Rätsel um den König: Zur religionsgeschichtlichen Herkunft des König-Titels im Johannesevangelium." In *Johannes aenigmaticus: Studien zum Johannesevangelium für Herbert Leroy*, ed. Stefan Schreiber and Alois Stimpfle, 45-70. Biblische Untersuchungen 29. Regensburg: Friedrich Pustet, 2000.

Schröter, Jens. "Die Evangelien als Augenzeugenberichte? Zur Auseinandersetzung mit Richard Bauckham." *Theologische Rundschau* 2008 (73): 219-33.

Schwankl, Otto. "Aspekte der johanneischen Christologie." In *Theology and Christology in the Fourth Gospel: Essays by the Members of the SNTS Johannine Writings Seminar*, ed. Gilbert van Belle, Jan G. van der Watt, and P.J. Maritz, 347-76. Bibliotheca ephemeridum theologicarum lovaniensium 184. Leuven: Peeters, 2005.

Schwartz, Eduard. "Aporien im vierten Evangelium." *Nachrichten von der Königlichen Gesellschaft der Wissenschaften zu Göttingen* 14 (1907): 342-72; 15 (1908): 115-88, 497-560.

Scott, Ian W. "Is Philo's Moses a Divine Man?" *Studia philonica Annual* 14 (2002): 87-111.

Scott, James. "Jesus' Vision for the Restoration of Israel as the Basis for a Biblical Theology of the New Testament." In *Biblical Theology: Retrospect and Prospect*, ed. Scott J. Hafemann, 129-43. Downers Grove: InterVarsity, 2002.

Séd, Nicolas. "Le Mēmar samaritain: Le Sēfer Yesīrā et les trente-deux sentiers de la Sagesse." *Revue de l'histoire des religions* 170 (1966): 159-84.

Seebass, Horst. "Die Stämmeliste von Dtn. XXXIII." *Vetus testamentum* 27 (1977): 158-69.

Seifrid, Mark A. "The 'New Perspective on Paul and Its Problems." *Themelios* 25, no. 2

(February 2000): 4-18.
— "Paul's Use of Habakkuk 2:4 in Romans 1:17: Reflections on Israel's Exile in Romans." In *History and Exegesis: New Testament Essays in Honor of Dr. E. Earle Ellis for His 80th Birthday*, ed. Sang-Won Son, 133-49. London: T & T Clark, 2006.
Seitz, Christopher R. "Christological Interpretation of Texts and Trinitarian Claims to Truth: An Engagement with Francis Watson's *Text and Truth*." *Scottish Journal of Theology* 52 (1999): 209-26.
— "Two Testaments and the Failure of One Tradition History." In *Biblical Theology: Retrospect and Prospect*, ed. Scott J. Hafemann, 195-211. Downers Grove: InterVarsity, 2002.
Sevrin, Jean-Marie. "Le commencement du quatrième évangile: Prologue et prélude." In *La Bible en récits*, ed. Daniel Marguerat, 340-49. 2nd ed. Le Monde de la Bible 48. Genève: Labor et Fides, 2005.
Seybold, Klaus. "Der Hilfe - und Huldigungsruf: Hosianna." In *Der Segen und andere liturgische Worte aus der hebräischen Bibel*, 97-103. Zurich: Theologischer, 2004.
— "Dimensionen und Intentionen der Davidisierung der Psalmen: Die Rolle Davids nach den Psalmenüberschriften und nach dem Septuagintapsalm 151." In *Composition of the Book of Psalms*, ed. Erich Zenger, 125-40. Bibliotheca ephemeridum theologicarum lovaniensium 238. Leuven: Peeters, 2010.
Sills, Deborah. "Vicious Rumors: Mosaic Narratives in First Century Alexandria." *The Society of Biblical Literature Seminar Papers* 31 (1992): 684-94.
Silva, Moisés. "The New Testament Use of the Old Testament: Text, Form, and Authority." In *Scripture and Truth*, ed. D.A. Carson and John D. Woodbridge, 147-65. Grand Rapids: Zondervan, 1983.
Simmers, Gary. "Who is 'The Angel of the Lord?'" *Faith and Mission* 17 (2000): 3-16.
Ska, Jean-Louis. "La sortie d'Egypte (Ex 7-14) dans le récit sacerdotal (Pg) et la tradition prophétique." *Biblica* 60 (1979): 191-215.
Smend, Friedrich. "Die Behandlung alttestamentlicher Zitate als Ausgangspunkt der Quellenscheidung im 4. Evangelium." *Zeitschrift für die neutestamentliche Wissenschaft* 24 (1925): 147-50.
Smend, Rudolf. "Methoden der Moseforschung." In *Gesammelte Studien*. Vol. 2 of *Zur ältesten Geschichte Israels*, 45-115. Beiträge zur evangelischen Theologie 100. Munich: Kaiser, 1987.
Smith, D. Moody. "The Life Setting of the Gospel of John." *Review and Expositor* 85 (1988): 433-44.
Smyth, Matthieu. "La figure de Moïse dans les sources gnostiques." In *Interprétations de Moïse: Égypte, Judée, Grèce et Rome*, ed. Philippe Borgeaud, Thomas Römer, and Youri Volokhine, 247-67. Jerusalem Studies in Religion and Culture 10. Leiden: Brill, 2010.
Söding, Thomas. "Die Schrift als Medium des Glaubens: Zur hermeneutischen Bedeutung von Joh 20:30f." In *Schrift und Tradition: Festschrift für Josef Ernst zum 70. Geburtstag*, ed. Knut Backhaus and Franz Georg Untergassmair, 343-71. Paderborn: Ferdinand Schöningh, 1996.
— "Kreuzerhöhung: Zur Deutung des Todes Jesu nach Johannes." *Zeitschrift für Theologie und Kirche* 103 (2006): 2-25.
— "Die Tempelaktion Jesu." *Trierer theologische Zeitschrift* 101 (1992): 36-64.
Songer, Harold S. "John 5-12: Opposition to the Giving of True Life." *Review and Expositor* 85 (1988): 459-72.

— "'Was kann aus Nazareth schon Gutes kommen?' (Joh 1.46): Die Bedeutung des Judeseins Jesu im Johannesevangelium," *NTS* 46 (2000): 21-41.
Sprinkle, Joe M. "Is There Truth in the Law (John 1:17)?: On the Gospel of John's View of the Mosaic Revelation." In *Biblical Law and Its Relevance: A Christian Understanding and Ethical Application for Today of the Mosaic Regulations*, 29-40. Lanham: The University Press of America, 2006.
Staley, Jeffrey L. "The Structure of John's Prologue: Its Implications for the Gospel's Narrative Structure." *Catholic Biblical Quarterly* 48 (1986): 241-64.
— "What Can a Postmodern Approach to the Fourth Gospel Add to Contemporary Debates about Its Historical Situation?" In *Jesus in Johannine Tradition*, ed. Robert T. Fortna and Tom Thatcher, 47-58. Louisville: Westminster/John Knox, 2001.
Starcky, Jean. "Les Maîtres de Justice et la chronologie de Qumrân." In *Qumrân: Sa piété, sa théologie et son milieu*, ed. M. Delcor, 249-56. Bibliotheca ephemeridum theologicarum lovaniensium 46. Louvain: Louvain University Press, 1978.
— "Les quatre étapes du messianisme à Qumran." *Revue biblique* 70 (1963): 481-505.
Stegemann, Ekkehard W. "Die Tragödie der Nähe: Zu den judenfeindlichen Aussagen des Johannesevangeliums." *Kirche und Israel* 4 (1989): 114-22.
— and Wolfgang Stegemann. "König Israels, nicht König der Juden?: Jesus als König im Johannesevangelium." In *Messiasvorstellungen bei Juden und Christen*, ed. Ekkehard W. Stegemann, 41-56. Stuttgart: W. Kohlhammer, 1993.
Steiger, Johann A. "Nathanael—Ein Israelit, an dem kein Falsch ist: Das hermeneutische Phänomen der Intertestamentarizität aufgezeigt an Joh 1,45-51." *Berliner theologische Zeitschrift* 9 (1992): 50-73.
Stemberger, Günter. "Hermeneutik der Jüdischen Bibel." In *Hermeneutik der Jüdischen Bibel und des Alten Testaments*, ed. Christoph Dohmen and Günter Stemberger, 23-74. Kohlhammer Studienbücher Theologie 1/2. Stuttgart: Kohlhammer, 1996.
— "Pesachhaggada und Abendmahlsberichte des Neuen Testaments." *Kairos* 29 (1987): 147-58
Sterling, Gregory E. "The Place of Philo of Alexandria in the Study of Christian Origins." In *Philo und das Neue Testament: Wechselseitige Wahrnehmungen, 1. Internationales Symposium zum Corpus Judaeo-Hellenisticum 1.—4. Mail 2003, Eisenach/Jenaeds*, ed. Roland Deines and Karl-Wilhelm Niebuhr, 21-52. Wissenschaftliche Untersuchungen zum Neuen Testament 172. Tübingen: Mohr Siebeck, 2004.
Stettler, Hanna. "Die Gebote Jesu im Johannesevangelium (14,15.21; 15,10)." *Biblica* 92 (2011): 554-79.
Stiglmair, Arnold. "Der Durchbohrte: Ein Versuch zu Sach 12." *Zeitschrift für katholische Theologie* 116 (1994): 451-56.
Stowasser, Martin. "Die johanneische Tempelaktion (Joh 2,13-17): Ein Beitrag zum Verhältnis von Johannesevangelium und Synoptikern." In *Im Geist und in der Wahrheit: Studien zum Johannesevangelium und zur Offenbarung des Johannes sowie andere Beiträge, Festschrift für Martin Hasitschka SJ zum 65. Geburtstag*, ed. Konrad Huber & Boris Repschinski, 41-60. Neutestamentliche Abhandlungen 52. Münster: Aschendorff, 2008.
Straub, Esther. "Alles ist durch ihn geworden: Die Erschaffung des Lebens in der Sabbatheilung Joh 5,1-18." In *Studien zu Matthäus und Johannes: Festschrift für Jean Zumstein zu seinem 65. Geburtstag*, ed. Andreas Dettwiler and Uta Poplutz, 157-67. Abhandlungen zur Theologie des Alten und Neuen Testaments 97. Zürich: Theologischer, 2009.

Strotmann, Angelika. "Relative oder absolute Präexistenz?: Zur Diskussion über die Präexistenz der frühjüdischen Weisheitsgestalt im Kontext von Joh 1,1-18." In *Israel und seine Heilstraditionen im Johannesevangelium: Festgabe für Johannes Beutler SJ zum 70. Geburtstag*, ed. Michael Labahn, Klaus Scholtissek, and Angelika Strotmann, 91-106. Paderborn: Schöningh, 2004.

Strugnell, John. "Apocryphon of Moses." In *Parabiblical Texts*, part 2 of *Qumran Cave 4, XIV*, ed. Joseph A. Fitzmyer and James A. Vanderkam, 111-36. Discoveries in the Judaean Desert 19. Oxford: Clarendon, 1995.

— "Notes en marge du volume V des Discoveries in the Judaean desert of Jordan." *Revue de Qumran* 7 (1970): 163-276.

Stuckenbruck, Loren T. "'Angels' and 'God': Exploring the Limits of Early Jewish Monotheism." In *Early Jewish and Christian Monotheism*, ed. Loren T. Stuckenbruck and Wendy E.S. North, 45-70. Journal for the Study of the New Testament Supplement Series 263. London: T & T Clark, 2004.

Stuhlmacher, Peter. "Das Gesetz als Thema biblischer Theologie." *Zeitschrift für Theologie und Kirche* 75 (1978): 251-80.

— "Isaiah 53 in the Gospels and Acts." In *The Suffering Servant: Isaiah 53 in Jewish and Christian Sources*, ed. Bernd Janowski and Peter Stuhlamcher, 147-63. Grand Rapids: Eerdmans, 2004.

Sundberg, Albert C. "Christology in the Fourth Gospel." *Biblical Research* 21 (1976): 29-37.

Tabor, James D., and Michael O. Wise. "4Q521 'On Resurrection' and the Synoptic Gospel Tradition: A Preliminary Study." *Journal for the Study of the Pseudepigrapha* 10 (1992): 149-62.

Tal, Abraham. "Samaritan Literature." In *The Samaritans*, ed. Alan D. Crown, 413-67. Tübingen: Mohr Siebeck, 1989.

— "The Samaritan Targum of the Pentateuch." In *Mikra: Text, Translation, Reading and Interpretation of the Hebrew Bible in Ancient Judaism and Early Christianity*, ed. Martin Jan Mulder, 189-216. Compendia rerum iudaicarum ad Novum Testamentum 2/1. Assen: Van Gorcum; Philadelphia: Fortress, 1988.

Tenney, Merrill C. "The Old Testament and the Fourth Gospel." *Bibliotheca Sacra* 120 (1963): 300-8.

Termini, Cristina. "Philo's Thought within the Context of Middle Judaism." In *The Cambridge Companion to Philo*, ed. Adam Kamesar, 95-123. Cambridge: Cambridge University Press, 2009.

Thatcher, Tom. "Remembering Jesus: John's Negative Christology." In *The Messiah in the Old and New Testaments*, ed. Stanley E. Porter, 165-89. McMaster New Testament Studies. Grand Rapids: Eerdmans, 2007.

Theobald, Michael. "Der Johannesprolog im 20. Jahrhundert." In *Die Fleischwerdung des Logos: Studien zum Verhältnis des Johannesprologs zum Corpus des Evangeliums und zu 1 Joh*, 54-161. Neutestamentliche Abhandlungen (New Series) 20. Münster: Aschendorff, 1988.

— "Der Tod Jesu im Spiegel seiner 'letzten Worte' vom Kreuz." *Theologische Quartalschrift* 190 (2010): 1-30.

Thiel, Winfried. "Character and Function of Divine Sayings in the Elijah and Elisha Traditions." In *Eschatology in the Bible and in Jewish and Christian Tradition*, ed. Henning Reventlow, 189-99. Journal for the Study of the Old Testament Supplement Series 243. Sheffield: Sheffield, 1997.

Thoma, Albrecht. "Das Alte Testament im Johannes-Evangelium." *Zeitschrift für wissenschaftliche Theolgie* 22 (1879): 18-66, 171-223, 273-312.
Thomassen, Einar, and Marvin Myer. "The Treatise on Resurrection." In *The Nag Hammadi Scriptures: The International Edition*, ed. Marvin Meyer, 49-56. New York: Harper Collins, 2007.
Thompson, Marianne Meye. "'They Bear Witness to Me': The Psalms in the Passoin Narrative of the Gospel of John." In *The World Leaps the Gap: Essays on Scripture and Theology in Honor of Richard B. Hays*, ed. J. Ross Wagner, C. Kavin Rowe and A. Katherine Grieb, 267-283. Grand Rapids: Eerdmans, 2008.
Thyen, Hartwig. "Ich bin das Licht der Welt: Das Ich- und Ich-Bin-Sagen Jesu im Johannesevangelium." *Jahrbuch für Antike und Christentum* 35 (1992): 19-46.
Trafton, Joseph L. "Commentary on Genesis A (4Q252=4QcommGenA=4QPBless)." In *Pesharim, Other Commentaries, and Related Documents*, vol. 6B of *The Dead Sea Scrolls: Hebrew, Aramaic, and Greek Texts with English Translations*, ed. James H. Charlesworth. The Princeton Theological Seminary Dead Sea Scrolls Project. Tübingen: Mohr Siebeck, 2002.
Trier, Daniel J. "Biblical Theology and/or Theological Interpretation of Scripture?" *Scottish Journal of Theology* 61 (2008): 16-31.
Trocmé, Etienne. "Jean-Baptiste dans le Quatrième Évangile." *Revue d'histoire et de philosophie religieuses* 60 (1980): 129-51.
Tromp, Johannes. "The Davidic Messiah in Jewish Eschatology of the First Century BCE." In *Restoration: Old Testament, Jewish, and Christian Perspectives*, ed. James M. Scott, 180-201. Supplements to the Journal for the Study of Judaism 72. Leiden: Brill, 2001.
——— "Taxo, the Messenger of the Lord." *Journal for the Study of Judaism in the Persian, Hellenistic and Roman Period* 21 (1990): 200-09.
Tucker, Gene. "Deuteronomy 18:15-22." *Interpretation* 41 (1987): 292-97.
Tuckett, Christopher. "Moses in Gnostic Writings." In *Moses in Biblical and Extra-Biblical Traditions*, ed. Axel Graupner and Michael Wolter, 227-40. Beiheft zur Zeitschrift für die alttestamentliche Wissenschaft 372. Berlin: Walter de Gruyter, 2007.
Turner, John D. "Sethian Gnosticism and Johannine Christianity." In *Theology and Christology in the Fourth Gospel: Essays by the Members of the SNTS Johannine Writings Seminar*, ed. G. van Belle, J.G. van der Watt, and P. Maritz, 399-434. Bibliotheca ephemeridum theologicarum lovaniensium 184. Leuven: Leuven University, 2005.
Ulrichsen, Jarl H. "Jesus—der neue Tempel?: Ein kritischer Blick auf die Auslegung von Joh 2,13-22." In *Neotestamentica et Philonica: Studies in Honor of Peder Borgen*, ed. David E. Aune, Torrey Seland, and Jarl H. Ulrichsen, 202-14. Supplements to Novum Testamentum 106. Leiden: Brill, 2003.
Umoh, Camillus. "The Temple in the Fourth Gospel." In *Israel und seine Heilstraditionen im vierten Evangelium: Festgabe für Johannes Beutler SJ zum 70. Geburtstag*, ed. Michael Labahn, Klaus Scholtissek, and Angelika Strotmann, 314-33. Paderborn: Schöningh, 2004.
Vahrenhorst, Martin. "Johannes und die Tora: Überlegungen zur Bedeutung der Tora im Johannesevangelium." *Kerygma und Dogma* 54 (2008): 14-36.
Vaiss, Paul. "L'interprétation juive des prophéties messianiques de l'Ancien Testament de l'époque hellénistique aux Talmuds et aux premiers Midrashim." *Transversalités*

96 (2005): 105-38.

Vahrenhorst, Martin. "Johannes und die Tora: Überlegungen zur Bedeutung der Tora im Johannesevangelium." *Kerygma und Dogma* 54 (2008): 14-36.

Vermes, Geza. "La Figure de Moïse au tournant des deux Testaments." In *Moïse: L'homme de l'alliance*, ed. Henri Cazelles, 63-92. Paris: Desclée, 1955.

— "The Qumran Interpretation of Scripture in Its Historical Setting." *Leeds University Oriental Society Annual* 6 (1966-68): 85-97.

Vollenweider, Samuel. "Der Logos als Brüke vom Evangelium zur Philosophie: Der Johannesprolog in der Relektüre des Neuplatonikers Amelios." In *Studien zu Matthäus und Johannes: Festschrift für Jean Zumstein zu seinem 65. Geburtstag*, ed. Andreas Dettwiler & Uta Poplutz, 377-97. Abhandlungen zur Theologie des Alten und Neuen Testaments 97. Zürich: Theologischer, 2009.

Voorwinde, Stephen. "John's Prologue: Beyond Some Impasses of Twentieth-Century Scholarship." *Westminster Theological Journal* 64 (2002): 15-44.

Walker, William O. "John 1:43-51 and 'The Son of Man' in the Fourth Gospel." *Journal for the Study of the New Testament* 56 (1994): 31-42.

— "The Son of Man: Some Recent Developments." *Catholic Biblical Quarterly* 45 (1983): 584-607.

Waal, C. van der. "The Gospel according to John and the Old Testament." In *Essays on the Jewish Background of the Fourth Gospel: Proceedings of the Sixteenth Meeting of the New Testament Society of South Africa*, 28-47. Neotestamentica 6. Bloemfontein, South Africa: The New Testament Society of South Africa, 1972.

Wahlde, Urban C. von. "Literary Structure and Theological Argument in Three Discourses with the Jews in the Fourth Gospel." *Journal of Biblical Literature* 103 (1984): 575-84.

— "'You Are of Your Father the Devil' in Its Context: Stereotyped Apocalyptic Polemic in John 8:38-47." In *Anti-Judaism and the Fourth Gospel: Papers of the Leuven Colloquium, 2000*, ed. Reimund Bieringer, Didier Pollefeyt, and Frederique Vandecasteele-Vanneuville, 418-44. Jewish and Christian Heritage Series 1. Assen: Royal Van Gorcum, 2001.

Walter, Nikolaus. "Zur theologischen problematik des christologischen 'Schriftbeweises' in Neuen Testament." *New Testament Studies* 41 (1995): 338-57.

Waltke, Bruce K. "Micah." In *Obadiah, Jonah, Micah, Nahum, and Habakkuk*, vol. 2 of *The Minor Prophets*, ed. Thomas E. McComiskey, 591-764. Grand Rapids: Baker, 1993.

Waschke, Ernst-Joachim. "Mose und David: Ein überlieferungs- und redaktionsgeschichtliche Desiderat?" In *Auf dem Weg zur Endgestalt von Genesis bis II Regum: Festschrift Hans-Christoph Schmitt zum 65. Geburtstag*, ed. Martin Beck and Ulrike Schorn, 217-30. Beihefte zur Zeitschrift für die alttestamentliche Wissenschaft 370. Berlin: Walter de Gruyter, 2006.

Watson, Francis. "Authors, Readers, Hermeneutics." In *Reading Scripture with the Church: Toward a Hermeneutic for Theological Interpretation*, ed. A.K.M. Adam et al., 95-118. Grand Rapids: Baker, 2006.

— "Hermeneutics and the Doctrine of Scripture: Why They Need Each Other." *International Journal of Systematic Theology* 12 (2010): 118-43.

Watt, Jan G. van der. "Salvation in the Gospel according to John." In *Salvation in the New Testament: Perspectives on Soteriology*, ed. Jan G. van der Watt, 101-31. Supplements to Novum Testamentum 121. Leiden: Brill, 2005.

Watts, James W. "The Legal Characterization of Moses in the Rhetoric of the Pentateuch." *Journal of Biblical Literature* 117 (1998): 415-26.
Wedderburn, Alexander J. M. "Jesus' Action in the Temple: A Key or a Puzzle?" *Zeitschrift für die neutestamentliche Wissenschaft und die Kunde der älteren Kirche* 97 (2006): 1-22.
Weder, Hans. "Die Menschwerdung Gottes: Überlegungen zur Auslegungsproblematik des Johannesevangeliums am Beispiel von Joh 6." In *Einblicke ins Evangelium: Exegetische Beiträge zur neutestamentlichen Hermeneutik*, 363-400. Göttingen: Vandenhoeck & Ruprecht, 1992.
— "Mein hermeneutisches Anliegen im Gegenüber zu Klaus Bergers Hermeneutik des Neuen Testaments." *Evangelische Theologie* 52 (1992): 319-31.
Weinfeld, Moshe. "God Versus Moses in the Temple Scroll: 'I Do Not Speak on My Own But on God's Authority' (Sifrei Deut sec 5; John 12, 48f)." *Revue de Qumran* 15 (1991-1992): 175-80.
Weinreich, Otto. "Antikes Gottmenschentum." In *Römischer Kaiserkult*, ed. Antonie Wlosok, 55-81. Wege der Forschung 372. Darmstadt: Wissenschaftliche Buchgesellschaft, 1978.
Wells, M. Jay. "Figural Representation and Canonical Unity." In *Biblical Theology: Retrospect and Prospect*, ed. Scott J. Hafemann, 111-25. Downers Grove: InterVarsity, 2002.
Wendland, Paul O. "Is Allegorizing a Legitimate Manner of Biblcial Interpretation?" *Wisconsin Lutheran Quarterly* 103 (2006): 163-94.
Wengst, Klaus. "Der jüdische Mose: Die Gestalt des Mose im rabbinischen Judentum." *Bibel und Kirche* 66 (2011): 19-24.
Wieder, Naftali. "The 'Law-Interpreter' of the Sect of the Dead Sea Scrolls: The Second Moses." *Journal of Jewish Studies* 4 (1953): 158-75.
Wilckens, Ulrich. "Gott, der Drei-Eine: Zur Trinitätstheologie der johanneischen Schriften." In *Der Sohn Gottes und seine Gemeinde: Studien zur Theologie der Johanneischen Schriften*, 9-28. Forschungen zur Religion und Literatur des Alten und Neuen Testaments 200. Göttingen: Vandenhoeck & Ruprecht, 2003.
— "Monotheismus und Christologie," In *Der Sohn Gottes und seine Gemeinde. Studien zur Theologie der Johanneischen Schriften*, 126-35. Forschungen zur Religion und Literatur des Alten und Neuen Testaments 200. Göttingen: Vandenhoeck & Ruprecht, 2003.
Wilcox, Max. "The Aramaic Background of the New Testament." In *The Aramaic Bible: Targums in Their Historical Context*, ed. D.R.G. Beattie and M.J. McNamara, 362-78. Journal for the Study of the Old Testament Supplement Series 166. Sheffield: JSOT, 1994.
Williams, Catrin H. "Isaiah in John's Gospel." In *Isaiah in the New Testament*, ed. Steve Moyise and Maarten J.J. Menken, 101-16. London: T & T Clark, 2005.
— "Seeing the Glory: The Reception of Isaiah's Call-Vision in Jn 12.41." In *Judaism, Jewish Identities and the Gospel Tradition: Essays in Honour of Maurice Casey*, ed. James G. Crossley, 253-80. London: Equinox, 2010.
Williamson, H.G.M. "History." In *It is Written: Scripture Citing Scripture, Essays in Honour of Barnabas Lindars*, ed. D.A. Carson and H.G.M. Williamson, 25-38. Cambridge: Cambridge University Press, 1988.
Wilson, Robert McL. "Philo and the Fourth Gospel." *Expository Times* 65 (1953): 47-49.
Windisch, Hubert. "Joh I 51 und die Auferstehung Jesu." *Zeitschrift für die*

neutestamentliche Wissenschaft und die Kunde der älteren Kirche 31 (1932): 199-204.
Winter, Sean F. "The Rhetorical Function of John's Portrayal of the Jewish Law." In *Torah in the New Testament: Papers Delivered at the Manchester-Lausanne Seminar of June 2008*, ed. Michael Tait and Peter Oakes, 82-95. The Library of New Testament Studies 401. London: T & T Clark, 2009.
Witte, Markus. "'Mose, sein Andenken sei zum Segen' (Sir 45:1): Das Mosebild des Sirachbuchs." *Biblische Notizen* 107/108 (2001): 161-86.
Woude, Adam S. van der. "Melchisedek als himmlische Erlösergestalt in den neugefundenen eschatologischen Midraschim aus Qumran Höhle XI." *Oudtestamentische studiën* 14 (1965): 354-73.
Wright, R.B. "Psalms of Solomon." In *The Old Testament Pseudepigrapha*, ed. James H. Charlesworth, 2:639-50. The Anchor Bible Reference Library. New York: Doubleday, 1985.
Wyss, Beatrice. "Philon und die Philologen." *Biblische Notizen* 148 (2011): 67-83.
Xeravits, Géza G. "Moses Redivivus in Qumran?" *Qumran Chronicle* 11 (2003): 91-105.
— "Wisdom Traits in the Qumranic Presentation of the Eschatological Prophet." In *Wisdom and Apocalypticism in the Dead Sea Scrolls and in the Biblical Tradition*, ed. Florentino García Martínez, 183-92. Bibliotheca ephemeridum theologicarum lovaniensium 168. Leven: Leuven University Press, 2003.
Zamagni, Claudio. "Alexander Polyhistor et Artapan: Une Mise en perspective à partir des extraits d'Eusèbe de Césarée." In *Interprétations de Moïse: Égypte, Judée, Grèce et Rome*, ed. Philippe Borgeaud, Thomas Römer, and Youri Volokhine, 57-82. Jerusalem Studies in Religion and Culture 10. Leiden: Brill, 2010.
— "Eusèbe de Césarée et les traditions extra-canoniques sur Moïse en Ethiopie." In *La Construction de la Figure de Moïse*, ed. Thomas Römer, 145-56. Supplément à Transeuphratène 13. Paris: Gabalda, 2007.
Zangenberg, Jürgen. "Between Jerusalem and Galilee: Samaria in the Time of Jesus." In *Jesus and Archaeology*, ed. James H. Charlesworth, 393-432. Grand Rapids: Eerdmans, 2006.
Zetterholm, Karin Hedner. "Elijah and the Books of Kings in Rabbinic Literature." In *Books of Kings: Sources, Composition, Historiography and Reception*, ed. André Lemaire & Baruch Halpern, 585-606. Supplements to Vetus Testamentum 129. Leiden: Brill, 2010.
— "Elijah and the Messiah as Spokesmen of Rabbinic Ideology." In *The Messiah in Early Judaism and Christianity*, ed. Magnus Zetterholm, 57-78. Minneapolis: Fortress, 2007.
Zola, Nicholas J. "'The One Who Eats My Bread Has Lifted His Heel against Me': Psalm 41:10 in 1QHa 13.25-26 and John 13:18." *Perspectives in Religious Studies* 37 (2010): 407-19.
Zumstein, Jean. "Die Schriftrezeption in der Brotrede (Joh 6)." In *Israel und seine Heilstraditionen im Johannessevangelium: Festgabe für Johannes Beutler SJ zum 70. Geburtstag*, ed. Michael Labahn, Klaus Scholtissek, and Angelika Strotmann, 123-39. Paderborn: Ferdinand Schöningh, 2004.
— "Intratextuality and Intertextuality in the Gospel of John." In *Anatomies of Narrative Criticism: The Past, Present, and Futures of the Fourth Gospel as Literature*, ed. Tom Thatcher and Stephen D. Moore, 121-36. The Society of Biblical Literature Resources for Biblical Study 55. Atlanta: The Society of Biblical Literature, 2008.
— "La réception de l'écriture en Jean 6." In *Analyse narrative et Bible: Deuxième*

colloque international du RRENAB, Louvain-la-Neuve, avril 2004, ed. Camille Focant and André Wénin, 147-66. Bibliotheca ephemeridum theologicarum lovaniensium 191. Leuven: Leuven Univ Press; Peeters, 2005.
— "Le lavement des pieds (Jean 13,1-20): Un exemple de la conception johannique du pouvoir." *Revue de théologie et de philosophie* 132 (2000): 345-60.
— "Zur Geschichte des johanneischen Christentums." In *Kreative Erinnerung: Relecture und Auslegung im Johannesevangelium*, 1-14. 2nd ed. Abhandlungen zur Theologie des Alten und Neuen Testaments 84. Zürich: Theologischer, 2004.

Dissertations

Johnson, David Harlan. "Our Father Jacob: The Role of the Jacob Narrative in the Fourth Gospel Compared to Its Role in the Jewish Bible and in the Writings of Early Judaism." Ph.D. diss., Trinity Evangelical Divinity School, 1992.

Wallace, Eric M.E. "The Testimony of Moses: Pentateuchal Traditions and Their Function in the Gospel of John." Ph.D. diss., Union Theological Seminary and Presbyterian School of Christian Education, 2004.

Author Index

Abegg, M.G. 186, 190, 199-200, 227, 286
Achenbach, R. 215
Albertz, R. 43, 65
Alexander, L. 149
Alexander, P.S. 218-19, 323-24
Alkier, S. 49
Allegri, J.M.
Allegro, J.M. 187
Allison, D.C. 82, 107, 173-74, 216, 230
Amsler, F. 116
Anderson, H. 183
Anderson, P.N. 9, 11, 13, 16, 26, 141, 262, 271, 300
Anderson, R.T. 219, 222-23
Ashton, J. 27, 45, 53-54, 113, 232
Assis, E. 100
Atkinson, K. 136
Attridge, H.W. 290, 295
Augenstein, J. 86-87, 234, 252-53, 255
Auld, A.G. 129
Aune, D.E. 283, 293
Aurelius, E. 233
Avery-Peck, A.J. 89

Baarda, T. 245
Backhaus, K. 124
Baffes, M. 311
Bailey, D.P. 278
Bailey, R.C. 206
Baillet, M. 197
Baird, W. 54, 289, 291
Baker, D.L. 2-3, 7, 56, 157
Baldensperger, W. 115
Balentine, S.E. 193
Balfour, G. 310
Ball, D.M. 94
Ballhorn, E. 128
Barr, J. 3-4
Barrera, J.T. 103
Barrett, C.K. 13, 151, 158, 166, 168, 234, 255-56, 266, 292, 309, 311
Barnett, P.W. 299
Barth, G. 6
Barton, J. 2-3, 139

Baslez, M.-F. 43, 278
Bassler, J.M. 129, 131-32, 134, 139-40, 151
Bauckham, R. 7-8, 11, 13, 15-16, 26, 28, 30, 54, 60, 68, 88-89, 94, 102, 113, 190, 210-11, 268, 283, 287, 293
Bauer, D.R. 140
Bauer, J.B. 310
Bauer, W. 238
Bauernfeind, O. 111
Bauks, M. 206
Baumgarten, J.M. 187-89
Beale, G.K. 49, 51, 156
Beasley-Murray, G.R. 55, 67, 79, 151, 157, 164, 235-36, 246, 255, 307-08, 311
Becker, Joachim 284-85
Becker, Jürgen. 12, 70, 149, 151, 235, 238, 240, 266, 270, 293, 295
Becker, M. 104-05
Beentjes, P.C. 129
Bell, G. van 113, 146
Beltz, W. 103
Ben-Hayyim, Z. 220
Bennema, C. 87, 120
Berger, K. 46, 131, 205
Bergey, R. 184
Bergmeier, R. 9, 117
Bernard, J.H.A. 128, 256
Bernstein, M.J. 138
Betz, O. 19, 44-45, 83, 227, 301
Beutler, J. 12, 15, 61, 87, 239, 255, 262
Beyschlag, K. 117
Bhaldraithe, Eoin de 233
Bickermann, E.J. 290
Bieberstein, K. 89
Bieberstein, S. 89
Bieler, L. 21-22
Bieringer, R. 86, 269
Bindemann, W. 232
Bird, M.F. 26, 60, 113, 180
Bittner, W.J. 31-32, 113, 255
Black, M. 297
Blanchard, Y.-M. 9, 68, 71
Bloch, R. 214, 216

Author Index

Block, D.I. 132-33, 178, 282
Blomberg, C.L. 127
Blumenthal, C. 234
Böcher, O. 292-93
Bock, D.L. 108
Bockmuehl, M. 137
Bodi, D. 310
Boismard, M.-E. 31, 111, 173, 220, 223-24, 232, 259
Bond, H.K. 164
Borchert, G. 255
Bordreuil, P. 135
Borgeaud, P. 200, 214
Borgen, P. 23-24, 249, 262, 295
Bowley, J.E. 88, 186-88, 195-96
Bowman, J. 132, 220
Boyarin, D. 26, 113
Braude, W.G. 201
Bremmer, J.N. 116
Brett, M.G. 3
Britt, B. 192
Broadhead, E.K. 45
Brodie, T.L. 126
Broer, I.
Brooke, G.J. 71, 122, 129, 138, 175, 228-29, 286
Browlee, W.H. 130
Brown, R.E. 46, 74-75, 81, 85, 115, 119, 148-49, 157-58, 167, 216, 227, 234, 236, 256, 265-66, 283, 296, 299-300, 306, 308, 311
Bruce, F.F. 73, 139, 234, 242
Brueggemann, D.A. 3
Brueggemann, W. 3-4
Brunson, A.C. 5, 78, 91, 142, 145, 269-72
Bryan, S.M. 144, 252
Buchanan, G.W. 82, 220
Büchsel, F. 241
Bultmann, R. 21, 27, 47, 60, 75, 85, 124, 149, 158, 161, 164, 168, 234, 238, 255, 293-95, 302, 305-06, 309
Burge, G.M. 113, 302
Burger, C. 149
Burnett, F.W. 90
Burney, C.F. 71, 297
Burridge, R.A. 15
Busse, U. 146-47
Buth, R. 28

Bynum, W.R. 169-70

Calvert, N.L. 87
Calvert-Koyzis, N.L. 87
Camponovo, O. 202
Cangh, J.-M. van 140
Capes, D.B. 15
Capper, B.J. 26
Caquot, A. 186, 197
Carmignac, J. 228
Caron, G. 87
Carroll, J.T. 247
Carroll R., M.D. 133, 285
Carson, D.A. 47, 49, 78-79, 144, 156, 161, 163-65, 234-35, 246, 255, 258, 260, 307, 309, 311
Cartlidge, D.R. 117
Casey, M. 210-11, 287, 297
Cathcart, K.J. 150
Cebulj, C. 252
Chae, Y.S. 140
Chancey, M.A. 298-99
Chapman, D.W. 325
Charlesworth, J.H. 9-10, 16, 49, 57, 63, 81-82, 89, 122, 181, 188-89, 196, 219, 223, 281-85, 298, 299-300, 323
Chester, A. 10, 287
Childs, B.S. 2-4, 129, 205-06
Chilton, B.D. 58, 139, 160, 217-18, 297, 324-25
Cho, S. 173
Chouinard, L. 45
Christensen, D.L. 177, 203, 216
Ciampa, R.E. 7-8
Clark, D.K. 232
Clark, E.G. 88
Clark-Soles, J. 290
Clements, R.E. 203
Coakley, J.F. 153-55
Coggins, R.J. 219
Cohen, S.J.D. 290
Cohn, R.L. 216
Coloe, M.L. 79, 121
Collins, J.J. 2-3, 27, 57, 68, 101, 103-06, 132, 134, 155, 191, 202, 211-12, 215-16, 225, 260, 284-88
Collins, N.L. 209
Colpe, C. 294

Condra, E. 287
Conzelmann, H. 292, 294, 302
Coogan, M.D. 135, 180, 193-94
Cook, E.M. 186, 190, 219, 227
Corley, J. 135, 208
Cortés, J.B. 310
Coulot, C. 128
Cowan, C. 13
Craigie, P.C. 203, 216
Crawford, S.W. 224
Croatto, J.S. 174
Crom, D. de 190
Cross, F.M. 225-27
Crown, A.D. 219, 222
Cullmann, O. 109-10
Culpepper, R.A. 62, 78, 164, 166, 235, 238, 252, 262
Cunningham, J.A. 9

Dahmen, U. 228
Dahood, M. 201
Daise, M.A. 310
Daly-Denton, M. 33-34, 140-44, 152, 159-60, 162, 164-65, 169-70
D'Angelo, M.R. 174
Dapaah, D.S. 124
Das, A.A. 6
Daube, D. 271, 324
Dauer, A. 157, 165
Davies, M. 126, 141
Davies, P.R. 283
Davies, W.D. 73, 217, 296
Davila, J.R. 18, 186, 207
Day, J. 286
Deines, R. 212, 291, 295-99, 301
Delamarter, S. 216
Demke, C. 160
Dennis, J. 5, 156, 232, 263, 268
Derrett, J.D.M. 155, 199, 247-48
DeSilva, D.A. 90, 182-83
Dettwiler, A. 252
Deursen, W. von 229
Dewey, J. 46, 53
Dexinger, F. 220-21
Diehl, J. 15
Dietrich, W. 128
Dietzfelbinger, C. 35, 66, 70, 75, 82-83, 88, 94, 123, 147, 151-52, 161, 164, 166-67, 171, 231, 235, 238, 247, 250, 270-71
Dijkstra, M. 175
Di Lella, A.A. 207
Dimant, D. 106
Dodd, C.H. 72, 144, 157, 168, 256, 270, 295, 308
Dommershausen, W. 185
Donner, H. 215
Doran, R. 183, 185
Douglas, J.R. 103
Downing, F.G. 90
Dozeman, T.B. 178
Draper, J.A. 153
Driver, S.R. 203, 216
Dschulnigg, P. 60, 62, 75, 151
Duling, D.C. 140
Dumbrell, W.J. 237-38
Dunderberg, I. 264
Dunn, J.D.G. 1, 7, 9, 14-15, 17-18, 53, 66, 211, 284
Durham, J.I. 177, 205-06

Ebner, M. 15
Eck, W. 290
Edwards, M.J. 91
Edwards, R.B. 234 -35, 238, 242
Ehrlich, C.S. 175
Ehrman, B.D. 166, 291
Elledge, C.D. 89, 138
Ellens, J.H. 68-69
Ellis, E.E. 7, 13, 72, 292
Ellis, P. 46, 53
Enns, P. 158-59, 309
Epstein, I. 218
Ernst, J. 123
Eshel, E. 80, 199
Eschel, H. 80, 227
Evans, C.A. 16, 71, 128, 130, 134, 142, 148, 155, 157, 160, 218-20, 225, 233, 283-84, 287, 298, 303, 307, 324
Eynikel, E. 129

Fabry, H.-J. 208, 228-30, 282, 285
Faierstein, M.M. 107
Falk, D.K. 180, 186, 196
Farelly, N. 144
Fee, G.D. 310

Author Index

Feldman, L.H. 128, 208, 213, 291
Finegan, J. 302
Fitzer, G. 230-31
Fitzmyer, J.A. 29, 52, 57, 107, 130, 153, 218, 227, 296, 323
Flesher, P.V.M. 72, 76, 160, 218
Fletcher-Louis, C.H. 195, 197, 207
Flint, P.W. 130
Flusser, D. 228-29
Fohrer, G. 282
Ford, J.M. 168
Ford, W.A. 206
Förster, N. 117
Fortna, R.T. 60
Fossum, J. 117, 292
Fouts, D. 201
France, R.T. 49, 157
Frankemölle, H. 3, 108-09, 231
Freed, E.D. 91, 168, 220, 306
Frerichs, E.S. 285
Fretheim, T.E. 206
Frey, J. 8, 10, 16, 20, 86, 249, 283, 289, 292, 307
Freyne, S. 298-99
Friedland, E.L. 99
Fröhlich, I. 138
Frühwald-König, J. 265
Fuerst, W.J. 193
Fuglseth, K.S. 26
Fuhs, H.F. 148
Fuller, M.E. 132, 136-37
Fuller, R.H. 109

Garland, D.E. 164-65, 167, 169
Gawlick, M. 239, 246, 250, 270
Geller, S.A. 211
Gemünden, P. von 69
Gerstenberger, E.S. 289
Gese, H. 4-5, 63, 99, 108, 126
Giles, T. 219, 222-23
Gieschen, C.A. 8, 209
Gilman, F.M. 231-32
Glasson, T.F. 23-24, 31, 120, 141, 173, 247-49, 261
Gleßmer, U. 102
Gnilka, J. 69, 234, 260, 293
Goldstein, J.A. 185, 191, 291
Goppelt, L. 56

Goodenough, E.R. 213
Goodspeed, E.J. 295
Gordon, R.P. 128, 150
Gourgues, M. 162
Grabbe, L.L. 89, 291
Grappe, C. 78, 145-46, 218, 233
Graupner, A. 175
Grätz, S. 214
Grau, A. 249
Green, J.B. 247
Green, W.S. 285
Greenspoon, L.J. 183
Grelot, P. 91, 243
Grigsby, B.H. 310
Grob, F. 31-32
Gruen, E.S. 209
Grundmann, W. 17
Gruson, M.-O. 214
Guelich, R. 14
Gunawan, H.P. 110
Gundry, R.H. 12, 15, 70
Gunneweg, A.H.J. 285

Haar, S. 117
Haenchen, E. 91, 117
Hafemann, S. 5, 180, 184-85, 191-92, 194
Häfner, D. 99
Hägerland, T. 26, 113
Hahn, F. 1, 14-15, 17, 29, 60, 87, 109
Hakola, R. 86, 94, 252, 255, 271
Haldimann, K. 10
Halivni, D.W. 134
Ham, C. 29
Hamid-Khani, S. 12, 56, 158, 300-01, 309
Hamidovic, D. 187
Hamilton, V. 249
Hannah, D.D. 9
Hanson, A.T. 48, 73, 91, 147-48, 168, 177-78, 233, 240-41, 243, 305-06
Hanson, K.C. 290
Hare, D.R. 69
Harnack, A. von 300
Harner, P.B. 94
Harrington, D.J. 102
Harris, E. 234
Harris, J.R. 144
Harris, M.J. 241
Harstine, S. 22, 52, 175, 231

Harvey, J.E. 175
Hasel, G.F. 5
Hayes, J.H. 5
Hayman, P. 211
Hays, D.M. 231, 287
Hays, J.D. 133, 285
Hays, R. 50-51, 144, 146-47
Hayward, R. 102
Heil, C. 149-50
Helyer, L.R. 114
Hempel, C. 187, 190
Hengel, M. 14-15, 26, 34-34, 44-45, 51, 54, 59, 80, 93, 117-18, 169, 210, 233, 240, 245, 278, 288, 290, 292, 300-01, 303
Henry, P. 91
Henten, J.W. van. 180, 183, 195, 198-99, 207, 229
Herbert, A.S. 193
Herr, B. 184
Herr, M.D. 66
Herring, S.L. 192
Hesse, F. 193
Hezser, C. 54, 219, 325
Hiebert, R.J.V. 183
Higgins, A.J.B. 23
Hill, C.E. 303
Himbaza, I. 100
Hjelm, I. 219, 222
Höffken, P. 128-29
Hofius, O. 233, 238-40, 243
Hogeterp, A.L. 82, 89, 187
Holladay, C.R. 208-10
Holmén, T. 153
Holtz, G. 324
Hooker, M.D. 13, 121, 233
Horbury, W. 8, 15, 27, 55, 57, 202, 209, 211, 217-18, 285, 288
Horsley, R.A. 100, 102, 106-07, 110-11, 217-18, 223, 297
Horst, P.W. van der 222
Horst, R. van der 209
Hoskins, P.M. 73-74, 78, 145
Hoskyns, E. 125, 255
Hübenthal, S. 154
Huber, K. 308
Hübner, H. 2, 8, 243
Hultgård, A. 228

Hunn, D. 87
Hurst, L.D. 286
Hurtado, L.W. 8-9, 207, 210-11, 287, 292, 296, 304
Hyldahl, N. 183
Hylen, S. 269

Im, T.S. 128
Inowlocki-Meister, S. 211
Iverson, K.R. 52

Jacobs, M. 128
Jacobson, H. 197, 210
Janowitz, N. 191
Janowski, B. 2-3, 89, 287
Jensen, M.H. 298
Jeremias, J. 99, 108, 175, 193, 217, 230
Jipp, J.W. 133
Johnson, D.H. 71-72, 74, 96
Johnson, S.E. 272
Johnstone, W. 192
Jones, D.L. 111
Jones, F.S. 116
Jonge, H.J. de. 86-87
Jonge, M. de 27-28, 93, 112, 115, 139-40, 267, 285-86
Joosten, J. 178
Joynes, C.E. 98
Juel, D. 169
Justnes, Å. 104

Kaiser, O. 99
Kaiser, W.C. 98, 109
Kamesar, A. 212
Kartveit, M. 81
Käsemann, E. 294, 306
Kastner, J.M. 230
Katz, P. 184
Katz, S.T. 26, 113
Kaufman, S.A. 219, 323
Kaufmann, Y. 132-33, 139
Kealrly, F.F. 132
Keck, L.E. 27
Keener, C.S. 18-19, 30, 70-71, 79, 82, 91, 94, 122, 125, 165, 234, 242, 307, 311
Kierspel, L. 87, 272
Kilpatrick, G.D. 310
Kim, S. 28-29

Author Index

Kimelman, R. 26, 113
Kingsbury, J.D. 140
Kirk, D.R. 70, 72, 75
Klappert, B. 40, 173, 232, 239, 251-52, 255, 257
Klauck, H.-J. 41-42, 49-50
Klink, E.W., III. 1, 26, 113
Knapp, H.M. 310
Knibb, M.A. 190, 200, 283
Knight, J. 9
Knoppers, G.N. 131, 220, 285
Knox, J. 111
Koch, C. 2, 308
Koch, K. 27
Koester, C.R. 76, 233, 310
Koester, H. 153, 293, 302
Koet, B.J. 99
Kohler, H. 304
Kooij, A. van der 187, 215
Köstenberger, A. 26, 60, 70, 73, 75, 82, 85, 94, 126, 164, 235, 238, 246, 255, 296, 305, 307, 311-12, 325
Kotila, M. 46, 60, 238, 240, 258
Kowalski, B. 144, 148
Kraft, R.A. 49
Kraus, W. 35-37, 40, 58, 156, 167, 231, 251, 253, 305
Krause, A.E. 184
Krauter, S. 8
Kreuzer, S. 173
Kruck, G. 233
Kruger, P.A. 196
Kugel, J.L. 70, 130
Kügler, J. 48-49, 55, 213, 255, 259, 292
Kuhn, H.-J. 20-21, 33
Kuhn, K.G. 283
Kuhn, K.H. 310
Kuper, L.J. 233
Kvalbein, H. 155, 269
Kysar, R. 10, 26, 113

Laato, A. 285
Labahn, M. 12, 19, 34, 40-41, 75, 86, 91, 93, 95, 127, 147, 245, 252, 262-65
Lagner, C. 259
Lamb, D.A. 26
Lambrecht, J. 118
Lanfranchi, P. 213

Lang, M. 147
Lange, A. 227
Langner, C. 68-69
La Potterie, I. de 164, 244
Lasor, W.S. 286
Latour, É. 224
Laurin, R.B. 286
Layton, B. 103
Leaney, A.R.C. 196
Le Déaut, R. 297
Lee, A.H.I. 9
Leibner, U. 291
Lelièvre, A. 144
Leonhardt-Balzer, J. 243
Léon-Dufour, X. 38
Lerle, E. 140
Levenson, J.D. 1-2
Lichtenberger, A. 298
Lichtenberger, H. 8, 99, 115, 123, 188, 283, 286
Lierman, J. 8, 25, 174-75, 182, 185, 194, 200, 202, 204-05, 207, 209, 212-13, 217, 220, 231
Lieu, J.M. 89, 306
Lightfoot, J.L. 101
Lincoln, A.T. 13, 67-68, 235-36, 246
Lindars, B. 60, 70, 79, 91, 146-47, 157, 168, 234, 308, 311
Lindemann, A. 250, 292, 294, 302
Ling, T.J.M. 113
Loader, W. 38-40, 71, 75, 146, 244, 258
Lockett, D.R. 1
Loewenstamm, S.E.
Lohfink, N. 204
Lohse, E. 17, 87, 196
Loiseau, A.-F. 218, 247-48
Loisy, A.F. 295
Longenecker, R.N. 156
Longman, T., III. 134
Lowe, M.F. 86
Lowenstamm, S.E. 209
Lübbe, J. 227
Luc, D. 61
Lucass, S. 57
Lüdemann, G. 117, 248, 289, 292
Lunt, H.G. 73
Lust, J. 148, 286
Luz, U. 36, 61, 240

MacDonald, J. 222-23
Macchi, J.-D. 222
Maccoby, H. 217
Macgregor, G.H.C. 242
Mach, M. 211
Macina, R. 111
Magezi, V. 300
Maher, M. 72
Maier, J. 43, 55, 65, 111, 118, 219, 223-24, 323
Malina, B.J. 271
Manning, G.T. 51, 69
Manns, F. 116, 170-71, 218, 300
Manzanga, P. 300
Marcus, J. 156, 307, 310
Marguerat, D. 113
Markschies, C. 117
Marrs, R.R. 246-47
Marshall, I.H. 28-29, 48-49
Martens, E.A. 177, 249
Martin, D.B. 290
Martin, J.D. 101
Martin-Achard, R. 193
Martínez, F.G. 189-90, 195, 198-99, 228
Martyn, J.L. 23, 26-28, 109, 112, 173, 231, 247, 266
Mason, E.F. 195, 228
Mason, R. 132
Mason, S. 89
Matera, F.J. 6
Matson, M.A. 146
McBride, S.D. 178-79, 203
McCaffrey, U.P. 158
McCartney, D. 158-59, 309
McConville, J.G. 192, 204-05, 216
McDonald, N. 7
McGrath, J.F. 9, 11, 287
McHugh, J.F. 27, 80, 220
McKay, R.T. 49
McKeating, H. 191
McNamara, M. 71-72, 76, 81-82, 297, 323
Mead, J.K. 1, 3
Meeks, W. 23-27, 111, 117, 155, 173, 194-95, 199-200, 204, 208-09, 214, 216-17, 220, 232, 247, 249, 251, 255, 258, 261, 265-67
Mees, M. 118, 252

Meier, J.P. 114, 153
Menken, M.J.J. 31, 37-38, 93, 119, 122, 144, 155-56, 159, 162-63, 168-71, 265, 269-71, 310-11
Merkel, H. 211
Merrill, E.H. 203
Metzger, B.M. 136, 166, 291
Metzner, R. 252
Meyer, R. 102
Meyers, C.L. 170
Meyers, E.M. 170, 297-98
Meynet, R. 140
Michaelis, W. 74
Michaels, J.R. 73, 91, 151, 159, 169, 234, 255
Milgrom, J. 178
Milik, J.T. 227
Miller, E. 199
Miller, P. 43, 305
Miller, P.D. 203, 274
Miller, R.J. 109
Mitchell, D.C. 225, 278
Miura, Y. 129
Moessner, D.P. 174
Moloney, F.J. 10, 36, 148, 235, 239, 265
Mönikes, A. 179
Mor, M. 219-20
Morgan, R. 306
Morgen, M. 10, 73-74, 248
Morris, L. 234, 242, 246, 255, 261
Motyer, S. 2
Moule, C.F.D. 111
Moyise, S. 49, 51
Muddiman, J. 194
Mulder, M.J. 202
Müller, M. 29-30, 58-59, 123-25
Müller, U.B. 121
Mullins, T.Y. 140
Munnich, O. 134, 217
Mußner, F. 264
Myer, M. 103
Myers, J.M. 180

Nagel, T. 118, 294
Necker, G. 99
Neeb, J.H.C. 72
Nelson, R.D. 177, 203, 216
Netzer, E. 298

Author Index

Neufeld, D. 23, 31, 44, 281
Neusner, J. 58, 71, 89, 218, 285, 323
Newsom, C.A. 197-98
Neyrey, J.H. 71, 75, 79, 82, 84
Nickelsburg, G.W.E. 89, 184, 187
Niebuhr, K.-W. 212, 295-96
Niehoff, M. 175
Nielsen, H.K. 10
Nihan, C. 175
Nilson, T.D. 79
Nitzan, B. 284
Noam, V. 131
Noble, P.R. 3
Nodet, E. 81, 222
Noisette, C. 88
Nongbri, B. 302
North, W.E.S. 86
Novakovic, L. 140
Nützel, J.M. 99

Oakman, D.E. 290
Oberhänsli-Widmer, G. 175
Obermann, A. 34-36, 59, 148, 155, 234, 239, 251, 256, 305, 307
Oblath, M. 75
Odeberg, H. 71, 79, 94
Oegema, G.S. 57-58, 217, 223, 286
Öhler, M. 98-99, 104, 107-08, 117
O'Kane, M. 191-92
Okorie, A.M. 108
Okure, T. 79
O'Neill, J.C. 8, 70, 199-200
Oporto, S.J. 118-19
Orlov, A.A. 209-10
O'Rourke, J.J. 156, 308
Osborne, G.R. 325
Oswald, N. 99
Otto, E. 175-76, 200
Overholt, T.W. 99

Paddison, A. 86
Paffenroth, K. 140
Paganini, S. 224-25
Painter, J. 23, 30, 43, 232, 238, 262, 288
Pamment, M. 30, 73, 81-82, 223
Pannenberg, W. 1-2
Parker, S.B. 198
Parsons, M.C. 217

Patte, D. 297
Pemberton, E.G. 164
Peri, C. 211
Perrin, N. 5
Petersen, S. 10
Petrotta, A.J. 149
Petterson, A.R. 129, 154
Petzke, G. 21
Phillips, P.M. 113, 235
Philonenko, M. 215
Pichon, C. 109
Pilgaard, A. 283
Piper, O.A. 196
Plummer, A. 307
Poirier, J.C. 105, 286
Polhill, J.B. 21-22, 75, 77-78, 82, 111, 115, 117, 130
Pollefeyt, D. 86
Pomykala, K. 129, 132, 136-37, 139, 287
Porter, A. 298
Porter, J.R. 202
Porter, S.E. 49, 153
Porton, G.G. 324
Priest, J. 194
Propp, W.H.C. 205-06
Prussner, F.C. 5
Pryor, J.W. 78, 118, 300
Puech, É. 88-89, 105-06
Pummer, R. 81, 221
Purvis, J.D. 220

Qimron, E. 224
Quispel, G. 69

Radl, W. 17
Rahner, J. 147, 150
Rainbow, P.A. 195, 229
Räisänen, H. 15
Rakotoharintsifa, A. 10
Ramaroson, L. 93
Ramón-Díaz, J. 81
Rappaport, U. 190
Raurell, F. 208
Rebell, W. 158, 231, 309
Reed, D.A. 233
Reed, J.L. 297-98
Refoulé, F. 173
Regev, E. 298

Reicke, B. 13
Reif, S.C. 129
Reim, G. 23, 59-60, 75, 76, 118, 159, 250, 305-06
Reinhartz, A. 45
Reiterer, F.V. 219-20
Reitzenstein, R. 21
Rendtorff, R. 129, 191
Rengstorf, K.H. 17
Rensberger, D. 17
Resseguie, J.L. 45
Reumann, J.H.P. 4
Reventlow, H.G. 5, 193, 289
Reynolds, B.E. 73-74, 247
Rhodes, A.B. 193
Ribben, B.J. 56
Richard. E. 297
Richter, G. 30-31, 270-71
Richter, W. 192
Ridderbos, H.N. 75, 242, 311
Riesner, R.D. 299
Robberechts, E. 278
Roberge, M. 263
Robert, R. 244
Roberts, J.J.M. 133, 228-29
Robertson, R.G. 209
Robinson, J.A.T. 111
Robinson, J.M. 103
Rochais, G. 258
Roeslli, J.-M. 211
Rogers, C.L., Jr. 132, 140
Roloff, J. 146
Römer, T. 175, 200, 209, 267
Ronning, J.L. 94, 323-24
Rordorf, W. 76
Rose, M. 262
Ross, J.F. 176
Rothfuchs, W. 158
Roure, D. 140
Rowland, C. 71, 76
Rubenstein, J.L. 134
Ruckstuhl, E. 60, 263
Rudolph, K. 117
Runia, D.T. 208, 296
Rütersworden, U. 203

Sailhamer, J.H. 284
Saito, T. 230-31

Saldarini, A.J. 89, 219, 323
Salmon, V. 302
Salzmann, J.C. 114, 141
Sanday, W. 294-95
Sanders, E.P. 210, 284, 291, 298, 325
Sanders, J.A. 3, 130
Sanderson, J.E. 222
Sänger, D. 36, 174, 231-33, 239, 250
Schäfer, P. 25-26, 113
Schapdick, S. 230, 245, 250, 254, 256, 261, 270, 273
Schenck, K. 212
Schencke, H.M. 80
Schenke, L. 69, 88, 171, 235, 260, 263, 295
Schiffman, L.H. 137-38, 187, 196, 224, 227, 284
Schlatter, A. 234, 255, 296, 301
Schmidt, A. 291
Schmidt, W.H. 205
Schmithals, W. 10, 58, 295
Schmitz, B. 184
Schnackenburg, R. 70, 74, 91, 110, 123, 125, 149, 151, 164, 168, 234, 242, 246, 266, 296, 303, 307, 311
Schneider, G. 201
Schneider, J. 234
Schnelle, U. 10-11, 36, 41, 67, 69-70, 86, 146, 235, 238-39, 253, 255, 264, 294, 295, 302-03
Scholtissek, K. 10, 13-14, 18, 39-40, 59-61, 173, 232, 251, 254, 257, 262-65, 269
Schottroff, L. 293-95
Schräge, W. 36
Schreiber, S. 69, 147, 160, 260, 285
Schröter, J. 298
Schuchard, B.G. 53, 168
Schulz, S. 293
Schürer, E. 285
Schwankl, O. 11-12, 17, 58
Schwartz, D.R. 183-84, 189
Schwartz, E. 60
Schweizer, E. 11, 60, 139
Scobie, C.H.H. 2, 4, 220
Scott, I.W. 21-22, 208
Scott, J.M. 5-6, 23
Scrogie, W.G. 305
Seebaß, H. 99, 202
Séd, N. 220

Seeman, C.J. 299
Segal, A.F. 90
Seglla, G. 10
Segovia, F.F. 162
Seifrid, M. 6
Seitz, C.R. 3, 6-7, 8, 59-60
Selman, M.J. 286
Sénéchal, V. 193
Seters, J.V. 75
Setzer, C. 90
Sevrin, J.-M. 68, 119, 233
Seybold, K. 144, 153, 285
Silva, M. 56, 149
Simmers, G. 9
Simian-Yofre, H. 201
Sinclair, L.A. 129
Ska, J-L. 45, 79, 205
Skehan, P.W. 207
Sloyan, G. 10
Smalley, S.S. 19
Smend, R. 176
Smith, D.M. 25, 36, 151, 157-58, 308-09
Smith, J.M. 15
Smith, M. 55
Smyth, H.W. 239
Smyths, M. 174
Snaith, J.G. 207
Söding, T. 15, 36, 160, 170, 247-48, 250, 300
Sollamo, R. 190
Sprinkle, J.M. 234
Staley, J.L. 62-63, 237
Stamps, D.L. 49
Stanley, C.D. 49
Starky, J. 227, 286
Stauffer, E. 94
Stefanovic, Z. 80
Stegemann, E.W. 69, 158, 260, 309
Stegemann, W. 69, 231, 260
Steiger, J.A. 69
Stein, R.H. 45, 52-53
Stemberger, G. 89, 134, 201, 218, 323
Stendahl, K. 2
Stenschke, C. 290
Sterling, G.E. 296
Stettler, H. 162
Stibbe, M.W.G. 14-15, 265
Stiglmair, A. 169

Stone, M.E. 136-38
Stout, S.O. 26
Stowasser, M. 118, 123, 125, 145-47
Strange, J.F. 298
Straub, E. 252
Strauss, M.L. 140
Strawn, B.A. 131
Strotmann, A. 243
Strugnell, J. 105, 224
Stuckenbruck, L.T. 8, 284
Stuhlmacher, P. 4-5, 13, 42, 63, 278
Sullivan, S. 80
Swancutt, D.M. 5, 42, 232

Tal, A. 220, 223
Tantlevskij, I.R. 200, 229
Tate, M.E. 138
Taylor, J.E. 108
Taylor, M.A. 175
Taylor, V. 54
Tcherikover, V. 191
Teeple, H.M. 217, 271, 283, 293
Termini, C. 212
Thatcher, T. 10, 274
Theobald, M. 36, 41-43, 51, 73, 75, 77, 79, 84, 88, 91, 95, 120, 167, 232, 240, 244, 246, 263, 269-71
Thettayil, B. 79, 145, 219, 310-11
Thielman, F. 6, 13, 78, 83, 147
Thoma, A. 59
Thoma, C. 131, 134
Thomas, H. 52
Thomas, J.C. 217, 298, 300
Thomassen, E. 103
Thompson, J.A. 177
Thompson, M.B. 149
Thompson, M.M. 272
Thüsing, W. 13
Thyen, H. 121-23, 151, 234-35, 263, 270
Tigay, J.H. 177
Tigchelaar, E.J.C. 198, 228
Tilly, M. 108
Tov, E. 170, 198
Toy, C.H. 305
Trafton, J.L. 137
Trier, D.J. 3
Trocmé, E. 115
Tromp, J. 133, 139, 180, 194-95

Tsedaka, B. 80
Trudinger, P. 23, 31-32, 141, 155, 173
Tuckett, C. 50, 174

Ulrichsen, J.H. 146
Umoh, C. 145, 148
Untergaßmair, U. 11

Vahrenhorst, M. 305
Vaissi, P. 278
Vanderkam, J.C. 130, 184, 196
Veerkamp, T. 79
Vermes, G. 29, 187-88, 297, 325
Verseput, D.J. 140
Visotzky, B.L. 219, 323
Vollenweider, S. 61
Volgger, D. 183-84
Voorwinde, S. 232-33, 237

Waetjen, H.C. 140
Wahlde, U.C. von. 26, 67, 80, 85, 87, 252, 270, 294
Walker, W.O 29, 73
Wallace, D.B. 94, 239
Wallace, E.M.E. 32-36, 234
Waltke, B.K. 201
Waschke, E.-J. 132, 191
Washington, H.C. 297
Water, R. van de 209
Watson, F. 7
Watt, J.G. van der 232
Watts, J.W. 204
Wcela, E.A. 286
Wedderburn, A.J.M. 144, 148
Weder, H. 10-11, 238
Wegner, P.D. 1
Weinreich, O. 21
Weiser, A. 264
Weiss, J. 295
Wells, M.J. 30
Wengst, K. 67, 69-70, 75, 79-80, 82-83, 86, 88, 94, 121, 123, 149, 151, 159, 161, 164, 171, 175, 231, 233-34, 236, 240, 250, 260, 266
Werlitz, J. 99
Westcott, B.F. 307
Westermann, C. 290
Wevers, J.W. 70, 202

Whitsett, C.G. 140
Whitters, M.F. 108
Widengren, G. 285
Widmer. M. 191, 193
Wiebe, J.M. 184
Wieder, N. 188
Wiens, D.H. 304
Wilckens, U. 6, 41, 83, 233, 235, 238, 263, 266, 270
Wilcox, M. 296
Williams, C.H. 243
Williamson, H.G.M. 88, 182, 219-20
Wilson, R.M. 54, 117
Windisch, H. 75
Wink, W. 73, 108-09, 115, 124
Winter, S.F. 235
Wischmeyer, O. 58
Wise, M.O. 186, 190, 227
Witmer, S.E. 325
Witte, M. 208
Wolter, M. 175
Woude, A.S. van der 228
Wright, B.G. 297
Wright, N.T. 6, 17, 210
Wright, R.B. 135-36
Wyss, B. 212

Xeravits, G.G. 97, 99, 103-05, 107, 185, 196, 225, 227-29, 283, 286, 293

Yamauchi, E.M. 294
Yarbro-Collins, A. 211
Yarbrough, R.W. 7
York, A.D. 218, 323

Zamagni, C. 175
Zangenberg, J. 80, 290
Zeev, W. 298
Zeller, D. 99
Zenger, E. 175-76
Zetterholm, K.H. 99
Zimmermann, J. 105, 286
Zola, N.J. 160
Zumstein, J. 11, 45, 49, 52-53, 61-63, 161, 247, 263, 269

Scripture Index

Genesis
1:1	35
4:16-25	242
12:6-7	80
17:6	132
17:16	132
17:17	91
18:2-13	91
28:12	69-70, 76, 315
28:13-15	76
33:19	80
33:20	80
35:11	132
37:9-10	211
48:22	80
49:10	133, 137, 287

Exodus
1-15	209
3:14	94
4:1-17	192
4:16	207
4:20	200, 205
4:34	192
7:1	205-07
8:9	193
12:46	168, 314
19:9	254
24:12	178
32	193
32:30-32	193
33:11	177
33:12-34:35	254
33:12-34:8	243
33:20-23	177
33-34	233
34:6	233
34:29-35	178

Leviticus
24:16	94

Numbers
7:89	254
9:12	168, 314
11	193
12:6-8	177
12:8	177
14	193
21	193, 247
21:7	193
21:8	248
23:6-8	254
24:15-17	225, 227
24:17	133, 287
32	193

Deuteronomy
4:44-45	182
5	254
5:28-29	225, 227
6:10-11	
9	193
9:20	193
16:18-18:22	215
17:14-20	133
18	269
18:15	111, 205, 214-16, 219, 224-25, 228
18:15-18	217, 254, 257, 261
18:15-19	162
18:15-22	266
18:16-17	205
18:18	214, 221, 223, 259
18:18-19	31, 224-25, 227
32:1	87-88
32:36	184
33:1	173
33:1-5	202
33:2	203
33:2-3	203
33:4	203
33:4-5	201
33:5	202-03, 205
33:6-25	202
33:8-11	226, 227
33:26	203
33:26-29	202-03
33:28	203
33:29	203
34:10	177
34:11-12	192

Joshua
6:26	226, 227
14:6	173, 179
24:32	80

1 Samuel
2:1-10	133
10:10-11	205
12:12	280
15:23	142
16:1-13	142
19:23-24	205

2 Samuel
5:1-3	133
7	164
7:19	133
15-17	160
15:23	142
17:3	142

1 Kings
2:3	179, 181
8:9	179
14:6	179, 181

17	105	**Psalms**		11:12	248
17:1	97	2:2	133	12:3	82
17:1-18:46	105	2:6-8	133	13:2	248
18:6	179	16:10	130	18:3	248
18:12	179	18:25-26	154	35:4	313
19:6	104	18:50-51	133	40:3	122, 312
		21:2	200	40:9	313
2 Kings		22	143	40:26	210
4	105	22:15	314	43:10	94
21:8	179	22:18	163-64, 314	49:6	101
23:25	179	22:19	164	53	287
		34	169	53:1	313
1 Chronicles		34:20	168, 314	53:3	132
6:49	179	35:19	162, 314	54:13	312
15:15	179	40:10	159	56:7	147
22:13	179	41:9	159, 161, 314	61:1	104
23:14	173, 179	41:10	159	62:10	248
2 Chronicles		42:1	165	**Jeremiah**	
3:1	81	62:11	313	1:4-10	214
8:13	179	63:1	166	2:13	82
23:18	179, 181	68:10	143	7:11	147
25:4	179	69	143, 147	17:13	82
30:16	179, 181	69:4	144, 162	23:5-6	133
33:8	179, 181	69:5	314	31:31-34	162
34:14	179, 181	69:9	144-45, 312	33:15	132
35	181			33:21-22	132
35:6	179, 181	69:10	143	33:25-26	132
35:12	179	69:21	144		
36	181	69:22-23	144	**Ezekiel**	
		69:25	144	17:22	133
Ezra		78:24	312	19:11	200
1	181	82:6	312	19:14	200
3:2	173, 179, 181	89:20-21	133	20:35	178
4:7-14	181	89:27-28	133	34:23-24	132-33
6:18	179	90:1	173, 179	36:26-27	162
7:6	179, 181	110:2	200	37:22-25	133
		118:25-26	154, 315	37:24-25	132
Nehemiah		147:4	210	47	82
1:7	179				
1:8	179	**Isaiah**		**Daniel**	
8:1	179, 181	5:26	248	7	27
8:14	179, 181	6:10	158, 309, 313	9:11	179, 181
9:14	179	9:5-7	133	9:13	179, 181
10:29	179, 181	10:34-11:5	287	9:25-26	133
		11:1	132-33	**Hosea**	
				1:11	132

Scripture Index

2	79	22:45	140	1:6-8	120, 236-38
3:5	132-33	23:2	324		
12:13	192	26:61	147	1:6-9	236
		27:34	144	1:6-13	235
Amos		27:35	163	1:7	67, 121
9:11-15	132	27:42	261	1:7-15	126
				1:8	67, 124-25
Micah		**Mark**			
5:2	132, 148	1:7	127	1:8-9	142
5:2-5	133	9:11	107, 127	1:9-10	237
		9:13	108	1:9-11	236-37
Haggai		10:47-48	140	1:9-13	236
2:23	132	11:9	153	1:9-14	238
		11:10	140, 153	1:10-11	237, 243
Zechariah		11:17	147	1:10-12	236
3:8	133	11:18	147	1:11-13	237, 264
6:12	133	12:24-27	89	1:12-13	236-37
9-14	154	12:35	140	1:14	233, 236-37, 240
9:9	154, 313	14:58	147		
9:9-10	133	15:24	163	1:14-15	243
12:10	133, 167, 169-70, 172, 315	15:32	261	1:14-16	236
				1:14-17	237
13:7-8	133	**Luke**		1:14-18	235-36, 239
14:9	170	1:17	98, 109		
		1:54-55	66	1:15	120-21, 127, 236-38
Malachi		3:31	140		
3	110	9:52	222	1:16	237, 239-41
3:23	103	18:38-39	140		
3:24	104-05	20:41-44	140	1:16-17	232, 238-39, 242-44, 273
3:25	100	23:34	163		
4:4	179	23:36	144		
4:5-6	100			1:16-18	236-38, 241-42, 245
4:6	105	**John**			
		1	237, 240	1:17	35, 37, 83, 237-41, 245
Matthew		1:1	35		
1:6	140	1:1-2	125, 236, 237-38	1:17-18	236
2:5-6	148-49			1:18	35, 75, 237, 240, 243-44, 256
9:27	140	1:1-4	236		
11:14	108	1:1-5	235-38		
12:23	140	1:1-13	236	1:19	121
15:22	140	1:1-18	12, 85, 256	1:19-24	67
17:10	107			1:19-28	67, 121
17:12	108	1:3	237	1:19-34	120-21, 123, 125
20:31-32	140	1:3-5	236-37		
21:9	140, 153	1:4	257	1:19-36	120
21:13	147	1:4-5	237	1:19-51	112, 264
21:15	140, 153	1:5	236	1:19-12:50	85
22:42-43	140	1:6	119, 123	1:20	121, 261

1:20-21	124	2:16	147	4:5	80
1:20-23	97, 118	2:17	36, 141,	4:9	78
1:21	109-10		143, 146-48, 312	4:10	82
1:23	122, 280,	2:18-22	36	4:10-14	66, 77,
	312	2:19	147		83, 95, 276
1:25	110, 261	2:20	147	4:10-15	84
1:25-28	67	2:21	145, 147	4:10-26	84
1:26	117	2:22	36, 146	4:12	66, 78,
1:26-27	115	2:23-24	145		83-84, 88
1:27	280	2:24-25	151, 161	4:14	311
1:29-34	67, 119,	2:25	78	4:14-15	82
	121	3:1-15	145	4:19	78
1:29-36	261	3:1-21	246, 249	4:19-26	79
1:31	119, 142	3:2	246	4:23	264
1:32	121	3:3	246	4:25	17
1:32-33	123	3:3-9	246	4:26	78
1:33	123-24	3:3-12	246	4:30	78
1:34	121	3:10	316	4:39	78
1:35-37	67, 125	3:11	78, 246	4:43-54	85
1:35-51	259	3:12	246	4:41	256
1:35-42	20	3:12-21	249	4:42	78
1:35-51	20, 264	3:13	35, 112,	4:43-54	311
1:38	68, 259		246-47, 250	4:44	78
1:38-50	68	3:13-14	246	4:46-54	112
1:41	17, 112,	3:14	245,	4:50	256
	261		247-48, 272-73	4:54ff	77
1:43-49	112	3:14ff	250	5	265, 302
1:44-50	20	3:14-15	79	5:1-9	252
1:45	32, 37,	3:15-16	250	5:1-19	258
	223, 234, 251,	3:15-18	249	5:1-47	85, 263,
	256-61, 273, 316	3:15-21	247		311
1:48	257	3:16	37	5:1-10:39	264
1:49	68, 76,	3:17	123	5:10	253
	152, 259, 261, 266	3:18-19	246	5:10-18	252
1:50	66	3:22	110	5:15-29	150
1:51	66-68,	3:23-30	120-21	5:16	253
	74, 76-77, 83, 95,	3:26	78	5:17-19	253
	145, 147-48, 259,	3:28	119, 124	5:18	13, 253
	261, 276, 315	3:29	79, 119	5:19-29	151, 252
2	298	3:30	37, 125,	5:23	253
2:1-11	78, 112		145	5:24	255, 257
2:1-12	85, 311	3:32	78	5:26	256-57
2-7	85	3:34	123	5:31-38	253
2:1ff	77	3:39	119	5:31-47	252
2:1-4:54	264	4	84, 263	5:33-35	253-54
2:10	145	4:1-15	78	5:33-36	120-21
2:13-22	78, 143,	4:1-42	79	5:34	125, 151,
	145-46	4:3-4	222		253

Scripture Index

5:34-35	264	6:19	265	7:42	141, 148, 150-51, 315
5:35	125, 142	6:21	265	7:52	151
5:36	253-54, 256, 264	6:22	269	8	85
		6:22-59	150	8:5	36, 233
5:36-37	151	6:24	269	8:12	151
5:36-38	264	6:24-26	257, 264-65	8:13	150
5:36-47	261, 264			8:14-20	151
5:37	75, 264	6:27	264	8:16-19	95
5:37-38	254-56, 264	6:27-28	264	8:17	36
		6:30	264, 269	8:19	150
5:37-39	250, 254, 273	6:30-33	272	8:21-22	264
		6:31	270, 312	8:22	150
5:38	123, 255-56	6:31-32	264	8:23	151
		6:31-35	271	8:26	95
5:39	37, 126, 151, 254-58, 261, 316	6:32	37, 83, 244-45, 264, 267, 270-71	8:27	150
				8:29	95
		6:32-33	262	8:31	86
5:39-40	257, 264	6:32-40	151	8:31-38	86
5:39-46	251	6:35	83, 256	8:32-36	95
5:39-47	253-54	6:40	248	8:33	95, 150, 253
5:41	151, 253	6:41	264, 269		
5:42	257	6:42	259	8:38	95
5:43	264	6:45	256, 312	8:39	66, 253
5:43-44	264	6:46	75, 244, 256, 264	8:39-47	86
5:44	257			8:41	150
5:45	37, 261	6:46-51	271	8:42	95
5:45-46	156, 251	6:48-58	267	8:43	150
5:45-47	257-58, 316	6:52	264, 269	8:44-47	151
		6:59-61	256	8:46	150
5:46	254, 256	6:60-71	264	8:48	86, 150
5:46-47	257, 261, 264	6:63	151, 256	8:48-59	86
		6:66-69	272	8:51	87, 95
5:56	273	7	264, 302	8:51-58	84-86, 95, 276
6	36, 263-66, 269, 302	7:1-13	265		
		7:15-24	263	8:51-59	94
6:1	265	7:18-24	233, 258	8:52	86
6:1-14	112	7:28	166	8:52-53	87, 150
6:1-15	150, 265	7:31	311	8:52-55	86
6:1-59	258	7:34-36	264	8:53	66, 84, 88, 253
6:1-71	85, 263, 311	7:37	110		
		7:37-39	256	8:56	37, 66, 91, 93
6:2	269	7:37-52	24, 266		
6:5	269	7:38	82, 310, 315	8:56-58	86, 91, 243
6:13	266				
6:14-15	262, 264-66, 271	7:38-39	83	8:57	86
		7:40	256	8:58	93
6:15	152	7:40-41	85, 151	8:59	91, 94,
6:16-21	150, 265				

	150, 161	12:17-19	154	18:4	264
9:1-7	112	12:20ff	272	18:7-8	264
9:1-41	85, 265	12:20-26	142	18:11	166
9:28-29	150, 253	12:20-33	154	18:9	36, 156
9:40-41	150	12:21	264	18:28-19:22	24, 266
10	302	12:24-27	155	18:31	36-37
10:1-39	266-67	12:26	142	18:32	36, 156
10:10	257	12:31-32	246	18:33-38	266
10:19	256	12:32	261	18:37	160
10:19-21	150	12:34-35	150	19:7	37
10:24	150	12:37	150	19:24	163, 165, 314
10:25	253	12:37-40	157		
10:30	11, 13, 161	12:37-41	158	19:28	36, 144, 156, 165, 167, 314
		12:38	313		
10:31	150	12:39	150	19:30	167
10:33	13	12:39-41	158, 309, 313	19:33-37	168-69
10:34	36-37, 312			19:36	167, 314
		12:41	243	19:36-37	167
10:35	40, 257	13-20	157	19:37	169-70, 248, 315
10:38	256	13:1f	160		
10:39	150, 161	13:1-17	160	20:8	36
10:40-42	120-21, 125	13:1-20:31	85	20:9	36, 156, 316
		13:18	156, 159, 163, 314		
10:41	125			20:11-18	264
11:1-44	112	13:19	160	20:24	272
11:1-57	85	13:31-32	161	20:30-31	12
11:7-16	265	13:33	264	20:31	260
11:12-13	150	13:34	37	21:1-25	85
11:16	150	13:34-35	160	21:24-25	157
11:25	256	13:36	264		
11:27	13, 260	14-16	160	**Acts**	
11:50	142	14:6	256	1:20	144
11:50-52	266	14:9-11	256	2:30	129
11:54-57	265	14:20	256	2:30-31	130
11:56	264	14:26	123	3	110
12	157, 308	15:1-17	162	3:12-26	110
12:1-8	154	15:3	144	3:22	110
12:9-11	154	15:18	162	7:37	110
12:12-16	154	15:22	163	13:22-23	139
12:12-19	266	15:25	36, 144, 156, 162-63, 314	18:24-19:7	115
12:13	141, 152-53, 315			19:1-7	124
		15:26	123		
12:13-15	154	16:1	163	**Romans**	
12:13-16	152	17	160	1:3-4	139
12:14-15	313	17:11	161	4:1	66
12:15	36	17:12	161, 315	11:9-10	144
12:16	36, 146, 150, 154	17:21-23	256	15:3	144
		18:1	142		

1 Corinthians
1:23   157

Revelation
5:5   139
22:16   139

Index for Other Ancient Sources

Apocrypha

1 Esdras
1:1-33	181
1:6	180-81
1:11	180
1:34-58	181
2:1-14	181
2:15-30	181
5:49	173, 179-80
7:9	180
8:1	181
8:3	180
9:39	180-81

2 Esdras
7:108	131

4 Esdras
7:106	194

Tobit
1:8	180-81
7:13	181

Judith
4:4	221
5:16	221
9:2-4	221

Wisdom of Solomon
11-19	194
11:1	194

Sirach
297
15:3	82
24:21	82
24:23	182
26:15	242
44:19	88
45:1-3	207
45:1-5	207
45:3	193
45:3-5	180, 183
45:5	180
47:3	131
47:22	135
48:3	105
48:5	105
48:10	100
48:11	105

Baruch
2:2	180-81
2:28	180

Susanna
1:3	180-81
1:62	180-81

1 Maccabees
2:57	131, 135
14:41	215
14:41-49	215

2 Maccabees
2:10	193-94
5:23	221
6:12	221
7:1-6	185-86
7:6	184-85
7:30	180,-81
	185

4 Maccabees
89
1:1	183
1:7	183
7:6	183
7:18-19	90
7:30	183
9:2	182
16:25	90

Pseudepigrapha

1 Enoch
37-71	27
48:1	82

3 Enoch
46:12	210

Sibylline Oracles
102, 211-12
2:187-204	101
11:35-40	212

4 Ezra
139
3:14	92
12:31-34	136
13	27

2 Baruch
4:4	92

Coptic Apocalypse of Elijah
102
4:7-20	102
5:32-35	101

Apocalypse of Abraham
1-8	92
9-32	92

Testament of Levi
221
18:1-9	107

Index for Other Ancient Sources

Testament of Judah		17:32	135-36	**Zechariah**	
24:1-6	107	18:5	136	12:10	170
		18:7	136	14:9	170
Testament of Benjamin		**Theodotus**		**Malachi**	
9:2	217	221		3:25	100

Assumption of Moses
1:14	180, 195
3:12	180
10:1-2	195
10:2	195
11:11	194
11:14	194
11:16-17	195
11:17	194-95
12:6	194-95

Letter of Aristeas
4-5	191
16	191
31	191
139	191
147-53	191
161	191
168	191
171	191
240	191
313	191

Jubilees
15:17	91
30	221
49:16-21	221

Pseudo Philo, L.A.B.
18:5	92
48	102
51:4	142

Lives of the Prophets
21:1	102

Ladder of Jacob
1:5	73

Psalms of Solomon
139

Ezekiel the Tragedian
209-11
68-82	209

The Samaritan Pentateuch

Genesis
12:6-7	80
33:20	80

Deuteronomy
18:15	219
18:18	221

The Septuagint

Numbers
21:8	248

Deuteronomy
18:15	214
32:36	184
33:4-5	202

2 Chronicles
35:6	181

Psalms
35:19	162
40:10	159
68:10	143
69:4	162

Isaiah
40:3	122

Dead Sea Scrolls

1QDM (1Q22)
198, 224
1-3	198
1 i	186
4 i-iii	198

1QS
1 ii-iii	181
1 iii	186
5 vii-x	188
9 i	107
9 xi	225

1QSa (1Q28a=*Rule of the Congregation*)
2 xxii-xxiii	287

1Q29 (Liturgy of the Three Tongues of Fire)
224

1QM (1Q33)
10 vi	186

1QHa (1Q35)
17 xii	186

2Q21 (2QapMoses)
197

4Q156 (4QtgLev)
324

4Q157 (4QtgJob)
324

4Q161 (4QpIsa^a)
137

4Q171 (4QpPs[a])		2 ix	186	**4Q397** (4QMMT)	
2 ii-iii	187			4 x	186
2 xiv	187	**4Q270** (*Damascus Covenant*)			
2 xxii	187			**4Q398** (4QMMT)	
3 xv	225	6 ii 6	188	1 v	186
		11 i 20	186		
4Q174 (*Florilegium*)				**4Q418** (*sapiential work*)	
137, 186, 189		**4Q271** (*Damascus Covenant*)		103 iii 6	81
2 ii 3	186				
3 x-xii	189	2 ii 3-4	187	**4Q427** (*Hymns[a]*)	
		2 ii 6	188	7 i 11	199
4Q175 (4QTestimonia)					
		4Q285 (*Rule of War*)		**4Q491** (*War Scroll[a]*)	
196, 224-25, 227		137		11	199
1 i	186			11 i 13	199
1-8	225	**4Q368** (4QapocrPent)			
9-13	226	1	197	**4Q504** (*Words of the Luminaries[a]*)	
14-20	226				
21-30	226	**4Q374** (4QapocrMos A)		1 ii 8-11	197
		207		1 v 14	186
4Q177		7 ii	197	2 ix-x	186
2 v	189				
		4Q375 (4QapocrMos B)		**4Q521** (*Messianic Apocalypse*)	
4Q252 (4QPBless or 4QpGen[a])					
		196, 224		2 ii 1	104
139, 189				2 ii 7-8	104
1 iv 2	186	**4Q376** (*Liturgy of the Three Tongues of Fire*)		2 ii 11-13	104
5 i-vii	137			2 iii 2	104-05
		196, 224			
4Q255 (4QS[a])				**4Q558** (4QVision[c])	
1 iii	186	**4Q377** (4QapocrMos C)		103	
		229			
4Q259 (4QS[e])		2 ii	188	**8QHevXIIgr**	
1 iii 6	186	2 ii 2	186	169	
4Q266 (*Damascus Covenant*)		**4Q378** (4QPssJosh[a])		**11QPs[a]** (11Q5)	
		199		27 ii-xi	130
3 ii	188	26	198-99		
3 ii 1-15	189	26 ii	173	**11Q10** (11QtgJob)	
3 ii 19	186			324	
8 i-ii	190	**4Q379** (4QPssJosh[b])			
17 i 3	187	226		**11QMelch** (11Q13)	
18 v 1-2	186			224, 228-30	
18 v 14-16	188	**4Q381** (*Noncanonical Psalms*)		13 xviii-xix	195
				18-19	229
4Q267 (*Damascus Covenant*)		24 iv	173		
2 v-vi	186				

Index for Other Ancient Sources   409

11QTemple^a (11Q19)
196
54 viii-xviii   224
60 xxi   224
61 i-v   224

CD (Cairo Genizah)
6 xi   189
12 xxiii   225
15 ix   187

CD-A
3 xvi-xvii   81
6 iv   81

Philo
89

Quod deterius potiori insidari solet (The Worse Attacks the Better)
160-62   208

De Posteritate Caini (On the Posterity of Cain)
145   242

De mutatione nominum (On the Change of Names)
154-75   91
177   92

De somniis (On Dreams)
1.3   75

De Abrahamo (On Abraham)
55   90

De vita Mosis (On the Life of Moses)
1.1   175
1.155   208

1.158-59   208
1.162   208
1.334   212-13
2.1-2   213
2.187   213

De virtutibus (On the Virtues)
70   213

De praemiis et poenis (On Rewards and Punishments)
54   212

Quod Omnis Probus Liber sit (That Every Good Man Is Free)
43-44   208

Josephus

Against Apion
2.165   214

Jewish War
2.165   89
2.232-33   222

Jewish Antiquities
18.16-17   89
4.202   94
20.118-38   222

Rabbinic Writings

Babylonian Talmud
Bava Batra
14-15   129

Berakhot
3   129
7   131

Ḥullin
91   76

Megillah
17   134

Pesaḥim
117   129

Sanhedrin
98   131, 134
106   160

Soṭah
9   105
11   131
49   131

Midrashim
Genesis Rabbah
73
28:12   71

Mishnah
Aboth
6.3   160

Baba Mesia
1:8   98
2:8   98
3:4   98
3:5   99

Eduyyyot
8:7   98

Ṭeharot
1:6   129
24:3   129
25:1   131
40:2   131
51:1   131
51:3   131

Targums
Neofiti on Genesis
324
28:12   72

Onkelos to Genesis
91, 323-24
28:12   73, 75

Pseudo-Jonathan on
Genesis
28:12   72

Pseudo-Jonathan on
Deuteronomy
32:1   87-88

*Targum of the Minor
Prophets*
149-50

Targum of Psalms
55   160

Targum Yerušalmi I
Ex 6:18   102
Num 25:12   102

**Other Rabbinic
Writings**
Midrash Tehillin
5.4   134
18:27   134
21:2   200-01

Numbers Rabbah
18:17   160

*Pesiqta de Rab
Kahana*
76   105

Pirqe Rabbi Eliezer
35   81

Rabba
68:12   76

Gnostic Writings
102-03

**Treatise on the
Resurrection** (The
Epistle to Rheginos)
102
46:23-29   102-03
47:9-10   103
48:3-20   103

**New Testament
Apocrypha and
Pseudepigrapha**

Pseudo-Clementines
Recognitions
1.54.8   116
1.60.1-2   116
1.60.1-11   116

Homilies
2.23   116

**Ancient Christian
Writings**

Didache
10:6   153

Justin Martyr
Apology
35:1   114

Dialogue with Trypho
8:4   114-15
88:7   118

www.ingramcontent.com/pod-product-compliance
Lightning Source LLC
Chambersburg PA
CBHW072117290426
44111CB00012B/1686